1955	1956	1957	1958	1959	1960	1961	1962	1963	1964	1965	1966	1967
109.7	111.0	112.3	113.7	115.3	117.2	118.8	120.2	122.4	124.5	126.5	128.1	129.9
65.0	66.6	66.9	67.6	68.4	69.6	70.5	70.6	71.8	73.1	74.5	75.8	77.3
59.3	60.0	59.6	59.5	59.3	59.4	59.3	58.8	58.7	58.7	58.9	59.2	59.6
87.6	87.6	86.9	86.6	86.3	86.0	85.7	84.8	84.4	84.2	83.9	83.6	83.4
35.4	36.4	36.5	36.9	37.0	37.6	38.0	37.8	38.3	38.9	39.4	40.1	41.1
58.7	59.4	59.1	58.9	58.7	58.8	58.8	58.3	58.2	58.2	58.4	58.7	59.2
64.2	64.9	64.4	64.8	64.3	64.5	64.1	63.2	63.0	63.1	62.9	63.0	62.8
62.2	63.8	64.1	63.0	64.6	65.8	65.7	66.7	67.8	69.3	71.1	72.9	74.4
2.9	2.8	2.9	4.6	3.7	3.9	4.7	3.9	4.1	3.8	3.4	2.9	3.0
4.4	4.1	4.3	6.8	5.5	5.5	6.7	5.5	5.7	5.2	4.5	3.8	3.8
4.2	3.8	4.1	6.8	5.2	5.4	6.4	5.2	5.2	4.6	4.0	3.2	3.1
4.9	4.8	4.7	6.8	5.9	5.9	7.2	6.2	6.5	6.2	5.5	4.8	5.2
3.9	3.6	3.8	6.1	4.8	5.0	6.0	4.9	5.0	4.6	4.1	3.4	3.4
8.7	8.3	7.9	12.6	10.7	10.2	12.4	10.9	10.8	9.6	8.1	7.3	7.4
11.0	11.1	11.6	15.9	14.6	14.7	16.8	14.7	17.2	16.2	14.8	12.8	12.9
1.71	1.80	1.89	1.95	2.02	2.09	2.14	2.22	2.28	2.36	2.46	2.56	2.68
39.6	39.3	38.8	38.5	39.0	38.6	38.6	38.7	38.8	38.7	38.8	38.6	38.0
153	158	158	157	164	165	167	172	175	178	183	184	185
5.4	3.1	.1	−.4	4.1	.7	1.4	3.0	1.7	1.8	2.7	.6	.2
.75	1.00	1.00	1.00	1.00	1.00	1.00	1.15	1.15	1.25	1.25	1.25	1.40
4.0	1.0	2.5	3.1	3.2	1.5	3.3	3.8	3.7	4.3	3.5	3.1	2.3
2.5	6.5	6.5	4.4	4.3	4.2	3.8	4.6	3.7	5.2	3.9	7.0	5.3
−1.4	5.5	3.9	1.3	1.0	2.7	.5	.7	.0	.8	.3	3.8	3.0
16.8	17.5	17.4	17.0	17.1	17.0	16.3	16.6	16.5	16.8	17.3	17.9	18.4
24.7	25.7	24.9	24.2	24.1	23.6	22.3	22.6	22.2	22.2	22.4	22.7	22.7
363	287	279	332	245	222	195	211	181	246	268	321	381
.16	.20	.07	.13	.43	.09	.07	.08	.07	.11	.10	.10	.18
68.0	70.2	70.4	70.4	69.8	70.9	70.8	70.4	70.2	70.1	69.3	70.0	71.2

1970–1984   ᶜdays idle in strikes involving 1000 or more workers divided by total estimated working time

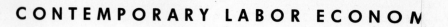

CONTEMPORARY
LABOR
ECONOMICS

CAMPBELL R. McCONNELL

Professor of Economics
University of Nebraska, Lincoln

STANLEY L. BRUE

Professor of Economics
Pacific Lutheran University

McGraw-Hill Book Company

New York St. Louis San Francisco Auckland Bogotá Hamburg Johannesburg London Madrid
Mexico Montreal New Delhi Panama Paris São Paulo Singapore Sydney Tokyo Toronto

CONTEMPORARY LABOR ECONOMICS

1 2 3 4 5 6 7 8 9 0 D O C D O C 8 9 8 7 6 5

ISBN 0-07-044911-2

This book was set in Meridien by Bi-Comp, Incorporated.
The editors were Patricia A. Mitchell, Paul V. Short, and Edwin Hanson;
the designer was Anne Canevari Green;
the production supervisor was Diane Renda.
The drawings were done by Fine Line Illustrations, Inc.
R. R. Donnelley & Sons Company was printer and binder.

Library of Congress Cataloging-in-Publication Data

McConnell, Campbell R.
    Contemporary labor economics.

    Includes indexes.
    1. Labor economics.   I. Brue, Stanley L.,
date   . II. Title.
HD4901.M15 1986   331   85-16662
ISBN 0-07-044911-2

ABOUT THE AUTHORS

Campbell R. McConnell earned his Ph.D. from the University of Iowa after receiving degrees from Cornell College and the University of Illinois. He is currently Carl Adolph Happold Professor of Economics at the University of Nebraska–Lincoln, where he has taught since 1953. He is also the author of *Economics,* currently in its ninth edition and the leading introductory economics textbook. His primary areas of interest are economic education and labor economics. He has an impressive collection of jazz recordings and enjoys reading jazz history.

Stanley L. Brue did his undergraduate work at Augustana College (SD) and received his Ph.D. from the University of Nebraska–Lincoln, where he was a student of Professor McConnell's. He has taught at Pacific Lutheran University since 1971. He is coauthor (with D. R. Wentworth) of *Economic Scenes: Theory in Today's World* and his main areas of specialization are labor economics and the history of economic thought. For relaxation he enjoys salmon fishing and skiing trips with his family.

To Mem
and
Terri and Craig

CONTENTS

13   THE PERSONAL DISTRIBUTION OF EARNINGS . . . 353

14   MOBILITY, MIGRATION, AND EFFICIENCY 379

PREFACE

BACKGROUND AND PURPOSE

There can be no doubt that the winds of change have permeated the field of labor economics. Labor economics has increasingly become an area for the application of micro and macro theory. To make room for such analytical applications, economists are making less and less use of the extensive historical, legal, and institutional materials which dominated the field two or three decades ago. Labor economics has become less and less an area tangential to the core of analytical economics and increasingly a major component of that core.

It is the fundamental purpose of the present volume to capture the content and the attendant excitement of these changes. To put it bluntly, we strive for a logically organized and clearly presented statement of the "new" labor economics. This is not to say that such topics as labor law and the structure of unions and collective bargaining have been entirely crowded out. These subjects remain, but only in a context which explains their impact upon the functioning of labor markets.

The level of analysis is tailored for the undergraduate student who has completed a reasonably rigorous sequence on macro and micro principles. The book is designed for a one-semester or one-quarter course, although appropriate supplementation can make it usable as the focal point of a two-semester course.

ORGANIZATION AND CONTENT

The subject matter generally proceeds from micro to macro topics. Figure 1-1 and the Overview section of Chapter 1 outline the organizational framework in some detail. Hence, our synopsis at this point will be brief.

Chapters 2 to 6 are designed to provide students with a no-nonsense, barebones understanding of how orthodox or neoclassical economists conceive of labor markets. Specifically, Chapters 2 to 4 explore the supply side and Chapter 5 the demand side of labor markets. Chapter 6 combines supply and demand to delineate a variety of labor market models, emphasizing the efficiency aspects of each.

Chapters 7 to 11 introduce institutions which influence the functioning of individual labor markets. Hence, Chapters 7 and 8 add unions and collective bargaining to the discussion and stress the effects of unions upon wages, efficiency, and the distribution of earnings. Chapters 9 and 10 embody a systematic and comprehensive analysis of the direct and indirect impacts of government upon labor markets. Chapter 11 is devoted to the institution of discrimination and the many ways it affects the functioning of labor markets.

In Chapters 12 to 14 we concentrate primarily upon labor market outcomes. Chapter 12 explores the general character of the wage structure which labor markets yield. Similarly, the personal distribution of earnings is examined in Chapter 13. In Chapter 14 we examine the geographic movement of labor resulting from the system of incentives inherent in labor markets and assess how that movement relates to efficiency over time.

While it is accurate to say that our approach is "orthodox," "neoclassical," or "mainstream," we feel that it is important for students to be aware of alternative conceptions of labor markets. Hence, in Chapter 15 we summarize the "old" institutionalism of the immediate post-World War II period, outline the "new" institutionalism of internal labor market theory, and explore the theory of dual or segmented labor markets.

Chapters 16 to 19 are mainly, but not exclusively, macro. The issue of labor productivity is accorded extensive treatment in Chapter 16. Chapter 17 embodies a rigorous discussion of several theories of labor's share of the national income. The next two chapters are devoted to the core macro topics of unemployment and inflation. Chapter 18 features a simplified job search model. In Chapter 19 we have resisted a generalized discussion of inflation in order to concentrate upon the relationship between wage determination and the price level.

Chapter 20 might be regarded as optional, although we feel an overview of the labor sector in the Soviet Union enhances a student's appreciation of labor markets and labor issues in the United States.

Finally, Chapter 21 serves as a springboard for students desiring to supplement their newly acquired knowledge of labor economics. The chapter should also prove useful to students doing term papers or projects in this or related courses. By delineating sources of labor-related data, listing and discussing the major journals and nontechnical publications in the field, and citing closely related books, it should help the interested student to avoid obsolescence of his or her human capital investment in labor economics!

DISTINGUISHING FEATURES

At the hazard of immodesty, we feel that this volume embodies a number of features which distinguish it from other books in the field.

Content. In the area of subject matter the emphasis in Chapter 6 upon allocative efficiency is both unique and desirable. The efficiency emphasis makes students realize that *society* has an interest in how labor markets function. The systematic and comprehensive analysis of government's impact upon labor markets found in Chapters 9 and 10 also set this book apart. Chapter 13 confines its focus almost entirely to the personal distribution of *earnings,* as compared to the usual discussion of the distribution of *income* and the poverty problem. While we recognize that the preferences of instructors vary on this matter, we believe our approach to be more relevant for a textbook on *labor* economics. In our treatment of the critiques of orthodoxy in Chapter 15 we have taken care to treat the "old" institutionalism, internal labor market theory, and labor market segmentation as logical outgrowths of one another, rather than as disparate topics. Indeed, we observe that many competing books give these topics only fleeting mention. The critical topic of labor productivity has been largely ignored or treated in a piecemeal fashion in other books. We have upgraded this topic by according it extensive treatment in Chapter 16. Chapters 18 and 19 on unemployment and wages and inflation embody the modern aggregate supply and demand model now common in principles texts to discuss the contending views of economists concerning search versus cyclical unemployment and wage-push versus demand-pull inflation. And, to our knowledge no other labor text embodies a separate analytically oriented chapter on the labor sector of the U.S.S.R. Finally, Chapter 21 provides a comprehensive discussion of information sources which can be used as a springboard to widen and deepen the reader's understanding of the field.

Organization and Presentation. We are aware that this book will face intense competition from similar texts authored by distinguished labor economists. Our basic strategy for meeting this competition has been to put great stress upon the logical organization of subject matter, not only chapter by chapter but within each chapter. It is our hope that our earlier discussion of Organization and Content and a reading of the Overview section of Chapter 1 will convince most instructors that we have given a great deal of thought to the sequence of chapters. What the world does *not* need is a new labor text comprised of twenty or so disparate and unrelated chapters. Hence, we have sought to develop the subject matter logically from micro to macro, from simple theory to real-world complications, and from analysis to policy. Similarly, considerable time has been spent in seeking the optimal arrangement of topics within each chapter. Chapter subheadings have been used liberally; our feeling is that the student should always be aware of the directional flow of the subject matter.

Many of the key topics of labor economics will be intellectually challenging for most students. We have tried not to impair student understanding with clumsy or oblique exposition. Our purpose is to communicate effectively with students. To this end we have taken great care that our writing be clear, direct, and uncluttered. It is our goal that the material contained herein be highly accessible to the typical college undergraduate.

Pedagogical Features. We have included a variety of pedagogical devices which we feel will make significant contributions to student understanding. First, the introduction of each chapter contains a paragraph or so stating the goals of the chapter and, in many cases, relating it to prior or future chapters. Second, end-of-chapter summaries provide a concise, pointed recapitulation of each chapter. Third, ample lists of questions are provided at the end of each chapter. These range from questions on basic terminology and "open-ended" discussion questions to numerical problems which permit students to test their understanding of basic analytical concepts. Fourth, a list of basic references is provided at the end of each chapter for those ambitious students who seek greater breadth and depth of understanding. Fifth, we have utilized the inside covers of the book to present relevant historical statistics which we hope will be valuable to both students and instructors. Furthermore, as indicated previously, the final chapter of the book lists and discusses various avenues by which the interested reader can update statistical materials found in the book and continue the learning process beyond the course. Finally, we have included short minireadings under the heading "Time and One-Half" at the close of each chapter. Some are special applications or cases pertinent to the chapter's subject matter. Others present views which contrast with or dissent from positions presented in a chapter. Others are simply in-depth extensions of subject matter. The Time and One-Half minireadings are purposely located at the end of each chapter so as not to interrupt the continuity of the text material.

To our knowledge *Contemporary Labor Economics* is the only text in the field which is accompanied by a comprehensive *Student Workbook,* which has been prepared by Professor Norris Peterson of Pacific Lutheran University. The *Workbook* contains behavioral objectives and a chapter-by-chapter glossary in addition to problems, exercises, and multiple-choice questions. The philosophy of the workbook is captured by the Chinese proverb inside its cover: "I hear and I forget, I see and I remember, I *do* and I understand." It is our belief that the *Student Workbook* will prove to be a valuable aid both to the instructor and to students. Professor Peterson's considerable expertise is also reflected in the *Instructor's Manual* which he has authored. Among other features, it contains chapter outlines and learning objectives, answers to selected end-of-chapter text questions, answers to the problems and multiple-choice questions in the *Workbook* (answers to odd-numbered questions also are contained in the *Workbook* itself), and several sample examinations comprised of essay and multiple-choice questions.

ACKNOWLEDGMENTS

We would like to express our thanks for the many useful comments and suggestions provided by colleagues who reviewed all or portions of this text during the course of its development, especially to Clive Bull, New York University; Robert Catlett, Emporia State University; David H. Ciscel, Memphis State University; Michael D. Harsh, Randolph-Macon College; Carl P. Kaiser, Washington and Lee University; John Marcis, Virginia Commonwealth University; J. Peter Mattila, Iowa State University; Norris Peterson, Pacific Lutheran University; Jerry Petr, University of Nebraska–Lincoln; Blair Ruble, Social Science Research Council; Robert Simonson, Mankato State University; Wade Thomas, Ithaca College; William Torrence, University of Nebraska–Lincoln; and Ronald S. Warren, Jr., University of Georgia.

This has truly been a joint endeavor. Hence, we see no gracious means by which either author can avoid the traditional responsibility for errors of commission or omission.

Campbell R. McConnell
Stanley L. Brue

LABOR ECONOMICS: INTRODUCTION AND OVERVIEW

The core problem of economics permeates all of its specialized branches or subdivisions. As you will undoubtedly recall from your principles of economics course, this problem is that productive resources are relatively scarce or limited. Society's material wants—the desires of consumers, businesses, and governmental units for goods and services—exceed our productive capacity. Stated differently, our economic system is incapable of providing all of the products and services which individuals and institutions would like to have. Given that absolute material abundance is not possible, society must make choices as to what goods and services should be produced, how they should be produced, and who should receive them. *Economics* is concerned with the discovery of rules or principles which indicate how such choices can be rationally and efficiently rendered. Since resources are scarce and wants are virtually unlimited, society is obligated to manage its resources as efficiently as possible so as to achieve the maximum fulfillment of its wants. Labor, of course, is one of society's scarce productive resources, and this book centers upon the problem of its efficient utilization.

IMPORTANCE OF LABOR ECONOMICS

How can a special field of economics which is concerned solely with labor be justified? What makes labor economics important as an area of inquiry? There are several answers to these questions.

In the first place, evidence of the importance of labor economics is all around us. One need simply glance at the newspaper headlines: "Inflation erodes paychecks"; "Postal workers threaten strike"; "Robots replace autoworkers"; "Labor productivity plunges"; "Teamsters gain wage hike"; "Regulations improve plant safety"; "More women enter labor force"; "Imports threaten jobs"; "Unemployment reaches postwar peak"; and so on. Many of the most compelling socioeconomic issues of the day center upon the labor sector of our economy.

A second justification for labor economics is quantitative. As we shall discover in Chapter 17, about three-quarters of the national income flows to workers in the form of wages and salaries. Ironically, in the various capitalistic economies of the world the bulk of the national income is received, not as capitalist income (profit, rent, interest), but as wages! The primary source of income for the vast majority of households in the United States is from the provision of labor services. The obvious implication is that quantitatively labor is our most important economic resource.

Finally, the markets in which labor services are "bought" and "sold" embody special characteristics and peculiarities which call for separate study. Labor market transactions are a far cry from product market transactions. More technically stated, the concepts of supply and demand must be substantially revised and reoriented when applied to labor markets. Specifically, on the supply side we will find that the labor services one "rents" to an employer are obviously inseparable from the worker. Because one must spend 40 or so hours per week on the job delivering labor services, the nonmonetary facets of a job become extremely significant. Aside from remuneration, the worker is interested in a job's health and safety features, the arduousness of the work, stability of employment, opportunities for training and advancement, and so forth. These nonmonetary characteristics may well be as important as the amount one earns. Indeed, even one's social status is related to the kind of work one performs. All of this means that the supply decisions of workers are more complex than the supply concept which applies to product markets. Similarly, while the demand for a product is based upon the satisfaction or utility it yields, labor is demanded because of its contribution—its productivity—in creating goods and services. Indeed, the demands for particular kinds of labor are derived from the demands for the products they produce. Society has a demand for automobile workers because there is a demand for automobiles. The demand for labor is therefore an indirect or "derived" demand. For present purposes the point to be underscored is that an understanding of labor markets presumes an appreciation of the special attributes of labor supply and demand. Needless to say, unique institutional considerations, such as labor unions and collective bargaining, the minimum wage, occupational licensing, and discrimination, all affect the functioning of labor markets and require special attention.

THE "OLD" AND THE "NEW"

The field of labor economics has long been recognized as a legitimate area of study. But the content or subject matter of the field has changed rather dramatically in the past two decades or so. If you were to go to the library and examine a labor text published 15 or 20 years ago, you would find its orientation to be highly descriptive and historical. Its emphasis would be upon the history of the labor movement, a recitation of labor law and salient court cases, the institutional structure of labor unions, the scope and composition of collective bargaining agreements, and so forth. In short, the "old" study of labor was highly descriptive, emphasizing historical developments, facts, institutions, and legal considerations. A primary reason for this approach was that the aforementioned complexities of labor markets seemed to make them more or less immune to economic analysis. To be sure, labor markets and unemployment were accorded some attention, but the analysis was typically minimal and superficial.

This state of affairs has changed dramatically in recent years. Economists have achieved important analytical breakthroughs in studying labor markets and labor problems. As a result, economic analysis has tended to crowd out historical, institutional, legal, and anecdotal material. Labor economics increasingly has become applied micro and macro theory. The present volume focuses upon the techniques and understandings associated with the "new" labor economics. This is not to say, however, that all nonanalytical aspects of the field have been discarded. As noted earlier, the unique institutional features of labor markets are a part of the justification for a special field of economics devoted to labor. Yet the focal point of our approach is upon the application of economic reasoning to labor markets and labor issues. This orientation becomes evident as we now outline the subject matter of this book.

OVERVIEW

Before plunging into the details of specific topics, it is valuable to pause for a brief overview of our field of study. This overview is useful for two closely related reasons. First, it provides us with a sense of direction. More specifically, it reveals the logic underlying the sequence of topics which comprise each chapter. Second, the overview yields insights as to how the subject matter of any particular chapter relates to other chapters.

Figure 1-1 is helpful in presenting the overview. Reading from left to right, we note that most aspects of labor economics can be fitted without too much arbitrariness under the headings of "microeconomics" or "macroeconomics." As you probably remember from your principles course, *microeconomics* is concerned with the decisions of individual economic units and the functioning of specific markets. On the other hand, *macroeconomics* is concerned with the economy as a whole or with basic aggregates which comprise the economy. Hence, the determination of the wage rate and the level of employment in a particular market—carpenters in Oshkosh or retail clerks in Okoboji—are clearly microeconomic matters. In contrast, the consideration of the average level of real wages, the aggregate levels of employment and unemployment, and the overall price level are issues in macroeconomics. Because some topics straddle micro- and macroeconomics, the subject matter of individual chapters will sometimes pertain to both aspects of economics. However, it is fair to say that Chapters 2 to 15 address topics that are "mainly micro." Similarly, Chapters 16 to 19 are "mainly macro."

Figure 1-1 reemphasizes that microeconomics stresses the functioning of individual markets. The task of Chapters 2 to 6 is to develop and bring together the concepts which underlie labor supply and demand. Specifically, in Chapter 2 we examine the simple theory of labor supply from the perspective of an individual. Here we analyze the basic factors which determine whether or not a person will participate in the labor force and, if so, the number of hours that individual

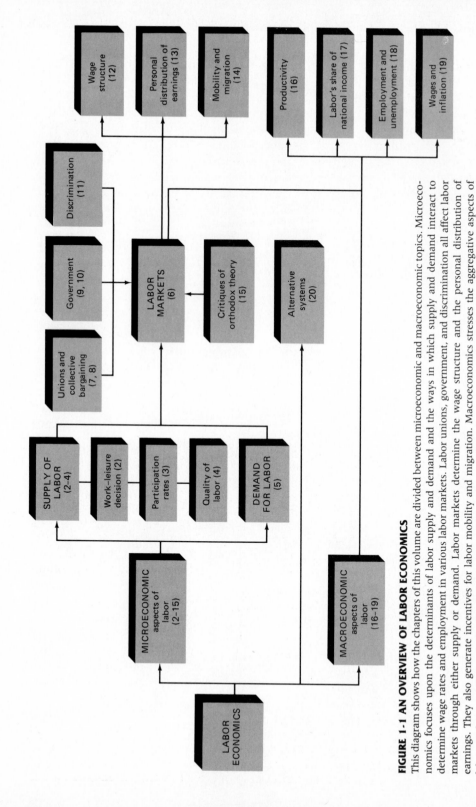

FIGURE 1-1 AN OVERVIEW OF LABOR ECONOMICS

This diagram shows how the chapters of this volume are divided between microeconomic and macroeconomic topics. Microeconomics focuses upon the determinants of labor supply and demand and the ways in which supply and demand interact to determine wage rates and employment in various labor markets. Labor unions, government, and discrimination all affect labor markets through either supply or demand. Labor markets determine the wage structure and the personal distribution of earnings. They also generate incentives for labor mobility and migration. Macroeconomics stresses the aggregative aspects of labor markets and, in particular, labor productivity, labor's share of the national income, the overall level of employment, and the impact of wages upon the price level.

would prefer to work. We also consider how various pay schemes and income maintenance programs might affect one's decision to supply labor services. In Chapter 3 we shift our attention from the individual to the household or family in order to better understand the labor supply decisions of various demographic groups, for example, married women, young males, prime-aged males, and older males. Our concern here is not only with secular trends in labor force participation, but also with the ways in which the business cycle affects decisions to work.

While Chapters 2 and 3 treat the supply of labor from a purely quantitative standpoint, Chapter 4 introduces a qualitative dimension to labor supply. A worker can provide more productive effort if he or she has more education and training. Hence, in Chapter 4 we examine the decision to invest in human capital—that is, in education and training—and explain why it is rational for different individuals to invest in different quantities of human capital.

We turn to the demand side of the labor market in Chapter 5. Here we systematically derive the short-run labor demand curve, explaining how the curve varies between a firm which is selling its product competitively and one which is not. The notion of a long-run demand curve is also explored, as is the concept of wage elasticity of demand.

Chapter 6 is a capstone chapter in that it combines labor supply and labor demand to explain how the equilibrium wage rate and level of employment are determined. An array of market models is presented, ranging from a basic perfectly competitive model to a relatively complex bilateral monopoly model. Given our earlier comments concerning the obvious importance of using scarce resources prudently, the emphasis in Chapter 6 is upon the efficiency with which labor is allocated. Is the "socially desirable" or "right" amount of labor employed in a particular labor market? If not, what is the efficiency loss to society?

As Figure 1-1 suggests, Chapters 7 to 11 focus upon a variety of real-world considerations that have a pervasive and profound impact upon the functioning of labor markets. Specifically, in these chapters we examine in some depth how labor unions, government, and discrimination affect the functioning of labor markets. Using the unionized models of labor markets in Chapter 6 as a springboard, Chapters 7 and 8 are concerned with unions and collective bargaining. In Chapter 7 we explore the demographics of trade union membership, discuss the size and institutional structure of the labor movement, note the unique characteristics of the collective bargaining transaction, and present a model of the bargaining process. Chapter 8 is devoted to the impact of unions and collective bargaining on the operation of labor markets. The discussion focuses upon the impact of unions upon wage rates, efficiency and productivity, and the distribution of earnings.

The direct and subtle ways by which government influences labor markets are the subject matter of Chapters 9 and 10. Chapter 9 considers government as a direct employer of labor and explores how government's fiscal functions affect labor markets. More specifically, we seek to determine how governmental expenditures and taxes alter the functioning of labor markets. In Chapter 10 our attention shifts to the impact of the legislative and regulatory functions of government upon labor markets. What are the implications, for example, of minimum wage legislation and regulations concerning worker health and safety?

In addition to labor unions and government, the "institution" of discrimination greatly affects labor markets. Thus Chapter 11 introduces several models of race and sex discrimination which enable us to see how discrimination might alter labor market results.

Looking to the far right of Figure 1-1, our attention moves from those factors which might alter labor market outcomes to those micro and macro outcomes per se. In Chapter 12 we confront the complex topic of the wage structure. Why do different workers receive different wages? We find that wage differences are traceable to such factors as the varying working conditions and skill requirements of jobs, differences in the human capital and job preference of workers, and imperfections in both worker mobility and the flow of job information. Attention is also given to the manner in which the wage structure changes secularly and cyclically.

The personal distribution of earnings is the subject of Chapter 13. Here we discuss alternative ways of portraying the overall earnings distribution and measuring the degree of observed inequality. We then offer explanations for the pattern of earnings and discuss related topics such as the degree of mobility within the earnings distribution and the impact of unions and government on inequality of earnings.

Chapter 14 examines the movement of labor that results from the information and incentives generated by labor markets. We discover that geographic mobility can be analyzed as an investment in human capital and that labor migration has a variety of economic ramifications.

Chapter 15 is a special chapter. While the present volume is predicated upon the notion that economic analysis is the most revealing approach to understanding the labor sector of our economy, this view is not universally accepted. Hence, we observe below the "labor markets" box of Figure 1-1 that the orthodox or mainstream economic analysis of this book is not without criticism. Chapter 15 is devoted to alternative conceptions of how labor markets work and, in particular, to institutional views of such markets. Here we summarize the "old" institutionalism of the immediate post-World War II era and present the "new" institutionalism of internal labor market theory. This logically leads to a discussion of the theory of dual or segmented labor markets. The common theme here is that economic forces are subordinate to institutional considerations in determining how labor markets function.

The remaining chapters deal primarily with macroeconomic aspects and outcomes of labor markets. In Chapter 16 we consider productivity for the important reason that the average level of real wages and, hence, living levels are intimately related to it. The factors which contribute to the growth of productivity are examined, as are the systematic changes in productivity which occur over the course of the business cycle. The relationship of changes in productivity to the price level and the level of employment are also explained.

Having considered the personal distribution of earnings in Chapter 13, our attention in Chapter 17 shifts to functional shares or, in simpler terms, the division of national income among wages, rent, interest, and profits. Our concern is naturally with labor's share. After noting some of the problems in measuring labor's share, we present three different models of labor's share and explain cyclical changes in labor's share.

The two core topics of the macroeconomics of labor are reserved for Chapters 18 and 19. Chapter 18 is devoted to the problem of unemployment. The procedures and problems associated with measuring aggregate unemployment and in defining full employment are first examined. An aggregate demand–aggregate supply model is then introduced to explain how the levels of employment and unemployment are determined. Distinctions are made between job search unemployment, structural unemployment, and cyclical unemployment. The distribution of unemployment by occupations and by demographic groups is considered, as are a variety of public policies designed to alleviate unemployment.

Chapter 19 addresses the difficult question of whether wage setting is a cause of inflation. Do wage increases cause higher prices? Or do wage increases merely transmit inflationary pressures whose ultimate causes are unrelated to labor markets? Both wage-push and demand-pull models of inflation are examined, and the impact of the inflationary expectations of workers is taken into account. The chapter concludes with a discussion of income policies, that is, wage-price guideposts and controls.

Contemporary labor economics also increasingly includes the study of alternative ways that labor resources are allocated globally. Chapter 20 examines one such alternative system—the Soviet Union. An understanding of how wages are determined and labor allocated in a centrally planned economy helps to deepen one's understanding of labor markets and labor problems in our own economy. Included are discussions of the relative freedom of Soviet workers, the use of wage differentials by planners in seeking the desired industrial and geographic allocation of labor, the role of Soviet labor unions, the impending labor shortage, labor productivity, and the status of Soviet women in the labor market.

Chapter 21 falls outside of Figure 1-1's overview, but is important to those who wish to stay apprised of future developments in labor economics and to continue their study of the field. The chapter lists and discusses sources of labor-related statistics; discusses bibliographic, technical, and nontechnical journals in the field; and cites advanced textbooks in labor economics along with books in the closely related fields of labor relations, collective bargaining, and labor law. Those doing term papers in labor economics will benefit by reading this chapter at the outset. Table 21-1 lists numerous potential term paper topics which may be of interest.

PAYOFFS

What benefits might you derive from studying labor economics? The payoffs from a basic understanding of the field may be both personal and social. On the one hand, labor economics yields information and develops analytical tools which may be useful in making personal and managerial decisions relevant to labor markets. Furthermore, a grasp of the field puts one in a better position as a citizen and voter to develop informed positions on labor market issues and policies.

At the personal level, the vast majority of readers will become labor market participants. Hence, many of the concepts embodied in this book which may seem to be somewhat abstract soon will become realities. Such issues as inflation, unemployment, migration, discrimination, unionism, and labor productivity, to enumerate only a few, will take on new meaning and relevance. For example, if you become a public schoolteacher or a state employee, what might you personally expect to gain in terms of salary and fringe benefits by unionization? To what extent does a college education contribute to higher earnings? That is, what rate of return can one expect from investing in higher education? What are the peculiarities of labor markets for college-trained workers? If you are a woman or member of a minority group, how might discrimination affect your access to specific occupations and your earnings? Similarly, a few of you will find yourselves in managerial positions with responsibilities for personnel and labor relations. The background and analytical perspective provided by an understanding of labor economics should be useful in making rational managerial decisions concerning the hiring, firing, promotion, training, and remuneration of workers.

From a social perspective a knowledge of labor economics should help make you a more informed citizen and more intelligent voter. The issues here are broad in scope and impact. Should unionization be encouraged or discouraged? Are unions on balance positive or negative forces in our society? Should wage increases be restricted by government persuasion or by law in the interest of curtailing inflation? How might a given change in the tax structure—for example, the change from a progressive to a flat-rate federal income tax—affect incentives to work? Should government subsidize worker mobility? Should United States immigration policies be liberalized or made more restrictive? Should "comparable worth" legislation be passed to guarantee that women and minorities are paid the same wages as white males receive on "comparable" jobs? Should formal education and vocational training be provided with more or less public support? Is a "teenwage" desirable? That is, is it a good idea to allow employers to pay wage rates to teenagers which are less than the legislated minimum wage? While detailed and definitive answers to such questions cannot be guaranteed, an understanding of labor economics should provide valuable insights which should be helpful in formulating your opinions on these and similar issues.

A final comment: The analytical approach of economic theory stressed herein does not make for an easy textbook. But we are convinced that this approach yields a far greater payoff—a deeper understanding of labor issues from both personal and social perspectives—than do available alternatives.

SUMMARY

1. The relative scarcity of labor and other productive resources provides an incentive for society to use such resources efficiently.
2. The importance of labor economics is reflected in (*a*) current socioeconomic issues and problems, (*b*) the quantitative dominance of labor as a resource, and (*c*) the unique characteristics of labor supply and demand.
3. In the past two decades the field of labor economics has put greater emphasis upon economic analysis and has deemphasized historical, institutional, and legal aspects.
4. This volume examines a series of pertinent microeconomic and macroeconomic topics as outlined in Figure 1-1.
5. An understanding of the content and analytical tools of labor economics contributes to more intelligent personal and social decisions.

QUESTIONS AND STUDY SUGGESTIONS

1. Key terms and concepts to remember: microeconomics; macroeconomics.
2. Why is economics a science of choice? Explain the kinds of choices which confront workers and employers in labor markets.
3. Why must the concepts of supply and demand as they pertain to product markets be modified when applied to labor markets?
4. What is the relative importance of labor as an economic resource?
5. Briefly compare the "old" and the "new" labor economics.
6. Briefly state your position on each of the following proposals:
    a. Women and minorities should be paid the same wage as white males, provided the work is comparable.
    b. The United States should close its boundaries to all immigration.
    c. The federal government should take measures to achieve the 4 percent unemployment rate specified by the Humphrey-Hawkins Act of 1978.
    d. So-called "right-to-work laws," which specify that workers who refuse to join unions cannot thereby be deprived of their jobs, should be repealed.
    e. Conditions of worker health and safety should be determined by the labor market, not by governmental regulation.
7. What benefits might accrue to you from studying labor economics?

SELECTED REFERENCES

ADDISON, JOHN T., and W. STANLEY SIEBERT: *The Market for Labor: An Analytical Treatment* (Santa Monica, Calif.: Goodyear Publishing Company, Inc., 1979), chap. 1.

FEARN, ROBERT M.: *Labor Economics: The Emerging Synthesis* (Cambridge, Mass.: Winthrop Publishers, Inc., 1981), intro.

FLEISHER, BELTON M., and THOMAS J. KNIESNER: *Labor Economics: Theory, Evidence, and Policy*, 3d ed. (Englewood Cliffs, N.J.: Prentice-Hall, Inc., 1984), chaps. 1–2.

T I M E   A N D   O N E - H A L F

THE CHOICE/THEORETIC ASSUMPTIONS

The "new" labor economics employs a choice/theoretic approach in analyzing labor market activity and outcomes. What are the implicit assumptions underlying this approach?

Contemporary labor economics employs theories of *choice* to analyze and predict the behavior of labor market participants and the micro- and macroeconomic consequences of labor market activity. Thus, it attempts to answer such questions as: Why do some prospective labor market participants choose to delay their labor force entry to attend college? Why do some people decide to work while others do not? Why do some employers choose to employ few workers and much capital while others select differing combinations? Why do employers lay off some workers during recessions but retain others?

Labor economists also examine the *outcomes* of the myriad of choices made in the labor market. Why do some workers earn $3.35 an hour while others are paid, say, $20 per hour? Why has the share of national income received by labor been relatively constant over the decades? Under what circumstances can wage determination contribute to inflation?

In short, contemporary labor economics focuses its attention on choices—why they are made and how they generate particular outcomes. It therefore is important to be aware of three implicit assumptions which underly this choice/theoretic approach.

1. *Relative scarcity.* Economists view land, labor, capital, and entrepreneurial resources as being scarce, or limited, relative to the many individual and collective wants in society. This relative scarcity dictates that society must choose how and for what purpose labor and other resources should be allocated. Similarly, individuals face a relative scarcity of time and spendable income. They must choose, for example, how much time to devote to jobs, to work in the home, and to leisure. They must choose how much present income (goods and services) to forgo for the prospect of obtaining higher future earnings. They must decide what to buy and, conversely, what not to buy. Relative scarcity—of time, personal income, and societal resources—then, is a basic element of the choice/ theoretic approach to labor economics.

2. *Purposeful behavior.* Because relative scarcity keeps us from having everything we want, we are forced to choose among alternatives. For every choice, say to work longer hours or to expand the number of people in the military, something is gained and something else is sacrificed. This sacrifice—forgone leisure, forgone private-sector output—is an *opportunity cost.*

The choice/theoretic approach assumes that people compare costs with expected benefits. For example, a worker will compare the extra utility (income) gained from added hours of work with the opportunity cost of the lost leisure. A firm will compare the added revenue from hiring a worker with the extra wage cost, and so forth. Thus, contemporary labor economics looks for purpose, or rationality, in labor market behavior and, for that matter, in labor market institutions. Relative scarcity necessitates that choices be made; the choice/theoretic approach assumes that these choices will be made purposefully, rather than randomly or in a chaotic way.

To say that labor market participants behave rationally, however, is not to say that they always achieve their intended goals. Information is imperfect or imperfectly processed, unforeseen events occur, choices made by others positively or adversely affect the outcomes of our own choices. But even those choices which in retrospect were "poor" choices are assumed to have been made on the *expectation* of net gain.

3. *Adaptability.* Because relative scarcity forces people to make choices, and because choices are made purposefully, labor market participants respond to changes in perceived costs and benefits. For example, some workers will adjust the number of hours they desire to work when the wage rate they receive changes. Fewer people will decide to obtain a specific skill when the cost of so doing rises or when the wage paid to those already possessing the skill falls. Firms will adjust their hiring when the demand for their product changes. Some workers will migrate from lower-paid regions to areas which have experienced a significant rise in labor demand and therefore in wage rates. Union officials will adjust their wage demands downward when the economy encounters recession and large portions of their members are unemployed. Restated, the choice/theoretic approach assumes that workers, employers, and other labor market actors *adapt, adjust,* or *alter* their behaviors in response to changes in expected costs and expected gains. Contemporary labor economics attempts to sort out these responses, to look for predictable patterns, and by so doing, to add to our understanding of an important element of the overall economy.

THE THEORY OF INDIVIDUAL LABOR SUPPLY

When viewed from the perspective of the economy as a whole, the concept of labor supply has many dimensions. As a glance ahead at Figure 3-1 indicates, the aggregate of labor services available to a society depends upon (1) the size and demographic composition of the population; (2) the labor force participation rate, that is, the percentage of the working-age population which is actually working or seeking work; (3) the number of hours worked per week or year; and (4) the quality of the labor force.

It is impractical to deal with all of these aspects of labor supply simultaneously. Hence, we want to restrict our focus. Because our subject matter is labor economics and not demography, we will be content to take the size and composition of the population as given.[1] The three other aspects of labor supply will be examined in Chapters 3 and 4. Chapter 3 is concerned primarily with participation rates, with some attention given to the long-term trends of the workweek and workyear. Chapter 4 is devoted to the quality of the work force. The present chapter focuses upon the basic theory of labor supply which is prerequisite to an understanding of all the various facets of labor supply.

More specifically, our discussion in this chapter is organized as follows. First, we introduce a basic model of work-leisure choice to understand the critical variables which determine an individual's optimum combination of work and leisure. Second, by manipulating the wage rate confronting the worker we use the basic model to derive a short-run labor supply curve for the individual. Third, we extend our basic model by delineating a number of applications. In particular, we explain the case of labor force nonparticipation, that is, the circumstances which might cause a person to choose zero hours of labor market work. Next, the implications of the situation in which the individual worker is confronted with a standard workday are discussed. Then we inquire whether different pay schemes affect the number of hours an individual might choose to work. And, finally, the basic model is modified to analyze the impact of an income maintenance program upon work incentives.

---

[1]There will be a few exceptions to this statement, for example, our later discussion of the international migration of labor.

THE WORK-LEISURE DECISION: BASIC MODEL

Imagine an individual with a certain amount of education and labor force experience and, therefore, a given level of skills. That individual, having a fixed amount of time at his or her disposal, is confronted with the decision as to how that time should be allocated among work ("labor market activity") and leisure ("nonlabor market activity"). The term "leisure" is used here in a broad sense to include all kinds of activities for which the person does not get paid, for example, work within the household and time spent on consumption, education, commuting, rest, relaxation, and so forth. In analyzing the work-leisure decision, we make the traditional assumption that the individual engages in work to obtain money and real income (goods and services) which provide utility. Similarly, we assume that all nonmarket activities—all uses of leisure—are sources of utility.

Two sets of information are necessary to determine the optimal distribution of an individual's time between work and leisure. First, we require *subjective* information concerning the individual's work-leisure preferences. This information is embodied in an **indifference map.** Secondly, we need the *objective* information which is reflected in a **budget constraint.**

Indifference Curves. As applied to the work-leisure decision, an *indifference curve shows the various combinations of real income and leisure time which will yield some given level of utility or satisfaction to the individual.* Curve I_1 in Figure 2-1 is illustrative. Note that we measure daily income on the vertical axis and hours of leisure, or nonlabor market activities, from left to right on the horizontal axis. The second horizontal axis simply reminds us that, given the fixed 24 hours available each day, we may measure the number of hours of work from right to left. According to the definition of indifference curves, each combination of income and leisure designated by any point on I_1 is equally satisfactory; that is, each point on the curve yields the same level of utility to the individual.

Why does the indifference curve slope downward? And why is it convex as viewed from the origin? It slopes downward because real income from work, on the one hand, and leisure, on the other, are both sources of utility or satisfaction. Hence, in moving southeast down the curve some amount of real income—that is, of goods and services—must be given up to compensate for the acquisition of more leisure in order for total utility to remain constant. But a downward-sloping curve can be concave, convex, or linear. An indifference curve is *convex* (bowed inward) to the origin; the absolute value of its slope diminishes as one moves down the curve. Why so? The answer is rooted in two considerations. First, the slope of the curve reflects an individual's subjective willingness to substitute between leisure and income. And, second, the individual's willingness to substitute leisure for income, or vice versa, varies with the amounts of leisure and income one initially possesses. In technical terms, the slope of an indifference curve is measured by the **marginal rate of substitution of leisure for income** (MRS L, Y). By definition, MRS L, Y is the amount of income one must give up to compensate for the gain of one more unit (hour) of leisure. Although the slope of the indifference curve shown in the figure is obviously negative, it is convenient to ignore the negative sign and think of the slope as an absolute value. In these terms, MRS *L, Y* is large—that is, the slope of the indifference curve is steep—in the northwest or upper left range of the curve. This is so because in this range the individual has much income and very little leisure. Hence, the subjective relative value of income is low at the margin and the subjective relative value of leisure is high at the margin. Therefore, the individual is willing to forgo a large number of units of income, say 4, for one additional unit of leisure. Mathematically, the ratio of the number of units of income forgone for each unit of leisure gained measures the slope of the curve. We observe that the slope of the northwest portion of the curve is steep, in this case ⁴/₁ or 4. That is, MRS *L, Y* is 4.

In moving down the indifference curve to the southeast, the quantities of income and leisure change at each point so that the individual now has less income and more leisure. This means that relatively abundant leisure now has less value at the margin and increasingly scarce income has more value at the margin. Hence, the individual is willing to forgo only a small amount of income—1 unit in this instance (Figure 2-1)—for an additional unit of leisure. MRS *L, Y*, or slope, is only ¹/₁ or 1. The slope, or MRS *L, Y*, is obviously smaller at some point on the indifference curve where the individual has more leisure and less income. The basic point is that MRS *L, Y*, which measures the slope of the indifference curve, declines as one moves down the curve. Any curve whose

FIGURE 2-1 AN INCOME-LEISURE INDIFFERENCE CURVE
The indifference curve shows the various combinations of income (goods) and leisure which yield some given level of total utility. The curve slopes downward because the additional utility associated with "more" leisure must be offset by "less" income in order that total utility remain unchanged. The convexity of the curve reflects a diminishing marginal rate of substitution of leisure for income.

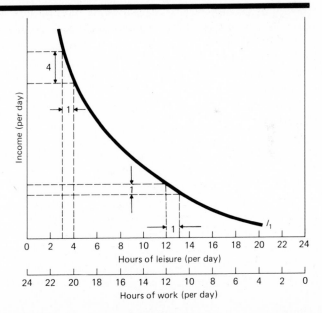

slope declines as one moves southeast along it is, by definition, convex to the origin.

It is both possible and useful to consider an indifference map, which is a whole family or field of indifference curves as shown in Figure 2-2. Each curve reflects some different level of total utility much like each contour line on a topographical map reflects a different elevation. Figure 2-2 illustrates only three of a potentially unlimited number of indifference curves. Every possible combination of income and leisure will lie on some indifference curve. Also, curves further from the origin indicate higher levels of utility. This can be demonstrated by drawing a 45° diagonal from the origin and noting that its intersection with each successive curve denotes larger amounts of *both* income and leisure. The y_2l_2 combination of income and leisure is preferred to the y_1l_1 combination because the former indicates larger amounts of *both* income and leisure. Similarly, the y_3l_3 combination entails greater total utility than does y_2l_2, and so on. It is evident that an individual will maximize his or her total utility by achieving a position on the highest attainable indifference curve.

It is important to note that, just as the tastes of various consumers for specific goods and services vary greatly, so do preferences for work and leisure. Thus Figure 2-2 is for a particular person with given work-leisure "tastes." Someone else who places a higher value on leisure (and a lower value on work) will have steeper indifference curves than does the individual we have portrayed. Conversely, the indifference curves of an individual who places a lower value on leisure (and a higher value on labor market work) will have flatter indifference curves than those shown in Figure 2-2.

FIGURE 2-2 AN INDIFFERENCE MAP FOR INCOME AND LEISURE
An indifference map is comprised of a number of indifference curves. Each successive curve to the northeast reflects a higher level of total utility.

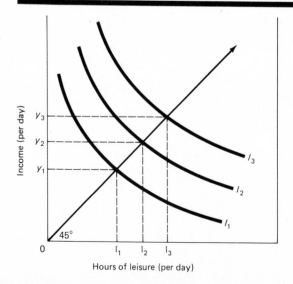

Budget Constraint. Our assertion that the individual maximizes utility by achieving a position on the highest *attainable* indifference curve implies that his or her choice of curves is constrained. Specifically, the individual is constrained by the amount of money income which she or he has available. Let us assume for the moment that an individual's only source of money income is from work, that is, from participating in the labor market. In other words, we are assuming the individual has no nonlabor income, no accumulated savings to draw upon, and no possibility of borrowing funds. Let us also make the reasonable assumption that the wage rate which confronts this person in the labor market is "given" in that the individual cannot alter the wage paid for his or her services by varying the number of hours worked.[2] Thus we can draw a ***budget (wage) constraint line*** which, by definition, *shows all the various combinations of income (goods) and leisure which a worker might realize or obtain, given the wage rate.* For example, if we suppose that the going wage rate is $1, we can draw a budget line from 24 hours on the horizontal leisure axis to $24 on the vertical income axis in Figure 2-3. That is, given the $1 wage rate, at the extremes an individual could obtain (1) 24 hours of leisure and no real income or (2) $24 worth of real

---

[2]This assumption permits us to deal with a linear budget constraint.

FIGURE 2-3 BUDGET CONSTRAINTS
A budget constraint (line) can be drawn for each possible wage rate. The wage rate determines the slope of each budget line. Specifically, budget lines fan out clockwise from the right origin as the wage rate increases.

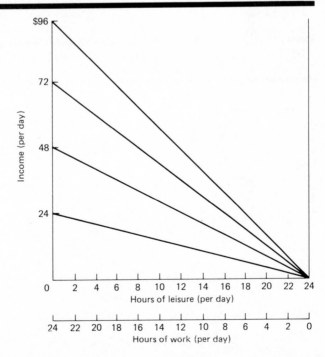

income and no leisure! The line connecting these two points reveals all other attainable options, for example, $8 of real income and 16 hours of leisure, $12 of income and 12 hours of leisure, and so forth. Observe that the absolute value of the slope of this budget line is 1, reflecting the $1 wage rate. In moving northwest along the line, 1 hour of leisure must be sacrificed to obtain each $1 of real income. This is true for the obvious reason that the wage rate is $1. Similarly, we note that, if the wage rate is $2, the appropriate budget line would be anchored at 24 hours of leisure and $48 of real income. The slope of this line is 2, again reflecting the wage rate. The budget constraints for wage rates of $3 and $4 are also shown in Figure 2-3. We observe that the budget lines fan out clockwise from the right origin as the wage rate goes up. It is very important to stress that in each case the wage rate—the slope of the budget line—reflects the "objective" or market rate of exchange between income and leisure. For example, if the wage rate is $1, an individual can exchange 1 hour of leisure (by working) and obtain $1 worth of real income. If the wage rate is $2, 1 hour of leisure can be exchanged in the labor market for $2 worth of real income. And so forth.[3]

Utility Maximization. The individual's optimum or utility-maximizing position can be determined by bringing together the subjective preferences embodied in

[3]In equation form the budget constraint is $Y = WH$, where Y = income, W = wage rate, and H = number of hours of work. Hence $Y = W(24 - L) = 24W - WL$, where L = number of hours of leisure and the slope of the budget line is $-W$.

FIGURE 2-4 UTILITY MAXIMIZATION: THE OPTIMUM CHOICE BETWEEN LEISURE AND INCOME
The optimum or utility-maximizing combination of leisure and income for the worker is at point u_1 where the budget constraint is tangent to the highest attainable indifference curve, I_2.

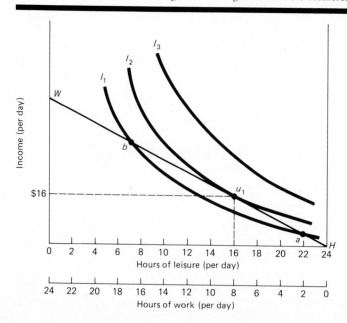

the indifference curves and the objective market information contained in each budget line. This is accomplished in Figure 2-4 where we assume that the wage rate is $2.

Recall that the farther the indifference curve is from the origin, the greater the person's total utility. Therefore, an individual will maximize total utility by attaining the highest possible indifference curve. Given the $2 wage rate, no leisure–real income combination is attainable outside—that is, to the north-east—of the resulting HW budget constraint. This particular budget constraint allows one to realize the highest attainable level of utility at point u_1 where the budget line just touches (is tangent to) indifference curve I_2. Of all the attainable positions on the various indifference curves, point u_1 is clearly on that curve which is farthest from the origin and therefore yields the highest achievable level of total utility. We observe that the individual will choose to work 8 hours, thereby earning a daily income of $16 and enjoying 16 hours of leisure. It is important to recognize that, at this optimum position, the individual and the market are in agreement as to the relative worth of leisure and real income at the margin. Put technically, at u_1 the slope of indifference curve I_2 and the slope of the budget line are equal. In other words, the individual's preferences are such that he or she is subjectively willing to substitute leisure for income at precisely the same exchange rate as the objective information of the labor market requires. The *optimum work-leisure position* is achieved where MRS L, Y (slope of the indifference curve) is equal to the wage rate (the slope of the budget line). By definition, these slopes are only equal at the point of tangency. The reader is urged to draw upon the above discussion to explain why attainable points a and b are *not* optimum positions.

Wage Rate Changes: Income and Substitution Effects. Will an individual choose to work more or fewer hours as the wage rate changes? It depends. Figure 2-5 (a) repeats the u_1 utility-maximizing position of Figure 2-4, but adds four more budget lines and indicates the relevant optimum positions associated with each. We observe that, for the wage rate increase which moves the budget line from W_1 to W_2, the optimum position moves from u_1 to u_2. The individual chooses fewer hours of leisure and, obviously, more hours of work. Similarly, the wage rate increase which shifts the budget constraint from W_2 to W_3 also entails more hours of work and fewer of leisure at u_3 than is the case at u_2. But the further wage rate boost reflected by the shift of the budget line from W_3 to W_4 produces an optimum at u_4 which involves less work and more leisure than the prior optimum u_3. Similarly, the wage increase depicted by the increase in the budget line from W_4 to W_5 causes a further reduction in hours of work at u_5. This analysis suggests that, for a specific person, *hours of work may for a time increase as wage rates rise, but beyond some point, further wage increases may lead to fewer hours of labor being supplied.* Indeed, we can translate the hours of work–wage rate combinations associated with the five optimum positions of Figure 2-5 (a) into a diagram such as shown in Figure 2-5 (b) which has traditional axes—wage rates on the vertical axis and hours of labor supplied measured left to right on the horizontal axis. In so doing we find that this individual's labor supply curve is forward-rising for a time and then backward-bending. This curve is known as a *backward-bending labor supply curve,* the forward-rising portion being expected or taken for granted. We can envision an individual labor supply curve for each person in the economy. But keep in mind that each individual's preferences for work versus leisure are unique, and hence the exact location, shape, and point of the backward bend of the curve varies from person to person.

Why is a backward-bending labor supply curve a realistic possibility? The possibility can be explained in terms of the income and substitution effects. When the wage rate increases, these two effects tend to alter one's utility-maximizing position. The *income effect* is based upon the fact that a higher wage rate means that a larger money income is obtainable from a given number of hours of work. We would expect an individual to use a part of this enhanced income to buy goods and services, for example, a new stereo, movie tickets, and so on. But if we make the reasonable assumption that leisure is a *normal good,* that is, a "good" of which more is consumed as income rises, then we can expect that a part of one's expanded income might be used to "purchase" leisure. It is obvious that consumers do not derive utility from goods alone, but from combi-

FIGURE 2-5 DERIVATION OF THE BACKWARD-BENDING LABOR SUPPLY CURVE

In (a) higher wage rates result in a series of increasingly steep budget lines whose tangencies with indifference curves locate a series of utility-maximizing positions. The movement from u_1 to u_2 and u_3 reveals that for a time higher wage rates are associated with longer hours of work, while the shifts from u_3 to u_4 and u_5 indicate that still higher wage rates entail fewer hours of work. The overall result is a backward-bending labor supply curve as shown in (b).

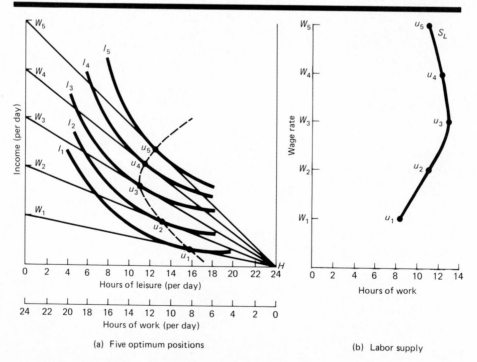

(a) Five optimum positions

(b) Labor supply

nations of goods and time. A stereo or movie tickets yield satisfaction only if one has the time to enjoy them. How does one "purchase" leisure or nonwork time? In a unique way: by working fewer hours. This means that when wage rates *rise,* and leisure is a normal good, the income effect reduces the number of hours one wants to work.[4]

The **substitution effect,** however, will tend to increase the optimum number of hours of work. When the wage rate increases, the relative price of leisure is altered. Specifically, an increase in the wage rate causes the "price" or opportunity cost of leisure to rise. Because the wage rate is higher, one will now forgo more income (goods) for each hour of leisure consumed (not worked). The basic theory of economic choice implies an individual will purchase less of any normal good when it becomes relatively more expensive. In brief, the higher price of leisure prompts one to consume less leisure or, in other words, to work more. The substitution effect merely reflects that, when wage rates rise and leisure becomes more expensive, it is sensible to substitute work for leisure. Hence, for a wage *increase,* the substitution effect causes the person to desire to work more hours.[5]

An alternative way to express the substitution effect is to say that a higher wage rate causes the "price of income" to fall since it now takes a smaller amount of work time to obtain $1 worth of goods. For example, when the wage rate is $2 per hour, the "price" of $1 worth of income is ½ an hour of work time. But if the wage rate increases to $4 per hour, the "price" of $1 worth of income falls to ¼ of an hour. Now that income is cheaper, it makes sense to purchase more of it. This purchase is made by working more hours and thereby taking less leisure.[6]

The overall effect of an increase in the wage rate upon the number of hours an individual wants to work depends upon the relative magnitudes of these two effects. Economic theory does not predict the outcome. If the substitution effect

---

[4]In mathematical terms:

$$\text{Income effect} = \frac{\Delta H}{\Delta Y}\ \Big|\ \bar{W} < 0$$

Where:
- H = hours of work
- Y = income
- $\bar{W}$ = constant wage

[5]In mathematical terms:

$$\text{Substitution effect} = \frac{\Delta H}{\Delta W}\ \Big|\ \bar{Y} > 0,$$

Where:
- H = hours of work
- W = wage
- $\bar{Y}$ = constant income

[6]The classic article is Lionel Robbins, "On the Elasticity of Demand for Income in Terms of Effort," *Economica,* June 1930, pp. 123–129.

dominates the income effect, the individual will choose to work more hours when the wage rate rises. Dominance of the substitution effect is reflected in shifts from u_1 to u_2 to u_3 in Figure 2-5 (a) and the upward-sloping portion of the labor supply curve in Figure 2-5 (b). But if the income effect is larger than the substitution effect, a wage increase will prompt the individual to work fewer hours. The movements from u_3 to u_4 and u_5 in Figure 2-5 (a) and the backward-bending portion of the labor supply curve in Figure 2-5 (b) are relevant in this case.

Note that the above discussion has been couched in terms of an *increase* in the wage rate. It is important to understand that the impact of the income and substitution effects upon hours of work is reversed if we assume a wage *decrease*. For a wage decline, the income effect increases hours of work. That is, a decline in the wage rate will reduce an individual's income from a given number of hours of work, and we can expect the individual to purchase less leisure and therefore choose to work more hours. Similarly, in terms of a wage decline, the substitution effect decreases work hours. A reduction in the wage rate makes leisure cheaper, prompting one to consume more of it. Once again, the final outcome depends upon the relative strength of the two effects.

Isolating Income and Substitution Effects. Figure 2-6 permits us to isolate graphically the income and substitution effects associated with a wage rate increase for a specific person. Remember that the substitution effect reflects the change in desired hours of work which is due solely to the fact that an increase in the wage rate alters the relative prices of income and leisure. Therefore, to isolate the substitution effect we must control for the increase in income created by the increase in the wage rate. Recall, too, that the income effect indicates the change in the hours of work which occurs solely because the higher wage rate means a larger total income from any number of hours of work. In portraying the income effect we must hold constant the relative prices of income and leisure.

Consider Figure 2-6. As the wage rate increases and shifts the budget line from HW_1 to HW_2, the resulting movement of the utility-maximizing position from u_1 on I_1 to u_2 on I_2 is the consequence of the combined income and substitution effects. The *income effect* is isolated by drawing the budget line nW' which is parallel to HW_1 and tangent to I_2 at point u_2'. The vertical distance Hn measures the amount of *nonlabor* income which would be required to make the individual just as well off (that is, attain the same total utility) at u_2' as at u_2. But by moving the individual from curve I_1 to curve I_2 with *nonlabor* income, we have left the wage rate, that is, the relative prices of leisure and goods, unchanged.[7] Hence, there is no substitution effect involved here. The movement from u_1 to u_2' therefore measures or isolates the income effect. As noted earlier, this effect reduces work hours when analyzed from the vantage point of an

---

[7]Note that the slopes of HW_1 and nW' are the same; that is, the lines are parallel. Hence, the wage rate embodied in both budget lines is the same.

increase in wage rates and hence in income. Specifically, the income effect would cause the individual to want to work $h_1 h_2'$ fewer hours.

The *substitution effect* is isolated as follows. The substitution effect is due solely to the fact that the slope of the budget line—the relative prices of income and leisure—has been altered by the assumed increase in the wage rate. We are concerned with budget lines nW' and HW_2 because their comparison involves no change in the individual's well being, that is, they pertain to the same indifference curve I_2. Line nW' however, reflects the original wage rate (also embodied in HW_1), while HW_2 mirrors the new higher wage rate. The movement from u_2' to u_2 on curve I_2 is the substitution effect. It is solely the result of a change in the relative prices of leisure and goods or, specifically, the fact that goods have become cheaper and leisure more expensive. It is no surprise that this prompts a substitution of work (goods) for leisure. For a wage rate increase, the substitution effect increases hours of work. In this case, the substitution effect would cause the individual to want to work $h_2' h_2$ more hours.

Keep in mind that the individual does not actually "move" to a new optimum position in two distinct steps, but rather goes directly from u_1 to u_2. We have conceptually isolated the income and substitution effects to stress that there are two ways in which a wage increase affects the worker: by increasing money income *and* by changing the relative prices of income (goods) and leisure.

FIGURE 2-6 THE INCOME AND SUBSTITUTION EFFECTS OF A WAGE RATE INCREASE
Assuming leisure is a normal good, the income effect associated with a wage increase will always reduce hours of work. It is shown here as a reduction in work time of $h_1 h_2'$ hours. The substitution effect, stemming from a rise in the wage rate, increases hours of work. The increase in hours of work of $h_2' h_2$ hours shows the substitution effect. In this instance the substitution effect outweighs the income effect, and the worker chooses to work $h_1 h_2$ additional hours as a result of the higher wage rate.

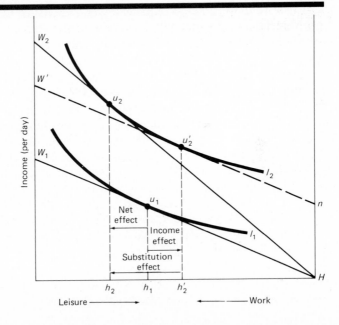

To summarize: In this instance the income effect is represented by the rightward horizontal movement from u_1 to u_2', that is, from Hh_1 to Hh_2' hours of work. The substitution effect is shown by the leftward horizontal movement from u_2' to u_2, that is, from Hh_2' to Hh_2 hours of work. In this case the substitution effect (increased work hours) is larger than the income effect (reduced work hours). The net effect is an increase in hours of work from Hh_1 to Hh_2; at the higher wage rate, the individual wants to work h_1h_2 additional hours. This individual is clearly on the upward-sloping segment of his or her labor supply curve; the wage rate and the desired hours of work are directly related. It is a worthwhile exercise for the reader to diagram and explain the case in which the income effect is larger than the substitution effect, causing the labor supply curve to be backward-bending. Question 3 at the end of this chapter also embodies a relevant exercise.

Rationale for Backward-Bending Supply Curve. From Figure 2-5 we remember that for a time wage rate increases are initially associated with the desire to work more hours. Specifically, for the wage increases which shift the budget line from W_1 through W_3, the absolute value of the substitution effects must be greater than that of the income effects, yielding the forward-rising segment of the labor supply curve. But further increases in the wage rate which shift the budget line from W_3 through W_5 are associated with the choice to work fewer hours. The income effects associated with these wage rate increases are greater than the substitution effects, yielding the backward-bending segment of the labor supply curve.

Question: What is the rationale for this reversal? The answer is that points u_1 and u_2 are at positions on indifference curves where the amount of leisure is large relative to the amount of income (goods). That is, u_1 and u_2 are located on relatively flat portions of indifference curves where MRS L, Y is small because the individual is willing to give up substantial amounts of leisure for an additional unit of income or goods. This means that the substitution effect is large—so large that it dominates the income effect. Hence, the individual's labor supply curve is forward-rising; higher wage rates induce more hours of work. But points $u_3, u_4,$ and u_5 are reached only after a substantial amount of leisure has been exchanged in the labor market for income. At these points the individual has a relatively large amount of income and relatively little leisure. This is reflected in the relative steepness of the indifference curves. In other words, MRS L, Y is large, indicating that the individual is only willing to give up a small amount of leisure for an additional unit of income. This means that the substitution effect is small and in this case is dominated by the income effect. Consequently, the labor supply curve of the individual becomes backward-bending; rising wage rates are associated with fewer hours of work.

Empirical Evidence. What do empirical studies reveal about labor supply curves? The evidence differs rather sharply between males and females. Specifically, Killingsworth made an exhaustive survey of empirical work which led him to the conclusion that "male labor supply is much less sensitive to wage changes than is female labor supply. Indeed, the male labor supply curve appears to be gently backward bending with respect to the wage, whereas the female schedule . . . is strongly positive sloped."[8] Apparently for men the income effect slightly dominates the substitution effect when wage rates rise. For women the substitution effect seems to dominate substantially the income effect.

Individual studies report various magnitudes of the labor supply responses of males and females. However, a careful review of nine empirical studies has led Borjas and Heckman to estimate that a 10 percent *increase* in male wage rates would *decrease* the amount of labor supplied by approximately 1 to 2 percent.[9] Keeley has offered the same general estimate for males as have Borjas and Heckman, but also suggests that a 10 percent increase in wages would increase the hours of work of married women by about 10 percent.[10]

How might one explain the apparent differences in the labor supply responses of males and females to a wage change? The answer may have to do with traditional differences in the use of nonlabor-market time by men and married women. Specifically, for many married women work in the home and in the labor market are highly substitutable. That is, household work may be accomplished by doing it oneself *or* by working in the labor market and using a portion of one's earnings for hiring housecleaning help, babysitters, and so forth. Thus when wage rates increase, a relatively large number of married women substitute labor market work for work in the home. In other words, a strong substitution effect occurs which implies an upward-sloping labor supply curve for married women. Most males, however, have traditionally performed very limited work within the home. Hence, for such men the choice in response to a wage rate increase is between labor market work and leisure, which are less substitutable than labor market work and household work. The result is a smaller substitution effect for men and a nearly vertical or perhaps backward-bending labor supply curve.

Elasticity versus Changes in Labor Supply. To this point, we have been discussing the extent to which wage changes cause an individual to alter the hours of work which he or she wishes to supply. Stated differently, our discussion has focused on the wage elasticity of labor supply. More precisely, wage elasticity is defined as follows:

[8]Mark R. Killingsworth, *Labor Supply* (Cambridge: Cambridge University Press, 1983), p. 102. Also see Michael C. Keeley, *Labor Supply and Public Policy* (New York: Academic Press, 1981), chap. 4.

[9]George J. Borjas and James J. Heckman, "Labor Supply Estimates for Public Policy Evaluation," *Proceedings of the Industrial Relations Research Association* (Madison, Wis.: Industrial Relations Research Association, 1978), p. 331.

[10]Keeley, op. cit., p. 104. However, Link and Settle have suggested that the labor supply curves of married nurses might be backward-bending. See Charles R. Link and Russell F. Settle, "Wage Incentives and Married Professional Nurses: A Case of Backward Bending Supply?", *Economic Inquiry*, January 1981, pp. 144–156.

$$E_s = \frac{\text{percentage change in quantity of labor supplied}}{\text{percentage change in the wage rate}} \qquad (2\text{-}1)$$

Over specific ranges of an individual's labor supply curve, the elasticity coefficient given in equation (2-1) may be zero (perfectly inelastic), infinite (perfectly elastic), less than one (relatively inelastic), greater than one (relatively elastic), or negative (backward-bending). The elasticity will depend on the relative strengths of the income and substitution effects *generated by a wage rate change*. But these movements *along* an existing individual labor supply curve should not be confused with *shifts* in the entire supply curve. These shifts—increases or decreases in labor supply—occur in response to changes in either of two factors which we have heretofore held constant. First, changes in *nonlabor income* may shift an individual's labor supply curve. For example, receiving a large inheritance, qualifying for a pension, or becoming eligible for welfare benefits may shift one's labor supply curve leftward, that is, cause a decrease in labor supply. Or conversely, the layoff of one's spouse or a significant decline in dividend income may produce an increase (rightward shift) in labor supply. Second, a change in a person's *indifference map*—that is, in work-leisure preferences—may cause a shift in the labor supply curve. For example, an improvement in working conditions, availability of child care, or large medical bills may change one's indifference map in ways that increase a person's labor supply. Working in the opposite direction, the purchase of a product which requires leisure to enjoy or the attainment of a culturally acceptable retirement age may alter one's indifference map such that labor supply declines.

To summarize: As Figure 2-5 suggests, given work-leisure preferences and nonlabor income, a change in wage rates traces out or locates the individual's labor supply curve. The elasticity of this curve for any particular wage change—that is, the sensitivity of hours one wants to work to a change in wages—depends upon the relative sizes of the income and substitution effects. In contrast, changes in work-leisure preferences or in nonlabor income cause the location of one's labor supply curve to change.

APPLYING AND EXTENDING THE MODEL

The basic model just developed outlines the logic of the work-leisure decision, provides a rationale for an individual's backward-bending labor supply curve, and helps us understand changes in labor supply. Our goal now is to extend, embellish, and apply the basic work-leisure model. Specifically, we want to show that the work-leisure model is useful in delineating reasons for nonparticipation in the labor force, in explaining how a standard workweek might cause certain workers to feel overemployed or underemployed, and in comparing the impact which various pay schemes and income maintenance programs might have upon work incentives.

Nonparticipants. Figure 2-7 portrays the case of a nonparticipant, that is, an individual who decides *not* to be in the labor force. Note the following characteristics in Figure 2-7. First, the person's indifference curves are very steep, indicating that leisure (nonmarket time) is valued very highly relative to income. Stated technically, the marginal rates of substitution of leisure for income are high, meaning that the individual is very willing to forgo real income for leisure or nonlabor market time. This might reflect the preferences of, say, a 20-year-old who deems it important to devote time and efforts to attending college. Second, we note the availability of nonlabor income HN. Perhaps this takes the form of an "intrahousehold transfer" to the young student from the earned income of his or her parents. Finally, the relative flatness of the NW budget line indicates that the wage rate which this individual can earn in the labor market is relatively low. For example, the student may have modest skills and little or no labor market experience and therefore is not yet able to command a high wage rate by working.

The optimum position in Figure 2-7 is based on the same principle employed in Figure 2-4: Choose that position which puts one on the highest attainable indifference curve. In this case the highest level of utility is achieved at point

FIGURE 2-7 NONPARTICIPATION: THE COLLEGE STUDENT
A very high subjective evaluation of nonwork time (reflected in steep indifference curves), the availability of nonlabor income (HN), and low earning ability (NW is relatively flat) are all factors which are conducive to not participating in the labor force.

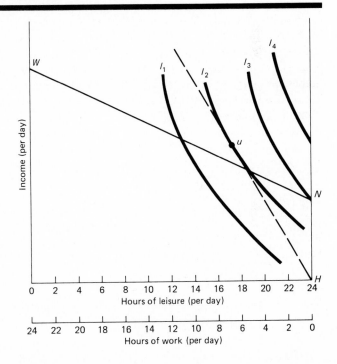

N. Here the budget constraint *HNW* touches I_3. At this point the individual is *not* participating in the labor market; all of this person's time is devoted to nonlabor market activities. The technical reason is that, at all points within the axes to the diagram, the person's indifference curves are more steeply sloped than is the budget constraint. In other words, at all points within the diagram the individual values leisure (nonlabor market time) more highly at the margin than does the market. Note that, in contrast to Figure 2-4, the optimum outcome at *N* is *not* a tangency position, but rather is a "corner" solution. At *N* the wage rate is less than MRS *L,Y*, which means that the individual values nonlabor market time more highly than does the market. But, given the fact that the individual is a nonparticipant, there is no further possible substitution of leisure for work to be made.

The importance of low earning capacity in the labor market and the availability of nonlabor income can be understood if we replace the original budget line *HNW* in Figure 2-7 with the broken line from the right origin. This new budget line reduces nonlabor income to zero *and* assumes a much higher wage rate can be garnered in the labor market. Suppose, for example, that our student is a highly skilled computer programmer who has immediate employment opportunities at a high wage. Or, to make the point even more graphic, suppose that the student is a premier college basketball player who is sought by the National Basketball Association. We find that under these new conditions the individual would prefer to participate in the labor force. The optimum position will now be at *u* where the person will want to work 6 or 7 hours per day.

Figure 2-8 illustrates another common instance of nonparticipation in the labor force. Here we assume that a rather elderly worker is initially participating in the labor force, working about 9 hours per day at optimum position *u* on indifference curve I_1. Suppose now that when the worker reaches age 65 a private or public pension of *HN* becomes available, *provided* the individual retires fully from work. In other words, the choice is between budget line *HW* and the associated optimum position at *u or* budget line *NN'* and the corner solution at point *N*. Obviously, *N* is preferable to *u* because it is associated with the higher indifference curve, I_2. In this case the availability of a pension—for example, social security benefits—induces the individual to become a nonparticipant. Stated differently, it shifts his or her labor supply curve leftward such that no labor is supplied at the market wage. Note that the decision to be a nonparticipant entails a *reduction* in money income, but a more than compensating *increase* in leisure. The individual is better off at *N* than at *u*, even though he or she has less income.

Empirical research confirms several generalizations which can be inferred from our discussions of Figures 2-7 and 2-8. First, other things being equal, full-time college attendance *is* a deterrent to labor force participation. This is also true of such things as the personal desire to provide child care to one's preschool children. Stated alternatively, those who attach great marginal utility to nonlabor market time (college attendance, child care) are more likely to be nonparticipants in the labor force. Second, other things being the same, the higher the nonlabor income available to a person from parents, spouses, social security pensions, private pensions, welfare, and other sources, the less likely it is the person will be a labor force participant. Finally, all else being equal, the greater the opportunity cost of not working—that is, the higher the wage one could obtain in the labor market—the more likely it is a person will be a labor force participant.[11]

Standard Workday: Overemployment and Underemployment.
Our discussion thus far has implicitly assumed that each worker can determine the number of hours he or she works. This is typically not the case. What may happen when

[11]Numerous studies confirm these conclusions. For example, for a listing and review of the studies which examine the impact of social security (nonlabor income) on the participation decision, see Sheldon Danziger, Robert Haveman, and Robert Plotnick, "How Income Transfers Affect Work, Savings, and the Income Distribution," *Journal of Economic Literature*, September 1981, pp. 975–1028. This source also surveys studies on the labor supply impact of other sources of nonlabor income such as disability payments, unemployment compensation, and Aid to Families with Dependent Children benefits. For an analysis of the impact of preschool children, education (market wage), and husband's income on the labor force participation of married females, see T. Aldrich Finegan, "Participation of Married Women in the Labor Force," in Cynthia B. Lloyd, (ed.), *Sex, Discrimination, and the Division of Labor* (New York: Columbia University Press, 1975), pp. 30–31.

FIGURE 2-8 NONPARTICIPATION: PENSIONS AND THE ELDERLY
An elderly worker whose wage rate yields the budget line *HW* will be a labor force participant at *u*. However, when a pension of *HN* becomes available at, say, age 65, the individual will prefer to become a nonparticipant at point *N*.

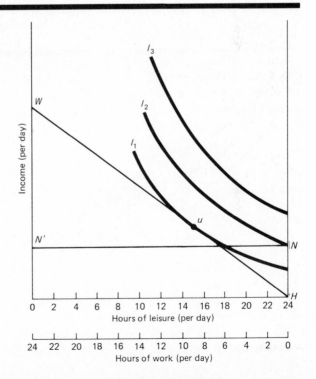

a worker is confronted with a standard workday of *HD* hours as illustrated in Figure 2-9? Consider first the solid indifference curves for Smith shown in the lower right-hand portion of the diagram. Smith's optimum position is at u_s where he prefers to work only Hh_s hours per day. But this is not a relevant choice; Smith can either work *HD* hours or not at all. That is, the relevant choice is between working the standard workday at *P* or being a nonparticipant at *N*. What to do? In this instance, it is preferable to work the standard workday for the simple reason that it entails a higher indifference curve, I_{s2}, as opposed to I_{s1}. Note once again that this is not a tangency position. At *P* the slope of I_{s2} is greater than the slope of the budget line *NW*. In technical terms the marginal rate of substitution of leisure for income exceeds the wage rate, which means that the worker values leisure more highly at the margin than does the market. Clearly Smith would be better off at u_s with more leisure and less work per day. Simply put, at point *P* Smith will feel **overemployed.** Faced with a standard workday which denies him added leisure, Smith may compensate by engaging in absenteeism; he may more or less habitually miss a day of work every week or so. In fact, 1 in 15 workers is absent at least one day during a typical week in the United States. Many of these workers are absent without pay. Or, this worker may have a relatively high rate of job turnover. The worker obtains more leisure by frequently being "between jobs." Of course, we have purposely ruled out the possibility of part-time employment, which would obviously appeal to this overemployed worker.

FIGURE 2-9 OVEREMPLOYMENT AND UNDEREMPLOYMENT

When confronted with a standard workday of *HD*, Smith (solid indifference curves) will feel overemployed while Jones (broken indifference curves) will feel underemployed.

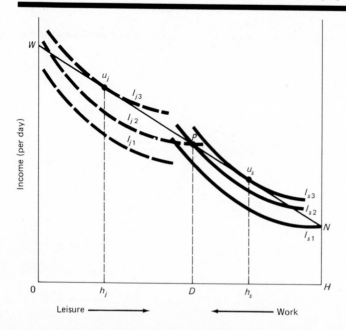

The broken indifference curves in the upper left-hand portion of Figure 2-9 portray the position of Jones, an **underemployed** worker. Jones would prefer to be at u_j where she would work the long work day of Hh_j hours as opposed to the shorter standard work day of HD hours. Note again that P is not a tangency position. At P the slope of Jones' indifference curve I_{j2} is less than the budget line. Jones' marginal rate of substitution of leisure for income is less than the wage rate. Simply stated, at the margin Jones values leisure less highly than does the market. This means that Jones will feel *underemployed* at P. Jones may realize her desire for more work and less leisure by "moonlighting," by taking a second job. The reader should use Figure 2-9 to demonstrate that Jones might be willing to take a second job even if the wage rate were less than that paid on the primary job. In fact over 5 million workers—approximately 5 percent of total employees—currently moonlight.

Premium Pay versus Straight Time. While we ordinarily think of a worker receiving the same wage rate regardless of the number of hours worked, this is not always the case. Indeed, the Fair Labor Standards Act of 1938 specifies that those workers covered by the legislation must be paid a premium wage—specifically, time and one-half—for hours worked in excess of 8 per day or 40 per week. What impact does this premium pay provision have upon the work-leisure decision? And how does it compare with a straight-time equivalent wage rate which provides an identical daily or weekly income from the same number of hours of work? Does it make any difference with respect to work incentives to pay $4 per hour for the first 8 hours of work and $6 per hour for an additional 2

FIGURE 2-10 PREMIUM WAGES AND STRAIGHT-TIME EQUIVALENT
Premium wage rates for overtime work will be conducive to more hours of work (Hh_2) than will a straight-time wage rate which would yield an equivalent daily income (Hh_3).

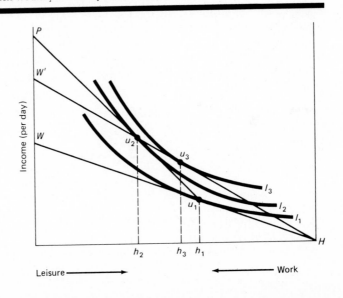

hours of overtime *or* to pay $4.40 per hour for each 10 hours of work? Since both payment plans yield the same daily income of $44, one is inclined to conclude it makes no difference. But with the aid of Figure 2-10, we find that it *does* make a difference.

We assume in Figure 2-10 that a worker is initially at the optimum point u_1 where HW is tangent to indifference curve I_1. At u_1 the individual chooses to work Hh_1 hours which we will presume to be the standard workday. Let us now suppose that the employer offers additional hours of overtime work at premium pay. This renders the u_1W segment of HW irrelevant and the budget constraint now becomes Hu_1P. We observe that the optimum position will move to u_2 on the higher indifference curve I_2 and that the worker will choose to work h_1h_2 additional hours. Daily earnings will be u_2h_2.

Consider now the alternative of a straight-time equivalent wage, that is, a standard hourly wage rate which will yield the same daily income of u_2h_2 for the Hh_2 hours of work. The straight-time equivalent wage can be shown by drawing a new budget line HW' through u_2. The budget lines Hu_1P and HW' will both yield the same money income of u_2h_2 for Hh_2 hours of work. The important point is that if confronted with HW', the worker will want to move from u_2 to a new optimum position at u_3 where fewer hours are worked. Stated differently, at u_2 indifference curve I_2 cuts HW' from above; that is, MRS L,Y is greater than the wage rate. This means that the worker subjectively values leisure more highly at the margin than does the market, and hence, u_2 is no longer the optimum position under a straight-time pay arrangement; our worker will feel overemployed when working Hh_2 hours on a straight-time pay plan (recall Figure 2-9). Conclusion: Premium wage rates for overtime work will call forth more hours of work than will a straight-time wage rate which yields the same income at the same number of hours as that actually chosen by an individual paid the overtime premium. Why the difference? The use of premium pay will have a relatively small income effect because it applies only to hours worked in excess of Hh_1. In comparison the straight-time equivalent wage will have a much larger income effect because it applies to *all* hours of work.[12] In simpler terms, Figure 2-10 is essentially the labor market analog of price discrimination in the product market. You might recall from elementary economics that the seller of a product can obtain more revenue by charging different prices for different quantities of output. In the present analysis we are simply observing that an employer can obtain a greater amount of labor for a given outlay by paying different wage rates for different hours of work.[13]

---

[12]Figure 2-10 is drawn so that for the straight-time equivalent wage the substitution effect dominates the income effect, and therefore, the individual is on the forward-rising portion of his labor supply curve. This is the reason u_3 entails more hours of work than does u_1. Such an outcome is not necessary. The diagram could have been drawn so that u_3 was to the right of u_1, in which case our basic conclusion would be even more evident.

[13]Kenneth E. Boulding, *Economic Analysis*, vol. 1, 4th ed. (New York: Harper & Row, Publishers, 1966), p. 616. Our conclusion holds only if we restrict the employer from hiring additional workers.

Income Maintenance Programs. Let us now consider the possible effects of *income maintenance programs* upon work incentives.

Three basic features. Although details vary greatly, most income maintenance programs in the United States—for example, Old Age and Survivors Insurance, Aid to Families with Dependent Children, and food stamps—have three basic features.

1. *The income guarantee or basic benefit, B.* This is the amount of public subsidy an individual or family would be paid if no earned income was received.[14]

2. *The benefit-loss rate, t.* This refers to the rate at which a family's basic benefit is reduced as earned income increases. For example, if *t* is .50, then a family's basic benefit will be reduced by $.50 for every $1.00 of wage income earned. This obviously means that, if the market wage rate is $5.00, the family's *net* wage rate will be just $2.50 when the benefit-loss provision is taken into account. The critical point is that the benefit-loss rate reduces one's net gain from work. Economists often refer to the benefit-loss rate as an "implicit tax rate" because *t* has the same impact upon the net income of a person participating in an income maintenance program as income tax rates have upon the earnings of individuals not in the program.

3. *The break-even level of income, Y_b.* The basic benefit and the benefit-loss rate permit the calculation of the break-even level of income. This is the level of earned income at which the actual subsidy payment received by an individual or family becomes zero. Stated differently, it is that level of earned income at which an individual is dropped from an income maintenance program. As we shall see in a moment, the break-even income depends upon the sizes of the basic benefit and the benefit-loss rate.

A simple numerical illustration might be helpful in relating these concepts to one another. The *actual subsidy payment, S,* received by an individual can be determined by the following formula:

$$S = B - tY \qquad (2\text{-}2)$$

Where:

B = basic benefit
t = benefit-loss rate
Y = level of earned income

Thus, for example, if B is $2000, t is .50, and Y is $2000, then the actual subsidy payment received will be $1000. That is:

$$\$1000 = \$2000 - .50(\$2000)$$

---

[14]We simplify by assuming that no nonwage income in the form of, say, interest or dividends is received.

Furthermore, the break-even level of income can be calculated quite readily. A glance back at equation (2-2) suggests that S will become zero—that is, the break-even income will be reached—when earned income Y is equal to B/t.[15] For our illustrative numbers, B is \$2000 and t is .50, so B/t—the break-even level of income—is therefore \$2000/.50 or \$4000. We verify this by substituting the relevant numbers into equation (2-2):

$$\$0 = \$2000 - .50 \ (\$4000)$$

Let us now incorporate these concepts into Figure 2-11 to examine the impact of an income maintenance program upon work incentives. The HW line shows us the budget constraint confronting the individual in the absence of an income maintenance program. The resulting optimum position is at u_1. For

[15]The algebra is simple. By setting $S = 0$ in equation (2-2) we get:

$$0 = B - tY$$

Therefore:

$$tY = B \text{ and } Y = B/t$$

FIGURE 2-11 INCOME MAINTENANCE AND INCENTIVES TO WORK
An income maintenance program which incorporates both a basic benefit and a benefit-loss rate will alter the budget constraint from HW to HBY_bW. This alteration moves the utility-maximizing position from u_1 to u_2 and thereby reduces hours of work.

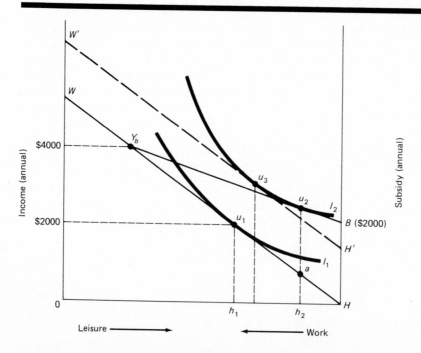

simplicity's sake let us assume that the wage rate is $1.00 per hour and that the individual chooses to work 40 hours per week. Over the 50-week workyear his or her earned income would be $2000 as shown on the left, vertical axis. Now suppose that an income maintenance program with the characteristics just described is enacted. The impact of this program is to change the budget constraint from HW to HBY_bW. Note that HB on the right vertical axis is the basic benefit; it is the amount of income subsidy the individual would receive if he or she had no earned income. The BY_b segment of the new budget constraint reflects the influence of the benefit-loss rate. Specifically, the slope of the BY_b segment is measured by the *net* wage rate, that is, the market wage rate as it is reduced by the benefit-loss rate. Thus, while the absolute value of the slope of HW is 1.00 (reflecting the $1.00 wage rate), the slope of BY_b is only .50 (reflecting the $.50 *net* wage rate).[16] The vertical distance between HW and BY_b is equal to S, the actual subsidy received. Point Y_b indicates the break-even level of income because at this point the individual's earned income is sufficiently large ($4000 in this case) so that the application of the .50 benefit-loss rate causes the actual subsidy payment S to become zero [see equation (2-2)].

We observe in Figure 2-11 that the new optimum position is at u_2 where HBY_bW is tangent to indifference curve I_2. While the individual's total money income has obviously increased (from h_1u_1 to h_2u_2), *earned* income and the number of hours worked have both declined (from h_1u_1 to h_2a and from Hh_1 to Hh_2, respectively). In our earlier analysis of a wage *increase* (Figure 2-6) we found that the net effect upon hours of work (work incentives) depended upon the relative sizes of the income effect (reduction in hours of work) and the substitution effect (increase in hours of work). *In the present case the income and substitution effects both reduce hours of work.* The tendency for the income effect to reduce hours of work is no surprise. The income maintenance program increases money income and, assuming leisure is a normal good, some of that income is "spent" on leisure and therefore fewer hours are worked. But, curiously, the substitution effect also reduces hours of work. The reason is that the presence of the benefit-loss rate *reduces* the *net* wage rate; that is, it makes BY_b flatter than HW. Even though the basic benefit raises total money income, the benefit-loss feature means there has been an effective decrease in wage rates. This means that leisure is now cheaper—one sacrifices only $.50 by not working an hour rather than $1.00—and therefore leisure is substituted for work.

Recalling our earlier diagrammatic separation of the income and substitution effects (Figure 2-6), we can draw the broken line $H'W'$ parallel to HW and tangent to I_2 at u_3. The horizontal distance between u_1 and u_3 is the income effect, and the horizontal distance between u_3 and u_2 is the substitution effect. We observe that both tend to reduce the amount of work supplied.

---

[16]As noted, the slope of BY_b reflects the *net* wage rate w_n, which is the wage rate w multiplied by $(1 - t)$; that is, $w_n = (1 - t)w$. In our example the slope of BY_b is .50 = $(1 - .5)1$. If the benefit-loss rate were .25, the net wage rate and slope of BY_b would be .75 = $(1 - .25)1$. If the benefit-loss rate were 1.00, BY_b would be horizontal.

Controversy. The various income maintenance programs have long been surrounded by controversy. This stems in part from fundamental ideological differences among policy makers. But it also reflects the fact that the accepted goals of income maintenance programs tend to be in conflict with one another and that it is easy to disagree as to the proper or "optimum" tradeoffs. In particular, it is generally agreed that income maintenance programs should (1) effectively get poor people out of poverty, (2) maintain incentives to work and (3) achieve goals 1 and 2 at a "reasonable" cost. Figure 2-11 is a useful point of reference in explaining these goal conflicts.

Our analysis of Figure 2-11 has just made it clear that goals 1 and 2 are in conflict. The imposition of an income maintenance program triggers income and substitution effects, both of which are negative with respect to work. Furthermore, we might improve the effectiveness of the program in eliminating poverty by increasing the basic benefit, that is, by shifting the BY_b line upward in Figure 2-11. But this will clearly make the program more costly. On the one hand, a larger basic benefit would relocate point Y_b to the northwest on line HW and thereby cause additional families to be eligible for subsidies. On the other hand, with a higher basic benefit, people already in the income maintenance program will each receive larger subsidy payments. Goal 1 conflicts with goal 3. Finally, given the basic benefit, one might want to reduce the benefit-loss rate—that is, increase the slope of BY_b line—in order to stimulate incentives to work. A reduction in the benefit-loss rate increases the net wage rate, thereby boosting the "price" of leisure and inducing the substitution of work for leisure. The higher net wage rate may also prompt individuals who are currently not in the labor force to become participants (see Figure 2-7). However, the resulting increase in the slope of the BY_b line will extend point Y_b to the northwest along HW, making more families eligible for subsidies and therefore increasing program costs. An increase in the slope of the BY_b line will also boost costs by increasing the actual subsidy received for any given number of hours worked. Goal 2 conflicts with goal 3.

Evidence. Several direct experimental tests of the impact of income maintenance programs upon labor supply were conducted in the late 1960s and throughout the 1970s. The first of these was the New Jersey–Pennsylvania experiment in which 1216 "intact" households were selected to participate. During the 1967–1969 period, a portion of these families were selected as an experimental group and were subjected to eight different income maintenance plans wherein basic benefits ranged from 50 to 125 percent of poverty levels and benefit-loss rates varied from 30 to 70 percent. The remaining families received no income transfers from the plan and were used only as a control group.

The initial analysis of the experiment found that (1) hours worked per week by males declined an average of 2.4 hours for whites and 7.3 hours for Spanish-speaking persons but actually *increased* slightly for blacks; (2) the labor force participation rate of wives declined by 20 percent; and (3) at the 50 percent benefit-loss rate, the overall reduction in labor supply was approximately 7 percent. Subsequent analysis of the experimental data found that the work hour reduction for white males was about 5 to 7 hours per week, rather than in the lower 2 to 3 range.[17]

The New Jersey–Pennsylvania experiment had numerous shortcomings. For example, it focused only on "intact" families when in fact much poverty is concentrated in families headed by a single parent. Also, participants understood the program to be temporary, and actual subsidy payments were too small to support large families adequately. It is likely that the temporary character of the income subsidies prompted individuals to retain their labor market ties to a greater extent than if the subsidies were permanent. Furthermore, the state of New Jersey liberalized its eligibility for welfare payments during the income supplement test. As a result of these shortcomings and a desire to ascertain more about labor supply responses, three similar experiments were carried out. The experiments in rural North Carolina and Iowa (1970–1972); Gary, Indiana (1971–1974); and Seattle and Denver (1970–1976 in Seattle; 1971–1981 in Denver) tested differing income supplement schemes, populations, and support services. The Time and One-Half segment of this chapter summarizes the findings from the Seattle-Denver experiments.

SUMMARY

1. In the work-leisure choice model an indifference curve shows the various combinations of real income and leisure which will yield a given level of utility to an individual. Indifference curves are convex to the origin, reflecting a diminishing marginal rate of substitution of leisure for income. Curves further from the origin indicate higher levels of utility.
2. The budget (wage) constraint line shows the various combinations of real income and leisure which are obtainable at a given wage rate. The absolute value of the slope of the budget line reflects the wage rate.
3. The individual achieves an optimum or utility-maximizing position by selecting that point which puts him or her on the highest attainable indifference curve.
4. Changing the wage rate and observing predicted changes in one's optimum position suggest the possibility of a backward-bending individual labor supply curve.
5. The impact of a wage change upon hours of work depends upon the size of the income and substitution effects. The income effect measures that portion of a total change in desired hours of work which is due solely to the change in real income caused by the wage change. The substitution effect is the portion of a total change in desired hours of work which is due solely to the wage rate change, the level of real income or utility being held constant. For a wage increase (decrease) the income

---

[17] For a review of the earlier New Jersey—Pennsylvania findings see Harold W. Watts and Albert Rees (eds.), *The New Jersey Income-Maintenance Experiment*, vol. 2: *Labor Supply Responses* (New York: Academic Press, 1977). For the updated estimates see John F. Cogan, *Negative Income Taxation and Labor Supply: New Evidence for the New Jersey–Pennsylvania Experiment* (Santa Monica, Calif.: Rand Corporation, 1978). The New Jersey–Pennsylvania experiment, as well as three later experiments (Rural North Carolina/Iowa, Gary, Denver-Seattle) are described in Robert Ferber and Werner Z. Hirsch, "Social Experimentation and Economic Policy: A Survey," *Journal of Economic Literature*, December 1978, pp. 1379–1444.

effect decreases (increases) while the substitution effect increases (decreases) desired hours of work.

6. Empirical evidence suggests that women are significantly more responsive in their labor supply decisions to a wage change than are men.

7. The responsiveness of the quantity of labor supplied to a given change in wage rates is measured by the elasticity of labor supply. It is calculated as the percentage change in quantity of labor supplied divided by the percentage change in the wage rate. In contrast, changes in nonlabor income or work-leisure preferences alter the location of an individual's labor supply curve.

8. The case of nonparticipants—individuals who choose not to do labor market work—is portrayed by a corner solution on the right vertical axis of the work-leisure model.

9. A worker may be overemployed or underemployed when forced to conform to a standard workday. A worker is overemployed (underemployed) when for the standard workday one's marginal rate of substitution of leisure for income is greater (less) than the wage rate.

10. A system of premium pay, for example, time and one-half for overtime work, has a more positive effect upon work incentives than does the straight-time wage rate which would yield an equivalent income for the same hours of work.

11. Most income maintenance programs entail a basic benefit and a benefit-loss rate from which the break-even level of income can be calculated. Because (*a*) the basic benefit causes only an income effect and (*b*) the benefit-loss rate *reduces* the net wage rate, the income and substitution effects both contributed to a decline in hours of work.

12. Experimental studies tend to confirm the effects of income maintenance programs upon labor supply which the work-leisure model predicts.

QUESTIONS AND STUDY SUGGESTIONS

1. Key terms and concepts to remember: indifference curve; marginal rate of substitution of leisure for income; budget constraint; optimum work-leisure position; income effect; substitution effect; backward-bending labor supply curve; overemployment; underemployment; income maintenance program; basic benefit; benefit-loss rate; break-even income.

2. Indicate in each of the following instances whether the specified circumstances will cause a worker to want to work more or fewer hours.
   a. The wage rate increases and the substitution effect is greater than the income effect.
   b. The wage rate decreases and the income effect is greater than the substitution effect.
   c. The wage rate decreases and the substitution effect is greater than the income effect.
   d. The wage rate increases and the income effect is greater than the substitution effect.

3. Employ a diagram similar to Figure 2-4 to show an individual's leisure-income choices before and after a wage rate *decrease*. Isolate the income and substitution effects, indicate whether each increases or decreases hours of work, and use the two effects to explain the overall impact of the wage decline upon hours of work. Is your

worker on the forward-rising or backward-bending portion of the labor supply curve?

4. Suppose Lauren is confronted with two options by her employer. First option: she may choose her own hours of work and be paid the relatively low wage rate implied by budget line HW_1 shown in the accompanying diagram. Second option: she can work exactly HR hours and be paid the relatively high wage rate implied by budget line HW_2. Which option will she choose? Justify your answer.

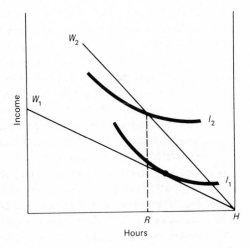

5. Discuss the possible effects upon desired hours of work which the imposition of a 20 percent tax on earned income would entail. Supply-side economists contend that tax cuts will stimulate incentives to work. Does your analysis confirm this view? Explain: "Supply-side economists envision a strong substitution effect, but ignore the possible impact of the income effect."

6. What set of circumstances will tend to cause an individual to choose not to participate in the labor force? What generalizations can you formulate on the basis of (a) education; (b) the presence of preschool children; (c) level of husband's income; (d) race; (e) location of a household (urban or rural) on the one hand, and the probability that a married woman will be a labor force participant on the other.

7. Using Figure 2-9, demonstrate that Smith has a stronger "taste" for leisure and a weaker "taste" for work than does Jones. What factor(s) might underlie this difference in tastes?

8. Use Figure 2-10 to explain the following statement: "Although premium wage rates for overtime work will induce workers to work longer hours than would a straight-time equivalent wage rate, the latter will entail a higher level of well-being."

9. If an income maintenance program entails a $3000 basic benefit and a benefit-loss rate of .30, what will be the size of the subsidy received by a family which earns $2000 per year? What will be the family's total income? What break-even level of income does this program imply?

10. Redraw Figure 2-11 on the assumption that the benefit-loss rate is 1.00 and show how this might cause an individual to become a labor force nonparticipant. "The higher the basic benefit and the higher the benefit-loss rate, the weaker the work incentive." Do you agree?

11. One way of aiding low-income families is to increase the minimum wage. An alternative is to provide a direct grant of nonlabor income. Compare the impact of these two options upon work incentives.
12. Evaluate the following statements:
    a. "An employer might reduce worker absenteeism by changing from a standard wage rate to premium pay for hours which exceed a fixed minimum."
    b. "A worker who feels underemployed may 'moonlight' even though the wage rate is somewhat lower than the one paid on her first job."
    c. "Given the wage rate, an individual will always prefer a job on which the worker, as opposed to the employer, selects the number of hours worked."

SELECTED REFERENCES

CAIN, GLEN G., and HAROLD W. WATTS (eds.): *Income Maintenance and Labor Supply* (Chicago: Rand McNally, 1973).

Final Report of the Seattle-Denver Income Maintenance Experiment, vol. 1 (Menlo Park, Calif.: SRI International, 1983).

FLEISHER, BELTON M., and THOMAS J. KNIESNER; *Labor Economics: Theory, Evidence, and Policy,* 3d ed. (Englewood Cliffs, N.J.: Prentice-Hall, Inc., 1984), chap. 4.

KEELEY, MICHAEL C., *Labor Supply and Public Policy* (New York: Academic Press, 1981).

KILLINGSWORTH, MARK R.: *Labor Supply* (Cambridge: Cambridge University Press, 1983).

T I M E   A N D   O N E - H A L F

THE SIME/DIME EXPERIMENTS*

A number of income maintenance experiments have been conducted in the United States in an attempt to determine whether the provision of an income guarantee involving a benefit-loss rate will generate work disincentives as suggested by Figure 2-11.

The most recent and most comprehensive income maintenance study was the Seattle and Denver Income Maintenance Experiments, popularly known as SIME/DIME. Carried out over the 1970–1981 period, SIME/DIME involved almost 5000 families and a number of combinations of income guarantees (basic benefits) and benefit-loss rates. The program lasted 3 years for some families, while other families were in a 5-year program. The basic benefits were relatively generous, providing families on the average with incomes which were 115 percent of the poverty level. One major purpose of SIME/DIME was to compare the labor supply response of families in the program with those of a "control" group who did not receive benefits.

*Based upon Office of Income Security Policy of the U.S. Department of Health and Human Services, *Overview of the Seattle-Denver Income Maintenance Experiment Final Report,* May 1983, pp. 12–17.

The accompanying table summarizes the labor supply responses of husbands. In part A of the table we note the percentage difference in hours worked between the experimental group and the control group. For those families in the 3-year program, the maximum decline in annual hours worked by husbands was 7.3 percent and occurred in both the second and third years. For those in the 5-year program, the maximum decline in the number of hours worked by husbands was 13.6 percent and happened in the fourth year. In absolute terms these declines represent reductions in the number of hours worked of approximately 133 and 234 hours per year respectively. The third row combines the 3- and 5-year groups and indicates that the work disincentive effect for husbands was about 9 percent of total hours in both the second and third years. Note, too, that for husbands in the 3-year program, the hours of work returned essentially to the same level as those in the control group in years 4 and 5. This strongly suggests that the reduction in hours which occurred during the experiment were attributable to the program, and that once the program ended husbands fairly quickly adjusted their labor supply to altered economic incentives. Furthermore, a disaggregation of the data (not shown) indicates there were no statistically significant differences between white, black, and Chicano husbands in their average work reductions.

Labor Supply Response of Husbands

A. Overall response (percentage difference in annual hours worked)

	Year				
	1	2	3	4	5
Three-year program	−1.6	−7.3	−7.3	−0.5	−0.2
Five-year program	−5.9	−12.2	−13.2	−13.6	−12.3
Combined programs	−3.1	−9.0	−9.3		

B. Second year response by plan (percentage difference in annual hours worked)

Basic Benefit	Benefit-Loss Rate	
	50 percent	70 percent
$3,800	−6.7	−5.6
$4,800	−8.8	−1.5
$5,600	−11.8	−10.4

Source: Office of Income Security Policy of the U.S. Department of Health and Human Services, *Overview of the Seattle-Denver Income Maintenance Experiment Final Report*, May 1983, p. 13.

What was the form of the reduction in hours? Did husbands in the experimental group work fewer hours per week? Or did they spend more time unemployed? The answer is the latter. That is, the availability of the income guarantee caused male workers who were out of work to spend more time between jobs than men in the control group.

Part B of the table breaks down the aggregate figures to show how differences in the basic benefit and the benefit-loss rate affected the size of the percentage decline in hours worked. The data here generally, although not uniformly, confirm the predictions of Figure 2-11. Given the benefit-loss rate, an increase in the basic benefit generates an income effect which is negative with respect to work. Hence, other things being equal, the larger the basic benefit, the larger the negative income effect and the larger the reduction in hours worked. On the other hand, we observe that the higher 70 percent benefit-loss rate is associated with a smaller reduction in hours than is the smaller 50 percent benefit-loss rate. At first glance this is surprising. Figure 2-11 would suggest that, as compared to the 50 percent benefit-loss rate, the 70 percent rate would result in a smaller *net* wage rate and therefore a larger substitution effect. Recall that in the income maintenance case this substitution effect is negative with respect to work. The explanation of this minor mystery lies in the fact that the higher benefit-loss rate also reduces the break-even level of income and thereby reduces the number of people in the experimental group subject to the work disincentives associated with the program.

Wives also responded to SIME/DIME by reducing hours of work outside the home. In fact, the relative decline was larger than for husbands. For example, the decline for wives in the second year of the combined programs was 20.1 percent as compared to 9.0 percent for husbands. However, this translated into a smaller absolute decline in hours because on the average women work outside the home fewer hours per year than do men. Finally, the relative decline in hours for females who were family heads also exceeded that of married men. The second-year decline for the combined group of female family heads was 14.3 percent.

To recapitulate: Overall the SIME/DIME experimental study confirmed the major predictions embodied in Figure 2-11's analysis of the work disincentive effects of income maintenance programs.

LABOR FORCE PARTICIPATION RATES AND HOURS OF WORK

The total productive effort available in the economy depends upon a variety of factors, the most prominent of which are enumerated in Figure 3-1. We observe that the total of available labor services depends upon (1) population size, which in turn depends upon births, deaths, and net immigration; (2) the labor force participation rate of the population; (3) the average number of hours worked weekly and annually by the labor force; and (4) the quality of labor. We will be content to delegate explanations of population size to demographers.[1] Furthermore, labor quality is the topic of Chapter 4. We simply note at this point that, other things being equal, a qualitatively superior labor force— one that is more experienced, more educated, and better trained—will be capable of supplying a larger quantity of useful productive effort than would one of inferior quality. Hence, in this chapter attention will be focused upon participation rates and hours of work.

Our discussion will proceed as follows. First, we will pause to reorient our perspective from that of the individual to that of the household or family. Next, we will briefly consider how participation rates are defined and measured. The third and major segment of this chapter is concerned with the long-run or secular trend of participation rates. We will find that in recent history the aggregate participation rate has been quite stable, although the participation rates of various subgroups making up the aggregate have changed significantly. Fourth, we will consider short-run or cyclical changes in participation rates. Finally, we will present and attempt to explain long-run trends in hours of work. Through-

---

[1]However, we will be concerned with industrial fatalities (Chapter 10) and immigration (Chapter 14) which obviously do affect population size. It should also be noted that Figure 3-1 conceals some interesting interactions between population growth and labor force participation rates. Thus the decision to have children may lower the participation rates of women and, conversely, the decision by women to be more-or-less permanent labor force participants—to pursue a labor market career— may influence women to delay (or forgo) marriage or to have few (if any) children. More generally, this chapter's Time and One-Half minireading assesses the importance of economic factors in the decision to have children.

out this chapter our discussion will draw upon and extend the theory of labor supply as presented in Chapter 2.

BECKER'S MODEL: THE ALLOCATION OF TIME

In Chapter 2 we introduced a simple model in which an *individual* was making a choice between labor market work and leisure. While this model proved useful in generating an understanding of the work-leisure decision and a number of its implications, the model has been generalized and expanded by Becker and others.[2] This generalized *model of the allocation of time* is particularly useful in understanding the topic at hand, namely, labor force participation.

Two Fundamental Changes. The basic work-leisure choice model can be extended in two fundamental ways.

1. Household perspective. The first change is that it is frequently more informative to think of the household as the basic decision-making unit rather than the individual. Most persons are in fact members of households, and decisions as to how they spend their time are strongly influenced by the decisions of other household members. Decision making is interrelated in that, for example, a wife's decision as to whether she should seek labor market work may depend upon whether her husband is currently employed.

2. Multiple uses of time. In Becker's model of household allocation of time the traditional work-leisure dichotomy is replaced by a more complex categori-

[2]The landmark article is Gary Becker, "A Theory of the Allocation of Time," *Economic Journal,* September 1965, pp. 493–517. See also Staffan B. Linder's *The Harried Leisure Class* (New York; Columbia University Press, 1970).

FIGURE 3-1 DETERMINANTS OF THE TOTAL LABOR SERVICES AVAILABLE
The total amount of labor services available in an economy depends upon population size, the labor force participation rate, the length of the workweek and workyear, and the quality of the labor force.

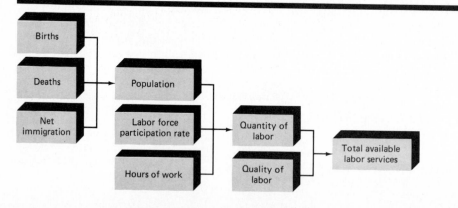

zation of the uses of time. As Becker sees it, a household should be regarded as an economic unit that is *producing* utility-yielding "commodities." These utility-yielding *commodities* are produced by the household by combining *goods* (goods and services) with *time*. More generally, a household can use the time available to it in at least three basic ways. Time can be (*a*) sold in the labor market to obtain the money income required to purchase goods and services (labor market time), (*b*) used in household production (household production time), and (*c*) used in the actual consumption of goods and services (consumption time). Hence, for the typical household, the commodity we call a meal is produced by combining certain goods acquired through the provision of labor market time (food bought at the supermarket) with household production time (the time it takes to prepare these goods as an edible meal) and consumption time (the time it takes to eat the meal). Because the total amount of time available to the household is obviously limited, the alternative uses of time are competitive with one another. Hence, for example, other things being equal, the family in which both spouses engage in labor market work will have less time available for household production and consumption than will the family with one non-working spouse.

Commodities have two characteristics which are of considerable significance for any discussion of how a household might allocate its time in general and how it might make labor market participation decisions in particular. First, some commodities are relatively **time-intensive**, while others are relatively **goods-intensive**. Stated differently, some commodities are comprised of a large amount of time and a small amount of goods. Examples include such "pure" leisure activities as watching the sunset at the beach or dozing in a hammock.[3] Other commodities require quite large amounts of goods and little time, for example, a meal at a fast-food restaurant. One obvious implication of this distinction is that, as one's time becomes more valuable in the labor market (if wage rates increase), then a household may sacrifice time-intensive commodities in favor of goods-intensive commodities in order to devote more time to labor market work.

The second characteristic of commodities is that, within limits, time and goods are usually substitutable in producing them. Thus, a specific commodity can be produced by the household with a great deal of time and a small amount of goods or vice versa. At one extreme a household can produce a meal with home-grown, home-prepared food. At the other extreme it can purchase a meal at a restaurant. The former is obviously a highly time-intensive commodity, while the latter is a goods-intensive commodity.

Within the context of the Becker model, the household has a number of questions to answer as it seeks to maximize its utility. First, what commodities does it want to consume? Second, how does it want to produce these commodities? That is, to what extent should commodities be provided through labor

---

[3]In the Becker model we can think of leisure as the pleasurable consumption of time per se wherein the amount of goods required is nil.

market work as opposed to production in the home? Third, how should individual family members allocate their time among labor market work, home production, consumption, and other possible uses?

The third question clearly is most relevant for the topic at hand.[4] The general principle employed in deciding how each household member should allocate his or her time is that of comparative advantage. The principle of comparative advantage simply says that an individual should specialize in that productive endeavor which he or she can perform with the greatest relative efficiency, or in other words, with the least opportunity cost. That is, in apportioning its available time a household should compare the productivity of each family member in all of the various market and nonmarket activities which need to be performed in producing commodities. The basic rule is that the more productive or proficient one is in a certain activity as compared to other family members, the greater the amount of one's time that should be devoted to that activity. Given that each family member has different characteristics with respect to age, sex, educational attainment, and previous labor market and nonlabor-market experience, we can expect that at any point in time the various family members will differ substantially in the relative efficiency with which they can "produce" commodities (utility) from market and nonmarket activities. At the risk of being obvious, there is no question that the wife has a biologically determined comparative advantage in childbearing! Also, through socialization (role definition by society) or because of preferences, or both, many females develop a comparative advantage in other aspects of household production, for example, in homemaking activities such as cleaning, food preparation, and caring for children. Furthermore, we will find evidence in Chapter 11 which suggests that women are often discriminated against in the labor market. Hence, other things (such as education, job training, and labor market experience) being equal, many husbands can obtain more money income and therefore more goods for the household from a given amount of labor market work than can the wife. Conse-

---

[4]The second question will be treated in the ensuing discussion of the participation rates of the various subaggregates of the population. With regard to the first question we will simply assume the household's preferences for commodities are given, noting that in Becker's model the theory of consumer behavior must be modified to account for the economic value of time. More precisely, you may remember from your introductory economics that a household will be purchasing the utility-maximizing combination of goods ($a, b, \ldots n$) when the marginal utility of the last dollar spent on each is the same. Algebraically stated, utility is maximized when

$$MUa/Pa = MUb/Pb = \ldots = MUn/Pn$$

where MU is marginal utility and P is product price. Becker contends that the appropriate prices to be used are *not* simply the market prices of each good, but rather the "full price," that is, the market price of a good *plus* the market value of the time used in its consumption. Thus, if good a is a 2-hour concert whose price is $8 and your time is worth $10 per hour in the labor market, then the full price of the concert is $28 = $8 + (2 × $10). Taking the value of time into account, the full prices of highly time-intensive goods will rise relatively and those of less time-intensive goods will fall relatively, generating a different utility-maximizing combination of goods than if only market prices were used.

quently, for many households the principle of comparative advantage leads husbands to devote much of their time to labor market work, while their wives engage in nonmarket work within the home. Similarly, we will find in Chapter 4 that children tend to have a comparative advantage in acquiring education. That is, education is an investment in human capital and, other things being equal, the rate of return on that investment varies directly with the length of time a person will be in the labor market after his or her education is completed.

Income and Substitution Effects Revisited. It is helpful in understanding Becker's model to reexamine the income and substitution effects within its more general framework. Assume there is an increase in wage rates. The *income effect* indicates that the household now realizes a larger money income for any number of hours of labor market work, and therefore the consumption of most goods will increase.[5] But the consumption of additional goods requires more time. Remember that goods must be combined with time to produce utility-yielding commodities. Hence, with consumption time increasing, hours of work will tend to fall. Although the rationale is different, the income effect reduces hours of work as it did in the simpler model of Chapter 2. There is also a more complex *substitution effect*. A higher market wage rate means that time is more valuable not only in the labor market but also in both the production and consumption activities which occur within the household. On the one hand, the household will tend to substitute goods for time in the *production* of commodities as the wage rate rises. This implies that the household will produce commodities in less time-intensive ways. For example, the family may patronize fast-food restaurants with greater frequency and therefore spend less time in meal preparation within the home. On the other hand, with respect to *consumption* the household will alter the mix of commodities which it consumes, shifting away from time-intensive commodities to goods-intensive commodities as the wage rates increase. Such time-intensive activities as vacations and playing golf may give way to the purchase of a work of art or racquetball. Or alternatively, a week's skiing in Colorado can be made less time-intensive for a Chicagoan by flying to the resort rather than driving. These adjustments in both the production and consumption of commodities release time for paid work in the labor market. Therefore, as in our simpler model, this more complex substitution effect increases hours of work when wage rates rise. Again, as in our simpler model, the net impact of the income and substitution effects upon the hours of labor market work could be either positive or negative, depending upon their relative magnitudes.

The alleged superiority of Becker's model lies in the fact that it embodies a more comprehensive and more realistic portrayal of the uses of time. People do not merely divide their time between the assembly line and the hammock as a narrow interpretation of the simpler model might imply. As noted earlier, the

---

[5]The exception, of course, is *inferior goods*, that is, goods whose purchases decline as incomes increase.

Becker model is a useful tool for understanding labor force participation rates, the topic to which we now turn.

PARTICIPATION RATES: DEFINED AND MEASURED

The labor force participation rate is determined by comparing the actual labor force with the potential labor force or what is sometimes called the "age-eligible population."

In the United States we consider the *potential labor force* or age-eligible population to be the entire population *less* (1) young people under 16 years of age and (2) people who are institutionalized. Children—those under 16—are excluded on the assumption that schooling and child labor laws keep most of them out of the labor force.[6] Furthermore, that segment of the population which is institutionalized—in penal or mental institutions, nursing homes, and so on—is also not available for labor market activities.[7] The *actual labor force* consists of those people who are either (1) employed or (2) unemployed but actively seeking a job.[8] Thus in percentage form we can say that the *labor force participation rate* is:

$$\frac{\text{actual labor force}}{\text{potential labor force}} \times 100$$

or

$$\frac{\text{noninstitutional population}\atop\text{16 years or over in the labor force}}{\text{noninstitutional population}\atop\text{16 years or over}} \times 100$$

In January of 1985, for example:

$$\frac{116,572,000}{179,081,000} \times 100 = 65.1\%$$

[6]Although excluded from the official definition of the labor force, many persons under 16 years of age do engage in labor market activities. For example, in 1981, almost 18 percent of all 14- to 15-year-olds were employed or were seeking employment.

[7]Since 1983 all armed forces personnel stationed in the United States have been considered to be members of the labor force, the rationale being that joining the military is a voluntary decision and therefore represents a viable labor market alternative. Prior to 1983 members of the military were not counted as a part of the labor force.

[8]More precise definitions will be introduced in Chapter 18. It should be noted that all part-time workers are included in the labor force.

Participation rates can be similarly determined for various subaggregates of the population, for example, married women, black teenage females, and so forth.

SECULAR TREND OF PARTICIPATION RATES

Let us now turn to the long-run or secular trend of participation rates in the United States as portrayed in Table 3-1. The reader should be forewarned that the factors affecting participation rates are varied and complex; some are economic variables, while others are of an institutional, legal, or attitudinal nature. Hence, while the Becker model is useful in explaining many of the important changes in participation rates, it cannot be realistically expected to provide a complete understanding of all the forces at work.

Column 2 of Table 3-1 reflects the generalization that, despite substantial growth of our population and significant changes in its demographic makeup, the aggregate participation rate has been quite stable over time. Specifically, the participation rate has hovered around 60 percent since World War II with perhaps a slight upward drift in the past few years. Furthermore, columns 3 and 4 make it clear that this overall stability is the consequence of simultaneous declines in male and increases in female participation rates. We observe that male and female participation rates are tending to converge. Over the 1947–1985 period the male participation rate fell from 86.8 to 76.9 percent, while the

TABLE 3-1

Labor Force Participation Rates by Sex, Selected Years (1947–1985), and Projections

(1) Year	(2) Both Sexes, %	(3) Males, %	(4) Females, %
1947	58.9	86.8	31.8
1953	60.2	86.9	34.5
1959	59.3	83.7	37.1
1965	58.9	80.7	39.3
1971	60.2	79.1	43.4
1976	61.6	77.5	47.3
1981	63.9	77.0	52.1
1985*	65.1	76.9	54.3
1990**	68.3	77.7	59.7
1995**	68.9	77.3	61.3

*Data are for January and include resident armed forces.

**Data for 1990 and 1995 are Department of Labor "intermediate growth" projections.

Source: Employment and Training Report of the President.

female rate rose from 31.8 to 54.3 percent. Let us consider the trends in female and male participation rates in more detail.

Rising Female Participation Rates. Most of the increase in female participation rates shown in Table 3-1 has been accounted for by married women. For example, the total number of females in the labor force increased by approximately 32 million over the 1947–1984 period. Of this total increase over 21 million were married women. In one sense this is a surprising phenomenon. From the perspective of a household one might have expected that the participation rate of married women would have declined since World War II as a consequence of the rising real wage rates and incomes of married males. And, indeed, cross-section (point-in-time) studies reveal that the participation rates of married women do in fact vary inversely with the husband's income. Our analysis in Chapter 2 suggests the reason why: If leisure is a normal good, then a household will "purchase" more leisure as its income rises. Historical evidence suggests that this purchase of leisure is likely to be in the form of the wife's nonparticipation in the labor market. In terms of Figure 2-7, as the husband's income rises, an expanding intrahousehold transfer of income is available to the wife and the consequent income effect induces her to be a nonparticipant. Put bluntly, this line of reasoning suggests that wives in lower-income families are likely to work in the labor market because of economic necessity, but as the husband's income increases more families will enjoy the luxury of having the wife produce "commodities" at home.

How can this reasoning be squared with the fact that the participation rates of married women have actually increased over time? The answer lies essentially in the fact that cross-section studies do not have a time dimension and, therefore, ignore or hold constant certain variables other than the husband's income which might have an impact upon a wife's decision to participate in the labor force. That is, a number of factors besides the husband's rising income have been influencing the participation rates of married women over time. These other factors have so strongly influenced women to enter the labor market that they have overwhelmed the negative effect on labor market work of the rising incomes of husbands.

What are these "other factors"? The list is well-known:[9]

1. Rising relative wage rates for women. There has been a long-run increase in the real wage rates which women can earn in the labor market. This is primarily a consequence of the fact that women have acquired more skills through education. As already noted, higher wage rates will generate both income and substitution effects within the framework of Becker's model. While the income effect will act to reduce hours of work, the substitution effects related

---

[9]See T. Aldrich Finegan, "Participation of Married Women in the Labor Force," in Cynthia B. Lloyd (ed.), *Sex, Discrimination, and the Division of Labor* (New York: Columbia University Press, 1975), pp. 28–29, and *Economic Report of the President, 1973* (Washington, D.C., 1973), chap. 4.

to both production- and consumption-related activities within the home will tend to increase them. Goods will be substituted for time in the production of commodities, *and* goods-intensive commodities will be substituted for time-intensive goods in the household's mix of consumer commodities. Both types of adjustments will free up the wife's time from household activities so that she may spend more time in the labor market. Presumably the substitution effect has dominated the income effect for many women, causing their participation rates to rise. The income effect for married women may be small because its size will vary directly with the amount of time they are already devoting to labor market work. For example, the income effect of a rise in wage rates will be negligible for a married woman who is not currently participating in labor market work.

2. Changing preferences. Rising female participation rates may also be the result of a fundamental change in female preferences in favor of labor market work. First, the feminist movement of the 1960s may well have had the effect of altering the career objectives of women toward labor market participation. Similarly, antidiscrimination legislation of the 1960s which specifies "equal pay for equal work" and presumably has made "men's jobs" more accessible also *may* have made labor market work more attractive in comparison to work in the home.[10] Furthermore, aside from its positive impact upon wage rates, greater education for women may have enhanced their "tastes" or preferences for labor market careers. Finally, growing marital instability has undoubtedly underscored the importance to women of achieving and sustaining contact with the labor market as a potential source of economic security.

Reference to Figure 2-7 is helpful in distinguishing between how higher wage rates, on the one hand, and changing preferences, on the other, affect female participation rates. We note that the availability of higher wage rates increases the slope of the budget line which, given preferences, encourages labor market participation. Similarly, given the wage rate, a change in preferences favorable to market work makes the indifference curves flatter, which is also conducive to participation.

3. Rising productivity in the household. As we shall discover in Chapter 16, the use of more and technologically superior capital goods by businesses over time has been an important factor in increasing the productivity of work time and therefore in raising real wage rates. Larger amounts of improved machinery and equipment permit workers to produce a unit of output with less time. Similarly, the availability of more and better capital goods for household use has permitted households to reduce the amount of time needed to accomplish both production and consumption within the home. For example, supermarkets and the availability of home refrigerators and freezers greatly reduce the

---

[10]It must be noted that there is considerable disagreement as to whether gender discrimination has diminished significantly. For example, a glance ahead at Table 11-1 indicates that the ratio of the earnings of full-time female workers to full-time male workers has *not* increased significantly.

amount of time devoted to grocery shopping. The supermarket permits one-stop shopping, and refrigerators and freezers further reduce the number of shopping trips needed per week. Similarly, microwave ovens, vacuum cleaners, automatic clothes washers and dryers, and dishwashers have greatly reduced the amount of time involved in food preparation and housecleaning. Fast-food restaurants circumvent the time-intensive activity of food preparation in the home. By providing direct and convenient transportation, the automobile has reduced the time required to attend a concert, movie, or football game. In terms of Becker's model, the increased availability of such household capital goods has increased productivity in the home, thereby freeing time from household production and consumption and allowing many women to engage in part- and full-time employment in the labor market.

4. Declining birth rates. The presence of children—and particularly preschool children—is associated with low participation rates for wives. Child care is a highly time-intensive household productive activity which keeps many wives out of the labor force. While baby-sitters, nurseries, husbands, and child care centers can substitute for wives in caring for children, the expense and opportunity cost involved often discourage such substitutions. What has happened over time is that the widespread availability and use of birth control techniques, coupled with changing lifestyles, has reduced birth rates *and* compacted the span of time over which a family's children are born. Women are having fewer children and having them over a shorter period of time. Fewer children obviously reduce associated homemaking responsibilities and free married women for labor market work. Furthermore, the compression of the time span over which children are born reduces the amount of time which many women are absent from the labor force for child-raising responsibilities and is therefore more conducive to their pursuit of a labor market career.

It is also worth noting that higher wage rates are associated with lower fertility rates. More-educated women who can command relatively high wage rates in the labor market tend to have fewer children than do less-educated women for whom wages are low. Becker's model provides one explanation for this relationship. Child rearing is a highly time-intensive activity and hence the opportunity cost of children—the income sacrificed by not being in the labor market—is higher for more-educated than for less-educated women. The Time and One-Half minireading at the end of this chapter explores this topic in greater depth.

5. Expanding job accessibility. In addition to the aforementioned decline in sex discrimination, a variety of other factors have made jobs more accessible to women. First, since World War II there has been a great expansion both absolutely and relatively in the kinds of employment which have traditionally been "women's jobs," for example, clerical and secretarial work, retail sales, teaching, and nursing. Second, there has been a long-run shift of the population from farms and rural regions to urban areas where jobs for women are more abundant and more geographically accessible. Third, the average length of the workweek has declined in full-time jobs, *and* the availability of part-time jobs has increased. These latter two developments have made it easier for women to reconcile labor market employment with housekeeping tasks.

Relative Importance. Recently Fuchs has perceptively analyzed the various factors which may have contributed to rising female participation rates with a view to discerning their comparative significance.[11] He discounts the importance of such considerations as antidiscrimination legislation and the feminist movement, largely on the basis that their timing is bad. That is, the growth of female participation rates predates both the feminist movement and the passage of antidiscrimination laws (Chapter 11). The problem with attributing rising participation rates for women to the availability of time-saving household goods and related innovations is that cause and effect are unclear. Did innovations such as clothes washers, freezers, fast-food restaurants, and supermarkets simply appear and thereby free up time which married women could devote to labor market work? Or were these innovations made largely in response to needs which arose when women decided for other reasons to enter the labor force? Noting the absence of supermarkets and fast-food restaurants in low-income countries, Fuchs is inclined to believe that their growth in the United States is the *result* of the rising value of time and of rising female participation rates rather than a causal factor.

More positively, Fuchs feels that rising real wage rates and the expansion of "women's jobs" in the service industries are the most important reasons for rising female participation rates. Better control of fertility is also deemed significant, but once again cause and effect are difficult to unravel. Do women first decide on labor force participation and, as a consequence of this decision, determine to have fewer children? Or does the decision to have smaller families precede the decision to enter the labor force? Fuchs also contends that the growing probability of divorce compels women to achieve and maintain their ties to the labor market.

Racial differences. It is worth noting that, although the participation rates of both black and white women have increased in the post-World War II period, the participation rates of black women have consistently been greater than those of white women. How might the greater participation of black women be explained? Cain[12] has offered the following arguments. First, black women may have encountered less discrimination in the labor market than do black men, which suggests that it has been rational for a black family to make some substitution of market work by the wife for market work by the husband. Second, the greater degree of marital instability in black families may have encouraged black women to maintain a stronger and more continuous link

---

[11]Victor R. Fuchs, *How We Live* (Cambridge, Mass.: Harvard University Press, 1983), pp. 127–133.

[12]Glen Cain, *Married Women in the Labor Force* (Chicago: University of Chicago Press, 1966), pp. 77–83.

with the labor market as a source of economic security. Finally, black women have often been members of extended families, where grandparents, cousins, or aunts and uncles are present. This increases the likelihood that "free" or "built-in" child care would be available to black wives, reducing the out-of-pocket cost of their labor market participation.

Postscript: Although the participation rate of black women has exceeded that of white women, the participation rate of white women has increased more rapidly than that of black women. For example, in the mid-1950s the difference between the participation rates of adult black and white women was on the order of 12 to 15 percentage points. Currently the difference is about 4 percentage points. The decline in this difference may be a critical factor in explaining why the ratio of black to white family incomes has increased only modestly in the past two decades or so. The income gains to black families which may have resulted from antidiscrimination legislation and more enlightened attitudes toward minorities may have been largely offset by the fact that relatively larger numbers of white married women have entered the labor force.

Declining Male Participation Rates. In some senses the reasons for the decline in male participation rates are more complex than are the causes of the increasing participation rate of females. Table 3-2 shows the participation rates for males by age and race for 1949 and 1984. It is informative to examine what has happened to the participation rates of (a) teenage males, (b) prime-aged males (25–54), and (c) older males.

TABLE 3-2

Male Participation Rates by Age and Race, 1949 and 1984*

(1) Age	Percent All Males		Percent White Males Only		Percent Black** Males Only	
	(2) 1949	(3) 1984	(4) 1949	(5) 1984	(6) 1949	(7) 1984
16–17	51.2	52.9	50.1	56.1	60.4	39.1
18–19	75.4	74.3	74.8	76.3	80.8	64.4
20–24	86.8	88.2	86.5	89.2	89.7	84.0
25–34	95.8	95.1	95.9	96.0	94.1	90.3
35–44	97.9	95.1	98.0	95.7	97.3	90.0
45–54	95.6	91.7	95.6	92.6	95.6	82.8
55–64	87.5	68.6	87.6	69.9	86.0	56.9
65 & over	47.0	16.1	46.6	16.3	51.4	13.2
Total 16 & over	86.4	77.6	86.4	78.2	87.0	72.8

*Data are for August 1984.

**Includes other minorities.

Source: Department of Labor, *Employment and Earnings.*

Teenage males. Concentrating on columns 1 through 3 for the moment, we observe that overall there has been no dramatic change in the participation rates of teenagers. Much of the 16–17 age group is occupied full time with school. While a substantially higher percentage of the 18–19 age group is at work, many of these hold part-time jobs. Columns 4 and 5 indicate that there has been no dramatic shift in the participation rates of white teenage males. However, in columns 6 and 7 we observe that the participation rates of black teenagers have fallen sharply. This reflects in part the fact that education is a normal good and, therefore, black families have purchased more education as their incomes have risen. Perhaps more important, increasing numbers of black youths have become discouraged in their futile attempts to gain employment and have ceased to look for jobs. Hence, they are neither "employed" nor "unemployed but actively seeking work" and therefore are not labor force participants. This discouragement effect is reinforced by the fact that the jobs which are available to black youths are typically menial, dead-end jobs.

In a real sense, black and white middle-class youth can psychologically afford to engage in "temporary" menial labor, for they are able to be relatively confident that better days are ahead. But the aspiring and often unskilled ghetto youth with a sense of sharply limited job opportunities lacks faith in the prospect of "better days ahead"—the "menial" job symbolizes and promises a bleak future which is all too real in the here and now. With meaningful employment often out of reach, the black youth in the urban area finds the streets to be an alternative source of self-esteem.[13]

A number of researchers have also suggested that increases in the minimum wage may be an important factor in restricting employment opportunities for black youths (Chapter 10). To summarize: There has been no substantial overall change in the participation rates of teenagers in the aggregate over the 1949–1984 period.

Prime-aged males. As Table 3-2 indicates, the participation rates for prime-aged males—those in the 25–54 age group—is very high. Notice that the rate is on the order of 95 or 96 percent. The underlying reason for such high rates is quite obvious: The vast majority of men in this age group are married and, given the role specialization discussed earlier, bear primary responsibility for supporting a family. Indeed, the participation rate of *married* males in the prime labor force is approximately 97 to 98 percent. In contrast, the participation rate of *unmarried* prime-aged males is about 85 percent. One's first thought is to attribute the lower rate to diminished economic responsibility; the unmarried male is "footloose and fancy-free," and a part of this freedom may involve periodic

[13]Elijah Anderson, "Some Observations on Black Youth Employment," in Bernard E. Anderson and Isabel V. Sawhill (eds.), *Youth Employment and Public Policy* (Englewood Cliffs, N.J.: Prentice-Hall, Inc., 1980), p. 79.

nonparticipation in the labor market. But the situation may be more complex. For some people being unmarried and being a nonparticipant may both be the result of other causes such as inadequate education, low intelligence, health or personality problems, a lack of motivation and self-discipline, and so on.

Racial differences are evident in Table 3-2. The participation rate of white prime-aged males in 1984 was 6 or 7 percentage points higher than that for prime-aged black males. Why the lower participation rates for blacks? Several closely related reasons might be offered. First, the difference may be partially attributable to inferior labor market opportunities as reflected in relatively lower wage rates and poorer prospects for finding employment. On the average blacks in this age group have less education and education that is allegedly of inferior quality in comparison to whites. Discrimination as embodied in lower wages, less desirable dead-end jobs, and the tendency for blacks to be the "last hired and first fired" are all inducements for blacks to remain outside of the labor force.[14] Second, the relatively lower participation rate for black married males may also be a reflection of the relatively high participation rate of black wives noted earlier. In terms of Becker's model black women may incur less discrimination in the labor market than do black men, making it rational for relatively more black women and relatively fewer black men to participate in labor market work. Finally, we found in Chapter 2 that the increased availability and enhanced generosity of public income maintenance programs tend to encourage income receivers of all races to withdraw from the labor force (see Figure 2-11 in particular). Because blacks are disproportionately represented among the lowest-income groups in our society, we would expect the participation rates of blacks to be less than those of whites.[15]

Older males. The most important conclusion to be drawn from Table 3-2 is that the participation rates of older workers have declined sharply. We observe in columns 1 through 3 that the participation rate of males 65 years of age or older has declined precipitously from 47 percent in 1949 to 16.1 percent in 1984. While less dramatic, the participation rate of males 55 to 64 years of age has declined by almost 19 percentage points in the same period. A variety of factors have been cited to explain these declines.

First, it has become increasingly common in the United States to mandate retirement and, at least until recently, at an earlier age. Many business firms and

---

[14]For more on this see the discussion of secondary labor markets in Chapter 15.

[15]This final point is stressed by Richard Butler and James J. Heckman, "The Government's Impact on the Labor Market Status of Black Americans: A Critical Review," in Leonard J. Hausman (ed.), *Equal Rights and Industrial Relations* (Madison, Wis.: Industrial Relations Research Association, 1977), pp. 235–281. It is interesting to note that Butler and Heckman argue that the increase in the ratio of black to white average earnings which has occurred in recent years (Chapter 11) is *not* attributable to government antidiscrimination policies, but rather to income maintenance programs which reduce the supply of black labor market participants to the extent that their average wage rates have increased in comparison to those of whites.

most public agencies encourage retirement at age 65. Declining participation rates for the 55–64 age group undoubtedly reflect the fact that many private and public pension plans allow retirement with full or partial benefits upon completion of a specified number of years—say, 20 or 30—of employment. Second, the Old Age, Survivors, Disability, and Health Insurance (OASDHI) component of our social security system has been characterized by both expanded coverage and increasingly generous benefits, thereby providing an important source of nonlabor income which has induced many older workers to withdraw from the labor force (see Figure 2-8).[16] Two other aspects of OASDHI have contributed to lower participation rates for older males. On the one hand, retirement benefits are subject to a substantial benefit-loss rate—that is, an implicit tax on earned income—which enhances the incentive of older workers to withdraw from the labor force. Recall from Figure 2-11 that both the income *and* the substitution effects associated with social security tend to reduce the hours of work. On the other hand, there is evidence to suggest that the disability program under OASDHI has become increasingly generous and is progressive in the sense that low-wage workers receive relatively larger benefits than do high-wage workers. As a result, low-wage workers are more inclined to seek disability benefits as an alternative to labor market participation. Because black workers are generally lower-income workers, this consideration may explain the larger decline in the participation rates of older black workers as compared to older white workers.[17] It must also be added that the increasing availability of private pension plans and the favorable tax treatment accorded various deferred compensation plans both have the same general impact upon participation rates as does OASDHI.

The long-term growth of real incomes is a third and more general consideration in explaining the declining participation rates of older workers. The declining participation rates of older workers predate the Social Security Act of 1935. The secular increase of real incomes has simply allowed many workers to accumulate sufficient wealth to retire at an earlier age.

Let us consider a fourth and final factor which may account for the declining participation rates of older males. You may have recognized that the factors discussed thus far have centered upon the income effect. The availability of nonlabor income in the form of public or private pensions, disability payments, deferred compensation, or income from accumulated wealth generates a pure income effect which is sufficient to induce many older males to become nonparticipants. Some economists feel that a kind of substitution effect is also at work in encouraging older workers to get out of the labor force. In particular, they observe that the real earnings of many workers rise until they reach, say, their mid-fifties, and then earnings gradually decline. A glance ahead at Figure 4-1 seems to confirm this trend of earnings. The alleged basic reason for the decline

---

[16]Recent evidence indicates that the negative effect of social security upon participation rates is considerably stronger for older males than for older females. See James E. Duggan, "The Labor Force Participation of Older Workers," *Industrial and Labor Relations Review*, April 1984, pp. 416–430.

[17]See Donald O. Parsons, "Racial Trends in Male Labor Force Participation," *American Economic Review*, December 1980, pp. 911–920.

in the earnings of older workers is that their formal education and on-the-job training tend to become obsolete and their mental and physical capabilities tend to decline. This means that, in allocating time over one's lifetime, it is rational to work continuously and for long hours during one's younger years for the simple reason that one's earnings potential is high and therefore leisure is expensive. Conversely, as one grows older, the earnings potential becomes smaller and leisure becomes relatively cheaper; hence, one is inclined to substitute leisure for work. In the extreme this substitution is complete and one chooses to retire.

Causal or Spurious? A reasonable interpretation of Table 3-1 is that the overall labor force participation rate in the United States has been relatively stable in the 1947–1985 period. We have seen that this stability is the consequence of two offsetting trends: (1) the increasing participation rates of women and, more specifically, married women and (2) the falling participation rates of older males. The obvious question to ponder is whether there is a causal relationship between the expanding participation rate of women and the declining participation rate of men. More precisely, is the increase in the participation rate of married women causally related to the decline in the participation rate of older males?

In his pioneering study of participation rates in five market-oriented economies, Long reached the conclusion that for the 1890–1951 period the participation rates of these countries "did not change materially during peacetime periods of rising income and high employment. . . ."[18] More relevant for present purposes, Long contended that this stability was the systematic result of a push-pull phenomenon. Specifically, Long argued that the expanding participation rate for women has been the result of circumstances whereby (1) women "push" men from the labor force by successfully competing for available jobs and (2) women are "pulled" into the labor force to fill the vacuum left by males who decide to leave for reasons such as the availability of OASDHI benefits. This hypothesis is consistent with simple economic theory. By lowering wage rates, an increase in the supply of female labor may "push" some males from the labor force. Similarly, declining male participation rates will reduce the supply of labor, increase wage rates, and "pull" females into the labor force.

Long's participation-rate–stability hypothesis has been the subject of considerable controversy and it is fair to say that no general consensus exists among labor economists as to whether causally related changes in the participation rates of various demographic subgroups have brought about the relative participation rate stability evidenced for the population as a whole.[19]

[18]Clarence D. Long, *The Labor Force under Changing Income and Employment* (Princeton, N.J.: National Bureau of Economic Research and Princeton University Press, 1958), pp. 230.
[19]The interested reader should consult Lowell E. Gallaway, *Manpower Economics* (Homewood, Ill.: Richard D. Irwin, Inc., 1971), chap. 2.

CYCLICAL CHANGES IN PARTICIPATION RATES

Although the secular trend of labor force participation rates reflects considerable stability, cyclical changes in participation rates do occur. Let us consider how cyclical fluctuations might impact upon a family in which one spouse currently engages in labor market work while the other performs productive activities within the home. Assume that a recession occurs, causing the employed spouse to lose her or his job. The net effect upon overall participation rates depends upon the size of the added-worker effect and the discouraged-worker effect.

Added-Worker Effect. The *added-worker effect* is the notion that, when the primary breadwinner in a family loses his or her job, other family members will enter the labor force in the hope of finding employment to offset the decline in the family's income. The rationale involved is highly reminiscent of Chapter 2's income effect. Specifically, one spouse's earned income may be treated as *nonlabor* income from the standpoint of the other spouse. In our illustration the nonemployed family member receives an intrahousehold transfer of some portion of the employed spouse's earnings. From the perspective of the person working in the home, this transfer is *nonlabor* income. In terms of Figure 2-7 the spouse's job loss will reduce nonlabor income as measured on the right vertical axis. As we concluded in Chapter 2, other things being equal, a decrease in nonlabor (transfer) income tends to cause one to become a labor force participant. This is the underlying rationale of the added-worker effect.

Discouraged-Worker Effect. The *discouraged-worker effect* works in the opposite direction. The discouraged-worker effect suggests that during a recession some unemployed workers (for example, the unemployed spouse in our illustration) become so pessimistic about finding a job with an acceptable wage rate that they cease to actively seek employment and thereby temporarily become nonparticipants. This phenomenon can be explained in terms of Chapter 2's substitution effect. Recessions generally entail declines in the real wages available to unemployed workers and new job seekers, increasing the "price" of income (that is, increasing the amount of work time which must be expended to earn $1 of goods) and decreasing the price of leisure. This causes some workers to substitute leisure (nonparticipation) for job search. Recalling our discussion of Figure 2-7 once again, other things being equal, a decrease in the wage rate will tend to cause some individuals to withdraw from the labor force now that the wage rate available to them is lower. Remember that the substitution effect suggests that a *decline* in the wage rate available to a worker will lead to a *decrease* in the incentive to engage in labor market work.

Procyclical Labor Force Changes. These two effects obviously influence participation rates and labor force size in opposite ways. The added-worker effect tends to increase, and the discouraged-worker effect to decrease, participation rates and labor force size during an economic downturn. Which effect is dominant? Stated differently, what actually happens to participation rates over the business cycle? Empirical research generally indicates that the discouraged worker effect is dominant, as is evidenced by the fact that the aggregate labor force participation rate varies inversely with the unemployment rate. When the unemployment rate increases, the participation rate tends to fall and vice versa. Why does the discouraged-worker effect apparently outweigh the added-worker effect? Why does the size of the labor force vary in a procyclical fashion?

The conventional wisdom is that the discouraged-worker effect applies to many more households than does the added-worker effect. For example, if the nation's unemployment rate rises from, say, 6 to 9 percent, only those 3 percent or so of all families who now contain an additional unemployed member will be subject to the added-worker effect. On the other hand, worsening labor market conditions evidenced by the increase in the unemployment rate and decline in real wages may have a discouraging effect upon actual and potential labor force participants in *all* households. Thus, for example, young persons who are deciding whether to continue school or to drop out in order to seek employment will take note that wage rates are less attractive and jobs more difficult to find. Hence, many of them will decide to stay in school rather than participate in the labor force.

Procyclical changes in the labor force size also have been explained in terms of the *timing* of labor force participation by some individuals. For example, many married women are marginally attached to the labor force in that they plan to engage in labor market work for, say, only one-half of their adult years. The other half of their time will be spent in household production. Given this planned overall division of time, it is only rational for such women to participate in the labor force in prosperous times when jobs are readily available and real wages are relatively high and, conversely, to be nonparticipants when unemployment is high and available wage rates are low.[20]

The procyclical changes in labor force size are of more than idle academic interest. Such changes have a significant bearing upon the magnitude of the official unemployment rate and, hence, indirectly upon macroeconomic policy (Chapter 18). The apparent dominance of the discouraged-worker effect over the added-worker effect means that the labor force shrinks (or at least grows at a below-normal rate) during recession, and the official unemployment rate understates unemployment. During the prosperity phase of the cycle, the discouraged-worker effect becomes an "encouraged-worker" effect and the added-worker effect becomes a "subtracted-worker" effect. The former dominates the latter and the labor force expands as a result. This means that there is a larger-than-normal increase in the labor force during an economic expansion which tends to keep the official unemployment rate higher than would otherwise be the case. In

[20]See Jacob Mincer, "Labor-Force Participation and Unemployment: A Review of Recent Evidence," in R. A. Gordon and M. S. Gordon (eds.), *Prosperity and Unemployment* (New York: John Wiley & Sons, Inc., 1966), pp. 73–112.

short, cyclical changes in participation rates tend to cause the official unemployment rate to understate unemployment during a cyclical downswing and to overstate it during an upswing.

Postscript: Despite the fact that cyclical changes in the labor force have been studied by economists for over four decades, there remains considerable disagreement as to the magnitude of such changes.[21] The reader should also be aware that unanimity does not exist with respect to the conclusion that the discouraged worker effect is dominant.[22]

HOURS OF WORK: TWO TRENDS

We obviously have neglected an important aspect of aggregate labor supply, namely, the hours of work. Observe in Figure 3-1 that the total amount of labor supplied in the economy depends not only upon the number of labor force participants, but also upon the average number of hours worked per week and per year by those participants.

Table 3-3 provides an overview of secular changes in the average workweek. The data show decade averages of the workweek and the workyear for production workers in United States manufacturing industries. Two important observations are apparent. First, hours of work declined steadily from 1900 to

---

[21]For a recent estimate, see T. Aldrich Finegan, "Discouraged Workers and Economic Fluctuations," *Industrial and Labor Relations Review,* October 1981, pp. 88–102.

[22]See, for example, Michael C. Keeley, "Cyclical Unemployment and Employment: Effects of Labor Force Entry and Exit," *Economic Review* (Federal Reserve Bank of San Francisco), Summer 1984, pp. 5–25. This article contains a useful review of theory and evidence and an extensive bibliography.

TABLE 3-3

Decade Averages of Weekly and Yearly Hours of Work for Production Workers in Manufacturing

Period	Workweek (hours)	Workyear (hours)
1910–1919	49.4	2630
1920–1929	44.7	2473
1930–1939	38.1	1971
1940–1949	41.5	2111
1950–1959	40.2	1991
1960–1969	40.6	2007
1970–1976	40.1	1955

Source: John Brack and Keith Cowling, "Advertising and Labour Supply: Workweek and Workyear in U.S. Manufacturing Industries, 1919–1976." *Kyklos,* Number 2, 1983, pp. 285–303.

World War II. Note that the average workweek fell by almost 16 percent [(49.4–41.5)/49.4] over the 1910–1919 to 1940–1949 period.[23] Second, the average workweek and workyear changed very little after the 1940s. While there is no universally accepted explanation of these trends, interesting and plausible theories have been put forth.

Workweek Decline, 1900–1940. The pre-World War II decline in the workweek is explainable in terms of the basic work-leisure model described in Chapter 2. The essential contention is that the declining workweek is simply a supply response to historically rising real wages and earnings. More precisely, given (1) worker income-leisure preferences, (2) nonwage incomes, and (3) the assumption that leisure is a normal good, rising wage rates over time will reduce the number of hours individuals will want to work, provided the income effect exceeds the substitution effect. And, in fact, a substantial amount of empirical evidence indicates that the net effect of wage increases upon hours of work is negative.[24]

Post-World War II: Workweek Stability. But how does one explain the relative constancy of the workweek in the postwar era?[25] Real wages have continued to rise, but either the substitution effect has somehow acted to offset the income effect, or perhaps some additional factors have been at work in recent decades to offset the tendency of higher wage rates to reduce the workweek. Let us survey a number of hypotheses.

1. Higher tax rates. One possible explanation is that marginal tax rates on income rose rapidly during and after World War II with the result that given increases in gross (before-tax) wage rates have translated into smaller increases in net (after-tax) wage rates. Hence, the negative supply, or hours of work, response has simply been much smaller in the postwar era than in earlier decades.

---

[23]The shorter hours of the 1930s are largely explainable in terms of the Great Depression; the shorter workweek was widely instituted to spread the smaller demand for labor among more workers.

[24]For a good discussion of these studies, see John T. Addison and W. Stanley Siebert, *The Market for Labor: An Analytical Treatment* (Santa Monica, Calif.: Goodyear Publishing Company, Inc., 1979), pp. 85–90.

[25]It should be noted that the alleged post-World War II stability of the work*year* has been questioned recently. Herbert R. Northrup and Theresa Diss Greis, "The Decline in Average Annual Hours Worked in the United States, 1947–1979," *Journal of Labor Research,* Spring 1983, pp. 95–113, present data which suggest that paid time off for workers—for example, vacations, sick leave, jury duty, bereavement leave, and so forth—has increased rapidly. The result is that the stable work*week* conceals a declining work*year*.

2. Education. Kniesner[26] has hypothesized that the supply of labor over time is positively related to education. Furthermore, he notes that increases in educational attainment have been much greater in the postwar period than in the prewar period; in the 1910–1940 period the increase in median years of schooling completed was only about 6 percent as compared to a 34 percent increase in the 1940–1970 period. Kniesner argues that these differences in educational attainment account for the two trends evidenced in Table 3-3.

Why might more education tend to increase or sustain hours of work? First, a change in preferences may be involved. Education is a means of enhancing one's earning power in the labor market. Decisions to acquire more education may therefore reflect a change in tastes favoring a stronger commitment to labor market work. Second, as we shall find in Chapter 4, more-educated workers generally acquire more-pleasant jobs, that is, jobs which are less physically demanding, less structured, more challenging, and so forth. Other things being equal, such job characteristics would make workers less willing to reduce the workweek. Finally, a more-educated work force may increase employer resistance to a declining workweek. The reason for this is that employers incur more fixed-cost expenditures in recruiting more-educated workers and in training them over their job tenures as compared to less-educated workers. A shorter workweek will increase these fixed costs per worker hour and hence will increase the overall hourly cost of any given quantity of labor. Thus, as their labor forces have become more educated, employers have stiffened their resistance to a shorter workweek.[27]

3. Advertising. More recently Brack and Cowling[28] have tested the notion that advertising has induced the labor force to work longer hours than it otherwise would. Their argument is that advertising has both grown quantitatively and increased in effectiveness (largely because of television) in the post-World War II period. This has increased the desires of workers for more goods and services and therefore induced them to work more hours than would otherwise be the case.

In more technical terms, the cumulative impact of advertising allegedly has been to generate a reemergence of a substitution effect powerful enough to prevent the continued fall in the workweek in the postwar period. This strengthening of the substitution effect has occurred because advertising has increased the marginal valuation of goods relative to leisure. In terms of the analysis in

---

[26]Thomas J. Kniesner, "The Full-Time Workweek in the United States, 1900–1970," *Industrial and Labor Relations Review,* October 1976, pp. 3–5. See also Ethel B. Jones, "Comment," and Kniesner, "Reply," *Industrial and Labor Relations Review,* April 1980, pp. 379–389.

[27]Employer resistance to a shrinking workweek may be reinforced by the greater growth of fringe benefits which has occurred in the postwar period (Chapter 8). Employer expenditures for such fringes as worker life and health insurance are also fixed costs on a per worker basis and, as with recruitment and training costs, a shortened workweek would entail higher hourly labor costs.

[28]John Brack and Keith Cowling, "Advertising and Labour Supply: Workweek and Workyear in U.S. Manufacturing Industries, 1919–1976," *Kyklos,* Number 2, 1983, pp. 285–303.

Chapter 2 (see Figure 2-4, for example), advertising has made worker indifference curves flatter, with the consequence that a given increase in wage rates may now leave desired hours of work unchanged, rather than reduced. Brack and Cowling conclude that "the growth in advertising . . . has exercised a cumulative impact on the desire to acquire goods and in consequence has created a reluctance to substitute leisure for income as the real wage rises."[29] They suggest that advertising has caused the workweek to be approximately 27 percent longer than it otherwise would have been.

4. "Catching up." Still another explanation of the postwar stability of the workweek has been offered by Owen.[30] He reminds us that the postwar period followed a decade and a half of depression and war. During the depression era of the 1930s most families were forced to curtail greatly their expenditures for consumer goods. And during the war years of the early 1940s many consumer durables were simply not available. Furthermore, birth rates declined in the 1930s because many couples found they simply could not afford children. Owen contends that in the immediate postwar period American households attempted to "catch up" on both consumption and childbearing and that, as a result, there was little demand for further reductions in the workweek. Hence, the immediate postwar period was characterized by both a consumer buying binge and a "baby boom." The latter was particularly significant because, unlike the purchase of a car or a television, the decision to have more children imposes higher household costs which extend over some two decades. Furthermore, the extension of the years of schooling during the postwar period added substantially to the cost of rearing each child. In short, Owen contends that catching up in terms of consumer goods and family size, coupled with more schooling, have made a declining workweek—and the attendant loss of earnings—less attractive.

SUMMARY

1. Given population size, the aggregate quantity of labor supplied depends upon the labor force participation rate and the number of hours worked weekly and annually.
2. It is fruitful to examine and explain participation rates in terms of Becker's time allocation model. This model views households as "producing" utility-yielding commodities by combining goods and time. In this context household members allocate their time to labor market work, household production, and consumption on the basis of comparative advantage.
3. The labor force participation rate is simply the actual labor force as a percentage of the potential or "age-eligible" population.
4. In the post-World War II period the aggregate participation rate has been quite

---

[29]Ibid., p. 300.

[30]John D. Owen, "Workweeks and Leisure: An Analysis of Trends, 1948–75," *Monthly Labor Review,* August 1976, pp. 3–8.

stable, varying only between 59 and 65 percent. This stability reflects offsetting increases in the participation rates of married women and decreases in the participation rates of older men.

5. Rising participation rates for married women have been caused by (*a*) rising relative wage rates for women, (*b*) stronger female preferences for labor market work, (*c*) rising productivity within the household, (*d*) declining birth rates, and (*e*) the greater accessibility of jobs. The participation rates of black women have been greater than those of white women, although the rates have tended to converge over time.

6. Most of the decline in male participation rates is due to older males. The declining participation rates of older males is attributed to (*a*) mandatory retirement policies, (*b*) the increased coverage and increasingly generous benefits provided by OASDHI, (*c*) the secular increase in real earnings and accumulated wealth; and (*d*) age-earnings profiles which suggest that the cost of leisure may decline for older workers.

7. Economists disagree as to whether or not there is a causal relationship between the changes in the participation rates of women and men.

8. Cyclical changes in participation rates reflect the net impact of the added-worker and discouraged-worker effects. The added-worker effect suggests that, when a family's primary breadwinner loses his or her job, other family members will become labor market participants in order to sustain the family's income. The discouraged-worker effect indicates that during recession some unemployed workers will become pessimistic as to their prospects for reemployment and will therefore withdraw from the labor force. Empirical studies suggest that the discouraged-worker effect is dominant with the result that the aggregate labor force participation rate tends to vary inversely with the unemployment rate.

9. The average workweek and workyear declined during the 1910–1940 period, but since World War II both have been quite stable. The earlier workweek and workyear declines have been explained in terms of the income effect's domination of the substitution effect as real wage rates have risen historically. The post-World War II stability of the workweek and workyear has been variously attributed to (*a*) higher income tax rates, (*b*) increases in education, (*c*) the effect of advertising, and (*d*) the desire of households to catch up with respect to the low levels of consumption and the low birth rates of the pre-World War II era.

QUESTIONS AND STUDY SUGGESTIONS

1. Key terms and concepts to remember: Becker's model of the allocation of time; time-intensive and goods-intensive commodities; potential and actual labor force; labor force participation rate; added-worker and discouraged-worker effects.

2. In what specific ways does Becker's model of the allocation of time differ from the simple work-leisure choice model? Compare the functioning of the income and substitution effects in each of the two models. Do the two effects have the same impact upon labor market work in both models?

3. In 1982 our economy had a population of 232 million, of which 57 million were either under 16 years of age or institutionalized. Approximately 110 million people were either employed or unemployed but actively seeking work. What was the participation rate in 1982?

4. What has happened to the aggregate labor force participation rate in the post-World War II period? Despite the rising real earnings of husbands, the participation rates of

married women have increased. What factors account for this increase? How might one explain that participation rates for black women are higher than for white women?

5. "The ratio of the incomes of black families to the incomes of white families has increased quite slowly in the past two or three decades, despite legislation and a variety of public policies to ameliorate discrimination. One may therefore conclude that government programs have failed to lessen racial discrimination." Discuss critically.

6. "Empirical evidence for the United States suggests a negative sensitivity of labor force participation to unemployment." Do you agree? Explain in terms of the discouraged-worker and added-worker effects.

7. "The added-worker effect can be explained in terms of the income effect, while the discouraged-worker effect is based upon the substitution effect." Do you agree?

8. What has happened to the length of the workweek and workyear during this century? Explain any significant trends.

9. The accompanying diagram restates the basic work-leisure choice model as presented in Chapter 2. Use this diagram to explain the declining workweek which occurred in the pre-World War II period, making explicit the assumptions underlying your analysis. We noted in the present chapter that the stability of the workweek in the post-World War II era has been attributed by various scholars to such considerations as (a) higher taxes on earnings, (b) acquisition of more education, (c) advertising, and (d) compensation by households for low levels of consumption and low birth rates experienced in the pre-World War II period. Make alterations in the indifference curves or budget line of the diagram to indicate how *each* of these four factors might contribute to a relatively stable workweek despite rising before-tax real wages.

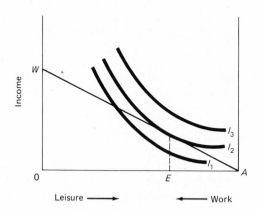

SELECTED REFERENCES

Bowen, William G., and T. Aldrich Finegan: *The Economics of Labor Force Participation* (Princeton, N.J.: Princeton University Press, 1969).

Cain, Glen G.: *Married Women in the Labor Force* (Chicago: University of Chicago Press, 1966).

Finegan, T. Aldrich: "Participation of Married Women in the Labor Force," in Cynthia B. Lloyd (ed.), *Sex, Discrimination, and the Division of Labor* (New York: Columbia University Press, 1975).

GREIS, THERESA DISS: *The Decline of Annual Hours Worked in the United States since 1948* (Philadelphia: The Wharton School, 1984).

KILLINGSWORTH, MARK: *Labor Supply* (Cambridge: Cambridge University Press, 1983), chaps 2 and 3.

T I M E   A N D   O N E - H A L F

ECONOMICS AND FERTILITY

In the past decade or so some economists have attempted to explain birthrates in terms of the benefit-cost calculations of microeconomic analysis.

Gary Becker's economic view of the family, summarized at the outset of the present chapter, has been extended to other areas such as criminal behavior, marriage and divorce, and fertility and childbearing. The latter topic is of present interest. Becker* and others contend that the decision to have children is analogous to a market transaction wherein one purchases a capital good or a consumer durable good. Considered as a "capital good" a child may yield *benefits* in the form of future income flows for the parents. That is, the child may provide labor and hence income for a family farm or business. Or the child may provide transfer income when the parents are elderly and retired. As "consumer goods" children presumably yield a future stream of satisfactions or benefits in the same sense as does an automobile or video recorder. On the other hand, the decision to have a child implies both *direct* and *indirect* (opportunity) *costs*. The former involve expenditures for food, shelter, health care, day care, education, and so forth. The latter entail the cost or value of the time which parents devote to a child's care. One of the primary costs here often is the forgone labor market income of the mother who remains out of the labor market to care for the child. In terms of Becker's time allocation model of this chapter, children are very time-intensive "goods." Presumably, if the future stream of benefits are estimated to exceed the stream of costs, a couple will decide in favor of having a child. But if the costs exceed benefits, the couple will choose to forgo having the child.

Proponents of this microeconomic explanation of fertility argue that it explains why birth rates decline with economic growth. That is, high-income families (nations) tend to have fewer children (lower rates of population growth) than do poor families (nations). Income and substitution effects are again relevant. Children are considered to be normal "goods," so that rising real incomes per se can be expected to *increase* birthrates. Wealthier families can afford to "purchase" more children. But this tendency is more than offset by the substitution effect. Specifically, the "price" of children has increased significantly, reflecting not merely higher direct costs but also higher opportunity costs due to the rising labor market wages available to wives. Furthermore, Becker contends there is a quality-quantity trade-off for children just as there is for other goods. As incomes have risen, couples have opted for higher-quality (healthier, better-educated) children in the same way they have purchased higher-quality stereos and housing. This

*See in particular Gary S. Becker, *The Economic Approach to Human Behavior* (Chicago: University of Chicago Press, 1976), part 6. Victor R. Fuchs, *How We Live* (Cambridge, Mass.: Harvard University Press, 1983), chap. 2, is also relevant.

choice has entailed the expenditure of more money and more time per child. For all of these reasons the cost or "price" of children has increased substantially with a consequent large substitution effect. Put bluntly, the higher price of children has induced higher-income couples to substitute other goods and to therefore "buy" fewer children.

Let us consider several of the many implications of this economic interpretation of fertility. First, the theory calls attention to some of the important interrelationships or feedbacks implicit in Figure 3-1. For example, birthrates affect, and are affected by, the participation rate, hours of work, and overall labor market opportunities of women. Similarly, the quality of labor is positively related to incomes. A second implication has to do with economic policy. The more-or-less traditional view of economists is that underdeveloped countries must first lower birthrates before they can expect per capita living levels to rise. The economic view of the family turns this perception on its head, implying that rising real incomes will alter perceived benefits and costs so that couples will freely choose to have fewer children. Finally, the analysis suggests that the decision of high-income couples to have fewer children of higher quality may contribute to the perpetuation of income inequality through time. If high-income couples "invest" more in the health and education of their children, those higher-quality children are likely to have greater earning capacity than the lower-quality children of lower-income families. The children of the well-to-do will also divide a larger inheritance of wealth among a smaller number of offspring.

Let us briefly note several of the criticisms which the economic view of fertility has elicited.† First, the market for children is fictional; the magnitude of the variables which would be relevant to a rational "purchasing" decision are simply not knowable when the decision is made. For example, the "quality" of a child cannot be predetermined and, hence, future benefits are unknown. Similarly, future costs—what must be given up in obtaining a child—cannot be accurately estimated. It simply strains the imagination to think that people behave "as if" they are buying a consumer durable good when they decide whether to have a child. A second and related criticism is that the economic view of fertility is too narrow in that it omits important sociological and cultural variables which apparently bear upon fertility. One can argue that fertility decisions are shaped in part by social norms and group lifestyles. Indeed, the inverse relationship between incomes and birthrates may simply reflect a better understanding of the effective use of birth control technologies by higher-income families, rather than changing benefit-cost relationships. Finally, even if one admits that benefit-cost analysis is relevant to the fertility decision, it is not at all clear that costs will rise sufficiently with incomes so as to generate the dominant substitution effect predicted by the economic view of fertility. For example, one can argue that the indirect or opportunity cost of children may be *relatively* greater for low-income than high-income families. The poor family can less afford the loss of the wife's income than can a well-to-do family. Indeed, the higher absolute wages presumably available to wives in high-income families may be irrelevant as an opportunity cost because for cultural reasons such wives are not likely to be labor force participants. And even if they do work, the net opportunity cost is not their forgone earnings, but rather much lower baby-sitting costs. High-income families should be more able to bear baby-sitting costs than are low-income families; therefore, we might expect them to have more, rather than fewer, children!

---

† See Harvey Leibenstein, "An Interpretation of the Economic Theory of Fertility: Promising Path or Blind Alley?", *Journal of Economic Literature*, June 1974, pp. 457–479, and Isabel V. Sawhill, "Economic Perspectives on the Family," *Daedalus*, Spring 1977, pp. 115–125.

LABOR QUALITY: INVESTING IN HUMAN CAPITAL

I n Chapters 2 and 3 our attention focused primarily upon the decision of whether one should participate in the labor market. Our emphasis there was upon the work-leisure decision and the various participation rates of subaggregates of the population. In this chapter we turn from quantitative to qualitative aspects of labor supply. Workers bring differing levels of educational attainment and skills to the labor market. They also acquire substantially different amounts of on-the-job training. Obviously, a more-educated, better-trained worker will be capable of supplying a larger amount of useful productive effort than will one with less education and training.

Any activity which increases the quality (productivity) of labor per se may be considered an investment in human capital. Thus human capital investments include not only expenditures on formal education and on-the-job training, but also expenditures on health and migration. Workers can become more productive by improving their physical or mental health and also by moving from locations and jobs where their productivity is relatively low to other locations and jobs where their productivity is relatively high. In fact, in Chapter 14 human capital theory will be the core concept used to analyze labor migration.

In the present chapter our focus is upon investment in education and on-the-job training. Our plan of attack is as follows. First, we want to justify the notion that expenditures on education and training merit consideration as investment and to present some simple data which show the statistical relation between education and worker earnings. Second, we will present a basic model which will demonstrate how the rate of return on a human capital investment can be estimated. Next, some important implications of the human capital model will be outlined. Fourth, the concept of the investment demand for human capital will be derived from the human capital model and combined with the supply of investment funds to explain why different individuals find it rational to invest in substantially different amounts of education. Fifth, we will digress slightly to consider some of the peculiarities of the markets for college-trained workers. Sixth, we will briefly consider on-the-job training as a human capital investment. Finally, we will present some of the criticisms and shortcomings of human capital theory.

INVESTMENT IN HUMAN CAPITAL: CONCEPT AND DATA

When a firm invests in physical capital it is acquiring some asset which is expected to enhance the firm's flow of net profits over a period of time. Hence, a company might purchase new machinery designed to increase output and therefore sales revenues over, say, the 10-year projected useful life of the machinery. The unique characteristic of investment is that *current* expenditures or costs are incurred with the intent that these costs will be more than compensated for by enhanced *future* revenues or returns. Analogously, investments are made in human capital. When a person (or one's parents or society at large) makes a current expenditure on education or training, it is anticipated that one's knowledge and skills and therefore future earnings will be enhanced.[1] The important point is that expenditures on education and training can be fruitfully treated as **investment in human capital** just as expenditures on capital equipment can be understood as investment in physical capital.

Pertinent data reveal two things. First, the educational attainment of the labor force has increased rather dramatically over time. For example, in 1962 over 22 percent of the civilian labor force had achieved less than 9 years of schooling, while a mere 11 percent had completed 4 or more years of college. Similar figures for 1980 were 7 and 18 percent respectively. Second, investments in education do apparently result in an enlarged flow of earnings. The **age-earnings profiles** of Figure 4-1 show the lifetime earnings patterns of male workers who have attained various educational levels. For present purposes the most obvious conclusion to be drawn from these profiles is that for each age group the median incomes of more-educated workers exceed those of less-educated workers. Closer scrutiny also reveals that the earnings profiles of more-educated workers rise more rapidly than do those of less-educated workers. There is thus a tendency for differences in the earnings of more- and less-educated workers to widen as workers grow older.[2]

---

[1]As will be noted later, the payoff from an investment in education may also take nonmonetary forms, for example, obtaining a more pleasant job or a greater appreciation of literature and art.

[2]The fact that the age-earnings profiles ultimately decline must be interpreted with some care. While one is tempted to attribute the declining incomes of older workers to such considerations as diminished physical vigor and mental alertness, the obsolescence of one's education and skills, or the decision to work shorter hours, the decline may be largely due to the character of the data. In particular, these data do *not* track the earnings of specific individuals through their lifetimes. Rather, these cross-sectional data show the earnings of different individuals of different ages in some particular year. Longitudinal data which do trace the earnings of specific persons over time indicate that earnings continue to increase until retirement. The declining segments of the age-earnings profiles in Figure 4-1 may be due to the fact that the U.S. economy has been growing and therefore each succeeding generation has tended to earn more than the preceding one. Hence, the average 45-year-old college-educated worker has higher earnings as shown in the age-earnings profiles simply because he or she is a member of a more recent "generation" than a 65-year-old college-educated worker.

THE HUMAN CAPITAL MODEL

Let us now introduce a simple model through which we might analyze the decision to invest in, say, a college education. Assume you have just graduated from high school and are trying to determine whether to go to college. From a purely economic standpoint, a rational decision will involve a comparison of the associated costs and benefits. The monetary costs incurred in the purchase of a college education are of two general types. On the one hand, there are *direct* or *out-of-pocket costs* in the form of expenditures for tuition, special fees, books and supplies, and so forth. Expenditures for room and board are *not* included as a part of direct costs because presumably you would need food and shelter regardless of whether you attend college or enter the labor market. On the other hand, the *indirect* or *opportunity cost* of going to college is the earnings one forgoes by not entering the labor market upon completing high school. For example, estimates suggest that indirect costs may account for as much as 60 to 70 percent of the total cost of a college education, at least for public universities. The economic *benefit* of investing in a college education, as we know from Figure 4-1, is an enlarged future flow of earnings.

FIGURE 4-1 AGE-EARNINGS PROFILES BY YEARS OF EDUCATION
Age-earnings profiles (in this case for males in 1982) indicate that education "pays" in that more-educated workers obtain higher annual earnings than do less-educated workers of the same age group.

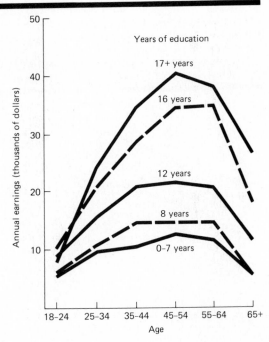

This simple conception of a human capital investment decision is portrayed graphically in Figure 4-2. Curve *HH* represents your earnings profile if you decide not to attend college, but rather enter the labor market immediately upon the completion of high school at age 18. The *CC* "curve" is your cost-earnings profile if you decide to undertake a 4-year college degree before entering the labor market. We note that area 1 below the horizontal axis represents the direct or out-of-pocket costs (the "negative income") incurred in attending college. Area 2 reflects the indirect or opportunity costs, that is, the earnings you forgo while attending college. The sum of areas 1 and 2 show the total cost—one's total investment—in a college education. Area 3 shows the gross *incremental* earnings which you will realize by obtaining a college degree; it shows how much *additional* income you will realize as a college graduate over your work life as compared to what you would have earned with just a high school diploma. Your work life in this case is presumed to extend over the 43-year period from age 22 to age 65.

Discounting and Net Present Value. We know that to make a rational decision you will want to compare costs (areas 1 and 2) with benefits (area 3). But a complication arises at this point. The costs and benefits associated with investing in a college education accrue at different points in time. This is important be-

FIGURE 4-2 AGE-EARNINGS PROFILES WITH AND WITHOUT A COLLEGE EDUCATION
If an individual decides to enter the labor market upon graduation from high school at age 18, the age-earnings profile will be *HH* in comparison with the *CC* profile if she or he had gone to college. Attending college entails both direct costs (tuition, fees, books) and indirect costs (forgone earnings). But upon entering the labor market at age 22 the college graduate will enjoy a high level of annual earnings over her or his working life. To determine whether it is economically rational to invest in a college education one must find its net present value by discounting costs and benefits back to the present (age 18).

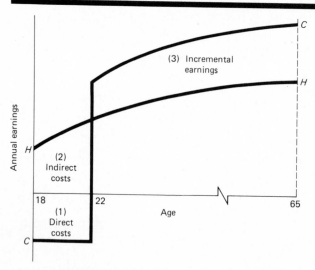

cause dollars expended and received at different points in time are of different value. Hence, a meaningful comparison of the costs and benefits associated with a college education requires that these costs and benefits be compared in terms of a common point in time, for example, the present. What we seek to determine from the vantage point of an 18-year-old youth is the net present discounted value, or simply the **net present value,** of the future costs and future benefits of a college education.

Why do dollars earned (or expended) have a different value a year, or 2 or 3 years, from now than they have today? The immediate answer is that a positive interest rate is paid for borrowing or "renting" money. But this raises an additional question: *Why* is interest paid for the use or "rent" of money? The answer lies in the notion of **time preference,** that is, the idea that, given the choice, most people prefer the pleasure of indulgence today rather than the promise of indulgence tomorrow. Most individuals prefer present consumption to future consumption because, given the uncertainties and vagaries of life, the former seems more tangible and therefore more valuable. Time preference, in short, is the idea that people are impatient and subjectively prefer goods in the present over the same goods in the future. It follows that an individual must be "bribed" or compensated by an interest payment to defer present consumption or, alternatively stated, to save a portion of one's income. Thus, if an individual equates $100 worth of goods today with $110 worth of goods a year from now, we can say that his time preference rate is 10 percent. The individual must be paid $10 or 10 percent as an inducement to forgo $100 worth of present consumption.

Because the preference for present consumption necessitates payment of a positive interest rate, a dollar received a year from now is worth less than a dollar obtained today because a dollar received today can be loaned or invested at some positive interest rate and thereby be worth more than a dollar a year from now. Thus if the interest rate is 10 percent, one can lend $1 today and receive $1.10 at the end of the year; the $1.10 is comprised of the original $1 plus $.10 of interest. This can be shown algebraically as follows:

$$V_p(1 + i) = V_1 \qquad\qquad (4\text{-}1)$$

Where:
   V_p = present or current value, that is, $1.00 today
   V_1 = value (of the $1.00) one year from now
   i = interest rate

The $(1 + i)$ term indicates that one receives back the original or present value ($1.00) *plus* the interest. Substituting our illustrative numbers, we have

$$\$1.00\ (1.10) = \$1.10$$

This formulation tells us that, given a 10 percent interest rate, $1.10 received next year is the equivalent of $1.00 in hand today.

Equation (4-1) focuses upon determining the *future* value of the $1.00 one has today. As indicated earlier, our goal is to determine the *present* (today's) value of expenditures and revenues incurred and received in the future. We can get at this by restating our original question. Instead of asking how much $1.00 obtained today will be worth a year from now, let us inquire how much $1.10 received a year from now would be worth today. In general terms the answer is found simply by solving equation (4-1) for V_p. Thus

$$V_p = \frac{V_1}{(1 + i)} \tag{4-2}$$

Equation (4-2) is simply a **discount formula** for a one-year period. Inserting our illustrative numbers:

$$\$1.00 = \frac{\$1.10}{1.10}$$

That is, $1.10 received a year from now is worth only $1.00 today if the interest rate is 10 percent.

Observing in Figure 4-2 that both costs and benefits are incurred, not simply next year, but over a number of years, we can extend the discounting formula of equation (4-2) as follows:

$$V_p = \frac{E_1}{(1 + i)} + \frac{E_2}{(1 + i)^2} + \frac{E_3}{(1 + i)^3} + \cdot \cdot \cdot + \frac{E_n}{(1 + i)^n} \tag{4-3}$$

where the E's represent a stream of incremental earnings (E_1 being the additional income received in the first year, E_2 the additional income received in the second year, and so forth); n is the duration of the earnings stream or, in other words, the individual's expected working life;[3] and i is the interest rate.[4] Observe that the denominator of the second term is squared, the third is cubed, and so forth. The reason for this, of course, is that E_2 and E_3 must be discounted back 2 and 3 years respectively. That is, the value of E_2 is discounted back to year 1 by dividing E_2 by $(1 + i)$, but *that* value must be divided again by $(1 + i)$ to find its present value, V_p.

Figure 4-2 reminds us that the decision to invest in a college education entails both costs and benefits (enhanced earnings). How can both be accounted for in equation (4-3)? The simplest answer is merely to treat costs as negative earnings. Hence, the "earnings" for the 4 years the individual is in college (E_1, E_2, E_3, and E_4) will be the negative sum of the direct and indirect costs incurred in each of those years. For each succeeding year until retirement, incremental

---

[3]In Figure 4-2, n would be 47 (= 65 − 18) for a high school graduate.

[4]We are sidestepping the troublesome problem of deciding which interest rate is appropriate. A small difference in the rate actually used can have a very substantial impact upon one's calculation of present value.

earnings will be positive. Thus, we are actually calculating the *net* present value of a college education in equation (4-3).

The relevant investment criterion or decision rule based upon this calculation is that the individual should make the investment if its net present value is greater than zero. A positive value tells us that the present discounted value of the benefits exceed the present discounted value of the costs and when this is so—when benefits exceed costs—the decision to invest is economically rational. If the net present value is negative, then costs exceed benefits and the investment is not economically justifiable.

A truncated example may be helpful at this point. Assume that upon graduating from high school Carl Carlson contemplates enrolling in a 1-year intensive course in data processing. The direct costs of the course are $1000 and the opportunity cost is $5000. Upon completion of the course, he has been promised employment with the Computex Corporation. Expecting to receive a large inheritance, he plans to work only 3 years and then retire permanently from the labor force. The incremental income he anticipates earning because of his data processing training is $2500, $3000, and $3500 for the 3 years he intends to work. The relevant interest rate at this time is 10 percent. Is the decision to enroll in the data processing course rational? By substituting these figures in equation (4-3), we have

$$V_p = \frac{E_1}{(1 + i)} + \frac{E_2}{(1 + i)^2} + \frac{E_3}{(1 + i)^3} + \frac{E_4}{(1 + i)^4}$$

$$V_p = \frac{-\$6000}{(1.10)} + \frac{\$2500}{(1.10)^2} + \frac{\$3000}{(1.10)^3} + \frac{\$3500}{(1.10)^4}$$

$$V_p = -\$5455 + \$2066 + \$2254 + \$2391$$

$$V_p = \$1256$$

Our formula tells us that the present value of the benefits (the incremental earnings) totals $6711 (= $2066 + $2254 + $2391) and exceeds the present value of the costs of $5455 by $1256. This positive net present value indicates that it *is* economically rational for Carlson to make this investment in human capital.

Internal Rate of Return. An alternative means of making an investment decision involves calculating the **internal rate of return** r on a prospective investment and comparing it with the interest rate i. *By definition, the internal rate of return is that rate of discount at which the net present value of a human capital investment will be zero.* Thus, instead of using the interest rate i in equation (4-3) to calculate whether the net present value is positive or negative, one determines what particular rate of discount r will equate the present values of future costs and benefits so that the net present value is zero. Hence, we must modify equation (4-3) as follows:

$$V_p = \frac{E_1}{(1 + r)} + \frac{E_2}{(1 + r)^2} + \frac{E_3}{(1 + r)^3} + \cdots + \frac{E_n}{(1 + r)^n} = 0 \qquad (4\text{-}4)$$

Instead of solving for V_p as in equation (4-3), we solve for r, given the values of the E's and assuming V_p is zero. A moment's reflection makes clear that r indicates the maximum rate of interest which one could pay on borrowed funds to finance a human capital investment and still break even.

The investment criterion or decision rule appropriate to this approach involves a comparison of the internal rate of return r with the interest rate i. If r exceeds the market i, the investment is profitable and should be undertaken. For example, if one can borrow funds at a 10 percent interest rate and make an investment which yields 15 percent, it is obviously profitable to do so. But if r is less than i, the investment is unprofitable and should not be undertaken. If one can borrow money at a 10 percent rate and the prospective investment only yields 5 percent, it is clearly not profitable to invest. If faced with a series of human capital investments—for example, successive years of schooling—whose rates of return are arranged in declining order, it will be profitable to invest up to the point at which $r = i$.

Generalizations and Implications. The explanatory power of the human capital model is considerable. Let us pause at this point to consider several generalizations which stem from the basic model as presented in Figure 4-2 and equations (4-3) and (4-4).

1. Length of income stream. Other things being equal, the longer the stream of postinvestment incremental earnings, the more likely the net present value of an investment in human capital will be positive. Or, alternatively stated, the longer the earnings stream, the higher the internal rate of return. A human capital investment made later in life will have a lower net present value (and a lower r) for the simple reason that fewer years of work life and, hence, of positive incremental earnings, will remain upon completion of the investment. This generalization helps explain why it is primarily young people who go to college[5] and why younger people are more likely to migrate—that is, to invest in geographic mobility—than are older people (see Chapter 14). It also explains a portion of the earnings differential that has existed between women and men. In many cases the participation of women in the labor force has been discontinuous. That is, many women worked for a few years after the completion of formal schooling, then married and stayed out of the labor force for a time to bear and

---

[5]While perhaps not rational on investment grounds, the decision of older people to return to college may be justified in terms of consumption (utility) criteria.

raise children. They then reentered the labor force sometime after the last child began school. The average absence of married women from the labor force was about 10 years. In terms of equations (4-3) and (4-4) this obviously meant an abbreviated stream of earnings. This dampened the economic incentive of females to invest in their own human capital by lowering the net present value or the rate of return. Furthermore, the fact that their labor force participation was likely to be interrupted inhibited employers from investing in their on-the-job training. One estimate suggests that as much as 50 percent of the difference in hourly earnings between males and females might be explained by differences in schooling and on-the-job experience.[6]

2. Costs. Other things being equal, the lower the cost of a human capital investment, the larger the number of people who will find that investment to be profitable. Hence, if the direct or indirect costs of attending college were to fall, we would expect enrollment to rise. Illustration: The GI Bill provided public subsidies to World War II veterans who decided to attend college. By reducing the private direct cost[7] of a college education, the GI Bill induced a sharp upsurge in college enrollments. Similarly, the state of the economy may influence college enrollments through its effects on the indirect or opportunity costs of attending college. For example, if recession reduces the earnings which high school graduates can achieve or, alternatively, reduces the probability of obtaining a job, the opportunity costs of attending college will fall and enrollments will rise. Lower costs increase the net present value of a college education, making the investment in education "profitable" for some who previously found it to be unprofitable. In fact, recession does tend to have a positive effect upon college enrollments.[8] A more subtle point ties in with our previous generalization that older individuals are less likely to invest in human capital. Our age-earnings profiles (Figure 4-1) tell us that earnings rise with age. Hence, the opportunity cost of attending college will be greater for older workers and, other things being equal, the net present value and the internal rate of return associated with human capital investments will be lower. In other words, there are two reasons

[6]Solomon W. Polachek, "Discontinuous Labor Force Participation and Its Effects on Women's Market Earnings," in Cynthia B. Lloyd (ed.), *Sex, Discrimination, and the Division of Labor* (New York: Columbia University Press, 1975), pp. 90–122.

[7]Of course, there is no free lunch. Taxpayers (society as a whole) paid the costs associated with the GI Bill subsidy. But in calculating the cost of a college education from a *private* (as opposed to *social*) perspective the GI Bill reduced the costs to the individual enrollee and increased the private net present value associated with a college education.

[8]J. Peter Mattila, "Determinants of Male School Enrollments: A Time-Series Analysis," *Review of Economics and Statistics*, May 1982, pp. 242–251. In examining cyclical changes in male school enrollment, Mattila notes that a recession imposes both a discouraged-worker effect and an added-worker effect (Chapter 3) upon young people. The former indicates that, when jobs are unavailable, one may decide to attend school. The latter effect suggests that, when a parent becomes unemployed, a youth may be unable to afford staying in school. Mattila finds that the discouraged-worker effect exceeds the added worker effect for males 16–19, but there is no clear impact upon males 20–21 years old.

why older people are less likely to invest in a college education: (1) the length of their future earnings stream will be relatively short, and (2) their opportunity costs of attending college will tend to be high.

3. Earnings differentials. Not only is the *length* of the incremental earnings stream critical in making a human capital investment decision, but so is the *size* of that differential. The obvious generalization is that, other things being equal, the larger the college–high school earnings differential, the larger the number of people who will invest in a college education. Empirical evidence tends to confirm this generalization. Freeman has argued that in about 1970 the labor market for college graduates changed from one characterized by shortages to one characterized by surpluses. One of the manifestations of this change was that the *college premium,* that is, the incremental earnings associated with a college education, declined sharply. "Among all men in 1969, college graduates earned 53% more than high school graduates and 99% more than grade school graduates; in 1974 the premiums stood at 35% and 74% respectively."[9] One of the responses to this decline in earnings differentials was that in the early 1970s the proportion of young persons enrolling in college declined significantly. In 1969 some 60 percent of male high school graduates decided to go to college; by 1974 only 49 percent were enrolling in college. "Despite a 20% increase in the number of persons of college age, enrollment of 18- to 19-year-old men fell from 1,397,000 in 1969 to 1,262,000 in 1974."[10]

Rate-of-Return Studies. There have been numerous empirical studies which estimate the returns of human capital investments at all educational levels. Here we concentrate upon those which show private rates of return on investments in a college education. Speaking very generally, most such studies have estimated such rates of return to be on the order of 10 to 15 percent. For example, in his classic work Becker estimated the internal rate of return to be 14.5, 13.0, and 14.8 percent in 1939, 1949, and 1958 respectively.[11] Hanoch calculated a 9.6 percent return in 1959.[12] Similarly, Mattila has estimated rates of return to males on the order of 10 to 13 percent for the entire 1956–1979 period.[13] Estimates by Freeman for males are summarized in columns 1 and 2 of Table 4-1. The decline

[9]Richard B. Freeman, *The Overeducated American* (New York: Academic Press, 1976), p. 13.

[10]Ibid., p. 34. The indicated declines were undoubted influenced by changes in military conscription laws. A young man could obtain a draft deferment by attending college in 1969, but by 1974 the draft was inconsequential as a determinant of college attendance.

[11]Gary Becker, *Human Capital,* 2d ed. (New York: National Bureau of Economic Research, 1975), chap. 4.

[12]Giora Hanoch, "An Economic Analysis of Earnings and Schooling," *Journal of Human Resources,* Summer 1967, pp. 310–329. For an excellent summary of empirical research on the private monetary returns to higher education, see Howard Bowen, *Investment in Learning* (San Francisco: Jossey-Bass Publishers, 1977), chap. 12.

[13]Mattila, op. cit., p. 244.

in the rate of return over the 1969–1974 period reflects Freeman's aforementioned contention that Americans are becoming overeducated and that the market for college graduates changed from one of shortages to one of surpluses in about 1970.

But all such estimates must be interpreted with some care. First, one has no way of accurately predicting the future. One cannot estimate with a great deal of accuracy what the future earnings of a new college graduate will be. Hence, data used in research studies to calculate rates of return on human capital investments are *historical* data; that is, the data are the age-earnings profiles of *past* college graduates who obtained their education as far back as, say, 1940 or even earlier. The observation that college graduates in the labor market in 1985 received on the average $4000 more per year than the typical high school graduate is no guarantee that this difference will persist into the future. By 1990 or 2000 the amount of incremental income might have widened or diminished. In this regard it is notable that, while incremental earnings affect the decision to invest in a college education, the decision to invest in a college education also affects incremental earnings! If college graduates have enjoyed a high earnings differential in comparison with high school graduates in the recent *past,* an increasing proportion of new high school graduates will find it rational to invest in a college education. But the fact that they do so will increase the supply of college as opposed to high school graduates and tend to reduce the *future* earnings differential or college premium. A high rate of return in the recent past could contribute to a decreasing rate of return in the future.

Second, it must be recognized that the historical data used in human capital studies are in the form of *average* (median) earnings *and* that the distribution of earnings by educational level around the average is wide. Hence, while a given study may calculate that the average rate of return on a college education is 10 percent, some individuals may earn 30 or 50 percent, while to others the return may be negative. For example, Lester Thurow has pointed out that "approximately 28 percent of those with college educations had incomes [in 1972] below the median high school income (negative gross rates of return), and approxi-

---

TABLE 4-1

Rates of Return to College Training for Men

(1) Year	(2) Private Rate of Return, %	(3) Social Rate of Return, %
1959	11.0	10.5
1969	11.5	11.1
1972	10.5	9.5
1974	8.5	7.5

Source: Richard B. Freeman, "Overinvestment in College Training?" *Journal of Human Resources,* Summer 1975, p. 296.

mately 21 percent of those with high school educations had incomes above the median college income."[14]

Private versus Social Perspective. To this point we have viewed the human capital investment decision from a *private* or *personal* **perspective.** That is, we have viewed benefits and costs strictly from the standpoint of an individual who is contemplating a human capital investment. It is important to recognize that the investment decision also can be viewed from a *social* or *public* **perspective.** In changing perspectives we can retain equations (4-3) and (4-4); however, we must alter our conceptions of costs and benefits. The private approach only includes those costs and benefits which accrue to the individual. But from the social perspective the scope of relevant costs and benefits must be broadened. In particular, the private perspective excludes any public subsidies to education in calculating costs for the simple reason that, by definition, such subsidies are obviously *not* paid by the individual. Similarly, benefits (incremental earnings) should be calculated on an *after-tax* basis from the personal point of view. From the standpoint of society, costs should obviously include any public subsidies to education, and benefits should be in terms of *before-tax* incremental earnings. Presumably the part of incremental earnings taxed away by government will be used to finance public goods and services which will be of benefit to society as a whole.

Furthermore, most economists believe that education entails substantial *external* or *social benefits,* that is, benefits which accrue to parties other than the individual acquiring the education. From a social perspective these benefits should clearly be included in estimating the rate of return on human capital investments. What are these social benefits? First, it is well known that more-educated workers have lower unemployment rates than do less-educated workers. Having high unemployment rates, poorly educated workers receive unemployment compensation and welfare benefits with greater frequency and may also find crime a relatively attractive alternative source of income. This means that society might benefit from investing in education by having to pay less taxes for social welfare programs, crime prevention, and law enforcement. Second, political participation and, presumably, the quality of political decisions might improve with increased literacy and education. More education might mean that society's political processes would function more effectively to the benefit of society at large. Third, there are intergenerational benefits in the sense that the children of better-educated parents grow up in a more desirable home environment and receive better care, guidance, and informal preschool education. Fourth, the research discoveries of highly educated people might yield large and widely disbursed benefits to society. Jonas Salk's discovery of an effective and economic polio vaccine is illustrative.[15]

[14]Lester C. Thurow, *Generating Inequality* (New York: Basic Books, Inc., Publishers, 1975), pp. 68–69.

[15]For a more detailed discussion see Burton A. Weisbrod, "Investing in Human Capital," *Journal of Human Resources,* Summer 1966, pp. 1–21.

Why is our distinction between private and social rates of return on human capital investments significant? In the first place, the difference between the private and the social perspective is of potential importance because efficiency demands that the economy's total investment outlay be allocated so that rates of return on human and physical capital should be equal at the margin. For example, if a given amount of investment spending is currently being allocated so that the rate of return on human capital investment is, say, 12 percent, while that on physical capital is only 8 percent, then society would benefit by reallocating investment from physical to human capital. In making this kind of comparison it is correct to use the social, rather than the private, rate of return. Hence, if we were to find that the *private* rate of return on human capital was in fact equal to the rate of return on physical capital, it would not necessarily be correct to conclude that investment resources were being efficiently divided between human and real capital. If the *social* rate of return was higher (lower) than the private rate, resources would have been underallocated (overallocated) to human capital investments. Incidentally, most studies of social rates of return yield rates which are quite comparable to those found in studies estimating private rates of return. Table 4-1 is relevant. A second reason why the distinction between the private and social perspectives is important has to do with policy. The social or external benefits associated with education provide the rationale for the subsidization of education with public funds. In the interest of allocative efficiency, the size of these public subsidies to education should be determined on the basis of the magnitude of the associated social benefits.

MARKETS FOR THE COLLEGE-TRAINED WORK FORCE

Having explored the human capital model in terms of the decision to invest in a college education, we now examine briefly the rather unique characteristics of markets for college-trained persons. In particular, the supply adjustments in the job markets for such people are sluggish and delayed in response to a change in demand, with the result that alternating periods of relative labor shortages and surpluses may occur.

The basic characteristics of the relevant model are as follows.[16] First, young people are highly sensitive to labor market conditions (for example, relative salaries and job opportunities) in making their educational and career decisions. Thus, as Figure 4-3 indicates, if market conditions for, say, engineers are favorable in 1985—perhaps because of increased military spending or the emergence of computer technologies which increase the demand for engineers—many students will enroll in engineering programs. Second, because we are considering highly skilled personnel, there will be a 4- or 5-year delay in the labor market response to 1985's favorable market conditions. Students enrolling in engineer-

---

[16]Our discussion is based upon Freeman, *The Overeducated American*, chap. 3.

ing schools in 1985 will not graduate and enter the labor market until 1990. Hence, we note in Figure 4-3 that the unusually large increase in the supply of engineers in 1990 causes the labor market for engineers to become depressed. Third, the excess supply and depressed salaries do *not* elicit an immediate decline in the supply of engineers to improve salaries and job availability. The reason is that those who have trained for a professional position are not likely to abandon their career in response to lower relative salaries and reduced job opportunities. The long working life of college-trained workers in their chosen professions means that the relative surplus of workers will persist. Therefore, the depressed market for engineers in 1990 has its effect primarily upon diminished enrollments in engineering programs in 1990, as indicated in Figure 4-3. This results in a relatively small number of graduates in 1995 which in turn generates a favorable market for engineers. Young people respond by enrolling in engineering programs in unusually large numbers and the process repeats itself. Instead of moving smoothly to an equilibrium position, the market is characterized by alternating periods of surpluses and shortages occurring every 5 years.

HUMAN CAPITAL INVESTMENT AND THE DISTRIBUTION OF EARNINGS

Why do people vary significantly in the amounts of human capital which they acquire? Why is Anderson a high school dropout, Brooks a high school gradu-

FIGURE 4-3 THE DYNAMICS OF LABOR MARKETS FOR COLLEGE GRADUATES
Because (1) student decisions about college attendance and curriculum are highly responsive to labor market conditions and (2) there is a 4- to 5-year time lag in the completion of a student's training, the labor markets for many kinds of college-level positions are subject to alternating periods of labor shortages and surpluses. [*Richard Freeman, The Overeducated American (New York: Academic Press, 1976), p. 60.*]

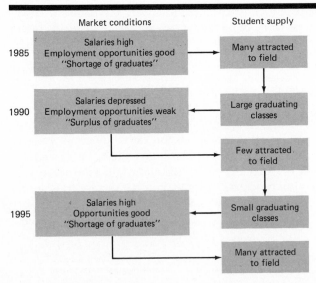

	Market conditions	Student supply
1985	Salaries high / Employment opportunities good / "Shortage of graduates"	Many attracted to field
1990	Salaries depressed / Employment opportunities weak / "Surplus of graduates"	Large graduating classes
		Few attracted to field
1995	Salaries high / Opportunities good / "Shortage of graduates"	Small graduating classes
		Many attracted to field

ate, and Chapman a Ph.D.? The reasons are many and complex, but by presenting a simple model of the demand for and the supply of human capital, we can gain valuable insights pertinent to the question. In so doing we shall also achieve some understanding as to why earnings are quite unequally distributed.

Diminishing Rates of Return. In Figure 4-4 we plot the marginal internal rate of return—the extra return from additional education—for a specific individual for successive years of education. Why do the rates of return diminish? The answer is essentially twofold. On the one hand, investment in human capital (education) is subject to the law of diminishing returns. On the other hand, as additional education is undertaken, the attendant benefits fall and the associated costs rise so as to cause the internal rate of return to decline.

1. One can argue that investment in education is subject to the law of diminishing returns (Chapter 5). That is, the extra knowledge and skills "produced" by education or schooling become smaller and smaller as the amount of schooling is increased. This means that the incremental earnings from each additional year of schooling will diminish and therefore so will the rate of return. Explanation: Think of the individual as analogous to a firm which combines fixed resources with variable inputs to generate a certain output. An individual combines certain genetically determined physical and mental characteristics with inputs of education or schooling in order to generate outputs of labor market skills. The individual's physical and mental characteristics—IQ, motor coordination, and so forth—are essentially fixed resources; these characteristics are determined by genes and the home environment. To these fixed resources we add variable inputs in the form of years of schooling. As with any other situation wherein a variable input is added to some fixed input, the resulting increases in the amount of human capital produced—the new knowledge and

FIGURE 4-4 RATES OF RETURN FROM SUCCESSIVE YEARS OF SCHOOLING
The rate of return from investing in successive years of schooling diminishes because (1) such investment is subject to the law of diminishing returns and (2) costs rise and benefits fall as more education is obtained.

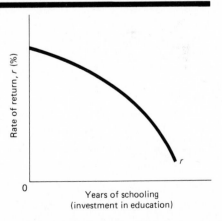

skills acquired by the individual—will ultimately decline. And diminishing returns will mean that the rate of return on successive human capital investments will also diminish.

2. We have already touched upon the second reason why the internal rate of return will decline as additional education is acquired. Costs tend to rise and benefits tend to fall for successive years of schooling. In addition to having essentially fixed mental and physical characteristics, the individual also possesses a fixed amount of time, that is, a finite work life. It follows that the more years one invests in education, the fewer one has during which one can realize incremental income from that investment and, hence, the lower will be the rate of return. The rate of return also declines because the costs of successive years of schooling tend to rise. On the one hand, the opportunity cost of one's time increases as more education is acquired. That is, an additional year of school has a greater opportunity cost for the holder of a bachelor's degree than it does for someone who has only a high school diploma. Similarly, it is also true that the private direct costs of schooling increase. Public subsidies make elementary and high school education essentially free, but a substantial portion of the cost of college and graduate school are borne by the individual student. Studies in fact confirm that the rate of return on schooling diminishes as the amount of schooling increases.

Demand , Supply, and Equilibrium. Next question: Why have we identified the curve labelled r as a *demand for human capital curve* (D_{hc}) in Figure 4-5? This

FIGURE 4-5 DERIVING THE DEMAND FOR HUMAN CAPITAL CURVE

Application of the $r = i$ rule reveals that the marginal rate of return curve is also the demand for human capital curve. Each of the equilibrium points (1, 2, 3) indicates the financial "price" of investing (i) on the vertical axis and the quantity of human capital demanded on the horizontal axis. By definition, this information on price and quantity demanded constitutes the demand curve for human capital.

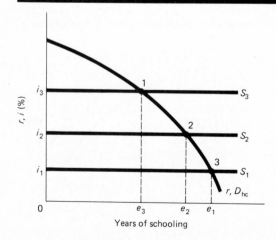

Years of schooling

identification is simply the result of applying the previously discussed decision rule which says that investment is profitable if $r > i$ and unprofitable if $r < i$. Or, in the context of Figure 4-5, it is profitable to invest in human capital or schooling up to the point at which the marginal rate of return equals the interest rate or, in short, where $r = i$. Thus in Figure 4-5 we assume that the individual is a "price taker" in borrowing funds for educational purposes and that needed amounts of money capital can be borrowed at a given interest rate. Hence, the horizontal line drawn at, say, i_2 indicates that the individual is faced with a perfectly elastic **supply of investment funds** S_2 at this interest rate. Our $r = i$ rule indicates that e_2 is the most profitable number of years of schooling in which to invest. Similarly, *if* the market rate of interest were higher at i_3, the application of the $r = i$ rule would make only e_3 years of schooling profitable. *If* the interest rate were lower at i_1, then it would obviously be profitable to invest in e_1 years of schooling. By applying a selection of possible interest rates or money capital prices to the marginal rate of return curve, we locate a number of equilibrium points (1, 2, 3) which indicate the financial "price" of investing (various possible interest rates) on the vertical axis *and* the corresponding quantities of human capital demanded on the horizontal axis. Any such curve which contains such information on price and quantity demanded is, by definition, a demand curve—in this case the demand curve for human capital or schooling.

Differences in Human Capital Investment. The demand and supply curves of Figure 4-5 can be used to explain why different people invest in different amounts of human capital *and,* therefore, realize substantially different earnings. Our emphasis is upon three considerations: (1) differences in ability, (2) differing degrees of uncertainty concerning the capacity to transform skills and knowledge into enhanced earnings due to discrimination, and (3) differing access to borrowed funds for human capital investment.

1. Ability differences. Figure 4-6 embodies two different demand curves for human capital, D_A and D_B for Adams and Bowen respectively, and a common supply curve. The common supply curve indicates that money capital for investment in schooling is assumed to be available to Adams and Bowen on identical terms. The key question is why Bowen's demand curve for human capital (D_B) is to the right of Adams' (D_A). The answer may be that Bowen has greater natural abilities—better mental and physical talents and perhaps greater motivation and self-discipline—which cause any given input of schooling to be translated into a larger increase in labor market productivity and earning ability. That is, Bowen is more able than Adams to obtain enhanced earnings for each year of schooling; Bowen is capable of "getting more out of education" that is useful in the labor market than is Adams. Hence, the rate of return on each year of schooling is higher, and Bowen's demand curve for human capital is therefore further to the right. Given the interest rate and the perfectly elastic supply of financial capital, this means that Bowen will invest in e_B years of schooling, while Adams will choose to invest in only e_A years.

Note that because it is rational for more-able people to obtain more education than less-able people, earnings differentials tend to be compounded. That is, given the same amount of schooling, we would expect Bowen to earn more than Adams because of the former's greater innate ability. Because it is rational for Bowen to obtain more education than Adams, we would anticipate a further widening of the earnings differential.

2. Discrimination: uncertainty of earnings. Let us now assume that Adams and Bowen are identical in terms of ability. But let us suppose that Adams is black or female and therefore is more likely to encounter discriminatory barriers to selling in the labor market the higher productivity acquired through education. In other words, Adams may encounter various forms of discrimination (see Chapter 11) which reduce the likelihood of transforming the labor market skills acquired through education into incremental earnings. In terms of equations (4-3) and (4-4) discrimination creates the probability that the flow of E's to black (female) Adams will be smaller than those accruing to white (male) Bowen from the same amount of education. This means lower rates of return on education to Adams than to Bowen. Referring to Figure 4-6 once again, Adams' demand for human capital is less than Bowen's. Given equal access to funds for the financing of education, (the iS curve in Figure 4-6), Bowen will again find it rational to invest in more human capital than will Adams. Discrimination which reduces wages and earnings also has the perverse impact of reducing the incentive for those discriminated against to invest in human capital.

FIGURE 4-6 ABILITY, DISCRIMINATION, AND INVESTMENT IN HUMAN CAPITAL
If Bowen has greater ability to translate schooling into increased labor market productivity and higher earnings than does Adams, then Bowen's demand curve for human capital (D_B) will lie further to the right than does Adams' (D_A). Given the interest rate, it will be rational for Bowen to invest in more education than does Adams. Similarly, if Adams and Bowen are of equal ability but discrimination reduces the amount of incremental income Adams can obtain from additional education, it will be rational for Adams to invest in less education than Bowen.

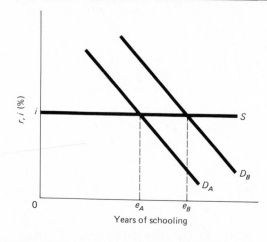

3. Access to funds. This brings us to a final consideration. Figure 4-7 portrays the situation where the demand for human capital curves for Adams and Bowen are identical, but Bowen can acquire money capital on more favorable terms than can Adams. Why the difference? Bowen may simply be from a wealthier family which is in a position to pledge certain financial or real assets as collateral and therefore obtain a lower interest rate. Under these conditions it is obviously rational for Bowen to invest in more years of schooling than Adams.

The basic point to be made is that differences in ability, the impact of discrimination, and varying access to financial resources are all reasons why various individuals find it rational to obtain different amounts of education. Recalling the age-earnings profiles in Figure 4-1, these differences in educational attainment are important in generating inequality in the distribution of earnings. In fact, the factors which explain educational inequality may interact to generate greater earnings inequality than our discussion would suggest. For example, discrimination may not only influence the demand side of the human capital market to reduce the demands of blacks and females for education, but may also appear on the supply side. If a lender reasons that discrimination makes it less likely that a black or a female will be able to achieve employment in the occupation for which they are training, the lender will compensate for this greater risk by charging a higher rate of interest. This causes the supply of human capital curve for blacks and women to shift upward as in Figure 4-7, and the amount of education acquired will obviously be further diminished. Similarly, individuals with greater ability may also enjoy lower financial costs. Greater ability may stem, not simply from one's genetic inheritance, but also from the quality of one's home environment. The child fortunate enough to be born into a high-

FIGURE 4-7 ACCESS TO FUNDS AND HUMAN CAPITAL INVESTMENT
If Bowen has access to financial resources on more favorable terms than does Adams, it will be rational for Bowen to invest in a larger amount of education.

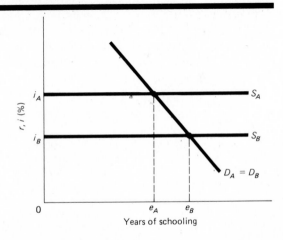

income family is likely to enjoy more and better preschool education, have greater motivation and self-discipline, and place a higher value on education in general. These considerations mean the child has greater ability to absorb education and to increase his or her labor market productivity and earnings. Being born into a high-income family also means a greater ability to finance education on favorable terms.[17]

Capital Market Imperfections. The capital market may include certain biases or imperfections which cause it to favor investment in physical, rather than human, capital. Specifically, funds may be less readily available, or accessible only on less favorable terms, for investment in human capital as compared to real capital or the purchase of consumer durables. Perhaps the primary reason for this is that human capital is obviously embodied in the borrower and therefore is not available as collateral on a loan. If one defaults on a house mortgage or an automobile loan, there is a tangible asset which the lender can repossess and sell to recover losses. But in a nation which rejects slavery and indentured servitude, there is no designated asset for the lender to seize if the borrower fails to repay an educational loan. This increases risk to the lender and prompts the inclusion of a risk premium in the interest rate charged. Furthermore, we have noted that, other things being equal, it is more rational for young people to make human capital investments than it is for old people. But young people are less likely to have established credit ratings or collateral assets to allow them to borrow on reasonable terms. Finally, the variation in returns on human capital investments tends to be very large. Recall that, although college graduates *on the average* earn substantially more than high school graduates, many college graduates earn less than the average high school graduate! This uncertainty of return may inflate the risk premium charged for human capital loans.[18]

The relative unsuitability of the capital market to educational loans has one or two important consequences. First, given the problems and uncertainties just noted, financial institutions may simply choose *not* to make human capital loans. This in turn means that the amount of human capital investment which individuals can undertake will depend upon their, or their families', income and wealth. Thus, well-to-do families can finance the college educations of their children by the relatively painless process of reducing their volume of saving. But poor families cannot save and, therefore, the financing of a college education implies a possibly severe cut in living standards.[19] These circumstances may

---

[17]For an interesting discussion of how parents affect the earnings of their children, see Paul Taubman, *Income Distribution and Redistribution* (Reading, Mass.: Addison-Wesley Publishing Company, 1978), chap. 5.

[18]For a further discussion of capital market imperfections, see Lester Thurow, *Investment in Human Capital* (Belmont, Calif.: Wadsworth Publishing Company., Inc., 1970), pp. 77–83.

[19]Even publicly supported colleges and universities which feature very minimal tuition and fees may attract relatively few students from low-income families for the simple reason that their families may not be able to afford the opportunity costs (see Figure 4-2). That is, a very poor family may not be able to forgo the income which a son or daughter can earn by entering the labor market immediately upon graduating from high school. Federal education loan programs have mitigated this problem in recent years.

tend to perpetuate a vicious circle. Individuals and families with little human capital (education) tend to be poor; being poor, it is extremely difficult for them to finance the acquisition of additional human capital.

Capital market imperfections have a second important implication. If it is in the social interest to achieve a balance or equilibrium between investment in real capital and human capital, then government may have to offset the imperfections by subsidizing or providing human capital loans. Ideally, an equilibrium between investment in real and human capital would occur when the last dollar spent on human capital contributes the same amount to the national output as does the last dollar expended on real capital. But the higher interest rates charged for educational loans will restrict expenditures on human capital so that its relative contribution to the national output will exceed that of real capital. This indicates that investment resources are being underallocated to human capital. It is in part this rationale which lies behind the loan guarantees and financial resources which government has provided to stimulate educational loans.

ON-THE-JOB TRAINING

Much of the usable labor market skills which workers possess are acquired, not through formal schooling, but rather through *on-the-job training.* Such training may be somewhat formal; that is, workers may undertake a structured trainee program or an apprenticeship program. On the other hand, on-the-job training is often highly informal and therefore difficult to measure or even detect. Less experienced workers often engage in "learning by doing"; that is, they acquire new skills by simply observing more skilled workers, filling in for them when they are ill or on vacation, or engaging in informal conversation during coffee breaks.

General and Specific Training. On-the-job training may be categorized by two polar types. At one extreme, *general training* refers to the creation of skills or characteristics which are equally usable in *all* firms and industries. Stated differently, general training enhances the productivity of workers to all firms. At the other end of the continuum, *specific training* is training which can be used *only* in the particular firm which provides that training. Specific training, in other words, increases the worker's productivity only in the firm providing that training. In practice, most on-the-job training contains elements of both general and specific training, and it is therefore difficult to muster unequivocal examples. Nevertheless, we might venture that the capacity to concentrate upon a task for a reasonable period of time; to show up for work regularly and be punctual; to read, to perform simple mathematical manipulations, and to follow instructions —all constitute general training. The ability to perform an assembly procedure unique to a firm's product exemplifies specific training.

The distinction between general and specific training is important for at least two reasons. First, it is helpful in explaining whether the worker or the employer is more likely to pay for on-the-job training. Second, it is useful in understanding why employers might be particularly anxious to retain certain of their trained workers.

Distributing Training Costs. Assuming competition prevails, the worker will usually pay for general training through lower wages during the initial weeks or months of employment. On the other hand, the firm must bear the cost of specific training. Given the definitions of general and specific training, these two hypotheses are intuitively obvious. General training provides a worker with skills and understanding which are transferable; that is, they can be sold to other firms at a higher wage rate. If the employer were to bear the cost, the worker might leave the firm's employment upon completion of the training and thus deprive the employer of any return on the training investment. Therefore, if general on-the-job training is undertaken, it is usually paid for by the worker in the form of a reduced wage rate. On the other hand, a specific skill is not transferable or salable by a worker. Hence, the worker will not pay for such training. If a worker is fired or laid off at the end of a period of specific training, the worker has gained nothing of value to sell in the labor market. The cost is usually borne by the employer. This typically means that the employer will pay a wage rate in excess of the worker's marginal revenue product during the training period.

Figures 4-8 (a) and (b) are useful in elaborating these generalizations. Figure 4-8 (a) shows the case of general training. Here W_u and MRP_u indicate the wage rate and marginal revenue product for an untrained worker. As we shall explain in Chapter 5, marginal revenue product is the amount which a worker adds to the firm's total revenue. The wage rate and marginal revenue product *during* training are represented by W and MRP, while W_t and MRP_t are the posttraining wage rate and marginal revenue product. MRP is below that for an untrained worker because during the training period the worker is presumably diverting time from production to learning. It is important to stress that the higher post-training marginal revenue product (MRP_t) is relevant *to all firms* because the training is general. Firms will therefore bid up the wage rate of this trained worker until it is equal to MRP_t. It is precisely for this reason—that the post-training wage rate will be competed upward into equality with the posttraining marginal revenue product—that the employer will *not* be willing to pay for general training. There is no opportunity for the employer to obtain a return on his training investment by paying a wage rate which is less than the worker's marginal revenue product. Why should the employer bear general training costs when the benefits accrue to the trained employee in the form of higher wages? To repeat: The worker usually pays for general training costs by accepting a wage below that of the untrained worker (W as compared to W_u) during the training period. Incidentally, the fact that competition will bid a worker's wage rate up into equality with his or her higher posttraining marginal revenue product (MRP_t) and thereby preclude a return to the employer explains why general education typically occurs in schools and not on the job.

Figure 4-8 (b) pertains to specific training. Again, W_u and MRP_u are the wage rate and marginal revenue product of an untrained worker, and MRP and MRP_t respectively show marginal revenue productivity during and after specific training. In contrast to Figure 4-8 (a), the posttraining marginal revenue product applies *only to this firm*. The worker has acquired specific training which will increase productivity in *this* firm; but by definition specific training is *not* transferable or useful to other firms. Because specific training is not transferable—that is, it will not allow the worker to obtain a higher wage rate as the consequence of labor market competition for his or her services—the worker will refuse to pay for such training and not accept a lower wage during the training period. Note that during the training period the wage rate will remain at W_u, which means that the employer must bear the cost of the training by paying a wage rate which is in excess of the worker's marginal revenue product (MRP). However, because specific training is not transferable—that is, it does not increase the worker's marginal revenue product to other firms—the employer need not increase the wage rate above W_u in the posttraining period. Hence, from the employer's standpoint, training imposes a flow of costs (W_u exceeds MRP) in the training period which is followed by a flow of benefits or incremental revenues (MRP_t exceeds W_u) in the posttraining period. Recalling equa-

FIGURE 4-8 WAGE RATES AND MARGINAL REVENUE PRODUCTS FOR GENERAL AND SPECIFIC TRAINING

(a) Because general training is salable to other firms and industries ($W_t = MRP_t$), workers must pay for any such training a firm provides. This payment is in the form of a reduced wage ($W < W_u$) during the training period. (b) Specific training is not transferable to other firms; therefore, the employer must pay for such training. During the training period the employer pays a wage rate in excess of the worker's marginal revenue product ($W_u > MRP$). In the posttraining period the employer receives a return on specific training because the worker's marginal revenue product will exceed his wage rate ($MRP_t > W_u$). Because the employer's return on specific training varies directly with the length of the posttraining period, the employer might voluntarily pay an above-competitive wage (W_t' as compared to W_u) in order to reduce worker turnover. [*Adapted from John T. Addison and W. Stanley Siebert, The Market for Labor: An Analytical Treatment (Santa Monica, Calif.: Goodyear Publishing Company, 1979), p. 114.*]

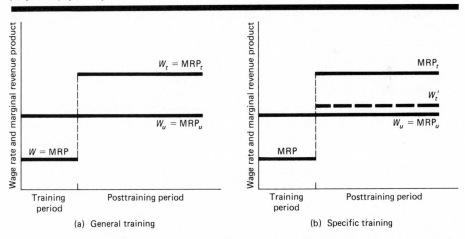

(a) General training

(b) Specific training

tion (4-3), if the net present value of these flows is positive, the firm will find it profitable to undertake a given program of specific training for its workers. Indeed, you have undoubtedly noticed that Figure 4-8 (b) resembles Figure 4-2.

Worker Retention. Figure 4-8 (b) merits modification in one rather important way. We have observed that in the posttraining period the employer realizes a return from specific training by paying a wage (W_u) which is less than each worker's contribution to the firm's total revenue (MRP_t). It is obvious that the total amount of revenue or profit derived from this discrepancy will vary directly with the length of time the worker remains employed by the firm. In short, the employer has an obvious financial interest in lowering the turnover or quit rates of workers with specific training. How might this be accomplished? By voluntarily paying a wage rate somewhat higher than the worker could obtain elsewhere, for example, W_t' rather than W_u. We note that specific training is one of a number of considerations which changes labor from a variable input to a *quasi-fixed* factor of production.[20]

A final comment: On the average, those individuals who receive the largest amount of formal education also tend to receive more on-the-job training. This is not surprising. A person who has demonstrated his or her trainability by completing, say, a college degree is more likely to be selected by an employer for on-the-job training than is someone with only a high school diploma. Why? Because that individual will be trainable at a lower cost. Indeed, Figure 4-8 (b) implies that on-the-job training will have a higher rate of return to employers when workers can absorb training in a short period of time. A college degree is evidence of the capacity to absorb training quickly. The fact that persons with more formal education tend to receive more on-the-job training helps explain why age-earnings profiles of more highly educated workers rise more rapidly than those of less-educated workers (see Figure 4-1).

CRITICISMS OF HUMAN CAPITAL THEORY

A number of criticisms have been made of the human capital model and its applications. The first two criticisms are concerned essentially with measurement problems and suggest that estimates of the rates of return on investments in education are likely to be biased. Although the remaining two criticisms have implications for measuring the rate of return on human capital investments, they are more profound in that they challenge the very concept or theory of investing in human capital.

---

[20]The classic study is Walter Oi, "Labor as a Quasi-Fixed Factor," *Journal of Political Economy*, December 1962, pp. 538–555.

Investment or Consumption? One criticism of measuring the rate of return on human capital investment is that it is *not* correct to treat all expenditures for education as investment because, in fact, a portion of such outlays are consumption expenditures. The decision to attend college, for example, is based upon considerations which are broader and more complex than simply expected increases in labor productivity and enhanced earnings. Some substantial portion of one's expenditures on a college education yields consumption benefits either immediately or in the long run. Expenditures for courses on Shakespeare, ceramics, music appreciation, and so forth yield both immediate and long-run consumption benefits by enlarging an individual's range of interests, tastes, and activities. It is true, of course, that a course in nineteenth-century English literature yields not only consumption benefits, but also enhances one's capacity to express oneself orally and in writing. And the ability to express oneself has value in the labor market and tends to increase one's productivity and earnings. The problem, however, is that there is no reasonable way of determining what portion of the expense on a literature course is investment and what part is consumption. The main point is that by ignoring the consumption component of educational expenditures and thereby considering *all* of such outlays as being investment, empirical researchers understate the rate of return on educational investments.

Nonwage Benefits. In calculating the internal rate of return most researchers simply compare the differences in the earnings of high school and college graduates. But the jobs of high school and college graduates differ in other respects. First, the fringe benefits associated with the jobs obtained by college graduates are more generous—both absolutely and as a percentage of earnings—than those received by high school graduates. Hence, by ignoring fringe benefits, empirical studies tend to understate the rate of return on a college education. Second, the jobs acquired by college graduates are generally more pleasant and interesting than those of high school graduates. This means that a calculated rate of return based upon incremental earnings understates the total benefits accruing from a college education.

The Ability Problem. Two other related criticisms, labelled the ability problem and the screening hypothesis, question the very concept of human capital investment. We first consider the *ability problem.*

   It is widely recognized that average incomes vary directly with the level of education. But it is less well accepted that a strong, clearcut cause-effect relationship exists between the two. Critics of human capital theory doubt that the observed income differential is solely—or even primarily—the result of the additional education. To state the problem somewhat differently, the *ceteris paribus* or "other things being equal" assumption underlies the simple model of Figure 4-2 and the conclusions derived therefrom. Critics of human capital theory contend that "other things" in fact are not likely to be equal. It is widely acknowledged that those who have more innate ability (higher IQs), more self-discipline, and greater motivation—not to mention more family wealth and better job market "connections"—are more likely to go to college. Hence, if we could somehow blot out all of the knowledge and understanding which college graduates acquired in college, we would still expect this group to earn larger incomes than those who decided *not* to attend college. Thus one can argue that, although college graduates earn higher incomes than do high school graduates, a substantial portion of that incremental income is *not* traceable to the investment in a college education. In other words, people with high innate abilities tend to do well in the labor market; the fact that they also attend college is somewhat incidental to this success. "The only reason that education is correlated with income is that the combination of ability, motivation, and personal habits that it takes to succeed in education happen to be the same combination that it takes to be a productive worker."[21] This criticism implies that, if a substantial portion of the incremental earnings enjoyed by college graduates is attributable to their *ability* and not to their *schooling*, then estimated rates of return on investing in a college education will be overstated.

Accepting the validity of the criticism, a number of researchers have tried to determine what portion of incremental earnings is due to human capital investment as opposed to differences in ability and other personal characteristics. For example, a study of white male twins[22] about age 50 concludes that as much as two-thirds of the observed differences in earnings were due to differences in ability. A variety of similar studies suggest that ability differences account for smaller, but still substantial, portions of the earnings differentials between "more" and "less" educated workers.

It is also worth observing that the causal relationship between education and earnings has important implications for public policy. *If* human capital theorists are correct in arguing that education is the sole or primary cause of higher earnings, then it obviously makes sense to provide more education to low-income groups if society chooses to reduce poverty and the degree of income inequality. On the other hand, *if* high incomes are caused primarily by ability and motivational factors, then a policy of increased spending on the education of low-income groups may be of limited success in increasing their incomes and alleviating income inequality.

The Screening Hypothesis. The *screening hypothesis* is closely related to the ability problem. This hypothesis suggests that education affects earnings, not

---

[21]Alice M. Rivlin, "Income Distribution—Can Economists Help?" *American Economic Review*, May 1975, p. 10.

[22]By studying twins one can control for much of the differences in genetic endowments and family background which obviously complicate comparisons of unrelated individuals. See Paul Taubman, "Earnings, Education, Genetics and Environment," *Journal of Human Resources*, Winter 1976, pp. 447–461.

primarily by altering the labor market productivity of students, but by grading and labeling students in such a way as to determine their job placement and thereby their earnings.[23] It is argued that employers use educational attainment—for example, the possession of a college degree—as an inexpensive means of identifying workers who are likely to be of high quality. A college degree or other credential thus becomes a ticket of admission to higher-level, higher-paying jobs wherein opportunities for further training and promotion are good. Less-educated workers are screened from these positions, not necessarily because of their inability to perform the job, but simply because they do not have the college degree to give them access to the position. The incremental income enjoyed by college graduates might be a payment for being credentialed rather than a reward for being more productive.

Viewed from a private perspective, screening should have no effect upon the internal rate of return. Whether one is admitted to a higher-paying position because of the knowledge and skills acquired in college or because one possesses the necessary credential (a college degree), the fact remains that having attended college typically results in higher earnings. But from a social perspective, screening is very important. One might well question the expenditure of over $215 billion (in 1983) on elementary, secondary, and higher education if the payoff is merely to signal employers that certain workers are above-average in terms of intelligence, motivation, and self-discipline. To the extent that a college graduate's incremental earnings stem from screening, the social rate of return of investing in a college education will be overstated.

To what extent are the higher earnings of more-educated workers due to education augmenting the productivity of workers, as the human capital view suggests? Similarly, to what degree are the higher earnings of such individuals attributable to the screening hypothesis, which indicates that schooling serves the function of merely identifying more productive workers? Does schooling produce skills or merely serve to identify preexistent skills? Empirical evidence is mixed. For example, research by Taubman and Wales suggests that as much as 50 percent of the effect of education upon earnings might be due to screening.[24] On the other hand, studies by Wolpin and Wise question the importance of screening. Wolpin has reasoned that, if education is a screening device, workers who are to be screened in the process of job acquisition will be prone to purchase more schooling than those workers who are not screened. He notes that, while salaried workers are obviously screened, self-employed workers are not. Therefore, if schooling is a screening device, salaried workers will tend to purchase more schooling than the self-employed. But he finds in fact the two groups of workers acquire about the same amount of education which Wolpin regards as "evidence against a predominate screening interpretation" of the positive associ-

---

[23]Michael Spence, "Job Market Signaling," *Quarterly Journal of Economics*, August 1973, pp. 355–374.

[24]Paul Taubman and Terence Wales, "Higher Education, Mental Ability and Screening," *Journal of Political Economy*, January–February 1973, pp. 28–55.

ation between schooling and earnings.[25] Similarly, Wise has argued that, if education does affect worker productivity as the human capital theory suggests, then college degrees of differing quality *and* student performance while attending college should be reflected in salary differentials. That is, if human capital theory is correct, workers with bachelor degrees from high-quality institutions *and* workers who achieved higher grade point averages should be more productive and therefore earn higher salaries. Examining data for some 1300 college graduates employed by Ford Motor Company, Wise found a "consistent positive relationship between commonly used measures of academic achievement [institutional quality and grade point average] and rates of salary increase." Wise concludes that a "college education is not only a signal of productive ability, but in fact enhances this ability."[26]

Recapitulation: There is no question that human capital theory has been the basis for important insights and the cornerstone for a myriad of revealing empirical studies. But as the ability problem and the screening hypothesis suggest, human capital theory is not universally accepted, and some who accept it do so only with reservations. While there is almost universal agreement as to the positive association between education and earnings, there is disagreement as to the *reasons* for this association. Unfortunately, human capital theory has not been tested directly in that no one has been able to determine whether education and training actually do increase one's labor market productivity. Instead, the empirical testing is indirect in that it is first determined that those with more education and training have higher earnings, and then it is *inferred* that the additional education and training are the cause of the enhanced earnings. But the issue remains: Does education increase one's productivity? Or do those who acquire more education earn more simply because they are more able and more motivated? Does education simply identify productive workers? To complicate matters we will find in Chapter 15 that some economists feel that productivity lies more in jobs than it does in workers. That is, a worker's productivity and earnings may be determined more by the job the individual holds than by the amount of schooling one has acquired. Hence, it is fair to say that human capital theory cannot be used uncritically as a basis for public policy. For example, as noted earlier, if earnings in fact depend upon innate ability, then expenditures on education to alter the distribution of income may prove to be an ineffective policy.[27]

---

[25]Kenneth Wolpin, "Education and Screening," *American Economic Review*, December 1977, pp. 949–958.

[26]David A. Wise, "Academic Achievement and Job Performance," *American Economic Review*, June 1975, pp. 350–366.

[27]For an excellent elaboration of the criticisms of human theory, see Bobbie McCrackin, "Education's Contribution to Productivity and Economic Growth," *Economic Review* (Federal Reserve Bank of Atlanta), November 1984, pp. 8–23.

SUMMARY

1. Expenditures on education and training which increase one's productivity and future earnings in the labor market can be treated as a human capital investment decision.
2. The decision to invest in a college education entails both direct (out-of-pocket) and indirect (forgone earnings) costs. Benefits take the form of future incremental earnings.
3. There are two basic methods of comparing the benefits and costs associated with a human capital investment. The net present value approach uses a discounting formula to compare the present value of costs and benefits. If net present value is positive, it is rational to invest. The internal rate of return is the rate of discount at which the net present value of the investment is zero. If the internal rate of return exceeds the interest rate, it is rational to invest.
4. Most empirical studies suggest that the rate of return on investing in a college education has ranged from 10 to 15 percent, but declined in the 1970s.
5. From a private perspective the human capital decision excludes public subsidies to education, considers after-tax earnings, and ignores any social or external benefits associated with education. The social perspective includes public subsidies and external benefits and considers before-tax earnings.
6. Largely because of delayed supply responses to market conditions, labor markets for college-trained workers are frequently characterized by alternating periods of surpluses and shortages.
7. The demand for human capital curve and the supply of investment funds curve can be combined to explain why various people invest in different amounts of human capital. Ability differences, discrimination, and varying access to financial resources all help explain differences in education and earnings among individuals.
8. The money market may provide funds for human capital investment on less favorable terms than for investment in physical capital, thereby providing some justification for public subsidization of human capital investments.
9. It is useful to distinguish between general and specific on-the-job training. General training generates worker skills which are useful in all firms and industries. Specific training is useful only in the specific firm providing that training. Given competitive markets, workers usually will pay for general training provided by a firm by accepting lower wages during the training period. However, employers typically pay for specific training.
10. Criticisms of human capital theory include the following: (a) By failing to recognize that a part of the expenditures on education are consumption rather than investment, empirical studies understate the rate of return on education; (b) empirical studies understate the rate of return on a college education by not taking into account that the jobs of college graduates are more pleasant and entail superior fringe benefits than do the jobs of high school graduates; (c) to the extent that the incremental earnings of college graduates are due to their greater ability and not to schooling per se, the rate of return on a college education will be overstated; (d) if a portion of the incremental earnings of college graduates is attributable to screening, the social rate of return on a college education will be overstated.

QUESTIONS AND STUDY SUGGESTIONS

1. Key terms and concepts to remember: human capital investment; age-earnings profiles; net present value; time preference; discount formula; internal rate of return; college premium; private and social perspective; demand for human capital; supply of investment funds; capital market imperfections; on-the-job training; general versus specific training; the ability problem; the screening hypothesis.

2. Why might the decision to undertake an educational program be treated as an investment?

3. From a private perspective, what are the costs and benefits associated with obtaining a college education? What are the costs and benefits from a social perspective? Explain why it is necessary to determine the net present value of costs and benefits in making a rational human capital investment decision.

4. What is the internal rate of return on a human capital investment? Given the internal rate of return, what is the appropriate investment criterion? Compare this to the criterion relevant to the present value approach.

5. Floyd is now working on a job which pays $8000 per year. He is contemplating a 1-year automobile mechanics course which entails costs of $1000 for books and tuition. Floyd estimates that the course will increase his income to $13,000 in each of the 3 years following completion of the course. At the end of the 3 years Floyd plans to retire to a commune in Boulder, Colorado. The current interest rate is 10 percent. Is it economically rational for Floyd to enroll in the course?

6. Comment on each of the following statements:
   a. Given the work-life cycle of the "traditional" woman, it may be rational for women to invest in less human capital than men.
   b. Older workers are less mobile geographically than are younger workers.
   c. An economic recession tends to stimulate school enrollments.
   d. If you think education is costly, try ignorance.

7. Carefully explain the characteristics of the market for college graduates. What assumptions or premises underlie the workings of this market?

8. Assume that a recent high school graduate reads in a magazine that the rate of return on a college education has been estimated to be 15 percent. What advice would you give the graduate in using this information as she decides whether or not to attend college?

9. Why is the internal rate of return from human capital investment subject to diminishing returns? Explain the rationale for identifying the "diminishing rate of returns to education curve" as the "demand for human capital curve." Combine the demand for human capital curve with a "supply of investment funds curve" to explain why various individuals find it rational to invest in different amounts of human capital. What are the implications of your answer for the personal distribution of income? Do you think that the educational system in the United States contributes to more or less equality in the distribution of earnings? Explain. If you wanted to reduce the degree of inequality in the distribution of earnings, what policy recommendations would you make?

10. Why might funds be available on less favorable terms for human capital investments than for physical capital investments? In your judgment does this difference justify public subsidy in the form, say, of federal guarantees of loans to college students?

11. As the following diagram indicates, the distribution of "ability" (as measured by IQ scores) is normal or bell-shaped, but the distribution of earnings is skewed to the right. Can you use human capital theory to reconcile these two distributions?

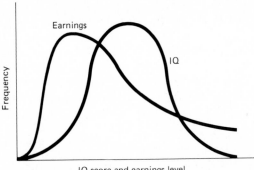

IQ score and earnings level

12. Distinguish between general and specific on-the-job training. Who pays for general training? Specific training? Why the difference?

13. Suppose the federal government reformed the personal income tax so that, instead of a system of progressive marginal tax rates running from 11 to 50 percent on earnings, a flat-rate tax was introduced so that earnings were taxed at, say, 15 percent regardless of the size of one's earnings. What impact might this reform have upon college enrollments? Explain.

14. What are some of the external benefits associated with education? Do you feel that these benefits justify public subsidies to education? Can you provide a rationale for the argument that public subsidies should diminish as students advance to higher and higher educational levels?

15. Data show that the age-earnings profiles of women are lower and flatter than those for men. Can you explain these differences?

16. Indicate the implications of each of the following for estimates of the rate of return on a college education: (*a*) the screening hypothesis, (*b*) the possibility that a portion of one's expenditures on college should be considered as consumption rather than investment, (*c*) the fact that people who go to college are generally more able than those who do not, and (*d*) the jobs acquired by college graduates generally entail larger fringe benefits than the jobs of high school graduates. What implications do the ability problem and the screening hypothesis have for public policy towards education?

SELECTED REFERENCES

BECKER, GARY S.: *Human Capital*, 2d ed. (New York: National Bureau of Economic Research, 1975).

BOWEN, HOWARD R.: *Investment in Learning* (San Francisco: Jossey-Bass Publishers, 1977).

FREEMAN, RICHARD B.: *The Overeducated American* (New York: Academic Press, 1976).

SCHULTZ, T. W.: "Investment in Human Capital," *American Economic Review*, March 1961, pp. 1–17.

TAUBMAN, PAUL: *Income Distribution and Redistribution* Reading, Mass.: Addison-Wesley Publishing Company, 1978), chaps. 3 and 4.

THUROW, LESTER: *Investment in Human Capital* (Belmont, Calif.: Wadsworth Publishing Company, Inc., 1970).

T I M E   A N D   O N E - H A L F

THE MARXIAN CRITIQUE OF HUMAN CAPITAL THEORY*

Marxian economists have developed a critique of human capital theory which is decidedly different from those explained in this chapter.

The Marxian critique of human capital theory is largely a philosophical attack which, while not rejecting the notion that schooling affects worker productivity, contends that schooling influences productivity much differently than hypothesized by human capital theory. Marxists insist that a highly educated, highly skilled work force is *not* necessarily a profitable work force. Profitable production in a capitalist system requires that, in addition to technical skills, workers have "appropriate" attitudes and personality traits. More specifically, the capitalist system needs workers who will submit to hierarchical systems of authority and control, accept a structure of unequal economic rewards, and respond positively to the incentive mechanisms through which enterprises extract useful labor from them. To Marxists the function of schooling—of human capital investment—is to inculcate these kinds of attitudes and values which are consistent with and therefore tend to sustain and perpetuate the capitalist system. Put bluntly, the function of schooling in the United States is to generate a disciplined, obedient, and well-motivated work force which accepts the capitalist ideology and fits the needs of capitalist enterprises. According to Marxists, human capital theorists fail to recognize that a basic function of education is "social reproduction," that is, the preservation of the capitalist system and the class distinctions peculiar to it. Human capital theory is therefore held to be incomplete, superficial, and quite irrelevant in explaining the amounts and kinds of education which we have in the United States.

How do schools develop those attitudes and personality traits which capitalist employers desire? First, Marxists point out that American schools embody systems of authority, control, and motivation which parallel those found in the job structures of business enterprises. "Good" students are those who, instead of thinking for themselves, accept the authoritarian hierarchy of teachers and administrators found in schools. Discipline, punctuality, responsibility, and dependability are earmarks of superior students and later of superior workers. Similarly, the system of grading which rewards certain classroom behaviors and penalizes others, ostensibly on the basis of merit, conditions students to acquiesce in the unequal structure of economic rewards which they will later encounter in the labor market. Thus the education system functions so that individuals with lower grades, lower test scores, and smaller amounts of education come to believe that their subsequent lower earnings are fair.

Not surprisingly, the implications drawn by Marxists and human capital theorists from their respective views of schooling are quite different. For example, human capital

---

*This synopsis is based upon Samuel Bowles and Herbert Gintis, "The Problem with Human Capital Theory: A Marxian Critique," *American Economic Review,* May 1975, pp. 74–82; Samuel Bowles and Herbert Gintis, *Schooling in Capitalist America* (New York: Basic Books, Inc., Publishers 1976); Herbert Gintis, "Education, Technology, and the Characteristics of Worker Productivity," *American Economic Review,* May 1971, pp. 266–279; and Samuel Bowles, "Unequal Education and the Reproduction of the Hierarchical Division of Labor," in R. C. Edwards, M. Reich, and T. E. Weisskopf (eds.), *The Capitalist System* (Englewood Cliffs, N. J.: Prentice-Hall, Inc., 1972), pp. 218–229.

theory is important from the social perspective because education presumably increases worker productivity, which then accelerates the growth of the gross national product. Indeed, numerous empirical studies do suggest that schooling has contributed significantly to economic growth. But some Marxists argue to the contrary. They contend that there are alternative economic systems which are potentially more productive than capitalism. Hence, by sustaining the capitalist order, investment in schooling in the United States on balance may have lessened growth. The problem, according to Marxists, is that human capital theorists only take into account the impact of education upon worker skills and productivity, but overlook the "social reproduction" function of schooling. Marxists ask: How much more growth might have occurred under an alternative economic system based on individual creativity and autonomy as opposed to submissiveness and conformity?

Finally, let us return to the issue of economic inequality. Human capital theory implies an obvious means by which society can, if it so desires, mitigate income inequality. That means, of course, is to increase educational opportunity for lower-income classes. In other words, education is a potential equalizing force which can be used to offset or ameliorate the distributional inequities inherent in the market system. But the Marxian view is much different. They argue that the educational system not only generates a justification and tolerance for inequality, but also plays a positive role in generating income and class inequalities. The contention is that, in fact, the children of well-educated, high-income parents are much more likely to complete high school and attend college than are the children of less-educated, low-income parents. Furthermore, the quality of educational institutions available to the children of high-income parents are superior to those of low-income parents. For example, elementary and secondary school education in the United States is financed largely from local tax revenues. Given that residences are segregated by income levels, this means that the children of high-income classes receive much better education than do the offspring of low-income classes. Children attending the wealthy suburban schools enjoy smaller classes, individualized attention by teachers, opportunities for creative work, and a broader curriculum. The resulting education prepares these students for the independent, autonomous jobs found in the upper (managerial) levels of the occupational hierarchy. Conversely, with fewer resources children in relatively poor school districts are confronted with the opposite situation: large classes, a limited curriculum, and academic regimentation. The education received by these working-class children prepares them for jobs similar to those held by their parents. "The children of managers and professionals are taught self-reliance within a broad set of constraints; the children of production line workers are taught obedience."†

†Bowles, "Unequal Education," pp. 227–228.

CHAPTER 5

THE DEMAND FOR LABOR

The previous three chapters have focused upon labor supply. In the present chapter our attention shifts to the demand side of the labor market. Then in Chapter 6 our understanding of labor supply and demand will be combined to explain how wage rates are determined.

The main goals of the present chapter are as follows. Our first and major objective is to explain how the short-run demand curve for labor is derived. In this discussion we note how a firm's short-run demand curve relates to the marginal physical productivity of labor and the way in which it varies according to whether a firm is selling its output in a competitive or noncompetitive product market. Next, the long-run demand for labor is presented and compared with the short-run demand curve. Third, we examine the process by which the labor demand curves of individual firms are summed to obtain the market demand curve for a particular type of labor. Fourth, the principal factors which influence the elasticity of demand for labor are enumerated and explained. Finally, we discuss the factors which cause the market demand for labor curve to shift leftward or rightward.

It should be noted at the outset that the demand for labor, or for any other productive resource, is a *derived demand*. This simply means that the demand for labor depends upon, or is derived from, the demand for the product which it is producing. With the exception of some services—for example, those provided by barbers, physicians, or lawyers—workers do not directly satisfy the wants of consumers. Rather, labor is demanded for the contribution it makes to the production of such products as automobiles, television sets, or loaves of bread. Hence, a decrease in the demand for, say, automobiles will reduce the demand for automobile workers.

The fact that the demand for labor is a derived demand correctly implies that the strength of the demand for any particular type of labor will depend upon (1) how productive that labor is in helping to create some product and (2) the market value of that product. If type A labor is highly productive in turning out product X, and if product X is highly valued by society, then there will be a great demand for type A labor. Conversely, the demand will be small for some kind of labor which is relatively unproductive in producing a good which is not of great value to society. These observations point the way for our discussion. We will find that the immediate determinants of the demand for labor are labor's marginal productivity and the value (price) of its output. Let us begin by examining the short-run production function for a typical firm and then introduce the role of product price.

A FIRM'S SHORT-RUN PRODUCTION FUNCTION

A *production function* is a relationship between quantities of resources (inputs) and the corresponding production outcomes (output). We will assume that the production process entails just two inputs—labor L and capital K; that is, that output is a function of L and K. To simplify further, let us suppose that a single type of labor is being employed or, in other words, that the firm is hiring homogeneous inputs of labor. Furthermore, initially we examine the firm as it operates in the *short run*. The short run refers to a situation in which the firm's stock of capital—its plant, machinery, and equipment—is fixed. Restated, in the short run the firm is adding variable quantities of labor L to a fixed amount of capital K.

What happens to the total product (output) as successive inputs of labor are added to a fixed plant? The answer is provided in Figure 5-1 (a) and (b) where the upper graph (a) shows a short-run production function or total physical product (TP) curve and the lower graph (b) displays the corresponding curves for the marginal physical product of labor (MP) and the average physical product of labor (AP). *Total physical product* (TP), measured on the vertical axis in (a), is simply the total output that is produced by each combination of the *variable* resource, labor, shown on the horizontal axis, and the *fixed* amount of capital. The *marginal physical product* (MP) of labor is the change in TP associated with the addition of one more unit of labor. It is the absolute change in TP and can be found by drawing a line tangent to the TP curve at any point and then determining the slope of that line. For example, notice line mm' which is drawn tangent to point Z on the TP curve. The slope of mm' is zero, and this is the marginal product MP as shown at point z on the MP curve in the lower graph. The *average physical product* (AP) of labor is TP divided by the number of labor units. Geometrically, it is measured as the slope of any straight line drawn from the origin to or through any particular point on the TP curve. For example, notice line $0a$ which radiates from the origin through point Y on TP. The slope ($\Delta TP/\Delta L$) of $0a$ tells us the AP associated with this particular combination of TP and labor input L. For example, if TP were 20 at point Y, and L were 4, then AP obviously would be 5 ($= 20/4$). This is the value of the slope of line $0a$, which as measured from the origin is the *vertical* "rise" ($= 20$) divided by the *horizontal* "run" ($= 4$). If we assume that labor units are labor hours, rather than workers, then this slope measures output per worker hour.

It is important to understand clearly the relationships between total, marginal, and average physical products. To show these relationships *and* to permit us later to isolate the region in which the firm will operate if it decides to operate at all, we have divided the total physical product curve (TP) into three stages, but have also subdivided stage I into two parts. Notice that over segment $0X$ of the TP curve—or stated alternatively, within part IA of stage I—the total product curve is increasing at an *increasing* rate. As observed in the lower graph, this implies that MP ($= \Delta TP/\Delta L$) necessarily is rising. For example, suppose that the TP's associated with the first three workers were 3, 8, and 15, respectively. The corresponding MP's would be 3 ($= 3 - 0$), 5 ($= 8 - 3$), and 7 ($= 15 - 8$), respectively. Note, too, from the lower graph that because MP exceeds average physical product (AP), the latter also is rising. This is a simple matter of arithmetic necessity: Whenever a number which is greater than the average of some total is added to that total, the average must rise. In the present context, marginal product is the addition to total product while average product is the average of total product. Hence, when MP exceeds AP, then AP must rise.[1]

[1]You raise your cumulative grade point average by earning grades in the most recent (marginal) semester which are higher than your current average.

FIGURE 5-1 A FIRM'S SHORT-RUN PRODUCTION FUNCTION

As labor is added to a fixed amount of capital, total product will eventually increase by diminishing amounts, reach a maximum, and then decline as shown in (a). Marginal products in (b) reflects the changes in total product associated with each additional input of labor. The relationship between marginal product and average product is such that MP intersects AP where AP is at its maximum. The *yz* segment of the MP curve in stage II is the basis for the short-run labor demand curve.

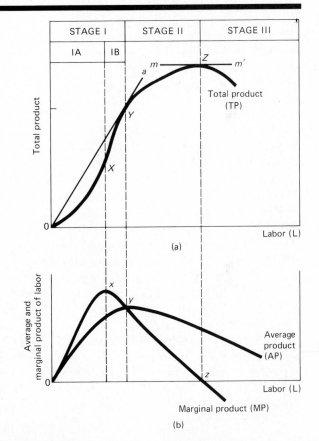

Next, observe segment *XY*—or stage IB—of the production function in Figure 5-1 (a). The total product curve is now such that TP is still increasing as more workers are hired, but at a *decreasing* rate, and therefore MP (graph b) is declining. Notice that MP reached its maximum at point *x* in the lower graph and that this point corresponds to point *X* on the production function. But beyond points *X* and *x*, MP falls. We see, however, that even though MP is now falling, it still is above AP, and hence AP continues to rise. Finally, observe that the end of range IB of stage I is marked by the point at which AP is at its maximum and just equals MP (point *y*). The fact that AP is at a maximum at point *Y* on the TP curve is confirmed by ray 0*a*. The slope of 0*a*, which, remember, measures AP, is greater than would be the slope of any other straight line drawn between the origin and a specific point on the TP curve.

In stage II, which we later will refer to as the zone of production, notice that total product continues to rise at a diminishing rate. Consequently, MP also continues to decline. But now AP also falls because MP finally is less than AP. Again, simple arithmetic tells us that when a number (MP) which is less than the current average is added to a total (TP), then the average (AP) must fall.

At the dividing line between stages II and III, TP reaches its maximum at point *Z* and MP becomes zero (point *z*), indicating that beyond this point additional workers detract from total product. In stage III, TP falls and MP is therefore negative, the latter causing AP to continue to decline.

Why do TP, MP, and AP behave in the manner shown in Figure 5-1 (a) and (b)? It is *not* because the quality of labor declines as more of it is hired; remember that we assumed all workers were identical. Rather the reason is that, as labor is added, the fixed amount of capital is initially underutilized relative to labor and then ultimately overutilized. Imagine a firm that possesses a fixed amount of machinery and equipment. If this firm hires just a few workers, total physical product (TP) and output per worker (AP) are low. Why so? Because each worker has a variety of tasks to perform, and gains in efficiency from worker specialization are unattainable. Time is lost as workers scramble from one job operation to another, and output is forgone as capital equipment stands idle much of the time. Production is inefficient because there is too little labor relative to capital; in other words, *capital* is underutilized. These difficulties are resolved as more workers are added and the fixed plant is used at, or near, its designed capacity. Workers can now specialize, and machinery is more fully utilized. Thus for a time the extra or marginal product of each worker increases. But these efficiency gains—as reflected in rising MP and AP—cannot be realized indefinitely. As still more labor is added, diminishing marginal returns result. Recall from your previous economics course(s) that the **law of diminishing marginal returns** indicates that, as successive units of a variable resource (labor) are added to a fixed resource (capital), a level of total product is reached beyond which the marginal physical product of that variable input declines. Restated, at some point labor becomes so abundant relative to the fixed capital that additional workers cannot contribute much to output. For example, workers may be forced to wait in line to use the machines, thereby causing *labor* to be underutilized. At the extreme, the continuous addition of labor could so overcrowd the plant that the MP of still more labor would become negative, causing total product to decline (stage III).

The characteristics of TP, MP, and AP just discussed are summarized in Table 5-1. In reviewing the table, notice that stage II of the production function is designated as the *zone of production*. To see why, let us establish that the left-hand boundary of stage II in Figure 5-1 is where the efficiency of labor—as measured by its average product—is at a maximum. Similarly, the right-hand boundary is where the efficiency of the fixed resource capital is maximized. Notice first that, at point Y on TP and y on AP and MP, total product *per unit of labor* is at its peak. This is shown both by ray $0a$, which is the steepest line that can be drawn from the origin to any point on TP, and by the AP curve, since AP is TP/L. Next, note that at point Z on TP and z on MP, total physical product is at a maximum. Because capital (K) is fixed, this implies that the average product of K is also at a maximum! That is, total product *per unit of capital* is greater at the right-hand boundary of stage II than at any other point. The generalization here is that if a firm chooses to operate at all, *it will wish to produce at a level of output where changes in labor contribute to increasing efficiency of either labor or capital.*

This is *not* the case in either stage I or III. In stage I, additions to labor *increase* both the efficiency of labor *and* the efficiency of capital. The former can easily be seen by the rising AP curve; the latter is true since K is constant and TP is rising, thereby increasing the average product of K $(= \text{TP}/K)$. The firm therefore will desire to move at least to the left-hand boundary of stage II.

What about stage III? Inspection of Figure 5-1 (a) and (b) shows that the addition of labor *reduces* the efficiency of *both* labor and capital. Notice that the AP curve is falling *and* that, because there is less total product than before, the TP/K ratio also is declining. Stated differently, the firm will not operate in stage III because it can *add* to its efficiency and to total product by *reducing* employment!

Conclusion? The profit-maximizing or loss-minimizing firm that chooses to operate will face a marginal physical product curve indicated by line segment yz

TABLE 5-1

Production Function Variables: A Summary

				Total Product, TP_L	Marginal Product, MP_L	Average Product, AP_L
		STAGE I	IA	Increasing at an increasing rate	Increasing and greater than AP	Increasing
			IB	Increasing at a decreasing rate	Declining but greater than AP	Increasing
Zone of Production		**STAGE II**		Increasing at a decreasing rate	Declining and less than AP	Declining
		STAGE III		Declining	Negative and less than AP	Declining

in Figure 5-1 (b). *This MP curve is the underlying basis for the firm's short-run demand for labor curve.*

SHORT-RUN DEMAND FOR LABOR: THE PERFECTLY COMPETITIVE SELLER

To see how segment *yz* in Figure 5-1 (b) relates to labor demand, let us next (1) transform the TP and MP information in that figure to hypothetical numbers via a table, and (2) convert our analysis from real to monetary terms. Employers, after all, make their decisions on how many workers to hire in terms of *revenues* and *costs,* rather than in physical terms.

Consider Table 5-2. Columns 1 to 3 are merely numerical illustrations of the relationships within the zone of production, showing total and marginal product but omitting average product. To simplify we assume here that diminishing marginal physical productivity sets in with the first unit of labor hired. Recalling our earlier discussion of the demand for labor as a derived demand, note that column 4 shows the price of the product that is being produced. The fact that this $2 price does not decline as more output is produced and sold indicates that the firm is selling its output in a perfectly competitive market. In technical terms, the firm's *product* demand curve is perfectly elastic; the firm is a "price taker." Multiplying column 2 by column 4 we obtain total revenue (sometimes called "total revenue product") in column 5. From these total revenue data we can easily compute **marginal revenue product** (MRP) which, *by definition, is the increase (change) in total revenue resulting from the hire of each additional worker.* These figures are shown in column 6. The MRP schedule shown by columns 1 and 6 is strictly proportionate to the MP schedule, shown by columns 1 and 3. In this case MRP is *twice* as large as MP.

Our task is to demonstrate that columns 1 and 6—the MRP schedule— constitute the firm's **short-run labor demand curve.** To justify and explain this assertion we must first understand the rule which a profit-maximizing firm will apply in determining the number of workers to employ. *A profit-maximizing*

TABLE 5-2

Demand for Labor: Firm Selling in a Perfectly Competitive Product Market (Hypothetical Data)

(1) Units of Labor, L	(2) TP	(3) MP	(4) Product Price, P	(5) Total Revenue, TR	(6) MRP ($\Delta TR/\Delta L$)	(7) VMP (MP × P)
1	15	15	$2	$30	$30	$30
2	27	12	2	54	24	24
3	36	9	2	72	18	18
4	42	6	2	84	12	12
5	45	3	2	90	6	6
6	46	1	2	92	2	2

employer should hire workers so long as each successive worker adds more to the firm's total revenue than he or she adds to total costs. We have just noted that the amount which each successive unit of labor adds to total revenue is measured by MRP. The amount which a worker adds to total costs is measured by **marginal wage cost,** MWC, which is defined as the change in total wage cost resulting from the hire of one more worker. Hence, we can abbreviate our rule by saying that the profit-maximizing firm should hire units of labor up to the point at which MRP = MWC.[2] If at some level of employment, MRP exceeds MWC, it will be profitable to employ more labor. If for some level of employment MWC exceeds MRP, the firm will increase its profits by hiring less labor.

Let us now assume that the employer for whom Table 5-2 is relevant is hiring labor under purely competitive conditions. This means the firm is a "wage taker" in that it employs a negligible portion of the total labor supply and therefore exerts no perceptible influence upon the wage rate. The wage rate is "given" to the employer and it follows that total wage cost (the wage bill) increases by the amount of the wage rate W for each additional unit of labor hired. In other words, the wage rate and marginal wage cost are equal. We can thus modify our MRP = MWC rule for the firm which is hiring competitively and restate it as the MRP = W rule. That is, the profit-maximizing firm which is a perfectly competitive employer of labor should hire units of labor up to the point at which the marginal revenue product MRP equals the wage rate W.

We now can apply the MRP = W rule to demonstrate our earlier assertion: the MRP schedule shown in columns 1 and 6, which we recall is derived directly from the MP data from the zone of production, *is* the firm's short-run labor demand curve. The MRP data from columns 1 and 6 are graphed in Figure 5-2 to demonstrate this point. This schedule and curve indicate how many units of labor this firm would demand at several separate competitively determined wage rates. First, let's suppose that the wage rate is $23.9\overline{9}$, an amount which is infinitesimally less than $24. This firm will decide to employ 2 units of labor because the first unit contributes $30 to total revenue and the second, $24. Hence the firm either adds to profits or subtracts from losses by hiring these two units of labor. But the firm will not employ the third, fourth, and further units, because MRP < W for each of them.

Next suppose that the wage rate falls to $11.9\overline{9}$. The MRP = W rule indicates that the firm will now also hire the third and fourth units of labor. If the wage rate falls further to, say, $1.9\overline{9}$, it will employ 6 units of labor. We conclude then that *the MRP curve in Figure 5-2 is the firm's short-run labor demand curve,* because each point on it indicates the quantity of labor which a firm will demand at each possible wage rate that might exist. Any curve which embodies this information on wage rate and quantity of labor demanded is, by definition, the firm's labor

---

[2]The rationale for this rule is essentially the same as that for the marginal revenue equals marginal cost (MR = MC) rule which identifies the profit-maximizing output in the product market. The difference, of course, is that the MRP = MWC rule is in terms of *inputs* of labor, while the MR = MC rule is couched in terms of *outputs* of product.

demand curve. Under perfectly competitive conditions in the sale of the product, the labor demand curve's downward slope is due solely to the diminishing marginal physical product of labor.

One further point needs to be made before leaving this topic. Notice that the demand for labor curve D_L in Figure 5-2 is labeled VMP, as well as MRP. The *value of marginal product* (VMP) is the extra output and income in dollar terms that accrues to *society* when an additional unit of labor is employed. Notice that the VMP schedule is shown by columns 1 and 7 in Table 5-2 *and* that VMP (column 7) equals MRP (column 6) in this case. The MRP data are found by calculating the change in total revenue (column 5) associated with the employment of one more unit of labor. The VMP data are determined by *multiplying* MP (column 3) by the product price (P). In this case, MRP = VMP because the extra revenue, or *marginal revenue,* gained by selling an extra unit of the product is equal to the product price. Conclusion: Where there is perfect competition in the sale of products, MRP = VMP; that is, the extra *revenue* to the firm from hiring an additional labor unit equals the social *value* of the extra output.

SHORT-RUN DEMAND FOR LABOR: THE IMPERFECTLY COMPETITIVE SELLER

Most firms in our economy do *not* sell their products in purely competitive markets. Rather they sell under imperfectly competitive conditions; that is, the firms are monopolies, oligopolies, or monopolistically competitive sellers. The

FIGURE 5-2 THE LABOR DEMAND CURVE OF A PURELY COMPETITIVE SELLER
Application of the MRP = W rule reveals that the MRP curve is the firm's short-run labor demand curve. Under perfect competition in the product market MRP = VMP and the labor demand curve slopes downward solely because of diminishing marginal productivity.

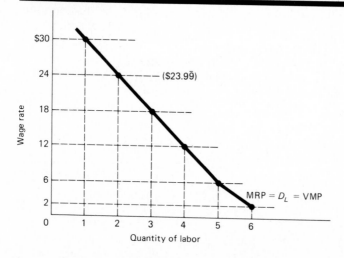

change in assumptions about product market conditions from pure competition to imperfect competition alters our analysis in one important respect. Because of product uniqueness or differentiation, the imperfectly competitive seller's product demand curve is downsloping, rather than perfectly elastic, and this means that the firm must lower its price to sell the output contributed by each successive worker. Furthermore, because we assume that the firm cannot engage in price discrimination, it must lower the price not only on the last unit produced but also on all previous units which otherwise could have been sold at a higher price. Hence, the MRP or labor demand curve of the purely competitive seller falls for a *single* reason: Marginal physical product diminishes. But the MRP or labor demand curve of the imperfectly competitive seller declines for *two* reasons: Marginal physical product falls *and* product price declines as output increases. Table 5-3 takes this second consideration into account. The production data of columns 1 to 3 are precisely the same as in Table 5-2, but in column 4 we recognize that product price must be lowered to sell the marginal physical product of each successive worker.

It is worth reemphasizing that the lower price which accompanies each increase in output applies not only to the output produced by each additional worker, but also to all prior units which otherwise could have been sold at a higher price. For example, the second worker's marginal product is 12 units, and these 12 units can be sold for $2.40 each or, as a group, for $28.80. Recall that this is the value of the marginal product (VMP) of labor, that is, the value of the added output from society's perspective (column 7). But the MRP of the second worker is only $25.80. Why the $3.00 difference? The answer is that in order to sell the 12 units associated with the second worker, the firm must accept a $.20 price cut on *each* of the 15 units produced by the first worker—units which could have been sold for $2.60 each. Thus the MRP of the second worker is only $25.80 [= $28.80 − (15 × $.20)]. Similarly, the third worker's MRP is only $14.40. Although the 9 units he or she produces are worth $2.20 each in the market and therefore their VMP is $19.80, the worker does *not* add $19.80 to the firm's total revenue when account is taken of the $.20 price cut which must be taken on the 27 units produced by the first two workers. Specifically, the third

TABLE 5-3

Demand for Labor: Firm Selling in an Imperfectly Competitive Product Market (Hypothetical Data)

(1) Units of Labor, L	(2) TP	(3) MP	(4) Product Price, P	(5) Total Revenue, TR	(6) MRP (ΔTR/ΔL)	(7) VMP (MP × P)
1	15	15	$2.60	$39.00	$39.00	$39.00
2	27	12	2.40	64.80	25.80	28.80
3	36	9	2.20	79.20	14.40	19.80
4	42	6	2.10	88.20	9.00	12.60
5	45	3	2.00	90.00	1.80	6.00
6	46	1	1.80	87.40	−2.60	1.80

worker's MRP is $14.40 [= $19.80 − (27 × $.20)]. The other MRP figures in column 6 of Table 5-3 are similarly explained. Comparison of columns 6 and 7 reveals that at each level of employment, VMP—the value of the extra product to buyers—exceeds MRP—the extra revenue to the firm. The efficiency implications of this difference will be examined in Chapter 6.

As in the case of the purely competitive seller, application of the MRP = W rule to the MRP curve will yield the conclusion that the MRP curve *is* the firm's labor demand curve. However, by plotting the imperfectly competitive seller's MRP or labor demand curve D_L in Figure 5-3 and comparing it with the demand curve in Figure 5-2, we find visual support for an important generalization: All else being equal, the imperfectly competitive seller's labor demand curve is steeper and less elastic than that of the purely competitive seller. It is not surprising that the firm which possesses monopoly power is less responsive to wage rate changes than is the purely competitive seller. The tendency for the imperfectly competitive seller to add fewer workers as the wage rate declines is merely the labor market reflection of the firm's tendency to restrict output in the product market. Other things being equal, the seller possessing monopoly power will find it profitable to produce less output than would a purely competitive seller. In producing this smaller output, it will employ fewer workers.

Finally, notice that the VMP schedule which is also plotted in Figure 5-3 lies

FIGURE 5-3 THE LABOR DEMAND CURVE FOR AN IMPERFECTLY COMPETITIVE SELLER
Under imperfect competition in the product market the firm's demand curve will slope downward because marginal product diminishes as more units of labor are employed *and* because the firm must reduce the product price on all units of output as more output is produced. Also, the MRP (= MR × MP) for the imperfect competitor is less than the VMP (= P × MP) at all levels of employment beyond the first unit.

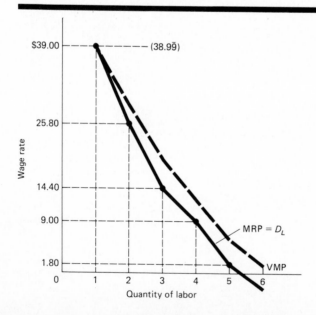

to the right of the firm's D_L = MRP curve. This visually depicts the conclusion stated previously: The marginal revenue accruing to an imperfectly competitive seller when it hires an additional unit of labor is *less than* the market value of the extra output that the unit of labor helps produce [(MRP = MR × MP) < (VMP = P × MP)].

THE LONG-RUN DEMAND FOR LABOR[3]

Thus far, we have derived and discussed the firm's short-run demand for labor, which presupposes that labor is a variable input and the amount of capital is fixed. We now want to understand the **long-run labor demand curve** which shows us the amount of labor which will be demanded at each possible wage rate when both labor and capital are variable inputs. Intuitively, we would expect the demand for labor to be more elastic in the long run than in the short run. The longer the amount of time a firm has to adjust to a wage rate change, the greater will be the firm's employment response. And this is in fact the case. In the long run, a change in the price of labor will induce changes in the quantities of other inputs employed. These changes in quantity will in turn have a feedback effect upon the demand curve for labor. The task is to detail the nature of these changes and to explain why the long-run demand curve for labor is more elastic than the short-run curve.

In Figure 5-4 the equilibrium wage rate and equilibrium quantity of labor employed are shown by W_1 and Q at point *a* on D_{L1}. Note that at *a* the wage rate W_1 is equal to labor's marginal revenue product, indicating that the firm is using the profit-maximizing amount of labor Q. We assume that the firm is at similar profit-maximizing positions with respect to capital and other inputs. Now suppose that the wage rate declines from W_1 to W_2. Because MRP now exceeds the wage rate at the Q level of employment, the firm will find it profitable to increase employment. Indeed, we know that the firm's new *short-run* equilibrium would be at point *b* where Q_1 units of labor are employed. But, in the long run, the employment of this additional labor will affect the quantities of capital and other inputs which the firm might want to employ, *and* these quantitative changes will in turn affect the marginal product (MP) of labor.

Nonlabor resources—let's concentrate upon capital—may be related to labor as either complementary or as substitute inputs. By definition, labor and capital are **complementary** if an increase (decrease) in the amount of either input increases (decreases) the marginal product of the other input. Similarly, labor and capital are **substitute** inputs if an increase (decrease) in the quantity of either one decreases (increases) the marginal product of the other. We first assume that labor and capital are complementary inputs. In Figure 5-4, this means that a decline in the wage rate from W_1 to W_2 will increase the amount of labor

---

[3]The appendix of this chapter provides a more sophisticated derivation of the long-run demand for labor curve.

employed from Q to Q_1, which then will increase the marginal product and, hence, the MRP of capital. Just as the MRP of labor *is* the firm's short-run demand for labor, the MRP of capital *is* the firm's demand for capital (labor being constant). Given the price of capital, the firm will now find it profitable to employ more capital. What impact will this increase in capital have on the firm's demand for *labor*? Recalling our assumption that capital and labor are comple-ments, we conclude that this increase in the quantity of capital will increase the MP and therefore the MRP or demand curve for labor. This is shown in Figure 5-4 by the rightward shift from D_{L1} $(= MRP_1)$ to D_{L2} $(= MRP_2)$. This increase in the demand for labor makes profitable an even further increase from Q_1 to Q_2 in the quantity of labor employed. While the short-run adjustment is from a to b, the additional long-run adjustment is from b to c. The locus of all long-run adjustment points such as a and c determines the location of the long-run de-mand curve. As observed in Figure 5-4, the long-run curve, D_{LR}, is more elastic than any given short-run labor demand curve.

While not intuitively obvious, the general character of the labor market adjustments will be the same if labor and capital are related as *substitute* or rival inputs. Recall that an increase (decrease) in the quantity of a substitute input will decrease (increase) the marginal product of the other resource. With this in mind, let us reconsider the analysis. Once again the assumed wage reduction from W_1 to W_2 will prompt the firm to use more (Q_1 rather than Q) labor. But this increase in the quantity of labor will *reduce* the MP of capital and, given the price of capital, *decrease* the amount employed. Given the definition of substitute inputs, this decrease in the quantity of capital will *increase* the MP of labor,

FIGURE 5-4 THE LONG-RUN DEMAND FOR LABOR

The long-run demand for labor is more elastic than the short-run demand because the long run allows for appropriate alterations in the quantity of complementary and substitute inputs such as capital.

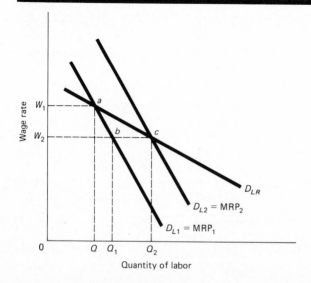

shifting the demand for labor curve from D_{L1} to D_{L2} as before. Again, while the short-run adjustment is from *a* to *b*, the added long-run adjustment is from *b* to *c*. In the case of complementary inputs, the firm uses more capital; in the situation where labor and capital are substitutes, less capital is used. But in *both* cases *more* labor is employed after the firm has had time to adjust its stock of capital! The firm's long-run demand curve for labor, D_{LR} is therefore more elastic than the short-run curve. To reinforce this conclusion, the reader is urged to analyze the short- versus long-run employment effects of, say, a union-negotiated *increase* in the wage rate.

THE MARKET DEMAND FOR LABOR

We have now demonstrated that the MRP curve derives from the MP curve in the firm's zone of production and *is* the firm's short-run demand curve for labor. We also have established that a firm's long-run demand for labor is more elastic than the short-run demand. Let us next turn our attention to the market demand for labor. At first thought we might reason that the total or **market demand** for any particular type of labor can be determined by simply summing (horizontally on a graph) the labor demand curves of all firms which employ this kind of labor. Thus if there were, say, 200 firms with labor demand curves identical to the firm portrayed in Table 5-2, we would simply multiply the amounts of labor demanded at the various wage rates by 200 and thereby determine the market

FIGURE 5-5 THE MARKET DEMAND CURVE FOR LABOR
The market demand curve for labor is less elastic than the simple horizontal summation of the labor demand curves of the individual employers. A lower wage induces all firms to hire more labor and produce more output, causing the supply of the product to increase. The resulting decline in product price shifts the firms' labor demand curves to the left. Consequently, total employment rises from *C* to *D* in graph (b), rather than from *C* to *D'*.

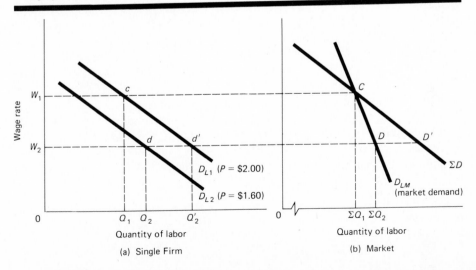

(a) Single Firm

(b) Market

demand curve. However, this simple process ignores an important aggregation problem. The problem arises from the fact that certain magnitudes (such as product price), which can be correctly viewed as constant from the vantage point of the *individual firm,* must be treated as variable from the standpoint of the *entire market.*

To illustrate, let us suppose there are, say, 200 competitive firms each with a labor demand curve identical to that shown earlier in Figure 5-2. Assume also that these firms are all producing a given product which they are selling in competition with one another. From the perspective of the *individual firm,* when the wage rate declines, the use of more labor will result in a *negligible* increase in the market supply of the product and, therefore, no change in product price. But because *all firms* experience the lower wage rate and respond by hiring more workers and increasing their outputs, there will be a *substantial* increase in the supply of the product. This in turn will reduce the product price. This point is critical because, as was shown earlier in Table 5-2, product price is a determinant of each firm's labor demand curve. Specifically, a lower product price will reduce MRP and therefore shift the labor demand curve of each firm to the left. This implies that the market demand curve for labor is in fact *less elastic* than that yielded by a simple summation of each firm's labor demand curve.[4]

Consider Figure 5-5 in which the diagram on the left (a) shows labor demand for one of the 200 firms and the diagram on the right (b) shows the market demand for labor. The individual firm is initially in equilibrium at point *c* where the wage rate is W_1 and employment is Q_1. The labor demand curve D_{L1} is based on a product price of $2.00 as shown in column 4 of Table 5-2. If the wage rate falls to W_2, *ceteris paribus,* (other things being equal), the firm would now find it profitable to move to a new equilibrium at d' where it would hire Q_2' workers. But our *ceteris paribus* assumption does *not* hold in the context of a number of firms which are hiring this kind of labor to produce some particular product. The lower wage induces *all* of the firms to hire more labor. This increases output or product supply, which then causes a decline in product price. This lower price— say $1.60 as compared to the original $2.00—feeds back to the labor demand curve for each firm, shifting those curves leftward as indicated by the move from D_{L1} to D_{L2} in Figure 5-5 (a). In effect, each firm then recalculates its MRP or labor demand using the new lower price. Hence, each firm achieves equilibrium at point *d* by hiring only Q_2, as opposed to Q_2', workers at the wage rate W_2. The market demand curve in Figure 5-5 (b) is therefore *not* curve CD', which is the simple horizontal summation of the demand for labor curves for all the 200 firms. Rather, the market demand curve is the horizontal summation of all quantities, such as Q_1 at wage rate W_1 on D_{L1}, *and* the summation of all quantities, such as Q_2 at wage rate W_2, which fall on the "price adjusted" market demand curve that cuts through points CD in Figure 5-5 (b). As seen in that

---

[4]If *all* employers are monopolists in their distinct product markets, our conclusion does not hold. As pointed out in the discussion of Figure 5-3, the monopolist's labor demand curve already incorporates the declines in product price which accompany output increases. Hence, to get the market labor demand curve one simply can sum the various labor demand curves of the monopolists.

graph, the correct "price adjusted" market demand curve CD is *less elastic* than the incorrect "simple summation" CD' curve.

ELASTICITY OF LABOR DEMAND

We have concluded that the long-run labor demand curve is *more* elastic than the short-run curve and that the market demand for labor is *less* elastic than a curve derived by a simple summation of labor demand curves of individual firms. These references to elasticity raise an important unanswered question: What determines the *sensitivity* of employment to a change in the wage rate, that is, the **elasticity of labor demand?** Let us examine this topic in more detail.

The Elasticity Coefficient. The sensitivity of the quantity of labor demanded to wage rate changes is measured by the wage elasticity coefficient E_d, as shown in equation (5-1).

$$E_d = \frac{\text{percentage change in quantity of labor demanded}}{\text{percentage change in the wage rate}} \qquad (5\text{-}1)$$

Demand is *elastic*—meaning that employers are quite responsive to a change in wage rates—if a given percentage change in the wage rate results in a larger percentage change in the number of workers demanded. In this case the absolute value of the elasticity coefficient will be greater than 1.[5] Conversely, demand is *inelastic* when a given percentage change in the wage rate causes a smaller percentage change in the amount of labor demanded. In this instance E_d will be less than 1, indicating that employers are relatively insensitive to changes in wage rates.

Empirical evidence reveals a wide range of elasticities of labor demand. For example, Clark and Freeman estimate that the elasticity of labor demand for all of U. S. manufacturing is 0.95.[6] This implies that labor demand is nearly unitary; that is, a 10 percent increase in the wage rate will cause a nearly equal percentage decline in employment. Similarly, the wage elasticity coefficient in public education is estimated by Ashenfelter and Ehrenberg to be 1.06.[7] Other esti-

---

[5]Since the wage rate and the quantity of labor demanded are inversely related, the elasticity coefficient will always be negative. By convention the minus sign is taken as understood and therefore is ignored. Also, in computing actual elasticity coefficients economists use a "midpoint" formula:

$$E_d = \frac{Q_2 - Q_1}{(Q_2 + Q_1)/2} \div \frac{W_2 - W_1}{(W_2 + W_1)/2}$$

[6]Kim B. Clark and Richard B. Freeman, "How Elastic Is the Demand for Labor?" *Review of Economics and Statistics,* November 1980, pp. 509–520.

[7]Orley Ashenfelter and Ronald G. Ehrenberg, "The Demand for Labor in the Public Sector," in Daniel Hamermesh (ed.), *Labor in the Public and Nonprofit Sectors* (Princeton, N. J.: Princeton University Press, 1975), p. 71.

mates of labor demand elasticity include coefficients of 0.3 in printing, 1.5 in petroleum, 0.1 in furniture manufacturing, and 2.4 in fabricated metals.[8]

The Total Wage Bill Rules. The reader may recall from basic economics that one can determine the price elasticity of demand for a *product* by observing what happens to total revenue when the product price changes. Similar rules, called the total wage bill rules, can be applied to determine the wage elasticity of demand. This is apparent in Figure 5-6, which displays two separate labor demand curves, D_{L1} and D_{L2}. Suppose initially that the wage rate is $8, at which the firm hires 5 units of labor. The *total wage bill* (TWB), defined as $W \times Q$, in this case is $40 (= 8×5). This also happens to be the *total wage income*, as viewed by the 5 workers. Now let us suppose that the wage rate rises to $12. This increase produces two opposing effects on the wage bill. The higher wage rate obviously tends to increase the wage bill, but the decrease in employment tends to reduce it. In the case of D_{L1}, the firm responds to the $4 higher wage rate by

[8]Roger N. Waud, "Man-Hour Behavior in U.S. Manufacturing: A Neoclassical Interpretation," *Journal of Political Economy*, May–June 1968, pp. 419–20. For a review of several elasticity of labor demand studies see Daniel Hamermesh, "Econometric Studies of Labor Demand and Their Applications to Policy Analysis," *Journal of Human Resources*, Fall 1976, pp. 507–525.

FIGURE 5-6 THE TOTAL WAGE BILL RULES

If a change in the wage rate causes the total wage bill ($W \times Q$) to change in the opposite direction, then labor demand is elastic. This is the case along the $8 to $12 segment of D_{L1}, where the total wage bill falls from $40(= 8×5) to $24(= 12×2) when the wage rate rises from $8 to $12. In the case of labor demand, D_{L2}, however, this same wage increase causes the total wage bill to rise from $40 to $48(= 12×4). This second situation supports the generalization that, when demand is inelastic, the wage rate and the total wage bill change in the same direction.

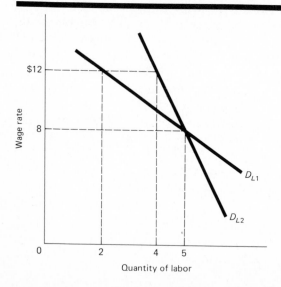

cutting back the amount of labor employed from 5 to 2 units. The wage increase results in a rise in the wage bill of $8 (= $4 × 2), while the decline in employment lowers it by $24 (= $8 × 3). The net effect is that the wage bill *falls* by $16 from $40 (= $8 × 5) to $24 (= $12 × 2). *When labor demand is elastic, a change in the wage rate causes the total wage bill to move in the opposite direction.* On the other hand, notice that for labor demand D_{L2} the $4 higher wage adds more to the wage bill (= $16) than the 1-unit decline in employment subtracts (= $8), causing the total wage bill to *rise* from $40 (= $8 × 5) to $48 (= $12 × 4). A second generalization emerges: *When labor demand is inelastic, a change in the wage rate causes the total wage bill to move in the same direction.* Finally, *where labor demand is unit elastic (= 1), a change in the wage rate leaves the total wage bill unchanged.* The reader is urged to confirm the first two of these three generalizations by using the equation in footnote 5 to compute the actual elasticity *coefficients* for the segments of D_{L1} and D_{L2} represented by the $8 to $12 wage increase. The reader is also reminded that elasticity is a percentage magnitude and hence is not the same as the slope of a demand curve.

We will find in subsequent chapters of this text that the elasticity of labor demand is of great importance. For example, a union will be in a much more advantageous bargaining position if its employer's demand for labor is inelastic. In this case, a relatively large increase in wage rates will be accompanied by only a relatively small loss in jobs, and the total amount of income realized by union workers will increase. But, if demand is elastic, a boost in the wage rate will cause a relatively large decline in employment, and the total income of the unionized workers will diminish. As a second example, if the demand for low-skilled labor is highly elastic, then an above-equilibrium minimum wage will cause considerable unemployment. On the other hand, all else being equal, if the demand is highly inelastic, then little unemployment will be observed. These points are pursued in this chapter's Time and One-Half section.

Determinants. What determines the elasticity of the market demand for labor? The theoretical generalizations are as follows:[9]

1. Elasticity of product demand. Because the demand for labor is a derived demand, the elasticity of demand for labor's output will influence the elasticity of demand for labor. Other things being equal, *the greater the price elasticity of product demand, the greater will be the elasticity of labor demand.* It is quite simple to see why this is so. If the wage rate falls, the cost of producing the product will decline. This means a decline in the price of the product and an increase in the quantity demanded. *If* the elasticity of *product* demand is great, that increase in the quantity of the product demanded will be large and, therefore, will necessi-

---

[9]These generalizations were developed in 1890 by Alfred Marshall in his *Principles of Economics* (London: Macmillan Publishing Company, 1964) and refined by John R. Hicks, *The Theory of Wages*, 2d ed. (New York: St. Martin's Press, 1966), pp. 241–247. For this reason they are often referred to as the "Marshall-Hicks rules of derived demand."

tate a large increase in the quantity of labor in order to produce that additional output. This implies an elastic demand for labor. But *if* the demand for the product is inelastic, the increase in the amount of the product demanded will be small, as will be the increase in the quantity of labor demanded. This suggests that the demand for labor would be inelastic.

This generalization has two noteworthy implications. First, other things being equal, the greater the monopoly power an individual firm possesses in the product market, the less elastic is its demand for labor. This is confirmed by Figures 5-2 and 5-3, which we discussed previously. Recall that in Figure 5-2 the firm is selling its product in a perfectly competitive market, which implies that it is a price-taker facing a *perfectly* elastic product demand curve. The resulting demand for labor curve slopes downward solely because of diminishing returns. Contrast that curve to the one for the imperfectly competitive seller shown in Figure 5-3. This firm's product demand curve is *less* elastic, as evidenced by the fact that its marginal revenue is less than its price (Table 5-3). Hence, the labor demand curve in Figure 5-3 also is less elastic; it slopes downward not only because of diminishing marginal productivity, but also because of the less than perfectly elastic product demand.

A second implication is that labor demand will be more elastic in the long run than in the short run. Why so? Apart from the factors cited in the previous section, wage elasticity is likely to be greater in the long run simply because price elasticity of product demand is greater in the long run. Consumers are often creatures of habit and only slowly change their buying behavior in response to a price change. Coffee drinkers may not immediately reduce their consumption when the price of coffee rises, but given sufficient time, some may acquire a taste for, say, tea. Another factor at work here is that some products are mainly used in conjunction with costly durable goods. For example, when the price of electricity rises, people who have electric furnaces and other appliances do not respond by *greatly* reducing their consumption of electricity. But as time transpires, the elasticity of the demand for electricity—*and the elasticity of the derived demand for workers in that industry*—becomes greater. People eventually replace their electrical furnaces and perhaps other appliances with devices which use natural gas, solar energy, wood, or even coal.

2. Ratio of labor costs to total costs. In general, all other things being the same, *the larger the proportion of total production costs accounted for by labor, the greater will be the elasticity of demand for labor.*[10] The rationale here is straightforward. Compare these two cases. Case one: If labor costs were the only production cost—that is, if the ratio of labor to total costs were 100 percent—then a 20 percent increase in the wage rate would increase unit costs by 20 percent. Given product demand, this large cost increase eventually would cause a considerable increase in product price, a sizeable reduction in sales of output and, therefore, a

[10]This proposition assumes that the product demand elasticity is greater than the elasticity of substitution between capital and labor (Chapter 17). See John R. Hicks, op. cit., pp. 241–247.

large decline in the employment of labor. Case two: If labor costs were only 10 percent of total cost, then the same 20 percent increase in the wage rate would increase total unit costs by only 2 percent. Assuming the same product demand as in case one, this relatively small cost increase will generate a relatively modest decline in employment. Case one implies a more elastic demand for labor than case two. The same 20 percent wage increase caused a larger percentage decline in employment in case one then it did in case two.

3. Substitutability of other inputs. Other things being equal, *the greater the substitutability of other inputs for labor, the greater will be the elasticity of demand for labor.* If technology is such that capital is readily substitutable for labor, then a small increase in the wage rate will elicit a substantial increase in the amount of machinery used and a large decline in the amount of labor employed. Conversely, a small drop in the wage rate will induce a large substitution of labor for capital. The demand for labor will tend to be elastic in this case. In other instances, technology may dictate that a certain amount of labor is more or less indispensable to the productive process; that is, the substitution of capital for labor is highly constrained. In the extreme, the production process may involve fixed proportions; for example, three airline pilots—no more and no less—may be required to fly a commercial airliner. In this case a change in the wage rate will have little short-run effect upon the number of pilots employed, and this implies an inelastic demand for labor.

It is worth noting that *time* plays an important role in the input substitution process, just as it does in the previously discussed process through which consumer goods are substituted for one another. Recall from the discussion of Figure 5-4 that the longer the period of time which has elapsed since the wage rate was changed, the more elastic labor demand curves tend to be. For example, a firm's truck drivers may obtain a substantial wage increase with little or no immediate decline in employment. But over time, as the firm's trucks wear out and are replaced, the company may purchase larger trucks and thereby be able to deliver the same total output with significantly fewer drivers. Alternatively, as the firm's trucks depreciate, it might turn to entirely different means of transportation for delivery. Or, in the case of airline pilots, new aircraft may be developed that require only two pilots, rather than three. The Boeing 737-300 is a case in point.

4. Supply elasticity of other inputs. The fourth determinant of the elasticity of demand for labor is basically an extension of the third determinant. The generalization is that, other things being equal, *the greater the elasticity of the supply of other inputs, the greater the elasticity of demand for labor.* In discussing our third generalization we implicitly assumed that the prices of nonlabor inputs, say, capital, are unaffected by a change in the demand for them. But this may not be realistic. To illustrate, assume once again that an increase in the wage rate prompts the firm to substitute capital for labor. This increase in the demand for capital will leave the price of capital unchanged only in the very special case where the supply of capital is perfectly elastic. But, let us suppose that the supply of capital slopes upward, so that an increase in demand would increase its price. Furthermore, the less elastic the supply of capital, the greater will be the increase in the price of capital in response to any given increase in demand. Any resulting change in the price of capital is important because it will tend to retard or dampen the substitution of capital for labor and thereby reduce the elasticity of demand for labor. More specifically, if the supply of capital is inelastic, a given increase in the demand for capital will cause a large increase in the price of capital, and this will greatly retard the substitution process. This implies that the demand for labor will tend to be inelastic. Conversely, if the supply of capital is highly elastic, the same increase in demand will cause only a small increase in the price of capital which only dampens the substitution process slightly. This suggests that the demand for labor will tend to be elastic.

CHANGES IN DEMAND FOR LABOR

The movement *along* a labor demand curve implied by the concept of elasticity is quite distinct from an *increase* or *decrease* in labor demand. The latter imply *shifts* of the demand for labor curve either rightward or leftward. What factors will cause such shifts? Our derivation of the labor demand curve for an individual firm and the discussions of (1) the market demand for labor and (2) substitute versus complementary resources provide the background required to generate a list of *determinants of labor demand*.

1. Product demand. *A change in the demand for the product that a particular type of labor is producing, all else being equal, will shift the labor demand curve in the same direction.* For example, suppose that in Table 5-2 and Figure 5-2 an increase in product demand occurs causing the product price to rise from $2 to $3. If we plotted the *new* MRP data onto Figure 5-2, we would observe that the demand for labor curve shifted rightward. A decline in the demand for the product would likewise shift the labor demand curve leftward.

2. Productivity. *Assuming that it does not cause a fully offsetting change in product price, a change in the marginal product of labor, MP, will shift the labor demand curve in the same direction.* Again return to Table 5-2 and Figure 5-2. Suppose that technology improves, causing the entire production function (column 2 in relationship to column 1 in Table 5-2) to shift upward. More concretely, let us assume that the total product produced by each worker in combination with the fixed capital *doubles*. Clearly, MP in column 3 and consequently MRP in column 6 would increase. If the new MRP data were plotted in Figure 5-2, we would observe that labor demand had shifted rightward. Conversely, a decline in labor productivity would shift the labor demand curve leftward.

3. Number of employers. Recall that the *market* demand for labor in Figure 5-5 was found by summing horizontally the "price-adjusted" labor demand curves possessed by individual employers. *Assuming no change in employment by other firms, a change in the number of firms employing a particular type of labor will change the demand for labor in the same direction.* In terms of Figure 5-5, D_{LM} will shift rightward if additional firms enter this labor market to hire workers, and shift leftward if firms leave, all else being equal.

4. Prices of other resources. In Figure 5-4 we observed that the elasticity of labor demand would be greater in the long run than in the short run, owing to the fact that changes in the *quantity of labor demanded* caused changes in the marginal products of substitute and complementary inputs. We now wish to consider the impact of *changes in the prices* of other inputs on the *location* of the labor demand curve.

Suppose, as an example, that the price of capital falls while the prices of labor and other inputs remain constant. Also, assume initially that capital and labor are substitutes in the production process. The decline in the price of capital will generate two opposing effects: a *substitution effect* and an *output effect*. Firms will substitute the now lower-priced capital for labor and, taken alone, this substitution effect will cause a decline in the demand for labor. But, the reduced price of capital also lowers the cost of producing the product. Having lower costs, firms will find it profitable to produce and sell greater levels of output. This output effect, taken alone, will cause the demand for labor to rise; that is, firms will need to hire more workers to produce the greater output. Hence, the net impact on labor demand will depend on the relative sizes of the two opposing effects. To generalize: *If the substitution effect outweighs the output effect, a change in the price of a substitute resource will cause the demand for labor to change in the same direction; if the output effect swamps the substitution effect, a change in the price of a substitute resource will cause the demand for labor to change in the opposite direction.*

This indeterminacy does not exist when labor and capital are complementary inputs. The decline in the price of capital will unambiguously increase the demand for labor. Because labor and capital are not substitutable for one another, there will not be a substitution effect. But, because the firm's costs are now lower, it will increase its output, thereby increasing its demand for labor. Our generalization? *A change in the price of a complementary resource will cause labor demand to change in the opposite direction.*

SUMMARY

1. The demand for labor is a derived demand and therefore depends upon the marginal productivity of labor and the price or market value of the product.
2. The segment of the marginal product curve which is positive and lies below the average product curve is the basis for the short-run labor demand curve. More specifically, the short-run demand curve for labor is determined by applying the MRP = W rule to the firm's marginal revenue product data.
3. Other things being equal, the demand for labor curve of a perfectly competitive seller is more elastic than that of an imperfectly competitive seller. This difference occurs

because the imperfectly competitive seller must reduce product price to sell additional units of output, while the purely competitive seller does not. This also means that the imperfectly competitive seller's marginal revenue product curve lies to the left of the corresponding value of marginal product curve, while marginal revenue product and the value of the marginal product are identical for the perfectly competitive seller.

4. A firm's long-run labor demand curve is more elastic than its short-run curve because in the long run the firm has sufficient time to adjust nonlabor inputs such as capital. The long-run curve is more elastic regardless of whether capital and labor are complementary or substitute inputs.

5. The market demand for a given type of labor is less elastic than a simple horizontal summation of the short- or long-run demand curves of individual employers. The reason for this is that as employers as a group hire more workers and produce more output, product supply will increase significantly and product price will therefore decline.

6. The elasticity of labor demand is measured by comparing the percentage change in the quantity of labor demanded with a given percentage change in the wage rate. If the elasticity coefficient is greater than one, demand is relatively elastic. If it is less than one, demand is relatively inelastic. When demand is elastic, changes in the wage rate cause the total wage bill to change in the *opposite* direction. When demand is inelastic, changes in the wage rate cause the total wage bill to move in the *same* direction.

7. The demand for labor generally is more elastic (a) the greater the elasticity of product demand, (b) the larger the ratio of labor cost to total cost, (c) the greater the substitutability of other inputs for labor, and (d) the greater the elasticity of supply of other inputs.

8. The location of the labor demand curve depends upon (a) product demand, (b) the marginal productivity of labor, (c) the number of employers, and (d) the prices of other inputs. When any of these determinants of demand change, the labor demand curve tends to shift to a new location.

QUESTIONS AND STUDY SUGGESTIONS

1. Key terms and concepts to remember: derived demand; production function; law of diminishing marginal returns; marginal revenue product; value of marginal product; marginal wage cost; zone of production; short-run labor demand; complementary and substitute resources; long-run labor demand; market demand for labor; elasticity of labor demand; total wage bill rules.

2. Graph a short-run production function (one variable resource) showing the correct relationships between total product, average product, and marginal product.

3. Explain how marginal revenue product is derived. Why is the MRP curve the firm's short-run labor demand curve? Explain how and why the labor demand curves of a perfectly competitive seller and an imperfectly competitive seller differ.

4. "Only that portion of the MP curve which lies below AP constitutes the basis for the firm's short-run demand curve for labor." Explain.

5. Given the following data, complete the labor demand schedule shown at the right. Contrast this schedule to the value of marginal product schedule which would exist given this data. Explain why the labor demand and VMP schedules differ.

Inputs of Labor	Total Product	Product Price	Labor Demand Schedule	
			Wage Rate	Quantity Demanded
0	0	$1.10		
1	17	1.00	$18	
2	32	.90	14	
3	45	.80	11	
4	55	.70	6	
5	62	.65	2	
6	68	.60	1	

6. Assuming labor and capital are complementary inputs, distinguish graphically between the short-run and long-run labor demand curves. Which is more elastic?
7. "It would be incorrect to say that an industry's labor demand curve is simply the horizontal sum of the demand curves of the individual firms." Do you agree? Explain.
8. Suppose that marginal productivity tripled while product price fell by one-half in Table 5-2. What would be the net impact on the location of the short-run labor demand curve in Figure 5-2?
9. Use the concepts of substitute versus complementary inputs and substitution versus output effects to assess the likely impact of the rapid decline in the price of computers, word processors, and related office equipment on the labor demand for secretaries.
10. Explain through illustrations or examples the determinants of the elasticity of demand for labor. Can you think of any tactics which a union might use to make the demand for its labor less elastic?
11. Use the total wage bill rules and the labor demand schedule in question 5 to determine whether demand is elastic or is inelastic over the $6 to $11 wage rate range. Compute the elasticity coefficient using the "midpoint" formula provided in footnote 5.
12. The physical productivity of farm labor has increased very substantially since World War II. How can this be reconciled with the fact that labor has moved from agricultural to nonagricultural occupations over this period?

SELECTED REFERENCES

FLANAGAN, ROBERT J., ROBERT S. SMITH, and RONALD G. EHRENBERG: *Labor Economics and Labor Relations* (Glenview, Ill.: Scott, Foresman and Company, 1984), chap. 4.

FLEISHER, BELTON M. and THOMAS J. KNIESNER: *Labor Economics: Theory, Evidence, and Policy,* 3d ed. (Englewood Cliffs, N.J.: Prentice-Hall, Inc., 1984), chap. 3.

GISSER, MICHA: *Intermediate Price Theory: Analysis, Issues, and Applications* (New York: McGraw-Hill Book Company, 1981), chaps. 5 and 14.

HAMERMESH, DANIEL S.: "Econometric Studies of Labor Demand and Their Application to Policy Analysis," *Journal of Human Resources,* Fall 1976, pp. 507–525.

HICKS, JOHN R.: *The Theory of Wages,* 2d ed. (London: Macmillan Publishing Company, 1964) chap. 1.

ROTHSCHILD, K. W.: *The Theory of Wages* (New York: Augustus M. Kelly, 1967), chap. 2.

T I M E   A N D   O N E - H A L F

ESTIMATES OF THE ELASTICITY OF LABOR DEMAND

A large number of empirical studies have attempted to estimate the elasticity of labor demand for particular industries, occupations, and demographic groups.

In a 1968 study Waud* estimated the elasticity of labor demand for a number of durable and nondurable goods industries. For eight nondurable good industries, he found that the average value of the elasticity of labor demand was 0.72. This implies that a 10 percent increase in real wages would be expected to reduce employment by about 7 percent. Labor demand elasticities for specific industries in this category ranged from a low of 0.27 in the printing industry to a high of 1.53 in the petroleum industry. Elasticities for the food, apparel, and chemical industries were estimated to be 0.51, 0.29, and 0.65 respectively. Waud found the average of the demand elasticities for eight durable good industries to be 1.51, ranging from a low of 0.12 in the furniture industry to a high of 2.37 in fabricated metals. Estimates for primary metals, nonelectric machinery, and other machinery were 0.31, 2.10, and 2.14 respectively. In 1976 Hamermesh† summarized and compared more than a dozen studies of manufacturing and private nonfarm workers, concluding that the short-run (one-year) elasticity of labor demand was about 0.32.

   Of what practical significance are such figures? The answer is that private and public policies might be greatly affected by the size of the wage rate–employment tradeoff suggested by elasticity of labor demand estimates. In the private sphere a union's bargaining strategy might be influenced by the elasticity of labor demand for its workers. To illustrate, if Waud's figures are correct, other things being the same, we might expect unions in nondurable goods industries (where labor demand is inelastic) to bargain more aggressively for higher wages than would unions in durable goods industries (where labor demand is elastic). The reason? A given percentage increase in wage rates will give rise to a smaller decline in employment in nondurable than in durable goods industries. Similarly, Waud's estimates suggest that higher wage rates will cause employment to decline very little in the furniture and printing industries, but by relatively large amounts in the fabricated metals and machinery industries.

   The impact of government policies may depend upon the elasticity of labor demand. For example, economists have conducted empirical studies concerning the extent to which increases in the minimum wage might reduce employment. Most of this research has focused upon teenagers because they are relatively inexperienced, low-wage workers who are most likely to be affected by boosts in the minimum wage. The policy implication is clear. Generally speaking, the more elastic the demand for teenage labor, the less desirable will be increases in the minimum wage. Brown, Gilroy, and Kohen†† analyzed almost three dozen studies of the employment effects of the minimum wage. The consen-

---

*Roger N. Waud, "Man-Hour Behavior in U.S. Manufacturing: A Neoclassical Interpretation," *Journal of Political Economy*, May–June, 1968, pp. 407–421.

†Daniel S. Hamermesh, "Econometric Studies of Labor Demand and their Application to Policy Analysis," *Journal of Human Resources*, Fall 1976, pp. 507–525.

††Charles Brown, Curtis Gilroy, and Andrew Kohen, "The Effect of the Minimum Wage on Employment and Unemployment," *Journal of Economic Literature*, June 1982, pp. 487–582.

sus estimate derived from this survey is that the demand for teenage (16–19) workers is quite inelastic: "On balance, a 10 percent increase in the minimum wage is estimated to result in about a 1–3 percent reduction in total teenage employment." For young adults (20–24), there is an even lower demand elasticity. Specifically, a 10 percent increase in the minimum wage is estimated to lower unemployment for this group by less than 1 percent. If these estimates are reasonably accurate, an increase in the minimum wage would create income gains for teenagers and young adults who remain employed which will exceed the income losses of those who would lose their jobs. Were the demand for teenage and youth labor elastic, the reverse would be true and any argument for increasing the minimum wage would be weakened.§

A P P E N D I X   T O   C H A P T E R   5

ISOQUANT-ISOCOST ANALYSIS OF THE LONG-RUN DEMAND FOR LABOR

A more sophisticated derivation of the firm's long-run downward-sloping labor demand curve is based on (1) isoquant and (2) isocost curves.

ISOQUANT CURVES

An *isoquant curve* shows the various possible combinations of two inputs that are capable of producing a specific quantity of physical output. By definition then, output is the same on all points on a *single* isoquant. For example, total output is 100 units of some product or service on curve Q_{100} in Figure 5-7 both when 20 units of capital are combined with 7 units of labor *or* when 10 units of capital and 15 units of labor are employed.* Isoquants—or equal output curves—possess several other characteristics.

1. Downward slope. Assuming that capital and labor are substitute inputs, if less of capital (K) is used, then to maintain a given level of output, more labor (L) must be employed. Conversely, in order to hold total output constant, using less of L will require employing more of K. Therefore there is an *inverse* relationship between K and L at each output level, implying a downward-sloping isoquant curve.

2. Convexity to the origin. Isoquants are convex to the origin because capital and labor are not *perfect* substitutes for one another. For example, an

§The economics of the minimum wage will be considered in detail in Chapter 10. The more general issue of youth unemployment is explored in Chapter 18's Time and One-Half minireading.

*For simplicity we will assume that the only two resources are capital and labor *and* disregard all combinations of capital and labor that are not within a firm's zone of production.

excavating company can substitute labor and capital to produce a specific level of "output," say, clearing 1000 acres of wooded land in a fixed amount of time. But, labor and capital are not perfectly substitutable for this purpose. To understand this and see why this firm's isoquant curve is convex to the origin, compare the following circumstances. First, suppose that the firm is using a single bulldozer and hundreds of workers. Clearly, an extra bulldozer would compensate, or substitute, for a large number of workers in producing this "output". Contrast that to a second situation in which the firm has, say, 100 bulldozers but only relatively few workers. The addition of still another machine would have a relatively low substitution value; that is, it would compensate for perhaps only one or two workers. Why? The firm already has numerous bulldozers; it needs people to operate them, supervise the operation, and cut down the trees that cannot be bulldozed.

This same concept can be viewed in the opposite way. When the firm is employing only a small amount of labor and a large amount of equipment, an extra worker will possess a relatively high substitution value, that is, compensate for the reduction of a large amount of capital. But as more labor is added, the decrease in capital permitted by an added unit of labor will decline. Stated in technical terms, the absolute value of the ***marginal rate of technical substitution*** of labor for capital will fall as more labor is added. This MRTS is shown symbolically in equation (5-2), and it is the absolute value of the slope of the isoquant at a given point.

$$MRTS = \frac{\Delta K}{\Delta L} \tag{5-2}$$

FIGURE 5-7 ISOQUANT CURVES
Every point on a specific isoquant represents some combination of inputs—in this case capital and labor—which produces a given level of total output. Isoquants, or "equal output curves," further to the northeast indicate higher levels of total output.

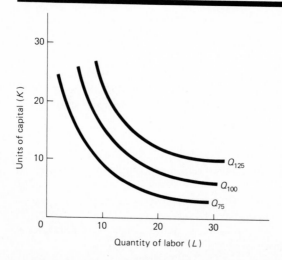

Returning to Figure 5-7 we see that each isoquant shown is convex to the origin. Notice that as one moves along, say, Q_{75}, from left to right, the absolute value of the slope of the curve declines; in other words, the curve gets flatter. By definition, a curve which gets flatter (whose absolute slope declines) as one moves southeast is convex to the origin.

3. Higher output to the northeast. Each isoquant further to the northeast reflects combinations of K and L which produce a greater level of total output than the previous curve. Isoquant Q_{125} represents greater output than Q_{100}, which in turn reflects more output than Q_{75}, and so forth. Two other points are relevant here. First, we have drawn only three of the many possible isoquant curves. Second, just as "equal elevation" lines on a contour map never intersect, neither do these "equal output" lines.

ISOCOST CURVES

A profit-maximizing firm will seek to minimize the costs of producing a given output. To accomplish this task, it will need to know the prices of K and L. These prices will enable the firm to determine the various combinations of K and L that are available to it for a specific expenditure. For example, if the prices of K and L are $6 and $4 per unit, respectively, then the input combinations that can be obtained from a given outlay, say, $120, would be $6 times the quantity of K plus $4 times the quantity of L. Then one possibility would be to use 20 units of

FIGURE 5-8 AN ISOCOST CURVE
An isocost, or "equal expenditure," curve shows the various combinations of two inputs—in this case capital and labor—which can be purchased with a specific dollar outlay, given the prices of the two inputs. The slope of an isocost line measures the price of one input divided by the price of the other.

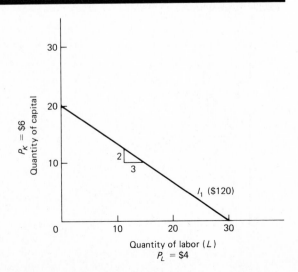

K (= \$120 = \$6 × 20) and no labor. At the other extreme, this firm could use zero units of capital and 30 units of labor (= \$120 = 30 × \$4). Another such combination would be $10K$ and $15L$. In Figure 5-8 we plot these three points and connect them with a straight line. This line is an **isocost curve;** it shows all the various combinations of capital and labor which can be purchased by a particular outlay, given the prices of K and L. Note that the absolute value of the slope of this "equal expenditure" line is the ratio of the price of labor to the price of capital; that is, the slope is $2/3$ (= \$4/\$6).

The location of a particular isocost curve obviously depends on (1) the total expenditure and (2) the relative prices of L and K. Given the prices of K and L, the greater the total expenditure, the further the isocost curve will lie outward from the origin. For example, if the total outlay were enlarged from \$120 to \$150, and the prices of K and L remained unchanged, then the isocost curve shown in Figure 5-8 would shift outward in a parallel fashion. Similarly, a smaller outlay would shift it inward. Second, the location of an isocost curve depends on the relative prices of L and K. Given the total expenditure, the higher the price of L relative to the price of K, the *steeper* will be the isocost curve; the lower the price of L relative to the price of K, the *flatter* the curve.

THE COST-MINIMIZING COMBINATION OF CAPITAL AND LABOR

By overlaying the isocost curve in Figure 5-8 onto the isoquant "map," we can determine the firm's cost-minimizing combination of K and L for a given quantity of total output. Stated somewhat differently, this allows us to determine the lowest cost *per unit of output*. This **least-cost combination of resources** occurs at

FIGURE 5-9 THE LEAST-COST COMBINATION OF CAPITAL AND LABOR
The least-cost combination of capital and labor used to produce 100 units of output is at point A, where the isocost line is tangent to isoquant Q_{100}. At A, the marginal rate of technical substitution (MRTS) equals the ratio of the price of labor to the price of capital. In this case the firm will use 10 units of capital and employ 15 units of labor and in the process expend \$120.

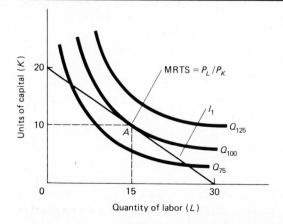

the *tangency point* of the isoquant curve, Q_{100}, and the isocost curve, I_1 (point A) in Figure 5-9. At point A the slope of the isoquant, which is the MRTS, just equals the ratio of the prices of labor and capital—the slope of the isocost curve. The firm will use 10 units of capital and employ 15 units of labor. This expenditure of $120 is the minimum outlay that is possible in achieving this level of output. To reinforce this proposition, the reader should determine why combinations of K and L represented by other points on Q_{100} are *not* optimal.

DERIVING THE LONG-RUN LABOR DEMAND CURVE

Earlier in this chapter we derived a *short-run* labor demand curve by holding capital constant, adding units of labor to generate a marginal product schedule, multiplying MP times the extra revenue gained from the sale of additional product, and graphing the resulting marginal revenue product schedule. By applying the $W = $ MRP rule we demonstrated that the MRP curve *is* the short-run labor demand curve. Now, we derive a *long-run* labor demand curve directly from our isoquant-isocost analysis. In Figure 5-10 (a) we reproduce our $120 isocost line, I_1, and the isoquant, Q_{100}, which is tangent to it at point A. We then drop a perpendicular dashed line down to the horizontal axis of graph (b), which also measures units of labor, but measures the price of labor, or wage rate, vertically. Recall that the price of L is assumed to be $4, at which the optimum level of employment is 15 units of labor. This gives us point a in the lower graph.

Now suppose that some factor, say out-migration, reduces labor supply and causes the price of labor to increase from $4 to $12. Our task is to ascertain graphically the effect of this increase of the wage rate on the quantity of labor demanded. To accomplish this, let us proceed in several steps. First, we must draw a new isocost curve, reflecting the new ratio of the price of L to K. Inasmuch as the price of labor is now $12 while the price of K is assumed to remain constant at $6, the new isocost curve will have a slope of 2 (= $12/$6). Because we wish initially to hold the level of output constant at Q_{100}, we construct isocost curve I_2 which has a slope of 2 and is tangent to Q_{100}.

Our next step is to determine the new combination of K and L which would be used *if* output were to be held constant. This is shown at point B where the marginal rate of technical substitution on isoquant curve Q_{100} equals the slope of isocost curve I_2. Notice what has happened thus far: In response to the higher wage rate, the firm has substituted more capital ($+10$) for less labor (-8). This is the **substitution effect** of the wage increase. As used here the substitution effect is defined as the change in the quantity of an input demanded resulting from a change in the price of the input, with the output remaining constant.

The final step is to acknowledge that the increase of the price of labor from $4 to $12 will cause the firm to reassess its profit-maximizing level of output. In particular, production costs are now higher and, given product demand, the firm will find it profitable to produce less output. Let us assume that this reevaluation results in the firm's decision to reduce its output from Q_{100} to Q_{75}. Given the new $12 to $6 price ratio of L and K, we simply push the I_2 line inward in a parallel fashion until it is tangent with this lower isoquant. Notice that the new tangency position is at *C*. This ***output effect*** further reduces the cost-minimizing quantity of labor; that is, not as much labor is needed to produce the smaller quantity of output. This effect is defined as the change in employment of an input resulting from the cost change associated with the change in the input's price. Dropping a dashed perpendicular line downward from point *C*, we derive point *c* in the

FIGURE 5-10 (a) AND (b) DERIVING THE LONG-RUN LABOR DEMAND CURVE
When the price of labor rises from $4 to $12, the substitution effect causes the firm to use more capital and less labor, while the output effect reduces the use of both. The labor demand curve is determined in (b) by plotting the quantity of labor demanded before and after the increase in the wage rate from $4 to $12.

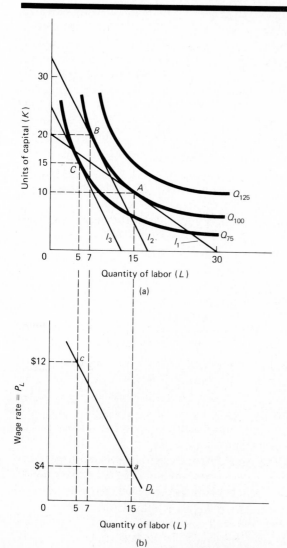

lower graph. At the new wage rate of $12, the firm desires to hire only 5 units of labor. By finding a series of points such as A and C in the upper graph and a and c in the lower one, and then by determining the locus of these latter points, we derive a long-run labor demand curve such as D_L in graph (b). This curve slopes downward because of both a *substitution effect* (−8 labor units) and an *output effect* (−2 units).

SUMMARY

1. An isoquant curve shows the various possible combinations of two inputs that are capable of producing a specific quantity of physical output.
2. An isocost curve shows the various combinations of two inputs which a firm can purchase with a given outlay or expenditure.
3. The firm's cost-minimizing combination of inputs in achieving a given output is found at the tangency point between the isocost and isoquant curve, that is, where the marginal rate of technical substitution (slope of isoquant curve) equals the ratio of the input prices (slope of the isocost curve).
4. Changing the price of either input while holding the price of the other resource and the level of output constant produces a new isocost curve that has a new tangency position on the given isoquant curve. This generates a *substitution effect* that results in the use of less of the resource which rose in price and more of the resource that did not experience a price change.
5. An increase in the price of a resource also increases the cost per unit of the product. This creates an *output effect* tending to reduce the employment of both labor and capital.
6. A downward-sloping labor demand curve can be derived by plotting the wage rate–quantity combinations associated with changing the price of labor (wage rate).

QUESTIONS AND STUDY SUGGESTIONS

1. Key terms and concepts to remember: isoquant curve; marginal rate of technical substitution; isocost curve; least-cost combination of resources; substitution effect; output effect.
2. Explain why isoquant curves (a) are negatively sloped, (b) are convex to the origin, and (c) never intersect.
3. Suppose that the quantity of capital is *fixed* at 10 units in Figure 5-7. Explain, by drawing a horizontal line rightward from 10K, the short-run law of diminishing marginal returns discussed in the body of this chapter. Hint: observe the distance between the isoquants along your horizontal line.
4. Explain how each of the following, other things being equal, would shift the isocost curve shown in Figure 5-8: (a) a decrease in the price of L, (b) a simultaneous and proportionate increase in the prices of both K and L, and (c) an increase in the total outlay, or expenditure, from $120 to $150.
5. Explain graphically how isoquant-isocost analysis can be used to derive a long-run labor demand curve. Distinguish between the *substitution* and *output* effects.

6. By referring to Figure 5-10 (a), explain the impact of the increase of the *price of labor* on the cost-minimizing quantity of *capital*. What can you conclude about the relative strengths of the substitution and output effects as they relate to the demand *for capital* in this specific situation?

7. Is labor demand (a) elastic, (b) unit elastic, or (c) inelastic over the $4 to $12 wage rate range of D_L in Figure 5-10 (b)? Explain by referring to the total wage bill rules (Figure 5-6) and the midpoint formula for elasticity (footnote 5).

WAGE DETERMINATION AND RESOURCE ALLOCATION

I
n Chapter 2 we explained how individuals make labor supply decisions based on their preferences for income and leisure in relationship to their wage opportunities. Then in Chapter 4 we extended the analysis of labor supply by examining how people decide on the types and amounts of human capital to obtain. In Chapter 5 our discussion turned to labor demand and hiring decisions by firms. We now *combine* supply and demand to demonstrate how wages are determined under a variety of product and labor market conditions and how labor resources get allocated to various employments.

This chapter is structured as follows. First, we will examine the elements of a perfectly competitive labor market, focusing on wage and employment determination, the hiring decision by the individual firm, and allocative efficiency. Second, we will assess the impact of product market monopoly on a firm's hiring conduct and on allocative efficiency. The third section of the chapter will explore a labor market in which there is a single firm hiring labor. Next, we will examine the ways in which unions alter labor supply or demand and thereby increase wage rates. Finally, we will develop a bilateral monopoly model in which power exists on both the buyer and seller sides of the labor market.

THE THEORY OF A PERFECTLY COMPETITIVE LABOR MARKET

A perfectly competitive labor market has the following distinct characteristics which contrast it with other labor markets: (1) a large number of firms competing with one another to hire a specific type of labor to fill identical jobs; (2) numerous qualified people who have identical skills and who independently supply their labor services; (3) "wage-taking" behavior; that is, neither workers nor firms exert control over the market wage; (4) perfect, costless information and labor mobility.

Let us examine the components, operation, and outcomes of this type of labor market in some detail. Specifically, we will divide our discussion into three subsections: the labor market, the hiring decision by an individual firm, and allocative efficiency.

The Labor Market. The competitive market for a specific type of labor can best be analyzed by separating it into two parts: labor demand, which reflects the behavior of employers; and labor supply, which derives from the decisions of workers. Recall from the previous chapter (Figure 5-5) that the market demand for a particular type of labor is found by summing over a range of wage rates the "price adjusted" amounts of labor that employers desire to hire at each of the various wage rates. Also remember, specifically from Chapter 2, that *individual* labor supply curves are normally backward-bending. Can we then conclude that the *market* supply of a particular grade of labor is also backward-bending? In most labor markets this is not the case; market supply curves generally slope upward and to the right, indicating that *collectively* workers will offer more labor hours at higher *relative* wage rates. Why is this so?

Figure 6-1 helps explain the positive relationship between the wage rate and the quantity of labor hours found in most labor markets. Graph (a) displays five separate backward-bending *individual* labor supply curves in a specific labor market, while graph (b) sums the curves horizontally to produce a *market* labor supply curve.[1] Notice from their respective labor supply curves S_A and S_B, that at wage W_1 Adams will offer 4 hours of labor and Bates 6 hours. We simply sum

[1]We are assuming that, while all these workers have identical skills, they have differing preferences for leisure, differing levels of nonwage income, and so forth. Thus, their individual labor supply curves differ.

FIGURE 6-1 THE MARKET SUPPLY OF LABOR
Even though specific individuals normally have backward-bending labor supply curves, market labor supply curves generally are positively sloped over realistic wage ranges. Higher relative wages attract workers away from leisure or their previous jobs. The height of the market labor supply measures the opportunity cost of using the marginal labor hour in this employment. The shorter the time period, the less elastic this curve.

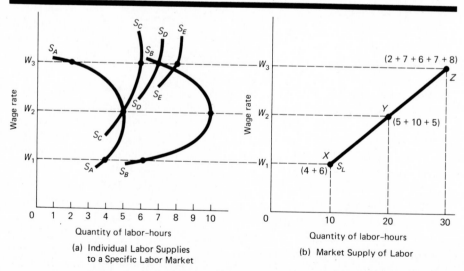

(a) Individual Labor Supplies
to a Specific Labor Market

(b) Market Supply of Labor

these outcomes (4 + 6) to get point X at wage W_1 on the market labor supply curve shown in graph (b). Now let us suppose the wage rate rises from W_1 to W_2 *in this labor market* while all other wage rates remain constant. Adams will increase her hours from 4 to 5 and Bates will work 10 hours rather than 6. We know from previous analysis that this implies that, for these two workers, substitution effects exceed income effects over the W_1 to W_2 wage range. But also notice that at W_2, a third worker—Choy (S_C)—chooses to participate in this labor market, deciding to offer 5 hours of labor. Presumably, he is attracted away from either another labor market, household production, or from leisure by the W_2 wage rate. Thus the total quantity of hours supplied is 20 (= 5 + 10 + 5), as shown by point Y in the right-hand graph. Finally, observe wage rate W_3, at which Adams and Bates choose to work *fewer hours* than previously, but Choy decides to offer 6 hours, and two *new workers*—Davis (S_D) and Egan (S_E)—now enter this labor market. The total number of hours, as observed at point Z on the market labor supply curve, is now 30 (= 2 + 7 + 6 + 7 + 8). Conclusion? Even though specific people may reduce their hours of work as the market wage rises, labor supply curves of specific labor markets generally are positively sloped over realistic wage ranges. Higher relative wages *attract workers away from either household production, leisure, or other labor markets and toward the labor market in which the wage increased.*

The vertical height of the market labor supply curve XYZ measures the opportunity cost of employing the last labor hour in this occupation. For example, point Y on S_L in Figure 6-1 (b) indicates that wage rate W_2 is necessary to entice the twentieth hour of labor. In the theoretical world of competition in product and labor markets, perfect information, and costless migration, the value of the alternative activity which that hour previously produced—either in the form of utility from leisure or output from work in a different occupation—is equivalent to W_2. To attract 30 hours of labor compared to 20, the wage must rise to W_3 (point Z). Why? The reason is that the twenty-first through thirtieth hours generate *more than* W_2 worth of value to workers and society in their alternative uses. To attract these hours to this labor market, these opportunity costs must be compensated for via a higher wage rate. To repeat: In perfectly competitive product and labor markets, labor supply curves measure marginal opportunity costs.

One final point needs to be emphasized concerning market labor supply. The shorter the time period and the more specialized the variety of labor, the less elastic the labor supply curve. In the short run, increases in the wage may not result in significant increases in the number of workers in a market but, in the long run, human capital investments can be undertaken which will allow greater responsiveness to the higher relative wage (Chapter 4).

Figure 6-2 combines the market labor demand and supply curves for a specific type of labor and shows the equilibrium wage W_0 and the equilibrium quantity of labor Q_0. If the wage were W_{es}, an *excess supply*, or surplus, of labor ($B - A$) would occur, driving the wage down to W_0; if instead the wage rate were W_{ed}, an *excess demand*, or shortage ($D - C$), of workers would develop, and the wage would increase to W_0. Wage W_0 and employment level Q_0 are the only levels that clear the market. That is, at W_0 the number of hours offered by labor suppliers just matches the number of hours that firms desire to employ.

The supply and demand curves in Figure 6-2 are drawn holding all factors other than the wage rate for this variety of labor constant. But, a number of other factors—or **determinants of labor supply and demand**—can change and thereby cause either rightward or leftward shifts in the curves. Many of these factors were discussed in Chapters 2 and 5; we simply formalize them in Table 6-1 here. The distinction made in the principles of economics course between "changes in demand" versus "changes in quantity demanded" *and* "changes in supply" versus "changes in quantity supplied" apply to the labor market as well as the product market. Changes in the determinants of labor demand and supply shown in the table cause the *entire curves to shift.* Changes in the wage rate, on the other hand, cause movements *along* demand and supply curves; that is, the *quantity* of labor demanded or supplied changes. But in the short run, changes in the wage rate *do not* cause shifts of the curves themselves.

To demonstrate how a competitive market for a particular type of labor operates and to emphasize the role of the determinants of supply and demand, let us suppose that the labor market in Figure 6-3 is characterized by labor demand D_0 and labor supply S_0, which together produce equilibrium wage and employment levels W_0 and Q_0 (point C). Next, assume that demand declines for the *product* produced by firms hiring this kind of labor, causing a fall in the price of the product and a corresponding drop in the **marginal revenue product** (MRP) of the labor (demand determinant 1, Table 6-1). Also, let us suppose that simultaneously the federal government releases findings of a definitive research

FIGURE 6-2 WAGE AND EMPLOYMENT DETERMINATION

The equilibrium wage rate W_0 and level of employment Q_0 occur at the intersection of labor supply and demand. A surplus, or excess supply, of labor would occur at wage rate W_{es}, a shortage, or excess demand, would result if the wage were W_{ed}.

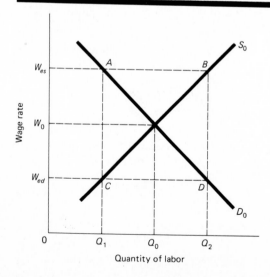

study which concludes that the considerable health and safety risks which were heretofore associated with this occupation are in fact minimal. Taken alone, this information will increase the relative nonwage attractiveness of this type of labor and shift the labor supply curve rightward—say from S_0 to S_1 (supply determinant 4, Table 6-1).

Now observe that at the initial wage rate W_0, the number of workers seeking jobs in this occupation (point B) exceeds the number of workers which firms wish to hire (point A). How will the market adjust to this surplus? Because wages are assumed to be perfectly flexible, the wage rate will drop to W_1 where the labor market will once again clear (point E). Figure 6-3 illustrates two generalizations. First, taken alone, a decline in labor demand causes *both* the

---

TABLE 6-1

The Determinants of Labor Supply and Demand

Determinants of Labor Supply

1. **Other Wage Rates**
   An increase (decrease) in the wages paid in other occupations for which workers in a particular labor market are qualified will decrease (increase) labor supply.
2. **Nonwage Income**
   An increase (decrease) in income other than from employment will decrease (increase) labor supply.
3. **Preferences for Work versus Leisure**
   A net increase (decrease) in people's preferences for work relative to leisure will increase (decrease) labor supply.
4. **Nonwage Aspects of the Job**
   An improvement (worsening) of the nonwage aspects of the job will increase (reduce) labor supply.
5. **Number of Qualified Suppliers**
   An increase (decrease) in the number of qualified suppliers of a specific grade of labor will increase (decrease) labor supply.

Determinants of Labor Demand

1. **Product Demand**
   Changes in *product* demand that increase (decrease) the product *price* will raise the marginal revenue product (MRP) of labor and therefore increase (decrease) the demand for labor.
2. **Productivity**
   Assuming that it does not cause an offsetting decline in product price, an increase (decrease) in productivity will increase (decrease) the demand for labor.
3. **Prices of Other Resources**
   If the substitution effect outweighs the output effect, a change in the price of a *substitute* resource will cause the demand for labor to change in the *same* direction. If the output effect swamps the substitution effect, a change in the price of a *substitute* resource will cause the demand for labor to change in the *opposite* direction.
   An increase (decrease) in the price of a *complementary* resource will cause labor demand to decline (increase).
4. **Number of Employers**
   Assuming no change in employment by other firms hiring a specific grade of labor, an increase (decrease) in the number of employers will increase (decrease) the demand for labor.

wage rate and quantity of labor to *fall*. Second, an increase in labor supply—also viewed separately—produces a *reduction* in the wage rate and an *increase* in equilibrium quantity. In this case, the net outcome of the simultaneous changes in supply and demand is a decline in the wage rate from W_0 to W_1 and a fall in the quantity of labor offered and employed from Q_0 to Q_1. The latter occurred because the decrease in demand *was greater than* the increase in labor supply. At W_1, the Q_1Q_0, workers formerly employed in this market were not sufficiently compensated for their opportunity costs and they left this occupation for either leisure, household production, or other jobs.

The Hiring Decision by an Individual Firm. Given the presence of, say, market wage W_0 or W_1 in Figure 6-3, how will a *firm* operating in a perfectly competitive labor and product market decide on the quantity of labor to employ? The answer can be found in Figure 6-4. Graph (a) portrays the labor market for a specific occupational group, and graph (b) shows the labor supply and demand curves for an *individual firm* which is hiring this grade of labor. Because this particular employer is just one of many firms in this labor market, its decision on how many workers to employ will not have an impact on the market wage. Instead, this firm is a "wage taker" in the same sense that a perfectly competitive seller is a "price taker" in the product market. The single employer in (b) has no incen-

FIGURE 6-3 CHANGES IN DEMAND, SUPPLY, AND MARKET EQUILIBRIUM

Changes in labor supply and demand create initial shortages or surplus in labor markets, followed by adjustments to new equilibrium wage rates and employment. In this case, the decline in demand from D_0 to D_1 and increase in supply from S_0 to S_1 produce an initial excess supply of AB at wage W_0. Consequently, the wage rate falls to W_1, and because the decline in demand is large relative to the increase in supply, the equilibrium quantity declines from Q_0 to Q_1.

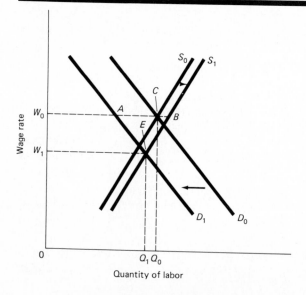

tive to pay more than the equilibrium wage W_0 because at the W_0 wage it can attract as many workers as it wants. On the other hand, if it offers a wage below W_0, it will attract *no* employees. All workers who possess this type of skill have marginal opportunity costs of at least W_0; they can get a minimum of W_0 in alternative employment. Consequently, the horizontal wage line W_0 in Figure 6-4 (b) *is* this firm's labor supply curve (S_L). You will observe that it is perfectly elastic.

Curve S_L in graph (b) also indicates this firm's *average wage cost* (AWC) and *marginal wage cost* (MWC). To see why, suppose that the firm hires 100 labor hours at $8 per hour. The total hourly wage bill will be $800 (= $8 × 100). What will be the average wage cost and marginal wage cost? Answer: AWC = $8 (= $800/100); MWC (extra cost of the last worker hour) = $8 (= $800 − $792). And if the firm hires 200 labor hours? Answer: total wage cost = $1600; AWC = $8 (= $1600/200); MWC = $8 (= $1600 − $1592). Hence, for all levels of employment, $W = $8 = MWC = AWC = S_L in this labor market.

How will this firm determine its profit-maximizing level of employment? Recall from Chapter 5 that in the short run a firm's demand for labor curve is its marginal revenue product curve. Thus, this firm can compare the additional revenue (MRP) obtained by hiring one more unit of labor with the added cost (MWC) or, in this case, the wage rate ($W = $ MWC). If MRP $>$ W, it will employ the particular hour of labor; on the other hand, if MRP $<$ W, it will not. To generalize: The profit-maximizing employer will obtain its optimal level of employment where MRP = MWC. We label this equality the **MRP = MWC rule.**

The profit-maximizing quantity is Q_0 in Figure 6-4 (b). To confirm this, observe level Q_1 where MRP, as shown by the vertical distance AC, exceeds MWC (distance AB). Clearly this firm will gain profits if it hires this unit of labor, because it can sell the added product produced by this worker for more than the wage W_0 (= MWC). This is true for all units of labor up to Q_0, where MRP and MWC are equal (distance DE). Beyond Q_0, diminishing returns finally reduce marginal physical product (MP) to the extent that MRP (= MP × P) lies below the market wage W_0 (= MWC). Thus this firm's total profit would fall if it hired more than Q_0 worker hours.

Allocative Efficiency. An efficient allocation of resources occurs when society obtains output—or national income—of greatest value from its available resources. The model of perfect competition presented in Figure 6-4 yields this outcome. To see why, we need to explain two closely interrelated propositions: (1) firms economize in using scarce resources by adjusting their inputs so as to minimize the cost of producing each level of output, and (2) firms operating in a perfectly competitive product and labor market employ resources such that resource prices (opportunity costs in alternative employment) equal the *value of the marginal products* (VMPs) of the resources in their present uses.

    1. Least-cost production. From a firm's perspective the total cost of any level of output is *minimized* when the marginal *physical* product (MP) per dollar cost of each resource used is the same. For simplicity let us assume there are only two resources: labor (L) and capital (K). Then the cost-minimizing position is shown in equation (6-1)

$$\frac{MP_L}{MRC_L} = \frac{MP_K}{MRC_K} \qquad (6\text{-}1)$$

where MP_L and MP_K are the marginal physical products of labor and capital and MRC_L and MRC_K are the marginal costs of each resource. In perfectly competitive labor markets, of course, the marginal cost of labor equals the wage rate. To demonstrate equation (6-1), let us suppose that the price of labor and capital are each \$1 but that MP_L is 5 and MP_K is 2; hence MP_L/MRC_L is $5/1$ and MP_K/MRC_K is $2/1$. This combination of L and K is inefficient, because *more* total output can be obtained for the *same* total cost. Stated alternatively, the same total output can be achieved at less total cost. For example, suppose the firm spends a dollar less on capital and instead purchases a dollar's worth of labor. It will lose 2 units of output by hiring less capital, but will gain 5 units from the employment of the extra dollar's worth of labor. Net output will increase by 3 units (= 5 − 2), and total cost will remain unchanged. As additional units of *labor* are employed, diminishing returns will dictate that the MP of labor will fall; and as fewer units of *capital* are used, the MP of capital will increase. Eventually, the conditions stated in equation (6-1) will be fulfilled; that is, $MP_L/MRC_L = MP_K/MRC_K$.

But will the *firm's* cost-minimizing combination of labor and capital also

FIGURE 6-4 PERFECT COMPETITION: THE LABOR MARKET (a) AND THE INDIVIDUAL FIRM (b)
In a perfectly competitive labor market, the equilibrium wage rate W_0 and quantity of labor Q_0 are determined by supply and demand, as shown in (a). The individual firm (b) hiring in this market is a "wage taker"; its labor supply curve, $S_L = MWC = AWC$, is perfectly elastic at W_0. The firm maximizes its profits by hiring Q_0 units of labor ($MRP = MWC$). Assuming competition in the product market, this employment level constitutes an efficient allocation of resources.

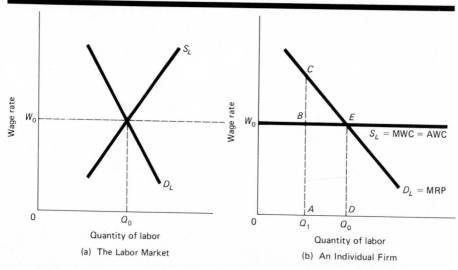

(a) The Labor Market

(b) An Individual Firm

minimize the cost to *society* of producing a given level of output? In the case of perfectly competitive markets the answer is "yes." We know that in perfect competition the marginal resource cost of labor—MWC_L or MRC_L—equals the wage rate. This wage rate represents the opportunity cost, or alternative output sacrificed, when the unit of labor is employed in a particular way and hence can be thought of as society's price of labor (P_L). Therefore the incremental cost of labor paid by the firm (MRC_L) equals the price of labor (P_L) as viewed by society. Similarly, the firm's marginal cost of capital (MRC_K) matches society's opportunity cost of using the unit of capital (P_K) in this way. Thus, when competitive firms employ the *cost-minimizing combination of resources* in achieving a specific level of output (equation 6-1), they also combine labor and capital resources in a way that minimizes the cost of that output from society's perspective. This latter condition is shown in equation (6-1').

$$\frac{MP_L}{P_L} = \frac{MP_K}{P_K}$$ (6-1')

The only difference between equation (6-1) and (6-1') is in the denominators. But in perfect competition, $MRC_L = P_L$ and $MRC_K = P_K$. Hence, in this circumstance, the firms' interests are identical to society's.

2. Profit-maximizing combination of resources. To maximize profits it is not enough simply to minimize costs. While different levels of output can be produced using equation (6-1), there is only a single output that will maximize profits. Let us examine how a profit-maximizing firm which is employing labor and capital will determine not only the optimal *mix* of each input but also their appropriate *levels*.

Recall from Figure 6-4 (b) that an employer will maximize profits by hiring labor at the level where the marginal *revenue* product of the last unit employed equals the marginal resource (wage) cost ($MRP_L = MRC_L$). The same rationale applies to hiring any other resource—say capital. The firm will employ capital in the profit-maximizing amount where $MRP_K = MRC_K$. We can alternatively state these rules as indicated in equation (6-2).

$$\frac{MRP_L}{MRC_L} = \frac{MRP_K}{MRC_K} = 1$$ (6-2)

Two examples will help clarify this equation. First, suppose that $MRP_L = \$20$, $MRC_L = \$10$, $MRP_K = \$6$, and $MRC_K = \$8$. By substituting these values into equation (6-2), we discover that the firm will want to employ more labor ($\$20/\$10 = 2$) and use less capital ($\$6/\$8 = .75$). But as the firm increases labor inputs, diminishing returns reduce the marginal physical product of labor and therefore MRP_L. And as less capital is used, the marginal physical product of capital and MRP_K will rise. Eventually, the profit-maximizing combination of the two resources will emerge; that is, MRP_L ($= \$10$)/$MRC_L$ ($= \$10$) will equal MRP_K ($= \$8$)/$MRC_K$ ($= \$8$), and both ratios will equal 1.

Let us try a second example. This time suppose that MRP_K is $16 rather than $6, but that all other values are at their initial levels. Now the firm will find it advantageous to increase the employment of *both* resources ($20/$10 > 1 and $16/$8 > 1). This points out that profit maximization requires more than simply having the MRPs of two resources *proportionate* to their MRCs ($20/$10 = $16/$8); they must be *equal* to their MRCs!

Thus far, we simply extended the profit-maximization rules discussed previously to include more than one variable resource. Of special interest to us, however, is whether the profit-maximizing position in equation (6-2) produces an efficient allocation of society's resources. Again the answer is "yes." Why is this so? Recall that perfect competition in the product market yields MRPs of labor which are identical to VMPs. The same is true for the MRPs of capital. To summarize: $MRP_L = VMP_L$ and $MRP_K = VMP_K$. We also know that in perfectly competitive *resource* markets, the MRCs of labor and capital equal the respective social prices of these inputs (opportunity costs as viewed by society). Hence, $MRC_L = P_L$ and $MRC_K = P_K$. Conclusion? By hiring resources in the profit-maximizing combination shown in equation (6-2), the competitive firm also combines resources and uses them at levels which maximize the total value of output to society:

$$\frac{VMP_L}{P_L} = \frac{VMP_K}{P_K} = 1 \qquad (6\text{-}2')$$

The VMPs of labor and capital measure the marginal gain in the value of society's total output that accrues from the employment of these resources in a particular use. On the other hand, the prices of L and K reflect the opportunity cost, or the value of the output sacrificed, by society from that employment. Hence equation (6-2') demonstrates allocative efficiency; no further reallocation of labor and capital among alternative uses *adds* more to the value of society's total output than it *subtracts* in the form of sacrificed output.

To summarize: A competitive labor market imparts wage information to market participants which (1) allows them to make profit-maximizing employment decisions and (2) generates an efficient allocation of labor resources. Workers receive wage rates equal to the marginal revenue gained by the employment of the last worker hired ($W = MRP$). This wage rate also equals society's valuation of that output ($W = VMP$). Capital and labor resources are combined in a manner which (1) minimizes costs of each level of output ($MP_L/MRC_L = MP_K/MRC_K$), (2) maximizes profits ($MRP_L/MRC_L = MRP_K/MRC_K = 1$), and (3) creates allocative efficiency ($VMPL/P_L = VMP_K/P_K = 1$).

As with all theoretical models, perfect competition purposefully abstracts from reality; it *greatly* simplifies the complex real world. But even though few labor markets are *perfectly* competitive, most labor markets contain *elements* of competition, and thus understanding this model helps one analyze the conduct of workers and employers *and* predict wage and employment outcomes in real-world labor markets. This model also provides a useful *yardstick* for measuring the costs of labor market distortions created by such things as product market monopoly, lack of competition in the hiring of labor, unionization, occupational licensure, discrimination, minimum wages, and barriers to mobility.

WAGE AND EMPLOYMENT DETERMINATION: MONOPOLY IN THE PRODUCT MARKET

To this point we have assumed that the employers hiring labor in a perfectly competitive labor market also are "price takers" in the product market; that is, they do not possess monopoly power. But recall from Chapter 5, specifically Table 5-3 and Figure 5-3, that if a firm is a monopolist in the sale of its product, it will face a downward-sloping product demand curve. This means that increases in its output will require price reductions, and because the lower prices will apply to all the firm's output, its marginal revenue (MR) will decline even faster than price. Consequently, MRP_L ($= MP \times MR$) will fall for two reasons: (1) MP will decline because of diminishing returns (also true for perfect product market competition), *and* (2) MR will decline as more workers are hired (in perfect competition MR is constant and equals product price P).

The labor market consequences of product market monopoly are shown in Figure 6-5. Here we assume that the labor market is perfectly competitive but that one particular firm hiring this type of labor is a monopolist in the sale of its

FIGURE 6-5 WAGE RATE AND EMPLOYMENT DETERMINATION: MONOPOLY IN THE PRODUCT MARKET
Because a product market monopolist faces a downward-sloping demand curve, increased hiring of labor and the resulting larger output forces the firm to lower its price. And, because it must lower its price on all units, its marginal revenue (MR) declines faster than the price. Hence the firm's MRP curve (MP $\times$ MR) lies below the VMP curve (MP $\times$ P), and this employer hires Q_m rather than Q_c units of labor. This creates an efficiency loss to society of BCD.

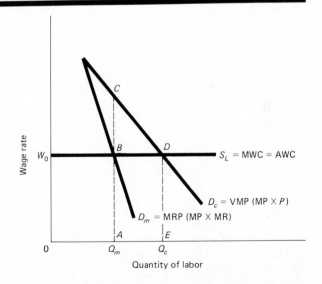

product. Restated, this type of labor is used by thousands of firms, not just this monopolist, and thus there is competition in the labor market.

Figure 6-5 indicates that this monopolist is a "wage taker" and therefore faces the perfectly elastic labor supply curve shown as S_L. This supply curve coincides with the firm's marginal wage cost (MWC) and its average wage cost (AWC), just as it did in our previous model.

Labor demand curve D_c is the MRP curve that would have existed had there been competition rather than monopoly and therefore no decline in marginal revenue as the firm increased its employment and output. This MRP curve is equal to VMP; that is, the firm's gain in revenue from hiring one more worker would equal society's gain in output. On the other hand, demand curve D_m is the *monopolist's* MRP curve. In this case MRP *does not equal* VMP. The value of the extra output of each worker to the monopolist is less than the value to society. The reason again: The extra output reduces the market price, which when applied to all the units of output, reduces the monopolist's marginal revenue even faster. Hence, MRP ($= \text{MR} \times \text{MP}$)—the value to the firm—is less than VMP ($= P \times \text{MP}$)—the value to society.[2]

Several noteworthy outcomes of monopoly in the product market are evident in Figure 6-5. First, the monopolist's labor demand curve D_m obviously is *less elastic* than the competitive curve D_c. Second, the monopolist behaves in the same way as the competitor by determining its profit-maximizing level of employment where MRP = MWC. Notice, however, that this produces a lower level of employment—Q_m in this case—than would occur under competitive product market conditions (Q_c). Third, the wage paid by the monopolist is the same as that paid by competitive firms. In the absence of unions, both are "wage takers."[3] Fourth, labor resources are misallocated. To understand why, recall that in a perfectly competitive labor market the price of labor (wages) reflects the marginal *opportunity cost* to society of using a resource in a particular employment. Also remember that the VMP of labor is a measure of the added *contribution* to output of a worker in a specific employment. Notice in the figure that VMP $> P_L(W_0)$ for the Q_m through Q_c workers. This implies that *too few* labor resources are being allocated to this employment and therefore that *too many* are allocated somewhere else. Assuming costless labor mobility, if Q_mQ_c (or BD) workers were reallocated from alternative activities and toward work in this industry, the *net* value of society's output would rise by area BCD. This is the case because these workers would contribute output valued at $ACDE$ in this employ-

[2]If still confused on this point, review Table 5-3 and Figure 5-3, Chapter 5.

[3]For evidence supporting this theoretical prediction see Leonard W. Weiss, "Concentration and Labor Earnings," *American Economic Review*, March 1966, pp. 96–117.

The less elastic labor demand curve possessed by the monopolist, however, may increase the collective bargaining power of unions and result in a higher wage for workers in monopolized product markets (Chapter 7). For evidence of a positive impact of monopoly power on wages, see James A. Dalton and Edward J. Ford, "Concentration and Labor Earnings in Manufacturing and Utilities," *Industrial and Labor Relations Review*, October 1977, pp. 45–60 and John E. Kwoka, "Monopoly, Plant and Union Effects on Worker Wages," *Industrial and Labor Relations Review*, January 1983, pp. 251–257.

ment—the value of the total product added—while they previously contributed output valued at area *ABDE*—the opportunity cost to society of using them here.[4]

MONOPSONY

Thus far, we have assumed that the labor market is perfectly competitive. Now we wish to analyze a labor market in which either a single firm is the sole hirer of a particular grade of labor or two or more employers collude to fix a below-competitive wage. These market circumstances are called *pure monopsony* and *joint monopsony*, respectively. For purposes of simplicity, our discussion will be confined to pure forms of monopsony, but keep in mind that monopsony power, much the same as monopoly power, extends beyond the *pure* model to include weaker forms of market power.

We will again assume that (1) there are numerous qualified, homogeneous workers who act independently to secure employment in the monopsonized labor market, and (2) information is perfect and mobility is costless. But, unlike perfect competition, we will discover that the monopsonist is a "wage setter"; it can control the wage rate it pays by adjusting the amount of labor it hires, much as a product market monopolist can control its price by adjusting its output.

Table 6-2 contains the elements needed to examine labor supply and demand, wage and employment determination, and allocative outcomes in the monopsony model. Comprehension of the table will greatly clarify the graphic analysis which follows.

Notice in Table 6-2 that columns 1 and 2 simply indicate that the firm must increase the wage rate it pays in order to attract more units of labor toward this

[4]We are assuming that the monopoly firm cannot "price discriminate." If it could charge purchasers the exact price they would be willing to pay rather than go without the product, MRP would coincide with VMP in Figure 6-5. Hence, the firm would now find it profitable to hire Q_c (rather than Q_m) workers and labor resources would be allocated efficiently (Q_c).

TABLE 6-2

Wage and Employment Determination: Monopsony (Hypothetical Data)

(1) Units of Labor	(2) (AWC) Wage	(3) TWC	(4) MWC	(5) (VMP) MRP
1	$1	$1	$1	$7
2	2	4	3	6
3	3	9	5	5
4	4	16	7	4
5	5	25	9	3
6	6	36	11	2

market and away from alternative employment opportunities. We assume that this firm cannot "wage discriminate" when hiring additional workers; it must pay the higher wage *to all workers;* including those who could have been attracted at a lower wage. This fact is reflected in column 3, where total wage cost (TWC) is shown. Notice that the values for TWC are found by *multiplying* the units of labor times the wage rate, rather than by summing the wage column. For example, if the monopsonist hires 5 units of labor it will have to pay $5 for each, for a total of $25. Next, notice the marginal wage cost (MWC) shown in column 4. The *extra* cost of hiring, say, the fifth unit of labor ($9) is more than the wage paid for that unit ($5). The reason? Each of the 4 labor units which could have been attracted at $4 must now also be paid $5. The $1 extra wage paid for each of these workers (= $4 total) plus the $5 paid for the extra worker yields the $9 MWC in column 4. To generalize: The monopsonist's marginal wage cost exceeds the wage rate because it must pay a higher wage to attract more workers, and it must pay this higher wage to all workers.

Finally, note column 5 in Table 6-2. This column shows the marginal revenue product (MRP) of labor, and we know from previous discussion that the MRP schedule is the firm's short-run demand for labor curve. In this case, we avoid unnecessary complexity by assuming that the monopsonist is selling its *product* in a perfectly competitive market, and therefore MRP = VMP. We will soon discover, however, that the monopsonist will disregard this MRP schedule once it selects its profit-maximizing level of employment.

Figure 6-6 shows the monopsony model graphically. The labor supply curve slopes upward because the monopsonist is the only firm hiring this type of labor and hence faces the market labor supply curve. Notice that S_L is also the firm's average wage cost (AWC) curve (total wage cost/quantity of labor). Marginal wage cost (MWC) lies above and rises more rapidly than S_L because the higher wage rate paid to attract an additional worker must also be paid to all workers already employed. As we previously indicated, the marginal revenue curve MRP is the competitive labor demand curve and also measures the value of the marginal product of labor, VMP.

What quantity of labor will this monopsonistic firm hire and what wage will it pay? To maximize profits, the firm will equate MWC with MRP, as shown at point A, and employ Q_1 units of labor. To see this, suppose that the firm employed Q_c units of labor rather than Q_1. The MWC of the Q_c unit is shown by point B on the MWC curve, but the MRP of the extra labor is only C. Hence the firm would lose profits equal to area ABC by its action. To repeat: The monopsonist, like the perfect competitor, finds its profit-maximizing employment level where MRP equals MWC.

What wage will this firm pay? Having decided to hire Q_1 units of labor, the monopsonist's effective labor demand becomes a single point D rather than the entire curve D_L. Notice that this point lies along the market labor supply curve S_L, allowing the firm to *set* the wage at W_1. The market clears at this wage; that is, the quantity of labor demanded by the firm, Q_1, just equals the amount of labor that suppliers are willing to offer. This equilibrium wage corresponds to that in Table 6-2 (circled row of data). Notice from point F on the MRP = VMP curve in Figure 6-6, however, that this monopsonist would prefer to hire Q_2 units of labor *if* it could pay each unit with a W_1 wage. Thus, the monopsonist may *perceive* a shortage of this type of labor. It would like more units of labor at the W_1 wage than it can get, but its self-interest keeps it from *raising* the wage above W_1. This may explain why monopsony markets, such as the one for nurses, are characterized by chronically unfilled job vacancies.[5]

If we transformed this labor market into a perfectly competitive one, the equilibrium wage and quantity of labor would be W_c and Q_c units, respectively (point C). But as previously indicated, it simply is not profitable for this monopsonist to hire the Q_c units of labor and pay W_c to *all* Q_c workers. Instead, it restricts the quantity of labor hired and pays (1) a lower than competitive wage (W_1 compared to W_c) and (2) a wage below *the MRP* of the last unit of labor employed (D as opposed to A).

It is easy to see the basic divergence between the monopsonist's profit-maximizing goal and society's desire to maximize the total value of its output. Indeed, MRP equals MWC at Q_1 units of labor, *but* VMP is greater than the price of labor, W_1 ($= Q_1D$). Remember that the market labor supply curve reflects the price of labor in terms of the value of the output which the labor can produce in

---

[5]See Richard Hurd, "Equilibrium Vacancies in a Labor Market Dominated by Non-Profit Firms: The 'Shortage' of Nurses," *Review of Economics and Statistics,* May 1973, pp. 234–240.

FIGURE 6-6 WAGE RATE AND EMPLOYMENT DETERMINATION: MONOPSONY
The firm's MWC lies above the S_L = AWC curve in a monopsonistic labor market. This monopsonist equates MRP with its MWC at point A and chooses to hire Q_1 units of labor. To attract these workers it need only pay W_1 an hour, as shown by point D. The firm thus pays a lower wage rate (W_1 rather than W_c) and hires fewer units of labor (Q_1 as compared to Q_c) than would firms in a competitive labor market. Society loses area *DAC* because of allocative inefficiency.

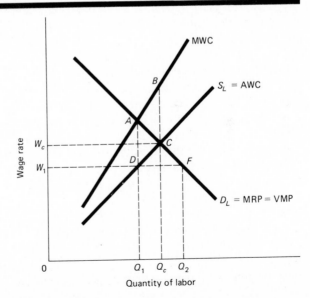

the next best employment opportunity. We observe that along segment AC of the VMP curve, the value of the marginal product of the Q_1Q_c labor units exceeds the opportunity cost to society of using that labor in this specific employment (shown by DC on the supply of labor curve). Hence, if society reallocated this labor from the alternative employments and to this particular market it would gain output of more value than it would forgo. The labor would contribute total output shown by area Q_1ACQ_c in Figure 6-6. Society would forgo area Q_1DCQ_c of national product elsewhere and thus the *net* gain would be area DAC. This latter triangle then identifies the allocative cost to society of the monopsonized labor market.

Several attempts to identify and measure monopsony power in real-world labor markets have been made. For example, economists have discovered monopsony situations in such diverse labor markets as those for professional athletes, nurses, public school teachers, newspaper employees, and some building trades.[6] But, monopsony outcomes are not widespread in the U.S. economy. There are a large number of potential employers for most workers, particularly when these workers are occupationally and geographically mobile (Chapter 14). Also, strong labor unions counteract monopsony power in many labor markets (Chapter 7 and 8).

UNION TECHNIQUES TO RAISE WAGES

We assumed throughout the previous discussion that workers *independently* supplied their labor services and therefore competed for available jobs. But obviously in many labor markets workers have organized into unions to "sell" their labor services *collectively*. These unions can increase the wage rate paid to those members who have jobs by (1) increasing the demand for labor, (2) restricting the supply of labor, and (3) "monopolizing" labor supply to set—or bargain for—an above-equilibrium wage.

Increasing the Demand for Labor. To the limited extent that a union is able to increase the demand for labor, it can raise *both* the market wage rate and the quantity of labor hired. This is shown in Figure 6-7, in which an increase in labor demand from D_0 to D_1 results in a rise in the wage rate from W_0 to W_1 and an increase in employment from Q_0 to Q_1. The more elastic the supply of labor, the less the increase in the wage rate relative to the rise in employment.

But how can a union increase labor demand? It can accomplish this through

[6]For a sampling of studies on monopsony, see C. R. Link and J. H. Landon, "Monopsony and Union Power in the Market for Nurses," *Southern Economic Journal,* April 1975, pp. 644–659; G. W. Scully, "Pay and Performance in Major League Baseball," *American Economic Review,* December 1974, pp. 915–930; R. L. Bunting, *Employer Concentration in Local Labor Markets* (Chapel Hill, N.C.: University of North Carolina Press, 1962); J. H. Landon and R. N. Baird, "Monopsony in the Market for Public School Teachers," *American Economic Review,* December 1971, pp. 966–971.

actions which *alter one or more of the determinants of labor demand* (Table 6-1). More specifically, it can try to (1) increase product demand, (2) enhance labor productivity, (3) influence the price of related resources, and (4) increase the number of "buyers" of its specific labor services. Let us analyze these actions and cite examples of each.

1. Increasing product demand. Unions do not have direct control over the demand for the product which they help produce, but they can influence it through (*a*) product advertising and (*b*) political lobbying.

First, unions can advertise the product which they help make. One example is the activity of the locals of the International Ladies Garment Workers Union (ILGWU) which have joined their employers in financing advertising campaigns to bolster the demand for their products. The ILGWU also participated in a multimedia campaign to persuade consumers to "look for the union label." A second example is the $2 million "Call or Buy Union" campaign begun by the Communications Workers union (CWA) in 1984. The purpose is to convince telephone users to choose the long distance services provided by AT&T Communications and Western Union Corporation, which together provide nearly 100,000 CWA jobs. If effective, that advertising increases the demand for, and price of, union-produced goods and services and thereby boosts the demand for union workers.

Of considerably more significance is political lobbying by unions to increase the demand for union-made goods and services. For example, unions often actively support proposed legislation which would increase *government purchases*

FIGURE 6-7 UNION TECHNIQUES: INCREASING THE DEMAND FOR LABOR
To the extent that unions can increase the demand for union labor (D_0 to D_1) they can realize higher wage rates (W_0 to W_1) and increased employment (Q_0 to Q_1).

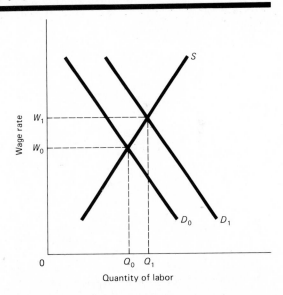

of the products they make. It is not surprising to see construction unions lobbying for new highway projects, urban mass transit proposals, plans to revitalize urban areas, or flood control and related water projects. Nor is it unusual to discover teachers' organizations pushing for legislation to increase government spending on education.

For similar reasons, unions also lobby for legislation that bolsters *private-sector* demand for union-made products. For example, aerospace industry unions strongly supported legislation which granted interest rate subsidies to foreign purchasers of commercial airplanes produced in the United States.

Still another way unions may increase product demand is through their political support for laws which *increase* the price of goods which are close *substitutes* for those made by union members. For instance, the United Auto Workers (UAW) joined the major U. S. auto companies in proposing tariffs and import quotas on imported motor vehicles. These trade barriers increase the price of a substitute good, thereby adding to the demand for (and price of) domestically produced autos. This then raises the demand for UAW members.

Finally, some unions recognize that they can enhance the demand for their own labor by lobbying successfully for legislation which *reduces* the price of goods or services that are *complements* to the services they render. For example, unions representing restaurant employees often resist attempts to increase city excise taxes levied on hotels and motels. The lower lodging prices help attract convention business, which increases the demand for restaurant meals and the derived demand for restaurant workers.

2. Enhancing productivity. We know from previous discussions that the strength of labor demand in a specific occupation depends partly on productivity (MP). Firms control most of the factors which determine worker productivity. But two possible ways in which unions might be able to influence output per worker hour are participation in joint labor-management committees on productivity—sometimes called "quality circles"—and "codetermination," which consists of direct worker participation in the decision processes of the firms. The latter also is sometimes called "worker democracy." The purpose of both approaches is to improve internal communication within the firm and increase productivity through more emphasis on teamwork and profit incentives. To the extent that either approach raises the marginal physical product of labor to a greater degree than it lowers product price, labor demand will rise, and given a fixed labor supply, so too will the wage rate.[7]

3. Influencing the prices of related inputs. If output effects are slight, unions can bolster the demand for their own labor by raising the relative price of

---

[7]For one recent study that finds a positive impact on productivity from cooperative union-management programs, see Michael Schuster, "The Impact of Union-Management Cooperation on Productivity and Employment," *Industrial and Labor Relations Review,* April 1983, pp. 415–430.

substitute resources. Again, unions have no direct control over these alternative prices, but there are examples of political actions by unions which might fit into this category. First, unions—generally being populated by higher paid, skilled workers—may support increases in the minimum wage as a way to raise the relative price of substitutable less-skilled, nonunionized labor. As a *simple* example, suppose that two less-skilled workers can produce the same amount of output in an hour—say one unit—as one skilled *union* laborer, but that the hourly pay for the unskilled workers is $2 while the union scale is $5. Obviously, firms would hire unskilled workers (per unit wage cost of output = $4). Now assume that unions successfully lobby for a $3 per hour *minimum* wage for all workers. Assuming that skilled and unskilled workers are substitute resources and that "output" effects are small, this increase in the price of unskilled workers will increase the demand for skilled, union workers. The reason is that now each unit of the product can be produced at less cost by hiring one union worker at $5 an hour rather than employing two unskilled workers at $6 (= 2 × $3).

The **Davis-Bacon Act** (1931) and its amendments provide another example of how unions might be able to increase the price of a substitute resource—in this case the price of *skilled nonunion* labor. The act, which has strong union support, requires contractors engaged in federally financed projects to pay "prevailing wages." The latter, in effect, are union wages since the formula for determining prevailing wages mandates that the wage rate which occurs with the greatest frequency be observed. Because nonunion firms normally pay their workers less than the union scale, the act has the effect of raising the price of nonunion labor, thereby increasing the demand for union labor and enabling unions to negotiate higher wages without fear of losing federal work to nonunion contractors.

Unions also can increase the demand for their labor through support of government actions which *reduce* the price of a complementary resource. As one example, affected unions occasionally argue against rate increases proposed by electric or natural gas utilities, particularly when the industries in which they work use substantial amounts of these energy sources. Where labor and energy inputs are complementary, these price increases might reduce the demand for labor through an output effect (higher production costs).

4. Increasing the number of employers. Unions can increase the demand for their labor by lobbying for government programs which encourage new employers to establish operations in a local area. For example, unions might favor the issuing of industrial revenue bonds to build industrial parks and property tax breaks to attract domestic or foreign manufacturers.

As a more specific example, the United Auto Workers (UAW) strongly lobbied Congress to pass "domestic content" legislation which would require that substantial portions of automobiles sold in the United States be produced here. This would restrict U. S. auto firms from moving the manufacture of major auto components abroad and would encourage foreign firms to locate operations in the U. S. In both cases, the domestic demand for U. S. unionized auto workers would be strengthened.

Restricting the Supply of Labor. Unions also can boost wages by reducing the *supply* of labor. By referring back to Figure 6-2, the reader will observe that a union can obtain a higher wage rate if it can shift the labor supply curve leftward. However, the union must accept a decrease in employment in achieving this wage hike. Fortunately for the union, the restriction of labor supply is more likely to occur in a *dynamic* context wherein the effect is merely to restrict *the growth of* job opportunities.

In Figure 6-8 we depict a *dynamic* labor market wherein increases in labor demand are occurring—say because of increases in product demand and productivity—as well as expansions of labor supply. The latter, for example, might be caused by increases in population and the number of persons qualified to supply this type of labor. In the absence of the union, the increases in demand (D_0 to D_1) and supply (S_0 to the broken line S_1) would raise the wage rate and level of employment from W_0 to W_1 and Q_0 to Q_1, respectively (point A to C).

Now let us introduce the union and suppose that it takes actions which keep labor supply from expanding to S_1. The result? The market wage will rise to W_u, not W_1, and the quantity of labor hired will be Q_u, as opposed to Q_1. It is clear from the figure that this union has increased the wage rate by restricting the growth of labor supply. It also demonstrates that in this case the action slows the growth rate of employment—$(Q_u - Q_0)/Q_0$ compared to $(Q_1 - Q_0)/Q_0$. The greater the elasticity of labor demand, of course, the greater the negative employment impact of a given supply restriction. Finally, note that the union action

FIGURE 6-8 UNION TECHNIQUES: RESTRICTING THE SUPPLY OF LABOR

In a dynamic labor market characterized by normal expansions of labor demand and supply, such as D_0 to D_1 and S_0 to S_1, a union or professional organization may be able to increase wage rates (W_1 to W_u) through actions which restrict the increase in labor supply that normally would occur (S_0 rather than S_1). However, these actions also slow the rate of growth of union employment [$(Q_u - Q_0)/Q_0$ compared to $(Q_1 - Q_0)/Q_0$].

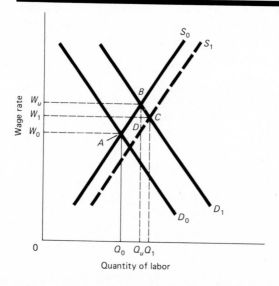

Quantity of labor

causes an efficiency loss of triangle DBC. If the Q_uQ_1 workers had been employed here they would contribute more to the value of society's output (segment BC of D_1) than they would contribute in their best alternative employment (segment DC of S_1).

Unions can restrict labor supply by taking actions or supporting government policies *which alter one or more of the determinants of labor supply* (Table 6-1). One of these factors in particular—reducing the number of qualified suppliers—is most easily influenced by unions. Two others—influencing nonwage income and boosting other wage rates—are also of some significance. Let us examine actions which fit into these three categories.

1. Reducing the number of qualified suppliers of labor. One way that unions in general can limit the supply of qualified workers in a specific labor market is to restrict the overall "stock" of qualified workers in the nation. This partially explains why organized labor has strongly supported (*a*) limited immigration, (*b*) child labor laws, (*c*) compulsory retirement, and (*d*) shorter workweeks.

Unions also can restrict labor supply for a particular grade of labor by limiting entry into the occupation itself. For example, craft unions comprised of workers of a specific skill, such as plumbers, carpenters, or bricklayers, and some professional groups such as the American Medical Association allegedly have controlled the access to training and established extraordinarily long apprenticeship programs to limit labor supply. Hence, this type of unionism is sometimes refered to as *exclusive unionism*; the supply restriction derives from actions which "exclude" potential workers from participating in the trade or profession.

Of perhaps even greater importance, unions and professional groups have been able to limit entry to certain occupations by encouraging government entities to enact laws which force practitioners of a trade to meet certain requirements. These requirements may specify the level of educational attainment or amount of work experience needed and may also include the passing of an examination to obtain a license. State licensing boards have wide discretion in establishing the tests and standards needed to qualify for a license. In fact, there is evidence that suggests that some boards adjust the "pass rate" as a way to control the rate of entry into the licensed occupation.[8] Furthermore, the licensing requirements may include a minimum residency stipulation which tends to inhibit the flow of qualified workers between states. Hence, *occupational licensure* restricts labor supply and increases the wage rate, as shown in Figure 6-8.

In the United States there are now 1500 separate state licensing boards, 600 licensed occupations, and another 400 occupations subject to some other form of state regulations.[9] Table 6-3 provides a partial list of occupations requiring licenses in one state.

---

[8]Alex Maurizi, "Occupational Licensing and the Public Interest," *Journal of Political Economy*, March/April 1974, pp. 399–413.

[9]*Employment and Training Report of the President*, 1982 (Washington: U.S. Government Printing Office, 1983), p. 94.

TABLE 6-3

Selected Licensed Occupations: State of Washington

Accountants	Dentists	Osteopaths
Agricultural brokers	Dispensing opticians	Oyster farmers
Aircraft pilots	Egg dealers	Pesticide applicators
Ambulance drivers	Embalmers	Pharmacists
Architects	Engineers	Physical therapists
Auditors	Fish dealers	Physician assistants
Barbers	Funeral directors	Physicians and surgeons
Beauticians	Harbor pilots	Proprietary school agents
Blasters	Insurance adjusters	Psychologists
Boathouse operators	Insurance agents	Real estate brokers
Boiler workers	Landscape architects	Real estate salesmen
Boxers	Law clerks	Sanitarians
Boxing managers	Lawyers	Security advisors
Chiropodists	Librarians	Security brokers
Chiropractors	Livestock dealers	Surveyors
Commercial fishermen	Marine pilots (inland)	Teachers
Commercial guides	Milk vendors	Veterinarians
Dairy technicians	Naturopaths	Wrestlers
Debt adjustors	Nurses	Weighers and graders
Dental hygienists	Optometrists	Well diggers

Source: Employment Security Department, State of Washington

A final means by which unions may limit labor supply to an occupation is through sexual or racial discrimination. For instance, some predominantly male craft unions and professional organizations have explicitly or implicitly argued that their particular type of work is "too physical" or "too stressful" to be performed by females, and then have taken such actions as instituting overly rigorous physical requirements to make it difficult for women to enter the trade or occupation. Some "craft" unions also have engaged in racial segregation. Perhaps this results from the direct economic self-interest evident in Figure 6-8.[10]

2. Influencing nonwage income. How might unions and professional organizations improve their wages by affecting the "nonwage income" determinant of labor supply? Examples are limited but unions may be able to accomplish this through legislation which provides income to unemployed workers, partially disabled workers, and older citizens. Stated differently, among the several reasons why labor unions generally support *increased* unemployment compensation, workers compensation, and social security retirement benefits is that these sources of nonwage income reduce labor force participation (Chapter 2) and therefore raise the before-tax wages to those employed. This is *not* to suggest

---

[10]For evidence of discrimination by unions, see Orley Ashenfelter, "Discrimination and Trade Unions," in Orley Ashenfelter and Albert Rees (eds.), *Discrimination in Labor Markets* (Princeton, N.J.: Princeton University Press, 1973). The economic aspects of labor market discrimination will be examined in detail in Chapter 11.

that this is a *primary* reason for such support; after all, union members must join others in paying for government transfers through higher taxes (lower after-tax wages), but it *is* to imply that such support is *consistent* with Figure 6-8.

3. Boosting alternative wages. By supporting actions which raise the wage rate paid to other similarly skilled workers—say in submarket B—unions may be able to decrease labor supply in their own submarket A. This will increase the wage rate in A, as indicated in Figure 6-8. Let us offer two examples. First, unions in the *private* sector may lend their considerable political clout to efforts to raise wages for their counterparts in the *public* sector. Second, by honoring picket lines and engaging in boycotts and other actions, unionized workers may aid closely related *private* sector employees in their attempts to raise wages. In either situation, any increases in the wage rate paid for the alternative jobs can be expected to attract workers away from submarket A to closely related submarket B. The consequence? Labor supply will decline in A causing the wage there to rise also. Thus there may be more to "union solidarity" than simply "class consciousness."[11]

"Monopolizing" Labor Supply. In addition to restricting labor supply to an occupation—that is, shifting the market labor supply curve leftward—unions try to gain full control over the existing labor pool in an industry or occupation. By "monopolizing" labor supply, or achieving "full occupancy" of the labor market by including all available workers, these *industrial* or *inclusive* unions can threaten to withhold the entire labor supply unless employers agree to the union's terms. Thus, unions can engage in such "exclusive" union tactics as occupational licensure and long apprenticeships while simultaneously employing such "inclusive" union techniques as negotiating for union shops (all workers must join the union within 30 days after being hired) and hiring through "union halls." The United Auto Workers (UAW) and the United Steelworkers of America (USA) are two unions particularly noted for successfully "monopolizing" the "sale" of particular labor services in the United States.[12]

The impact of "full control" over labor supply by a union is shown graphically in Figure 6-9. Suppose that employers in this labor market act independently and that in the absence of the union the competitive equilibrium wage rate and quantity of labor are W_c and Q_c. Now suppose that a union forms, gains a union shop arrangement, and demands and receives the higher, above-equilibrium wage rate W_u. This in effect makes the labor supply curve perfectly elastic

---

[11]The possibility of an opposite impact also exists here. If union A helps workers in submarket B negotiate a higher wage, employers in B *may* reduce employment. Some of these displaced workers may seek work in labor submarket A, increasing labor supply and depressing wage rates there.

[12]It is important to note that we are using the term *monopolization* conceptually here. Legally, labor unions are not monopolists and not subject to the antitrust laws when engaged in their normal activities. Congress and the courts have declared that "labor is not an article of commerce" and therefore not subject to antitrust.

over the W_uD range. If employers hire any number of workers within this range, they must pay the union scale W_u or the union will withdraw *all* labor via a strike. If the employers desire more than D workers, however, say because of a major expansion of labor demand during the life of the union contract, they will need to pay wages above the union's scale in order to attract workers away from alternative jobs which pay more than W_u.

Notice the *postunion* employment outcome in Figure 6-9. Employers respond to the union-imposed wage rate W_u by discharging BC workers (Q_cQ_u). Furthermore, the higher wage attracts DC additional job seekers to the occupation. Thus, excess labor supply BD exists at the union-imposed wage. The greater the elasticity of demand, the wider the range BC. The more elastic the preunion supply of labor, the greater the gap DC.

This model enables us to understand several observed labor market phenomena and union actions. First, it explains why some unionized labor markets are characterized by chronic "waiting lists" for jobs. Second, and closely related, it clarifies why labor organizations place great emphasis on gaining *union security* provisions in labor contracts. It is important for unions to ensure that the BD workers in Figure 6-9 are either union members or will become union members if turnover and attrition enable them to gain employment in the market. Otherwise, the competition for jobs by these people could undermine the union's control over labor supply and drive the wage down to equilibrium wage W_c. For

FIGURE 6-9 UNION TECHNIQUES: "MONOPOLIZING" THE SUPPLY OF LABOR
By organizing all available workers and securing closed, union, or agency shops, inclusive unions may impose a wage rate, such as W_u, which is above the competitive wage rate W_c. The effect is to make the labor supply curve perfectly elastic between W_u and point D (MWC = AWC = S_L), to reduce employment from Q_c to Q_u, and to create an efficiency loss of area EBA. The more elastic the labor demand, the greater the employment and allocative impact.

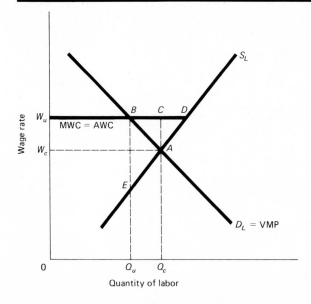

example, the firm might "break" a strike by replacing strikers with nonunion workers. **Closed shops** (in which union membership is required as a condition of employment) are illegal in most industries, but **union shops** (defined previously) and **agency shops** (where workers need not join the union but must pay union dues) are second- and third-best alternatives which help preserve union control over the entire labor supply. Union and agency shops are *illegal* in 21 states which have "right-to-work" laws. Not surprisingly, unions strongly support repeal of Section 14b of the National Labor Relations Act. That section permits states to outlaw union and agency shops. Unions intuitively understand what empirical evidence confirms: Compulsory union membership clauses enable unions to negotiate significantly greater wage increases.[13]

Third, the distance *BC* in Figure 6-9 sheds light on why unions are interested in securing contract provisions which reduce the *elasticity* of labor demand. The lower this elasticity, the less will be the number of displaced workers from any given wage increase. Recall from Chapter 5 that one major determinant of the elasticity of labor demand is the substitutability of other inputs. What contract provisions might reduce the substitution of capital for union labor? What provisions might limit the substitution of nonunion labor for union workers? Examples of the first include provisions limiting new technology, requiring redundant labor ("featherbedding"), and providing for supplementary unemployment benefits (SUBs). By dictating the pace of the introduction of new technology, and engaging in featherbedding, the union can temporarily reduce the elasticity of labor demand—that is, slow the substitution of capital for labor in response to wage increases. SUBs and severance pay provisions perform a similar function; if high enough, they raise the "effective price" of any capital which is used to *replace* union labor. Examples of contract provisions which reduce the substitutability of nonunion and union labor include clauses which prevent subcontracting and plant relocation. Both are sometimes used to "economize" on the use of union labor following union-imposed wage increases. But by preventing such actions, the union at least temporarily reduces the elasticity of labor demand.

The employment impact of the union-imposed above-equilibrium wage in Figure 6-9 will be greater as time transpires. For example, the firm may resist continuing the contract provisions which keep the short-run demand curve inelastic. Alternatively, foreign or nonunion competition may arise in response to the high product prices in unionized industries. On the other hand, in a growing economy the demand curves for most types of labor gradually shift rightward over time. Instead of an *absolute decline* in the number of jobs in the unionized labor market, the outcome may simply be a slower *rate of growth* of job opportunities. In this respect, no specific *layoff* of existing union workers is observed. This may explain why some union leaders have in the past erroneously concluded that demand for labor curves are highly inelastic.

A final observation from Figure 6-9 is that, given homogeneous workers, a

---

[13]Sandra Christensen and Dennis Maki, "The Wage Effect of Compulsory Union Membership," *Industrial and Labor Relations Review,* January 1983, pp. 230–238. Right-to-work laws are discussed in more detail in the Time and One-Half section of Chapter 10.

union-imposed above-equilibrium wage creates a misallocation of labor resources. Notice that the value of the marginal product B exceeds the marginal opportunity cost of labor E at wage W_u and quantity Q_u. If Q_cQ_u workers were transferred from competitive labor markets to this one, society would experience a net gain in the value of its output equal to area EBA.[14]

BILATERAL MONOPOLY

In the previous section we assumed that a union had gained complete control over the supply of labor in an otherwise competitive labor market. But what if a monopsonist and a strong industrial union coexist in a labor market? This situation is common in many U. S. labor markets. For example, in the eastern coal industry the United Mine Workers (UMW) union confronts a "multiemployer" bargaining unit in negotiating a standard labor contract. In the labor market for automobile workers, the UAW bargains individually with the "Big Three" U.S. auto manufacturers. Similarly, the Communication Workers union negotiates with regional telephone service monopsonists, and the players' associations of various professional sports bargain against unified team owners. Will the wage be below or above the competitive equilibrium wage in these **bilateral monopoly** situations? The answer is that the wage outcome is *indeterminate*; the negotiated wage rate may either be above, below, or just equal to the competitive wage rate. Let us explore why.

In Figure 6-10 we combine the monopsony model (Figure 6-6) and union "monopoly" model (Figure 6-9) to illustrate bilateral monopoly. For simplicity, we once again assume that the product is sold in a perfectly competitive market (MRP = VMP). If monopsony alone existed in this market, the wage rate would be W_m and the level of employment would be Q_1. On the other hand, if the union could set any wage rate it desired, it *might* select W_u.[15] But neither the employer nor the union can impose its desired wage on the other in this situation. If the monopsonist offers W_m, the union will threaten to withhold the supply of labor via a strike. If the union demands W_u, the monopsonist *may* resist, believing that it is too costly to pay the wage rate relative to the expected costs associated with either allowing the strike or locking out workers. Thus we are left with a *range* of possible wage outcomes—W_m to W_u—and the mutual interest of the two parties will normally result in a negotiated wage rate acceptable to each. The final wage will depend on the relative bargaining strength and prowess of each party (Chapter 7).

Careful scrutiny of the bilateral monopoly situation shown in Figure 6-10 reveals several interesting points. First, it is entirely possible that the negotiated wage will be at or near the wage rate W_c which would have occurred if *neither* monopsony nor union power existed in the market! In that case, the quantity of

---

[14]A more complete analysis of the efficiency losses created by unions is provided in Chapter 8.

[15]We will analyze the criteria that a union might use to determine this wage rate in Chapter 7.

labor hired would be Q_c (point B). The perfectly elastic segment of S_L would now be W_cB, which means that the coincident MWC intersects MRP at the Q_c level of employment. And because perfect competition is assumed to exist in the product market, labor resources would be efficiently allocated.

Second, the union may be able simultaneously to increase (1) the wage rate, (2) the level of employment, and (3) allocative efficiency. Notice that any increase in the wage above W_m but below W_u causes the firm to increase its employment beyond Q_1. The reason? Once the firm agrees to one of these wage rates, its incentive to restrict employment disappears; at the negotiated wage, its marginal wage cost (MWC) and average wage cost (AWC) become perfectly horizontal overlaying lines. Therefore, the firm equates the negotiated wage (MWC) with the marginal revenue product (MRP) and hires more workers than it would if its MWC exceeded its AWC. For example, if the negotiated wage rate is W_c, and this happens to be $6 an hour, then from the firm's perspective, the MWC and AWC are also $6 per hour. The firm will operate where MRP and this wage rate are equal and hire B rather than A units of labor. Notice also that area ACB portrays the efficiency loss associated with either wage rate W_m *or* W_u. If the union negotiates a wage above W_m *but below* W_u, this area will diminish. In the case of W_c it disappears! Hence the presence of unions in monopsonized labor markets *may* enhance allocative efficiency.

A final observation from Figure 6-10 is that, even though the low monop-

FIGURE 6-10 BILATERAL MONOPOLY IN THE LABOR MARKET

When a monopsonistic employer must "buy" labor services from a "monopolistic" union, the wage rate and employment outcomes are indeterminate. However, if the union negotiates a wage above W_m but below W_u, employment will increase and allocative efficiency will improve relative to the situation under monopsony alone (W_m, Q_1).

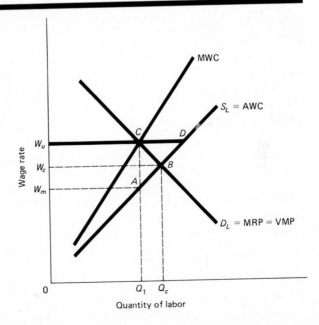

sony wage W_m and the high union wage W_u result in the same employment level, Q_1, at wages W_m through W_c, the labor market clears (although there may be a "perceived" shortage). But for wages above W_c, unemployment occurs. For example, at wage W_u the firm hires only C units of labor, but D units are supplied. Some of the CD suppliers may be willing to *wait* for job turnover to enable them to gain employment in this market. Since they are in the labor force and seeking work, they are officially unemployed.

EXTENDING THE ANALYSIS

The labor market models presented in this chapter are complicated in one sense: They are not easy to understand without careful study. But in a more important way, the models are quite simple. They purposely reduce complex labor market interactions and outcomes to their basic rudiments and in the process focus attention on fundamental relationships and major principles of labor economics. But labor markets in the real world are far richer in complexity and diversity than the basic models might imply. In the chapters which follow we embellish, modify, and broaden the analysis of labor market activity and wage and employment determination. In fact, each remaining chapter builds on the simple foundation laid in this and previous chapters.

Understanding the models in this chapter and their underlying components constitutes a *necessary* condition for being able to analyze the economics of real-world labor markets. The *sufficient* condition is comprehending the numerous extentions, nuances, and modifications which are still to follow.

SUMMARY

1. In a competitive labor market, the demand for labor is a "price adjusted" summation of labor demand by independently acting individual employers, and the supply of labor is a summation of the responses of individual workers to various wage rates. Market supply and demand determine an equilibrium wage rate and level of employment.
2. The vertical height of the market labor supply curve measures the opportunity cost to society of employing the last worker in this use (P_L). The vertical height of the labor demand curve indicates the extra revenue the employer gains by hiring that unit of labor (MRP) and, given perfectly competitive product markets, the value of that output to society (VMP).
3. The locations of the supply and demand curves in the labor market depend upon the determinants of each (Table 6-1). When one of these determinants changes, the affected curve either shifts rightward or leftward, altering the equilibrium wage and employment levels.
4. The individual firm operating in a perfectly competitive labor market is a "wage taker." This implies that its MWC equals the wage rate W; that is, the supply of labor is perfectly elastic. This firm maximizes its profits by hiring the quantity of labor at which MRP = MWC, or MRP = W.

5. Perfectly competitive product and resource markets create allocative efficiency. Workers receive wage rates equal to the marginal revenue gained by the employment of the last worker hired (W = MRP). This wage rate also equals society's valuation of that output (W = VMP). Capital and labor resources are thus combined in a manner which (a) minimizes costs of each level of output (MP_L/MRC_L = MP_K/MRC_K), and (b) maximizes profits (MRP_L/MRC_L = MRP_K/MRC_K = 1).

6. Monopoly in the product market causes marginal revenue to fall faster than product price as more workers are hired and output is expanded. Because product price P exceeds marginal revenue MR, it follows that MRP (= MP × MR) is less than VMP (= MP × P). The result is less employment and an underallocation of labor resources relative to the case of perfect competition in the product market.

7. Under monopsony, MWC > S_L (or P_L) because the employer must bid up wages to attract a greater quantity of labor and it must pay the higher wage to *all* workers. Consequently, it will employ fewer workers than under competitive conditions and pay a wage rate below the MRP of labor. This underallocation of labor resources (VMP > P_L) reduces the total value of output in the economy.

8. Unions can increase the wage rate paid to those members who are employed by (a) increasing the demand for labor, (b) restricting the supply of labor, and (c) "monopolizing" labor supply. To increase the demand for labor, unions try to influence one or more of the determinants of labor demand. To restrict labor supply, unions attempt to affect the number of qualified suppliers, nonwage income, and alternative wages. To "monopolize" labor supply, unions organize "inclusively" and bargain for closed and union shops.

9. Bilateral monopoly is a labor market situation in which a union which has a "monopolized" labor supply faces a monopsonistic employer or coalition of employers. Although the wage rate and employment outcomes are indeterminant, the possibility arises that through collective bargaining a union may be able to enhance simultaneously (a) its wage rate, (b) the level of employment, and (c) allocative efficiency.

QUESTIONS AND STUDY SUGGESTIONS

1. Key terms and concepts to remember: perfectly competitive labor market; determinants of labor supply and demand; marginal revenue product; average wage cost; marginal wage cost; MRP = MWC rule; allocative efficiency; cost-minimizing combination of resources; profit-maximizing combination of resources; monopsony; Davis-Bacon Act; occupational licensure; closed, union, and agency shops; bilateral monopoly.

2. List the distinct characteristics of a perfectly competitive labor market and compare them to the characteristics of monopsony.

3. Explain why most *market* labor supply curves slope upward and to the right, even though individual labor supply curves are presumed to be backward-bending. How does the height of a *market* labor supply curve relate to the concept of opportunity costs?

4. What effect will each one of the following have on the market labor demand for a specific type of labor?
   a. An increase in product demand which increases product price
   b. A decline in the productivity of this type of labor
   c. An increase in the price of a substitute resource

  d. A decline in the price of a complementary resource
  e. The demise of several firms which hire this labor
  f. A decline in the market wage rate for this labor
  g. A series of mergers which transforms the product market into a monopoly
5. Predict the impact of each of the following on the equilibrium wage rate and level of employment in labor market A:
  a. An increase in the market wage rate in labor market B, which employs the same kind of labor as A
  b. An increase in labor demand and supply in labor market A
  c. The transformation of labor market A from a competitive to a monopsony market
6. The American Medical Association (AMA) has declared that there will be a large surplus (excess supply) of physicians in the United States in the 1990s. Use labor market supply and demand graphics to depict this supposed outcome. Speculate as to the "solutions" that the AMA proposes for this situation.
7. Suppose the productivity of capital (K) and labor (L) are as shown below. Also assume that the two resources are neither complements nor substitutes and that firms employ both resources under perfectly competitive conditions at a price of $6 for K and $4 for L. Finally, suppose that the output of these resources sells in a perfectly competitive product market for $2 per unit.

Units of K	MP of K	MRP of K	Units of L	MP of L	MRP of L
1	24		1	22	
2	21		2	18	
3	18		3	16	
4	15		4	14	
5	9		5	12	
6	6		6	8	
7	3		7	2	
8	1		8	1	

  a. Fill in the MRP data for K and L. What is the profit-maximizing combination of K and L? What is the level of *total* physical output at this production level?
  b. Explain why this profit-maximizing combination of K and L is also the least-cost way to produce the profit-maximizing level of total physical output.
  c. Suppose that the employed combination of K and L were 3 units of K and 5 units of L. Explain why this would produce an inefficient allocation of resources.
8. Complete the following table for a single firm operating in labor market A and product market AA.

Units of Labor	Wage Rate (W)	Total Wage Cost	MWC	MRP	VMP
1	$10			$16	$16
2	10			14	15
3	10			12	14
4	10			10	12
5	10			8	10
6	10			6	8

    a. What, if anything, can one conclude about the degree of competition in labor market A and product market AA?

    b. What is the profit-maximizing level of employment? Explain.

    c. Does this profit-maximizing level of employment yield allocative efficiency? Explain.

9. Under what elasticity of labor demand conditions could a union restrict the supply of labor—that is, shift the supply inward—and thereby increase the collective wage income (wage bill) of those workers still employed?

10. Use graphic analysis to explain how a union in a monopsonized labor market might simultaneously enhance (*a*) its wage rate, (*b*) employment, and (*c*) allocative efficiency.

11. Explain why there may be an "appearance" of chronic shortages in some monopsonized labor markets, while in some bilateral monopoly markets chronic surpluses exist.

12. Explain how each one of the following contract provisions might affect the *elasticity* of labor demand during the period of the labor contract.

    a. Layoff and severance pay

    b. Prevention of subcontracting

    c. The limiting of plant shutdown or relocation

SELECTED REFERENCES

Bellante, Don, and Mark Jackson: *Labor Economics: Choice in Labor Markets,* 2d ed. (New York: McGraw-Hill Book Company, 1983), chap. 10.

Bunting, Robert L.: *Employer Concentration in Local Labor Markets* (Chapel Hill, N.C.: University of North Carolina Press, 1962).

Fleisher, Belton M., and Thomas J. Kniesner: *Labor Economics: Theory, Evidence, and Policy,* 3d ed. (Englewood Cliffs, N.J.: Prentice-Hall, Inc., 1984), chaps. 5 and 6.

Greene, Karen, and Robert Gay: *Directory of State Regulated Occupations* (Great Falls, Va.: Akipan Associates, Inc., 1982).

Rima, Ingrid H.: *Labor Markets, Wages, and Employment* (New York: W. W. Norton and Company, 1981), chaps. 5 and 6.

Rottenberg, Simon (ed.): *Occupational Licensure and Regulation* (Washington, D.C.: American Enterprise Institute for Public Policy Research, 1980).

Yett, D. E.: *An Economic Analysis of the Nurse Shortage* (Lexington, Mass.: Lexington Books, 1975).

TIME AND ONE-HALF

PAY AND PERFORMANCE IN PROFESSIONAL BASEBALL

Professional baseball has provided an interesting "laboratory" in which the predictions of orthodox wage theory have been empirically tested.

Until 1976 professional baseball players were bound to a single team through the so-called "reserve clause" which prevented players from selling their talents on the open (competitive) market. Stated differently, the reserve clause conferred monopsony power upon the team which originally drafted a player. As we have seen in the present chapter, labor market theory would lead us to predict that this monopsony power would permit teams to pay wages less than a player's marginal revenue product (MRP). However, since 1976 major league players have been able to become "free agents" at the end of their sixth season of play and at that time can sell their services to any team. Orthodox theory suggests that free agents should be able to increase their salaries and bring them more closely into accord with their MRPs. Research tends to confirm both of the indicated predictions.

Scully* found that before baseball players could become free agents their salaries were substantially below their MRPs. Scully estimated a player's MRP as follows. First, he determined the relationship between a team's winning percentage and its revenue. Then he estimated the relationship between various possible measures of player productivity

*Gerald W. Scully, "Pay and Performance in Major League Baseball," *American Economic Review,* December 1974, pp. 915–930.

TABLE 1

Marginal Revenue Products and Salaries of Professional Baseball Pitchers, 1968–1969

(1) Performance*	(2) Marginal Revenue Product	(3) Salary
1.60	$ 57,600	$31,100
1.80	80,900	34,200
2.00	104,100	37,200
2.20	127,400	40,200
2.40	150,600	43,100
2.60	173,900	46,000
2.80	197,100	48,800
3.00	220,300	51,600
3.20	243,600	54,400
3.40	266,800	57,100
3.60	290,100	59,800

*Strikeout-to-walk ratio.

Source: Scully, op. cit., p. 923.

and a team's winning percentage. He found the ratio of strikeouts to walks for pitchers and the slugging averages for hitters (all nonpitchers) to be the best indicators of a player's contribution to the winning percentage. These two estimates were combined to calculate the contribution of a player to a team's total revenue.

Scully found that prior to free agency the estimated MRPs of both pitchers and hitters were substantially greater than player salaries. Table 1 shows the relevant data for pitchers. Column 1 indicates pitcher performance as measured by lifetime strikeout-to-walk ratio, a higher ratio being associated with a better pitcher. Column 2 indicates estimated MRP after player training costs are taken into account, and Column 3 shows actual average salary for pitchers in each quality class. As orthodox labor market theory predicts, the monopsony power provided by the reserve clause allowed the payment of salaries far less than MRPs. Even the lowest-quality pitchers (those with a 1.60 strikeout-to-walk ratio) received on the average salaries amounting to only about 54 percent of their MRPs. Observe, too, that the gap between MRP and average salary widens as player quality improves. "Star" players were exploited more than other players. The best pitchers received salaries which were only about 21 percent of their MRPs, according to Scully. The same general results applied to hitters. For example, the least productive hitters on the average received a salary equal to about 37 percent of their MRPs.

Sommers and Quinton† have recently assessed the economic fortunes of fourteen players who constituted the "first family" of free agents. In accordance with the predictions of labor market theory, their research indicates that the competitive bidding of free agency has brought the salaries of free agents more closely into accord with their estimated MRPs. The data for the five free-agent pitchers are shown in Table 2 where we find a surprisingly close correspondence between estimated MRPs and salaries. Although MRP and salary differences are larger for hitters, Sommers and Quinton conclude that the overturn of the monopsonistic reserve clause "has forced owners into a situation where there is a greater tendency to pay players in relation to their contribution to team revenues."

†Paul M. Sommers and Noel Quinton, "Pay and Performance in Major League Baseball: The Case of the First Family of Free Agents," *Journal of Human Resources,* Summer 1982, pp. 426–435.

TABLE 2

Estimated Marginal Revenue Products and Player Costs, 1977

(1) Pitcher	(2) Marginal Revenue Product	(3) Annual Contract Cost*
Garland	$282,091	$230,000
Gullett	340,846	349,333
Fingers	303,511	332,000
Campbell	205,639	210,000
Alexander	166,203	166,667

*Includes annual salary, bonuses, the value of insurance policies and deferred payments, etc.

Source: Sommers and Quinton, op. cit., p. 432.

LABOR UNIONS AND COLLECTIVE BARGAINING

n Chapter 6 we discussed ways in which workers can collectively influence wage rates through unionization. Our main objective in this and the following chapter is to deepen our understanding of unionism and collective bargaining.

In the present chapter we initially address such questions as: How large is the labor movement in the United States? What kinds of workers are most likely to be union members? In what industries are unions concentrated? Has the labor movement grown or declined in recent decades? Second, we ask what, if anything, unions attempt to maximize. What are the goals of unions? Third, we discuss how collective bargaining differs from ordinary market transactions, that is, how the "buying" and "selling" of labor *services* differ from the buying and selling of, say, a carton of milk at a supermarket. Finally, we inquire how wage rate indeterminacy (Figure 6-10) gets resolved through collective bargaining in situations where there is economic power on both sides of the labor market. More specifically, in the final section of this chapter we present and discuss a well-known bargaining model.

In Chapter 8 our concern turns to the economic impacts of collective bargaining. There we attempt to determine whether unions and bargaining are effective means for raising wages; whether unions have a positive or negative impact upon efficiency and productivity; and whether unions increase or diminish inequality in the distribution of earnings.

LABOR UNIONISM: FACTS AND FIGURES

Before analyzing the collective bargaining process and its economic implications, it is important that we gain a basic understanding of the scope and character of unionization in the United States. Specifically, let us discuss (1) the distribution of unionized labor by industry, occupation, sex, race, age, and location; (2) the structure of organized labor, and (3) the decline in the relative size of the unionized sector which has occurred since the mid-1950s.

Who Belongs to Unions? In 1984 approximately 17 million of the 113 million in the civilian labor force belonged to unions. In other words, about 15 percent of American workers were union members. But the likelihood that any given worker will be a union member depends upon the occupation and industry with which the worker is associated, personal characteristics (sex, race, and age), and geographic location.

1. Industry and occupation. Table 7-1 shows the percentage of wage and salary workers who are unionized by industry and occupational classification. It is clear that union membership is heavily concentrated in goods-producing industries (mining, construction, and manufacturing) and is relatively low in most service-oriented industries (wholesale and retail trade; finance, insurance, and real estate; and services). The exceptions are the low level of unionization in goods-producing agriculture and the high level in the service-providing transportation, communication, and public utilities industries. Also notable is the high level of unionization in public administration, which reflects the facts that almost three-fourths of all postal workers are organized and that there has been vigorous growth of public sector unionism at the state and local levels during the past few decades.

It is also evident from Table 7-1 that blue-collar workers are much more heavily unionized than are white-collar workers. The reasons for this include the following. First, some white-collar workers are managers, and under existing labor law employers are not obligated to bargain with supervisory employees. Second, on the average white-collar workers enjoy higher wages and better working conditions than do blue-collar workers; hence, the former may simply feel they have less need for unions.

With some important exceptions, the industrial-occupational pattern of unionization was established by the late 1940s. Industries which were heavily

---

TABLE 7-1

Union Membership by Industry and Occupation, 1984

Industry	Percent Union*	Occupation	Percent Union*
Goods-producing:		White collar:	
Agriculture	3	Professional and technical	23
Mining	18	Managers and administrators	6
Construction	18	Clerical workers	14
Manufacturing	26	Sales workers	6
Services-producing:		Blue collar:	
Transportation, communication,		Craft workers	30
and public utilities	39	Operatives	33
Wholesale and retail trade	8	Transportation	35
Finance, insurance, and		Nonfarm laborers	27
real estate	3		
Services	7		
Public administration	36		

*Percent of employed wage and salary workers who belong to unions.

Source: Department of Labor, Employment and Earnings, January 1985, p. 209.

unionized by that time remain so now. Today most workers do *not* become union members by organizing their employers, but rather join a union because they take a job with an already unionized employer. "A blue-collar worker who finds himself in the automobile industry will almost certainly work under a union contract. A worker who takes a job in banking almost certainly will not."[1]

2. Personal characteristics: sex, race, and age. Table 7-2 indicates that one's personal characteristics are associated with the likelihood of union membership. We observe that men are much more likely to be union members than are women. This difference is *not* attributable to any fundamental attitudinal differences based on gender, but rather is explained largely by the fact that women are disproportionately represented in industries and occupations which are less unionized. For example, many women are employed in retail sales, food service, and office work where the levels of unionization are very low. The fact that a larger proportion of blacks than whites belong to unions is also partly a reflection of the industrial distribution of workers. Specifically, a disproportionately larger number of blacks have blue-collar jobs. Another explanatory factor is that unionization results in larger relative wage gains for black workers than it does for white workers (Chapter 11). Blacks stand to benefit relatively more than whites by belonging to unions.

[1]Daniel J. B. Mitchell, *Unions, Wages, and Inflation* (Washington, D.C.: The Brookings Institution, 1980), p. 214.

TABLE 7-2

Union Membership by Sex, Race, and Age, 1984

Personal Characteristic	Percent Union*
Sex:	
Male	23
Female	14
Race:	
White	18
Black	26
Age:	
Under 25	8
25 and over	22

*Percent of employed wage and salary workers who belong to unions.

Source: Department of Labor, *Employment and Earnings,* January 1985, p. 210.

Table 7-2 also reveals that young workers (under 25 years of age) are less likely than older workers to have union cards. Once again, this is largely explainable in terms of the kinds of jobs young workers acquire. Specifically, as we shall see momentarily, the traditional blue-collar, goods-producing, unionized sectors of the economy have *not* been expanding rapidly in recent years and therefore have *not* been a major source of jobs to youths entering the labor force. Rather, the largely nonunion service sectors have been growing and providing more jobs. Today high school graduates are more likely to take jobs with nonunion fast-food chains; 25 years ago many high school graduates found work in unionized automobile manufacturing plants.

3. Location. To a considerable degree the labor movement in the United States is an urban phenomenon. Six heavily urbanized, heavily industrialized states—New York, California, Pennsylvania, Illinois, Ohio, and Michigan—account for approximately one-half of all union members.[2] Furthermore, the percentage of workers who are unionized in the south is only about two-thirds of what it is in the rest of the country. This may stem in part from the occupational and industrial makeup of jobs in the south, but it is also claimed that employers and the general populace simply are more inclined to be antiunion.

Structure of Organized Labor.[3] Figure 7-1 provides us with a thumbnail sketch of the structure of American labor organizations. You will observe that there are three major levels of union organizations: the federation, national unions,[4] and local unions. Let us comment briefly on each.

AFL-CIO. The *American Federation of Labor and Congress of Industrial Organizations,* better known as the *AFL-CIO,* is simply a loose and voluntary federation of independent and autonomous national unions. We note in Figure 7-1 that 102 national unions with a combined membership of about 12 million workers belonged to the AFL-CIO in 1982, while 101 national unions possessing an aggregate membership of about 5 million were independent of the AFL-CIO. The AFL-CIO does *not* engage in collective bargaining, but is the primary political organ of organized labor. The AFL-CIO formulates labor's view on a spectrum of political issues ranging from the minimum wage to foreign policy, publicizes labor's positions, and engages in political lobbying.[5] The AFL-CIO is

---

[2]Marten Estey, *The Unions,* 3d ed. (New York: Harcourt Brace Jovanovich, 1981), p. 10.

[3]The ensuing discussion draws upon ibid., chap. 3. For a discussion of the evolution of the labor movement and a more detailed consideration of its structure, see Gordon F. Bloom and Herbert R. Northrup, *Economics of Labor Relations,* 9th ed. (Homewood, Ill.: Richard D. Irwin, Inc., 1981), chaps. 2 and 3.

[4]Some national unions call themselves "international" unions—for example, the International Brotherhood of Electrical Workers (IBEW)—which usually means that there are some affiliated locals in Canada or Puerto Rico.

[5]For an analysis of organized labor's effectiveness in the political sphere, see Richard B. Freeman and James L. Medoff, *What Do Unions Do?* (New York: Basic Books, Inc., Publishers, 1984), chap. 13.

also responsible for settling jurisdictional disputes among affiliated national unions; that is, it determines which union has the "right" to organize a particular group of nonunion workers.

National unions. The *national unions* are federations of local unions which are typically in either the same industry ("industrial unions" such as the automobile or steel workers) or the same skilled occupation ("craft unions" such as carpenters and electricians). Table 7-3 lists the largest national unions and indicates which are, and which are not, affiliated with the AFL-CIO. Specifically, those not identified as independent are affiliated with the AFL-CIO.

A national union has two primary functions: (1) organizing the unorganized workers in its craft or industry and (2) negotiating collective bargaining agreements. Responsibility for the latter function, however, may be shared in some cases with local unions, depending upon the size of the local and the industry involved. For example, if the relevant product market is local (such as housing construction), the local carpenters, bricklayers, and other craft unions are likely to negotiate their own bargaining contracts. But where the product market is regional or national in scope (for example, textiles or automobiles) contract negotiation is usually performed by the national union rather than its locals. The reasons for this are twofold. Most importantly, the national union wants to standardize wages—to "take wages out of competition"—so that employers who would otherwise pay high union wages would not be penalized by losing sales to other firms paying low union wages. Furthermore, collective bargaining has become very complex and legalistic, requiring skilled negotiators, lawyers, and so forth. Consequently, it is likely that "economies of scale" are to be gained by relying on national negotiators.

FIGURE 7-1 THE INSTITUTIONAL ORGANIZATION OF THE AMERICAN LABOR MOVEMENT
Organized labor in the U.S. consists of the AFL-CIO and numerous independent unions. The AFL-CIO's basic function is to formulate and promote labor's views on a wide range of economic, social, and political issues. The national unions generally have responsibility for negotiating collective bargaining agreements, while the locals are concerned with administering those agreements.

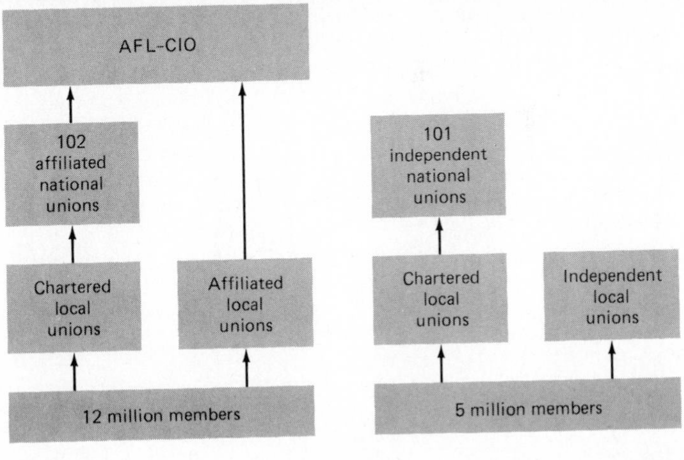

Local unions. Generally, the approximately 65,000 *local unions* are essentially branches or components of the respective national unions. We do observe in Figure 7-1, however, that some locals are directly affiliated with the AFL-CIO, and a few are unaffiliated with either a national union or the AFL-CIO. The relationship between the locals and the national unions is significantly different from that between the AFL-CIO and the nationals. When they join the federation, the national unions retain their sovereignty and autonomy over their internal affairs. But a local union is usually subservient to its national union. For example, locals are often required to clear a decision to strike with the national before undertaking such action. Furthermore, the national union has the power to suspend or to disband one of its locals.

This is not to downgrade the role of the local union. Locals perform the important function of administering or policing the bargaining contract and seeking the resolution of worker grievances which may arise in interpreting the contract. As Estey points out:

TABLE 7-3

Labor Organizations Reporting 100,000 Members or More, 1982* (In Thousands)

Labor Organization	Members	Labor Organization	Members
Teamsters (independent)	1,800	Electrical workers	190
National education association		Letter carriers	175
(Independent)	1,641	Graphic communication workers	165
Steelworkers	1,200	Painters	165
Auto workers	1,140	Firefighters	162
Food and commercial	1,079	Electrical workers (independent)	162
State, county	950	Nurses (independent)	160
Electrical	883	Police	160
Service employees	700	Iron workers	155
Carpenters	679	Bakery, tobacco	152
Machinists	655	Classified school (independent)	150
Communications workers	650	Mine workers (independent)	150
Teachers	573	Sheet metal workers	144
Laborers	450	Railway clerks	140
Clothing and textile workers	400	Oil, chemical workers	125
Hotel and restaurant	375	Bricklayers	120
Plumbers	353	Transit workers	120
Operating engineers	345	Boilermakers	117
Ladies' garment workers	276	Longshoremen	116
Paperworkers	263	Transportation	115
Musicians	260	Office and professional	112
Retail	250	Rubber workers	100
Postal workers	248		
Government workers	210		

*All organizations not identified as independent are affiliated with the AFL-CIO.

Source: Courtney D. Gifford, *Directory of U.S. Labor Organizations, 1984–1985 Edition* (Washington, D.C.: The Bureau of National Affairs, Inc., 1984), p. 3.

The local union is judged primarily on its handling of the grievance procedure, the process by which the collective bargaining agreement is administered and interpreted. It is the local-union officer, not the international representative or someone from the Federation, who gets the individual member's complaints about how he or she is treated in the plant. And it is the local-union officer who, in effect, is responsible for winning or losing the grievance for the worker. If the grievance is settled in favor of the worker, the local—and through it the national union and unions generally—looks good; and if the grievance is lost, unionism may suffer. . . .

Active, interested, and effective local leadership tends to produce a favorable reaction from the members, and vice versa. In short, the local union *is* the union to the members. Its performance is the basis for their opinions of unions.[6]

Diversity of bargaining structures. The term *bargaining structure* refers to the scope of the employees and employers covered by a collective bargaining agreement; the bargaining structure tells us who bargains with whom. In the United States there exists a great diversity of bargaining structures. The diversity is implicit in Figure 7-1 and in the fact that currently there are almost 200,000 collective bargaining agreements in force in the United States.

Many unions simply negotiate with a single-plant employer. Others bargain on a more centralized basis with multiplant employers. In this case firms with many plants negotiate a "master agreement" with one or more unions which then applies to workers in all of the firm's plants.[7] Still greater centralization is involved in *pattern bargaining* wherein the union negotiates a contract with a particular firm in an industry, and this contract—or a slightly modified version—comprises the demands which the union seeks to impose upon all other employers in that industry. In still other instances multiemployer bargaining occurs; employers in a given industry will form an employer's association (for example, the Bituminous Coal Owners Association) and bargain as a group with the union.

While the determinants of a bargaining structure are manifold and complex,[8] pragmatic considerations and perceived effects upon each party's bargaining power are important. For example, where employers are numerous and small and their markets are highly localized, unions are likely to bargain a citywide agreement with an employer's association. Both employers and the union may see advantages in such a bargaining structure. First, there may be some economies of scale in negotiations; it would be very costly for the union to have to negotiate separate agreements with a large number of employers. Second, employers may feel that they can enhance their bargaining power by negotiating

---

[6]Estey, op. cit., pp. 50–51.

[7]The master agreement is often supplemented by a local agreement which deals with issues and conditions unique to particular plants.

[8]For a systematic discussion of the determinants of bargaining structure, see Thomas A. Kochan, *Collective Bargaining and Industrial Relations* (Homewood, Ill.: Richard D. Irwin, Inc., 1980), chap. 4.

as a group rather than individually. Finally—and perhaps most importantly—by standardizing wage rates through a citywide agreement each employer avoids the risk of incurring a competitive disadvantage vis-a-vis other firms because of higher wage costs. Similarly, the union "takes wages out of competition" and avoids the problem of job loss in higher-wage union firms. Thus in building construction, hotels and motels, retail trade, and local trucking, citywide agreements are quite common. Regional multiemployer bargaining has also been practiced in over-the-road trucking, bituminous coal, and the basic steel industry, among others.

Single-company bargaining is common in many of the basic manufacturing industries wherein large oligopolistic corporations feel sufficiently strong to "go it alone" in negotiating with the union. But frequently the negotiation of a contract with one firm will establish a pattern for other firms in the same industry. The automobile industry is the most publicized example of pattern bargaining. When contracts terminate every three years, the United Auto Workers selects one of the "Big Three" manufacturers for contract renegotiation. The negotiated contract serves as the standard for dealing with the other automakers. This bargaining structure is advantageous to the union because lost wages during a possible strike will be less if only one firm is struck rather than the entire industry. Furthermore, the firm experiencing the work stoppage will lose sales to its nonstruck competitors, creating pressure upon the former to accept the union's demands. The basic point is that there is no such thing as a "typical" bargaining structure in the United States.

Unionism's Relative Decline. We noted earlier that some 17 million workers— about 15 percent of the civilian labor force—belonged to unions in 1984. Table 7-4 provides us with a historical overview of trends in union membership. Two points stand out. First, the unionized sector is clearly the minority component of the labor force. Union membership has never exceeded 26 percent of the total labor force. The United States, incidentally, is relatively "nonunion" compared to most other industrially advanced western economies. For example, estimates indicate that over 80 percent of all wage and salary workers are organized in Sweden. Comparable figures for Australia, West Germany, and Japan are 55, 40, and 35 percent respectively.

The second point is that over the past fifteen years or so the relative size of the unionized sector has been declining. Basically, the growth of union membership has failed to keep pace with the growth of the labor force, although we note that in the 1981–1984 high unemployment years, the absolute number of active union workers also fell sharply.

Why has this happened? There is no consensus on this issue, but it is revealing to consider three possible explanations. These explanations may well be complementary in the sense that each might explain some portion of the relative membership decline.

1. Structural changes. The traditional view, which we shall dub the *structural-change hypothesis,* is that a variety of structural changes have occurred both in our economy and in the labor force which have been unfavorable to the expansion of union membership. This view embraces a number of interrelated observations. First, consumer demand and therefore employment patterns have shifted away from traditional union strongholds. Generally speaking, national output has been shifting away from manufactured goods (where unions have been strong) to services (where unions have been weak). This change in the mix of industrial output may be reinforced by increased competition from imports in highly unionized sectors such as automobiles and steel. Growing import competition in these industries has curtailed domestic employment and therefore union membership. Second, an unusually large proportion of the increase in employment in recent years has been concentrated among women, youths, and part-time workers, groups which have allegedly been difficult to organize because of their less firm attachment to the labor force. Third, spurred by rising energy costs, the long-run trend for industry to shift from the northeast and the midwest where unionism is "a way of life" to "hard to organize" areas of the south and southwest may have impeded the expansion of union membership. A fourth and ironic possibility is that the relative decline of unionism may be in part a reflection of the greater success unions apparently have had in recent years in gaining a wage advantage over nonunion workers. As we shall find in the next chapter, there is some evidence to suggest that on the average union workers have been realizing a growing wage advantage over their nonunion counterparts. Confronted with a growing wage-cost disadvantage vis-a-vis nonunion employers, we would expect union employers to accelerate the substitution of capital for labor (or to subcontract more work to nonunion suppliers). This use of more capital-intensive production methods tends to reduce the

TABLE 7-4

Union Membership in the United States, Selected Years, 1900–1984

Year	Union Membership (1000s)	Percentage of Labor Force
1900	791	3
1910	2,116	6
1920	5,034	12
1930	3,632	7
1940	7,282	13
1950	14,823	23
1960	18,117	25
1970	21,248	26
1980	22,366	21
1982	19,763	18
1984	17,340	15

Sources: Bureau of Labor Statistics and Courtney D. Gifford, *Directory of U.S. Labor Organizations, 1984–1985 Edition* (Washington, D.C.: The Bureau of National Affairs, Inc., 1984). Data exclude Canadian members of U.S. unions.

growth of employment opportunities in the union sector as compared to the nonunion sector.

2. The substitution hypothesis. Neumann and Rissman have attempted to explain the relative decline in union membership in terms of what they label the substitution hypothesis. The *substitution hypothesis* is the notion that "the provision of certain social welfare benefits by government substitutes for the private provision by unions, thereby reducing the attractiveness of union membership."[9] The authors note that many of today's social programs that relate to the labor market—such as unemployment insurance, workers' compensation, social security, and health and safety laws—were once important goals of labor unions. Their empirical analysis leads them to conclude that historically government has been responsible for providing more and more "union-like" services, and this has simply lessened the need for workers to join unions.[10]

3. Managerial-opposition hypothesis. Freeman and Medoff have also challenged the structural-change explanation, arguing instead that intensified *managerial opposition* to unions has been a major deterrent to union growth.[11] They envision several problems with the structural-change hypothesis. First, other advanced capitalistic countries have experienced structural changes similar to those which have occurred in the United States, and their labor movements continue to grow both absolutely and relatively. Secondly, they point out that historically union growth has been realized in good measure by the unionization of groups of workers who were once regarded as traditionally "nonunion." The unionization of blue-collar workers in the mass production industries such as automobiles and steel in the 1930s and public sector workers more recently are cases in point. Given this history, why can't women workers, young workers, and southern workers be brought into the labor movement to spur its continued growth? Finally, surveys indicate that young and female workers—whom we found in Table 7-2 are now less unionized—are in fact as much or more prounion as are more heavily unionized older and male workers. Yet unions are losing an increasing proportion of National Labor Relations Board elections wherein workers vote to determine whether they want to be unionized.

More positively, Freeman and Medoff contend that in the past decade or so unions have increased the union wage advantage which they enjoy vis-a-vis nonunion workers (Chapter 8) and, as a result, union firms have become less profitable than nonunion firms. As a reaction, managerial opposition to unions

---

[9]George R. Neumann and Ellen R. Rissman, "Where Have All the Union Members Gone?" *Journal of Labor Economics,* April 1984. p. 175.

[10]From their empirical work Neumann and Rissman find that about half of the decrease in union membership which has occurred since 1956 is explainable in terms of changes in the structure of industry.

[11]Freeman and Medoff, op. cit., chap. 15.

has crystallized and become more aggressive. This opposition takes a variety of forms. In some cases, nonunion firms emulate the wage rates and fringe benefits of union employers in the hope of convincing their workers that unionization is unnecessary. A further strategy is to employ labor-management consultants who specialize in mounting aggressive antiunion drives to dissuade workers from unionizing or, alternatively, to persuade union workers to decertify their union.[12] Finally, Freeman and Medoff contend there has been a dramatic rise in the use of illegal antiunion tactics. In particular, they argue that it has become increasingly common for management to identify and dismiss leading prounion workers even though this is prohibited by the Wagner Act. Given these antiunion strategies and a reduction in resources devoted to organizing the unorganized, the labor movement has gone into relative eclipse.

Union responses: mergers. One of the basic responses of unions to the relative decline of organized labor has been for unions with similar jurisdictions to merge with one another. Of the eighty-six labor organization mergers which have occurred since the AFL and CIO combined in 1955, about 35 percent took place between 1979 and 1984. While it is true that trade union ideology stresses unity, practical considerations have clearly been paramount in recent mergers. Shrinking membership, declining income from dues, and the desire to achieve a strong and united voice in collective bargaining negotiations have all contributed to the recent impetus for merger.[13]

ARE UNIONS MAXIMIZERS?

Given some understanding of (1) the size of the labor movement, (2) the kinds of workers who are most likely to belong to unions, (3) the structure of organized labor, and (4) the possible causes of the relative decline in union membership, let us now turn to the thorny question of union objectives.

In Chapter 6 we considered how unions might increase wage rates by manipulating labor supply and demand. One of the "loose ends" in that discussion is the issue of union goals. For what ends does a union formulate its wage policy? What are unions trying to achieve in terms of wage and employment outcomes? In terms of Figures 6-7 and 6-8 in the previous chapter, the question is: To what extent and for what purposes will unions attempt to enhance labor demand or restrict labor supply? Or in terms of Figure 6-9: Why might the union seek the wage rate W_u rather than some higher or lower wage rate?

---

[12]A 1984 brochure from an organization called Executive Enterprises, Inc., boasts that it has had over 20,000 management representatives attend its seminars on "How to Maintain Non-union Status" and "The Process of Decertification."

[13]Larry T. Adams, "Labor Organization Mergers 1979–84: Adapting to Change," *Monthly Labor Review*, September 1984, pp. 21–27.

For better or worse, economists tend to think almost automatically that individuals and institutions attempt to maximize some magnitude or another. Thus, for example, in models of consumer behavior the goal is to maximize utility. Similarly, business firms presumably seek to maximize profits. Hence, it is not surprising that economists have attempted to apply the maximizing concept to unions in explaining their wage policies. As we shall now find, attempts to isolate single maximizing goals have *not* been particularly successful.

1. Wage rate. Samuel Gompers, founder of the AFL, is reported to have said that unions want "more, more, more!" But attempts by a union to maximize the wage rate per worker make no sense. Assuming a union is able to impose its wage demand unilaterally upon a totally submissive employer, the logical outcome would be the employment of one worker at an extremely high wage rate! Unions are concerned with their institutional survival and growth. And their members are concerned with having jobs. Given the reality of a downward-sloping labor demand curve as shown in Figure 7-2, a policy of aggressively pushing up wage rates obviously will cause unemployment among union members. And it is reasonable to suppose that in time these unemployed workers will seek and obtain alternative jobs and cease to be affiliated with the union. We can conclude that union wage demands eventually will be constrained by unemployment effects. Indeed, the widespread "concession bargaining" of the past several years, whereby unions have accepted wage freezes or have agreed to

FIGURE 7-2 ARE UNIONS MAXIMIZERS?
Simple maximizing objectives do not adequately describe union behavior. Concern about employment and institutional survival constrains unions from the goal of maximizing—or even dramatically increasing—wage rates. And, if the current combination of wage rate and employment were on the elastic segment of the labor demand curve, a union seeking to maximize the wage bill would need to reduce wages. Similarly, the maximization of employment and union membership would occur at the equilibrium wage rate, implying that a union is redundant.

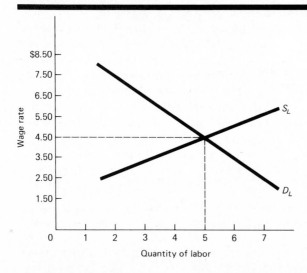

wage cuts, provides rather compelling evidence that unions and their members are concerned with being employed. Chapter 8's Time and One-Half minireading discusses in some detail the causes and quantitative significance of wage freezes and "givebacks" in the early 1980s.

2. Wage bill. Given concern with employment, another obvious goal might be to maximize the wage bill, that is, to maximize the wage rate multiplied by the number of employed workers. But this objective runs into difficulties where the demand for labor is elastic. In Figure 7-2 the labor demand curve is constructed so that demand is elastic at all wage rates above $4.50 and inelastic at all wage rates below $4.50. Now, if the union currently enjoys a wage rate above $4.50—say $6.50—it will be obligated to request a wage *reduction* in order to maximize the wage bill! Why so? Recall from Figure 5-6 that where the demand curve is elastic—as it is at $6.50—a reduction in the wage rate will *increase* the wage bill because the resulting percentage increase in employment will be larger than the percentage reduction in the wage rate per worker.[14] Given the labor supply curve in Figure 7-2, the union would maximize the wage bill at the equilibrium wage rate of $4.50. More precisely, by lowering the wage rate from $6.50 to $4.50 the union's wage bill will increase from $19.50 (= $6.50 × 3) to $22.50 (= $4.50 × 5). In this instance the union would be irrelevant insofar as wage determination is concerned because the market would yield the combination of wage rate and employment which would maximize the wage bill. Why should workers pay union dues when the market yields the desired result? "The goal of maximizing wages per member is deficient because it implies that unions have no concern for members who become unemployed and no interest in remaining in existence as organizations. The goal of maximizing the wage bill has the opposite difficulty—it implies that unions can be interested in increasing membership to the point of leaving the original members no better off than they would have been without a union."[15]

3. Employment and membership. Because unions are concerned with institutional survival and growth and because union leaders derive prestige and power from presiding over large organizations, perhaps unions seek to maximize the employment of their (dues-paying) members. If in Figure 7-2 we assume that all available workers are union members and, hence, the curves reflect the demand for and the supply of *union* workers, the realization of this goal would require the union to seek the competitive equilibrium wage of $4.50. At any higher wage rate the constraint of the demand curve would be pertinent and employment would fall below 5 workers. At any wage rate below $4.50 the restraint of the supply curve becomes relevant and employment again falls below 5. In other words, at any wage rate above equilibrium employers will choose to

[14]Remember from the discussion of the elasticity coefficient in Chapter 5 that, by definition, demand is elastic when the percentage change in the quantity of labor demanded is greater than the associated percentage change in the wage rate.

[15]Albert Rees, *The Economics of Trade Unions* (Chicago: University of Chicago Press, 1962), pp. 53–54.

employ fewer than the equilibrium number of workers. At any below-equilibrium wage rate fewer than the equilibrium number of workers will want to be employed in this market. Again, why have a union if the market will achieve your goal in the union's absence?

One can readily devise more complex models of union behavior.[16] For example, a union might be concerned with the wage and rate employment status not of its entire membership, but rather of some particular subgroup. Thus if older workers with considerable seniority dominate the union, then it might more aggressively seek higher wage rates because the consequent loss of jobs will be borne by younger workers who have less seniority. Such models rather quickly turn from economics to the internal politics of particular unions.

While unions are ordinarily concerned with both wages and employment, it is probably the former which is of paramount interest. While the notion of a tradeoff between wages and employment is taken for granted by economists, that relationship is not so evident to union workers and their leaders. To them the links between wage rates, production costs, product prices, and product sales are far from precise or dependable. For example, workers observe that fluctuations in a firm's sales and hence in employment seem to be linked to the general state of the economy and have little to do with the level of wage rates in their particular firm. Similarly, the decline in employment which results from the substitution of capital for labor may be interpreted by workers as the consequence of an "unfortunate" management decision rather than a response to higher wages. Furthermore, workers may feel that wage rates are a factor over which they can collectively exert some degree of control. Employment, on the other hand, depends upon the decisions of others and the general state of the economy.[17]

Our conclusion is that, while unions have goals—few would deny that unions engage in purposeful behavior—their goals are multidimensional and impossible to analyze through one-dimensional maximization assumptions. Indeed, by glancing at Table 7-5's synopsis of the contents of a typical collective bargaining agreement, one can see the multiplicity of areas which are of concern to unions. With this in mind let us turn to the unique characteristics of the collective bargaining transaction.

COLLECTIVE BARGAINING: A SPECIAL TRANSACTION

Economic transactions range from the exceedingly simple to the highly complex. Buying a loaf of bread at a supermarket or obtaining a Coke from a vending

---

[16] For an in-depth discussion of union objectives, see Allan M. Cartter, *Theory of Wages and Employment* (Homewood, Ill.: Richard D. Irwin, Inc., 1959), chap. 7.

[17] For more on the union view of the relationship between the wage rate and employment, see Mitchell, op. cit., pp. 64–68. The reader may also want to glance ahead at the section in Chapter 15 on "Institutional Economics and Wage Determination" which summarizes the view that economic calculus cannot be applied meaningfully to labor unions.

machine are clearly uncomplicated transactions. In contrast, the negotiation of a collective bargaining agreement is undoubtedly one of the most complex transactions which occurs in our economy. This complexity derives from a number of rather unique characteristics of the collective bargaining transaction.

1. Labor services are inseparably tied up with the worker who is "selling" or "renting" those services to an employer. While the buyer and seller of a used car may never see each other again after their transaction, the seller of labor services must spend 40 or so hours per week in an office or factory delivering those services to the buyer. Hence, collective bargaining obviously involves much more than wage determination. Working conditions, work rules, promotion and training, fringe benefits, and a spectrum of other issues must be mutually approved by the union and management. Table 7-5 illustrates the range and complexity of bargainable issues. While our discussion will focus upon the wage aspects of bargaining, it is important to keep in mind that in fact the bargaining agenda is extensive and that many of the bargaining subjects affect the cost of employing workers.

2. The relationship between labor and management is a long-term one. The parties will negotiate a contract this year, a new contract 2 or 3 years hence, and so forth. This long-term relationship is important in that what transpires in negotiating this year's contract may well have an impact upon succeeding agreements. For example, suppose in the present negotiations the union flatly threatens to strike if the employer does not double its contribution to the pension plan. If the employer rejects this demand and the union does *not* strike, the credibility of the union's threats will be diminished in future negotiations.

3. Many buyers and sellers confront each other on a simple "take-it-or-

---

TABLE 7-5

Abbreviated Contents of a Collective Bargaining Agreement

The Agreement and Its Administration	Job Security, Promotions, and Layoffs
Managerial rights and obligations	Seniority provisions
Union security and status	Hiring and layoff procedures
Contract enforcement	Training and retraining
Grievance procedure	Severance pay
Mediation and arbitration	Promotion procedures
Wage Determination	Allocation of overtime work
Basic wage rates and wage structure	**Fringe Benefits**
Incentive systems	Pension plans
Pay for overtime work	Health and insurance plans
Shift differentials	Sick leave
Cost-of-living adjustments	Vacations and holidays
Company Operations	Profit-sharing, stock-purchase plans
Work rules	
Disciplinary procedures	
Production rates and standards	
Safety and health	
Rest periods	
Technological change	

leave-it" basis. A supermarket manager will not negotiate the price of a loaf of bread, and a vending machine stands mute as you consider dropping in $.50 for a Coke. If you decide not to buy the bread or the Coke, no great damage is inflicted upon either potential buyer or seller.

But labor and management are highly dependent upon one another, and this changes their transaction from a "take-it-or-leave-it" situation to one of *negotiation*. If labor and management do not reach agreement and a strike therefore results, significant costs will be imposed upon both parties. More positively, collective bargaining involves what is called a **symbiotic relationship** between the two parties, that is, a relationship which simultaneously involves elements of both *cooperation* and *competition*. On the one hand, both parties gain by cooperating and reaching agreement. By agreeing, the two parties combine their resources in the production of some good or service and share the revenues derived therefrom. Hence, there is a strong mutual interest in reaching agreement. On the other hand, the two parties are in a competitive position because the "terms of trade" under which agreement is reached determine how the revenues stemming from their cooperative efforts in the production process will be shared between the two parties.

Given these several characteristics of the bargaining transaction, let us next examine the bargaining process. This process is a means through which the opposing interests of the union and the employer normally get resolved. We will see that the key to this resolution is the symbiotic relationship just described.

A MODEL OF THE BARGAINING PROCESS

Although there are numerous models of collective bargaining,[18] we will confine our attention to a conceptually simple, but very insightful, model of bargaining developed by Chamberlain.[19] This model focuses upon the determinants of bargaining power and the ways in which changes in these determinants lead to settlement in the majority of collective bargaining situations.

The Model. Chamberlain defines **bargaining power** as the ability to secure your opponent's agreement to your terms. Thus a **union's bargaining power** can be defined as management's willingness to agree to the union's terms or demands. But what determines the willingness (or unwillingness) of management to agree

---

[18]The ambitious reader may want to consult Charles Mulvey, *The Economic Analysis of Trade Unions* (New York: St. Martin's Press, 1978), chap. 7; Bevars D. Mabry, *Economics of Manpower and the Labor Market* (New York: Intext Educational Publishers, 1973), chap. 13; John G. Cross, *The Economics of Bargaining* (New York: Basic Books, Inc., Publishers, 1969); Richard B. Peterson and Lane Tracy, *Models of the Bargaining Process: with Special Reference to Collective Bargaining* (Seattle, Wash.: University of Washington, Graduate School of Business Administration, 1977).

[19]Neil W. Chamberlain, *A General Theory of Economic Process* (New York: Harper & Row, Publishers, 1955), particularly chaps. 6–8.

to the union's terms? The answer, according to Chamberlain, depends upon how costly disagreeing will be relative to how costly agreeing will be. That is:

$$\text{Union's bargaining power (UBP)} = \frac{\text{management's perceived cost of disagreeing with the union's terms (MCD)}}{\text{management's perceived cost of agreeing with the union's terms (MCA)}} \quad (7\text{-}1)$$

If management estimates that it is more costly to agree than to disagree (that is, if the union's bargaining power is less than one), management will choose to disagree and thereby reject the union's terms. If, however, management judges that it is more costly to disagree than to agree (that is, if the union's bargaining power is greater than one), management will choose to agree.

But what comprises the "cost of agreeing" and the "cost of disagreeing"? If we simplify by assuming that the wage rate is the only bargainable issue, then management's cost of disagreeing is the probable or estimated loss of profits during the strike which may follow its rejection of the union's stated wage demand. This perceived cost is probabilistic in that management's estimate of the cost of disagreeing depends both upon its estimate of (1) the probability that a strike will occur if the wage demand is rejected and (2) the probable length of the strike should it occur. Management's perceived cost of agreeing—that is, the cost of accepting the union's wage demand—is the estimated reduction in the flow of profits resulting from the payment of a higher than intended wage rate.

Management's bargaining power can be similarly defined:

$$\text{Management's bargaining power (MBP)} = \frac{\text{union's perceived cost of disagreeing with management's terms (UCD)}}{\text{union's perceived cost of agreeing with management's terms (UCA)}} \quad (7\text{-}2)$$

Once again, if the union believes it is more costly to agree than to disagree, the union will disagree with management's offer. Whenever the denominator is greater than the numerator in equation (7-2)—that is, whenever management's bargaining power is less than one—the union will choose to reject management's offer. Conversely, if the union judges it to be more costly to disagree than to agree, the union will choose to agree. In other words, when management's bargaining power is greater than one, the union will be willing to accept management's offer.

The union's costs of disagreeing and agreeing can be defined similarly to those of management. The union's perceived cost of disagreeing is the probable loss of wage income during a strike. This estimate depends upon the probability that a strike will occur *and* upon the estimated length of the strike. The union's cost of agreeing is a reduced flow of wage income. Given that the union seeks a higher wage rate than management is now willing to offer, the decision to accept the lower wage offered by management entails forgoing the larger flow of wage income to which the union and its constituents aspire.

Implications. A number of significant observations can be derived directly from these concepts of bargaining power.

1. Requirement for agreement. As our prior discussion suggests, the *necessary condition* for a settlement is simply that one party must be willing to agree to the terms put forward by the other party. More specifically, management (the union) will be willing to agree to the union's (management's) terms when management (the union) feels that the cost of disagreeing to those terms is greater than the cost of agreeing. As previously noted, in terms of the bargaining power ratios of equations (7-1) and (7-2), the ratio would have to exceed unity or one for agreement to be possible. To illustrate, suppose negotiations begin with the union asking for a $1.00 per hour wage increase. Consulting equation (7-1), if management perceives that the cost of disagreeing to this wage demand will exceed the cost of agreeing, then management will be willing to accept the union's wage demand. Needless to say, the $1.00 wage increase is presumably also acceptable to the union because it is the union's proposal! On the other hand, if management perceives that the costs of agreeing will exceed the costs of disagreeing, the union's wage demand will be unacceptable to management. At this point several things may happen: the union may alter (lower) its wage demand, management may put an alternative wage offer on the table for consideration by the union, or a stalemate (strike) may result. The implications of these developments are discussed below.

2. Relative bargaining power. Individuals normally think of the bargaining power of a union or an employer as being in some sense absolute. But Chamberlain's model correctly suggests that a party's bargaining power is *relative* in the sense that it will depend upon what is being demanded or offered. For example, equation (7-1) implies that the union's bargaining power will be much less when it is asking for, say, a $1.00 per hour wage increase than when it is asking for only $.20 more per hour. Why so? Because it is very costly for management to agree to a $1.00 wage increase, while it costs relatively little to agree to a $.20 per hour wage boost. In terms of equation (7-1) the denominator will be small for the $.20 wage demand, tending to cause the union's bargaining power to exceed unity and inducing management's acceptance of the union's terms. Conversely, the denominator of equation (7-1) will be large for the $1.00 wage demand, tending to cause the union's bargaining power to be less than unity so that the necessary condition for agreement is not realized. The important generalization is that the greater the union's wage demand, the greater the management's resistance to it and therefore the less will be the union's bargaining power.

3. "Unnecessary" strikes. We have stressed that the *necessary condition* for agreement is that one party must find it more costly to disagree than to agree with the other party's wage demand or offer. But this is not a *sufficient condition* for agreement. Work stoppages may arise because one party misjudges the other's position or because the parties become committed to irreconcilable positions during the negotiation process.

Misjudgment. Let us suppose that, in fact, management would be willing to grant a maximum hourly wage increase of, say, $.50 per hour. That is, $.50 is the maximum wage increase at which management perceives the cost of disagreeing to exceed the cost of agreeing. Similarly, suppose the union is willing to accept as little as a $.25 hourly increase. This is the minimum wage increase at which the union perceives the cost of disagreeing to exceed the cost of agreeing. Hence, we have a range or zone of potential agreement wherein the necessary condition for agreement is present. Either party would rather agree than disagree with the opponent's terms within the $.25 to $.50 range.

But the negotiation process occurs in an environment of incomplete knowledge. Specifically, the union does *not* know the maximum wage increase ($.50) to which management will agree because this depends upon *management's* estimates of the costs of agreeing and disagreeing to the union's wage demands. Similarly, management does *not* know the minimum wage increase ($.25) the union will accept. Now assume the union misjudges the maximum wage increase which management will concede. For example, suppose the exchange of information which occurs in the bargaining process leads the union to believe that management will eventually concede $.60 per hour rather than the actual $.50. Hence, if the union adamantly demands $.60 during negotiations, time may run out and the cost of this misjudgment will be an unwanted and unnecessary strike. A similar outcome would occur if management misjudged the lowest acceptable wage increase to the union to be, say, $.15.

Commitments. The other possibility is that the union and management might become "committed" to irreconcilable positions *within* the $.50 to $.25 range of potential agreements. That is, the parties may establish a wage demand and a wage offer from which neither can retreat without "loss of face" and the undermining of its credibility in future negotiations. For example, management might become committed to a $.30 wage increase on the grounds that it is noninflationary, and management accepts social responsibility to behave in a noninflationary manner. Conversely, the union may become committed to a $.40 hourly increase on the grounds that it is justified on the basis of "what other peer groups of workers are getting." These commitments, clearly tied to publicized "principles," may put both parties in a position wherein they cannot retreat from their stated terms without bringing into question the credibility of the positions they may take in future negotiations. We have here a range of mutually acceptable wage increases, but no actual agreement. By becoming committed the parties blunder into a strike which neither wants! To the layman it appears highly irrational to engage in a perhaps long and mutually costly strike over a few cents an hour. However, such an outcome is more understandable when one recognizes that if, for example, the union adamantly says it will strike provided it does not receive $.40 per hour and then fails to do so, its bargaining power in future negotiations will be decreased because the credibility of its demands has been diminished.[20]

4. Reaching agreement. Let us assume that initially the bargaining power of neither party exceeds unity. That is, at the outset of the negotiation period both parties feel it is more costly to agree than to disagree with its opponent's terms. As the bargaining process proceeds, two developments may occur which cause the parties to move toward agreement. In the first place, collective bargaining negotiations are characterized by a *deadline.* For example, the parties begin to bargain, say, 60 days prior to the termination of their current collective bargaining agreement. It is generally understood that, if no agreement is reached during the negotiating period, a work stoppage in the form of either a strike or a lockout will occur. The general rule is "no contract, no work." Now recall that an important ingredient of each party's perceived cost of disagreeing is the probability that a strike will occur. One can expect that as the strike deadline approaches, both parties will revise upward their estimate that a strike will in fact occur. In terms of equations (7-1) and (7-2), this means that as the prestrike negotiating period diminishes, the estimated costs of disagreeing for labor and management will increase, tending to increase the likelihood that the bargaining power of one or both parties will exceed unity and therefore create the necessary condition for agreement. The purpose of a deadline in collective bargaining is to create pressures upon both parties to reach agreement. In Chamberlain's model this function is reflected in upward revisions of the perceived costs of disagreeing for both parties.

The second and perhaps more obvious factor which may move the bargainers toward agreement is revision of the terms of both parties. Compromise demands and offers promote agreement. Specifically, the union may lower its wage demand and management may increase its wage offer. If the union lowers its wage demand, management's cost of agreeing is obviously reduced in equation (7-1), pushing the union's bargaining power toward unity and making for agreement. Similarly, an increase in management's wage offer will reduce the union's cost of agreeing in equation (7-2), driving management's bargaining power toward unity and thereby agreement.

There is, however, a potential problem with compromise offers and demands. While they reduce the opponent's costs of agreeing and thereby increase one's own bargaining power, there is the risk that a compromise offer or demand will be interpreted by the opponent as a sign of "weakness." Should this happen, the opponent's cost of disagreeing will also decrease, tending to reduce one's own bargaining power and thereby impeding agreement. For example, if the union reduces its wage demand, management might interpret this to mean that the union is very anxious to reach agreement and therefore a strike is less

[20]For a perceptive discussion of the "commitment" issue in particular and the bargaining process in general, see Carl M. Stevens, *Strategy and Collective Bargaining Negotiations* (New York: McGraw-Hill Book Company, Inc., 1963).

likely to occur than management had heretofore thought. Thus management revises its estimate of the cost of disagreeing downward. The point is that by reducing its wage demand the union may reduce *both* management's cost of agreeing and its cost of disagreeing. Declines in both the numerator and denominator of equation (7-1) do not necessarily move the negotiators toward agreement.

5. Negotiating tactics: coercion and persuasion. Chamberlain's model encompasses the use of negotiating tactics as a means of improving one's bargaining power. Given equations (7-1) and (7-2), either party can increase its bargaining power by increasing its opponent's perception of the cost of disagreeing *and* by decreasing the opponent's estimate of the cost of agreeing.

Tactics designed to *increase* the opponent's costs of *disagreeing* might be termed **coercive bargaining tactics** in that they suggest that some negative or undesirable outcomes, which have been either ignored or underestimated, will occur if the opponent does not agree to the other party's terms. Thus the union might take a strike vote or emphasize the availability of strike funds to induce management to increase its estimate of the probability that a strike will occur if it rejects the union's wage demand. If successful, management's estimate of the cost of disagreeing will increase and hence so will the union's bargaining power. Conversely, the company may threaten to automate or to close the plant to prompt the union to increase its estimate of the cost of disagreeing to management's wage offer.

Strikes and lockouts, of course, are coercive tactics in and of themselves. As the length of a work stoppage increases, the actual loss of wage income rises and this increases the union's cost of disagreeing. Similarly, the lengthening impasse increases the amount of revenues and profits lost by the firm and therefore increases its cost of disagreeing. Furthermore, during a strike coercive tactics may be employed in an attempt to increase a party's bargaining power. For example, unions may picket the firm to reduce patronage and to keep other employees from working. In both instances the picketing imposes higher costs of disagreeing upon the firm. It is important to note that in collective bargaining a strike or lockout can play a positive role in that it impels the two parties toward agreement by increasing their costs of disagreeing.

Tactics designed to *decrease* the opponent's estimate of the costs of *agreeing* can be labelled *conciliatory* or **persuasive bargaining tactics** because they imply that certain desirable outcomes, which have been ignored or underestimated, will occur if the opponent agrees to the other party's terms. Hence, the union may stress that higher wages will improve worker morale and productivity, enhance the prosperity of the community and hence of the firm itself, improve worker discipline, reduce turnover, and so forth. Similarly, management may argue that the acceptance of its wage offer will make the firm more competitive in its industry, thereby increasing employment security for workers and providing them with greater opportunities for overtime work. And, of course, we have already noted that either party can reduce the other's cost of agreeing by altering the wage demand or offer. The union can reduce management's cost of agreeing and thereby increase the probability of settlement by asking for a smaller wage increase; management can reduce the union's cost of agreeing by offering a larger wage increase. In fact, this process of compromise in wage demands and offers is typically involved in the resolution of strikes.

6. The economic environment. Economic forces are not circumvented by collective bargaining. On the contrary, the character of the economic environment within which workers and employers negotiate affects the bargaining power of the two parties. In our discussion we will consider (1) the overall condition of the national economy and (2) the structure of the employer's industry.

Prosperity and recession. Generally speaking, the bargaining power of a union is procyclical and that of an employer is anticyclical. That is, a strong economy enhances a union's bargaining strength while weakening the bargaining power of the employer. Let us see why this is the case.

If the economy has been prosperous and operating at, or close to, full employment for a period of time, we can expect the bargaining power of the union to be strong. In the first place, if workers actually strike the employer, they will have a good chance of obtaining alternative employment. This means that workers will be in a good position to prolong a strike. Conversely, the employer will have few alternative sources of labor in the event of a work stoppage. A second and related point is that a period of prosperity will have provided workers with an opportunity to build up their personal savings and their union an opportunity to enlarge its strike fund. Finally, if the firm has been operating at capacity for some time, its inventories will tend to be low. This means that, if a strike occurs, the firm will not be able to service its customers for any length of time. The employer will lose profitable business and, perhaps more importantly, may lose established customers to other producers who are not experiencing labor disputes. The impact of all of these considerations is to increase management's perceived cost of disagreeing to the union's terms (equation 7-1), which clearly has the effect of increasing the union's bargaining power.

When the economy is experiencing a recession, the tables will obviously be turned. In recession the employer is likely to have overly large inventories of unsold goods so that, at least for a time, customers could be served during a strike. In fact, a firm which is losing money by operating at a loss during a recession may find the cost of a strike to be virtually nil! Similarly, unemployed nonstriking workers may be readily available to operate the employer's plant in the event of a strike. And the high unemployment rate means that it will be difficult for striking workers to find alternative jobs. All of these factors suggest that the union's perceived cost of disagreeing with the employer's terms will be high in equation (7-2) and that management's bargaining power will therefore be enhanced.

Industry structure. There is no clear agreement among economists as to how industry structure affects bargaining power. Is bargaining power greater for firms functioning in a heavily concentrated, oligopolistic industry such as the automobile industry or in unconcentrated, more competitive environments such as the clothing and shoe industries? On the one hand, we would expect a corporate giant in a concentrated industry to have great financial resources to draw upon in meeting the costs associated with a strike. One could argue that a union, realizing this, will estimate the cost of disagreeing with the employer's terms to be high and, therefore, that management's bargaining power in equation (7-2) will be large. On the other hand, large firms in concentrated industries may possess a degree of monopoly power which enables them to practice administered pricing and to pass increases in labor costs on to consumers via higher product prices (Chapter 19). The exercise of market power enables management to "escape" union attempts to encroach upon profits. Such firms may find it convenient to acquiesce to the union's wage demand. If the union feels that the "will to resist" of such firms is weak, its perceived cost of disagreeing with management's terms will be small in equation (7-2) and so will management's bargaining power.

It should be added that the scope or coverage of a collective bargaining agreement *and* the extent to which an industry is unionized can also have important effects upon bargaining power. For example, if a union is bargaining simultaneously with all three or four firms in an oligopolistic industry, the resistance shown to the union's wage demand may be less than if the union were bargaining with one of the firms separately. For the firms as a group a 5 percent increase in labor costs and in product price will put none of the firms at a competitive disadvantage vis-a-vis its rivals. But a single firm might exhibit greater resistance when faced with the prospect of raising its price by 5 percent while its rivals do not. Similarly, when the degree of unionization in an industry is small, the union's bargaining power will tend to be weak. If only a few firms are organized in the industry, those firms will find themselves at an obvious competitive disadvantage vis-a-vis nonunion firms if they accept union wage demands significantly above those paid by nonunion firms. In equation (7-1) this competitive disadvantage may be regarded as increasing management's cost of agreeing to the union's terms and therefore reducing the union's bargaining power.

SUMMARY

1. Approximately 17 million workers—about one worker in seven—belong to a labor union. Generally speaking, membership is strong in goods-producing industries and weak in service-providing industries. Unionization is also relatively strong in the public sector.
2. Male, older, and black workers are more likely to belong to unions than are female, young, and white workers. These differences are largely explained in terms of the industrial and occupational affiliations of these demographic groups.
3. Labor unions are strongest in the heavily urbanized, heavily industrialized states and are relatively weak in the south.
4. The structure of the labor movement reveals three basic levels of union organization. The American Federation of Labor and Congress of Industrial Organizations (AFL-CIO) is concerned with formulating and expressing labor's political views and in

resolving jurisdictional disputes among national unions. The primary functions of the national unions are to organize unorganized workers and to negotiate collective bargaining agreements. The task of administering bargaining agreements falls primarily to the local unions. Bargaining structures are many and diverse.

5. Unionism has been declining relatively in the United States. Some labor economists attribute this to changes in the composition of national output and in the demographic structure of the labor force which have been uncongenial to union growth. Others feel that government programs have usurped a number of organized labor's traditional functions, thereby lessening workers' perceived need for union membership. Still others contend that employers, recognizing that unionization results in lower profitability, have more aggressively sought to dissuade workers from being union members.

6. Union bargaining behavior cannot be readily interpreted in terms of the maximization of such magnitudes as wage rates, the wage bill, or employment.

7. Collective bargaining embodies several unique characteristics: (a) Workers must deliver their labor services over time which makes working conditions, work rules, and a variety of other issues bargainable; (b) because a long-term relationship exists between management and a union, the negotiations involved in the present contract have an impact upon future negotiations; (c) a symbiotic relationship exists between the union and management in that both parties benefit from cooperating (agreeing) but simultaneously are competing for shares of the revenue they jointly produce.

8. Chamberlain has defined bargaining power as the ability to secure your opponent's agreement to your terms. The willingness of your opponent to accept your terms depends upon the comparative costs of disagreeing and agreeing. That is:

$$\frac{\text{Your bargaining}}{\text{power}} = \frac{\text{opponent's cost of disagreeing to your terms}}{\text{opponent's cost of agreeing to your terms}}$$

9. The Chamberlain bargaining power model has a number of salient implications: (a) At least one party must perceive disagreement to be more costly than agreement in order for agreement to occur; (b) one's bargaining power is relative in that it depends upon the size of the wage increase one is asking for or offering; (c) misjudgment of the maximum offer the employer will make (or the minimum offer the union will accept) or the commitment of the parties to irreconcilable positions may result in a strike even though a range of mutually acceptable settlements exists; (d) compromise offers (and demands) and the approach of the bargaining deadline both tend to move the parties toward agreement; (e) the model allows for coercive tactics (which increase your opponent's costs of disagreeing) and for persuasive tactics (which reduce your opponent's costs of agreeing); (f) the economic environment, including both the state of the macroeconomy and industry structure, can affect the bargaining power of the two parties.

QUESTIONS AND STUDY SUGGESTIONS

1. Key terms and concepts to remember: American Federation of Labor and Congress of Industrial Organizations (AFL-CIO); national unions; local unions; bargaining structure; pattern bargaining; structural-change hypothesis; substitution hypothesis; managerial-opposition hypothesis; symbiotic relationship; Chamberlain's bargain-

ing power model; union (management) bargaining power; union's costs of agreeing and disagreeing; management's costs of agreeing and disagreeing; coercive bargaining tactics; persuasive bargaining tactics.

2. To what extent is the civilian labor force unionized? Indicate the (a) industrial and (b) occupational distribution of union members. Why are relatively fewer white-collar workers organized than blue-collar workers? Briefly explain union membership differences as related to sex, race, and age. Evaluate: "Whether an individual worker is a union member depends, not so much upon the worker's feelings toward membership, but rather upon her or his occupational choice."

3. Summarize the organizational structure of the American labor movement, indicating the functions of the AFL-CIO, the national unions, and the local unions.

4. Describe the variety of bargaining structures which exist in the United States. What might be the advantages of multiemployer bargaining to a union? To employers? What is "pattern bargaining"?

5. Critically evaluate: "The relative decline of the American labor movement can be explained by the shift from goods-producing to service-providing industries, and the closely related shifts from blue- to white-collar occupations and from male to female employees."

6. In what ways does collective bargaining differ from most transactions between buyers and sellers? What is the nature of the "symbiotic relationship" which exists between a union and management?

7. What are some of the difficulties encountered in using maximizing models to explain trade union behavior? Specifically, using the elasticity of demand concept, explain how the goal of maximizing the wage bill might prompt a union to seek a wage cut.

8. How does Chamberlain define bargaining power from the union's point of view? From management's standpoint? Explain: "No agreement will be possible unless for at least one of the parties the cost of agreeing to the opponent's terms is less than the cost of disagreeing to those terms." Explain how coercive and persuasive tactics might be employed within Chamberlain's model.

9. Explain in terms of Chamberlain's model: "Bargaining power depends upon how much is demanded of the opponent." If there is no basis for agreement initially under the Chamberlain model, what developments might occur over time to create conditions favorable to settlement? Is it rational for a party to engage in coercive and persuasive tactics simultaneously?

10. Explain how a strike might occur even though a range of potential agreement exists.

11. Use Chamberlain's conception of a union's bargaining power to explain the rationale for each of the following union tactics:
    a. The union announces a strike vote wherein workers overwhelmingly endorse striking
    b. The union places a full-page newspaper ad explaining the reasonableness of its wage demand
    c. The union threatens to encourage a buyer's boycott of the firm's product
    d. The union pickets the firm
    e. The union promises to accept the removal of certain provisions of the old bargaining agreement which management claims impede productivity
    f. The union eliminates its demand for a 5-day increase in sick leaves
    g. The union reduces its hourly wage demand by $.20
    Indicate which of the above actions or tactics are coercive and which are persuasive.

12. "Negotiation deadlines and strikes play *positive* roles in collective bargaining." Do you agree? Explain.

13. How does the bargaining power of labor and management vary over the business cycle? What is the effect of industry structure upon the bargaining power of a union?
14. Explain the impact upon a union's bargaining power of (a) income maintenance programs and (b) federal commitment to maintain full employment.

SELECTED REFERENCES

BLOOM, GORDON F., and HERBERT R. NORTHRUP: *Economics of Labor Relations*, 9th ed. (Homewood, Ill.: Richard D. Irwin, Inc., 1981), pts. 2 and 3.

CHAMBERLAIN, NEIL W.: *A General Theory of Economic Process* (New York: Harper & Row, Publishers, 1955).

CODDINGTON, ALAN: *Theories of the Bargaining Process* (Chicago: Aldine Publishing Company, 1968).

ESTEY, MARTEN: *The Unions*, 3d ed. (New York: Harcourt Brace Jovanovich, 1981).

MULVEY, CHARLES: *The Economic Analysis of Trade Unions* (New York: St. Martin's Press, 1978).

ROWAN, RICHARD L. (ed.): *Readings in Labor Economics and Labor Relations*, 5th ed. (Homewood, Ill.: Richard D. Irwin, Inc., 1984), pts. 3 and 4.

STEVENS, CARL M.: *Strategy and Collective Bargaining Negotiation* (New York: McGraw-Hill Book Company, 1963).

T I M E   A N D   O N E - H A L F

THE AIRLINE UNIONS: DIMINISHED BARGAINING POWER?*

As suggested in this chapter, the economic conditions within an industry can critically affect the relative bargaining power of labor and management.

In the past decade the economic, legal, and institutional climate in which the nation's airlines operate has changed dramatically. These new product-market realities have had far-reaching effects upon relevant labor markets and, more pointedly, upon labor-management relations in the industry. The new environment has significantly and perhaps permanently reduced the bargaining power of the airline unions.

What are the major changes? Most importantly, the industry was substantially deregulated in 1978. Prior to deregulation the Civil Aeronautics Board in effect functioned as a legal cartel for domestic airlines. Specifically, the CAB limited entry to the industry, divided up the market among the various airlines by assigning routes, and controlled fares. With deregulation, however, new firms entered the industry, initiating a competitive scramble for the most lucrative routes and for customers. Competition shifted from service to price and the competitive "fare wars" became common. Many of the new

*This synopsis is based upon Herbert R. Northrup, "The New Employee-Relations Climate in Airlines," *Industrial and Labor Relations Review*, January 1983, pp. 167–181.

airlines were nonunion and consequently enjoyed a wage-cost advantage in comparison to the established unionized carriers. These competitive pressures were complicated by rising fuel costs, diminished traffic during the 1981-1982 recession, and the illegal strike of the Professional Air Traffic Controllers Organization (PATCO) in 1981.† The latter event was important because the federal government dismissed the striking air controllers and, as a consequence, the number of flights from the more congested terminals had to be curtailed. This new environment generated airline bankruptcies, forced consolidations, and, most importantly for our purposes, caused a significant decline in bargaining power for the various airline unions.

Prior to deregulation and the other events outlined above, airline unions possessed significant bargaining power relative to their employers. Airlines, after all, sell services which cannot be stockpiled. Furthermore, airline workers tend to be needed complements to capital rather than being easily substituted for by capital. Finally, even before deregulation, alternative carriers were usually available on the major trunk routes. Consequently, a work stoppage could be extremely costly to a given airline or, in terms of the Chamberlain bargaining model, management's perceived cost of disagreeing to union demands could be very high. Thus it is no surprise that, prior to deregulation and the other adverse developments, this union bargaining power resulted in wages and earnings for airline workers at or near the top of the interindustry scale. Flight attendants, mechanics, and ground crews, for example, realized earnings comparable to workers in the automobile, steel, and trucking industries. However, the new deregulated environment faced by the major airlines generated great pressure upon unions to moderate their demands, to accept wage and benefits cuts, and to eliminate restrictive work rules.

The airlines' changing labor relations with the Air Line Pilots Association (ALPA) is informative. ALPA members have perhaps a greater stake in the viability and prosperity of the airlines than any other group of workers in the industry. They are the highest paid and most prestigious group of workers, and their skills are not readily transferable to other industries. Furthermore, the ease with which new entrants to the deregulated industries were able to obtain qualified pilots made it clear that there existed no shortage of pilots. Hence, pilots for many major carriers have been forced to accept wage freezes or wage cuts (frequently on the order of 10 to 20 percent), to accept two- rather than three-member flight crews on many flights, to agree to the elimination of a variety of pay-for-not-working provisions, and to increase their flying time without additional pay. In varying degrees the other airline unions—the flight attendants, ground crews, and machinists—have had to make similar concessions. For example, in 1984 the Association of Flight Attendants at United Airlines agreed to a two-tier pay system under which pay rates for new workers were cut 25 percent during their first seven years of employment. Also in 1984 six unions at Republic Airlines agreed to a two-year extension of a 15 percent pay cut agreed to earlier. While a more prosperous economy and the gradual lifting of flight curtailments imposed by the PATCO strike may partially restore the bargaining power of the airline unions in the future, the continuing competition from the new nonunion carriers has probably precipitated a permanent diminution in their bargaining strength.

---

†For a perceptive discussion of the PATCO strike, see Herbert R. Northrup, "The Rise and Demise of PATCO," *Industrial and Labor Relations Review*, January 1984, pp. 167–184.

THE ECONOMIC IMPACT OF UNIONS

n the previous chapter we focused upon (1) the industrial, occupational and demographic characteristics of organized labor, (2) the institutional structure of the American labor movement, (3) the unique characteristics of collective bargaining negotiations, and (4) a well-known model of the negotiation process.

In this chapter we focus our attention upon the economic effects of unions and collective bargaining.[1] The three specific issues which we want to examine are as follows. First, are unions able to gain a wage advantage through collective bargaining? Other things being equal, do union workers in a given occupation receive higher wages than nonunion workers in the same occupation? And what of fringe benefits? Are they more or less generous when unions are present? Second, what are the implications of unions and collective bargaining for productivity and allocative efficiency? Is our economy more or less efficient because of the presence of unions? Third, what is the impact of union wage determination upon the distribution of earnings? Do unions cause wage income to be more or less equally distributed?

These three issues obviously do not exhaust the economic implications of unions which merit exploration. Hence, in Chapter 19 we will confront the very complex question of the impact of collective wage determination upon the price level. Similarly, one of the issues considered in Chapter 17 is whether unions have been able to increase the relative share of the national income going to labor.

THE UNION WAGE ADVANTAGE

Most people undoubtedly assume that union workers are paid more than nonunion workers. That is, they assume that unions gain a wage differential or *wage advantage* for their constituents. A union, after all, is able to deprive a firm of its

---

[1] Richard B. Freeman and James L. Medoff have recently done pioneering research on the various economic effects of unions. Hence, this chapter necessarily draws heavily upon their work. For a preliminary summary of their research findings, see ''The Two Faces of Unionism,'' *The Public Interest*, Fall 1979, pp. 398–415. A more detailed statement is found in *What Do Unions Do?* (New York: Basic Books, Publishers, Inc., 1984).

work force by striking and can thus impose associated costs upon the firm. Presumably an employer, within limits, will pay the "price" of higher wage rates to avoid the costs of a strike.

Preliminary Complications. But upon closer examination the issue is not so clear-cut. In the first place, envision a unionized employer in a perfectly (or at least a "highly") competitive industry. If rival firms in the industry are nonunion, other things being equal, this firm will *not* be able to survive if it pays a higher wage to its employees than competitors are paying to their nonunion workers. Despite its potential to impose strike costs on the employer, the union would be faced with the dilemma of "no wage advantage" or "no firm" in these circumstances! In addition to describing a situation wherein a union could not realize a wage advantage, this simple model implies two additional points. First, the model tells us why unions are anxious to organize not just single firms but entire industries. The United Automobile Workers' intense desire to organize workers of new automobile plants established by foreign manufacturers in the United States is prompted by much more than the goal of adding a few thousand workers to the UAW's ranks! Second, the model implies that unions may fare better in industries where product markets are imperfect, for example, the oligopolistic industries which dominate much of the manufacturing sector of our economy.

This leads us to a second complication. Suppose that we do find a positive association between the degree of unionization and the average level of wage rates in various industries. That is, we discover that strongly unionized industries do in fact pay higher wage rates than do weakly unionized industries. How do we know that unions are responsible for the higher wages? Put bluntly, do unions cause higher wages *or* are unions prone to organize industries that already pay high wages? The automobile industry, for example, was renowned for paying relatively high wages long before it was unionized in the late 1930s. In fact, one can cite considerations other than the presence of unions which might explain at least a part of the wage advantage which is enjoyed by highly unionized industries.[2] First, female workers generally constitute a larger proportion of the work force in weakly unionized industries than they do in strongly unionized industries. And we will find in Chapter 11 that women—due to discrimination and other considerations—are paid less than men. Hence, one can argue that at least some portion of the wage differential found between strongly and weakly unionized industries is due, not to the existence of unions, but to the differing demographic makeup of the work forces in these industries. Second, strongly unionized industries tend to have larger plants *and* to be more capital-intensive than weakly unionized industries. The fact that unionized plants tend to be larger raises the possibility that supervision may be more costly in such firms and that employers therefore seek out and hire "superior" workers who

[2]The following discussion is based upon Daniel J. B. Mitchell, *Unions, Wages, and Inflation* (Washington, D. C.: The Brookings Institution, 1980), pp. 83–85.

can work effectively with less supervision. Such workers would be paid relatively high wages even if the union were not present. Similarly, capital-intensive production often requires more highly skilled workers who naturally command higher wages.[3] Our basic point is that higher wages in unionized industries might be attributable—at least in part—to factors other than the existence of the union.

Measuring the Wage Advantage. Aside from the complications just discussed, there is also a basic conceptual problem in measuring the *pure* union-nonunion differential. This arises because unionization may affect wage rates in nonunion labor markets, pushing them upward or downward and creating a bias in the measurement of the union wage advantage.

To begin, the *pure union wage advantage A,* is defined as follows:

$$A = \frac{W_u - W_n}{W_n} \cdot 100 \tag{8-1}$$

where W_u is the union wage and W_n is the nonunion wage. The $(W_u - W_n)/W_n$ term is multiplied by 100 to express the union wage advantage as a percentage. Hence, if the union wage were \$6 per hour and the nonunion wage were \$5, the union wage advantage would be 20 percent $[(6 - 5)/5 \times 100]$.

Ideally, the union wage advantage should be determined under "laboratory conditions" wherein we compare union and nonunion wages with all other possible influences upon wages being held constant. Thus in Figure 8-1 we first would want to observe the level of wages "before" the presence of the union (W_n) and then to compare this with the wage rate "after" the union was added (W_u). We would then use the relevant numbers in our union wage advantage formula as just described. The problem, of course, is that we have no way of conducting such a controlled experiment. In particular, we cannot observe what the earnings of unionized workers–or for that matter, nonunionized workers– would be in a given labor market if the union did not exist. We must therefore make "real-world" comparisons of a more complex and tentative nature.

The best we can do in this regard is compare the wages of workers of a specific kind in unionized (or strongly unionized) markets with the wages of workers in nonunion (or weakly unionized) markets. But in making this kind of comparison our aforementioned conceptual difficulty intrudes. *Unions may influence the wage rates of nonunion workers as well as the wage rates of their own workers.* Furthermore, the potential influence of unions upon nonunion wages can take several different forms, so that the overall impact is ambiguous! We are theoretically uncertain whether an increase in union wages will cause nonunion wages to rise or fall. Let us briefly explore several different "effects" which describe

---

[3]Of course, one can push the causal relationship back one step further by arguing that highly unionized industries are capital-intensive *because* of union wage pressure which prompts employers to substitute capital for labor.

various means by which union wage setting may have an impact upon non-union wages.

1. Spillover effects. The *spillover effect* suggests that the higher wages achieved in the unionized sector of the labor market will be accompanied by a loss of jobs and that displaced workers will "spill over" into the nonunion sector and thereby depress nonunion wages.

The rudiments of the spillover effect are portrayed in Figure 8-2. Assume that both sectors are initially nonunion and that movement between the two sectors entails a common equilibrium wage rate of W_n for this type of labor. Now assume that sector 1 becomes unionized and that the union is successful in increasing the wage rate to W_u. We observe that the higher wage rate in this sector causes unemployment of $Q_1 Q_2$. The spillover effect is predicated on the assumption that all of these unemployed workers will seek and find employment in the nonunion sector. This movement of workers from the union to the nonunion sector will reduce the supply of labor in the union sector and increase the supply in the nonunion sector. If we assume downward flexibility of wages, then in time wages will fall in the nonunion sector to W_s.

To the extent that the spillover effect occurs, our **measured union wage advantage** will *overstate* the pure union wage advantage. This can be quickly grasped by comparing our hypothetical "laboratory experiment" of Figure 8-1 with the "real-world" comparison of Figure 8-2 embodying the spillover effect. Specifically, instead of comparing the union wage W_u with the nonunion wage W_n in Figure 8-1 to get the pure union wage advantage of 20 percent, we must compare the union wage W_u with the nonunion wage W_s. Because W_s is less than

FIGURE 8-1 THE UNION WAGE ADVANTAGE MEASURED UNDER IDEAL CONDITIONS
If we could compare wage rates in a given labor market, wherein all conditions were held constant except for the presence of the union, one could calculate a pure measure of the union's wage advantage. That pure advantage is $(W_u - W_n)/W_n \times 100$.

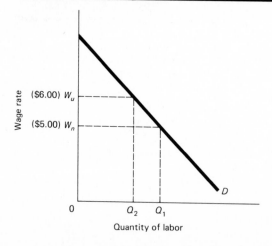

W_n due to the spillover effect, the measured wage advantage in this case is 50 percent [$(6 - 4)/4 \times 100$]. That is, because the spillover effect depresses observed nonunion wages, the measured union wage advantage is larger than the pure union wage advantage of 20 percent.

2. Threat effect. We shall find in Chapter 15 that some labor economists, labeled "institutionalists," argue that market forces, as described by the spillover effect, are largely subverted or set aside by collective bargaining and that wage rates are determined largely on the basis of "equitable comparisons." This implies that wages for any group of workers will be determined mainly on the basis of wages being paid to comparable workers.

More specifically, in contrast to the spillover effect, the ***threat effect*** holds that unions will have a *positive* effect upon the wage rates of nonunion workers in that occupation. The reasoning is that nonunion employers will feel increasingly threatened with unionization when workers in union firms obtain wage increases. An enlarged union-nonunion differential will increase the incentive for the workers in the nonunion firms to organize. To meet this threat, the nonunion employer will grant wage increases. Hence, if we start from the W_n equilibrium wage in both sectors once again (Figure 8-2), the wage increase from $5 to $6 resulting from the unionization of sector 1 might *increase* nonunion wages in Sector 2 from $5 to, say, $5.50. Now the measured union wage advantage will be about 9 percent [$(6 - 5.50)/5.50 \times 100$] rather than the pure advantage of 20 percent (Figure 8-1). To recapitulate: If the threat effect causes union wage increases to pull up nonunion wages, then the measured union wage advantage will *understate* the pure union advantage.

FIGURE 8-2 THE SPILLOVER EFFECT AND THE MEASURED WAGE ADVANTAGE
If a union is able to raise wage rates from W_n to W_u in sector 1, it will reduce employment by Q_1Q_2. Assuming downward wage flexibility, the reemployment of these workers in sector 2 will reduce wages there from W_n to W_s. The measured union wage advantage will be $(W_u - W_s)/W_s \times 100$, which overstates the pure advantage of $(W_u - W_n)/W_n \times 100$.

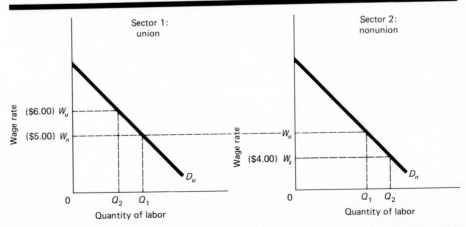

3. Other effects. Our brief discussions of the spillover and threat effects do not exhaust all of the possible avenues by which union wages may influence nonunion wages. For example, there may be a *product-market effect* whose impact would be similar to that of the threat effect. The product-market effect works as follows: a "union pay increase, through its effect on costs and prices, tends to shift demand to firms in the nonunion sector. The added demand for nonunion output is translated into added demand for nonunion labor, which could have a pay-raising influence."[4] Other economists question the relevance of the spillover effect by citing the phenomenon of *wait unemployment*. The argument here is that when the union achieves a wage increase in sector 1 of Figure 8-2, the resulting unemployed workers may well remain in sector 1 hoping to be recalled to their high-paying jobs. Encouraged perhaps by the availability of unemployment insurance, they might prefer the probability of being recalled at higher union wages to the alternative of accepting lower-wage jobs in the nonunion sector. If wait unemployment occurs, the downward spillover pressure on nonunion wages simply does not occur to any great degree in sector 2. This implies that the measured union wage advantage more accurately portrays the pure wage advantage. There is also the notion of the *superiorworker effect*. The idea here is that the higher wages paid by union firms will cause workers to queue up for these "good" union jobs. Given the availability of many job seekers, unionized employers will carefully screen these prospective workers for those who have the greatest innate ability, the most motivation, the least need for costly supervision, and other worker traits which contribute to high productivity. This means that in time high-wage union firms may acquire superior work forces in comparison to nonunion firms. Thus, in seeking to measure the union wage advantage accurately, the researcher is confronted with determining how much of an observed union wage advantage is due to the presence of the union as an institution and how much it reflects the presence of more highly productive workers in the unionized firms. To the extent that "superior workers" acquire the high-wage union jobs, the measured union wage advantage would be *overstated*. Finally, a part of the union wage advantage may be a "compensating wage differential" (Chapter 12), that is, a wage differential which compensates for the fewer amenities in the workplace encountered by union workers. Alternatively stated, some portion of the wage advantage enjoyed by union members may be compensation for the fact that their working conditions are more structured, working hours are less flexible, and the work pace is faster.[5]

Empirical Evidence. Given some appreciation of the practical and conceptual difficulties involved in estimating the union wage advantage, let us now turn to the available empirical evidence. Our approach will be to first examine in Table 8-1 a chronological listing of a number of important studies which have at-

---

[4]Ibid., p. 87.

[5]Greg J. Duncan and Frank P. Stafford, "Do Union Members Receive Compensating Wage Differentials?" *American Economic Review*, June 1980, pp. 355–371.

TABLE 8-1

Estimates of the Union Wage Advantage for the United States

Author	Time Period	Subject of Study (By Industry, Occupation, Race or Sex)	Union Wage Advantage (%)		
Lewis	1923–1929	*Industrial workers*	15–20		
	1931–1933		25+		
	1939–1941		10–20		
	1945–1949		0–5		
	1957–1958		10–15		
Weiss	1959	*Craftsmen*	7–8		
		Operatives	6–8		
Ashenfelter	1961–1966	*Firemen*	6–16		
Stafford	1966	*Craftsmen*	24		
		Operatives	26		
		Laborers	52		
		Clerical workers	18		
		Professional workers	−8		
Boskin	1967	*Professional workers*	19.0		
		Managers	−5.3		
		Clerical workers	9.1		
		Salespeople	2.3		
		Craftsmen	15.5		
		Operatives	15.2		
		Service workers	7.4		
		Laborers	24.7		
Schmenner	1962–1970	*Teachers*	12–14		
		Firefighters/Police	15		
Personick	1972	*Carpenters*	35–50		
		Laborers	40–65		
		Electricians/Plumbers	55–70		
		Cement Masons	35–50		
Ryscavage	1973	*All workers*	12		
		White men	8		
		Black men	27		
		White women	22		
		Black women	19		
Ashenfelter	1967		1967	1973	1975
	1973	*All workers*	12.0	15.0	17.0
	1975	*White men*	10.0	15.5	16.0
		Black men	21.5	22.5	22.5
		White women	14.0	13.0	17.0
		Black women	6.0	13.0	17.0

Source: C. J. Parsley, "Labor Union Effects on Wage Gains: A Survey of Recent Literature," *Journal of Economic Literature,* March 1980, Table 1a, pp. 6–7, condensed and rearranged.

tempted to measure the union wage advantage. Then we will employ Tables 8-2 and 8-3 to consider two recent studies which suggest that the union wage advantage has increased in the past decade or so.

Although there are no unassailable generalizations to be drawn from Table 8-1, the following comments seem to be reasonably defensible.

1. The most general observation is that unions almost invariably achieve a wage advantage for their members, but the size of that gain varies greatly according to industry, occupation, race, and sex.
2. Lewis's pioneering work[6] suggests that, although the union wage advantage varies over time, it is correct to say that union workers enjoyed a wage advantage on the order of 10 to 15 percent over the 1923–1958 period he examined.
3. Lewis's research also suggests that the union wage advantage varies cyclically. Specifically, the advantage tends to increase during depression (1931–1933 in Table 8-1) as union contracts provide a bulwark against wage cuts which is unavailable to nonunion workers. Conversely, during periods of

[6]H. Gregg Lewis, *Unionism and Relative Wages in the United States* (Chicago: University of Chicago Press, 1963).

TABLE 8-2

Union Wage Effects in Selected Industries, by Source of Unionization Data, 1974

Source of Unionization Data and Type of Compensation	Mean Union-Nonunion Compensation Difference as Percent of Nonunion Compensation
Contract file (77 industries)	
Straight-time hourly earnings	28
Private fringe benefits	80
Total compensation	33
Compensation survey (73 industries)	
Straight-time hourly earnings	28
Private fringe benefits	83
Total compensation	33
Current population survey (60 industries)	
Straight-time hourly earnings	31
Private fringe benefits	100
Total compensation	36

Source: Daniel J. B. Mitchell, *Unions, Wages, and Inflation* (Washington, D.C.: The Brookings Institution, 1980), p. 95.

demand-pull inflation, such as the immediate post-World War II period (1945–1949 in Table 8-1), the union wage advantage diminishes. The likely explanation is that during such periods of sharp and unanticipated inflation, union wages are locked into bargaining agreements which cannot be readily adjusted upward. At the same time, nonunion wages are free to respond to the bouyant labor market, and therefore nonunion wages rise relative to union wages.

4. A comparison of Personick's results with the remainder of Table 8-1 suggests that craft unions in the construction industry have achieved much larger than average union wage advantages.

5. The work by Ryscavage and the 1967–1975 study by Ashenfelter both suggest that black males tend to gain more from being union members than do other racial or sexual groups.[7] We will explore this point in more detail in Chapter 11.

6. The Stafford and Boskin studies suggest that unions achieve larger wage gains for blue-collar workers (craftsmen, operatives, laborers) than they do for white-collar workers (clerical workers, salespeople).

[7]More recent research by Mitchell, op. cit., pp. 100–101, suggests that the union wage gains for *both* black males and black females are greater than those for white males and white females.

TABLE 8-3

Estimates of the Impact of Unions on Wages

Source of Estimates:	Year	Number of Observations	Approximate Percentage Gain in Wages Due to Collective Bargaining
Data on individuals:			
May Current Population Survey, Bureau of Labor Statistics	1979	16,728	21
Panel Study of Income Dynamics, University of Michigan	1970–1979	11,445	26
Older Men, National Longitudinal Survey, Ohio State University	1976	1,922	25
Younger Men, National Longitudinal Survey	1976	2,335	32
Mature Women, National Longitudinal Survey	1977	1,724	25
Younger Women, National Longitudinal Survey	1978	2,068	21
Data on establishments:			
Expenditures for Employee Compensation Survey, Bureau of Labor Statistics	1972–1976	15,574	27

Source: Richard B. Freeman and James L. Medoff, *What Do Unions Do?* (New York: Basic Books, Inc., Publishers, 1984), p. 46.

Using Lewis's generalization that the union wage advantage was on the order of 10 to 15 percent during the 1923–1958 period as a benchmark, two recent studies suggest that the union wage advantage may have widened in the 1970s. Table 8-2 presents results derived from three different data sets by Mitchell. His estimates suggest that for 1974 the straight-time hourly earnings of union workers were 28 to 31 percent greater than those of nonunion workers. When the more generous fringe benefits accruing to union workers are taken into account, the union compensation advantage increases to 33 to 36 percent. Noting that these data are "probably upwardly biased," Mitchell settles for the conclusion that the union wage advantage in the 1970s was on the order of 20 to 30 percent. Similarly, Table 8-3 shows the union wage advantage calculated from a series of data sets for individuals and one set for enterprises by Freeman and Medoff. As did Mitchell, they conclude that "in the 1970s the archetypical union wage effect was on the order of 20 to 30 percent."[8]

The conclusion that the union wage advantage increased in the 1970s is of interest for at least two reasons. First, it enhances the possibility that union wage determination may contribute to inflation, a matter which we will examine in depth in Chapter 19. Second, given that the 1970s was the decade of "the great inflation," a widening union wage advantage would seem to be at odds with Lewis's previously cited conclusion that the union-nonunion wage differential declines during inflation. However, upon closer scrutiny we find that the inflations of the immediate post-World War II period and the 1970s were substantially different. The 1945–1949 inflation was essentially an *unanticipated* demand-pull inflation. The inflation of the 1970s differed from this in two important respects. First, "the great inflation" actually began in the mid-1960s and came to be *anticipated* or expected in the 1970s. Hence, unions built the expectation of continuing inflation into their wage demands. In fact, this expectation came to be institutionalized by incorporating cost-of-living adjustments (COLAs) into more and more bargaining agreements. Second, the 1970s was an era of stagflation, that is, of periods wherein real gross national product was stagnating and unemployment rising, despite the occurrence of price inflation. Thus it is possible that union workers, operating under long-term contracts which embodied deferred wage increases, were better able in the 1970s to protect their wages from the effects of loose labor markets than were nonunion workers.[9] Given these differences between the 1945–1949 inflation and the inflation of the 1970s, Lewis's conclusion, on the one hand, and the conclusions of Mitchell and of Freeman and Medoff, on the other, are not necessarily incompatible.

Finally, it is significant to note that Freeman and Medoff do *not* feel that the apparent increase in the union wage advantage is a permanent phenomenon. They observe that the increase in the union-nonunion differential has been a serious threat to many union jobs and that the much-publicized union "givebacks" of the early 1980s reflect a return to more normal and sustainable union-

[8]Freeman and Medoff, *What Do Unions Do?* p. 46.
[9]Ibid., pp. 53–54.

nonunion differentials.[10] These givebacks are considered in detail in this chapter's Time and One-Half section.

Total Compensation: Wages plus Fringe Benefits. We would be remiss not to examine the impact of unions upon fringe benefits. *Fringe benefits* include public (legally mandated) programs such as social security, unemployment compensation, and workers' compensation as well as a wide variety of private non-mandatory programs, including private pensions, medical and dental insurance, paid vacations and sick leave, and so forth. *Total compensation* is simply the sum of wage earnings and the value of fringe benefits. *If* union workers enjoy more generous fringe benefits than nonunion workers, then the overall economic advantage which union workers have over nonunion workers is obviously greater than the wage advantage suggests. On the other hand, *if* union wage gains are realized at the expense of fringe benefits and nonunion workers receive larger fringe benefits, then the union wage advantage overstates the economic advantage of union workers.

Fringe benefit growth. The first point to note is that there has been significant overall growth historically in the importance of fringe benefits as a component of total worker compensation. In Table 8-4 we find that fringe benefits for all workers—union and nonunion combined—have expanded from about 1 percent of total compensation in 1929 to 17 percent in 1984, with much of the growth occurring in the past 15 years. Absolute growth has been even more dramatic.

[10]Ibid., pp. 54–57.

TABLE 8-4

The Absolute and Relative Growth of Fringe Benefits, 1929–1984

Year	Supplements* to Wages and Salaries (Billions of Dollars)	Supplements as a Percent of Total Compensation
1929	0.6	1.2
1939	2.1	4.4
1949	6.6	4.7
1959	20.6	7.4
1969	57.2	10.0
1979	220.7	15.1
1984	369.0	17.0

*Supplements include employer contributions to social insurance and workers' compensation and to private pension, health, and welfare funds. Data are in current dollars.

Source: Economic Report of the President, 1985.

At first glance the growth of fringe benefits is surprising because most fringes are *in-kind benefits*; that is, they take the form of a specific kind of good or service. A moment's reflection suggests that a worker (consumer) should be better off with—and therefore would prefer—an additional dollar's worth of (cash) wages rather than an additional dollar's worth of some specific fringe benefit. The reason for this is that $1 in cash wages represents generalized purchasing power which can be spent on $1 worth of whatever good or service is most preferred by (yields the most marginal utility to) the consumer. An in-kind fringe benefit, on the other hand, ties the individual to the particular good or service and, in fact, that good or service may provide little or no marginal utility or satisfaction to particular workers. An on-the-job day care center yields little satisfaction to an unmarried worker or to an older worker whose children are grown. An older worker with false teeth may derive little or no utility from a program of dental insurance.

Causes of growth. The question then is how the apparent preference for cash wage income rather than in-kind fringe benefits can be squared with the growth of fringes as shown in Table 8-4? The answer involves two major considerations.

1. *Tax advantages.* Undoubtedly of greatest consequence, certain fringe benefits entail substantial tax advantages to both workers and employers. For example, workers do *not* pay taxes on the deferred income benefits embodied in private pension plans until these benefits are actually received. Because the worker's earned income will fall to zero at retirement, the income provided by the pension plan will be taxed at lower rates than would the same amount paid as wages during the worker's active work life. In short, pensions are a means of deferring income to achieve lower tax rates. The after-tax value of $1 of pension contributions is perceived to be greater than the after-tax value of $1 of current wage income. Similarly, premiums paid by employers for worker health and life insurance are not taxed at all. From the employer's standpoint, the amounts a firm must pay as social security taxes and as workers' compensation premiums are based upon total *wages* paid, not total compensation. Hence, these tax payments are reduced by increasing fringes and reducing cash wages as components of a given total amount of compensation.

2. *Scale economies.* There are usually substantial economies of scale in the collective purchase of fringe benefits which lower their prices to buyers. In particular, the administrative costs and agent fees are much less in purchasing medical, life, disability, or dental insurance on a group basis rather than an individual one. Like tax advantages, these "discount prices" increase the utility derived from each dollar spent on fringes and make them more attractive to workers.

Still other reasons may help explain the absolute and relative growth of fringe benefits. Employers who are interested in protecting their training investments in workers and in reducing their recruiting and training costs may regard fringe benefits as a means of tying workers to their firms and thereby reducing turnover. Expenditures on health insurance foster a healthier and more productive labor force and reduce sick leave. It may also be that certain fringe benefits are quite income-elastic; that is, they involve such services as medical and dental care whose purchases are quite sensitive to increases in income. Hence, as worker incomes have grown historically, it is not surprising that the "purchase" of such fringes has expanded.

Evidence. We now return to the basic question: How do union fringe benefits compare to those of nonunion workers? The answer is that union workers enjoy a greater variety and higher overall level of fringe benefits than do nonunion workers. A glance back at Table 8-2 is revealing. Column 1 indicates that, while union workers in the first ("contract file") sampling received wage rates 28 percent higher than nonunion workers, their private fringe benefits were 80 percent higher![11] Hence, total compensation of union workers was 33 percent greater than that of nonunion workers. You will observe that the other two samplings ("compensation survey" and "current population survey") show the same general results. More recent research done by Freeman and Medoff confirm that unions gain a large fringe benefit advantage than they do a wage advantage.[12]

Why do union members receive more generous fringe benefits than nonunion workers? Several interrelated reasons may be involved. First, union fringes may be higher for the same reason that union wage rates are higher. The union is able to deprive management of its work force, and the employer is willing to pay both higher wages *and* larger fringe benefits to avoid the costs of a strike. Second, union workers, by virtue of their higher earnings, may simply choose to "buy" more fringes than do lower-income nonunion workers. Third, as a collective-voice institution, a union may formulate fringe benefit proposals, inform its constituents of the details of such proposals, and crystallize worker preferences; the union then communicates these preferences to management. Finally, older workers are usually more active in the internal politics of a union and are therefore more influential in determining union goals. These older workers are typically more interested in pensions and insurance programs—and the tax advantages associated with them—than are younger workers.

EFFICIENCY AND PRODUCTIVITY

Are unions a positive or a negative force insofar as economic efficiency and productivity are concerned? How do unions affect the allocation of resources?

---

[11]Public (legally required) fringes, such as social security taxes and unemployment insurance premiums, are excluded in the comparisons of Table 8-2 because they obviously apply to union and nonunion employers alike.

[12]Freeman and Medoff, *What Do Unions Do?* chap. 4.

While there is a great deal of disagreement as to the efficiency aspects of unionism, it is instructive to consider some of the avenues through which unions might affect efficiency both negatively and positively. We will consider the negative view first.

Negative View. There are essentially three basic means by which unions might exert a negative impact upon efficiency.

1. Featherbedding and work rules. Some unions have undoubtedly diminished productivity growth by engaging in "make-work" or "featherbedding" practices and resisting the introduction of output-increasing machinery and equipment. These productivity-reducing practices often come into being against a backdrop of technological change. That is, labor and management may agree to a crew size which is reasonable and appropriate at the time the agreement is concluded. But labor-saving technology may then emerge which renders the crew "too large." The union is likely to resist the potential loss of jobs. For example, for many years the Brotherhood of Locomotive Firemen and Engineers was able to retain a fireman on train crews, even though his function was eliminated by the shift from steam to diesel engines. Similarly, union painters sometimes eschewed the use of spray guns and in some instances limited the width of paint brushes. In recent years, the typographers' unions have resisted the introduction of computers in setting type. Historically, the musicians' union insisted upon oversized orchestras for musical shows and required that a union standby orchestra be paid by employers using nonunion orchestras.

More generally, one can argue that unions are responsible for the establishment of work rules and practices which are not conducive to efficient production. For example, under seniority rules workers may be promoted in accordance with length of employment, rather than efficiency. Also, unions may impose jurisdictional restrictions upon the kinds of jobs which workers may perform. For example, sheetmetal workers or bricklayers may be prohibited from performing the simple carpentry work which is often associated with their jobs. Observance of such rules means, in this instance, that unneeded and underutilized carpenters must be available. Finally, it is often contended that unions constrain managerial prerogatives to establish work schedules, determine production targets, and freely make the myriad of decisions which contribute to productive efficiency.

This recitation of reasons why unions might impede efficiency merits modification in two respects. On the one hand, one must not make the mistake of assuming that productivity will necessarily be enhanced by "speeding up the assembly line." A speedup may in fact cause workers to tire and become demoralized, and hence be *less* efficient. On the other hand, it is also incorrect to associate featherbedding, unnecessarily large work crews, make-work rules and the like, solely with unionized workers. While unions may be responsible for codifying and enforcing such practices, the practices themselves are quite common to both union and nonunion sectors of the economy. Peer pressure and the threat of social ostracism can be as effective as a clause in a collective bargaining agreement in controlling the pace of production.[13]

2. Strikes. A second means by which unions may adversely affect efficiency is through strikes. If union and management reach an impasse in their negotiations, a strike will result and the firm's production will cease for the strike's duration. The firm will forgo sales and profits and workers will sacrifice income.

Simple statistics on strike activity suggest that strikes are relatively rare and the associated aggregate economic losses are relatively minimal. Table 8-5 provides data on major work stoppages, defined as those involving 1000 or more workers and lasting at least one full day or one work shift. Given that an estimated 80,000 collective bargaining agreements are negotiated each year, the number of major work stoppages is surprisingly small. Furthermore, most strikes last only a few days. Hence, we find in column 4 that for the 1960–1984 period, the amount of work time lost because of strikes has been consistently far less than one-half of 1 percent of total work time. In fact, over this period the amount of work time lost is typically less than two-tenths of 1 percent of total work time! This loss is the equivalent of 4 hours per worker per year, which is less than 5 minutes per worker per week![14]

But these data on time lost from work stoppages can be misleading as a measure of the costliness of a strike. On the one hand, employers in the struck industry may have anticipated the strike and worked their labor force overtime to accumulate inventories in order to supply customers during the strike period. This means that the overall loss of work time, production, profits, and wages is less than the work-time loss figures suggest. Similarly, other nonstruck producers in an industry may have increased their output to offset the loss of production by those firms engaged in a strike. In other words, while a strike may impose significant losses upon participants, the total *output* loss to the industry or to society at large may be minuscule or nonexistent. Note, however, that the production adjustments made in anticipation of, or as a consequence of, a strike may entail some *efficiency* losses. If firms which suffered a strike were able to anticipate perfectly the loss of output and sales and therefore accumulate inventories prior to the strike, this additional production would likely entail the overutilization of productive facilities and, hence, higher costs (less productive efficiency) per unit of output. Similar efficiency losses may be incurred by firms replacing the output of the firm that is struck. While the data on worker days lost because of strikes may overstate the output loss, a consequent efficiency loss may be concealed.

Furthermore, the amount of production and income lost because of a strike will be greater than that suggested by work-time loss data when a work stoppage in a particular industry disrupts production in associated industries. That is,

---

[13] See Paul A. Weinstein, (ed.), *Featherbedding and Technological Change*, (Boston: D. C. Heath and Company, 1965).

[14] Marten Estey, *The Unions*, 3d ed. (New York: Harcourt Brace Jovanovich, Inc., 1981), p. 140.

nonstriking workers in related industries may lose work time and the economy may lose their output if a strike deprives these industries of essential inputs and thereby forces them to curtail or cease operations. As a broad generalization, the adverse effects of a strike upon nonstriking firms and customers are likely to be greater when services are involved and less when products are involved. As Estey has pointed out, the impact on the public of strikes in durable goods industries tends to be negligible. For example, although the General Motors strike of 1970 resulted in the loss of 17.8 million worker days and contributed to an unusually high national work-time loss figure of .29 percent for loss of work time in that year (Table 8-5), the consuming public was not severely affected. The public was able to buy other makes of cars or purchase used cars which were

TABLE 8-5

Major Work Stoppages in the United States, 1960–1984

| | | | Days Idle | |
Year	(1) Work Stoppages (Number)	(2) Workers Involved (Number in Thousands)	(3) Number (in Thousands)	(4) Percent of Estimated Total Working Time
1960	222	896	13,260	.09
1961	195	1,031	10,140	.07
1962	211	793	11,760	.08
1963	181	512	10,020	.07
1964	246	1,183	16,220	.11
1965	268	999	15,140	.10
1966	321	1,300	16,000	.10
1967	381	2,192	31,320	.18
1968	392	1,855	35,567	.20
1969	412	1,576	29,397	.16
1970	381	2,468	52,761	.29
1971	298	2,516	35,538	.19
1972	250	975	16,764	.09
1973	317	1,400	16,260	.08
1974	424	1,796	31,809	.16
1975	235	965	17,563	.09
1976	231	1,519	23,962	.12
1977	298	1,212	21,258	.10
1978	219	1,006	23,774	.11
1979	235	1,021	20,409	.09
1980	187	795	20,844	.09
1981	145	729	16,908	.07
1982	96	656	9,061	.04
1983	81	909	17,461	.08
1984	62	376	8,499	.04

Source: Department of Labor, *Current Wage Developments,* March 1985, pp. 41–42.

readily available.[15] And, of course, within limits the purchase of consumer durables such as autos is postponable. In contrast, a strike of a major airline or a public transit system might impose significant economic costs upon consumers, workers, and businesses who are not party to the strike.

Overall it is appropriate to say that on the average the costs imposed upon the immediate parties to a strike and upon the general public are not as great as one might surmise. A recent study of some sixty-three manufacturing industries over the 1955-1977 period concluded that strike costs were significant in only nineteen of these industries.[16] Furthermore, in these nineteen industries the amount of output lost was typically a small fraction of 1 percent of total annual output. The ability of struck firms to draw upon inventories and the capacity of nonstruck firms to increase their output apparently make industry output losses minimal.

3. Wage advantage and labor misallocation. A third major avenue through which unions may adversely affect efficiency is the wage advantage itself. This can be easily envisioned through reconsideration and extension of the spillover model in Figure 8-2.[17] In Figure 8-3 we have drawn (for simplicity's sake) identical labor demand curves for the unionized and nonunion sectors of the labor market for some particular kind of labor. We assume that the relevant product market is purely competitive so that the labor demand curves reflect not only marginal revenue product (MRP), but also value of marginal product (VMP).[18] If there is no union present, then the wage rate which would result from competition in the hire of labor is W_n. Now assume a union comes into being in sector 1 and increases the wage rate from W_n to W_u. In accordance with our spillover effect analysis, the result is that the $Q_1'Q_2'$ workers who lose their jobs in the union sector move to nonunion sector 2 where we assume they secure employment. These additional workers depress the wage rate in the nonunion sector 2 from W_n to W_s.

Because we have kept the level of employment unchanged, this simple model allows us to isolate the efficiency or allocative effect of the union wage differential. The area $Q_2'abQ_1'$ represents the loss of national output caused by the $Q_1'Q_2'$ employment decline in the union sector. This area is simply the sum of the VMPs—the total contribution to the national output—of the workers displaced by the W_n to W_u wage increase achieved by the union. As these workers spill over into nonunion sector 2 and are reemployed, they add to the national output the

[15]Ibid., pp. 140–141.

[16]George R. Neumann and Melvin W. Reder, "Output and Strike Activity in U. S. Manufacturing: How Large Are the Losses?" *Industrial and Labor Relations Review*, January 1984, pp. 197–211.

[17]The reader should be forewarned that the basic analysis which follows will reappear in different contexts in the discussion of the minimum wage in Chapter 10 (see Figure 10-5) and in the examination of the economic effects of worker migration in Chapter 14 (see Figure 14-2).

[18]Recall from Chapter 5 that MRP measures the amount that an additional worker adds to a firm's total revenue, while VMP indicates the value of a worker's extra output to society. Stated differently, VMP tells us what an extra worker contributes to the national output.

amount indicated by the Q_1cdQ_2 area. Because $Q'_2abQ'_1$ exceeds Q_1cdQ_2, there is a net loss of national output. More precisely, because the shaded areas are equal in each diagram, the net loss of output attributable to the union wage advantage is equal to area $c'abd'$ as shown in the union sector diagram. Since the same amount of employed labor is now producing a smaller output, labor is obviously misallocated and inefficiently used. Viewed from a slightly different perspective, *after* the spillover of Q_1Q_2 workers from the union to the nonunion sector has occurred, workers will be paid a wage rate equal to their VMPs in both sectors. But the VMPs of the union workers will be higher than the VMPs of the nonunion workers. The economy will always benefit from a larger national output when any given type of labor is reallocated from a relatively low-VMP use to a relatively high-VMP use. But, given the union's presence and its ability to maintain the W_u wage rate in its sector, this reallocation from sector 2 to 1 will not occur.

We must acknowledge that our model of the allocative inefficiency stemming from a union wage advantage is very simplified. In the "real world" the degree of resource misallocation could be greater or less than our model suggests. For example, recalling our earlier comments on "wait unemployment," what if some of those workers who lost their jobs because of higher wages in the union sector decided to remain in that sector in the hope of reemployment? The obvious consequence is a net loss of output in excess of $c'abd'$ in Figure 8-3. The reason? While output would decline by area $Q'_2abQ'_1$ in the union sector, it would increase by *less than* Q'_1cdQ_2 in the nonunion sector. In the extreme, if the entire Q_1Q_2 displaced workers remained unemployed in the union sector, the

FIGURE 8-3 THE EFFECT OF THE UNION WAGE ADVANTAGE ON THE ALLOCATION OF LABOR
The higher wage W_u which the union achieves in sector 1 causes the displacement of $Q'_1Q'_2$ workers. The reemployment of these workers in nonunion sector 2 reduces the wage rate there from W_n to W_s. The associated loss of output in the union sector is the area $Q'_2abQ'_1$, while the gain in the nonunion sector is only area Q_1cdQ_2. Because the shaded areas are equal in each diagram, the net loss of output is area $c'abd'$.

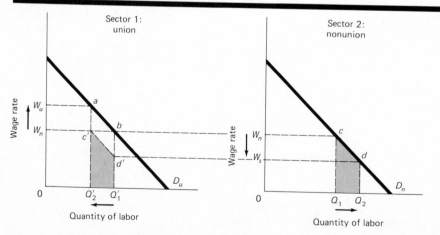

loss of output to society would be $Q_2'abQ_1'$. A second and related point is that our model understates the loss of output because it implicitly assumes that workers instantly and costlessly shift from the union to the nonunion sector. As Chapter 18 will reveal, job search by unemployed workers takes time and entails both out-of-pocket costs (paying for advertisements and for the services of employment agencies) and opportunity costs (earnings forgone during the search period). And, as we shall discover in Chapter 14, the geographic movement which may be involved in shifting from the union to the nonunion sector is also costly. On the other hand, our discussion tends to overstate the detrimental effect which unions may have upon allocative efficiency to the extent that unions engage in bargaining with monopsonistic employers. Recall from the discussion of the bilateral monopoly case in Figure 6-10 that union wage determination may in effect "correct" the underallocation of labor resources which a monopsonistic employer would find profitable.

How large is the output loss due to the allocative inefficiency associated with the wage gains of unions? In a pioneering study Rees assumed a 15 percent union wage advantage and estimated that approximately .14 percent—only about one-seventh of 1 percent—of the national output was lost![19] Similarly, a recent estimate by Freeman and Medoff indicates that "union monpoly wage gains cost the economy .02 to .04 percent of gross national product, which in 1980 amounted to about $5 to $10 billion dollars or $20.00 to $40.00 per person."[20]

Positive View. Other economists take the position that on balance unions make a positive contribution to productivity and efficiency.

1. Investment and technological progress. One may carry Figure 8-3's discussion of the labor misallocation that stems from the union wage advantage a step further and argue that union wage increases may *accelerate* the substitution of capital for labor and *hasten* the search for cost-reducing (productivity-increasing) technologies. That is to say, when faced with higher production costs due to the union wage advantage, employers will be prompted to reduce costs by using more machinery and by seeking improved production techniques which use less of both labor and capital per unit of output. In fact, if the product market is reasonably competitive, a unionized firm with labor costs which are, say, 15 to 20 percent higher than nonunion competitors will simply not survive unless productivity can be raised. In short, union wage pressure may inadvertently generate managerial actions which increase national productivity.

[19]Albert Rees, "The Effects of Unions on Resource Allocation," *The Journal of Law and Economics*, October 1963, pp. 69–78. More recently Robert H. DeFina has estimated that a 15 percent union wage advantage would result in only a .08 to .09 percentage loss of output. See his "Unions, Relative Wages, and Economic Efficiency," *Journal of Labor Economics*, October 1983, pp. 408–429.

[20]Freeman and Medoff, *What Do Unions Do?* p. 57.

2. Unions as a collective voice. Freeman and Medoff have recently stressed the view that on balance unions contribute to rising productivity within firms through their effects upon labor turnover, worker security, and managerial efficiency.[21] In their view the positive impact of unions upon productivity occurs in part because unions function as a *collective voice* for its members in resolving disputes, improving working conditions, and so forth. If a group of workers is dissatisfied with its conditions of employment, it has two potential means of response. These are the "exit mechanism" and the "voice mechanism." The *exit mechanism* simply refers to the use of the labor market—by leaving or exiting the present job in search of a better one—as a means of reacting to "bad" employers and "bad" working conditions. In contrast, the *voice mechanism* entails communication between workers and the employer to improve working conditions and resolve worker grievances. It may well be risky for *individual* workers to express their dissatisfaction to employers because employers may retaliate by firing such workers as "troublemakers." But unions can provide workers with a *collective* voice to communicate problems and grievances to management and to press for their satisfactory resolution. According to Freeman and Medoff, unions can positively affect productivity, not only through the voice mechanism, but in a variety of other ways.

Reduced turnover. There is substantial evidence that unionization reduces job quits and turnover. On the one hand, the collective voice of the union may be effective in correcting job dissatisfactions which otherwise would be "resolved" by workers through the exit mechanism of changing jobs. On the other hand, other things being the same, the union wage advantage will tend to reduce the quit rates of union workers.

A variety of studies by Freeman suggest that the decline in quit rates attributable to unionism is very substantial, ranging from 31 to 65 percent.[22] A lower quit rate increases efficiency by giving rise to a more experienced labor force within unionized firms and by reducing the firm's recruitment, screening, and hiring costs. Furthermore, the reduced turnover makes investments in specific training by employers more attractive. Reduced turnover increases the likelihood that the employer will capture a positive return on training (Chapter 4).

Seniority and informal training. Because of union insistence upon the primacy of seniority in such matters as promotion and layoff, worker security is enhanced. Given this security, workers are more willing to pass on their job knowledge and skills to new or subordinate workers through informal on-the-job training (Chapter 15). Obviously, this enhances labor quality and productivity.[23]

Managerial performance. Union wage pressure may precipitate a *shock effect* which is favorable to productivity. Confronted with a strong union and higher

---

[21]Freeman and Medoff, *What Do Unions Do?*, chap. 11.

[22]Ibid., pp. 95–96.

[23]The "lifetime" job security which some Japanese firms provide for a portion of their labor forces is often cited as an important determinant of their rapid productivity growth.

wage demands, firms may be forced to adopt better personnel and production methods to meet the union's wage demands and maintain profitability. For example, in his study of the impact of unionization on productivity in the cement industry, Clark observes that after unionization plant management was improved.[24] He documents a managerial shift to "a more professional, business-like approach to labor relations." Furthermore, after unionization greater stress was placed upon production goals and the monitoring of worker performance. "Perhaps the most cogent description of the differences in the management process before and after unionization was given by a plant manager who remarked: '. . . before the union this place was run like a family; now we run it like a business.'"[25] Finally, it is worth noting that collective bargaining provides a potential avenue of communication through which the union can point out to management ways of enhancing productivity.

Mixed Empirical Evidence. Freeman and Medoff have surveyed empirical evidence on the union productivity issue and find it generally supportive of their position that unionism has had a positive effect on productivity. In these studies, which are summarized in Table 8-6, attempts were made to control for labor quality, capital-labor ratios, and other variables aside from unionization which might have contributed to productivity differences. The dramatic turnaround from a substantial positive to an equally substantial negative productivity effect in the bituminous coal industry is attributed to seriously deteriorating industrial relations in the industry. Freeman and Medoff emphasize that: "If industrial relations are good, with management and unions working together to produce a

[24]Kim B. Clark, "The Impact of Unionization on Productivity: A Case Study," *Industrial and Labor Relations Review,* July 1980, pp. 451–469.
[25]Ibid., p. 467.

TABLE 8-6

Estimates of the Impact of Unionism on Productivity

Setting	Percent Estimated Increase or Decrease in Output per Worker Due to Unionism
All 2-digit Standard Industrial Classification (SIC) manufacturing industries	20 to 25
Wooden household furniture	15
Cement	6 to 8
Underground bituminous coal, 1965	25 to 30
Underground bituminous coal, 1975	−20 to −25

Source: Richard L. Freeman and James L. Medoff, "The Two Faces of Unionism, "*The Public Interest,* Fall 1979, p. 80.

bigger 'pie' as well as fighting over the size of their slices, productivity is likely to be higher under unionism. If industrial relations are poor, with management and labor ignoring common goals to battle one another, productivity is likely to be lower under unionism."[26]

Other research studies not included in Table 8-6 show mixed results. For example, Allen's[27] recent study of the construction industry is supportive. Holding constant such productivity-influencing variables as labor quality, the capital-labor ratio, and scale of production, he estimates that union workers are 20 percent more productive than nonunion workers. On the other hand, Ehrenberg, Sherman, and Schwarz[28] have found that unionization has *not* significantly affected productivity in municipal libraries. Pencavel[29] has presented evidence showing that in the 1900–1913 period the growth of trade unionism in the British coal industry contributed to declining productivity. Finally, in examining some nineteen manufacturing industries, Hirsch and Link[30] have concluded that productivity growth is slower in industries characterized by (1) a greater proportion of union coverage and (2) faster union growth.

There is obviously no neat summing up of this discussion of the efficiency effects of unions. Systematic analysis of the impact of unions upon productivity is a relatively new endeavor, and there are no unassailable conclusions. The relationship between unionism and productivity is multifaceted, complex, and imperfectly understood at this point in time.

DISTRIBUTION OF EARNINGS

There is also disagreement as to the impact of unions upon the distribution of earnings. Some economists reason that unions contribute to earnings inequality; others take precisely the opposite view.

Increasing Inequality. Perhaps the simplest argument in support of the position that unions enhance inequality is based upon the spillover effect. Recall once

---

[26]Freeman and Medoff, *What Do Unions Do?* p. 165.

[27]Steven G. Allen, "Unionized Construction Workers are More Productive," *Quarterly Journal of Economics,* May 1984, pp. 251–273.

[28]Ronald G. Ehrenberg, Daniel R. Sherman, and Joshua L. Schwarz, "Unions and Productivity in the Public Sector: A Study of Municipal Libraries," *Industrial and Labor Relations Review,* January 1983, pp. 199–213. Randall W. Eberts in his study of "Union Effects on Teacher Productivity," *Industrial and Labor Relations Review,* April 1984, pp. 346–358 concludes that, while unionization has a significant effect upon how teachers allocate their time, the overall effects upon their productivity are unclear.

[29]John H. Pencavel, "The Distributional and Efficiency Effects of Trade Unions in Britain," *British Journal of Industrial Relations,* July 1977, pp. 137–156.

[30]Barry T. Hirsch and Albert N. Link, "Unions, Productivity, and Productivity Growth," *Journal of Labor Research,* Winter 1984, pp. 29–37. John T. Addison, "Are Unions Good for Productivity?" *Journal of Labor Research,* Spring 1982, pp. 125–138, and W. H. Hutt, "The Face and Mask of Unionism," *Journal of Labor Research,* Summer 1983, pp. 197–211, both contend there are serious shortcomings in Freeman and Medoff's analysis of unionism.

again that the higher wage rates realized in the union sector of Figure 8-2 displace workers who seek reemployment in the nonunion sector. The result of this displacement is that nonunion wage rates are depressed. Hence, while we began with equal rates of W_n in both submarkets, the effect of unionism is to generate higher wage rates of W_u for union workers but lower wages of W_s for nonunion workers. Furthermore, the fact that unionization is more extensive among the more highly skilled, higher-paid blue-collar workers than it is among less-skilled, lower-paid blue-collar workers also suggests that the obtaining of a wage advantage by unions increases the dispersion of earnings.

Pettengill[31] has employed a more sophisticated set of arguments to reach the same general conclusion. The essence of his position is that when unions force employers to pay above-equilibrium wage rates, the long-run response of the latter is to hire higher-quality workers. This constitutes a shift in the structure of labor demand away from low-quality and towards high-quality workers. The net result is a widening of the dispersion of wages or, in short, greater wage inequality.

Pettengill elaborates his reasoning with the following example shown in Table 8-7. Here we assume that A, B, and C designate various levels of labor quality, say, high school graduates, high school dropouts, and workers with no high school education respectively, which are available to a nonunion employer. The productivity or output per hour of each quality level is given in column 2, and wage rates are specified in column 3. By dividing productivity into the wage rate we obtain wage cost per unit of output as shown in column 4. Given these options, the firm will hire B-quality labor at $4 per hour because the associated wage costs per unit of output are minimized.

Now suppose that the firm is unionized and the wages of B-quality labor are increased to $6. What are the consequences? In the short run the per unit cost of production rises to $1.50 and the lifetime earnings prospects of B-quality workers are enhanced. In the long run the normal attrition of B-quality workers through retirement, voluntary quits, deaths, and so forth will prompt the firm to replace such workers with A-quality workers. That is, if the union forces the

---

[31]John S. Pettengill, *Labor Unions and the Inequality of Earned Income* (Amsterdam: North-Holland Publishing Company, 1980).

TABLE 8-7

Labor Quality, Productivity, and Wage Rates

(1) Type of Labor	(2) Output per Hour	(3) Wage Rate	(4) = (3) ÷ (2) Wage Cost per Unit of Output
A	5	$6.00	$1.20
B	4	4.00	1.00
C	2	2.50	1.25

employer to pay $6 per hour for labor, then the firm will seek the best qualified workers obtainable at that wage rate. Specifically, the firm will now require all of its new employees to have a high school diploma. Note that when all *B* workers are eventually replaced with *A* workers at the $6 wage rate, labor costs per unit of output will have fallen from $1.50 to $1.20 because *A* workers are more productive.

If this scenario is repeated on a wide scale, we find that there has occurred an increase in the demand for high-quality *A* workers and a decline in the demand for lower-quality *B* workers. This causes the ratio of the "going wage" of high school graduates to increase relative to the "going wage" of high school dropouts, widening the dispersion of wages and increasing earnings inequality. Less obviously, the higher wages for high school graduates will reduce the incremental income received by college graduates in comparison with high school graduates (see Figure 4-2). This decline in the "college premium" will reduce the rate of return on an investment in a college education and in time reduce the supply of college graduates. As a result, the wages and salaries received by college graduates will tend to rise, further increasing the dispersion of wages and increasing earnings inequality.

Promoting Equality. But there are other aspects of union wage policies which suggest that unionism promotes greater, not less, equality in the distribution of earnings. What are these other ways through which unions tend to equalize wages?

1. Uniform wages within firms. In the absence of unions employers are apt to pay different wages to individual workers on the same job. These wage differences are based upon perceived differences in job performance, length of job tenure and, perhaps, favoritism. Unions, on the other hand, have a tradition of seeking uniform wage rates for all workers performing a particular job. In short, while nonunion firms tend to assign wage rates to *individual workers,* unions—in the interest of worker allegiance and solidarity—seek to assign wage rates to *jobs.* To the extent that unions are successful, wage and earnings differentials based upon supervisory judgments of individual worker performance are eliminated. An important side effect of this standard-wage policy is that wage discrimination against blacks, other minorities, and women is likely to be less when a union is present. Recall from our earlier discussion of Table 8-1 that black male workers tend to benefit more from unionization than does any other demographic group.

Wage and earnings inequality within a firm may be reduced by unionism for another reason. Industrial unions—that is, unions comprised of a variety of workers ranging from unskilled to highly skilled—frequently follow a wage policy of seeking equal *absolute* wage increases for all of their constituents. This means that larger *percentage* increases are realized by less skilled workers and the earnings gap between unskilled and skilled workers is reduced. Consider this simple illustration. Assume skilled workers are initially paid $10 and unskilled workers $5 per hour. Suppose the union negotiates equal $2 increases for both groups so that skilled workers now receive $12 and unskilled $7 per hour. Originally unskilled workers earned 50 percent (= $5/$10) of what skilled workers received. But after the wage increase unskilled workers get about 58 percent (= $7/$12) of skilled wages. Relative wage inequality has diminished.

Why would an industrial union adopt a policy of equal absolute wage increases for workers of different skills? The answer is twofold. On the one hand, it reflects their egalitarian ideology. On the other hand, it allows union leaders to largely sidestep politically awkward and potentially divisive decisions concerning the relative worth of various groups of constituents.

2. Uniform wages among firms. In addition to seeking standard wage rates for given occupational classes *within* firms, unions also seek standard wage rates *among* firms. The rationale for this policy is almost self-evident. The existence of substantial wage differences among competing firms may undermine the ability of unions to sustain and enhance wage advantages. For example, if one firm in a four-firm oligopoly is allowed to pay significantly lower wages to its union workers, the union is likely to find it difficult to maintain the union wage advantage in the other three firms. In particular, during a recession the high-wage firms are likely to put great pressure on the union to lower wages to the level of the low-wage firm. To avoid this kind of problem unions seek to "take labor (wages) out of competition" by standardizing wage rates among firms, thereby tending to reduce the degree of wage dispersion. You may recall from Chapter 7 that multiemployer bargaining which culminates in an industry-wide contract is in important means of standardizing wage rates.

3. Reducing the white-collar to blue-collar differential. In examining the empirical evidence on the union wage advantage (Table 8-1) we observed that unions achieve larger wage gains for blue-collar workers than they do for white-collar workers. Given the fact that on the average white-collar workers enjoy higher earnings than blue-collar workers, the larger wage gains which unions achieve for the latter tend to reduce earnings inequalities betwen blue- and white-collar workers.

What is the *net* effect of unionism upon the distribution of earnings? Although the issue remains controversial, Freeman and Medoff have used empirical analysis to conclude that the spillover effect *increases* earnings inequality by about 1 percent, but the standardization of wage rates within and among firms *decreases* inequality by about 4 percent. The net result is a 3 percent decline in earnings inequality due to unionism. Noting that only a relatively small percentage of the labor force is unionized, the authors contend that this 3 percent reduction in inequality should be regarded as "substantial."[32]

[32]Freeman and Medoff, *What Do Unions Do?*, pp. 90–93, and additional studies cited therein. See also Nguyen T. Quan, "Unionism and the Size Distribution of Earnings," *Industrial Relations*, Spring 1984, pp. 270–277.

OTHER ISSUES: INFLATION AND INCOME SHARES

Our discussion of the economic impact of unions is not complete. Specifically, we will later examine in detail the possible impact of union wage-setting upon the price level (Chapter 19) and the effect of unions upon the share of national income going to labor (Chapter 17). At this point we will simply make a few assertions concerning these two topics and defer detailed analyses to the indicated chapters.

Economists seem to be in general agreement that union wage-determination is *not* a basic cause of inflation. Most of our serious inflationary episodes can be associated with excess aggregate demand or supply-side shocks rather than wage-push considerations. More specifically, recent inflations can be attributed largely to expansionary fiscal or monetary policies or supply-side shocks such as the dramatic Organization of Petroleum Exporting Countries' (OPEC) oil price increases of the 1970s. On the other hand, we will find that wage-determination under collective bargaining may well perpetuate an ongoing inflation and therefore make it more difficult and more costly for anti-inflationary policies to be effective.

There is no significant evidence to suggest that unions have been able to increase labor's share and decrease the capitalist share of national income. The reasons for this are several. In the first place, as our analysis of the spillover effect implies, higher wages for union workers may come largely at the expense of the wages of nonunion workers (Figure 8-2) and not out of the capitalist share. Second, union wage increases may induce the substitution of capital for labor. Hence, the potential positive effect which higher union wages have upon labor's share in the unionized sector *may* be offset by the negative effect associated with fewer jobs. Finally, management may escape a redistribution of national income from capital to labor through productivity and price increases. The potential encroachment upon profits which stems from wage increases may simply be absorbed or offset by productivity increases (Chapter 16) or by price increases.

SUMMARY

1. Considerations other than the presence of unions may explain at least in part why strongly unionized industries pay higher wages than weakly organized industries. These factors include relatively fewer female workers, larger-scale plants, and more capital-intensive production methods in the strongly unionized industries.
2. The pure union wage advantage A is equal to $(W_u - W_n)/W_n \times 100$, where W_u is the union wage and W_n the nonunion wage.
3. In practice the pure union wage advantage is difficult to determine because an increase in union wages may decrease (through the spillover effect) or increase (through the threat effect) nonunion wages.
4. Research evidence consistently indicates that unions do achieve a wage advantage for their constituents, although the size of the advantage varies substantially by occupation, industry, race, and sex. Estimates by Lewis for the 1923–1958 period suggest that the average union wage advantage was on the order of 10 to 15 percent,

but that the advantage widens during depression and diminishes when unexpected inflation occurs. More recent studies suggest that the union wage advantage may have increased to 20 to 30 percent in the 1970s.

5. Union workers also generally receive a higher level and greater variety of fringe benefits, causing the union total compensation advantage to exceed the wage advantage.

6. There is disagreement whether the net effect of unions upon allocative efficiency and productivity is positive or negative. The negative view cites (a) the inefficiencies associated with featherbedding and union-imposed work rules; (b) the loss of output through strikes; and (c) the misallocation of labor to which the union wage advantage gives rise.

7. The positive view contends that (a) union wage pressure spurs technological advance and the mechanization of the production process and (b) as collective voice institutions unions contribute to rising productivity by reducing labor turnover, enhancing worker security, and inducing greater managerial efficiency.

8. Those who contend that unions increase earnings inequality argue that (a) unionization increases the wages of union workers but lowers the wages of nonunion workers; (b) unions are strongest among highly paid skilled blue-collar workers but relatively weak among low-paid unskilled blue-collar workers; and (c) union wage increases generate an increase in the demand for high-quality workers and a decline in the demand for low-quality workers. The opposing view is that unions contribute to greater earnings equality because (a) unions seek uniform wages for given jobs within firms; (b) unions favor uniform wages among firms; and (c) unions have achieved higher wage gains for relatively low-paid blue-collar workers than they have for relatively high-paid white-collar workers.

QUESTIONS AND STUDY SUGGESTIONS

1. Key terms and concepts to remember: pure versus measured union wage advantage, spillover effect; threat effect; product-market effect; wait unemployment; superior-worker effect; fringe benefits; in-kind benefits; collective voice; exit and voice mechanisms; shock effect.

2. What is the "commonsense" basis for expecting a union wage advantage? Explain how each of the following differences between union and nonunion firms might complicate one's determination of whether unions actually are responsible for an observed wage advantage: (a) the demographic makeup of the labor forces, (b) plant sizes, and (c) the amount of capital equipment used per worker.

3. Evaluate: "A union could not obtain a wage gain in a purely competitive industry unless it organized every firm in the industry."

4. How is the "pure" union wage advantage defined? If in a given labor market the wage rate would be $8 without a union and $10 with a union, then what is the pure union wage advantage? Explain how, and in what direction, each of the following might cause the "measured" union wage advantage to vary from the pure advantage: (a) the spillover effect, (b) the threat effect, (c) the product-market effect, and (d) the superior-worker effect.

5. Indicate the overall size of the measured union wage advantage. Does recent evidence suggest that the advantage has increased or decreased? Comment upon and explain cyclical changes in the union wage advantage.

6. Comment on each of the following statements:
   a. "Unions tie the hands of management and inhibit efficient decision making."
   b. "Unions contribute to economic efficiency in that union wage pressure hastens the weeding out of the high-cost, least-efficient producers in each industry."
7. Indicate the amount of work time lost each year because of strikes. Cite circumstances under which the amount of work time lost during a specific strike might be a poor indicator of the amount of lost output.
8. "There is an inherent cost to society that accompanies any union wage gain. That cost is the diminished efficiency with which labor resources are allocated." Explain this contention. Are you in agreement?
9. There is evidence to suggest that firms which sell their products in less competitive product markets are more likely to be unionized than firms selling in highly competitive markets. Recalling from Chapter 4 that the elasticity of product demand is an important determinant of the elasticity of labor demand, how might this affect (*a*) the elasticities of the union and nonunion demand curves in Figure 8-3 and (*b*) the net loss of output due to the union wage advantage?
10. In what specific ways might the presence of a union raise productivity within a firm? Use the "exit mechanism" and "voice mechanism" concepts in your response.
11. Explain the historical growth of fringe benefits as a percentage of total compensation. Compare the size of the fringe benefits received by union and nonunion workers and indicate possible reasons for any differences.
12. Assume Trans State Airways offers its employees the choice between a $200 annual wage increment or $200 worth of free air travel per year. Explain why, even though the latter option greatly restrains consumer choice, workers might prefer the gratis flights.
13. Describe the various avenues through which unions might alter the distribution of earnings. Evaluate: "Unions purport to be egalitarian institutions, but their effect is to increase earnings inequality among American workers."

SELECTED REFERENCES

BURTON, JOHN F, JR. ET AL, "Review Symposium on *What Do Unions Do?*" *Industrial and Labor Relations Review,* January 1985, pp. 244–263.

FREEMAN, RICHARD B., and JAMES L. MEDOFF: *What Do Unions Do?* (New York: Basic Books, Publishers, Inc., 1984).

HIRSCH, BARRY T., and JOHN T. ADDISON: *The Economic Analysis of Trade Unions* (London: Allen and Unwin, 1985).

LEWIS, H. GREGG: *Unionism and Relative Wages in the United States* (Chicago: University of Chicago Press, 1963).

MITCHELL, DANIEL J. B.: *Unions, Wages, and Inflation* (Washington, D.C.: The Brookings Institution, 1980), chap. 3.

PARSLEY, C. J.: "Labor Union Effects on Wage Gains: A Survey of Recent Literature," *Journal of Economic Literature,* March 1980, pp. 1–31.

PETTENGILL, JOHN S.: *Labor Unions and the Inequality of Earned Income* (Amsterdam: North-Holland Publishing Company, 1980).

REES, ALBERT: *The Economics of Trade Unions,* rev. ed. (Chicago: University of Chicago Press, 1977), chaps. 4 and 7.

REYNOLDS, MORGAN O.: *Power and Privilege: Labor Unions in America* (New York: Universe Books, Inc., 1984).

T I M E   A N D   O N E - H A L F

FREEZES AND "GIVEBACKS": WAGE BARGAINING IN THE 1980s*

In the early 1980s wage freezes and wage cuts ("givebacks") became almost as common as wage increases in major collective bargaining agreements.

In the past several years, a dramatic turnaround in union wage settlements has occurred. While it was customary in the 1970s for union workers to achieve substantial money wage increases based upon an "improvement factor" (that is, current and projected productivity increases) and rises in the cost of living, this is no longer the case. Wage freezes, wage cuts, and the paring back of fringe benefits have become common occurrences in the 1980s.

We are concerned with two major aspects of this turnaround. First, what is its magnitude? How many workers have been affected and to what degree? Second, how can the turnaround be explained? What forces have changed the 1970s environment of customary and substantial wage increases into a climate of freezes and cuts in the 1980s?

Scope. Since 1979, at least 3 million workers—one out of six—have accepted collective bargaining agreements which freeze or reduce wages and fringe benefits or alter work rules. Table 1 is informative, showing the percentage of union workers who accepted a wage decrease or freeze over the 1980–1984 period. The data here apply to all major collective bargaining agreements, that is, those covering 1000 or more workers. We observe in the top two rows that, while no workers covered by major new bargaining settlements accepted wage freezes or reductions in 1980, over two-fifths of all such workers received first-year freezes in 1982. In absolute terms an estimated 2.3 million workers accepted first-year wage cuts or freezes in 1982. Workers in the automobile,

---

* This is a synopsis of Robert S. Gay, "Union Settlements and Aggregate Wage Behavior in the 1980s," *Federal Reserve Bulletin,* December 1984, pp. 843–856.

TABLE 1

Distribution of Workers by First-Year Wage Adjustment in Major Collective Bargaining Settlements, 1980–1984 (in percents)

Wage Adjustment	1980	1981	1982	1983	1984*
Wage decrease	0	5	2	15	6
Wage freeze	0	3	42	22	21
Average wage adjustment	9.5	9.8	3.8	2.6	2.5

*First nine months.

Source: Bureau of Labor Statistics, *Current Wage Developments.*

trucking, and rubber industries were in the forefront of those whose wages were frozen in that year. In 1983 we note a significant shift from wage freezes to wage reductions. Collective bargaining agreements in the steel, airline, and meatpacking industries entailed wage declines on the order of 10 to 20 percent. An estimated 1.3 million workers were affected by the 1983 cuts and freezes. Despite the strong resurgence of economic activity and profits, wage cuts and freezes remained an important characteristic of collective bargaining in 1984. The bottom row of data in Table 1 documents the dramatic fall in the average size of the first-year money wage increases paid. Wage increases on the order of 10 percent in 1980 and 1981 gave way to 2.5 percent increments in 1983 and 1984.

Causal factors. The numerous factors precipitating the recent wave of wage freezes and cuts are interrelated and vary by industry. Certainly, the overall macroeconomic environment of the early 1980s was not conducive to large wage hikes. Back-to-back recessions spawned an unfavorable bargaining environment for unions, and the dramatic decline in the rate of inflation undermined the rationale for large money wage increases. On the other hand, prior post-World War II recessions did not generate wage cuts and freezes. Furthermore, while a decline in inflation might slow the rate of wage increases, it would not be expected to spawn freezes and cuts. Instead, a variety of interrelated factors, including a widening of the union-nonunion wage differential in the 1970s, the relative decline in United States productivity growth, the failure of certain heavily unionized industries to adjust quickly to changes in technology and consumer preferences, and institutional changes, all contributed to the collective bargaining turnaround. The net consequence of such factors was that many unionized industries were less able to compete with foreign producers and with domestic nonunion producers. As a consequence, union wage bargaining power was significantly eroded.

As noted in the body of this chapter, the union-nonunion wage differential increased significantly in the 1970s. A basic consequence of this was that unionized firms became less profitable and less competitive vis-a-vis domestic nonunion and foreign firms. It is not by chance that many of the union workers faced with wage cuts and freezes in the 1980s—those in the automobile, steel, rubber, and trucking industries, for example— were those who achieved the greatest wage gains in the 1970s. In the heavily unionized auto and steel industries the competition came from foreign producers. Foreign cars accounted for only 9 percent of United States auto sales in 1968, but for 28 percent in 1982. Steel imports rose from 12 to almost 22 percent of domestic sales in the same period. Of course, high union wages were not the only factor contributing to the difficulties experienced by the auto and steel industries. In the auto industry managements seriously misjudged the scope and apparent permanence of the shift in consumer preferences toward smaller, fuel-efficient cars. Technical considerations were also relevant. Many consumers concluded that imported autos were generally qualitatively superior to American products. In the steel industry there was a widespread failure to adopt more efficient production methods.

The inroads made by foreign producers in steel, automobiles, and other industries were exacerbated by two other considerations. First, beginning in the early 1970s the growth of United States labor productivity diminished significantly in comparison to that of most of our major international trading partners. As we shall discover in Chapter 16, productivity increases tend to offset or "absorb" increases in money wages. Hence, our relatively poor productivity performance enhanced upward pressure on costs and product prices, making many American goods less attractive to both domestic and foreign buyers. Second, foreign competition has been bolstered by the post-1980 rise in the foreign exchange value of the dollar. When the dollar becomes more expensive to foreigners, all American goods become more expensive to them and United States exports therefore decline.

In other industries, such as construction, meatpacking, and retail food stores, it was the competition of lower-wage nonunion domestic firms rather than foreign competition which eroded union bargaining power. As we saw in the Time and One-Half section of Chapter 7, in the case of air transportation deregulation generated a more highly competitive environment in which new low-cost nonunion firms have tended to prosper at the expense of union firms.

GOVERNMENT AND THE LABOR MARKET: EMPLOYMENT, EXPENDITURES, AND TAXATION

n the previous three chapters, we discussed the role of unions in influencing wage rates and employment levels in labor markets. We now turn our attention to another major institution—government—and the various ways it affects wages and employment throughout the economy. This chapter examines public-sector employment and the impacts of government spending and selected taxes on wages and employment in the private sector. Then in the following chapter we discuss examples of direct government intervention in labor markets via laws and regulations.

Our present discussion proceeds as follows. First, we examine the extent and growth of government employment and compare public-sector and private-sector pay. Next, the labor market aspects of the draft versus those of the voluntary army are analyzed. Third, we take a look at the labor market effects of government's nonpayroll spending, that is, its purchases of private-sector output and its transfers and subsidies. This is followed by a discussion of how the *presence* of publicly provided goods and services can influence labor supply and demand, independently of the hiring of workers needed to produce these items. The final three sections of the chapter analyze the labor market consequences of the personal income tax, the social security payroll tax, and selective excises. There we answer such questions as: Does the personal income tax affect wage rates and employment levels? Who bears the burden of the social security payroll tax? Do specific excise taxes affect labor demand?

PUBLIC-SECTOR EMPLOYMENT AND WAGES

Government is a major—or even the sole—employer of specific types of workers in many labor markets. For example, it hires military personnel, antitrust prosecutors, postal workers, air traffic controllers, park rangers, school teachers, agency managers, firefighters, and highway maintenance personnel. The demand for these employees is derived from society's demand for the public-sector

229

goods and services which these workers help provide. When government employs workers, it "exhausts" or "absorbs" economic resources. More precisely, government employment makes a direct claim on the nation's productive capabilities. For example, when government employs postal workers, those laborers are no longer available to produce other goods and services. Likewise, when the military either drafts personnel or persuades them to enlist voluntarily, society forgoes the private-sector output which those resources could have produced. Presumably, society values the public-sector output or services more highly than the alternative uses for these resources.

Government Employment: Extent and Growth. Table 9-1 demonstrates the extent and growth of government employment in the United States since 1950. Close examination of the columns in the table reveals several generalizations. First, the absolute number of federal civilian (column 2) and state and local government employees (column 4) increased over the 34-year period. This is not surprising because total employment in the economy (column 5) also rose considerably. Second, the growth of federal government employment was much less dramatic than the increase in state and local government employment. Clearly, most of the growth of employment in the public sector since 1950 occurred at the state and local levels of government. Federal civilian employment as a percentage of total employment (column 6) fell from 3.6 percent in 1950 to 2.7 percent in 1984. During those same years, state and local employment rose from 7.3 to 12.6 percent of total employment (column 7). Third, in 1950 one of ten U.S. workers was employed by government; by 1984, that figure had risen to about one of six workers. Finally, the number of active duty personnel in the armed services (column 3) varied between 1.5 and 3 million during these selected years.

The relative growth of public-sector employment over the past several decades occurred mainly because government's demand for labor grew disproportionately faster than private-sector demand. Economists cite several reasons for this relative growth of labor demand in the public sector. In the first place, the attendant needs and problems associated with population growth, urbanization, and urban sprawl increased the demand for many state and local government services. Furthermore, the age composition of the population dramatically changed over the 30-year period. The post-World War II "baby boom" caused a considerable increase in school-age children, which in turn caused a marked increase in the demand for public school teachers. A third factor at work was the growth of real income in the society, which increased the demand for such income-elastic government services as higher education, health services, parks, and a clean environment. Additionally, public-sector unions emerged as a more powerful and militant force in the public-sector labor market. Some observers contend that public employee unions and professional groups increasingly used their political power—via campaign contributions, organizational support, endorsements, and votes—to elect government officials who favored greater spending for governmentally provided goods and services. This may have in-

TABLE 9-1

Extent and Growth of Government Employment in the United States since 1950

(1) Year	Government Employment (millions)			(5) Total U.S. Employment (millions)	(6) Federal Civilian Employment as a Percent of Total U.S. Employment	(7) State and Local Employment as a Percent of Total U.S. Employment
	(2) Federal Civilian	(3) Armed Services*	(4) State & Local			
1950	2.1	1.5	4.3	58.9	3.6%	7.3%
1955	2.4	2.9	5.0	62.2	3.9	8.0
1960	2.4	2.5	6.4	65.8	3.6	9.7
1965	2.6	2.7	8.0	71.1	3.7	11.3
1970	2.9	3.0	10.1	78.7	3.7	12.8
1975	2.9	2.1	12.1	85.8	3.4	14.1
1980	2.9	2.1	13.3	99.3	2.9	13.4
1984	2.8	2.1	13.2	105.0	2.7	12.6

*Active duty personnel

Source: Compiled from U.S. Bureau of the Census, *Statistical Abstract of the United States*, 1984, Tables 487, 570, and 669; and *Economic Report of the President*, 1985, p. 267.

creased the derived demand for public employees.[1] Finally, government expanded its regulatory role in the economy, and this also increased the demand for government workers.

Public versus Private-Sector Pay. The increase in public-sector employment over the 1950-1984 period was accompanied by an increase in public-sector pay. In theory, most governmental units adhere to a *prevailing-wage rule* (or "comparable-wage" rule). That is, they attempt to set public employees' wages equal to those earned by comparably trained and employed private-sector workers.[2] In 1983, the average pay for full-time federal employees was $22,264, while the average for state and local public employees was $19,325. Both figures are higher than the $19,273 average earnings for that year among private-sector full-time workers. But these averages fail to adjust for such factors as differences in union status, education and training, and demographic characteristics (gender, race). Smith undertook a comprehensive study in the mid-1970s to test empirically whether public-sector employees did in fact achieve wages comparable to private counterparts, once accounting for these other factors.[3] Her study generated several interesting findings. First, in the year observed—1975— *federal* employees received wages which were 13 to 20 percent *higher* than those earned by comparably educated and experienced private-sector workers. Second, at the *state* level, female workers received 6 to 7 percent more and males 3 to 11 percent less than similar private-sector employees. Finally, *local* government workers appeared to earn wages nearly equal to their private-sector counterparts.[4] These findings may help explain why *federal* government job openings in the 1970s and early 1980s produced long waiting lists even during periods of relatively high national employment.

Two additional points concerning public- versus private-sector pay are noteworthy. The percent of total compensation paid in the form of fringe benefits is higher for public employees than for private workers. Hence, wage and salary comparisons alone may be misleading. Secondly, although average government pay is higher, the occupational wage structure within government is more egali-

---

[1]See Paul Courant, Edward Gramlich, and Daniel Rubinfeld, "Public Employee Market Power and the Level of Government Spending," *American Economic Review*, December 1979, pp. 806–817.

[2]The prevailing-wage principle was codified for federal workers in the Federal Pay Comparability Act of 1970. Many state and local governments have similar formal policies.

[3]See Sharon P. Smith, *Equal Pay in the Public Sector: Fact or Fantasy* (Princeton, N.J.: Princeton University Press, 1977).

[4]The Smith study compared wages of individuals while controlling for such personal characteristics as age, sex, education, race, and experience. But rates of return to such characteristics vary by *occupation*. Daniel J. B. Mitchell employed the Smith methodology on an occupational basis and found the results to be "at least qualitatively in line with those of Smith" at the federal level. But he concluded that state and local governments paid employees lower wages than those received by comparable private-sector workers. See Daniel J. B. Mitchell, "The Impact of Collective Bargaining on Compensation in the Public Sector," in Benjamin Aaron et al. (eds.), *Public Sector Bargaining* (Madison, Wis.: Industrial Relations Research Association 1979), pp. 118–149.

tarian than in the private sector (Chapter 13). Apparently, political considerations cause government to pay lower-skilled workers relatively more, and elected and appointed officials relatively less, than comparably trained and experienced private-sector workers.

THE MILITARY SECTOR: THE DRAFT VERSUS THE VOLUNTARY ARMY

As indicated earlier in column (3) of Table 9-1, the number of active duty military personnel employed by the United States during the selected years shown varied between a high of 3 million in 1970 to a low of 1.5 million in 1950. Prior to 1973, the United States used the selective service system—commonly called the "draft"—to compel people to serve in the military. These draftees worked alongside "volunteers," some of whom offered their labor services to the military rather than waiting to be drafted. Under this system of military conscription, wages were below those which many draftees and enlisted personnel could have earned in civilian-sector jobs. In 1973, the federal government abandoned the draft in favor of armed services staffed by people recruited voluntarily through wages and benefits which were sufficiently high to attract the required number of employees. In a sense, the armed services became a professional, market-based entity, much like the U. S. Postal Service, Federal Bureau of Investigation, and National Park Service.

The voluntary, wage-based army remains highly controversial. Critics argue that it produces an army drawn mainly from the ranks of low-income families, creates a racially imbalanced military force, reduces incentives to join the military reserves, generates persistent shortages of skilled personnel, and increases the cost of the military to taxpayers. Defenders of the voluntary approach counter that the professional army is better prepared to achieve its goals, minimizes society's overall cost of allocating labor to the services, promotes the use of a more efficient combination of labor and capital in the military, creates employment opportunities for low-skilled workers, provides on-the-job training that is transferable to the private sector, and maximizes individual freedom. These defenders also argue that it is more equitable to have taxpayers, rather than draftees, bear the costs of the armed services; that the voluntary army reduces the military's training costs by lessening the turnover of personnel; and that shortages of skilled personnel or reservists can be eliminated by simply raising wages in the areas where more personnel are needed.[5]

A comprehensive examination of these pros and cons is well beyond our present discussion. Because our interest is government's role in the labor market, we limit our analysis here to the *labor market* aspects of the two alternatives.

---

[5]For an annotated listing of publications which discuss the issues surrounding the draft and the voluntary army, see Martin Anderson (ed.), *Conscription: A Select and Annotated Bibliography* (Stanford, Calif.: Hoover Institution Press, 1976).

The Labor Economics of Military Conscription. Figure 9-1 shows labor supply and demand as viewed by the military. For sake of simplicity, we assume that the market from which the military drafts personnel is perfectly competitive and that the nation is not at war. Initially, disregard the labor demand curve labeled D_v and instead concentrate on curves S and D_d. The curve S is a conventional competitive supply curve *as viewed by an employer.* The perfectly inelastic demand curve D_d is drawn on the assumption that Congress authorizes the armed services to conscript or *draft* OG people and pay each of them wage rate OA. Initially, suppose that those drafted are the *specific* individuals who would have voluntarily enlisted had the wage rate been at the equilibrium level OB rather than OA.

Let us now address two questions. First, what is the total wage bill that the military (taxpayers) will have to pay under this draft authorization? Second, given our assumptions, what is the overall cost to society of drafting these specific OG workers? The answer to the first question is very simple and straightforward. The military's wage bill is the area $OAFG$ which is found by multiplying the authorized wage OA times the authorized employment level OG. Is this wage bill also the total cost to society? The answer is "no," and this can be understood by examining the labor supply curve. The vertical height of curve S measures the opportunity cost of using each unit of labor in this employment or, in other words, the forgone civilian earnings for each of the OG workers drafted. For example, suppose that these workers would earn $12,500 a year at wage rate OB

FIGURE 9-1 THE DRAFT VERSUS THE VOLUNTARY ARMY
If the military drafts the specific group of workers $0G$ and pays each of them $0A$, the wage bill to taxpayers ($0AFG$) will be less than the total opportunity costs to those drafted ($0BCG$). Under a voluntary, market-based system, the relevant demand curve becomes D_v, the cost to taxpayers increases ($0BEH$ as compared to $0AFG$), those who volunteer are fully compensated for their opportunity costs ($0BEH$), and the military is likely to reduce its total work force ($0G$ to $0H$). The true cost of employing any specific group of workers is *independent* of the wage bill.

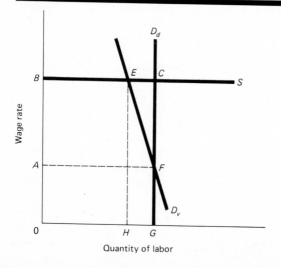

and only $5000 at the military wage rate OA. The annual income these individuals sacrifice and the output forgone by society from drafting them is $12,500 times OG draftees. The fact that the military pays these workers $5000 does *not* reflect the actual costs to either these individuals or to society. By drafting OG workers, the military imposes an opportunity cost on draftees and society equal to the area under the labor supply curve, $OBCG$. It pays the draftees $OAFG$ and imposes the remainder of the cost—$ABCF$—on those drafted. This cost is the difference between what draftees could earn as civilians and the amount earned in the military. To generalize: The true social cost of drafting any specific group of workers to the military is *independent* of the total wage rate that the military pays them. The actual cost consists of the income (output) sacrificed by draftees. Conscription at low pay reduces the military's (taxpayer's) personnel costs, but it does *not* lower the costs of the military to society. Rather, it shifts a portion of the true costs from taxpayers to those drafted.

Thus far, we have assumed that draftees are people who have opportunity costs which are reflected by the perfectly elastic supply curve in Figure 9-1. This assumes that government drafts only those from the low-skilled labor market—people who have low civilian earnings. But what if the military imposes a *lottery* to select the OG draftees? Many of those selected will have higher civilian wage opportunities than OB. Stated differently, the collective civilian wage opportunities of the OG draftees selected through a lottery will exceed area $OBCG$. The relevant generalization here is that the true cost to individuals and society of a lottery draft will exceed that of a draft of low-paid civilian workers.

The Voluntary, Market-Based Approach. We can analyze the economic implications of a *voluntary* or *market-based army* by turning to the demand curve D_v in Figure 9-1. Notice that we have drawn a typical downward-sloping demand curve, as opposed to the perfectly inelastic one used to analyze the draft. This downward-sloping curve reflects a realistic expectation that higher market wages for military personnel will cause the armed services to reduce the number of its employees. As seen by the intersection of D_v and S, the equilibrium military wage and quantity of labor will be OB and OH, respectively. The total wage bill to the military will be $OBEH$, which is considerably greater than $OAFG$, the total wage bill under the draft. Assuming that the military's demand for personnel is relatively inelastic, we conclude that a voluntary army will increase the money costs of military personnel to *taxpayers*. Notice that it transfers income from taxpayers to military personnel such that the latter are totally compensated for their opportunity costs $OBEH$.

Figure 9-1 shows us that, *if* the wage rate were at the draft level of OA, the voluntary army would hire the same number of employees that it previously drafted (OG). But the existence of the voluntary army with a market-determined wage rate reduces military employment from OG to OH. We assume that this occurs for two reasons. First, as the wage rises from OA to OB, the military will likely *substitute* capital for labor. More precisely, the ratio of the marginal physical product of capital (MP_K) to the price of capital (P_K) will now exceed the ratio of the marginal physical product of labor (MP_L) to the price of labor (P_L). Therefore, the military can lower its costs by engaging in such activity as purchasing dishwashing machines, procuring more weapons, and computerizing routine paperwork (recall equation 6-1). This will enable the armed services to economize on the use of the now higher-priced labor. Second, although the higher wage bill adds nothing to the true cost of the military, it does raise the price of the armed services *as perceived by Congress and taxpayers.* We would expect this increase in price to cause Congress to reduce its "output" of military services or reduce the *scale* of the total military establishment, which then would reduce military employment. The alert reader who has read the Appendix to Chapter 5 will recognize that we are here referring to both substitution and output effects.

To summarize: Government's conscription or hiring of personnel for the military is another example of how it influences specific labor markets in the economy. Labor market analysis suggests that (1) the true cost of allocating personnel to the military is independent of the wage paid to those workers; (2) the method used to obtain labor may affect the total cost of acquiring a given amount of military personnel; (3) a voluntary army is likely to raise the monetary cost to taxpayers; and (4) society is likely to allocate fewer labor resources to the military under a higher-pay voluntary system than a lower-pay compulsory one. Finally, while labor market analysis *can* help us understand the costs of public policy options, it *cannot* determine which option society should select.

NONPAYROLL SPENDING BY GOVERNMENT: IMPACT ON LABOR

We have established that government employment of civilian and military workers is a major factor in the overall labor market. But government's nonpayroll spending also indirectly influences wages and employment. This spending is substantial and takes two forms: (1) purchases of private-sector goods and services and (2) transfer payments and subsidies. In 1984 government spent $748 billion, about one-half of which was for goods produced by private industry. Government also made transfer payments of $407 billion. Let us briefly examine selected labor market impacts of each type of expenditure.

Government Purchases of Private-Sector Output. Government purchases include procurement of such items as word processors, tanks, medical supplies, textbooks, buses, submarines, paper clips, furniture, and weather satellites. This type of spending by government obviously creates a derived demand for specific kinds of private-sector workers. In some cases, it creates demands for labor which would not exist—or at least not be nearly as great—in the absence of government. We could expect such changes in demand to affect equilibrium wage rates and employment levels. For example, boosts in government spending on strategic missiles could be expected to increase the wages and employment levels of aerospace engineers. Similarly, increases in federal construction spending would likely increase the demand for—and the collective bargaining position of—a wide range of construction workers. In 1984 an estimated 7 to 8 million private sector jobs were directly created by government purchases from private industry.

Transfer Payments and Subsidies. Government payroll expenditures and nonpayroll spending for private-sector goods and services have one common feature. Both are *exhaustive* or resource-absorbing expenditures in that they account for the employment of labor and other economic resources. In contrast, transfer payments and subsidies are *nonexhaustive* because, as such, they do not directly absorb resources or account for production. More precisely, as their name implies, *transfer payments*—such as social security benefits to the retired, unemployment compensation, welfare payments, and veterans' benefits—merely transfer income from government to individuals and families. The recipients perform no current productive activities in return; hence, transfers are nonexhaustive. Similarly, a *subsidy* is a transfer payment to a firm, institution, or household which consumes or produces some specific product or service. Medicare for the elderly, price supports for farmers, and public education for youth are all examples of governmental subsidies.

Although transfers and subsidies do not directly exhaust or absorb labor or other resources, they do alter the structure of total demand in the economy and therefore affect the derived demands for specific types of labor. For example, cash and in-kind medical transfers provided to older Americans under provisions of the social security program increase the demand for products and services which older Americans tend to purchase. More specifically, the transfers increase the demand for such items as prescription and over-the-counter drugs, nursing home services, hospital care, and retirement property. This demand, in turn, increases the derived demand for workers who help produce, deliver, or sell these goods and services. In a similar sense, the cash transfers provided through the Aid to Families with Dependent Children (AFDC) program—the basic welfare program for low-income families—increase the demand for a variety of products, including children's clothing, toys, and foodstuffs. Other things being equal, these increases in product demand boost product prices, which then increase the demand for labor in the affected industries (demand determinant 1, Table 6-1).

Subsidies provided to private firms and nonprofit organizations also increase the demand for specific types of workers. For instance the U. S. government, through the Export-Import Bank, provides loans at below-market interest rates to some foreign buyers of U.S. exports. This reduces the effective price of U.S. exports while leaving the price charged by the exporters intact, thereby increasing foreign purchases and ultimately the derived demand for labor in the U.S. export sector. Similarly, the federal government provides subsidies to such nonprofit organizations as private universities which then demand more workers to deliver their services.

In addition to their impact on labor demand, transfer payments and subsidies affect short- and long-run labor supply. Recall from our discussion of individual labor supply in Chapter 2 that transfers generate an *income effect* which tends to reduce the optimal number of work hours offered by the recipient. Put simply, transfer income induces the recipient to buy more normal goods and services, including leisure (Figure 2-11). Also, if the amount of the cash transfer is inversely related to work income, that is, if a benefit-loss rate applies to earned income, then the program creates an accompanying *substitution effect* which further reduces work effort. By reducing the opportunity cost—or price—of leisure, the transfer payment encourages the substitution of the lower-priced leisure for the now relatively higher-priced work.

Transfers and subsidies also influence long-run labor supply decisions (Chapter 4). For example, the existence of cash and in-kind transfers *may* reduce incentives to invest in human capital. In essence, the present value of the *net* returns to the investor is reduced because future gains in earned income which result from the training or education are accompanied by the loss of future transfers. Other things being equal, the higher the benefit-loss rate of a transfer plan, the less the actual net rate of return on any given investment in human capital.

Not *all* transfer and subsidy programs, however, reduce long-run labor supply. Those transfers and subsidies which reduce the private *cost* of investing in human capital produce just the opposite effect. For example, government provides subsidized, below-market interest rates on loans to many college students. Recall that the economic rationale for these loans was outlined in Chapter 4. This subsidy reduces the supply price of investing in a college education which increases the private rate of return on this form of human capital. As a direct consequence, long-run labor supply in various skilled and professional labor markets increases. Thus, we see that government transfers and subsidies may either positively or negatively effect supply in specific labor markets.

LABOR MARKET EFFECTS OF PUBLICLY PROVIDED GOODS AND SERVICES

Thus far we have established that government employment and public-sector purchases of private-sector output influence wage rates and employment levels in specific labor markets. We next raise an interesting related question: Do publicly provided goods and services affect labor demand and supply *independently* of the public and private employment necessary to provide these items? Publicly provided goods and services range from **pure public goods,** whose benefits are indivisible and therefore impossible to deny to those who have not paid for them, to goods and services provided by government but also sold in the private sector. An example of the former is national defense, while an example of the latter is college education. It is clear that some publicly provided goods *do* affect private-sector *demand* for labor. It is also conceivable that these goods and services reduce overall labor *supply* in the economy. Let us examine each possibility.

Impacts on Demand. The provision of public-sector goods and services influences labor demand in a variety of ways. For example, suppose that government builds a major dam on a river. Assume that this project creates multiple benefits such as electricity generation, flood control, irrigation, and recreational opportunities. Government affects the labor market by employing labor and private-sector products to construct the dam, power station, irrigation network, and adjacent recreational areas. But, the *existence* of the dam also independently affects labor demand. For example, the irrigation system will likely increase the demand for farm workers; the new recreational opportunities will increase the demand for fishing boats, motors, and water skis which will increase the derived demand for workers who help produce these products; the availability of cheap electrical power may entice manufacturing firms to the area, thereby increasing the demand for specific skilled and unskilled workers; and the control of down-river flooding may actually *reduce* the demand for flood insurance agents and claims adjusters. In fact, we may generalize as follows: Other things being equal, the provision of a public good which is a *complement* in either production or consumption to a specific private good will *increase* the derived demand for workers who help produce the private good; the provision of a public good

FIGURE 9-2 IMPACT OF PUBLICLY PROVIDED GOODS ON INDIVIDUAL LABOR SUPPLY
If real income is defined as the total quantity of public and private goods and services obtainable from any specific level of work, then the presence of Y_{pu} public-sector goods or services shifts the effective budget constraint upward from WW' to W_1W_1'. Assuming leisure to be a normal good and disregarding the tax consequences of the increased public-sector provision, this creates an income effect which reduces the optimal number of hours worked by h_1h_2.

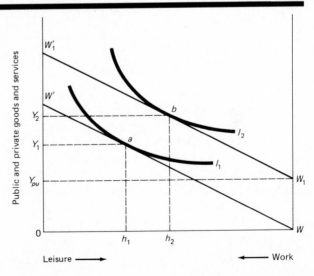

which is a *substitute* in production or consumption to a specific private good will *reduce* the derived demand for workers who help produce the private good.

Impacts on Supply. A modified version of the basic income-leisure model of short-run individual labor supply suggests that publicly provided goods and services may reduce the quantity of labor supplied. Recall from Chapter 2 that the basic model of income-leisure choice contains a preference map composed of indifference curves, each one of which shows the various combinations of real income and leisure which yield some specific level of utility. Also recall that it contains a wage rate, or budget, line which indicates the *actual* combination of income and leisure which the individual can obtain given his or her wage.

Figure 9-2 shows a modified version of the basic model. Notice from the vertical axis that we are defining real income as the total amount of private- and public-sector goods and services obtainable from any specific level of work. Suppose that Y_{pu} ($= WW_1$) of public-sector goods is available to Green regardless of how much he works. The real income available to him will be Y_{pu} plus the level of private goods which his work income will allow him to obtain. Prior to the provision of Y_{pu} public goods, Green's budget constraint was WW', but the existence of the publicly provided output means that his effective budget constraint is $W_1 W_1'$. This latter curve shows the combinations of leisure and goods (private- and public-sector) available to Green at each level of work, given his wage rate. The vertical distance between the two budget lines measures the value of the public goods available to Green.

If there were *no* public goods available to this individual, he would maximize his utility at *a* by working h_1 hours, from which he would earn Y_1 goods (real income). The existence of the public goods, however, creates an income effect which allows Green to "buy" more leisure. The provision of the public-sector goods Y_{pu} increases his *total* utility by moving him from *a* on indifference curve I_1 to *b* on curve I_2. But in achieving this gain in utility Green *reduces* his labor hours from h_1 to h_2. We thus conclude that the existence of publicly provided goods and services may reduce individual and overall labor supply in the economy. And as pointed out by two scholars of public finance,

> Paradoxically, the work incentive effect . . . will be more detrimental as expenditures are better designed to correspond to what consumers would otherwise wish to buy. . . . The depressing effect on work effort, moreover, will be stronger the more the public goods are complementary to leisure, e.g., ski slopes, marinas, or scenic highways. By the same token, effects will be less depressing if expenditures are work related (commuting roads). . . .[6]

[6]Richard A. Musgrave and Peggy B. Musgrave, *Public Finance in Theory and Practice*, 3d ed. (New York: McGraw-Hill Book company, 1980), pp. 665–666.

INCOME TAXATION AND THE LABOR MARKET

To this point our emphasis has been on government's influence on labor markets through its spending and hiring decisions. We now examine the effects of selected taxes on the labor market, beginning with a discussion of the personal income tax. Income from wages and salaries constitutes approximately 75 percent of national income in the United States (Chapter 17). Because a large portion of this income is subjected to the personal income tax, it is particularly important to ascertain the impact of this tax on labor markets. Specifically, do workers bear the full burden of the tax in the form of lower net, or after-tax, wage rates? Or is it possible that part or all of the tax is borne by employers who must pay higher market wage rates to attract profit-maximizing quantities of labor? What impact does the income tax have on employment?

The Income Tax: Impact on Wages and Employment. We shall discover from the following discussion that, given the elasticity of labor demand, the effects of the personal income tax on wages and employment depend principally on the elasticity of labor supply. Figure 9-3 (a) and (b) clearly demonstrate this proposition. The labor supply curve in graph (a) is perfectly inelastic, indicating that workers do not collectively change the extent of their labor force participation in

FIGURE 9-3 IMPACT OF THE PERSONAL INCOME TAX ON WAGES AND EMPLOYMENT
If the aggregate labor supply curve in the economy is perfectly inelastic as in (a), then the personal income tax—measured by the vertical distance between D and D_t—will not affect the market wage ($9), but will reduce the after-tax wage by the amount of the tax per hour. If the labor supply curve displays some elasticity as in (b), the tax reduces the quantity of labor hours supplied and raises the before-tax market wage—in this case from $9 to $10. Given labor demand, the greater the elasticity of labor supply, the greater the increase in the wage rate and the greater the reduction in employment resulting from the tax.

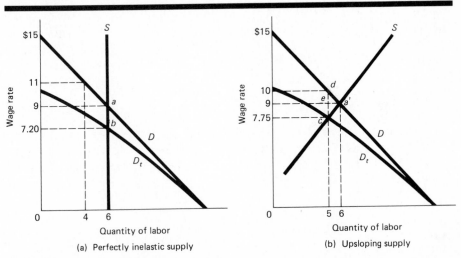

(a) Perfectly inelastic supply

(b) Upsloping supply

response to wage rate changes. In graph (b) the labor supply curve displays some elasticity; that is, people collectively increase their labor hour offerings when the wage rises and reduce them when it falls.

The demand curves in the two graphs are identical and reflect the *before-tax* wage rates and corresponding quantities of labor that firms will desire to employ. The curves labeled D_t lie below the conventional demand curves in each graph and show the *after-tax* wages as viewed by workers. The progressive income tax on labor earnings pivots the after-tax wage rate lines downward from D to D_t by the amount of the tax per hour of work. To better understand this crucial distinction between D and D_t, carefully examine Table 9-2. Notice that columns 1 and 2 represent the before-tax demand curve D; columns 2 and 4 establish the after-tax labor demand line D_t; and column 3 indicates the vertical distance between D and D_t. For example, suppose that the wage rate is $12. As observed in the table, the tax per hour of work is $3.25 and the net wage rate is $8.75. Column 5 of Table 9-2 shows the *average* hourly tax rate for each wage rate. Notice that the average tax rate rises as earnings per hour increase, indicating that this tax is progressive. In terms of Figure 9-3 (a) and (b) this progressivity is reflected in the fact that the distances between D and D_t increase as a percentage of the wage as the wage rises.

Let us now focus on graph (a) in Figure 9-3. The before-tax equilibrium market wage and quantity of labor are $9 and 6 units, respectively (point *a*). Once the tax is introduced, however, workers perceive their net wage to be only $7.20 (= $9.00 − $1.80), as shown by point *b*. But, because the supply of labor is perfectly inelastic, the income tax will not effect the collective quantity of labor supplied. Therefore, workers bear the entire burden of the tax; the before-tax wage rate remains at $9 and the after-tax hourly pay falls by the full amount of the tax, $1.80 (= $9.00 − $7.20).

TABLE 9-2

Before-Tax versus After-Tax Earnings per Unit of Labor (Hypothetical Data)

(1) W	(2) Q	(3) T	(4) W−T	(5) T/W(%)
$14	1	$4.25	$9.75	30.4
13	2	3.75	9.25	28.8
12	3	3.25	8.75	27.1
11	4	2.75	8.25	25.0
10	5	2.25	7.75	22.5
9	6	1.80	7.20	20.0
8	7	1.40	6.60	17.5
7	8	1.05	5.95	15.0
6	9	.75	5.25	12.5
5	10	.50	4.50	10.0
4	11	.30	3.70	7.5
3	12	.15	2.85	5.0
2	13	.05	1.95	2.5

To confirm this proposition, suppose that workers are angered by their *net* wage decline and try to shift the tax to their employers. If they demand, say, $11 (= $9 + $2), employers will seek only 4 units of labor, while workers will continue to offer 6 units. Assuming competition, the excess supply of workers will drive the before-tax wage down to $9 where the labor market will once again clear. It is evident that, if the labor supply curve is perfectly inelastic, employees will be unable to pass the tax forward to their employers and the tax will have no impact on either the market wage rate or equilibrium employment.[7]

We next turn our attention to graph (b) in Figure 9-3, wherein we discover a labor supply curve which displays a positive slope. This implies that workers collectively will respond to wage or income tax changes by adjusting the amount of labor supplied. In the absence of the income tax, the equilibrium wage rate and quantity of labor are $9 and 6 units (point a'). How will these workers react to a newly imposed income tax? As we see from the intersection of D_t and S, workers will reduce the amount of labor supplied from 6 to 5 units (point c). Employers will encounter a shortage of labor of 1 unit (= 6 − 5) *at the $9 market wage*. This excess demand will drive the wage to $10, and the market will again clear at point d—this time at 5 units of labor. Those still working following the tax will receive a before-tax wage rate of $10 rather than $9. The workers' after-tax wage will fall by $1.25 (= $9 − $7.75) to $7.75. Notice that this decline is less than the tax per hour of $2.25 (= $10 − $7.75). The reason is that $1 of the tax is borne indirectly by employers as higher wage rates. Restated, of the total tax dc in Figure 9-3, ec is borne by workers while ed is borne by employers.

To summarize: Other things being equal, if the overall labor supply curve slopes upward, a personal income tax will reduce the quantity of labor supplied, cause the wage rate to rise, and decrease employment. Given the elasticity of demand, the greater the elasticity of supply, the greater will be the portion of the income tax borne by employers in the form of a higher market wage. The reader might want to rework the analysis for a perfectly *elastic* labor supply curve to demonstrate that under these conditions the *entire* tax will be borne by employers and that the employment effect will be greater.

Which of the two graphs in Figure 9-3 best portrays reality? How elastic is the overall supply of labor? Economists have approached this question both theoretically and empirically.

The Income Tax and Individual Labor Supply. The income tax is similar in impact to a wage rate decrease—both reduce the actual return from an hour of work and lower total net income from any specific number of hours of work. The tax generates income and substitution effects which act in opposing direc-

---

[7]This is true even in the presence of a strong union, assuming that it has already bargained for its optimal contract package. If it has squeezed all it can extract from the employers, the sudden enactment of an income tax can do nothing to enhance its ability to gain still more.

tions. By reducing income at any specific level of work, the tax lowers consumption of all normal goods, including leisure, and therefore the incentive to work increases. But the tax also reduces the net return from work or, stated alternatively, decreases the opportunity cost (price) of leisure. This creates an incentive to substitute the relatively lower-priced leisure for the now relatively higher-priced work (work declines). Thus, the overall impact of the tax on the number of labor hours collectively offered is theoretically indeterminate.

Figure 9-4 illustrates this graphically. The figure shows the indifference maps and budget constraints for Smith (graph a) and Jones (graph b). Notice that each graph portrays two budget lines—*HW* which is linear and *HW_t* which lies below *HW* and increases at a diminishing rate as work hours increase from 0 to 24. The *HW* curves show the *before-tax* income for Smith and Jones at each level of work hours, and the *HW_t* curves depict the *after-tax* income from that specific work effort. The vertical distances between *HW* and *HW_t* measure the income tax paid at each work-income combination. These distances increase as a percentage of income as income rises, again indicating that the tax is progressive.

In the absence of the tax, Smith (graph a) will choose to work h_1 hours, earn income Y_b, and maximize his utility at point *a* on indifference curve I_2. Once the income tax is imposed, Smith's after-tax wage rate falls as shown by the downward shift of *HW* to *HW_t*, and he reacts by *reducing* work effort to h_2 (point *b*). At this level of work he earns a gross income of Y_g, pays a total income tax of $Y_g Y_a$,

FIGURE 9-4 THE IMPACT OF A PERSONAL INCOME TAX ON INDIVIDUAL LABOR SUPPLY
A personal income tax shifts the after-tax wage rate line downward to W_t and may cause either an increase or decrease in a person's optimal supply of labor hours. For Smith (a), the substitution effect generated by the tax overpowers the income effect, resulting in a *decrease* in work from h_1 to h_2. Alternatively, for Jones, the income effect swamps the substitution effect, leading her to *increase* work hours from h_1 to h_2. The overall effect of the tax on the quantity of labor supplied is indeterminate.

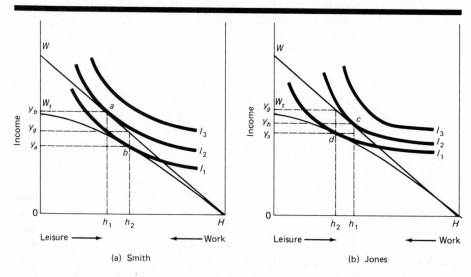

(a) Smith

(b) Jones

and receives an after-tax income of Y_a. For Smith, the income tax *reduces* the number of labor hours supplied by h_1h_2.

What is the outcome for Jones (graph b)? By employing the same logic, we find that she reacts to the tax by *increasing* her labor hours! Given her subjective preferences for income versus leisure, she discovers it to be in her interest to increase work from h_1 to h_2 (point d rather than c), earn a gross income of Y_g, pay a tax equal to the vertical distance Y_gY_a, and retain an after-tax income of Y_a. Hence, Figure 9-4 illustrates a basic point: The progressive income tax (and changes in tax rates) cause some workers to work less; others to work more; and still others to maintain their pretax level of work. For Smith (graph a), the substitution effect outweighs the income effect and he works less, but for Jones (graph b) the income effect swamps the substitution effect, leading her to work more. (Remember from Chapter 2 that the income effect increases hours of work and the substitution effect decreases hours of work when we are considering a *reduction* in wages.)

We have reached two general conclusions. First, the extent to which the U.S. income tax causes higher wages and reduces employment depends on the elasticity of labor supply in the economy. Second, the basic work-leisure theory of individual labor supply leaves one unable to predict whether the aggregate labor supply curve is negatively sloped, perfectly inelastic, or positively sloped. Thus we are uncertain as to whether the aggregate amount of labor supplied will increase or decrease in response to, say, an income tax reduction. Consequently, we must turn our attention to the empirical literature for further guidance.

Many economists have tried to measure the relative strengths of the income and substitution effects and thereby estimate the elasticity of aggregate labor supply in the economy. The task of designing these studies so that they incorporate and properly control for the many intercorrelated influences on labor supply behavior is extremely complex and difficult. The success of existing studies in accomplishing this task is subject to some debate, so the findings must be regarded with caution. Nevertheless, most of the studies conclude that the income effect slightly exceeds the substitution effect for adult males as a group. This implies that the supply curve for this group is negative; that is, tax increases (net wage decreases) cause males to increase their work hours slightly. For females, the substitution effect appears to dominate the income effect so that tax increases (wage decreases) create reductions in hours worked. The studies generally find that aggregating various individual labor curves yields an overall supply curve which is extremely inelastic. This empirical evidence leads most economists to conclude that the major portion of the income tax in the United States falls squarely on workers. Apparently the tax has a minimal net impact on work effort, the market wage rate, and equilibrium employment [Figure 9-3 (a)].

We must note, however, that this matter is not entirely settled. Recall from our previous analysis that government's provision of public goods theoretically can produce income effects which reduce labor hour offerings. These goods are financed partially through the personal income tax and are available to people independently of their work effort. Consequently, workers need not work as much to achieve a given level of real goods or total utility. This income effect may reduce labor hours offered and offset any added work effort generated by the income effect from the imposition of the tax. If so, only a substitution effect remains, and the overall outcome may be a reduced quantity of labor supplied.[8]

Federal and state income taxes may affect labor supply in several other ways. For example, an income tax may reduce the *net* rate of return from investment in human capital and therefore discourage such investments. Or, the tax may lead some workers who are paid on a piece-work or commission basis to reduce the intensity of their efforts. It also may entice people to retire early, induce workers to migrate form high- to low-tax geographic areas, and cause some salaried workers to switch to "underground" work activity to avoid paying income taxes.[9]

But the preponderance of evidence generated to date suggests that the personal income tax has a minor impact on the overall quantity of labor hours supplied. In fact, a case can be made that the exclusions, deductions, and credits which are part of the tax code do more to influence labor markets than does the tax itself. These tax preferences and tax expenditures influence spending patterns and thereby produce impacts in *specific* labor markets. For example, the tax deductability of interest paid on mortgages increases the demand for residential construction workers; the tax deduction for charitable contributions enables colleges to provide financial aid, which in turn increases the supply of graduates to such occupations as teaching, medicine, and law; the credit for child care expenses increases the demand for day care personnel and raises the labor force participation rate for females in the economy; and the complexity of the tax code increases the demand for tax accountants, tax lawyers, and IRS agents.

THE INCIDENCE OF THE PAYROLL TAX

The federal government levies flat rate taxes on all earnings below a set maximum to finance the Old Age, Survivors, Disability, and Health Insurance (OAS-DHI) and unemployment compensation programs. In 1984 employees and employers each paid a social security tax of 6.7 percent of the first $37,800 of wage or salary earnings. Employers also paid an unemployment compensation tax averaging 3.4 percent on the first $6000 of annual wages of each covered employee. Because these taxes are significant—they constituted about 30 percent of total federal tax receipts in 1984—and are levied directly on work earnings, labor economists have a keen interest in their impact on labor supply, wages, and employment.

---

[8]See Assar Lindbeck, "Tax Effects versus Budget Effect on Labor Supply," *Economic Inquiry*, October 1982, pp. 473–489. Also see Jerry A. Hausman, "Income and Payroll Tax Policy and Labor Supply," in Lawrence H. Meyer (ed.), *The Supply-Side Effects of Economic Policy* (St. Louis: Center for the Study of American Business, Washington University, 1981), pp. 173–202.

[9]See Harvey S. Rosen, "What is Labor Supply and Do Taxes Affect It?" *American Economic Review*, May 1980, pp. 171–176, and James E. Long, "Income Taxation and the Allocation of Labor," *Journal of Labor Research*, Summer 1982, pp. 259–276.

We will limit our analysis here to the social security tax under which the employer and employee legally are assessed equal taxes.[10] Figure 9-5 demonstrates the traditional analysis and conclusions concerning the question of who actually bears the burden of the tax. Notice that we simplify by assuming that the overall labor supply curve is perfectly inelastic, indicating that workers do not respond to the tax by reducing the collective quantity of labor supplied. The curve labeled D_1 in the figure is the conventional labor demand or marginal revenue product (MRP) curve. The pretax equilibrium wage is $10 and the equilibrium quantity is Q_1 units of labor. Let us assume that the employer is assessed a 7 percent payroll tax (one-half of 14 percent) on the pretax equilibrium wage. Because the true MRP of labor is now the initial MRP less the tax, the after-tax labor demand curve shifts downward to D_2. Note that, at the equilibrium quantity of Q_1 units of labor, the pretax wage and MRP are $10. But employers must pay a $.70 hourly tax (.07 × $10) for each labor hour employed. From their perspective, the effective MRP is only $9.30 ($10 − $.70). Thus the demand curve D_2 is the relevant one for making hiring decisions, and the vertical distance between D_1 and D_2 is the employer-paid tax. Given D_2 and S, the new equilibrium wage is $9.30. The overall labor *cost* for an hour of work

[10]We discuss selected labor market consequences of the unemployment insurance program in Chapter 18.

FIGURE 9-5 TAX INCIDENCE: A PAYROLL TAX

Given a perfectly inelastic supply of labor, the full incidence of a payroll tax is borne by workers in the form of a reduced net wage. Even though one-half of the 14 percent tax shown in this example ostensibly is paid by the employer, in reality all of the tax (= .14 × $10 = $1.40) is borne by the workers. In the absence of this payroll tax, the market wage would be $10; in its presence, the after-tax wage is $8.60.

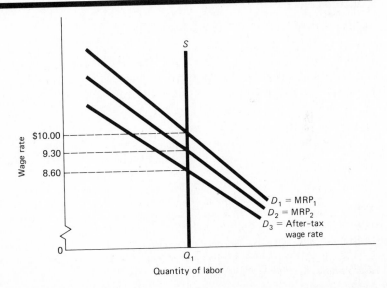

is still $10, but the composition of that cost has changed as follows: before taxes— $10 wage + 0 tax = $10; after taxes— $9.30 wage + $.70 tax = $10.

We also assume that *workers* pay a 7 percent tax on the full pretax wage. Curve D_3 shows the *after-tax* wage, which is calculated by subtracting the total 14 percent tax from D_1, or alternatively, subtracting a second 7 percent of $10 from D_2. As workers see it, their *net* hourly wage is $8.60. The payroll tax reduces their *market* wage from $10 to $9.30 and their actual after-tax wage from $10 to $8.60. On the surface, employers pay a tax of $.70 per hour, but in reality workers pay the entire $1.40 of tax.[11]

Empirical research conducted in the early 1970s by Brittain confirmed the conclusion drawn from Figure 9-5. According to his study, the full amount of the employer's share of the payroll tax tends to get shifted backward in the form of lower wages for employees.[12] More recent but highly controversial studies suggest that not all of the employer's portion of the tax is actually passed backward.[13] At least two explanations for these latter findings are possible. First, the labor supply curve may be somewhat elastic rather than perfectly inelastic. As the tax rises, spouses, teenagers, retired workers, and others who do not have strong attachment to the labor force may reduce their offerings of labor. If the overall labor supply in Figure 9-5 were somewhat elastic, employers would have to bear some of the tax imposed on them in order to continue to attract sufficient labor hours [recall our discussion of Figure 9-3, graph (b)]. Second, unions may accept net wage reductions deriving from the employee portion of the payroll tax, but may actively resist attempts by firms to shift the employer share backward to workers. Some corporations may conclude that it is less costly to pass portions of the payroll tax forward to customers than to attempt to pass it all backward to their unionized workers. If such forward shifting does occur, then the general price level will rise and the *real* wages received by all workers will fall.

EXCISE TAXATION AND LABOR MARKETS

Specific excises are a third type of tax that has a bearing on the labor market. These taxes are levied on the producers or sellers of such products as motor fuel, alcoholic beverages, tobacco products, fishing equipment, firearms, auto tires,

[11]As actually administered, the social security tax is levied against the actual wage paid to the worker—$9.30—and not against the wage which would have existed without the combined tax on the employer and employee—$10. This complication does not alter our basic conclusion: Given a perfectly inelastic labor supply curve, a worker will net an after-tax wage equal to the before-tax wage minus the combined amount of tax paid by the employer and the worker.

[12]See John A. Brittain, "The Incidence of Social Payroll Taxes," *American Economic Review*, March 1971, pp. 110–125; and *The Payroll Tax for Social Security* (Washington, D.C.: The Brookings Institution, 1972).

[13]Wayne Vroman, "Employer Payroll Tax Incidence: Empirical Tests with Cross Country Data," *Public Finance*, vol. 29, 1974, pp. 184–200; and J. H. Leuthold, "The Incidence of the Payroll Tax," *Southern Economic Journal*, February 1979, pp. 1208–1219.

telephone service, and amusement tickets. Under normal short-run supply and demand conditions, an excise tax *increases* the product price to the buyer and *lowers* the net or after-tax price to the seller. This can be observed in Figure 9-6 where the before-tax supply and demand for hypothetical product X yield an equilibrium price and quantity of $10 and 20 million units. Suppose that government imposes a $4 per unit excise tax on the sellers of product X. The tax increases the seller's marginal costs by $4 per unit and therefore shifts the supply curve upward vertically from S to S_t as shown in the figure. The after-tax equilibrium price rises to $12 and quantity falls from 20 to 16 million units. Notice that the net price to the seller falls from the original $10 to $8 (= $12 price − $4 tax). It is clear then that in this case the sellers bear $2 of the tax and the buyers pay the other $2. The reader should extend the analysis of Figure 9-6 to demonstrate the following two generalizations. First, given the supply curve of product X, the more inelastic the demand, the larger the portion of the tax paid by customers. Second, given the demand curve of product X, the greater the elasticity of supply, the larger the part of the tax paid by the seller.

The tax shown in Figure 9-6 is likely to have a direct impact in the market for the labor which helps produce product X. It also may produce secondary effects in other labor markets.

Direct Impact. Notice that the rise in price from $10 to $12 causes customers to reduce their purchases by 4 million units (= 20 − 16). This means that at a given

FIGURE 9-6 TAX INCIDENCE: A SELECTIVE EXCISE

A selective excise tax of $4 per unit increases marginal cost by $4 and shifts the supply curve upward by $4 at each quantity. The market price rises ($10 to $12), and the *net* price to the seller falls ($10 to $8). In this case, the sellers and buyers each bear part of the tax burden ($2 each).

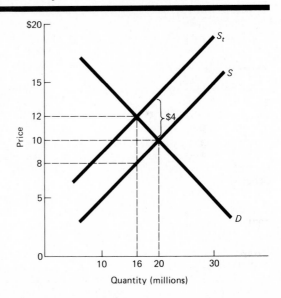

Quantity (millions)

wage rate, sellers will demand less labor than previously, or, stated more precisely, the derived demand for labor will decline. An alternative way to view this is to note the effect that the $4 tax has on the market MRP curve. Because the net price to sellers falls by $2 (= $12 − $10), MRP (= MP × P_p) falls by $2 *times* MP, with the result that firms demand fewer workers at each wage rate.

Figure 9-7 shows the impact of this decline in labor demand under three separate conditions of labor supply. If the supply is perfectly elastic as in (a), then the reduced demand caused by the excise tax will leave the wage rate unchanged but reduce employment from Q_0 to Q_t. If the supply of labor is perfectly inelastic as shown in (b), then the tax will cause no change in employment, but will cause the wage rate to decrease from W_0 to W_t. Finally, in the more realistic intermediate case where the supply of labor in the taxed industry is positively sloped (c), both the wage and quantity of labor hours will fall (W_0 to W_t and Q_0 to Q_t). We conclude that the portion of the excise tax on product X which initially falls on sellers may in fact impose costs on labor suppliers in the form of wage reductions or employment declines. Unions implicitly understand this and often vigorously oppose government attempts to impose or raise excise taxes on the products or services which they help produce. For example, a brewer's union might lobby against a proposal to increase an excise on beer, or communications workers might join with their employers to oppose a suggested increase in the excise tax on telephone services.

Secondary Effects. The market impacts of the $4 excise tax on product X may extend beyond the labor market for product X workers. In particular, the supply of, and demand for, labor may be affected in various other markets. In graphs (a) and (c) of Figure 9-7 we observed that the tax reduced employment. Where do

FIGURE 9-7 EXCISES, LABOR DEMAND, AND WAGE AND EMPLOYMENT IMPACTS
Other things being equal, the wage and employment impact of a decline in labor demand caused by a selective excise tax depends on the elasticity of labor supply in the specific industry. If supply is perfectly elastic as in (a), employment declines; if it is perfectly inelastic as shown in (b), the equilibrium wage rate falls; and if it displays an upward slope as in (c), both employment and the wage rate fall.

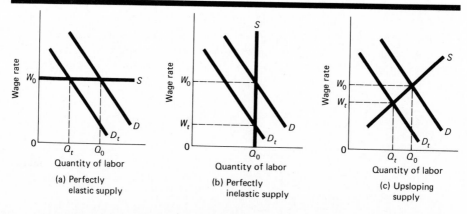

(a) Perfectly elastic supply

(b) Perfectly inelastic supply

(c) Upsloping supply

the discharged workers offer their labor services? Let us initially assume that they all enter a single closely related occupation. As a consequence, the supply of labor to that occupation would increase and, assuming a competitive market, the wage rate would tend to fall. Alternatively, and perhaps more likely, the workers who are displaced from industry X would scatter to various occupations and the impact on the labor supply in any one labor market would be slight. To summarize: A selective excise tax may cause a decline in labor demand in the taxed industry which in turn may produce increases in labor supply in nontaxed industries. The extent to which these effects occur depends upon elasticities of supply and demand.

To complicate things further, the excise tax on product X may influence the demand for labor in industries related to X. Suppose, for example, that product Y is untaxed and is a reasonable *substitute* for product X. For example, X might be one type of alcoholic beverage while Y is another. The higher price for X might cause buyers to shift their purchases to the relatively cheaper Y, thereby increasing the demand for the labor which produces Y. Or suppose, as a second example, that product X is used as a *complement* to product Z. For example, X might be firearms while Z is ammunition. The higher price for X (firearms) ultimately might reduce the demand for Z (ammunition) and consequently cause the demand for labor in industry Z to fall.

The reader who is familiar with general equilibrium analysis will recognize that the final labor market effects of the $4 tax on product X are difficult to ascertain. Thus some of the impacts that we have cited may be mitigated or completely offset by still further secondary effects. For example, when the wage rate of a specific occupation falls, the net present value of new investment in human capital required for that occupation declines (Chapter 4). In the long run this will reduce supply in this particular labor market, which will then reduce some of the initial wage rate decline. As another example, if government uses the tax revenue from the excise to build public goods which are *complements* to the taxed product X, then the product and labor demand for X may increase, causing an increase in the derived demand for labor. For example, the revenues from the federal excise tax on gasoline are earmarked for road construction and maintenance. Taken alone, this increases the demand for gasoline and the derived demand for refinery workers.

Fortunately—at least for the sake of analytical simplicity—present excise taxes are levied mainly on products for which demand is highly inelastic. Therefore most of the tax impact falls on buyers who do not respond by substantially cutting their purchases. Hence the labor market impacts in the taxed industry are greatly reduced.

SUMMARY

1. Between 1950 and 1984, government employment increased both absolutely and as a percentage of total employment. The rate of growth of public-sector employment was greatest at the state and local levels of government.

2. The increase in demand for government workers over the 1950–1984 period increased wages in public-sector employment. Evidence suggests that, in the 1970s, federal workers may have achieved higher wage rates than comparably educated and experienced private-sector employees.

3. The total economic cost of allocating labor to the military consists of the total value of the alternative output (income) that is forgone. A "voluntary" army requires that economic costs be paid by taxpayers; a "drafted" army at below-market wage rates imposes much of the costs on those who are conscripted.

4. Taken alone, government's provision of goods and services may create an income effect which reduces one's optimal supply of hours of work.

5. Government transfer payments and subsidies affect the composition of labor demand in the economy and also influence labor supply decisions.

6. Other things being equal, the more elastic the overall labor supply in the economy, the greater the extent to which a personal income tax will cause (a) a decline in the hours of labor supplied, (b) an increase in the market wage, and (c) lower overall employment. Most economists, however, judge the aggregate labor supply curve to be highly inelastic.

7. The impact of an income tax on an individual's optimal supply of labor is theoretically indeterminate in that the tax generates income and substitution effects which work in opposite directions with respect to the quantity of labor supplied.

8. Traditional analysis of the incidence of the payroll tax concludes that the full burden of the tax—including that portion levied on the employer—is borne by workers in the form of reduced wage rates. Recent analysis suggests that a portion of the tax levied on employers may be borne by that group.

9. Selective excise taxes may reduce labor demand in directly affected industries and may either increase or decrease the demand for labor in industries which produce substitutes or complements to the taxed product.

QUESTIONS AND STUDY SUGGESTIONS

1. Key terms and concepts to remember: prevailing-wage rule; military conscription; volunteer or market-based army; government purchases; transfer payments; subsidies; pure public goods; income, payroll, and excise taxes.

2. List and discuss factors which help explain why public-sector employment has risen faster than private-sector employment over the past several decades. At what levels of government has public-sector employment increased most dramatically?

3. Comment: "In general, federal government employees are underpaid compared to similar private-sector workers. This is due to the monopsony power of government."

4. Speculate as to the political considerations which might cause local governments to pay less-skilled workers more, and more highly trained workers less, than comparably trained, experienced, and employed private-sector workers.

5. Explain why a voluntary army may be less expensive to society than an army composed of draftees. Which will likely be less expensive to taxpayers?

6. Explain why a draft system might cause the U.S. military to overemploy labor and underemploy capital (from society's perspective). Speculate as to why the army increasingly "contracts out" construction and maintenance work to private firms now that there is a voluntary army.

7. Assuming that "income" includes both private and public goods, and that leisure is a normal good, explain how a major reduction in governmentally provided goods might increase a person's optimum number of hours of work.

8. Explain how the existence of national, state, and city parks might affect
   a. labor demand in the recreational vehicle industry
   b. labor demand for workers who build and maintain equipment for private recreational "theme" parks
   c. the overall supply of labor

9. Use the following labor market data to determine the answers to (a) through (d).

(1) Wage Rate	(2) Quantity Demanded	(3) Quantity Supplied	(4) Tax Per Hour
$10	14	22	$3.33
8	18	22	2.67
6	22	22	2.00
4	26	22	1.33
2	30	22	.67

   a. Is this tax progressive? Explain.
   b. What is the before-tax equilibrium wage rate?
   c. What effect does the tax have on the number of hours of work supplied and the after-tax *market* wage rate?
   d. If the labor supply curve were highly elastic, rather than perfectly inelastic, how would your answers to (c) change?

10. In what way are the following two statements contradictory?
   a. "An increase in that portion of a payroll tax levied on the *employer* is simply a disguised tax on workers. It will be borne fully by employees in the form of reduced market wages."
   b. "An increase in the *employer*-paid portion of a payroll tax is highly inflationary."

SELECTED REFERENCES

ANDERSON, MARTIN (ed.): *Conscription: A Select and Annotated Bibliography* (Stanford, Calif.: Hoover Institution Press, 1976), chaps. 4 and 9.

BRITTAIN, JOHN A.: *The Payroll Tax for Social Security* (Washington, D.C.: The Brookings Institution, 1972).

BROWN, CHARLES V.: *Taxation and the Incentive to Work*, 2nd ed. (New York: Oxford University Press, 1983).

HAUSMAN, JERRY A.: "Labor Supply," in Henry J. Aaron and Joseph A. Pechman (eds.), *How Taxes Affect Economic Behavior* (Washington, D.C.: The Brookings Institution, 1981), pp. 27–72.

LEVINE, MARVIN J. (ed.): *Labor Relations in the Public Sector: Readings and Cases*, 2nd ed. (Columbus, Ohio: Grid Publishing, Inc., 1985).

MUSGRAVE, RICHARD A., and PEGGY B. MUSGRAVE: *Public Finance in Theory and Practice*, 4th ed. (New York: McGraw-Hill Book Company, 1984), chap. 13.

ROSEN, HARVEY S.: *Public Finance* (Homewood, Ill.: Richard D. Irwin, Inc., 1985), chap. 15.

SMITH, SHARON P.: *Equal Pay in the Public Sector: Fact or Fantasy* (Princeton, N. J.: Princeton University Press, 1977).

TIME AND ONE-HALF

INTEREST ARBITRATION IN THE PUBLIC SECTOR

Arbitration increasingly is being used to settle disputes involving government employees.

Nonmilitary federal employees and state and local workers in all but three states legally can join unions. Presently, about one-half of all federal workers belong to an affiliate of the AFL-CIO, and nearly one-half of all state and local government employees are represented by either labor unions or by professional associations which bargain collectively.

But unlike private-sector workers, most public employees cannot legally strike. The National Labor Relations Act prohibits work stoppages by employees of the United States or any of its agencies or wholly owned corporations. Violation of the law may result in loss of civil service status, discharge from one's job, and ineligibility for federal employment for 3 years. Most states have similar prohibitions, although a few states do allow strikes by nonessential government workers under specific circumstances.

Recall from Chapter 7's Chamberlain model that, in the private sector, the threat of the strike and the strike itself impose costs of disagreeing—lost profits and wages—on the parties to the dispute. Each party, therefore, has an incentive to reach a settlement. But this strike-induced incentive does not exist in the public sector where strikes are illegal. Consequently, alternative procedures often are needed to resolve bargaining impasses. One such procedure is *interest arbitration.*[1]

Interest arbitration involves the appointment of a professional arbitrator or a tripartite panel of labor, management, and public representatives to hear the final positions of the parties and then to make a binding determination of the contract terms. Interest arbitration takes two general forms: *conventional arbitration,* in which the arbitrator typically "customizes" the contract award by devising compromise solutions, and *final-offer arbitration,* wherein the arbitrator must select either the last position of the union or of the management with no compromises permitted.

Just how effective are these procedures? While there are numerous criteria by which effectiveness might be judged, the following are most often used.

1. *Preservation of collective bargaining.* Most labor relations experts contend that a "good" impasse procedure is one that rarely needs to be used. The added uncertainty associated with the outcome of the procedure ideally should replace the strike as an incentive for the parties to reach settlement on their own. Conventional interest arbitration does not grade highly on this criterion. Rather, arbitration of this sort tends to produce two effects which together discourage predeadline concession making.

Chilling Effect: Conventional arbitration "chills" bargaining by diminishing each party's incentive to offer concessions. This effect is particularly pronounced where the parties expect the arbitrator to "split the difference" between the final positions. There simply is no reason for one party to offer a concession if it assumes that the other side will fail to reciprocate and that eventually the arbitrator will produce an award which is midway between the final positions. Although arbitrators clearly do not uniformly "split the

---

[1]This is termed *interest* arbitration to distinguish it from *grievance* arbitration. The latter involves disputes that arise under the terms of *existing* contracts, while our focus is on arbitration involving attempts by differing interests to agree on *new* contracts.

difference" in devising compromise awards, several studies do confirm that conventional arbitration tends to produce a significant chilling effect on negotiations.[2]

Narcotic Effect: The evidence also indicates that arbitration creates a dependency upon the procedures, or a so-called "narcotic effect." For example, Kochan notes the repeated pattern of usage of arbitration by police and firefighters in municipalities covered by arbitration laws.[3] This dependency apparently occurs because union members and the public tend to equate the concession making required to achieve voluntary agreement with weak bargaining on the part of their negotiators. By turning the final outcome over to the arbitration board and then blaming it for the "unfair" award, negotiators can retain their reputations for toughness at the bargaining table.

In theory, final-offer arbitration should greatly diminish the chilling effect of arbitration. Recognizing that the arbitrator must select one or the other of the final positions, negotiators should prefer to modify their positions rather than risk having the other party's position accepted. This should increase the likelihood of prearbitration settlements. There is some evidence which does support this theory. But scholars also note the continued presence of the narcotic effect even under final-offer arbitration.

2. *Reduction of illegal strike activity.* Strikes by public-sector workers are prohibited because of the presumed severity of the costs imposed by the disruption of public services. Nevertheless, government employees occasionally are willing to risk being fired for striking when they judge the likelihood of being replaced to be slight. Finding qualified replacements for, say, police officers, firefighters, or nurses may be difficult, if not impossible, in the short run. A "good" impasse procedure therefore ought to reduce the incidence of these illegal strikes. Interest arbitration—both conventional and final-offer—accomplishes this goal quite admirably. For example, a national study of municipal police bargaining found that only 6.2 percent of all the police strikes occurring in the 5-year period under study happened in environments providing for binding arbitration.[4] While interest arbitration does not eliminate strikes in the public sector, it does clearly reduce their number and severity.

3. *Generation of equitable and efficient wage outcomes.* Some experts in labor relations contend that a "good" arbitration award is one that closely resembles the outcome that would have occurred in the absence of the strike prohibition and the arbitration procedure. How well does arbitration perform against this admittedly arbitrary standard? Olson found that wage increases received by firefighters in jurisdictions which had binding arbitration laws were significantly higher than in jurisdictions which did not.[5] What might explain this? One possibility is that, because arbitration adds uncertainty to the outcome of the negotiations, parties who are less averse to risks will have an advantage

[2]See, for example, Thomas Kochan, "Dynamics of Dispute Resolution in the Public Sector" in Benjamin Aaron et al. (eds.), *Public-Sector Bargaining* (Washington, D.C.: Bureau of National Affairs, Inc., 1979), pp. 176–177. Also see John M. Magenau, "The Impact of Alternative Impasse Procedures on Bargaining: A Laboratory Experiment," *Industrial and Labor Relations Review*, April 1983, pp. 361–377.

[3]T. Kochan, op. cit., pp. 171–177. For a finding that the narcotic effect may *lessen* as negotiators gain more *experience* with arbitration, see Richard J. Butler and Ronald G. Ehrenberg, "Estimating the Narcotic Effect of Public Sector Impasse Procedures," *Industrial and Labor Relations Review*, October 1981, pp. 3–20.

[4]Casey Ichniowski, "Arbitration and Police Bargaining: Prescriptions for the Blue Flu," *Industrial Relations*, Spring 1982, pp. 149–166.

[5]Craig A. Olson, "The Impact of Arbitration on the Wages of Firefighters," *Industrial Relations*, Fall 1980, pp. 325–389.

over those who are less more to risks. Perhaps public-sector negotiators are less willing to risk the consequences of a negative award by the arbitrator than are union negotiators. This may translate into less willingness on the part of government to retain present negotiating positions and therefore into more willingness to yield to union demands in advance of the deadline.

To summarize: Interest arbitration reduces strikes and the attendant disruption of public services, but also tends to reduce the incentive for the parties to bargain in good faith prior to the deadline and quite possibly may result in higher government wages. The increasing enactment of arbitration statutes across the nation indicates that state governments perceive the benefits from interest arbitration to outweigh the costs.

GOVERNMENT AND THE LABOR MARKET: LEGISLATION AND REGULATION

Besides directly employing labor, providing public goods and services, transferring income, and levying taxes (Chapter 9), government engages in the important task of establishing the legal rules for the economy. Many of these laws and regulations directly or indirectly affect wage and employment outcomes in labor markets. We examine such laws throughout the book—for example, in later chapters we analyze laws which outlaw discrimination, limit immigration, and promote full employment. Laws affecting labor markets are so numerous that we must be highly selective in our discussion. Therefore we limit our analysis here to four main topics. First, we discuss the influence of labor relations laws on union membership, bargaining power, and labor markets. Second, we examine the wage, employment, and income distribution effects of the federal minimum wage law. Next, our focus turns to the controversial Occupational Safety and Health Act of 1970 and the question of the proper role of the government in promoting workplace safety. This is an interesting example of the wide variety of ways in which government directly intervenes in the labor market. Finally, we discuss government laws which provide workers with increases in economic "rent." In this section we extend the discussion of occupational licensure presented in Chapter 6 and also look at the rent aspects of tariffs, quotas, and proposed "domestic content" laws.

LABOR LAW

Laws governing labor relations in general and collective bargaining in particular constitute a significant institutional factor which influences wages, employment, and resource allocation. The major laws in this category are summarized in Table 10-1. A careful reading of this table will complement the discussion which follows. The labor relations laws summarized in the table affect the labor market in diverse ways, two of which are: (1) by influencing the extent and growth of union membership, which in turn influences the ability of unions to secure wage gains; and (2) by establishing the rules under which collective bargaining transpires. Let us examine each.

257

Labor Law and Union Membership. We observe in Figure 10-1 that the absolute number of unionized workers grew from about a million in 1900 to approximately 22 million in 1980. Notice, however, that union membership stood at less than 4 million in 1930 before surging to 15 million two decades later. What accounted for the slow growth prior to the 1930s? What explains the dramatic rise in union membership in the two decades following that period? Let us see how labor law relates to each question.

TABLE 10-1

A Summary of Basic Labor Relations Laws

Norris-LaGuardia Act of 1932

1. Increased the difficulty for employers to obtain injunctions against union activity.
2. Declared that yellow-dog contracts were unenforceable. These contracts legally prohibited workers from joining a union as a condition of continued employment.

The Wagner Act of 1935 (National Labor Relations Act - NLRA)

1. Guaranteed the "twin rights" of labor: the right of self-organization and the right to bargain with employers engaged in interstate commerce.
2. Listed a number of "unfair labor practices" on the part of management. Specifically, it (a) forbids employers to interfere with the right of workers to form unions; (b) outlaws company unions; (c) prohibits antiunion discrimination by employers in hiring, firing, and promoting; (d) outlaws discrimination against any worker who files charges or gives testimony under the act; and (e) obligates employers to bargain in good faith.
3. Established the National Labor Relations Board (NLRB) which was given the authority to investigate unfair labor practices occurring under the act, to issue cease-and-desist orders, and to conduct elections by workers on whether or not they desire union representation.
4. Made strikes by federal employees illegal and grounds for dismissal.

The Taft-Hartley Act of 1947 (Amendment to the NLRA of 1935)

1. Established "unfair labor practices" on the part of unions. Specifically, it prohibits (1) coercion of employees to become union members, (2) jurisdictional strikes (disputes between unions over who is authorized to perform a specific job), (3) secondary boycotts (refusing to buy or handle products produced by another union or group of workers); (4) sympathy strikes (work stoppages by one union designed to assist some other union in gaining employer recognition or some other objective); (5) excessive union dues, and (6) featherbedding (forcing payment for work not actually performed).
2. Regulated the internal administration of unions; e.g., required detailed financial reports to the NLRB.
3. Outlawed the closed shop but made union and agency shops legal in those states which do not expressly prohibit them (state "right-to-work" laws).
4. Set up emergency strike procedures allowing the government to stop for up to 80 days a strike which imperils the nation's health and safety.
5. Created the Federal Mediation and Conciliation Service to provide mediators for labor disputes.

The Landrum-Griffin Act of 1959 (Amendment to the NLRA of 1935)

1. Required regularly scheduled elections of union officers and excluded Communists and those convicted of felonies from holding union office.
2. Held union officers strictly accountable for union funds and property.
3. Prevented union leaders from infringing on the individual worker's rights to participate in union meetings, to vote in union proceedings, and to nominate officers.

Although the reasons for the slow growth of unionism before the mid-1930s are many and varied, historians point to one as dominant: prior to the 1930s, union organizers and members were legally unprotected against reprisals by employers or even government itself. Stated bluntly, joining a union might involve job loss, fines, or bodily harm. Attempts to unionize were met with *discriminatory discharge* in many instances. Those dismissed often were placed on *blacklists* and therefore denied opportunities to gain alternative employment. Workers sometimes were required to sign *yellow-dog contracts* which, as a condition of continued employment, legally prohibited them from joining unions. Violation could result not only in discharge, but also in a lawsuit initiated by the employer and culminating in a court-imposed fine. Firms also used *lockouts* (plant closedowns) as a way to stop organizing attempts in their infancies. By closing down the plant for a few weeks, employers could impose high costs on those contemplating joining labor unions. Where workers did successfully organize and attempt to force their employers to bargain, firms often countered strikes by employing *strikebreakers* who sometimes clashed violently with union workers. The Homestead Strike of 1892 and the Pullman Strike of 1894 are cases in point. Often government intervened with police action on the side of employers during these confrontations.

Court hostility toward unionization was a related factor explaining the low union membership during this period. In the absence of labor laws, courts relied on common law interpretations. This placed unions in the weak position of

FIGURE 10-1 UNION MEMBERSHIP, 1900–1980
Union membership grew in absolute numbers from about a million in 1900 to 22 million in 1980. Most of this growth occurred after the passage of prolabor legislation in the mid-1930s.

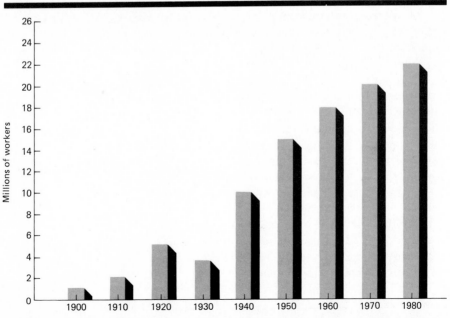

seeking new legal rights for labor at the expense of long-standing property rights of firms. This court hostility manifested itself in several ways, including (1) their interpretation of antitrust laws and (2) *injunctions.* For example, the Supreme Court held that the Sherman Antitrust Act of 1890 applied to unions, even though the intent of the legislation was clearly directed toward prohibiting price fixing and monopolization by firms. Injunctions were readily dispensed as a way of stopping actions such as picketing, striking, and boycotting which employers claimed would reduce their profits. Lower profits would reduce the capitalized value of the firm's assets and, according to the courts, violate the firm's property rights.

To summarize: Prior to the 1930s, the *absence* of protective labor legislation allowed firms and the courts to repress union activity and growth. The low union membership translated into an inability of unions, in general, to make a significant impact on the overall labor market.

This changed dramatically in the 1930s. Recall from the summary of labor legislation in Table 10-1 that Congress enacted significant labor relations laws during this period. These laws—specifically, the Norris-LaGuardia Act of 1932 and the Wagner Act of 1935—placed a protective umbrella over the union movement and greatly encouraged growth of union membership. More precisely, by outlawing yellow-dog contracts, the *Norris-LaGuardia Act* significantly reduced the personal costs of becoming a union member and thus made it easier to organize a firm's work force. Previously, the opportunity costs of joining a union might be the loss of one's job! Also, the act's provision limiting the use of the court-issued injunction to halt normal union activities such as striking and picketing obviously increased the ability of unions to impose costs on firms as a way to obtain higher wage offers. Larger union wage gains, in turn, increased the *incentive* for workers to become union members.

The *Wagner Act* had even greater impact on union membership. In fact, one of the expressed purposes of this law was to promote the growth of unionism. A glance back at Table 10-1 reminds us that this legislation guaranteed unions (1) the right to self-organization, free of interference from employers, and (2) the right to bargain as a unit with employers. Furthermore, the act delineated several "unfair labor practices" which management previously had used successfully to thwart unionism. The Wagner Act enabled the American Federation of Labor (AFL) to solidify its power within various crafts and also permitted the rapid growth of industrial unions affiliated with the Congress of Industrial Organizations (CIO). These CIO unions organized millions of less-skilled workers employed in such mass production industries as steel, rubber, and automobiles. By the time of the merger between the AFL and CIO in 1955, union membership had risen to about 17 million.

The dramatic surge in union membership in the two decades following the prounion legislation of the mid-1930s strengthened the ability of unions to achieve dominance (Chapter 6) of many labor and product markets and hence secure improvements in wage rates and working conditions. That is, increases in union membership translated into increased union bargaining power and a greater overall impact of unionism on labor market outcomes.

Labor Law and Bargaining Power. The overall body of labor law and specific provisions of the law influence bargaining power independently of effects on the level of union membership. Stated succinctly, many provisions of labor law enhance the bargaining power of unions, thereby enabling unions to secure higher wage gains; other provisions strengthen the negotiating positions of employers.

There are as many examples to support this generalization as there are major provisions of the labor laws. Let us explore just three: (1) the aforementioned limitation of the use of the injunction, (2) the prohibition of many forms of secondary boycotts, and (3) the emergency strike provision of the Taft-Hartley Act of 1947. In discussing these topics, our purpose is not to sort out the pros and cons of the particular provisions but rather simply to provide examples of ways in which labor law influences bargaining power and labor market outcomes.

1. Limitation of the use of the injunction. A limitation on the use of court-issued injunctions to enjoin picketing, striking, and related union activities was placed into effect by the Norris-LaGuardia Act of 1932. This prohibition clearly strengthened union bargaining power. Because firms could no longer gain legal relief from, say, a work stoppage, threats by unions to strike now became more credible. Previously, firms knew they could get the courts to enjoin the strike once it began. In terms of the bargaining power model discussed in Chapter 7, the limitation on the issuance of these back-to-work orders caused management's costs of disagreeing to rise. This raised union bargaining power which, you will recall, is its ability to get management to accept the union's wage demand. This provision of the Norris-LaGuardia Act, then, confirms our basic point: Labor law influences labor market outcomes by affecting relative bargaining power.

2. Prohibition of secondary boycotts. *Secondary boycotts* are actions by one union to refuse to handle, or to get one's employer to refuse to buy, products made by a firm that is party to a labor dispute. Although the Taft-Hartley Act of 1947 presumably made these secondary pressures illegal, trucking unions continued to demand and obtain "hot cargo" clauses in their contracts. The courts ruled that such clauses technically did not constitute an illegal secondary boycott. What were these clauses and how did they affect union bargaining power?

Hot cargo clauses declared that trucking firms would not require unionized truckers to handle or transport products made by an "unfair" employer involved in a labor dispute. For example, suppose that a manufacturer of fabricated steel products was being struck by its employees. Unionized transportation firms governed by hot cargo provisions would refuse to transport these fabricated steel items while the labor dispute was in progress. In terms of equation (7-1), this would mean that the union representing the steel fabricators had more bargaining power than it might otherwise have possessed. The reason is that, as a result of the hot cargo provisions, the strike would effectively curtail all revenue to the firm, thus causing it to suffer losses; it could not maintain its sales and profits through such actions as hiring strikebreakers, using supervisory personnel, or selling from its inventory. Once struck by a union, the firm simply could not get its products transported to its customers. Hence, management's costs of disagreeing would increase, causing a corresponding rise in the union's bargaining power (equation 7-1).

The Landrum-Griffin Act of 1959 declared hot cargo contracts illegal. Specifically, the act stated that it was an unfair labor practice for a union and employer "to enter into any contract or agreement, express or implied, whereby the employer ceases or refrains or agrees to cease or refrain from handling; using; selling; transporting; or otherwise dealing in any products of any other employer, or to cease doing business with any other persons." Once passed and enforced, this prohibition reduced union bargaining power by reducing management's cost of disagreeing in many labor disputes. That is, many firms now could continue to maintain their profits during strikes by hiring strikebreakers, using supervisory personnel, or selling previously produced goods.

3. Emergency strike provisions. The Taft-Hartley Act of 1947 established procedures for direct government intervention to stop strikes which threaten the nation's health and safety. These *emergency strike procedures* enable the government to declare a "cooling off" period during which work resumes and the parties continue their negotiations. The specific procedures under the Taft-Hartley Act are as follows. First, if the president has reason to believe that a strike or lockout affecting an entire or substantial part of an industry will imperil the national health and safety, he or she can appoint a board of inquiry to study the situation. Upon receiving the report of the board, the president can then direct the U.S. attorney general to seek a court injunction to halt the strike. The injunction ends the strike for a maximum of 80 days. After the first 60 days, the National Labor Relations Board (NLRB) conducts an election by secret ballot of union workers on the last offer made by the firm. The NLRB then has 15 days to report the results, and the attorney general has 5 days to certify them. If there is still no settlement after 80 days (= 60 + 15 + 5), the procedure reaches an end and the strike legally may resume.

The net impact of the emergency strike procedure on relative bargaining strength is less certain than in our previous examples. However, many observers conclude that these procedures increase management's bargaining power. Why? The argument is that in industries where national health and safety are presumably involved—coal, aircraft engines, steel, longshoring and shipping, and so forth—management need not make compromise offers prior to the expiration of the existing contract (strike deadline). Firms, in effect, expect government to enjoin a threatened strike should it occur. Hence, management's costs of disagreeing with the union's demands remain low, and therefore the union's bargaining power also remains low. Furthermore, the status quo usually favors the firm; that is, normally the firm is resisting a demanded wage increase and the procedures allow production to continue for 80 days *at the lower wage scale* stated in the old contract. To be sure, once the 80-day cooling off period has expired, the strike legally may resume but, once having declared such a strike a national emergency, government is likely to place *extreme* pressure on the union to keep working. If successful, this pressure nullifies the union's strike threat and lessens the likelihood that it will achieve its wage demand. To summarize: The emergency strike provision eliminates the realistic threat and probability of a strike. Under such circumstances, it is difficult for the union to impose high costs of disagreeing on management; therefore, union bargaining power is lower than it otherwise might be. Consequently, it is not surprising that unions strongly opposed passage of the Taft-Hartley Act in general and the emergency strike procedures in particular. This opposition again highlights our central proposition that labor law is an important influence on bargaining power. In fact, the expressed purpose of labor law is to *balance* the bargaining power of unions and management so that wage settlements are generally consistent with the nation's overall equity and efficiency goals.

THE MINIMUM-WAGE LAW

The *Fair Labor Standards Act of 1938*, which established a minimum hourly wage of $.25 per hour, represents another way government legislation affects the labor market. Congress has amended the act many times to increase the legal minimum wage in monetary terms. In 1985, the legal minimum was $3.35 an hour. For most years since 1938, the minimum wage has remained roughly 40 to 50 percent of the average hourly wage in manufacturing.

Congress also has extended the coverage of the minimum-wage law over the years. The original legislation placed approximately 44 percent of all nonsupervisory workers under its coverage; in 1985 approximately 85 percent of all such employees were included. Statistics for 1980 show that 12.4 percent of all part-time and full-time U.S. workers earned the minimum wage or less. About 44 percent of all teenagers and 38 percent of workers 65 or older were in this category. Also, about 18 percent of black employees compared to 11 percent of white workers and 18 percent of females as contrasted to 8 percent of males earned the minimum wage or less in 1980. Finally, minimum-wage employment was found to be heaviest in agriculture, retail trade, and services.[1]

The minimum wage has been controversial since its inception. Proponents argue that it is needed to ensure that workers receive a "living wage," that is, one that will provide full-time workers an annual income sufficient to purchase the bare necessities of life. They also contend that this wage floor prevents monopsonistic employers from exploiting low-skilled labor, a disproportionate number of whom are minorities and women. Finally, proponents point to the possibility that the minimum wage "shocks" employers into greater technical efficiency, thereby raising labor productivity and mitigating much of the unemployment consequence predicted by conventional economic theory.

Opponents of the minimum wage, on the other hand, argue that it results in

---

[1] *Report of the Minimum Wage Study Commission* (Washington: U.S. Government Printing Office, 1981), pp. 9 and 20.

increased unemployment, particularly among teenagers, females, and minorities. Second, opponents cite the possibility that the legal wage floor causes declines in wage rates in those sectors of the economy which are not covered by the law. Finally, critics contend that the minimum wage is poorly targeted to reduce poverty; that is, it has little impact on the distribution of *family* income.

Economists have engaged in both theoretical analysis and empirical research to sort out the possible effects of the minimum wage. Our discussion of these efforts will proceed as follows. First, we will assume uniform, or complete, coverage under the minimum-wage law and analyze the wage and employment consequences in the low-wage labor market. Second, the potential consequence of a shock effect on the employment outcome will be explored. Next, we will extend the analysis by examining the impact of the legal minimum wage in a monopsonistic labor market. Then we will relax the assumption that coverage is complete and analyze the effects of the minimum wage in a two-sector model. Finally, a summary of the empirical findings on the impacts of the minimum wage will be provided.[2]

The Basic Model: Complete Coverage. In Figure 10-2 we assume that all employees in the economy are covered by the minimum-wage law and that

[2]Our organization roughly follows that used by Charles Brown, Curtis Gilroy, and Andrew Kohen in "The Effect of the Minimum Wage on Employment and Unemployment," *The Journal of Economic Literature,*" June 1982, pp. 487–528.

FIGURE 10-2 MINIMUM WAGE EFFECTS: BASIC MODEL
The above-equilibrium minimum wage W_m reduces employment in this low-wage labor market by ab and creates unemployment of ac. The more elastic the labor supply and demand curves, the greater the unemployment consequences of the law.

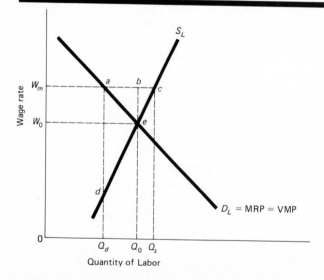

labor and product markets are perfectly competitive (MRP = VMP). The figure depicts the impact of a specific minimum wage W_m on a labor market in which the equilibrium wage and employment levels are W_0 and Q_0, respectively. One point needs to be stressed at the outset: If the minimum wage W_m is at or below the equilibrium wage W_0, which is the case for higher-wage labor markets, then the law is irrelevant and has *no* direct wage and employment consequence. That is, the actual wage and employment outcome will remain at W_0 and Q_0. But clearly this is not the situation in Figure 10-2 where W_m exceeds the equilibrium wage W_0.

What employment, unemployment, and allocation effects will this government-imposed minimum wage produce? First, observe that, at W_m, employers will hire only Q_d workers rather than the original Q_0. Stated differently, the marginal revenue product of the Q_d through Q_0 workers will be less than the minimum wage, and therefore profit-maximizing employers will reduce employment. Second, notice that the supply curve suggests that the minimum wage will attract Q_s as opposed to Q_0 workers to the market. The minimum wage changes the behavior of employers and labor suppliers such that employment declines by the amount ba, while unemployment increases by the larger amount ac.

Third, the minimum wage W_m causes allocative inefficiency. Notice from segment ae of the labor demand curve that the value of the marginal product (VMP) for each of the Q_d to Q_0 workers exceeds the supply price of these persons (as shown by segment de of S_L). This implies that society is giving up output of greater value ($Q_d a e Q_0$) than the $Q_d Q_0$ displaced workers can contribute in their next most productive employment ($Q_d d e Q_0$). The *net* loss of national output is shown then by area dae ($= Q_d a e Q_0 - Q_d d e Q_0$). The reader should use Figure 10-2 to verify the following generalizations: (1) other things being equal, the higher the minimum wage relative to the equilibrium wage, the greater the negative employment and allocation effects; and (2) the more elastic the labor supply and demand curves, the greater the unemployment consequences of the law.

The Shock Effect. We next examine the potential consequences of a shock effect on the outcome predicted by the competitive labor market model. Recall from our discussion in Chapter 6 that, under conditions of imperfect competition or productive inefficiency in product markets, unions might be able to force an increase in the wage rate without suffering the unemployment effects predicted by the standard model. This may also be true for a minimum wage which shocks the firm into improving its management, employing better technology, or undertaking any other actions which increase the marginal product of labor. As portrayed in Figure 10-3, the minimum wage may actually shift the demand for labor curve rightward. Notice that the increase in labor demand from D to D' mitigates some of the unemployment which otherwise would have resulted. In the absence of the shock effect, unemployment would be ac; in the presence of this effect it is only xc.

A shock effect produced by a minimum wage theoretically could *completely* offset any negative unemployment and resource allocation consequences, but most economists judge the likelihood of this outcome to be small. First, for inefficiency to exist, competition in the product market must be quite weak. In competitive product markets, inefficient firms—those who do not achieve minimum average cost—are driven out of business or acquired by firms who are efficient. Second, where inefficiency does exist, firms are just as likely to be *overemploying* labor as they are to be underutilizing capital and technology. Some economists point out that the minimum wage might shock firms into discharging redundant labor.[3]

Monopsony. Thus far we have assumed that the minimum-wage law covers all workers in the economy and that the low-wage labor market is perfectly competitive. We now relax the latter assumption and analyze the potential employment effects of the minimum wage under conditions of nondiscriminating monopsony. Figure 10-4 portrays a labor market in which there is only a single employer of labor services or where the several employers collude to set a below-competitive wage. Recall from Figure 6-6 that a monopsonist's marginal

[3]Brown, Gilroy, and Kohen, op. cit., p. 489. Also see E. G. West and Michael McKee, "Monopsony and the 'Shock' Arguments for Minimum Wages," *Southern Economic Journal*, January 1980, pp. 888–891.

FIGURE 10-3 MINIMUM WAGE EFFECTS: THE SHOCK EFFECT

A minimum wage such as W_m may "shock" firms out of their organizational inefficiency. As a result, the marginal product of labor may rise, shifting the labor demand curve rightward (D to D'). Consequently, a portion of the unemployment predicted by the basic model may be mitigated (xc rather than ac).

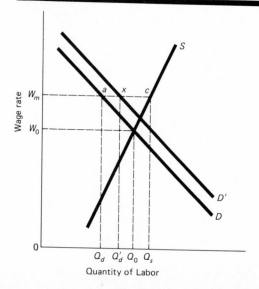

wage cost (MWC) exceeds its average wage cost (AWC) at each level of employment. Because it is the only buyer of labor services, the monopsonist faces the
typical upward-sloping market supply of labor curve. To hire more workers it
must attract them away from other occupations, and it accomplishes this by
raising the wage which it pays. But because the nondiscriminating monopsonist
must pay *all* of its workers the same wage, it discovers that its extra *cost* of hiring
one more worker (MWC) exceeds the higher *wage* payment to that worker alone
(AWC).

The monopsonist depicted in Figure 10-4 will use the profit-maximizing
hiring rule—MRP = MWC—and choose to employ Q_0 workers. As we see from
point c on the labor supply curve, to attract that number of workers it has to pay
a wage of W_0. But now suppose that government sets a minimum wage somewhere between W_0 and W_2—say W_1. In effect the labor supply curve becomes
perfectly horizontal at W_1 over the $0Q_1$ range of employment. Because the firm
can hire up to Q_1 extra workers at the minimum wage, its marginal wage cost
equals its average wage cost over this entire range. Contrast this to the previous
situation in which it had to raise the wage to attract more workers (MWC >
AWC). Given the legal minimum wage of W_1, the monopsonist becomes a
"wage taker" rather than a "wage setter" and maximizes its profits by hiring Q_1
workers. The additional Q_0 through Q_1 workers are now hired because their
MRPs exceed the minimum wage (MWC). Thus, in this case, the minimum

FIGURE 10-4 MINIMUM WAGE EFFECTS: MONOPSONY
In the absence of the minimum wage, this monopsonist will choose to hire Q_0 workers and pay a
wage equal to W_0. The imposition of any legal minimum wage above W_0 and below W_2 will
transform the firm into a "wage taker," and it will choose to increase its level of employment. For
example, if the minimum wage is W_1, this firm will hire the same number of workers as if competition existed in this labor market. Thus it is theoretically possible that a minimum wage might cause
employment to increase in some industries.

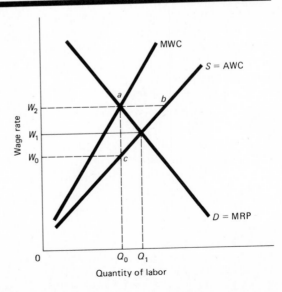

wage *increases* employment from Q_0 to Q_1 by perfectly countervailing the monopsony power of the employer. In fact, close scrutiny of Figure 10-4 shows that any legal wage above W_0 and below W_2 will increase employment above Q_0. It therefore is theoretically possible that a well-chosen and selectively implemented minimum wage might *increase employment* and improve allocative efficiency. This is the same analytically as Chapter 6's discussion of bilateral monopoly in which a union-imposed wage rate might increase employment and enhance efficiency (Figure 6-10).

But much caution is needed here. First, if government sets the minimum wage above W_2, employment will decline. Second, even though *employment* may be equal to or greater than Q_0 at minimum-wage levels above the monopsony wage W_0, *unemployment* clearly will be higher. For example, notice that b laborers seek employment in this market at wage rate W_2, while firms hire only a workers. Hence, at W_2, although *employment* is the same as at the monopsony wage W_0, the excess supply of workers—*unemployment*—rises from zero to ab. Third, being the only employer of a specific type of low-wage labor, a monopsonist might be able to discriminate, that is, to pay each worker a wage just sufficient to attract her or his employment. If this is the case, the MWC curve will coincide with the labor supply curve, and the firm's profit-maximizing level of employment (MRP = MWC) will be the competitive one, Q_1, rather than Q_0. This is true because the firm must pay the higher wage which is necessary to attract each extra worker only to that particular worker. Where discriminating monopsony exists, a minimum wage will either be ineffective or reduce employment; it cannot increase employment. Fourth, empirical studies done on this subject find little evidence of monopsony in most *low-wage* labor markets.[4]

Two-Sector Model: Incomplete Coverage. We next relax the assumption that all employers are covered under the minimum-wage law. Although coverage in the total nonfarm sector is approximately 85 percent, it is much less in such industries as agriculture and services. What impact might incomplete coverage have on the employment effects which we have discussed?

Figure 10-5 (a) and (b) portray two purely competitive labor markets for unskilled workers. One of these (a) is covered by the minimum-wage law and the other (b) is not. To simplify the analysis, assume that jobs are equally attractive in both markets and that the total quantity of labor hours supplied remains constant. In the absence of the minimum wage and the presence of costless migration and perfect information, workers will migrate between the two sectors until a single equilibrium wage, say W_0, emerges. Employment at that wage will be QC_0 in the soon-to-be "covered" sector (a) and QU_0 in the sector shown in graph (b). Now suppose that government establishes a mini-

[4]See Robert L. Bunting, *Employer Concentration in Local Labor Markets* (Chapel Hill, N.C.: University of North Carolina Press, 1962). Recall from Chapter 6 that there is considerable evidence of monopsony in some higher-wage labor markets (nursing, professional sports, teaching), but these markets are not directly affected by the minimum-wage rate.

mum wage of W_m for the covered sector (a) of the unskilled labor market. Assuming there is not a shock effect, firms in the newly covered sector will respond to the law by reducing employment from QC_0 to QC_1. Because of our assumption that the total level of worker hours remains constant, all of the displaced employees will then migrate to the uncovered sector where labor supply will shift rightward from S to S_1. This will increase the equilibrium employment from QU_0 to QU_1 $[QU_1 = QU_0 + (QC_0 - QC_1)]$ and drive down the equilibrium wage to W_u in the uncovered sector.

This spillover model is analytically the same as the union-nonunion spillover model discussed in Chapter 8. The overall outcomes can be summarized as follows. First, the minimum wage will benefit those workers in the covered sector who are fortunate enough to retain their jobs ($0QC_1$). Second, the law will reduce employment in the covered sector (QC_0 to QU_1), which in turn will increase employment in the uncovered sector (QU_0 to QC_1). The net employment effect will be zero. Third, the legal minimum will *reduce* the wage of unskilled workers in the uncovered sector (W_0 to W_u). Finally, the law will cause a misallocation of labor resources. Society will gain total output and income of area QU_0cdQU_1 in the uncovered sector (shaded area under the VMP_u curve) but will lose output and income equal to area QC_1abQC_0 in the covered sector. Since the shaded areas are equal in each graph, the *net* loss to society is area $c'abd'$ as shown in panel (a). A reallocation of the QU_0QU_1 workers from the uncovered

FIGURE 10-5 MINIMUM WAGE EFFECTS: A TWO-SECTOR MODEL WITH INCOMPLETE COVERAGE
The minimum wage W_m imposed in the covered sector of the low-wage labor market (a) reduces employment from QC_0 to QC_1. These displaced workers seek employment in the uncovered section (b). As a direct result, the supply of labor in the latter sector increases and the market wage falls from W_0 to W_u. Although total employment is unaffected, uncovered workers suffer a wage decline owing to the minimum wage. Also, labor resources are inefficiently allocated; that is, society suffers a net loss of national output and income equal to the area $c'abd'$ in graph (a).

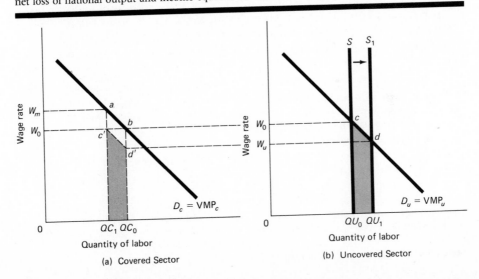

(a) Covered Sector

(b) Uncovered Sector

sector to the covered one where the VMP is higher would increase the total value of output in the economy.[5]

An Assessment of the Empirical Evidence. It should be evident from our discussion that the overall employment and unemployment effects of the minimum wage are theoretically ambiguous. Economists, therefore, have devoted considerable effort to examining statistically the employment consequences of the minimum wage. Additionally, they have sought to determine whether the minimum wage influences human capital investment decisions and whether it achieves its goal of creating more equality in the distribution of income. The results of these research efforts are summarized as follows.

1. The minimum wage reduces teenage employment. Overall, the minimum wage is estimated to reduce *male* teenage employment by about 7 percent.[6] A 10 percent increase in the minimum wage causes an estimated 1 to 3 percent decline in the number of jobs held by teenagers if all other factors are constant. This implies that the demand for teenage laborers is inelastic, and it means that more teenagers benefit from the minimum wage than are hurt. It also indicates, however, that the minimum wage is a source of teenage unemployment.[7]

2. The increase in *unemployment* caused by the minimum wage is less than the *reduction* in employment. Many teenagers who are unsuccessful at finding jobs withdraw from the labor force (for example, return to school) rather than continuing to search for work and remaining officially unemployed.[8]

3. Young adults aged 20 to 24 also suffer adverse employment effects from the minimum wage, but these impacts are even smaller than for teenagers.

4. "The direction of the effects [of the minimum wage] on adult employment is uncertain in empirical work, as it is in theory. While some adults are undoubtedly displaced by the minimum wage, others may be employed because the minimum wage protects them from teenage competition."[9]

5. The minimum wage appears to reduce on-the-job training but increases human capital gained through formal education. Recall from Chapter 4 that firms sometimes hire workers and provide them with *general* on-the-job training. To cover the expense, they pay a lower wage during the training period. But

---

[5] In reference to the foregoing outcomes, keep in mind that the assumptions of this model are quite rigid. In reality, as the wage sinks from W_0 to W_u, some workers may decide to withdraw from the labor force. Also, some workers may choose to "wait" for jobs to open at the minimum wage. Finally, as we will see in later chapters, both job search and geographic migration involve costs which may reduce the spillover effect shown in Figure 10-5(a) and (b).

[6] David Wise and Robert H. Meyer, "The Effects of the Minimum Wage on Employment and Earnings of Youth," *Journal of Labor Economics*, January 1983, pp. 66–100.

[7] Brown, Gilroy, and Kohen, op. cit., pp. 497–512.

[8] Jacob Mincer, "Unemployment Effects of Minimum Wages," *Journal of Political Economy*, August 1976 and C. Brown, C. Gilroy, and A. Kohen, "Time-Series Evidence of the Effect of the Minimum Wage on Youth Employment and Unemployment," *Journal of Human Resources*, Winter 1983, pp. 3–31.

[9] Brown, Gilroy, and Kohen, op. cit., p. 524.

the minimum wage places a floor on the wage which firms are able to offer. Therefore, some firms may decide against providing general job training under these circumstances, and hence the minimum wage may reduce the formation of this type of human capital. On the other hand, by reducing the number of jobs available to teenagers, the minimum wage keeps more youths in school and therefore increases the amount of human capital gained through education. The overall outcome of these opposing effects is uncertain.[10]

6. The minimum wage does not greatly alter the *overall* degree of income inequality in the society. This somewhat surprising conclusion rests on the empirical evidence that people who are paid a minimum wage are just as likely to be members of middle- or even high-income families as of low-income families. Many teenage minimum-wage recipients are the second or third income earners in these middle- or upper-income families. Thus, the minimum wage may be poorly targeted as an antipoverty weapon.[11]

Some final remarks: The minimum wage *does* offset monopsony power in some circumstances and *does* increase the earnings of many low-income persons. Therein lies its political and economic appeal. The debate over the minimum wage has moved away from the question of whether such a law should exist and toward the issue of how high it should be set. In particular, recent proposals have called for a **subminimum wage** for teenagers. It has been estimated that a youth subminimum wage set at $2.50 an hour could create as many as 370,000 jobs for teenagers. Proponents also contend that the subminimum wage would reduce racial discrimination by eliminating the surplus of teenagers applying for present minimum-wage jobs. This surplus allows biased employers to eliminate some black teenagers from employment consideration at no cost to the firm. Also, those who favor a subminimum wage argue that it would increase the amount of on-the-job training that employers would be willing to provide to their teenage workers.

Opponents of the youth subminimum wage counter that the proposal would decrease the price of teenage labor relative to adult low-skilled labor. This would result in a substantial substitution of teenagers for adult minimum-wage workers. The unemployment of adult minimum-wage workers would increase the amount of family poverty in the nation. Finally, opponents point out that the youth subminimum would depart from the important principle of equal pay for equal work.[12]

---

[10]Masanori Hashimoto, "Minimum Wage Effects of Training on the Job, *American Economic Review*, December 1982, pp. 1070–1087; Jacob Mincer and Linda Leighton, "Effects of Minimum Wages on Human Capital Formation" in Simon Rottenberg (ed.), *The Economics of Legal Minimum Wages* (Washington, D.C.: American Enterprise Institute, 1981).

[11]William Johnson and Edgar Browning, "The Distributional Effects of Increasing the Minimum Wage," *American Economic Review*, March 1983, p. 211. We discuss the effect of the minimum wage on the personal distribution of *earnings* in Chapter 13. For a critical review of minimum wage research, see Sar Levitan and Richard Belous, *More Than Subsistence: Minimum Wages for the Working Poor* (Baltimore: Johns Hopkins Press, 1979).

[12] These pros and cons are discussed in greater detail in the *Report of the Minimum Wage Study Commission*, Chap. 2.

OCCUPATIONAL HEALTH AND SAFETY REGULATION

Another important and controversial area of direct government intervention into the labor market is the regulation of occupational health and safety. This intervention has taken several forms, including state workers' compensation programs and the federal Occupational Safety and Health Act of 1970. The former mandated that firms purchase insurance that pays specified benefits to workers injured on the job. The latter, which will be our main focus, requires employers to comply with workplace health and safety standards established under the legislation.

Government regulation of workplace health and safety merits discussion for several reasons. First, statistics show that work is more dangerous than generally perceived. In 1983 over 11,000 workers died in job-related accidents in the United States, and nearly 2 million people incurred injuries that precluded work for a full day or more. As observed in Table 10-2, these accidents varied greatly by industry. Note, for example, that there were 50 deaths per 100,000 workers in "mining and quarrying" as compared to 5 deaths per 100,000 employees in "trade." Second, job safety—or lack thereof—is an important nonwage aspect of work, which in turn is an important determinant of labor supply (Chapter 6). Therefore, degrees of workplace safety help explain wage differentials among certain occupations (Chapter 12). Finally, just as with such labor market interventions as the minimum wage, affirmative action legislation (Chapter 11), and wage and price controls (Chapter 19), there is controversy over the appropriateness and effectiveness of regulation of workplace health and safety.

TABLE 10-2

Occupational Fatalities and Disabilities by Industry, 1983

Industry Group	Deaths		Number of Disabling Injuries* (1,000)
	Number (1,000)	Rate Per 100,000 Workers	
Total	11.2	11	1,900
Agriculture	1.9	55	200
Mining and quarrying	.5	50	40
Construction	2.0	37	200
Manufacturing	1.2	6	340
Transportation and utilities	1.3	25	140
Trade	1.1	5	330
Service	1.7	6	370
Government	1.5	10	280

*Defined as injuries resulting in death, physical impairment, or inability to perform regular duties for a full day beyond the day of injury.

Source: Statistical Abstract of the United States, 1985, Table 712.

This topic will be approached as follows. First, we will discuss how a profit-maximizing firm determines how much job safety to provide its workers. Then we will analyze why this level of protection against workplace hazards might be less than society's optimal amount. Finally, the controversies surrounding the Occupational Safety and Health Act of 1970 will be discussed.

Profit-Maximizing Level of Job Safety.[13] Competition in the product market will force a profit-maximizing firm to minimize its internal costs of producing any specific amount of output. One cost of production is the expenditure necessary to make the workplace safe. The "production" of job safety normally involves diminishing returns, which, translated into cost terms, means that each dollar of additional expenditure yields successively smaller increases in job safety. More concretely, firms will first use such relatively inexpensive techniques as disseminating safety information and issuing protective gear (say, hardhats) to make the job safer, but to make further gains, they may have to resort to such increasingly costly actions as purchasing safer equipment and slowing the work pace. Therefore, most firms, experience a rising *marginal cost of job safety*; successively higher amounts of direct expense, reduced output, or both, will be required to gain additional "units" of job safety. We depict a marginal cost of safety (MC_s) schedule for a typical firm in columns 2 and 3 of Table 10-3. Column 2 portrays the quantity of job safety (Q_s) and column 3 shows the rising marginal cost of each unit provided.

Given that job safety is costly to provide, why would a firm choose to offer workers *any* protection from workplace hazards? The answer is provided by column 1 in Table 10-3: An employer *benefits* from creating a relatively safe workplace; job safety reduces certain costs which the firm might otherwise incur. Notice from column 1, however, that as more units of job safety are produced by this firm, the *marginal benefit from job safety* (MB_s) falls.

Just what are these benefits to the firm? First, lower risks of injury or death enable employers to attract workers at lower wage rates. Because workers value job safety, they are willing to accept a lower wage for work performed in a healthy, relatively safe environment (Chapter 12). Second, a safer workplace reduces the amount of disruption of the production process that job accidents create. Workplace mishaps and the absence of key employees during rehabilitation often halt or slow the production process. Third, a safer workplace reduces the cost of recruiting, screening, and training workers. The fewer the number of workers injured on the job, the fewer the resources required to hire and train *new* employees. Fourth, workplace safety helps maintain the firm's return on its

[13]The basic analytical framework for this section and the section which follows was developed by Walter Oi in "An Essay on Workmen's Compensation and Industrial Safety," in *Supplemental Studies for the National Commission on State Workmen's Compensation Laws*, vol. 1, 1974, pp. 41–106. This framework also is employed by Belton M. Fleisher and Thomas J. Kniesner in *Labor Economics: Theory, Evidence, and Policy*, 3rd ed. (Englewood Cliffs, N.J.: Prentice-Hall, Inc., 1984), pp. 428–445.

specific investment in human capital. Job fatalities and injuries terminate or reduce the firm's returns on its previously financed specific formal and on-the-job training. Finally, fewer job-related accidents translate into lower workers' compensation insurance rates. Such rates are determined by the probability and types of accidents experienced in a given industry.

To determine the profit-maximizing level of workplace safety, the cost-minimizing firm will compare the marginal benefits of safety (MB_s) against the marginal costs (MC_s). In so doing, it will use the following decision rule: Provide additional job safety so long as the marginal benefits exceed the marginal costs (ideally to the point where MB = MC). Let us return to Table 10-3 to determine the profit-maximizing level of workplace safety for our hypothetical firm. Disregarding column 4 for the present, we note that our firm will choose to provide 3 units of job safety (circled data). The reason is that at 3 units, MB_s (= 8) is greater than MC_s (= 7); but at 4 units, MB_s (= 4) is less than MC_s (= 11). Conclusion? Even in the absence of government intervention, this firm will find it cost-effective and profitable to provide some degree of job safety. In this case, our firm will provide 3 units.

Another observation merits comment here. The popular perception that some jobs, say coal mining and professional football, are *inherently* dangerous while others, say accounting and teaching, are *innately* safe is somewhat misleading. A more accurate statement is that, given present technology, it is inherently *more costly* to provide job safety in some occupations than others. Hence, firms which have similar marginal benefit schedules but different marginal costs of safety will offer differing levels of job safety. To test your understanding of this, determine the optimum level of job safety for a firm that has the MB_s schedule shown in column 1 of Table 10-3, but has marginal costs of providing safety that are twice as great as those shown in column 3—that is, 4, 8, 14, 22, 32, and 48. How does this firm's optimal level of workplace safety Q_s compare to that of the firm in the previous example?

TABLE 10-3

Optimal Levels of Job Safety: The Firm versus Society

(1) MB_s	(2) Q_s	(3) MC_s	(4) MB_s'
$14	1	$ 2	$22
10	2	4	18
8	3	7	16
4	4	11	12
2	5	16	6
0	6	24	3

Society's Optimum Level of Job Safety. No assurances exist that the levels of workplace safety offered by firms are also optimal from society's perspective. As succinctly stated by Petersen,

> . . . there are reasons to believe that labor markets may not allocate suffi-
> cient resources to occupational health and safety. First is the problem of
> inadequate information. Data correlating job conditions and health and
> safety hazards are poor. In particular, many health risks appear years after
> the initial exposure. . . . A second concern is the difficulty that workers
> sometimes have, even with good data, in making rational decisions. Experi-
> mental and actual evidence suggests that individuals are not very adept at
> processing information involving small probabilities of risk. Unfortunately,
> the critical decisions relating to occupational health and safety often are
> characterized by events whose occurrence is improbable, but very costly.[14]

An important generalization emerges from this statement: *If* inadequate information or an inaccurate assessment of personal risk leads workers to *under-estimate* the actual likelihood of occupational fatality, injury, or disease, then the amount of job safety offered by employers will tend to be insufficient to achieve allocative efficiency.

This proposition can be demonstrated by referring again to Table 10-3. Recall that our profit-maximizing firm would employ the data in columns 1 through 3 and provide 3 units of job safety. However, if workers are either unaware of the job dangers or underestimate personal risks, then column 1 will *understate* the true marginal benefits to the firm and society from job safety. The marginal benefits which the firm would obtain *if* workers had perfect informa-tion and made perfect estimates of risk would be greater, for example like those shown in column 4 of Table 10-3. Why is this so?

To answer this question as simply as possible, let us suppose that workers and employers mistakenly judge the job to be risk-free when in reality one of the substances handled by workers is dangerous. *If* workers had knowledge of this health hazard and accurately assessed its risk, some would have chosen alterna-tive employment. Those willing to work in this hazardous occupation would have demanded and received (due to declines in labor supply) a substantial *wage rate premium* as compensation for this workplace disamenity. Consequently, the *firm's* marginal benefits from reducing the health hazard, that is, from providing a safer workplace, would have been greater than shown in column 1 of Table 10-3. More specifically, additional job safety would have *reduced the required wage rate premium* that this firm had to pay to attract workers. This would have conferred a benefit to the employer! For example, the firm might have been able to attract workers at $10 an hour rather than, say, $13 an hour.

[14]H. Craig Petersen, *Business and Government,* 2nd ed. (New York: Harper and Row, 1985), pp. 367–368.

From society's perspective, the *true* marginal benefits of each added unit of safety are those such as the ones shown in column 4 of Table 10-3. *Given full information and accurate assessment of job risks,* the profit-maximizing and allocatively efficient level of job safety would be 4 units, as indicated by the boxed data. This fourth unit of job safety generates marginal benefits (= $12 from column 4) which exceed marginal costs (= $11 from column 3). *In the absence of perfect information and accurate risk assessment,* the profit-maximizing firm simply has no incentive to provide this fourth unit. From *its* perspective the marginal benefit (= $4 from column 1) from this unit is less than the marginal cost (= $11 from column 3). Conclusion? A firm's profit-maximizing level of job safety may not always conform to society's optimal level of job safety.

The Occupational Safety and Health Act of 1970. The *Occupational Safety and Health Act of 1970* interjected the federal government directly into regulation of workplace hazards. The act's purpose was to reduce the incidence of job injury and illness by identifying and eliminating hazards found in the workplace. The Occupational Safety and Health Administration (OSHA) was given the responsibility of developing safety and health standards and enforcing them through workplace inspections and fines for violations.

OSHA was controversial when passed and remains subject to much debate today. Those who support the legislation contend that the costs of providing a healthy and safe workplace are legitimate business costs which should not be transferred to workers. According to this view, imperfect information, underestimation of risk, and barriers to occupational mobility prevent the labor market from making the adjustments which would produce adequate wage premiums for hazardous jobs. Hence, for reasons described earlier, government standards are needed to force firms to provide more job safety than is dictated by their own self-interests. Finally, supporters of OSHA regulation point out that much of the criticism has originated in the corporate community, where resistance is predictable and understandable. To see why, simply note in Table 10-3 that a minimum safety standard, say of 4 units, would force this firm to provide a unit of safety which from *its perspective* costs more to produce ($MC_s = \$11$) than it generates in private benefits ($MB_s = \$4$). It thus is not surprising that many corporations strongly object to OSHA standards and inspections.

Critics of OSHA counter that safety standards and inspections represent an unwarranted, costly government intrusion into the private sector. They point out that even though information about job hazards may be imperfect and workers may inaccurately assess personal risk, there is no a priori reason to expect that workers systematically will *underestimate* the risk of job hazards. Rather, workers could just as well *overestimate* the likelihood that they will be the unlucky party affected by occupational death, injury, or illness, just as many purchasers of state lottery tickets or sweepstake entrants overestimate the probability that *they* will win. According to this line of reasoning, it is possible that wage premiums for hazardous jobs are *greater* than they would be if there were perfect information and risk assessment. Restated, the perspective that "it will probably happen to me" may dissuade people from hazardous occupations, driving up the wage rate for those who perform such work. Recall that when such wage premiums exist, the firm's marginal benefits from reducing the job hazard are greater than otherwise, say column 4 rather than 1 in Table 10-3, and an underallocation of resources to job safety is not likely.

Critics of OSHA also assert that workplace standards often bear no relationship to reductions in injury and illness. They point to the numerous trivial standards—wall-height rules for fire extinguishers, specified shapes of toilet seats, and so forth—to support this assertion. Additionally, opponents of OSHA cite the complexity of determining just what the standards are. Murray Wiedenbaum notes OSHA's original definition of an "exit": "That portion of a means of egress which is separated from all other spaces of the building or structure by construction or equipment as required in this subpart to provide a protected way of travel to the exit discharge." Wiedenbaum contrasts this definition with one from a dictionary: An exit is "a passage or way out."[15]

The controversy over OSHA has been heightened by recent studies which suggest that OSHA standards and inspections have had little impact in reducing occupational accidents and injuries. Specifically, Viscusi found no significant effect of OSHA on industrial injury rates over the 1972–1975 period, and Smith and McCaffrey found no effects of OSHA inspections during the 1974–1976 period.[16] As these scholars point out, however, one must be cautious in interpreting the findings. For example, the findings may simply result from lack of enforcement of the law or inadequate penalties for firms which fail to meet the standards. Viscusi estimates that, on a per worker basis, fines for violations have averaged only $.34. But the studies have given credence to those who argue that the OSHA approach is inferior to other alternatives. For instance, evidence suggests that passage of workers' compensation laws by states between 1900 and 1940 significantly reduced industrial fatalities and injuries by forcing firms having higher accident rates to either pay higher insurance premiums or improve the safety of their workplaces.[17] This has led some economists to suggest that taxes or surcharges on worker compensation premiums might be superior to OSHA standards as a way to reduce job accidents. Other economists suggest that OSHA standards should be replaced by requirements that firms disclose all available information concerning employment hazards to their work forces.

[15]Murray L. Wiedenbaum, *Business, Government, and the Public* (Englewood Cliffs, N.J.: Prentice-Hall, Inc., 1977), pp. 64–65. In the face of criticism over trivial rules and bureaucratic language, OSHA revoked over 1100 standards in 1978 and attempted to rewrite remaining standards in plain English.

[16]W. Kip Viscusi, "The Impact of Occupational Safety and Health Regulation," *Bell Journal of Economics*, Spring 1978, pp. 117–140; Robert Smith and David McCaffrey, "An Assessment of OSHA's Recent Effect on Injury Rates," *Journal of Human Resources*, Winter 1983, pp. 131–145. The interested reader may also wish to see Viscusi's *Risk by Choice: Regulating Health and Safety in the Workplace* (Cambridge, Mass.: Harvard University Press, 1983), chap. 2.

[17]James Chelius, *Workplace Safety and Health: The Role of Workers' Compensation* (Washington, D.C.: The American Enterprise Institute, 1977).

What then can we conclude about the labor market impact of OSHA? The honest answer is that few widely accepted conclusions are possible. Nevertheless, the following generalizations seem warranted.

1. *If* OSHA is *not* effective in reducing job accidents and illnesses—either directly by setting standards or by providing information—then obviously the marginal costs to society (agency costs and compliance costs) exceed the marginal benefits (zero). Consequently, the legislation reduces society's well-being.

2. *If*, on the other hand, OSHA *is* effective at reducing job injuries and deaths, two differing outcomes are possible. In the case where information about job hazards is widely disseminated and fully understood, reductions in job hazards deriving from OSHA can be expected to reduce the existing wage differential between "hazardous" and "safe" occupations. In other words, the OSHA standards will make the "hazardous" jobs safer, reducing the disparity in job riskiness and pay among occupations. Why is this so? Recall from Chapter 6 that one of the determinants of labor supply to an occupation is the nonwage aspects of employment. Given a safer workplace, more people will be willing to work in a formerly hazardous job, eventually causing the wage premium there to fall. Thus in this first case, effective OSHA standards will tend simply to substitute more of the nonwage amenity "workplace safety" for less of the wage rate amenity "wage premium."

A second case yields a different conclusion. In situations where information about job hazards is imperfect or where personal assessment of risk leads to underestimation of the hazard, effective and appropriate OSHA regulations may increase the well-being of workers as a group and society as a whole. The existing wage premium, if any, will be too small to compensate workers for the true employment hazards. Notice from Table 10-3 that requiring 4 units of job safety by law rather than the 3 being provided adds more benefits (= $12 from column 4) than it adds costs (= $11 from column 3). If this net gain exceeds the agency's costs, society's well-being also rises.

GOVERNMENT AS A RENT-PROVIDER

Government influences wages and employment in labor markets in ways which are more subtle than establishing labor laws, imposing a legal minimum wage, or setting occupational safety standards. One such method is through providing economic rent to labor market participants. **Economic rent** *in the labor market is the difference between the wage paid to a particular worker and the wage which would be just sufficient to keep that person in his or her present employment.* Recall from Chapter 6 that a market labor supply curve such as the one shown in Figure 10-6 is essentially a marginal opportunity cost curve. The curve reflects the value of each worker's next best alternative, whether that be another job or leisure. Given the market wage of $8 in Figure 10-6, all employed workers with the exception of the marginal one, Q_0, receive economic rent, the total of which is area *ABC*. To clarify further, suppose Jones is the worker shown by Q_J and that her marginal cost is $6 an hour. We can see then that Jones is receiving a $2 per hour "rent" (= $8 − $6).

What would happen to Jones' economic rent if government passed a law which had the effect of increasing the market wage to $10 an hour? Obviously, she and all other workers who remain employed would receive an *increase* in economic rent of $2 (= $10 − $8). But why might government be interested in providing increases in economic rent to workers? According to some economic and political theorists, the main goal of politicians is to get and stay elected. Consequently, they offer and provide a wide range of publicly provided goods and services which enhance the utility of their constituents. One such service may be the provision or the enhancement of economic rents! According to this controversial theory, groups of workers—for example, professional groups or unions—have a demand for economic rent; that is, they are **rent seekers.** Elected officials respond to this demand by supplying the publicly provided service, economic rent; they are **rent providers.**[18]

Admittedly, care must be taken not to oversimplify here. Higher wages provided by law or regulation may produce lower market-determined wages for other workers, higher product prices for consumers, lower corporate dividends

---

[18]A political scientist once defined politics as "who gets what, when, and how." This view of politics has been formalized into a theory of regulation by several economists. See, for example, George J. Stigler, "The Theory of Economic Regulation," *The Bell Journal of Economics and Management Science,* Spring 1971, pp. 3–21.

FIGURE 10-6 ECONOMIC RENT IN LABOR MARKETS
At the market wage of $8, employers will hire Q_0 workers. The labor supply curve indicates that these Q_0 workers collectively receive economic rent equal to the area ABC. The Q_j worker receives a $2 per hour rent ($8 minus her opportunity cost of $6).

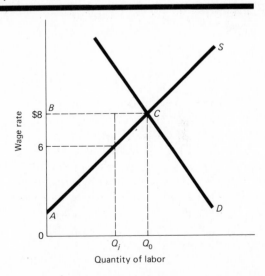

for common stockholders, or some combination of all three. These groups are interested in their own rents and may intervene politically to block the provision of rents to a group of workers. But because acquisition of information and political lobbying are costly, people have little incentive to try to block rent provision when they perceive their *personal* losses to be small. Hence, elected officials may find it beneficial to dispense economic rent to highly organized groups of workers.

This concept of rent provision is clearly observable in some instances of occupational licensure and in legislation which establishes tariffs, quotas, and "domestic content" laws.

Occupational Licensure. We first discussed occupational licensure in Chapter 6 as an example of a technique used by craft unions to increase wages. In many instances licensing of occupational groups (pharmacists, stockbrokers, surgeons) is held to be necessary to protect the public against fraud, injury, or illicit activity. In these circumstances governmental licensing may be the most efficient way to minimize the costs of obtaining information needed by consumers to make optimal buying decisions. But in other situations, the occupational groups themselves, not consumers, generate the demand for licensing. These groups may wish to restrict access to licenses as a way to obtain economic rent for licensees.

Figure 10-7 demonstrates how occupational licensure can confer economic rent. Suppose that the prelicensing equilibrium wage and employment level are $8 and 10,000 workers, respectively. Next assume that government restricts the

FIGURE 10-7 RENT PROVISION THROUGH OCCUPATIONAL LICENSURE

By setting a limit of 7000 licenses in this labor market, government indirectly increases the wage from $8 to $11, thereby providing licensees collectively an increase in economic rent of *ABCD*.

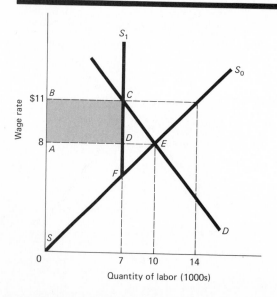

Quantity of labor (1000s)

total number of licensed workers to 7,000. In effect, the postlicensing labor supply curve is SFS_1, compared to the old curve of SS_0. Notice that licensing increases the market wage to $11 an hour and that total employment falls from 10,000 to 7,000. The $11 wage attracts another 4,000 workers (= 14,000 − 10,000) who would like to work in this occupation. These 14,000 workers seek 7,000 licenses, and those who get the licenses receive increases in economic rent of $3 for every hour worked. As a consequence, the government's action *raises* the total rent *to those employed* by $21,000. This can be determined by noting that the total rent was area *SAE* prior to the licensing. Following licensing, the total economic rent increases to *SBCF*. Thus, the *gain* in rent is *ABCD*—the shaded area in the figure—and the loss of rent to the workers displaced by the licensing is area *FDE*.

Close inspection of Figure 10-7 reveals that occupational licensure of a type which restricts labor supply creates an efficiency loss for society. In this case the loss is shown by triangle *FCE*. The 3,000 additional employees who would have been employed in this occupation would contribute more to the value of society's output in this employment (as shown by segment *CE* of the demand curve) than in their most productive alternative uses of time (as shown by segment *FE* of the supply curve). Additionally, society forgos the resources used up by those who seek to enact the licensing law and those who seek to obtain the individual licenses. To summarize: Occupational licensure of the type which restricts labor supply increases the market wage, confers economic rent to licensees, and

FIGURE 10-8 RENT PROVISION: TARIFFS, QUOTAS, AND DOMESTIC CONTENT LAWS
Import restrictions reduce labor demand in foreign nations and increase the demand for specific types of labor in the protected country. These restrictions, therefore, cause increases in wages in these specific labor markets. In this case, the wage rises from $10 to $12, and economic rent increases by the amount *BCDE*.

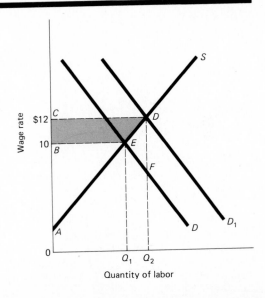

causes economic inefficiency. We might add that it is possible that the competition for the limited number of licenses will cause the new licensees to expend dollars in an amount equal to the expected rents. Hence, those who are automatically granted licenses at the time the law is passed and those who train potential licensees will be the major beneficiaries of the law.[19]

Tariffs, Quotas, and "Domestic Content" Rules. Collectively, tariffs, quotas, and domestic content rules provide a second example of governmental provision of economic rent to groups of workers. Tariffs are excise duties on imported products; import quotas are limits on the quantity or total value of imports; and domestic content rules are requirements that a specified portion of imported products contain domestically produced or domestically assembled components. These laws and regulations tend to increase the prices of foreign goods, raise the sales of the competing "protected" domestic products, and increase the derived demand for the U.S. workers who help produce the domestic goods. Assuming a competitive labor market in which there is a normal upward-sloping labor supply curve, the increased domestic demand for labor increases the equilibrium wage and employment. If the labor market is imperfectly competitive, the increase in labor demand enhances the bargaining position of the union and increases the probability that the union-negotiated wage will rise. It is therefore perfectly understandable why some U.S. unions, for example, the United Steelworkers and the United Auto Workers (UAW), strongly support tariffs, quotas, and domestic content rules. Quite simply, these laws increase economic rent for domestic workers at the expense of foreign producers and domestic consumers.

It is a fairly simple matter to portray this gain in economic rent graphically. Figure 10-8 depicts an initial equilibrium wage of $10 per hour at which firms hire Q_1 workers. The tariff, import quota, or domestic content law increases the derived demand for labor from D to D_1. The increase in labor demand raises the equilibrium wage from $10 to $12 an hour and causes the level of employment to rise to Q_2. Prior to the trade restriction, the total economic rent to workers was ABE. After the law, it is ACD. The workers in this market thus collectively gain an increase in economic rent equal to the shaded area $BCDE$.

SUMMARY

1. Labor laws constitute one of several factors explaining the growth of unionism in the United States. Thus, in an indirect way, these laws are an important force which influences labor markets and wage, employment, and allocative outcomes in the economy.

---

[19]For empirical evidence that more restrictive state licensing laws reduce immigration and, as a consequence, raise economic rent to incumbents within various occupations, see Morris M. Kleiner, Robert S. Gay, and Karen Greene, "Barriers to Labor Migration: The Case of Occupational Licensing," *Industrial Relations,* Fall 1982, pp. 383–391.

2. The absence of federal laws protecting union activities helps explain the slow growth of union membership before the mid-1930s. The passage of the Norris-LaGuardia Act of 1932 and the Wagner Act of 1935, on the other hand, gave impetus to the tremendous growth of union membership during the two decades following their passage. To the extent that union membership and union bargaining power are positively correlated, labor law influences the determination of wages and employment in labor markets.

3. Labor law in general and specific provisions of labor law in particular influence union bargaining power—and therefore labor market results—independently of impacts on union membership.

4. The basic model of a competitive labor market predicts that an above-equilibrium minimum wage will reduce employment in the covered industry. The more elastic the supply and demand for labor, the greater the resulting unemployment.

5. The presence of a "shock" effect, the existence of nondiscriminating monopsony, and the possibility that displaced workers will find employment in noncovered sectors each explain why the negative employment consequence predicted by the basic competitive model might not materialize.

6. Empirical evidence suggests that the minimum wage (a) reduces teenage employment, but that many teenagers who are unable to find jobs withdraw from the labor force rather than remain "officially" unemployed; (b) reduces the amount of on-the-job training offered to low-wage workers, but encourages school attendance for those unable to find work; and (c) has a minor equalizing impact on the *overall* degree of family income inequality in society.

7. Even though it is costly to "produce" job safety, profit-maximizing firms have an incentive to provide some amount of it because employers gain benefits (for example, lower wage rates) from having a safer workplace. Firms will compare marginal benefits with marginal costs of providing added safety and determine a profit-maximizing level of workplace safety where $MB_s = MC_s$.

8. Society's optimum level of job safety may be greater than the level willingly provided by profit-maximizing firms. The reasons for this divergence between private and societal interests include (a) imperfect information as to job risk, and (b) underestimation of personal probabilities of job injury or illness.

9. The Occupational Safety and Health Act of 1970 imposed a set of workplace safety standards on individual firms. The act is highly controversial and the debate over its provisions and enforcement methods has been heightened by several studies which fail to find reductions in work-related accidents which can be attributed to it.

10. Government affects wages and employment in specific occupations through its "rent provision" activities. Two examples are: (a) occupational licensure of the kind which restricts labor supply, and (b) tariffs, import quotas, and "domestic content" laws, which increase labor demand for protected domestic workers.

QUESTIONS AND STUDY SUGGESTIONS

1. Key terms and concepts to remember: discriminatory discharge; blacklists; yellow-dog contract; lockout; Norris-LaGuardia Act of 1932; Wagner Act of 1935; Taft-Hartley Act of 1947; Landrum-Griffin Act of 1959; secondary boycott; hot cargo clause, emergency strike procedures; Fair Labor Standards Act of 1938; minimum wage; subminimum wage; Occupational Safety and Health Act of 1970; marginal

cost of job safety; marginal benefit from job safety; economic rent in the labor market; rent-seeking and rent-providing activity.

2. Explain each of the following statements.

a. "The Wagner Act of 1935 reduced the costs of providing union services and thereby increased the number of union members."

b. "The Wagner Act of 1935 increased the demand for union services by increasing the relative bargaining power of unions. This increased union membership."

3. Use the Chamberlain bargaining power model (equations 7-1 and 7-2) to predict the impact of each of the following hypothetical changes in labor law on union bargaining power.

a. Legalization of all forms of secondary boycotts

b. Legislation making it an "unfair labor practice" to employ strikebreakers

c. Repeal of the prohibition against strikes by federal employees (recall the Time and One-Half discussion at the end of Chapter 9)

4. Show graphically how an increase in the minimum wage might affect employment in (a) a competitive labor market and (b) a labor market characterized by monopsony.

5. How might a subminimum wage for teenagers—say one which is two-thirds the adult minimum wage—increase teenage employment in the economy? Why might the overall level of employment increase less than the increase in teenage employment?

6. Explain how an increase in the minimum wage could:

a. reduce teenage employment, but leave the teenage unemployment rate unaffected;

b. reduce one type of investment in human capital, but increase another type.

7. Evaluate: "Profit-maximizing firms lack an incentive to provide job safety, and consequently the federal government must intervene legislatively to protect workers against the blatantly unsafe working conditions that will surely result."

8. Answer the questions below on the basis of the following information for a competitive firm.

Marginal Benefits from Safety	Amount of Safety Provided	Marginal Costs of Safety
$60	1	$ 1
40	2	3
20	3	6
10	4	9
6	5	15

a. What is the profit-maximizing level of job safety as viewed by the firm? Explain.

b. Assume that information is perfect and that workers accurately assess personal risk. What is the optimum level of job safety from society's perspective? Explain.

c. Suppose that government imposed a minimum safety standard of 5 units. Why would the firm object? Speculate as to why some workers might object.

d. Suppose that new technology reduced this firm's marginal cost data to $1, 2, 3, 4, and 5 for the first through fifth units of safety. How would this firm respond?

9. How might each one of the following be interpreted to be an example of "rent provision" by government?

a. State laws which require out-of-state big game hunters to be accompanied by one of a limited number of licensed in-state hunting guides.

b. An increase in the minimum wage which increases the likelihood that firms will hire skilled unionized labor rather than unskilled labor.

c. A state law which requires that graduates of dental schools pass a stringent examination, established by a panel of dentists, in order to practice dentistry.

SELECTED REFERENCES

BLOOM, GORDON F., and HERBERT R. NORTHRUP: *Economics of Labor Relations,* 9th ed. (Homewood, Ill.: Richard D. Irwin, Inc., 1981), chaps. 18–21.

BROWN, CHARLES, CURTIS GILROY, and ANDREW KOHEN: "The Effect of the Minimum Wage on Employment and Unemployment," *Journal of Economic Literature,* June 1982, pp. 487–528.

GOULD, WILLIAM B.: *A Primer on American Labor Law* (Cambridge, Mass.: The MIT Press, 1982).

LEVITAN, SAR, and RICHARD BELOUS: *More Than Subsistence: Minimum Wages for the Working Poor* (Baltimore: Johns Hopkins Press, 1979).

Report of the Minimum Wage Study Commission (Washington: U.S. Government Printing Office, 1981).

ROTTENBERG, SIMON (ed.): *Occupational Licensure and Regulation* (Washington, D.C.: American Enterprise Institute for Public Policy Research, 1980).

TAYLOR, B. J., and F. WITNEY: *Labor Relations Law,* 4th ed. (Englewood Cliffs, N.J.: Prentice-Hall, Inc., 1983).

VISCUSI, W. KIP: *Risk by Choice: Regulating Health and Safety in the Workplace* (Cambridge, Mass.: Harvard University Press, 1983).

T I M E   A N D   O N E - H A L F

STATE RIGHT-TO-WORK LAWS

Few topics in labor law are more controversial than the state laws which prohibit compulsory unionism. What are the pros and cons of these so-called right-to-work laws? What impacts do they have on union wage gains and membership?

Although federal law permits union shops whereby workers are required to join a union within a specified period of time after being hired, Section 14(b) of the Taft-Hartley Act allows individual *states* to enact laws prohibiting this form of compulsory unionism. Twenty-one states—most of them located in the south, midwest, and southwest—have enacted these right-to-work statutes.[1]

Proponents of right-to-work laws argue that union shops restrict individual freedom and violate the right of free association. They claim that a union shop clause is equivalent

[1] Alabama, Arizona, Arkansas, Florida, Georgia, Idaho, Iowa, Kansas, Louisiana, Mississippi, Nebraska, Nevada, North Carolina, North Dakota, South Carolina, South Dakota, Tennessee, Texas, Utah, Virginia, and Wyoming.

to a yellow-dog contract in reverse. Recall that yellow-dog contracts made *nonunion* status a condition for continued employment. The union shop does precisely the opposite. Supporters of right-to-work laws also point out that union shop clauses prevent disgruntled workers from withdrawing from the union as a way to protest leadership action. Some of the workers therefore may be forced to pay dues to an organization that espouses economic and political views which conflict with their own.

Those who support union shops and urge the repeal of Section 14(b) counter that unions are democratic institutions which provide a collective service to *all* workers in the bargaining unit. In the absence of union security arrangements such as the union shop, some workers will opt to become "free riders" who will gain the benefits of collective bargaining without paying union dues. Opponents of right-to-work laws also contend that union shops create a mature, stable labor relations environment which allows union leaders to turn their attention away from recruiting and retaining members and toward enforcing the labor contract and addressing genuine labor-management problems.

In light of these arguments, it is easy to see why the controversy continues. Economics seems better suited to assess the *impacts* of union shops and right-to-work laws than to settle the debate over whether or not union shops should be allowed. Hence, recent research has attempted to ascertain the effects of union shops and right-to-work laws on union wages and membership. The following are some of the more recent findings.

1. *Compulsory union membership clauses apparently do enable unions to negotiate greater wage increases than they might otherwise.* Christensen and Maki confirm this effect in a study involving fifty-four manufacturing industries.[2] Apparently a union shop increases the union's bargaining power by ensuring that a threatened strike will involve all of the workers, rather than some fraction of them.

2. *All else being equal, states with right-to-work laws have lower proportions of their labor forces unionized than states allowing union shops.* All twenty-one states with right-to-work laws have lower percentages of their labor forces unionized than the national average. Most of these states, however, are also less industrialized than states with higher rates of unionization. Therefore, it is necessary to correct for the differences in the industrial mix among states in attempting to ascertain the relationship between right-to-work laws and unionization rates. Studies which make this correction find that states having right-to-work laws average about a 5 percent lower rate of unionization than other states.[3]

3. *The evidence on whether or not right-to-work laws cause the observed lower incidence of unionism in states with right-to-work laws is inconclusive.* There are a number of plausible explanations for the lower incidence of unionism in states with right-to-work laws. First, the laws themselves may reduce the rate of unionism by creating the previously mentioned free-rider problem. Only 80 percent of workers covered by collective bargaining agreements are union members in states with right-to-work laws compared with 90 percent elsewhere.[4] Additionally, the wage gains resulting from the union shop clauses may make unionism, in general, more attractive to workers in the states which do not have right-to-work laws.

[2]Sandra Christensen and Dennis Maki, "The Wage Effect of Compulsory Union Membership," *Industrial and Labor Relations Review*, January 1983, pp. 230–238.

[3]For example, see Barry T. Hirsch, "The Determinants of Unionization: An Analysis of Interarea Differences," *Industrial and Labor Relations Review*, January 1980, pp. 147–161; and Thomas M. Carroll, "Right-to-Work Laws Do Matter," *Southern Economic Journal*, October 1983, pp. 494–509.

[4]Richard B. Freeman and James L. Medoff, *What Do Unions Do?* (New York: Basic Books Inc., 1984), p. 243.

But another interpretation is also possible. Perhaps workers in states with right-to-work laws simply have lower preferences or "tastes" for unionism than their cohorts in other states. Or, perhaps employers in states with right-to-work laws are more hostile toward unions than employers in other states. Put simply, interest groups and voters in these states may be more inclined to lobby for, and pass, right-to-work laws. In any case, these antiunion attitudes may explain *both* the existence of right-to-work laws *and* the lower incidence of union membership. Consequently, the laws themselves may not be a *cause* of the reduced extent of unionism.

Attempts to test these alternative interpretations have produced varied results. A few economists have found an independent impact of the right-to-work laws on union membership.[5] But other economists, using different techniques and data, find that the incidence of unionization in states with right-to-work laws and the presence of the laws are both explained by antiunion attitudes.[6]

So what can we conclude? Perhaps the clearest evidence from the combined studies is that, irrespective of whether right-to-work laws actually reduce unionization, these laws appear to be *less* important in explaining low rates of unionism in the states with right-to-work laws than are the underlying negative union attitudes held by workers and employers in these states.

[5] For example, Ronald S. Warren and Robert P. Strauss, "A Mixed Logit Model of the Relationship between Unionization and Right-to-Work Legislation," *Journal of Political Economy*, June 1979, pp. 648–655.

[6] Keith Lumsden and Craig Petersen, "The Effect of Right-to-Work Laws on Unionization in the United States," *Journal of Political Economy*, June 1979, pp. 648–655; Walter J. Wessells, "Economic Effects of Right-to-Work Laws," *Journal of Labor Research*, Spring 1981, pp. 55–76; and Henry S. Farber, "Right-to-Work Laws and the Extent of Unionization," *Journal of Labor Economics*, July 1984, pp. 319–352.

LABOR MARKET DISCRIMINATION BASED ON RACE AND SEX

F ew would seriously question the assertion that discrimination based upon race, sex, religion, and ethnic background is a fact of American life. There is abundant statistical evidence to suggest discrimination: comparisons of blacks and whites and of males and females reveal substantial differences in earnings, unemployment rates, allocations among various occupations, and accumulations of human capital.

Discrimination based upon race and sex is emphasized in this chapter. In the introductory section we define discrimination, delineate the various types of discrimination, and present data to suggest the severity of discrimination. Second, in the major portion of the chapter we present four important labor market models of discrimination. Next, brief consideration is given to the discriminatory role of labor unions. Fourth, the problem of distinguishing discrimination from other factors which might affect male-female and white-black earnings differentials is discussed. Finally, we examine antidiscrimination policies, note some of the controversies they have generated, and consider their effectiveness.

Several interrelated caveats must be made explicit at the outset. Discrimination is complex, multifaceted, and deeply ingrained in behavior. It is also difficult to measure or quantify. Furthermore, any reasonably complete explanation of discrimination must be interdisciplinary; economic analysis per se can only contribute insights rather than a full-blown explanation of the phenomenon. In fact, we shall find that within economics there are a number of contrasting explanations of discrimination, and these frequently imply different policy prescriptions. Bluntly stated, discrimination constitutes an untidy area of study which is characterized by controversy and a lack of consensus.

DISCRIMINATION AND ITS DIMENSIONS

Discrimination is easier to define than it is to discern. *Economic discrimination exists when female or minority workers, who have the same abilities, education, train-*

289

ing, and experience as white male workers, are accorded inferior treatment with respect to hiring, occupational access, promotion, or wage rate. Note that discrimination may also take the form of unequal access to formal education, apprenticeships, or on-the-job training programs, each of which enhances one's stock of human capital (Chapter 4).[1]

Types of Discrimination. This definition is sufficiently important so as to merit elaboration. Implicit in our definition, labor market discrimination can be classified into four general types.[2]

1. *Wage discrimination* means that female (black) workers are paid less than male (white) workers for doing the same work. More technically, wage discrimination exists when wage differentials are based upon considerations other than productivity differentials.
2. *Employment discrimination* occurs when, other things being equal, blacks and women bear a disproportionate share of the burden of unemployment. Blacks in particular have long faced the problem of being the last hired and the first fired.
3. *Occupational* or *job discrimination* means that females (blacks) have been arbitrarily restricted or prohibited from entering certain occupations, even though they are as capable as male (white) workers of performing those jobs, and conversely "crowded" into other occupations wherein they are frequently overqualified.
4. *Human-capital discrimination* is in evidence when females (blacks) have less access to productivity-increasing opportunities such as formal schooling or on-the-job training. Blacks in particular often obtain less education and education of inferior quality as compared to whites.

The first three categories of discrimination are frequently designated as *post-market* (also "current" or "direct") *discrimination* for the obvious reason that they are encountered *after* the individual has entered the labor market. Similarly, the fourth category is called *premarket* (also "past" or "indirect") *discrimination* because it occurs *before* the individual seeks employment.[3]

---

[1]Lloyd G. Reynolds, *Labor Economics and Labor Relations*, 7th ed. (Englewood Cliffs, N.J.: Prentice-Hall, Inc., 1978), p. 158.

[2]We are concerned here only with those kinds of discrimination which are relevant to the labor market. While discrimination in access to housing or consumer credit is obviously important, it is less germane to the subject matter of labor economics.

[3]On-the-job training poses a bit of a problem for our pre- and postmarket classification. While such training is obviously a form of human capital investment, people do not have access to it until they have entered the labor market. A very useful and more detailed taxonomy of discrimination is presented by Brian Chiplin and Peter J. Sloane, "Sexual Discrimination in the Labor Market," in Alice H. Amsden (ed.), *The Economics of Women and Work* (New York: St. Martin's Press, 1980), p. 285.

These distinctions among the various kinds of discrimination are useful for at least two reasons. First, the significance of the various kinds of discrimination varies among blacks and women. Generally speaking, blacks are subject to a much greater degree of employment discrimination than are women (see Table 11-2). And, although blacks and women are both subject to occupational segregation, this form of discrimination is especially relevant with respect to women (see Table 11-3). Second, awareness of the various forms of discrimination helps one understand how discrimination may be self-reinforcing and therefore tends to perpetuate itself. For example, if blacks and women anticipate that occupational discrimination will confine them to low-wage, dead-end jobs or that they will be exposed to frequent and prolonged periods of unemployment, they will rationally choose to invest less than otherwise in schooling (Chapter 4). That is, the expectation of postmarket discrimination will reduce the rate of return expected on investments in education and training which will aggravate the premarket condition of inadequate preparation for many jobs.

Indicators of Discrimination: Casual Evidence. It is not difficult to marshall empirical data which lead one to suspect the presence of discrimination based upon sex and race. For example, Table 11-1 shows the median weekly earnings of full-time workers on the basis of sex and race. We observe that the weekly earnings of female workers have been about 62 percent that of males, although that figure has increased slightly in the past few years. And, while the ratio of black to white weekly earnings has increased since the 1960s, a substantial earnings gap remains.

TABLE 11-1

Median Weekly Earnings of Full-Time Workers by Race and Sex for Selected Years, 1967–1984 (in Current Dollars)

| | Sex | | | Race | | |
| | | | Ratio of Female to Male | | | Ratio of Blacks to Whites |
Year	Males	Females	to Male	Whites	Blacks*	to Whites
1967	$125	$ 78	.62	$113	$ 79	.70
1969	142	86	.61	125	90	.72
1971	162	100	.62	142	107	.75
1973	188	116	.62	162	129	.80
1975	221	137	.62	190	156	.82
1977	253	156	.62	217	171	.79
1978	272	166	.61	232	186	.80
1981	345	217	.63	292	236	.81
1984	400	259	.65	339	256	.76

*Includes other nonwhites.

Source: Department of Labor, *Handbook of Labor Statistics, 1980,* p. 118; and *Employment and Earnings,* January 1985, p. 210.

Table 11-2 shows selected data on the distribution of unemployment over the past several decades. A comparison of columns 2 and 3 reveals that, while white females seem to have been at some disadvantage as compared to white males, the differential is not dramatic. In fact, in the recessionary year 1983 the unemployment rate for females dipped below that for males. Blacks, however, have consistently had unemployment rates which have been roughly twice as great as those of whites. Furthermore, the data understate the disadvantage of blacks because a larger percentage of blacks than whites have been discouraged workers (Chapter 3), that is, workers who have dropped from the labor force because of poor job prospects and are therefore not counted among the unemployed.

Substantial differences in the occupational distribution of workers by sex and race are revealed in Table 11-3. Women, who constitute about 44 percent of the employed labor force, have been disproportionately concentrated in the following occupations: nursing, public school teaching, clerical work, retail sales, services, and private household employment. All of these occupations rank low in terms of relative earnings. Nonwhites—blacks and other minorities—constitute about 10 percent of the total labor force and have also been concentrated in a limited number of low-paying jobs as laundry workers, cleaners and servants, hospital orderlies, and other manual workers. Conversely, note that women and blacks have both been underrepresented among such highly paid professionals as dentists and physicians.

Table 11-4 provides some basic insights into differentials in human capital accumulation, although the data provide no information with respect to access to apprenticeship programs and on-the-job training. We found in Chapter 4 that those individuals who acquire the most formal education also tend to receive the

TABLE 11-2

Unemployment Rates by Race and Sex, Selected Years, 1950–1984

(1) Year	(2) White Male	(3) White Female	(4) Black Male	(5) Black Female
1950	4.7%	5.3%	9.4%	8.4%
1955	3.7	4.3	8.8	8.4
1960	4.8	5.3	10.7	9.4
1965	3.6	5.0	7.4	9.2
1970	4.0	5.4	7.3	9.3
1975	7.2	8.6	14.8	14.8
1978	4.5	6.2	11.8	13.8
1981	6.5	6.9	15.7	15.6
1983	8.8	7.9	20.3	18.6
1984	6.4	6.5	16.4	15.4

Source: *Employment and Training Report of the President, 1982*, p. 190, and *Economic Report of the President, 1985*, p. 273.

most on-the-job training. The advantage which white males have enjoyed as compared to white females and blacks in obtaining a college education has been magnified through the greater access these white males have had to postmarket job training which has increased their productivity and earnings. Furthermore, studies indicate that the quality of education received by blacks has been generally inferior to that acquired by whites.

While it is tempting to conclude that Tables 11-1 through 11-4 prove the existence of wage, employment, occupational, and human capital discrimination respectively, the situation is in fact more complex than this. We will observe later in this chapter that a variety of factors other than discrimination may bear upon the differences shown in the tables. Also, the various "types" of discrimination are interrelated. For example, differences in human capital accumulation shown in Table 11-4 are undoubtedly an important causal factor in explaining the earnings, unemployment, and occupational differences revealed in the other three tables.

Finally, one might be inclined to infer from our tabular comparisons that the economic impact of discrimination is essentially distributional; that is, discrimination is a mechanism whereby males (whites) are able to gain income at the

TABLE 11-3

Occupational Distribution of Employed Workers by Sex and Race, 1984

Occupation	Percent Female	Percent Black
Total employment	44	10
Professional workers	49	6
Dentists	6	1
Physicians	16	5
Registered nurses	96	8
Elementary school teachers	85	10
Retail sales workers	69	7
Clerical workers	80	10
Secretaries	98	6
Typists	96	16
Receptionists	97	8
Laborers (nonconstruction)	18	15
Laundry and drycleaning	63	21
Pressing machine operators	66	31
Service workers	65	17
Waiters and waitresses	86	5
Child care (in homes)	97	10
Nursing aides and orderlies	90	29
Janitors and cleaners	28	23
Servants	95	44
Taxi drivers and chauffeurs	9	22

Source: Department of Labor, *Employment and Earnings*, January 1985, pp. 176–180.

expense of females (blacks). But as our later discussion of the crowding theory of discrimination will reveal, the *size* of the national output will also be adversely affected. Discrimination influences the distribution of a *diminished* national income. An understanding of basic economics suggests on intuitive grounds that this would be the case. Discrimination is like a tariff or any other artificial barrier to free competition which diminishes economic efficiency and causes the national output to be less than otherwise. Stated differently, discrimination arbitrarily restricts minorities and women from high-productivity, high-wage jobs and prohibits them from making their maximum contribution to national output and income.

One rather simple estimate suggests that the level of gross national product would be about 4.4 percent higher if *racial* discrimination were eliminated. In absolute terms this would amount to about $161 billion worth of goods and services in 1984! This estimate was made essentially by assuming that (1) the unemployment rate of blacks was reduced to the same level as whites and (2) the annual earnings of black workers was increased to the level received by whites.[4] A more sophisticated study has concluded that the elimination of *sexual* discrimination would increase national income by 2.57 percent.[5]

[4]Joint Economic Committee, *The Cost of Racial Discrimination* (Washington: U.S. Government Printing Office, 1980), pp. 2–5.

[5]Estelle James, "Income and Employment Effects of Women's Liberation," in Cynthia B. Lloyd (ed.), *Sex, Discrimination, and the Division of Labor* (New York: Columbia University Press, 1975), pp. 379–400.

TABLE 11-4

Selected Measures of the Educational Attainment of the Civilian Labor Force by Sex and Race, 1983

Average Years of School Completed	
White males	12.7
White females	12.6
Black males	12.2
Black females	12.2

Percent Completing 4 Years of High School or More	
White males	74.4
White females	73.3
Black males	56.5
Black females	57.2

Percent Completing 4 Years of College or More	
White males	24.0
White females	15.4
Black males	10.0
Black females	9.2

Source: Statistical Abstract of the United States, 1985, p. 134.

THEORIES OF LABOR MARKET DISCRIMINATION

As indicated earlier, there is no generally accepted economic theory of discrimination. There are undoubtedly a variety of reasons for this. First, the interest of economists in explaining the phenomenon of discrimination is relatively recent. The pioneering book in the field, Gary Becker's *The Economics of Discrimination*,[6] was published in 1957. Second, discrimination may assume a variety of guises and take different forms for different groups. For example, we have already cited evidence which suggests that blacks have been at a substantial disadvantage in obtaining employment, while women have had access to jobs but only in a restricted number of occupations. Finally, we noted at the outset that the roots of discrimination are diverse and complex, ranging beyond the boundaries of economics. A discipline such as economics, which predicates its analysis upon rational behavior, may be at a severe disadvantage in explaining a phenomenon which many regard as being irrational. Nevertheless, economists have contributed important analytical and empirical work on the problem of discrimination, and our immediate goal is to summarize several of the more prominent theories: (1) the taste-for-discrimination model; (2) the monopsony or market power model; (3) statistical discrimination; and (4) the crowding model. The reader should be aware that, for the most part, the models to be discussed apply to all types of discrimination. While we will present the market power model, for example, in terms of sexual discrimination, the model is also useful in explaining racial discrimination.

Taste-for-Discrimination Model. Becker's *taste-for-discrimination model* envisions discrimination as a preference or "taste" for which the discriminator is willing to pay. Becker uses an analogy based upon the theory of international trade. It is well known that a nation can maximize its national output by engaging in free trade based upon the principle of comparative advantage. But in fact nations obstruct trade through the use of tariffs, quotas, and a variety of other techniques. Nations are apparently willing to sacrifice economic efficiency for the sake of having certain goods produced domestically rather than imported. We seem to have a preference or taste for domestically produced goods, even though we must pay the "price" of a diminished national income in exercising that taste. Similarly, Becker argues that society also has a taste for discrimination and it is willing to forgo productive efficiency and, therefore, maximum output and profits, in order to exercise its prejudices. As noted earlier, the price—or opportunity cost—of racial discrimination alone may be on the order of 4 percent of the national output!

Becker's theory is general in the sense that it can be applied to, say, white (male) workers who discriminate against black (female) workers, *or* white consumers who discriminate against firms which employ black workers or salesper-

[6](Chicago: The University of Chicago Press, 1957).

sons, *or* white employers who discriminate against black workers. The latter aspect of this theory—white employers who exercise their taste for discrimination against black workers—is obviously the most relevant to our discussion, and therefore we will concentrate upon it. Why do employers discriminate? Employers' tastes for discrimination are based upon the notion that they and/or their employees need to maintain a physical or "social" distance from certain groups, here, that white employers and their workers do not want to associate with black workers. These employers may then choose not to hire black workers because they and their employees do not want to work alongside them.

The discrimination coefficient. Assuming that black and white workers are equally productive, a nondiscriminating employer will regard them as perfect substitutes, will hire them at random, and will pay the same wage rate to both. Note, in particular, that the nondiscriminating employer will regard the market wage rate W, the wage rate of white workers W_w, and the wage rate of black workers W_b all to be the same ($W = W_w = W_b$). On the other hand, an employer discriminates when, faced with a given market wage rate for equally productive black and white workers, she or he acts *as if* the wage rate for black workers were $W(1 + d)$. Becker calls d the **discrimination coefficient,** which is assumed to be zero or more.[7] For example, if the market wage were $4 and the employer's d is .50, then the employer would regard black wages as being $6 [$W_b = W(1 + d) = \$4(1 + .50) = \$6$]. This implies that this discriminating employer would pay a wage premium for whites in satisfying his taste or preference not to employ blacks. More precisely, if $d = .50$, the white employer would be willing to pay up to a $2 wage premium for whites (50 percent more than the $4 which actually must be paid for blacks) rather than hire blacks. Higher values of d indicate a stronger taste for discrimination, that is, a more prejudiced employer. An employer whose d is zero is an unbiased or "color blind" employer. An employer whose d was infinity would refuse to hire blacks at any wage rate.

Given a positive d, an employer will not discriminate between black and white workers when:

$$\frac{W_b}{W_w} = \frac{1}{1 + d} \qquad (11\text{-}1)$$

In this equation W_b/W_w is the ratio of black and white wage rates. For the nondiscriminating employer, d is zero and the employer will not discriminate between black and white workers so long as their wage rates are equal, that is, so long as the W_b/W_w ratio is equal to 1. But what of an employer who has a discrimination coefficient d of, say, .50? In this case $1/(1 + d)$ is $1/1.50$ or $2/3$. This means that the employer would hire black and white labor impartially only

---

[7]A negative d would indicate favoritism. That is, an employer who preferred to hire black workers would have a negative discrimination coefficient.

when the ratio of black to white wages was 2 to 3, for example, when the hourly wages for blacks and whites were $4 and $6 respectively. This discriminating employer would be willing to pay a $2 wage premium for white workers even though this would raise production costs and lower profits. Note that if in the labor market W_b/W_w were *greater* than 2/3—for example, if black wages were $5 and white wages $6—the competitive employer would not hire any blacks. On the other hand, if the actual W_b/W_w were *less* than 2/3—for example, if black wages were $3 and white wages $6—the competitive employer would hire only black workers *despite* having a positive taste for discrimination.

Demand and supply interpretation. Modified demand and supply analysis is useful in deepening our understanding of Becker's model and, more specifically, in explaining the prevailing wage differential between black and white workers. In Figure 11-1 we assume a competitive labor market for some particular occupation. The vertical axis differs from the usual labor market representation in that it measures the ratio of black to white wages W_b/W_w, and the horizontal axis shows the quantity of the *black* workers. The quantity of white workers and their wage rate are assumed to be given. The kinked demand curve for black workers D_b is constructed by arraying white employers left to right from lowest to highest discrimination coefficients. Recalling equation 11-1, the horizontal portion (*AB*) of the demand curve where W_b/W_w equals 1.00 reflects nondiscriminating white employers, that is, those whose d's are zero. These employers do not discriminate between black and white workers so long as the wage rates of the two groups are equal. The downward-sloping portion of the demand curve (*BD_b*) reflects discriminating employers whose d's increase as we move down that segment. On this segment of the curve W_b/W_w is less than 1.00 and diminishes as we move to the southeast.

FIGURE 11-1 WAGE DISCRIMINATION IN THE LABOR MARKET
The D_b and S_b curves show the demand for and the supply of black labor. Their intersection determines the black-white wage ratio and the number of black workers employed.

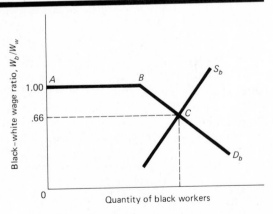

To this demand curve we now add the supply of black labor. Not surprisingly, this curve is upward-sloping; the quantity of black labor supplied increases as W_b/W_w increases. The intersection of the two curves establishes the actual W_b/W_w ratio—that is, the extent of wage discrimination—and the number of black workers who will be employed in this occupation. Using the numbers from our earlier illustration, we find that the wage ratio is .66 or $\frac{2}{3}$. This model suggests that nondiscriminating white employers (segment AB of the demand curve) and those whose d's are between 0 and .50 (segment BC) will hire all black workers in this occupation; those shown by the CD_b range of the demand curve will hire only whites.

Two generalizations. Two generalizations concerning the size of the black-white wage differential emerge from the taste-for-discrimination model.

1. A change in the shape or location of the demand curve will alter the W_b/W_w ratio. For example, suppose that a change in societal attitudes or affirmative action legislation has the effect of reducing the discrimination coefficient of employers. This will extend the horizontal portion of the demand curve further to the right *and* reduce the slope of the remaining downward-sloping segment. Given the supply of black labor, the effect will be to raise the equilibrium W_b/W_w ratio, that is, to reduce the discriminatory wage differential and increase the employment of black workers. For example, the equilibrium W_b/W_w ratio in Figure 11-1 may rise from .66 to, say, .80.

2. The size of the discriminatory wage differential varies directly with the supply of minority (black) workers. If the supply of black labor in Figure 11-1 were so small as to intersect the horizontal segment of the demand curve, there would be no discriminatory wage differential. If the supply of black labor increased to the position shown on the diagram, the differential would be .66 or $\frac{2}{3}$. A further increase in supply will obviously lower the W_b/W_w ratio, indicating a widening of the wage differential.

These two generalizations raise an interesting question: Is the greater observed wage differential between black and white workers in the south as compared to the north the consequence of a stronger taste for discrimination in the south, that is, a further leftward demand curve? Or, alternatively, is it merely the result of a greater relative supply of black workers in the south?

Gainers, losers, and the persistence of discrimination. Becker's taste-for-discrimination model indicates that white workers will gain from discrimination because their wage rates will be higher than otherwise. The reason for this is that, just as import restrictions reduce foreign competition to the benefit of domestic producers, the exercise of discrimination by employers protects white workers from the competition of black workers. Blacks, of course, are losers in that they receive lower wages because of discrimination. Finally, employers who discriminate injure themselves in that they will experience higher costs than are necessary. Let us explain why this is so.

Returning to Figure 11-1 once again, let us make the further assumption that all of the employers arrayed on the demand curve are producing the same product. All of the non- or less-discriminating employers on the demand curve to the left of the intersection point will find themselves with a competitive cost advantage relative to the more-discriminating employers on the segment of the demand curve to the right of the intersection. To illustrate: In equilibrium the W_b/W_w ratio is .66 or $2/3$ or, say, $4 to $6. Remembering the assumption that blacks and whites are equally productive workers, a nondiscriminating employer on the horizontal segment would hire a black labor force at $4 per hour, while a discriminator far down the demand curve would hire all white workers at $6 per hour. The discriminating employer will incur higher wage costs than the nondiscriminating employer. Therefore, nondiscriminating firms will have lower average total costs and product prices than discriminating producers.

One of the important implications of Becker's model is that competitive market forces will cause discrimination to diminish and disappear over time because the lower-cost nondiscriminating firms can gain a larger share of the market at the expense of less-efficient discriminating firms. In fact, in a highly competitive product market only nondiscriminating firms (least-cost producers) will survive; discriminators will have average total costs which will exceed product price. Hence, Becker's theory is consistent with a "conservative" or laissez-faire position toward discrimination; that is, in the long run the operation of the competitive market will resolve the problem of discrimination, and therefore the only governmental action required is that which promotes free occupational choice.[8]

A fundamental criticism of Becker's model is that in fact progress in eliminating discrimination has been modest. The functioning of the market has not eliminated employers' prejudices. Discrimination based on both race and sex has persisted decade after decade. Hence, alternative models have been proposed to explain why discrimination has continued.

Market Power or Monopsony Model. One alternative explanation rests upon the monopsonistic or market power of employers. A monopolistic seller of a product may be able to enhance profits by practicing *price* discrimination. Specifically, the seller will find it profitable to charge buyers whose demand for a given product is less elastic a higher price than those whose demand is more elastic. The monopsony or *market power model* is similar in that it suggests that an employer may find it profitable to practice *wage* discrimination, that is, to pay different wage rates to equally productive males and females (whites and blacks). As we shall see momentarily, in the case of wage discrimination the lower wage will be paid to those workers whose labor supply curve is less elastic. It should be noted that in this model the employer need not be prejudiced; that is, a white male employer need not dislike blacks or females as employees or on any other grounds. Wage discrimination simply "pays" in terms of maximizing profits.

---

[8]That government will be unsuccessful in eliminating discrimination is the major theme of Thomas Sowell, *Markets and Minorities* (New York: Basic Books, Inc., Publishers, 1981).

A disaggregation of the simple monopsony model presented in Chapter 6 to allow for payment of differing wages to different groups reveals the essence of this theory. Figure 11-2 then is simply one version of a "discriminating monopsony" model.[9] In panel (a) we have reproduced the monopsony model of Figure 6-6. The firm's total labor supply is represented by S_t, the associated marginal wage cost curve is MWC_t, and D_L is the demand for labor. Note that equilibrium is at point T where 9 workers are employed and the wage rate is $4.50. Now observe in panels (b) and (c) that we have disaggregated the monopsonist's total labor supply on the basis of gender. In panel (b) the supply and marginal wage cost curves of female workers are S_f and MWC_f. Similarly, S_m and MWC_m in panel (c) show these same curves for male workers. The labor supply curve for women is purposely drawn to be less elastic than that for men.

By extending the horizontal (dashed) line rightward from equilibrium point T in panel (a) we can show how total employment will be divided among men and women. That is, the dashed line reflects the MRP associated with the profit-maximizing total quantity of labor. Hence, its intersection with MWC_f and MWC_m tells us how many female and male workers respectively it is profitable to employ. Specifically, by dropping vertical (dashed) lines from equilibrium points F and M we find that the firm will employ 3 women and 6 men. The wage

[9]The discussion here is based upon Janice Fanning Madden, "Discrimination—A Manifestation of Male Market Power?" in Lloyd, op. cit., pp. 146–174.

FIGURE 11-2 THE MARKET POWER (MONOPSONY) MODEL OF DISCRIMINATION
Under monopsony the disaggregation of total labor supply (a) on the basis of sex (b and c) will result in lower wage rates for women, provided the labor supply curve for women is less elastic than for men. In this case the monopsonist will increase profits by hiring 9 workers (Q_t) of which 3 (Q_f) are females and 6 (Q_m) are males. Projecting these quantities off the female and male labor supply curves, S_f and S_m, we determine that the wage rates of females and males are $3 and $5 respectively.

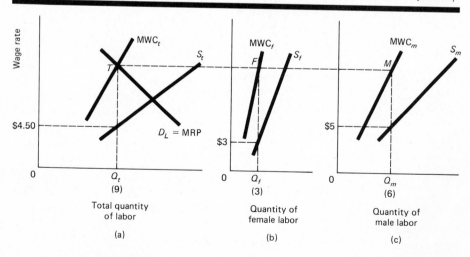

rates paid to women and men are determined where the vertical lines intersect the female and male labor supply curves S_f and S_m. That is, the discriminating monopsonist will pay wage rates equal to the supply prices of Q_f (3) females and Q_m (6) males. In this instance we find women are paid a $3 wage and men a $5 wage.

The implications of this model are both straightforward and interesting. First, the male wage rate is higher than it would be without sex discrimination ($5 as compared to $4.50). Second, the female wage of $3 is lower than both the male wage ($5) and the wage that would prevail in the absence of sex discrimination ($4.50). Third, the profits of the firm have increased. In discriminating the firm hires the same number of workers and, because female and male workers are assumed to be equally productive, realizes the same total output and total revenue. However, discrimination reduces total wage costs from $40.50 ($= 9 \times \$4.50$) to $39 [$= (3 \times \$3) + (6 \times \$5)$]. Unlike the Becker model, this model shows that it is profitable to discriminate. Fourth, assuming competition in the product market, if this firm does *not* engage in sex discrimination while its rivals do, it will have higher production costs and will ultimately be driven out of business by its discriminating rivals. Note that circumstances are precisely the reverse of those implicit in Becker's taste-for-discrimination model. In Becker's model nondiscriminators would drive discriminators out of business. In the monopsonist model discriminators would drive nondiscriminators from the market! Finally, a corollary of our fourth point is that, while the taste-for-discrimination model indicates that the pursuit of profits by employers will reduce discrimination over time, the market power model suggests that there is no necessary reason why market forces would cause discrimination to diminish. The monopsony model implies that public policy action is required to deal with discrimination.

As noted, these outcomes depend upon a situation wherein the female labor supply curve S_f is less elastic than the male supply curve S_m. There are two reasons why this *might* be the case. First, some women are less mobile than men both geographically and occupationally. If a woman's husband has a job in a particular locality, she may be unwilling to accept a job in another locality. Similarly, because of the prevalence of occupational segregation, women do not have access to as wide a range of occupations and job opportunities as men do. (Note that occupational mobility often involves geographic mobility as well). Because some women have less geographic and occupational mobility, if wage rates in this particular labor market were, say, reduced, we would expect more males than females to leave this work for alternative jobs. Given these conditions the conclusion might be that women are less responsive to wage changes than are men or, in technical terms, the supply curve of women is less elastic. Stated differently, there may be more employment alternatives for male workers than for female workers, making the supply curves of male workers more elastic. The end result would be that male workers would be paid more than equally productive female workers because the supply elasticity of female workers would be such that they would be willing to work for less.

A second reason for the less elastic supply curve for female workers has to do with unionization. Specifically, male workers are more likely to be unionized than are female workers. While 23 percent of male workers are unionized, only about 14 percent of all female workers belong to unions (Table 7-2). You may recall from Figure 6-9 that industrial unions establish a uniform wage which makes the labor supply curve perfectly elastic at that wage. The significance of this is that the union reduces the monopsonistic employer's ability to exploit workers. Thus in firms where men are unionized and women are not the labor supply of women will obviously be less elastic than for men, resulting in wage differentials that are unfavorable to women.[10]

Some economists find the monopsony model of discrimination to be unpersuasive, particularly as it relates to married women. Specifically, the critical assumption that the female labor supply is less elastic than that for males can be questioned. Although the job and occupational mobility of women may be less than those of men, women may perceive work within the home to be a more relevant alternative than do men. Hence, in terms of our earlier illustration, while discrimination may limit the reallocation of women to other jobs when wage rates fall, it does not prevent relatively large numbers of women from becoming nonparticipants. Therefore, when the option of work within the home is included, the quantitative response of women to a wage change could well be as large or larger than that of males. And, in fact, there is considerable empirical evidence to suggest that the supply responses of women to wage rate changes may be greater than those of men (Chapter 2).[11]

Theory of Statistical Discrimination. Still another theory centers upon the concept of *statistical discrimination*.[12] What is statistical discrimination? And why is it practiced? By way of definition we can say that statistical discrimination

> . . . occurs whenever an individual is judged on the basis of the average characteristics of the group, or groups, to which he or she belongs rather than upon his or her own personal characteristics. The judgments are correct, factual, and objective in the sense that the group actually has the characteristics that are subscribed to it, but the judgments are incorrect with the respect to many individuals within the group.[13]

[10]It is a worthwhile exercise to reanalyze Figure 11-2(a) on the assumption that a union of male workers is able to establish a wage which is above $4.50.

[11]Mark R. Killingsworth, *Labor Supply* (Cambridge, England: Cambridge University Press, 1983), p. 102.

[12]See Edmund S. Phelps, "The Statistical Theory of Racism and Sexism," *American Economic Review,* September 1972, pp. 659–661 and Dennis J. Aigner and Glen G. Cain, "Statistical Theories of Discrimination in Labor Markets," *Industrial and Labor Relations Review,* January 1977, pp. 175–187.

[13]Lester Thurow, *Generating Inequality* (New York: Basic Books, Inc., Publishers, 1975), p. 172. This entire section draws upon Chapter 7 of Thurow's work.

A commonplace non-labor market example of statistical discrimination involves automobile insurance. Insurance rates for teenage males are higher than those for teenage females. This rate differential is based upon accumulated factual evidence which indicates that on the average young males are more likely than females to be involved in accidents. However, many young male drivers are equally or less accident prone than the average of young females, and these males are discriminated against by having to pay higher insurance rates.

It is easy to understand how statistical discrimination would function in labor markets. Employers with job vacancies want to hire the most productive workers available to fill open positions. Hence, their personnel departments collect a variety of information concerning each job applicant, for example, an individual's age, education, prior work experience, and so forth. Employers supplement this information with scores on preemployment tests which they feel are helpful indicators of potential job performance. But two interrelated considerations pertain to this employee screening process. First, it is very expensive to collect *detailed* information about each job applicant; hence, only limited data are collected. Second, the limited information available to the employer from job application forms and test scores will *not* permit the employer to predict perfectly which of the job applicants will prove to be the most productive employees. As a consequence of these two considerations, it is common for employers to use "subjective" considerations such as race or sex or age in determining who is actually hired. Stated differently, in practicing statistical discrimination the employer is not satisfying a taste for discrimination, but rather is using sex or race as a proxy for production-related attributes which are not easily discernible. Sex, for example, may be used as a proxy for physical strength or job commitment.

To illustrate: An employer may be aware that *on the average* married women are more likely to quit their jobs within, say, two years after hire than are males because they may become pregnant[14] or their husbands may take a job in a different locality. All other things being equal, when confronted with a married female and a male job applicant, the employer will hire the male. Similarly, when considering the employment of a black or a white high-school graduate whose age, work experience, and test scores are identical, the white youth may be hired because the employer knows that *on the average* blacks receive schooling which is qualitatively inferior to that obtained by whites. Note what is happening here: Characteristics which apply to a *group* are being applied to *individuals*. *Each* married woman is assumed to behave with respect to employment tenure as does the "average" married woman. Similarly, *every* black youth is assumed to have the same quality of education as the "average" black youth. It is assumed that group or average differences apply in each individual case. As a result, married women who do not plan to have children (or do not plan to quit

---

[14]The increasing availability of child care facilities may be alleviating employers' fears that having children will seriously interrupt the work careers of married women. See Sheila B. Kamerman, "Child-Care Services: A National Picture," *Monthly Labor Review,* December 1983, pp. 35–39.

work if they do) and black youths who receive a quality education will be discriminated against.

Three further aspects of statistical discrimination merit comment. In the first place, unlike the taste-for-discrimination model, the employer is *not* harmed by practicing discrimination. On the contrary, the employer is a beneficiary. An employer will enhance profits by minimizing hiring costs. Given that the gathering of detailed information on each job applicant is costly, the application of perceived group characteristics to job seekers is an inexpensive means of screening employees. Some economists feel that the statistical discrimination theory which envisions employers as "gainers" is more plausible than the taste-for-discrimination model which conceives of them as "losers." Second, as suggested earlier, the statistical discrimination model does not necessarily indicate that an employer is being malicious in his or her hiring behavior. The decisions made may very well be correct, rational, and, as noted, profitable on the average. The only problem is that many workers who differ from the group average will be discriminated against. Finally, as noted at the outset, there is no compelling reason why statistical discrimination need diminish over time. In contrast to the taste-for-discrimination model, statistical discrimination may persist because those who practice it are beneficiaries.[15]

The Crowding Model: Occupational Segregation. We observed earlier in Table 11-3 that the occupational distributions of whites and blacks *and* of males and females are substantially different. We have also noted that job segregation is a factor underlying the less elastic female labor supply curve which is critical in explaining sex-based wage differences in the market power model. Thus it is no surprise to find that an entire theory of discrimination has been based upon the concept of occupational segregation. This *crowding model,* based upon simple supply and demand concepts, explores the consequences of confining women and blacks to a limited number of occupations.[16]

Assumptions and predictions. The following simplifying assumptions will facilitate our discussion of the crowding model.

---

[15]Our first and third points merit qualification in one important sense. To the extent that the average characteristics of any two groups converge over time—perhaps because of a decline in other aspects of discrimination—the application of statistical discrimination may become increasingly costly to employers. For example, suppose human capital discrimination diminishes and black youths now obtain high school educations of equal quality to those acquired by white youths. By applying statistical discrimination to employ only whites, the employer will now be making more hiring mistakes. These mistakes will be of two types: hiring more whites who are not qualified and failing to hire blacks who are qualified. The cost to the employer of such mistakes is that the most productive workers available are not being selected. Employers who make fewer mistakes will have lower production costs and will increase their market share at the expense of rivals.

[16]The following article by Barbara Bergmann, the leading exponent of the "crowding hypothesis," is relevant: "The Effect on White Incomes of Discrimination in Employment," *Journal of Political Economy,* March–April 1971, pp. 294–313.

1. The labor force is equally divided between male and female (or white and black) workers. Let us say there are 6 million male and 6 million female workers.
2. The total labor market is composed of three occupations, X, Y, and Z, each having identical labor demand curves as shown in Figure 11-3.
3. Men and women are homogeneous with respect to their labor force characteristics; males and females are equally productive in each of the three occupations.
4. Product markets are competitive so that the demand curves reflect not only marginal revenue product (MRP), but also value of marginal product (VMP) (Chapter 5).
5. We assume that, as a result of occupational segregation, occupations X and Y are "men's jobs" and occupation Z is a "woman's job." That is, women are confined to occupation Z and systematically excluded from occupations X and Y.

Men will distribute themselves equally among occupations X and Y so there are 3 million male workers in each and the resulting common wage rate for men is W_m. Assuming no barriers to mobility, any initially different distribution of males between X and Y would result in a wage differential which would prompt labor shifts from low- to high-wage occupations until wage equality was realized. Note that all 6 million women, on the other hand, are crowded into occupation Z and, as a consequence of this occupational segregation, receive a much lower wage rate W_f. Given the reality of discrimination, this is an "equilibrium" situation. Women *cannot*, because of discrimination, reallocate themselves to occupations X and Y in the pursuit of higher wage rates. Although men could presumably enter occupation Z if they so chose, they would obviously not want to do so in the face of Z's lower wage rates.

The net result of occupational segregation is intuitively obvious: Men realize

FIGURE 11-3 OCCUPATIONAL SEGREGATION: THE CROWDING MODEL
By crowding women into occupation Z, men will receive high wage rates of W_m in occupations X and Y while women receive low wage rates of W_f in occupation Z. The abandonment of discrimination will equalize wage rates at W_e and result in a net increase in the national output $[(ABCD + EFGH) - IJKL)]$.

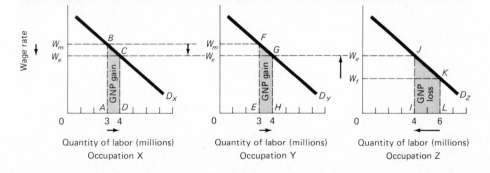

Quantity of labor (millions)
Occupation X

Quantity of labor (millions)
Occupation Y

Quantity of labor (millions)
Occupation Z

higher wage rates and incomes at the expense of women. Note, however, that women are not being disadvantaged as the result of exploitation; that is, they are *not* being paid a wage rate which is less than their marginal revenue product. In occupation Z women *are* being paid a wage rate equal to their MRP *and* to their contribution to society's output (VMP). Their problem is that, by being restricted to only occupation Z, their supply is great relative to demand and their wage rate is therefore low as compared to males.

Ending discrimination. Suppose that, through legislation or sweeping changes in social attitudes, discrimination disappears. What are the results? Women, attracted by higher wage rates, will shift from Z to X and Y. Specifically, if we assume occupational shifts are costless, 1 million women will shift into X and another 1 million into Y, leaving 4 million workers in Z. At this point 4 million workers will be in each occupation and wage rates will be equal to W_e in all three occupations, and therefore there is no incentive for further reallocation. This new, nondiscriminatory equilibrium is to the obvious advantage of women, who now receive higher wages, and to the disadvantage of men, who now receive lower wages.

If the elimination of occupational segregation results in both winners (women) and losers (men), it is only reasonable to ask whether the gains exceed the losses. That is, does society reap an economic gain by ending occupational segregation? A glance at Figure 11-3 reveals that there *is* a net gain to society. Our labor demand curves reflect value of marginal product, that is, the contribution of each successive worker to the national output. Hence, the movement of 2 million women out of occupation Z yields a *decrease* in national output shown by area *IJKL*. But the areas *ABCD* and *EFGH* for occupations X and Y show the *increases* in national output—the market values of the marginal products—realized by adding 1 million women to each of these occupations. By inspection we observe that the sum of the additions to national output in occupations X and Y exceeds the decline in national output that occurs when women leave occupation Z. The conclusion that society gains from the termination of occupational segregation is not unexpected. Women reallocate themselves from occupation Z where their VMP is relatively low to occupations X and Y where their VMPs are relatively high. This analysis underscores our earlier point that discrimination has both equity and efficiency connotations. Discrimination influences not only the distribution, but also the size, of the national income.

Index of segregation. How extensive is crowding or occupational segregation? An ***index of segregation*** has been devised to quantify occupational segregation. As applied to sex discrimination, this index is designed to show the percentage of women (or men) who would have to change occupations in order for women to be distributed among occupations in the same proportions as men. The hypothetical figures of Table 11-5 are instructive. Suppose that the occupational distributions of male and female workers are as shown in columns 2 and 3. To make the distributions identical *either* 30 percent of the total of *female* workers would have to move *from* occupation C (20 percent going to A and 10 percent to B) *or* 30 percent of the total of *male* workers would have to move *to* occupation C (20 percent coming from A and 10 percent coming from B). Because either 30 percent of female (or male) workers would have to change occupations in order for males and females to be distributed in the same proportions among occupations, the index of segregation is 30 percent, or simply .30. For more numerous occupational categories, the index can be calculated by determining the absolute value of the percentage differences for each occupation (without regard to sign) and summing these differences as shown in column 4. The resulting 60 percent is then divided by 2 because any movement of workers is counted twice, as a movement *out of* one occupation and as a movement *into* another occupation.

The conclusion from our simple hypothetical illustration is that 30 percent of the female (or male) labor force must change occupations in order for the proportions of men and women in each occupation to be the same. Note that this new distribution would result in an index of segregation of zero. The other extreme where, say, occupations A and B are each populated 50 percent by men and occupation C 100 percent by women yields an index of 100 percent or 1.00. Hence, the index of segregation may take on any value ranging from 0 to 1.00, and the higher the value, the greater the extent of occupational segregation.

What is the index of occupational segregation based upon sex for the United States? As stated by one researcher:

A review of historical trends indicates that not only is interoccupational segregation presently of considerable magnitude, it has also been a persistent and stable characteristic of female employment throughout the present century. According to census data, in both 1900 and 1960, well over half of all employed female workers were in detailed occupational categories in which women comprised 70 percent or more of total occupational employment. Moreover, the value of the index of segregation as computed in each census

TABLE 11-5

Determining the Index of Segregation (Hypothetical Data)

| (1) | (2) | (3) | (4) = (2) − (3) |
| | | | **Absolute** |
Occupation	**Male**	**Female**	**Differences**
A	50%	30%	20%
B	30	20	10
C	20	50	30
	100%	100%	60%

Index of segregation = $\dfrac{60\%}{2}$ = 30% or .30.

year between 1900 and 1960 has varied over a small range, 65.9 to 69.0, and has exhibited no secular trend toward a reduction in segregation.[17]

UNIONS AND DISCRIMINATION

In considering labor market discrimination it is only natural that our four theories have focused upon employers. It is obviously employers who have the greatest opportunity to practice discrimination as they make decisions in such areas as hiring and firing, promotion, salary determination, and on-the-job training. But we would be remiss not to give brief consideration to the discriminatory practices of labor unions. We will be concerned, first, with discrimination in union membership policies and, second, with the impact of unions upon black-white and male-female wage ratios.

Membership policies. Membership policies—both espoused and actual—vary greatly among unions. Some unions have been explicitly and blatantly discriminatory, while others have actively affiliated themselves with the civil rights movement. The obvious question is: Why the difference? Ashenfelter[18] has suggested that two factors strongly influence the discriminatory stances of labor unions with respect to membership: (1) the extent to which black workers constitute the union's jurisdiction both prior and subsequent to unionization and (2) whether the union is a craft or an industrial union. Let us pursue these considerations in the order stated.

1. *Composition of Work Force.* Clearly, if black workers make up a substantial fraction of the specific work force that a union is attempting to organize, it has little choice but actively to recruit black workers. To do otherwise would create a pool of substitutable black nonunion workers which would undermine the effectiveness of the discriminating union. The basic generalization here is that we would expect a union to be less discriminatory or more egalitarian the larger the proportion of blacks in its labor force jurisdiction. Ashenfelter suggests that the relatively nondiscriminatory policies of the United Mine Workers and the Packinghouse Workers, for example, can be attributed largely to the fact that large percentages of the workers in these industries were black prior to unionization.

---

[17]Francine D. Blau, "Sex Segregation of Workers by Enterprise in Clerical Occupations," in Richard G. Edwards, Michael Reich, and David M. Gordon (eds.), *Labor Market Segmentation* (Lexington, Mass.: D. C. Heath and Company, 1975), pp. 260–261. Blau also cites reasons why calculations based upon census data tend to understate the extent of occupational segregation.

[18]This section draws heavily upon Orley Ashenfelter's "Discrimination and Trade Unions" in Orley Ashenfelter and Albert Rees (eds.), *Discrimination in Labor Markets* (Princeton, N. J.: Princeton University Press, 1973), pp. 88–112. See also Duane E. Leigh, "Racial Discrimination and Labor Unions: Evidence from the NLS Sample of Middle-Aged Men," *Journal of Human Resources,* Fall 1978, pp. 568–577. The interested reader will also do well to consult Ray Marshall, *The Negro Worker* (New York: Random House, 1966).

To have excluded blacks would have been tantamount to having no effective union at all.

2. *Craft versus Industrial Unions.* The second important determinant of a union's discriminatory posture is simply the methods which it employs to influence wages, working conditions, and so forth. It is here that our earlier distinction between the tactics of craft (exclusive) unions and industrial (inclusive) unions becomes highly relevant (see Chapter 6). Recall from Figure 6-8 and the accompanying discussion that the bargaining power of craft unions derives from their ability to restrict labor supply by *excluding* workers from the occupation and the union and hence from employment. The "ideal" arrangement for a craft union is to enjoy closed or union shop status and to provide the apprenticeship program through which individuals acquire a particular skill. Under such circumstances the union becomes, in effect, a hiring agent for employers. Thus, for example, instead of hiring workers directly, a building contractor may simply call upon the local craft unions to provide the required number of bricklayers, carpenters, electricians, and so forth for a construction project. This arrangement obviously puts a union in a strategic position to discriminate against minorities and women as decisions are made about who is admitted to apprenticeship programs and hence to the union and to employment.

Similarly, Figure 6-9 reminds us that the bargaining power of industrial unions is based upon their ability to strike and deprive the employer of its work force. To pursue this tactic effectively the union must *include* as many workers as possible within its membership. A union which can deprive a mass-production firm of, say, only 10 percent of its labor force by striking will obviously have little bargaining power. From a slightly different vantage point, the hiring decision remains with the employer under industrial unionism, and therefore an industrial union which excludes, say, blacks from membership does not necessarily exclude them from employment in this occupation. An employer may simply hire nonunion black workers and thereby undermine the power and the effectiveness of the union.[19]

The overall generalization that industrial unions will tend to be less discriminatory than craft unions is supported by empirical data. Ashenfelter notes that in the construction industry, where skilled workers are organized solely along craft lines, approximately 54 percent of white male workers are unionized as compared to only about 27 percent of black males. In contrast, the proportions of whites and blacks unionized in all other (nonconstruction) industries are quite comparable.[20]

Impact upon wage ratios. What impact have unions had upon relative wage rates? Ashenfelter's calculations show that "the effect of unionism in the building construction (craft union) trades is to lower the ratio of black to white

---

[19]This is not to imply that an industrial union will not exert a discriminatory effect as it influences job assignment, promotion, and other employment conditions. While many blacks have been employed in the steel industry, they have been concentrated in the less-skilled, less desirable jobs.

[20]Ashenfelter, op. cit., pp. 100–102.

male wages by about 5 percent. . . . This does not result from differences in the wage advantage of black workers once they are in one of these unions, but from the fact that the likelihood of a black worker in the building trades gaining access to a union job is less than half the likelihood of a white worker gaining access to such a job."[21] In contrast, in the nonconstruction *blue-collar* occupations, where black workers have had greater access to membership, unions have had the effect of increasing the black-white wage ratio for males by approximately 4 percent. Furthermore, unionism has increased the black-white ratio for males in *white-collar* jobs by about 2.5 percent. Ashenfelter concludes that the overall impact upon the black-white wage ratio of all male workers has been to increase that ratio by almost 3.5 percent. What about females? Here Ashenfelter estimates the net effect has been to reduce the female-male wage ratio for white workers by about 2 percent for whites and by about 3 percent for blacks. The reason for these declines is that a much smaller percentage of females than males belong to unions. Ashenfelter underscores the modest magnitudes of these positive and negative effects on the black-white and the female-male wage ratios and concludes that "the presence of trade unionism is not a major factor affecting wage differentials between black and white workers or between male and female workers."[22]

CAUSE AND EFFECT: NONDISCRIMINATORY FACTORS

In analyzing discrimination economists have long been aware that a variety of factors other than discrimination may bear upon apparent black-white and male-female earnings differentials. To find that Ms. Smith earns $15,000 per year while Mr. Jones earns $20,000 annually is not necessarily evidence of sex discrimination. A variety of considerations which have nothing to do with prejudice may simply cause Jones to be more productive than Smith. More generally, cause and effect considerations are difficult to unravel in attempting to isolate the role of discrimination in explaining differences in socioeconomic status. Let us consider this issue in terms of sex discrimination.

Rational Choice. One can argue that the inferior economic position of women is basically the result of rational and freely rendered decisions by women. Let us examine two potentially relevant considerations: (1) the possible discontinuity

---

[21]Ibid., pp. 107–108.

[22]Ibid., p. 110. A recent study suggests that union membership has been of little benefit to blacks because those particular black workers who join unions enjoy "large unexplained wage premiums" prior to membership. That is, unionized employers may select black workers who have skill characteristics which provide them with high earnings prior to accepting union jobs. See Wesley Mellow, "Unions and Wages: A Longitudinal Analysis," *Review of Economics and Statistics,* February 1981, pp. 43–52.

of female labor force participation and (2) the potential role of heterogeneous jobs and male-female differences in job preferences.

1. Most women, it is contended, anticipate marriage and childbearing, which means that their participation in the labor market will be discontinuous and truncated. As Fuchs has pointed out:

> . . . although female participation in the labor force has increased enormously, less than half of the employed women work full time the year around. At ages 25–44 the proportion is even smaller. . . . Among whites in 1979 only one out of three women worked full time the year around, whereas three out of four men did. The percentage of white women who worked part time (either less than a full work week or less than a full year, or both) was actually larger than either the percentage working full time or not working at all.[23]

This fact has a variety of implications. First, given that women will work fewer lifetime hours, their expected rate of return on human capital investments (education and job training) will be lower than for men. Hence, it might be rational for women to choose to invest less in education and training. Because of smaller investments in human capital, the productivity and therefore the earnings of women will be less than for men. Similarly, anticipating greater turnover among female workers as they move from labor market work to work in the home, employers may act rationally in investing in less on-the-job training for women. Second, the stock of human capital which women possess may deteriorate during the period in which they are out of the labor force. For example, a professional nurse who temporarily withdraws from the labor force to have and to rear children may find that technological advances in medicine have rendered her skills largely obsolete during her 10- or 15-year absence from the labor market. Again, this means lower productivity and lower earnings. Third, it can be argued that occupational segregation is also the result of rational choice. Knowing they will not be in the labor force continuously, women may have a preference for occupations such as nursing or elementary schoolteaching which will have the greatest relevance or carryover value for productive activity within the home. The overall implication here is that some portion, if not all, of the male-female earnings differential is due to considerations other than discrimination.

2. We will discover in the discussion of wage differentials in Chapter 12 that wage and earnings differentials may arise because jobs and workers are heterogeneous. On one hand, jobs differ in terms of such factors as social status, location, and risk of accident or death. On the other hand, workers have different job preferences or "tastes." "Compensating wage differentials" arise in part as a consequence of these heterogeneities. *If* women put a high value on, say, job

---

[23]Victor R. Fuchs, *How We Live: An Economic Perspective from Birth to Death* (Cambridge, Mass.: Harvard University Press, 1983), p. 135.

safety and the location of jobs close to their homes, then the exercise of these preferences may result in lower wages and earnings for women. Stated differently, some portion of the higher earnings of males *may* be a wage differential which compensates them for performing more hazardous and inconveniently located jobs and thus is unrelated to sex discrimination.

Discrimination as a Cause. The "rational choice" view suggests that voluntary decisions by women concerning the amounts and types of education and training they receive and the kinds of jobs they choose *cause* them to realize lower earnings than men. Skeptics argue that it is equally, if not more, plausible to reverse the implied cause-effect sequence and thereby assign a primary role to discrimination in explaining male-female earnings differentials. To facilitate our discussion we will concentrate on the contention that women freely choose to truncate their labor market careers with the result that it is rational for employers and women themselves to invest less in human capital.

One can argue that women invest in less education and training or invest in types of training which have the greatest carryover value for household production *because* of labor market discrimination and manifest income disparities. For example, one can contend that the decision of many women to withdraw from the labor force for extended periods of time is the consequence of the low opportunity cost of nonparticipation, the latter being the result of low market pay due to discrimination. Poor labor market opportunities for women lower their earnings and thereby increase the relative attractiveness of work in the home. In more positive terms, if job opportunities and the earnings potential for women in the labor market were improved because of a decline in discrimination, more women might decide to remain single or to remain childless if they did marry. Or, if they marry and do have children, the higher earnings due to less discrimination might make it rational for them to employ domestic help or use child care facilities and remain continuously in the labor force. In this interpretation labor market discrimination *causes* women to choose the amounts and kinds of human capital investment which they do and to withdraw from the labor market for extended periods.

Those who feel that the lower socioeconomic status of women is the result of discrimination rather than rational choice point out that it is circular reasoning to argue that women earn less in the labor market because they spend so much time within the household *and* then to contend that women spend so much time in the household because they earn less in the labor market!

Which position is correct? Perhaps the most balanced response is that provided by Lloyd and Niemi:

> Do the lower earnings, higher unemployment, and occupational segregation of women result from their higher turnover and lack of continuous job experience? Or are discontinuous work histories and high turnover the inevitable result of being restricted to secondary occupations, characterized

by low earnings, unstable employment and little or no opportunity for advancement? The answer to both questions is *yes*. The same observed variables, such as occupation and work experience, simultaneously represent both different opportunities *and* different qualifications. Different opportunities arise in part because of employers' perceptions of the different qualifications of women and men, and different qualifications, in turn, are the result of different opportunities for skill acquisition.[24]

The point, of course, is that discrimination entails a complex intermingling of cause and effect. Differences in supply decisions with respect to human capital investment and occupational choice of males and females may *result* from labor market discrimination and existing earnings disparities and simultaneously be a *cause* of these earnings differentials.

Evidence. Despite the difficult cause-effect interrelationships involved, a large number of empirical studies have attempted to disaggregate male-female and white-black earnings differentials in the hope of determining what portion of these differentials is due to rational choice as opposed to discrimination per se. For example, Lloyd and Niemi have systematically reviewed twenty-one important studies of male-female earnings differentials wherein adjustments have been made for a wide range of factors other than sex per se which might be expected to affect worker productivity and therefore earnings. These adjustment factors include hours of work, age, education, occupation, amount and continuity of work experience, health, and so forth. The adjustments generally lower the male-to-female earnings ratio, indicating that the productivity of men is generally higher than women due to one or more of the enumerated factors. That is, part of the male-female earnings differential is explainable in terms of higher productivity for males. However, the differential by no means disappears. Lloyd and Niemi indicate that "the net earnings gap, unexplained after the adjustment, was still found to be at least 20 to 25 percent of male earnings in most of these studies. . . ."[25] Similarly, Oaxaca[26] has estimated that, on the average, whites earn wages 55 percent in excess of the wages earned by blacks. About three-fifths of this 55 percent wage gap can *not* be explained by differences in such factors as schooling, age, occupation, health, hours of work, and so forth. In other words, direct labor market discrimination accounts for approximately 60 percent of the 55 percent white-black wage differential.

[24]Cynthia B. Lloyd and Beth T. Niemi, *The Economics of Sex Differentials* (New York: Columbia University Press, 1979), p. 13.

[25]Ibid., p. 204.

[26]Ronald L. Oaxaca, "Theory and Measurement in the Economics of Discrimination," in Leonard J. Hausman et al. (eds.), *Equal Rights and Industrial Relations* (Madison, Wisc.: Industrial Relations Research Association, 1977), pp. 25–26.

ANTIDISCRIMINATION POLICIES

There are several avenues through which government might attack the problem of discrimination.[27] One very general policy is to achieve a tight labor market through the use of appropriate monetary and fiscal policies. On the one hand, an expanding economy makes it increasingly expensive for employers to indulge their "tastes for discrimination." On the other hand, tight labor markets help to overcome stereotyping. For example, the over-full employment of World War II simultaneously created new labor market opportunities for minorities and women and made it clear that females and blacks could effectively perform in jobs that heretofore had been closed to them. A second general policy is to improve the education and training opportunities of those who have been discriminated against. For example, by upgrading the quantity and quality of schooling received by blacks they can become more competitive with white workers. The third and most obvious means of dealing with discrimination is through direct governmental intervention. We will focus upon this latter aspect of policy.

Direct governmental intervention has stressed equal employment opportunities for minorities and for women. The purpose has been to deal directly with labor market inequalities by prohibiting certain practices in hiring, promotion, and compensation. Let us briefly consider the major pieces of legislation and policy decisions.

Equal Pay Act of 1963. This was the first major federal act to deal with sex discrimination. The act makes it illegal for employers to pay men and women different wage rates if they "do equal work on jobs, the performance of which requires equal skill, effort and responsibility, and which are performed under similar working conditions." While the Equal Pay Act was clearly a landmark piece of legislation, it did not comprehensively deal with all forms of sex discrimination. In particular, we have seen that women workers are plagued with the problem of occupational segregation as indicated by the crowding model. Hence, a discriminating employer could simply dodge the provisions of the act by practicing strict occupational segregation, that is, by *not* employing women and men on the same jobs. In fact, an employer with an all-male labor force would be in compliance with the law!

The *comparable worth doctrine* is in part a reaction to the reality of occupation segregation. Equal pay for the same jobs will be of little or no help to women and minorities if they are unable to gain access to the jobs now dominated by white males. The essence of the comparable worth doctrine is that female secretaries, nurses, and clerks should receive the same salaries as male truck drivers or construction workers if the levels of skill, effort, and responsibility in these disparate jobs are comparable. The controversy surrounding comparable worth is detailed in this chapter's Time and One-Half minireading.

[27]For a more detailed discussion of antidiscrimination policies see Lloyd and Niemi, op. cit., chap. 6.

Civil Rights Act of 1964. Title VII of the Civil Rights Act attempts to deal with not only discriminatory wages, but also discrimination in hiring and promotions. Specifically, the act made it illegal for any employer "to refuse to hire or to discharge any individual, or otherwise to discriminate against any individual with respect to his compensation, terms, conditions, or privileges of employment, because of such individual's race, color, religion, sex, or national origin." By requiring equal treatment in hiring, firing, promotion, and compensation (including fringe benefits), the ability of employers to practice overt discrimination legally was virtually eliminated. As amended, the act applies to all employers in interstate commerce with fifteen or more workers, to all labor unions with fifteen or more members, and to workers employed by educational institutions, state and local governments, and federal agencies. Enforcement rests primarily with the Equal Employment Opportunity Commission (EEOC).

Executive Orders and Federal Contracts. Executive orders issued in 1965 and 1968 attempted to eliminate all discriminatory policies which might be practiced by businesses and other institutions which hold government contracts. Thus the executive order of 1968 specifies,

> The contractor will not discriminate against any employee or applicant for employment because of race, color, religion or national origin. The contractor will take *affirmative action* to ensure that applicants are employed, and that employees are treated during employment, without regard to their race, color, religion, sex or national origin. Such action shall include, but not be limited to the following: employment, upgrading, demotion, or transfer; recruitment or recruitment advertising; layoff or termination; rates of pay or other forms of compensation; and selection for training, including apprenticeship.

As revised, the executive orders require firms with contracts totaling $50,000 or more to develop *affirmative-action programs.* If upon examination it is found that a firm underutilizes women and minorities in comparison to their proportions in the available labor force, the firm must establish a program embodying numerical goals and timetables for increasing its employment of women and minorities.

Controversy and Conflict. To say that government antidiscrimination legislation and policies have been controversial is an understatement. Making no pretense at being comprehensive, let us note some of the controversies and criticisms which surround antidiscrimination measures and their application.

A few economists take the position that direct governmental intervention is at best unnecessary and at worst counterproductive in eliminating discrimination. Friedman has argued that the competitive market system is quite capable of eliminating discrimination:

. . . there is an economic incentive in a free market to separate economic efficiency from other characteristics of the individual. A businessman or an entrepreneur who expresses preferences in his business activities that are not related to productive efficiency is at a disadvantage compared to other individuals who do not. Such an individual is in effect imposing higher costs on himself than are other individuals who do not have such preferences. Hence, in a free market they will tend to drive him out.[28]

Sowell has gone further to argue that in fact legislation and policies designed to aid disadvantaged groups have often worked to their detriment. He notes that American Indians, who have had the longest and most intimate involvement with the federal government, have persistently been on the lowest rung of the economic ladder. Furthermore, Sowell points out that some groups—for example, Jewish and Japanese Americans—have realized highly favorable socioeconomic positions in our society "despite a well documented record of anti-Semitism and anti-Oriental feelings, policies, and laws."[29] Sowell's view is that the socioeconomic positions of various racial and ethnic groups in our society are not due primarily to discrimination.

Others take the opposite view that the market has obviously failed to make reasonable progress in eliminating discrimination and that, while present laws and policies are helpful, they do not go far enough. For example, some critics contend that legislation and public policies have been too narrowly focused. As our enumeration of the various types of discrimination at the outset of this chapter suggests, discrimination is a multifaceted and deeply rooted problem which will not quickly be resolved by laws which apply primarily to compensation, hiring, and promotion. More specifically, these policies function only on the demand side of the labor market, while much of the problem lies on the supply side. Minorities and women have been discriminated against in acquiring the human capital—that is, the formal education and job training—required to compete on equal terms with white males. What good is a firm's affirmative-action program to hire more blacks and women for middle-management positions or a university's efforts to employ more black and female faculty if qualified candidates are simply not available? More generally, the argument is that discrimination assumes many forms and is highly institutionalized, and that the various types of discrimination tend to reinforce one another. Therefore, a more comprehensive and more aggressive government program against discrimination is required.

---

[28]Milton Friedman, *Capitalism and Freedom* (Chicago: University of Chicago Press, 1962), pp. 109–110.

[29]Thomas Sowell, op. cit., p. 126. Barry Chiswick in his "Analysis of the Earnings and Employment of Asian-American Men," *Journal of Labor Economics*, April 1983, pp. 197–214, concludes that American-born Chinese and Japanese men have enjoyed as much labor market success as have native white males, although Filipinos have been less successful. Chiswick has also found that, other things being the same, Jewish men have 16 percent higher earnings and a 20 percent higher rate of return from schooling than do non-Jewish white men. See Chiswick, "The Earnings and Human Capital of American Jews," *Journal of Human Resources*, Summer 1983, pp. 315–336.

Another related criticism is that *current* legislation and policies which are designed to create equal opportunities for all workers do little to correct the effects of *past* discrimination. While recent legislation may keep existing income differentials based upon sex and race from widening, they will allegedly do little to lessen those disparities in the foreseeable future. Minorities and women have been forced to carry the extra burden of discrimination in the "race" for socioeconomic status; hence, they find themselves far behind. To merely remove the discrimination burden does nothing to close the present gap in the socioeconomic race. It is argued that something more than equal opportunity—positive preferential treatment—is required if women and minorities are to catch up. For example, job segregation is currently so pervasive that it will persist for decades if we are content to accept only the marginal changes in the occupational allocation of labor which equal opportunity legislation allows. Furthermore, white male workers typically have achieved seniority which protects them from layoffs and thereby puts the burden of unemployment upon women and minorities. Those who accept this line of reasoning endorse affirmative action, quotas, and other forms of preferential treatment as appropriate means for hastening the elimination of discrimination. The counterargument is that such practices will frequently force employers to hire less qualified female or minority workers to achieve affirmative action targets or quotas and therefore economic efficiency will be impaired. Another counterargument is that quotas and preferential treatment are a form of "reverse discrimination." It is held that preferential treatment and discrimination are simply two ways of viewing the same phenomenon. Showing preference for A is to discriminate against B.

Empirical Evidence. Have antidiscrimination legislation and policies been effective? The simple answer is that empirical evidence is mixed and, therefore, opinions are divided. This lack of consensus is not surprising once it is recognized that it is extremely difficult to isolate the impact of antidiscrimination policies from other factors and policies which might have an impact upon measures of the relative economic status of blacks and whites *and* of males and females. For example, the increase in the ratio of black-to-white earnings shown in Table 11-1 might be interpreted as the result of, say, affirmative action which has presumably increased the demand for, and therefore the wages and earnings of, black workers. On the other hand, an alternative explanation might be that increases in the quantity and improvements in the quality of the education of black workers relative to whites have been the cause of the rising black-white earnings ratio. Or, as we shall see momentarily, the improved relative earnings of blacks may derive from labor supply adjustments which have little or nothing to do with antidiscrimination policies. Aware of such difficulties, let us touch upon some of the relevant empirical evidence.

An influential 1973 study by Freeman concluded that federal antidiscrimination efforts have been instrumental in reducing black-white income differentials. His analysis indicates that specific groups of black workers—women, young men, and young male college graduates—have realized very large economic gains since World War II, while the progress of older black workers has been more modest. Freeman estimates that overall the incomes of black males and black females were 15 and 22 percent higher, respectively, in 1971 than they would have been in the absence of the antidiscrimination laws and policies of the mid-1960s. Although the attainment of more education and the general economic boom of the late 1960s were undoubtedly helpful in improving the relative economic status of blacks, Freeman concludes that most of the relative gain realized by blacks during the 1960s was "the result of governmental and related antidiscriminatory activity associated with the 1964 Civil Rights Act."[30]

However, Butler and Heckman have critically examined Freeman's study, along with a number of others, and concluded that there is no real evidence that the tightening of the black-white earnings ratio is attributable to government's antidiscrimination activities.[31] Their basic argument is that, although black-white wage and earnings differentials did begin to decline in the mid-1960s when antidiscrimination legislation was put into place, the relationship is quite coincidental rather than causal. Butler and Heckman contend that the relative improvement in the economic status of blacks was attributable to a decline in the participation rates of low-income blacks (Chapter 3) caused by various income-maintenance programs which were inaugurated and expanded as a part of the War on Poverty in the 1960s. As our analysis in Chapter 2 suggests, the increased availability of more generous income-transfer payments encourages low-income receivers of both races to withdraw from the labor force. However, because relatively more blacks have low incomes than do whites, there occurred a greater relative decline in the supply of black workers which caused the average wages and earnings of blacks to increase in comparison to whites. After reviewing a number of other empirical studies in addition to Freeman's, Butler and Heckman conclude that "at our current level of understanding, the most honest summary of existing knowledge of government impact on the status of blacks is to say that there is no evidence that government antidiscrimination policy has had any impact on eliminating black-white wage differentials."[32]

Issue closed? Not at all. A very recent study of affirmative action is supportive of Freeman's position, concluding that it has led to a significant improvement in the employment opportunities of both minorities and females. Leonard[33] has made a statistical comparison of the changes in the demographic composition of the labor force of over 68,000 firms between 1974 and 1980.[34] Some 41,000 of

[30]Richard B. Freeman, "Changes in the Labor Market for Black Americans, 1948–72," *Brookings Papers on Economic Activity*, no. 1, 1973, pp. 67–120.

[31]Richard Butler and James J. Heckman, "The Government's Impact on the Labor Market Status of Black Americans: A Critical Review," in Leonard J. Hausman et al. (eds.), *Equal Rights and Industrial Relations* (Madison, Wisc.: Industrial Relations Research Association, 1977), pp. 235–281.

[32]Ibid., p. 267.

[33]Jonathon S. Leonard, "The Impact of Affirmative Action on Employment," *Journal of Labor Economics*, October 1984, pp. 439–463.

[34]The year 1974 was chosen because, although affirmative action came into being in 1965, provisions applying to females were first enforced in 1974.

these firms are federal contractors subject to affirmative action, while the other 27,000 firms (noncontractors) are not. After controlling for factors other than affirmative action which might have brought about changes in the demographic composition of the labor forces of the two groups of firms, Leonard concludes:

> The growth rates of females' and minorities' shares of employment are greater in contractor establishments obligated to undertake affirmative action than in noncontractor establishments with no such obligation. . . . In the contractor sector affirmative action has increased the demand relative to white males for black males by 6.5%, for nonblack minority males by 11.9%, and for white females by 3.5%. Among females, it has increased the demand for blacks relative to whites by 11%. For a program lacking public consensus and vigorous enforcement, this is a surprisingly strong showing.[35]

A final comment. We can be quite certain that controversy will continue to surround not only the scope and techniques of antidiscrimination policies, but also the question of their actual effectiveness. It is equally clear that discrimination influences labor supply and demand and, therefore, wage rates and the allocation of labor. An understanding of discrimination and antidiscrimination policies is essential to a realistic conception of how labor markets function.

SUMMARY

1. Discrimination occurs when female or black workers, who have the same abilities, education, training, and experience as male or white workers, are accorded inferior treatment with respect to hiring, occupational access, promotion, or wage rate.
2. Forms of labor market discrimination include (a) wage, (b) employment, (c) occupational, and (d) human capital discrimination.
3. Empirical data suggest that (a) the earnings of full-time black and female workers are substantially less than those of white male workers; (b) blacks and women have higher unemployment rates than white men; (c) occupational distributions differ significantly on the basis of sex and race; and (d) there are sexual and racial differences in human capital accumulation.
4. The effect of racial and sexual discrimination is to redistribute *and* diminish the size of the national income.
5. Becker's taste-for-discrimination model indicates that an employer will not discriminate between black and white workers when the ratio of black to white wage rates equals $1/(1 + d)$, where d is the employer's discrimination coefficient. In supply and demand form the model indicates that (a) a decline in the discrimination coefficient will increase the ratio of black to white wages and increase black employment and (b) the size of the black-white wage differential will vary directly with the supply of black workers.
6. Market power models indicate that employers with monopsony power will pay

---

[35]Ibid., pp. 457, 459.

female workers less than male workers. The reason is that the labor supply curve of female workers is allegedly less elastic than that of male workers because females have fewer alternative job opportunities due to occupational segregation.

7. The theory of statistical discrimination indicates that, because detailed information concerning the potential productivity of job applicants is costly to obtain, profit-seeking employers base employment decisions upon the perceived characteristics of groups of workers. The imputation of group characteristics to individuals discriminates against many individuals within those groups.

8. The crowding model focuses upon occupational segregation. Using supply and demand analysis, it demonstrates that occupational crowding results in lower wages for women, higher wages for men, and a net loss of national output. The index of occupational segregation measures the percentage of women or men who would have to change occupations in order for the occupational distribution of women to be the same as for men.

9. The extent to which unions discriminate with respect to membership depends primarily upon (*a*) the extent to which blacks constitute the labor force which a union seeks to organize and (*b*) whether the union is a craft or an industrial union. Overall the impact of unions upon black-white and female-male wage ratios has been modest.

10. There is disagreement as to the extent to which earnings differentials based upon sex or race are rooted in discrimination per se as opposed to rational decision making by women and blacks.

11. Governmental antidiscrimination legislation and policies involving direct labor market intervention include the Equal Pay Act of 1963, the Civil Rights Act of 1964, and executive orders applicable to federal contractors. Empirical evidence reveals no clear picture of the effectiveness of antidiscrimination policies.

QUESTIONS AND STUDY SUGGESTIONS

1. Key terms and concepts to remember: discrimination; wage, employment, occupational, and human capital discrimination; taste-for-discrimination model; discrimination coefficient; market power model; statistical discrimination; crowding model; index of segregation; Equal Pay Act of 1963; Civil Rights Act of 1964; affirmative-action programs; comparable worth doctrine.

2. In Becker's taste-for-discrimination model, what is the meaning of a discrimination coefficient of .80? Compare it to a coefficient of .65. In this model what effect would a decrease in the supply of black labor have upon the black-white wage ratio and the employment of black workers? Use the model to explain the economic effects of an increase in employer prejudice. What are the basic public policy implications of this model?

3. Use the market power model to explain why women might be paid lower wages than men. What assumption concerning the elasticity of the female labor supply curve is requisite to this conclusion? Do you feel this assumption is justified?

4. What is statistical discrimination and why does it occur? The theory of statistical discrimination implies that discrimination can persist indefinitely, while the taste-for-discrimination model suggests discrimination will tend to disappear. Explain the difference.

5. Use simple supply and demand analysis to explain the impact of occupational segregation or "crowding" upon the relative wage rates of men and women. Who gains and who loses as a consequence of eliminating occupational segregation? Is there a net gain or loss to society as a whole?

6. Assume that the occupational distribution of males and females is as follows:

Occupation	Male	Female
E	60%	5%
F	20	5
G	10	40
H	10	50

Calculate the index of segregation and explain its meaning. Compare the meaning of an index of .40 with 1.00 and 0. As applied to sex, has the index changed significantly over time?

7. There has been considerable controversy over the fact that certain pension plans into which males and females make equal contributions pay smaller monthly benefits to women than they do to men on the grounds that women live longer on the average than do men. Is this practice discriminatory? Explain.

8. It has been argued that in order to correct the inequalities of past discrimination blacks and females should be given preference in employment and promotion. Do you agree? In the celebrated Bakke case the plaintiff argued that he had been unjustly denied admission to medical school because less qualified black applicants were given preference under a quota system. Evaluate the plaintiff's argument.

9. "To discriminate in favor of one individual or group is necessarily to discriminate against some other individual or group." Do you agree?

10. "Wage differences between men and women do not reflect discrimination, but rather differences in job continuity and rational decisions with respect to education and on-the-job training." Do you agree?

11. Some economists have argued that the unemployment effects associated with the minimum wage have been greater for blacks than for whites. Can you explain why this might be the case?

12. What major factors seem to determine the membership policies of unions with respect to minorities? What has been the effect of unions upon wage differentials based upon race and sex?

13. Explain: "In the taste-for-discrimination model discrimination is practiced even though it is costly to do so. But in the monopsony and statistical discrimination models it is clear that discrimination pays."

SELECTED REFERENCES

AMSDEN, ALICE H. (ed.): *The Economics of Women and Work* (New York: St. Martin's Press, 1980).

ASHENFELTER, ORLEY, and ALBERT REES (eds.): *Discrimination in Labor Markets* (Princeton, N. J.: Princeton University Press, 1973).

BECKER, GARY: *The Economics of Discrimination* (Chicago: University of Chicago Press, 1957).

HAUSMAN, LEONARD J. et al. (eds.): *Equal Rights and Industrial Relations* (Madison, Wisc.: Industrial Relations Research Association, 1977).

KREPS, JUANITA M. (ed.): *Women and the American Economy: A Look to the 1980s* (Englewood Cliffs, N. J.: Prentice-Hall, Inc., 1976).

LAYARD, RICHARD, and JACOB MINCER (eds.), Proceedings of a conference on "Trends in Women's Work, Education, and Family Building," *Journal of Labor Economics*, January 1985.

LLOYD, CYNTHIA B., and BETH T. NIEMI: *The Economics of Sex Differentials* (New York: Columbia University Press, 1979)

MARSHALL, RAY: "The Economics of Racial Discrimination: A Survey," *Journal of Economic Literature*, September 1974, pp. 849–871.

SOWELL, THOMAS: *Markets and Minorities* (New York: Basic Books, Inc., Publishers, 1981).

STROMBER, ANN H., and SHIRLEY HARKESS (eds.): *Women Working* (Palo Alto, Calif.: Mayfield Publishing Company, 1978).

TIME AND ONE-HALF

COMPARABLE WORTH

Should the male-female earnings disparity be reduced by enlarging the "equal pay for equal work" doctrine to require "equal pay for dissimilar jobs of comparable worth?"

The Equal Pay Act of 1963 established the concept of equal pay for equal work under which an employer must provide equal pay to males and females who are doing the *same* job. Exceptions in the law allow for differences in pay resulting from differences in seniority, productivity, or merit.

Proponents of higher pay for female workers wish to expand this concept, claiming that employers discriminate against females by underpaying them for work which, although different from work performed mainly by males, is of comparable value to the employer. Advocates contend that comparable worth can be measured by assigning points to such job characteristics as knowledge and skill required, mental demands, accountability, and working conditions. Several states have conducted job evaluations and have assigned point totals to various public-sector jobs. As observed in Table 1, "mostly male" jobs tend to pay more than "mostly female" ones possessing similar point totals. Based on the comparable worth values shown in parentheses in the table, secretaries should be paid as much as carpenters and corrections officers, licensed practical nurses as much as painters, and laundry workers as much as truck drivers.

Proponents of comparable worth contend that these point scales, though admittedly imperfect, provide a better indication of female worth than existing market-determined wages. The latter are distorted by such institutional factors as unions, seniority provisions, statistical discrimination, barriers to occupational choice, imperfect information, and tradition. Thus, according to this view, it simply is incorrect to argue that existing earnings disparities between males and females largely reflect differences in productivity, varying degrees of job attachment, and differing job preferences. Supporters of comparable worth point out that numerous firms presently employ job evaluation techniques based on point assignment in setting their internal wage scales. Comparable worth, therefore, would merely extend an accepted practice to government and ultimately to the entire economy. Finally, and most importantly, those advocating this concept argue that it constitutes the quickest method for ending wage discrimination caused by occupational segregation.

Comparable worth is not without its critics. Opponents contend that comparable worth substitutes wage setting by job evaluation and bureaucrats for wage determination by supply and demand. Why should someone who is one of many suppliers of a particular skill be paid the same as one who is one of a fewer number of qualified suppliers? Does not the abundance of supply in the first case indicate greater preference for that type of work? Why should a firm be forced to pay a nonunion secretary an amount equal to a unionized truck driver? Should electrical engineers who typically have point totals in job evaluation studies equal to lawyers and accountants receive the same pay as the latter two groups? If so, how will a firm attract electrical engineers who are in short supply?

Critics of comparable worth point out that job evaluations are notoriously subjective and that no two evaluations seem to produce the same results. Detractors predict that, once wage scales are set through job evaluation by some government agency, occupational groups will bicker over the accuracy of the methods used to calculate point totals. Lawsuits are certain to follow. Also, to the degree that the point values deviate from true market worth, shortages of some types of workers will develop while surpluses of other types will result. In short, critics contend that, if applied to the entire economy, the comparable worth doctrine would render labor markets useless as mechanisms for allocating labor resources to their highest valued employment.

TABLE 1

Comparable Worth, Noncomparable Pay

Mostly Male Jobs (Points)	Monthly Salary		Mostly Female Jobs (Points)
Illinois			
Financial examiner (464)	$2,376	$2,104	Registered nurse (480)
Electrician (274)	2,826	1,298	Licensed practical nurse (278)
Mechanic (228)	1,681	1,135	Mental-health technician (236)
Corrections officer (198)	1,438	1,293	Secretary (203)
Minnesota			
Senior pharmacist (406)	$2,565	$2,041	Nursing administrator (406)
Communications sup. (199)	1,834	1,373	Typing pool sup. (199)
Painter (185)	1,707	1,307	Licensed practical nurse (183)
Grain sampler (136)	1,646	1,171	Clerk stenographer (135)
Washington			
Transportation engineer (345)	$2,170	$1,738	Registered nurse (345)
Carpenter (197)	1,781	1,230	Secretary (197)
Media technician (158)	1,654	1,087	Licensed practical nurse (158)
Truck driver (97)	1,499	849	Laundry operator (96)

Sources: State of Washington and the Minnesota and Illinois Commissions on the Status of Women.

Comparable worth opponents also argue that implementation of pay hikes for traditional female jobs will produce unintended negative effects. More precisely, these wage hikes will cause substitution and output effects (Chapter 5) which will reduce female employment. Additionally, the higher pay will attract even more females to traditional female occupations. One of the root causes of *market* wage disparities—occupational crowding—will be reinforced.

Opponents of comparable worth suggest that public policy might better be directed toward enforcement of existing laws—or enactment of stricter laws, if necessary—which grant and guarantee equal access for females, free from harassment, to job-training programs, employment opportunities, and job advancement in *all* occupations. Therefore, females desiring to enter the higher-paying "mostly male" occupations could do so. This would improve female pay directly and, by reducing labor supply to traditional female jobs, eventually would increase pay there as well. Any remaining differentials would reflect preferences for particular types of work, not discrimination. Proponents of comparable worth, however, quickly counter that this "equal access" approach has not reduced the male-female pay gap to date and that, even if it were more successful in the future, it would take decades to accomplish what comparable worth can quickly achieve. Conclusion? Comparable worth may prove to be *the* labor economics issue of the 1980s. The debate will surely continue!*

*For a fuller treatment of the pros and cons of this issue, including an extensive set of references to other sources, see Michael E. Gold, *A Dialogue on Comparable Worth* (Ithaca, N.Y.: ILR Press, 1983).

THE WAGE STRUCTURE

The previous four chapters focused on three factors—unions, government, and discrimination—which profoundly affect labor market functioning. Our attention now turns to several *outcomes* of labor markets. In this chapter we focus on the wage structure which labor markets generate and the factors which interact to produce wage differentials. Specifically, we analyze why wages differ among individuals and jobs, both *among* and *within* labor markets and both over *short* and *long* periods of time.

Our organizational strategy is as follows. In the first section we examine the wage structure which would result if *all* labor markets were competitive. Next, some data on the actual wage structure in the United States is presented. The remainder of the chapter discusses the factors which produce the observed wage differentials in the economy. More specifically, in the third section of the chapter we examine wage differences that are due to heterogeneous *jobs;* the fourth part looks at heterogeneous *workers* as a source of earnings differences; the fifth section then combines portions of the previous two sections into a "hedonic" model of wages; and the sixth segment discusses imperfect information and immobilities as each relates to observed wage differences. Finally, we analyze cyclical and secular changes in the pattern of wages in the United States.

PERFECT COMPETITION: HOMOGENEOUS WORKERS AND JOBS

In Chapter 6 we analyzed a perfectly competitive labor market for *a specific type of labor*. Let us now extend the assumption of **homogeneous workers and jobs** to *all* employees and firms in the economy. It is easy to see that if information is perfect and job searches and migration are costless, labor resources will flow among various employments and regions of the economy until *all workers* have the *same wage*.

The process whereby wages equalize is demonstrated in Figure 12-1. Initially assume that labor demand and supply are D_a and S_a in submarket A and D_b and S_b in submarket B, respectively. Notice that these supply and demand conditions produce a $10 hourly wage in submarket A as compared to a $5 wage in B. In each instance the wage rate equals the VMP of labor, but note that the VMP of the Q_b worker in submarket B is less than the wage rate and VMP of the Q_a employee in submarket A. The consequence? Workers will exit submarket B and take jobs in higher-paying A. The decline in labor supply in B from S_b to S_b' and the increase in A from S_a to S_a' will cause the equilibrium wage in A to drop from $10 to $7.50. The market-clearing wage in submarket B will rise from $5 to $7.50. Following the migration of workers between the two submarkets: (1) the wage rates will be equal ($7.50), (2) these wages will equal the VMPs in each submarket, and (3) the VMPs will equal each other. Symbolically, $W_a = W_b$; $W_a = VMP_a$ and $W_b = VMP_b$; and $VMP_a = VMP_b$.

We may thus summarize as follows: If all jobs and workers are homogeneous and there is perfect mobility and competition, the **wage structure**—defined as the array of wage rates paid to workers—will evidence no variability. The average wage rate will be the *only* wage rate in the economy.

THE WAGE STRUCTURE: OBSERVED DIFFERENTIALS

Casual observation of the economy reveals that in fact wage differentials *do* exist and that many of them *persist* over time. Some of these differences are dramatic. For example, some professional basketball players earn as much in one *week* as minimum-wage earners receive in a *year*. Most earnings differentials, of course, are far less spectacular. For example, as observed in Table 12-1, the median weekly earnings of managerial and professional workers in 1984 were $494, while precision production workers received $390 and service employees $209.

FIGURE 12-1 WAGE EQUALIZATION IN PERFECT COMPETITION
If labor supply and demand are S_a and D_a in labor submarket A and S_b and D_b in submarket B, a $5 wage differential (=$10 in A minus $5 in B) will emerge. Assuming that jobs and workers are homogeneous and information and mobility are costless, workers will leave submarket B for the higher-paying submarket A. The decline of labor supply in B from S_b to S_b' and the increase in submarket A from S_a to S_a' will cause the wage rates in each submarket to equalize at $7.50.

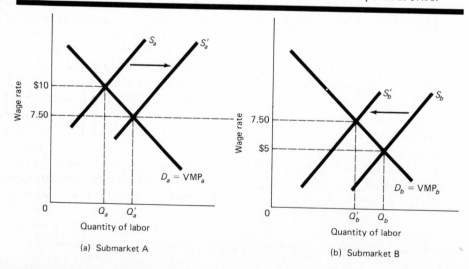

(a) Submarket A

(b) Submarket B

TABLE 12-1

Median Weekly Earnings of Full-Time Workers by Occupational Group, 1984

Occupational Group	Median Weekly Earnings
Managerial and professional workers	$494
Precision production workers	390
Technical, sales, and administrative support workers	302
Operators, fabricators, and laborers	294
Service workers	209
Farming, forestry, and fishing workers	205

Source: Bureau of Labor Statistics, *Employment and Earnings,* April 1985, p. 73. Data are for the fourth quarter of 1984.

Weekly earnings also vary *within* occupational categories such as those shown in Table 12-1. For example, under the category, "service workers," one would discover a difference in weekly earnings between people providing private household services and those providing protective services to, say, corporations. Also, the highest-paid service workers earn more than the lowest-paid workers who are classified as technical, sales, and administrative support workers, even though the median weekly salary is higher for the latter occupational group.

The occupational wage structure is just one of many wage structures that one can isolate for study. Notice from Tables 12-2 and 12-3 that average hourly gross earnings also differ greatly by industry and geographical location. For example, observe that hourly pay averaged $5.88 in retail trade in June of 1984 while it was $11.94 in construction. Also notice in Table 12-3 that production workers in Michigan earned an average of $12.24 per hour; in Mississippi, on the other hand, they received $6.94. Finally, recall from Chapter 11 that as of 1984 female earnings were less than two-thirds of male earnings and that pay for blacks was approximately three-fourths of that paid to whites.

TABLE 12-2

Average Hourly Earnings by Industry Group, June 1984

Industry Group	Average Hourly Earnings
Construction	$11.94
Mining	11.57
Transportation, public utilities	11.07
Manufacturing	9.14
Wholesale trade	8.90
Finance, insurance, real estate	7.58
Services	7.53
Retail trade	5.88

Source: Bureau of Labor Statistics, *Employment and Earnings.*

What causes these wage differentials and how can they persist? Why do some wage differences narrow over time while other remain? To answer these and related questions we need to abandon several assumptions made in the previous section of this chapter. More specifically, wage differentials occur because (1) jobs are heterogeneous, (2) workers are heterogeneous, and (3) labor markets are imperfect. Let us examine each reason in detail.

WAGE DIFFERENTIALS: HETEROGENEOUS JOBS

In Figure 12-1 we assumed that jobs were identical to one another in all respects. Utility-maximizing employees thus needed only to consider the wage rate itself in deciding where to work. Higher wages in one submarket would attract workers there. But, in reality, jobs are heterogeneous rather than homogeneous. In particular, *heterogeneous jobs* have differing nonwage attributes and require different types and degrees of skill. Additionally, employers vary with respect to such things as union status; firm size; strategies for attracting, screening, and retaining workers; and personal taste for discrimination.

Compensating Differentials. Nonwage aspects of jobs vary greatly and are the source of *compensating wage differentials*. These differentials consist of the extra pay that an employer must provide to compensate a worker for some

---

TABLE 12-3

Average Hourly Earnings of Production Workers in Manufacturing Industries by Selected States, June 1984

State	Average Hourly Earnings
Alaska	$11.63
California	9.75
Colorado	9.34
Hawaii	8.33
Maryland	9.34
Massachusetts	8.43
Michigan	12.24
Mississippi	6.94
New Mexico	7.93
New York	9.18
North Carolina	6.98
Pennsylvania	9.30
South Dakota	6.97
Texas	9.09
Vermont	7.90

Source: Bureau of Labor Statistics, *Employment and Earnings.*

undesirable job characteristic that does not exist in an alternative employment. Compensating wage differentials are thus *equilibrium wage differences,* since they do not cause workers to shift to the higher-paying jobs.

Figure 12-1 is useful in showing this concept. In our previous discussion of this figure we assumed that the jobs shown in labor submarkets A and B were homogeneous. Now let's suppose instead that the jobs in submarket A are performed outdoors in freezing weather throughout the year while the work in B occurs indoors in pleasant surroundings. Recall from Table 6-1 that one of the categories of determinants of labor supply consists of the nonwage attributes of employment. Because of the indicated differences in nonwage amenities between submarkets A and B, labor supply will be less in A relative to B. If, for example, S_a is the labor supply curve in submarket A while S_b portrays supply in B, the *equilibrium* wage rate in A will be $10 as contrasted to $5 in submarket B.

The extra $5 paid in A is called a wage premium, compensating wage differential, or equalizing difference. No movement of workers from B to A will occur, as happened when jobs were assumed to be homogeneous. This $5 wage differential will *persist;* it will change only in response to changes in the other determinants of supply and demand in either of the two labor markets.

Several additional points need to be highlighted here. First, the observed wage disparity—$5—does *not* reflect an actual difference in "net advantage" or net utility between the two jobs. Taking the nonwage characteristics of the two jobs into account, workers Q_a and Q_b are equally paid; that is, they both *net* $5 of utility from an hour of work: In A, $10 of wage minus $5 of extra disutility equals $5 net; in B, $5 of wage minus $0 of extra disutility equals $5 net.

Second, assuming demand is the same in both markets, employment will be lower where the compensating wage differential must be paid. Notice in Figure 12-1 that only Q_a workers are employed in A as contrasted to Q_b in B. Third, be aware that although the marginal revenue product (MRP) and the value of the marginal product (VMP) of worker Q_a in A exceeds the MRP (=VMP) in B, the reason for the difference is purely on the supply side. Note that S_a cuts D_a higher on the demand curve than S_b intersects D_b. The point is that workers in A receive $10 rather than $5 an hour because supply is small in that market, rather than because workers there are inherently more productive. Finally, it is clear that the compensating wage differential performs the socially useful function of allocating labor resources to a productive task which is not as pleasant as others.

Having established the basic principle of compensating wage differentials, we next examine the types of nonwage aspects of jobs which are thought to cause differing labor supply curves and therefore compensating payments. Specifically, let us examine each of the following sources of compensating differentials: (1) risk of job injury and death, (2) fringe benefits, (3) job status, (4) job location, (5) the regularity of earnings, (6) the prospect for wage advancement, and (7) the extent of control over the work place.

1. Risk of job injury or death. Recall from our discussion of occupational safety and health in Chapter 10 that we would expect that the greater the risk of being injured or killed on the job, the less the labor supply to a particular occupation. Hence, jobs which have high risks of accidents relative to others requiring similar skill will command compensating wage differentials. For example, Viscusi found the average earnings premium for risk of injury and death to be about 5 percent. While other studies have produced mixed findings, collectively they confirm the existence of compensating differentials, particularly those associated with higher probabilities of *fatal* injury on the job.[1]

2. Fringe benefits. Fringe benefits vary greatly among employers who hire similar workers and pay similar wage rates. How might this fact relate to wage differentials? Suppose that some firms which hire a specific grade of labor pay only $8 an hour while others pay the $8 plus provide such fringe benefits as sick leave, paid vacations, and medical and dental insurance. Obviously, other things being equal, workers will choose to offer their services to these latter employers. To attract qualified employees, the firms which do not provide fringe benefits will be forced to pay a compensating wage differential that in effect will equalize the gross hourly compensation between the two groups. In this regard, Schiller and Weiss examined the experience of approximately 14,000 workers in 133 large firms and found that less generous pension provisions were offset by higher wage rates.[2] This same principle applies in reverse to jobs in which gratuities are customarily received. Other things being equal, wage rates will be *lower* in those occupations than in similar ones in which no tips are paid.

3. Job status. Some jobs offer high status and prestige and hence attract a large number of willing suppliers; other employment carries with it the social stigma of being mundane, uninspiring, and dirty. As an extreme example, there is more status in being a semiskilled worker in the burgeoning electronics industry than in being a similarly skilled worker in, say, a sewage disposal plant. To the extent that labor supply behavior is affected by status-seeking, compensating wage differentials may emerge between low- and high-prestige work.

Status, of course, is defined culturally, and hence the degree of esteem society places upon various jobs is subject to change. For example, in the early 1970s working for the U.S. military commanded limited status, reflecting widespread disapproval of the Vietnam war. On the other hand, the successful U.S. military action in Grenada in 1983 boosted public esteem for those in the mili-

---

[1]W. Kip Viscusi, *Employment Hazards: An Investigation of Market Performance* (Cambridge, Mass.: Harvard University Press, 1979). Also see Charles Brown, "Equalizing Differences in the Labor Market," *Quarterly Journal of Economics,* February 1980, pp. 113–134; Richard Thaler and Sherwin Rosen, "The Value of Saving a Life," in Nestor Terleckyj (ed.), *Household Production and Consumption* (New York: National Bureau of Economic Research, 1975); Greg J. Duncan and Bertil Holmlund, "Was Adam Smith Right After All? Another Test of the Theory of Compensating Wage Differentials," *Journal of Labor Economics,* October 1983, pp. 366–379; and Stuart A. Low and Lee R. McPheters, "Wage Differentials and the Risk of Death: An Empirical Analysis," *Economic Inquiry,* April 1983, pp. 271–280.

[2]Bradley R. Schiller and Randall D. Weiss, "Pensions and Wages: A Test of Equalizing Differences," *Review of Economics and Statistics,* November 1980, pp. 529–538.

tary. One result was that the supply of labor to the military increased, enabling the armed services to meet recruitment goals more easily.

4. Job location. Similar jobs also differ greatly with respect to their locations, which in turn vary as to their *amenities* and their *living costs*. Cities noted for their "livability" may attract a larger supply of workers in a specific occupation than cities mainly noted for their smokestack industries. Consequently, compensating differentials may arise.[3]

Differences in price levels may also dictate equalization of real wages through the impact of the former on labor supply. Alaska is a good example. Because the general price level is so high there, a given money wage is not equal in purchasing power to the same wage in one of the lower forty-eight states. Therefore, the number of workers who are willing to supply a particular type of labor at each *money wage* is less in Alaska than elsewhere, and thus the equilibrium money wage is much higher. This wage differential is needed to equate *real* wages among the various labor markets.

5. Job security: regularity of earnings. Some jobs provide employment security for long periods and explicit or implicit assurances that one will work full weeks throughout the year. Other positions—for example, construction, consulting, and commissioned sales—are characterized by variability of employment, variability of earnings, or both. Since a specific paycheck is not assured each week of the year, fewer workers may find these occupations attractive and, all else being equal, people who do work in these jobs may receive a compensating wage differential. Restated, the hourly wage may be relatively high as compensation for the low probability that it will be earned 40 hours a week for the entire year. One study concludes that a compensating wage premium of as much as 14 percent may accrue in industries where the workers experience substantial anticipated unemployment and unemployment risk.[4]

Another study finds that unemployment insurance greatly reduces compensating wage differentials. In the absence of this insurance, an added percentage point of expected unemployment increases a worker's wage rate by about 2.5 percent.[5]

6. Prospect of wage advancement. Jobs are also heterogeneous with respect to the amount of firm-financed investment in human capital provided over

[3]For evidence on how locational factors such as crime rates and air pollution affect wage differentials, see Jennifer Roback, "Wages, Rents and the Quality of Life," *Journal of Political Economy*, December 1982, pp. 1257–1278.

[4]J. M. Abowd and Orley Ashenfelter, "Anticipated Unemployment, Temporary Layoffs, and Compensating Wage Differentials," in Sherwin Rosen (ed.), *Studies in Labor Markets* (Chicago: University of Chicago Press, 1981).

[5]Robert H. Topel, "Equilibrium Earnings, Turnover, and Unemployment: New Evidence," *Journal of Labor Economics*, October 1984, pp. 500–522.

the years. For example, someone entering the banking profession at age 22 might reasonably expect to receive rather continuous on-the-job training enabling her or him to be promoted to successively higher-paying positions over time. A person that same age who decides to be a carpenter is not as likely to experience as large an overall *increase* in earnings over the years. Assuming that people's time preferences for earnings are the same, *at any given wage* people will opt for jobs which have greater prospects for earnings increases. Hence labor supply will be greater to these jobs and less to employment characterized by flat lifetime earnings streams. This will necessitate a compensating wage differential for *entry level* pay in the latter type of occupation. In our example we would expect the beginning pay of the bank employee to be less than that of the carpenter. This type of a compensating differential is confirmed by research which finds that *lower* starting salaries across industries are systematically related to *higher* rates of wage *growth* as length of time on the job increases.[6]

7. Extent of control over the work pace. Some jobs provide less personal control of the work pace and less flexibility in work hours than other positions. More people are likely to prefer the latter jobs to the former, and therefore an equalizing wage differential may result. In fact, Duncan and Stafford estimate that two-fifths of the union-nonunion wage differential discussed in Chapter 8 is simply an equalizing difference necessitated by the structured work setting, inflexible hours, employer-set overtime, and fast work pace in union jobs.[7]

Differing Skill Requirements. We have established that one reason for wage differentials in a market economy is differing nonwage aspects of jobs. But jobs are clearly heterogeneous in a second major way: They widely differ as to their skill requirements. To illustrate, let us compare two hypothetical occupations. Suppose that these two jobs have identical nonwage attributes and that all workers have similar preferences for current versus future earnings. But suppose that job X requires 8 years of education beyond high school while job Y demands only a high school diploma. If these two occupations paid an identical wage rate, there would be *no* incentive for people making occupational choices to select employment X. Why is this so? The unsurprising answer is that occupation X is more costly to enter than Y. Occupation X necessitates much more investment in human capital to meet the skill requirement, and therefore if the hourly pay is the same in both occupations, the return on the investment for the extra 8 years of education is *negative* (Chapter 4). That is, the present value of the gained earnings is zero (one receives the same wage after investment as before invest-

[6]B. J. Chapman and H. W. Hong, "Specific Training and Inter-Industry Wage Differentials in U.S. Manufacturing," *Review of Economics and Statistics,* August 1980, pp. 371–378.

[7]Greg Duncan and Frank Stafford, "Do Union Members Receive Compensating Differentials?" *American Economic Review,* June 1980, pp. 355–371. For a criticism of this research and the author's rebuttal, see J. M. Barron and D. A. Black, "Do Union Members Receive Compensating Wage Differentials?: Comment" and G. J. Duncan and F. P. Stafford, "Reply," *American Economic Review,* September 1982, pp. 864–872.

ment), while the present value of the costs is positive and substantial (tuition, books, sacrificed earnings for 8 years).

The point is that wage equality between occupations X and Y is not sustainable; wage equality would create a disequilibrium situation. In order to attract a sufficient flow of people to occupation X, employers must pay these workers more than they pay people in occupation Y. Hence, an equilibrium wage differential will persist between the two occupations. The earnings difference created by this wage gap must be just sufficient to produce an internal rate of return r on the investment in 8 years of education equal to the cost of borrowing i as discussed in Chapter 4. If the wage differential and therefore r were greater than this i, more people would enter college and pursue the advanced degree. This eventually would expand labor supply, reduce the market wage in occupation X, lower the rate of return, and reduce the wage differential between the two occupations to a sustainable level. On the other hand, if the wage differential were insufficient between occupation X and Y, fewer people would enter occupation X and eventually the wage differential would rise to the equilibrium one.

To reiterate: Other things being equal, jobs which require large amounts of education and training will pay a higher wage rate than those which do not. The wide variety of skill requirements for various jobs constitutes a major source of wage disparity in the economy.

It is important to recognize that wage differentials created by differing skill requirements can either *increase, lessen,* or *reverse* wage variances produced by differences in nonwage aspects of jobs. For example, suppose that job A is characterized by a high risk of injury and hence pays a $3 hourly compensating wage premium relative to safe job B. Now, let us make two alternative assumptions about the **skill differentials** between the two jobs. First, suppose that the skills necessary to perform dangerous job A are greater than those needed in safe job B. Obviously the actual wage differential will *exceed* the $3 hourly wage premium paid for the risk of injury. Alternatively, suppose that the risky job A requires little skill while job B demands costly investment in human capital. In this second case, the actual wage differential between A and B will be *less than* $3 hourly and, depending on the size of the skill differential, may even reverse the pay such that safe job B pays more than dangerous job A.

Conclusion? The oft-made observation that higher-paid workers also seem to have more desirable working conditions does not refute the theory of compensating wage differentials. Rather, this observation simply indicates that in many cases the wage gap created by differences in skills *offsets* the compensating differential working in the opposite direction. Without the compensating differential, the actual wage gap would be even greater. Furthermore, if pleasant working conditions are a normal good (purchases of them rise with increases in income), then we would expect to find better working conditions and higher wages positively correlated. Workers who are more highly skilled can afford to "buy" better working conditions as part of their overall compensation package; they can afford to give up some of their relatively high direct wage for more nonwage job amenities.

Other Job or Employer Heterogeneities. Although differences in nonwage amenities and disamenities *and* variations in skill requirements of alternative employment are clearly the major heterogeneities of jobs which create wage differentials, several other job or employer differences may contribute to this phenomenon. For instance, employers or jobs differ as to such things as (1) union status, (2) tendency to discriminate, (3) absolute and relative firm size, and (4) strategies to recruit, monitor, and retain workers. We will discuss each difference briefly.

1. Union status. Recall from Chapter 8 that empirical evidence suggests that on the average unions generate a substantial wage advantage for their members. Part of this differential may be a compensating wage premium for the structured work setting, inflexible hours, employer-set overtime, and so forth which are characteristic of unionized firms. Another part may reflect the higher productivity which some economists attribute to unionized labor (Chapter 8). But most economists conclude that the union-nonunion wage differential involves something above a compensating wage premium or a productivity differential; it also includes a separate economic rent component (Chapter 10) deriving from the ability of unions to exert market power. In this latter respect, the existence of both union and nonunion jobs creates a *distinct* job heterogeneity which helps explain wage disparities.

2. Tendency to discriminate. We discovered in Chapter 11 that some economists contend that employers possess varying tastes for discrimination; that is, some employers are biased toward or against hiring certain classes of workers, say, blacks, females, or specific ethnic minorities. Hence direct wage discrimination may occur in some labor markets. The demand for workers for whom firms have positive preferences will increase; the demand for those whom firms possess negative "tastes" will decline; and an observable wage differential will emerge among whites and blacks, males and females, and other groups. Recall that there is much disagreement on whether or not these observed differentials will persist or be eroded by competitive market forces.

3. Absolute and relative firm size. Several studies indicate that firms which are large or have major market shares pay higher wages and salaries in general than do smaller firms. There are various possible explanations for this, some of which are simply the previously discussed job heterogeneities. First, large firms are more likely than small firms to be unionized. Second, workers in large firms may be more productive—that is, have higher skills—than otherwise comparable workers in small enterprises. This productivity may be due to (1) greater amounts and better quality of capital per worker, (2) more on-the-job training necessitated by skill specialization, or (3) the possibility that workers in large firms are "superior" employees who require less supervision than average workers.[8]

[8]For more on this topic, see Wesley Mellow, "Employer Size and Wages," *Review of Economics and Statistics*, August 1982, pp. 495–501, and Walter Oi, "Heterogeneous Firms and the Organization of Production," *Economic Inquiry*, April 1983, pp. 147–171.

A third possibility is that the higher pay observed in larger firms is a compensating wage premium. Larger firms may simply be more bureaucratic and less pleasant places to work than smaller companies, although the evidence on this is certainly mixed. Also, larger firms are more likely to be located in major metropolitan areas where overall living costs in addition to commuting and parking expenses are high.

Finally, firms possessing large market shares often make significant economic profits. This may increase union bargaining power and consequently enable unions to secure higher than usual wage rates.

4. Recruitment, supervision, and retention strategies. We observed in Chapter 6 that some firms have discretion over the wage rate they pay. Hence differing pay strategies among employers are possible. For instance, some employers may chose to pay high wage rates as a strategy to attract a large surplus of job applicants from which it can screen those whose personal attributes best match the firm's needs. This "high-wage" strategy is likely to (1) reduce recruitment costs, (3) lessen the quit rate, and (3) lower the cost of supervising workers. Other employers may chose to pay lower wages for similar work and accept the accompanying costs associated with higher recruitment, monitoring, and job turnover. Once again we see that job or employer heterogeneity can produce wage differentials.

WAGE DIFFERENTIALS: HETEROGENEOUS WORKERS

Having observed that heterogeneities among jobs and employers constitute a major source of wage disparities, we now turn to an equally important factor which influences the wage structure: *heterogeneous workers.* The wage equality initially predicted in Figure 12-1 relied on our assumption not only that all *jobs* were identical but also that all *workers* in the labor force were equally productive. In reality, people have greatly differing stocks of human capital as well as differing preferences for nonwage aspects of jobs.

Differing Human Capital: Noncompeting Groups. In the chapter which follows we discuss the personal distribution of earnings as it relates to such characteristics as age, years of education, quality of education, native ability, and family background. That approach points out an important reality: People obviously are not homogeneous! Of particular significance to our discussion of the wage structure is the fact that people possess differing stocks of human capital. Hence, at any point in time the labor force consists of numerous **noncompeting groups,** each one of which represents one or several occupations for which the members of the group qualify.

Differences in stocks of human capital may result from differing innate abilities to learn and perform. Few people possess the required intellectual or physical endowments to be a nuclear physicist, a professional football quarterback, a petroleum engineer, an opera singer, or a professional model. There is no effective competition in the labor market between these groups and larger groups of skilled or unskilled workers. Nor is there substitutability between nuclear physicists and professional athletes. In fact, even within occupational groups workers are not always perfectly substitutable. For example, some professional football players command salaries far in excess of the average pay for that occupation. The reason: Other players are only imperfect substitutes because of differences in innate abilities.

More significantly, noncompeting groups result from differences in the type, amount, and quality of education and training which people possess (Chapter 4). For instance, recent high school graduates have several employment options—being a farm worker, a gasoline station attendant, a member of the armed forces, an unskilled construction worker, or a fast-food employee. Each of these categories of workers can be classified into one broad group, because each is capable of doing the other jobs. But none of the workers in this group currently offers direct competition to, say, lawyers or accountants, who find themselves in other, more exclusive groups.

Workers can and do move from one noncompeting group to another by investing in human capital. The gasoline attendant may decide to attend college to obtain a degree in accounting. But this presupposes the person has the financial means and innate intelligence needed to pursue this degree successfully. To the extent that income, credit worthiness, and native learning skills are unequally distributed, wage differentials between noncompeting groups can persist. Also, bear in mind that the *quality* of education varies. A degree in accounting from a relatively unknown college may not generate the same postinvestment earnings as a degree from a more prestigious university.

To summarize: People have differing stocks of human capital according to native endowments and the type, amount, and quality of education and training they possess. Unsurprisingly, the result is a wide variety of groups, subgroups, or even individuals who are not readily substitutable for one another in the labor market. In the short run, these human capital heterogeneities produce wage differentials due to the varying productivity of workers. People can and do move toward the higher-paying positions in the long run, but the extent of the movement is limited by differing abilities to finance human capital investments and differing inherent abilities to absorb and apply education and training. Therefore, wage differentials remain.

Differing Individual Preferences. In addition to possessing differing stocks of human capital, people also are heterogeneous with respect to their preferences for such things as (1) present versus future income, and (2) various nonwage aspects of work.

Differences in time preferences. Some people are highly present-oriented; that is, they discount the future heavily or ignore it entirely. Other people have a great willingness or ability to sacrifice present satisfaction to obtain greater future rewards. In terms of the investment in human capital framework presented in Chapter 4, we are suggesting that people have differing discount rates—or "i's" in equation (4-3). Those persons who are *highly* present-oriented will have high discount rates, or i's. They will not be willing to sacrifice consumption today unless as a result they are able to obtain *substantially* more dollars in the future. The higher the i in equation (4-3), the lower the net present value of the prospective investment and the less the likelihood that one will undertake a given investment in human capital. On the other hand, people who are more future-oriented will be willing to forgo current consumption for the expectation of obtaining relatively small *additions* to earnings later. In technical terms, such people will have a low discount rates (i's) and will perceive a given investment in human capital to have a higher net present value. Consequently, they will obtain more human capital than the more present-oriented individuals.

These differences in time preferences have a significant implication for the theory of noncompeting groups. Specifically, they help explain why people who possess similar innate abilities and access to financing often choose to obtain differing levels of human capital. We have seen that the latter are a major source of wage differentials. Restated, differences in time preferences, which in themselves represent a worker heterogeneity, help explain an even more significant heterogeneity—differing stocks of human capital.

Tastes for nonwage aspects of jobs. We noted earlier that *jobs* are heterogeneous with respect to such nonwage features as probability of job accidents, fringe benefits, job status, location, regularity of earnings, prospects for wage advancement, and control over the work pace. People also differ as to their preferences for these nonwage amenities and disamenities; *workers* as well as jobs are heterogeneous in this regard. As examples, some workers value job safety highly while others are far less averse to risks; some people desire positions having paid vacations while others find vacations boring and would gladly forgo paid absences for higher hourly pay; and some individuals seek status while others do not care what people think of their occupations.

THE HEDONIC THEORY OF WAGES

The fact that both jobs *and* workers are heterogeneous is contained in the *hedonic theory of wages*.[9] The term "hedonic" derives from the philosophical concept of hedonism which hypothesizes that people pursue that which provides utility (pleasure), say wage income, and avoid that which creates disutility (pain), for example jobs having unpleasant working conditions. According to the hedonic theory, workers are interested in maximizing *net* utility and there-

[9]Sherwin Rosen, "Hedonic Prices and Implicit Markets," *Journal of Political Economy,* January/February 1974, pp. 34–55.

fore are willing to "exchange" that which produces utility to get reductions in something which yields disutility.

The Worker's Indifference Map. The hedonic wage theory often is portrayed in terms of a tradeoff between a "good" (the wage) and a "bad" (the probability of injury). However, the *absence* of a "bad" (probability that an injury will not occur) is indeed a "good," and therefore the theory can also be presented in terms of trading off wages and nonwage amenities. This allows the use of standard indifference curve analysis and avoids much of the complexity associated with the former representation of the hedonic theory.

It is reasonable to assume that the typical worker places a positive value on (1) the wage rate being paid, and (2) the nonwage amenities that a job offers. Hence, in a manner similar to the income-leisure analysis in Chapter 2, a worker faces a subjective tradeoff between two things which yield utility.

Figure 12-2 is illustrative. Note that the wage rate is measured on the vertical axis and a single nonwage amenity is shown on the horizontal axis. This nonwage amenity may be any one of several positive job attributes, for example, the monetary value of fringe benefits, the probability of *not* being injured on the job, the advantages associated with the job's location, or the expenses saved and leisure gained as commuting time declines.

Let us suppose that the particular nonwage amenity measured left to right on the horizontal axis is the degree of job safety (the probability of not being injured on the job). Each indifference curve shows the various combinations of wages and degrees of job safety which will yield some given level of utility or satisfaction to this worker. Recall from earlier discussions that each point on a specific indifference curve is equally satisfactory, but that total utility can be

FIGURE 12-2 AN INDIFFERENCE MAP FOR WAGES AND NONWAGE AMENITIES

The "hedonic" indifference map is comprised of a number of indifference curves. Each individual curve shows the various combinations of wage rates and a particular nonwage amenity (for example, job safety) which yields a specific level of total utility. Each successive curve to the northeast reflects a higher level of total utility.

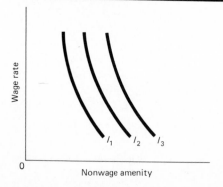

increased by getting to a higher indifference curve, that is, by moving northeasterly from I_1 to I_2 to I_3.

Notice that the indifference curves in Figure 12-2 are steep, implying that this individual is highly averse to risks. To understand this conclusion, observe curve I_1 and notice that this person places a high substitution value on extra degrees of job safety. A very large increase in the wage rate is necessary to compensate him or her for a small reduction in safety (small increase in the probability of job injury). But indifference maps vary from person to person; another worker may be far less averse to risk and therefore will have indifference curves which are relatively flat compared to those shown in Figure 12-2. Succinctly stated, workers are heterogeneous with respect to their preferences for nonwage amenities.

The Employer's Isoprofit Curves. It is reasonable to assume that an employer can take actions to reduce the probability of job injury or, alternatively stated, to increase the safety of the workplace. For example, the employer might provide education programs about job safety, purchase safer machinery, provide protective work gear, or slow the pace of work (Chapter 10). But, because these steps are costly, it is easy to see that the employer faces a tradeoff between the wages offered and the degree of job safety provided to workers. To maintain any *given* level of profits, the firm can either (1) pay lower wages and provide a high degree of job safety, or (2) pay higher wages and take fewer actions to reduce the risk of job-related accidents.

Figure 12-3 shows a family of *isoprofit curves,* each one of which shows the

FIGURE 12-3 ISOPROFIT CURVES
The employer's isoprofit map consists of a number of isoprofit curves. Each individual isoprofit curve portrays the various combinations of wage rates and job amenities (for example, job safety) which yield a given level of profit. Successive curves toward the origin represent higher levels of total profit. Competition among firms will result in only normal profits (zero-economic profit) in the long run; therefore, firms will be forced to make their "wage rate–job amenity" decisions along a curve such as P_2.

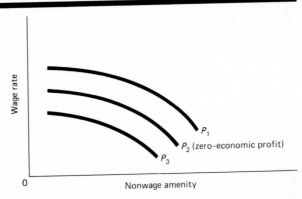

various combinations of wage rates and degrees of job safety which yield a given level of profits. Curve P_1 is illustrative of the employer's tradeoff. The concave shape of this isoprofit curve derives from the realistic assumption that each unit of added job safety comes at increasing expense, and therefore results in a successively larger wage reduction. Stated alternatively, successive units of expense (wage reduction) yield diminishing returns to job safety. Recall from Chapter 10 that marginal costs typically rise as more job safety is produced. Hence, as one moves *rightward* on P_1 the curve becomes increasingly steep.

But not all employers have identical isoprofit maps; they too are *heterogeneous*. The isoprofit curves in Figure 12-3 are relatively flat, indicating that this firm can "purchase" job safety at a relatively low incremental cost. Note from P_1 that large increments of job safety are associated with only small reductions in the wage. But other firms may not be so fortunate. Their technological constraints may make it extremely difficult to reduce the risk of accident and therefore will make it very costly to "produce" a safe work environment. These firms would face steep isoprofit curves.

Irrespective of the flatness or steepness of their isoprofit curves, firms desire to move southwesterly (toward the origin) on their isoprofit maps. The reason, of course, is that just as northeasterly indifference curves indicate higher levels of total utility for workers, each successive isoprofit curve *closer to the origin* represents a higher level of total profit. This is the case because less is being spent on wages *and* the nonwage amenity. Competition, however, will dictate a *specific* isoprofit curve among the many. For example, suppose that this competitive firm finds itself temporarily on curve P_3 but that curve P_2 represents a normal (zero-economic) profit. The above-normal profit at P_3 will attract new entrants to the industry and thereby increase product supply. This, in turn, will lower the product price and decrease the firm's profit to a normal one (P_2). On the other hand, this firm is incurring an economic loss when it is on P_1. As a result, firms will leave the industry until the remaining firms have isoprofit curves such as P_2. Conclusion? Although a competitive firm indeed faces a *family* of isoprofit curves, in the long run the zero-economic profit curve is the relevant one for its decision making with regard to wage amenities.

Matching Workers with Jobs. Figure 12-4 portrays the optimal combination of wage rate and job safety for two distinct sets of employers and workers. Workers A and B possess identical stocks of human capital, but have greatly different tastes for the nonwage amenity job safety. The isoprofit curves P_A in panel (a) and P_B in (b) show the highest profit levels attainable for firms A and B, given the competitive nature of their respective industries. Notice that the general slope of isoprofit curve P_A is less steep than that of P_B. This indicates that for technological reasons the marginal cost of producing job safety is more in firm B than in A. Restated, a specific increase in job safety reduces the wage rate more for firm B than for A.

Now observe the indifference curves I_A and I_B in graphs (a) and (b). These are the highest attainable indifference curves for each worker. Notice that curve

I_A is relatively steep, implying that person A is quite averse to the risk of job injury (he values job safety highly). On the other hand, the curve for person B is relatively flat, indicating that B is less concerned about job injury or death than A. Obviously, workers A and B have differing tastes for this particular job disamenity.

Each worker maximizes total utility where her or his highest indifference curve is tangent to the employer's zero-economic profit isoprofit curve. Worker A will choose to work for employer A and, as indicated by point *a* in the left-hand graph, will receive wage rate W_A. Along with this relatively low wage the person will gain a relatively large quantity of the amenity job safety. Job and worker heterogeneity therefore produce an optimal match between an individual who is highly averse to risk and an employer who has relatively low marginal costs of producing job safety. Similarly, worker B will match up with employer B and receive a higher wage rate, W_B, but will be employed in a relatively more dangerous work setting. The matching of laborer B and firm B maximizes the interests of both; employer B has a high marginal cost of producing job safety, and this worker is willing to trade off much of that amenity for a higher wage rate.

Labor Market Implications. The hedonic wage model has some interesting—and in some cases, controversial—implications. Let us sample a few.

1. The labor market will generate wage differentials among people who

FIGURE 12-4 MATCHING HETEROGENEOUS WORKERS AND JOBS
Panel (a) portrays an optimal job match between worker A who places a high valuation upon job safety at the margin and Firm A that can "produce" job safety at relatively low marginal cost. Panel (b) shows the utility-maximizing and profit-maximizing "wage rate–nonwage amenity" combination (point b) for a worker who is less averse to risk and a firm which has high marginal costs of making the workplace safer. Panel (c) plots the optimal "wage–job safety" combinations shown in (a) and (b). Line WS in panel (c) indicates the general relationship between wage rates and job safety in a labor market characterized by many—not just two—heterogeneous workers and jobs. Higher wage rates are associated with lower levels of nonwage amenities, other things being the same.

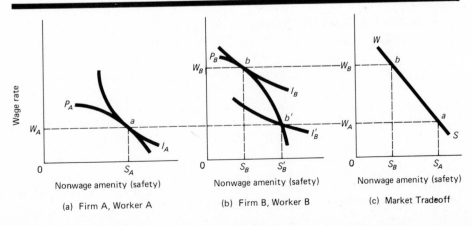

(a) Firm A, Worker A   (b) Firm B, Worker B   (c) Market Tradeoff

possess similar amounts of human capital. Other things being equal, higher wages will tend to be associated with fewer nonwage amenities. This is shown in graph (c) in Figure 12-4. Line *WS*, which connects points such as *a* and *b* in the two left-hand graphs, indicates the general inverse relationship between wage rates and job safety in a labor market characterized by many—not just two—heterogeneous workers and jobs. The wage differentials possible along this line are persistent, or equilibrium, differentials; they will not create movements of workers among the jobs.

2. Laws which set a minimum standard for nonwage job amenities may actually *reduce* the utility of *some* workers. This is easily shown through reference again to Figure 12-4. If, for instance, government forces firm B (graph b) to increase its job safety from S_B to, say, S_B' it will move from point *b* downward on P_B to *b'*, and worker B will be forced to indifference curve I_B', which clearly is below I_B.[10]

3. Part of the observed male-female earnings differential (Chapter 11) may reflect differing tastes for positive job amenities such as pleasant working conditions, a short commuting distance, and a low probability of job injury. In terms of Figure 12-4, *if* indifference curves for females as a group tend to be more on the order of I_A rather than I_B, women will match up to a greater extent than men with jobs which have lower pay, but also better nonwage amenities. According to some economists, this may explain a *portion* of the observed male-female earning differential among similarly trained workers.

WAGE DIFFERENTIALS: LABOR MARKET IMPERFECTIONS

Wage differences can be explained largely—but not *fully*—on the basis of heterogeneous jobs, employers, and workers. Wage differences also occur because of labor market imperfections which impede labor mobility. Such factors as imperfect information, costly migration, and various other barriers to mobility interact to create and maintain wage differentials.

Imperfect Labor Market Information. Labor market information was assumed to be perfect in Chapter 6, but in reality it is imperfect and costly to obtain. Recognizing that workers are heterogeneous, firms search the labor market to find those workers who are best suited for employment. Similarly, workers attempt to gather information about prospective job opportunities by scanning help wanted ads, writing letters, inquiring at business establishments, and so forth. These search efforts by firms and prospective employees therefore involve both direct costs and opportunity costs of time. Furthermore, the activity of

---

[10]This conclusion assumes that worker B has been provided full information about the risk of injury on job B and that she or he fully comprehends that information. We are not suggesting that such laws necessarily reduce society's well-being (Chapter 10).

gaining information eventually will yield diminishing returns. Translated into costs, this implies that the marginal cost of obtaining information will increase as more of it is sought. The fact that information is imperfect and increasingly costly to obtain has important implications for labor market activity and the wage structure.[11] Specifically, it implies that (1) a range of wage rates will exist for any given occupation, independently of compensating differentials, and (2) when changes in demand cause wage differentials, long-run supply adjustments are likely to be slow.

1. A wage rate distribution. In our earlier discussion of labor markets we assumed that a single equilibrium wage rate would emerge and that all homogeneous firms hiring this type of labor would pay this single wage to all qualified workers (Figure 6-1). Once costly information and job searches are introduced to the situation, this is no longer true. Rather than a single equilibrium wage, there will be an average wage rate, around which there is a distribution of other wage rates. Figure 12-5 portrays one of many possible wage rate distributions. The horizontal axis shows a range of wages, $6.00 through $7.80, and the vertical axis measures the relative frequency of the occurrence of each subrange of wages in the distribution. The area covered by the wage distribution equals 1; that is, there is a 100 percent probability that the wage will fall within the $6.00

[11]It also has important implications for unemployment. We formalize a job search model in Chapter 18.

FIGURE 12-5 A WAGE RATE DISTRIBUTION
Under conditions of costly information and job searches, competitive labor markets generate an equilibrium distribution of wage rates within a single occupation, rather than an equilibrium hourly wage. In this example, 20 percent of the workers receive a wage rate between $6.80 and $6.99 an hour, but some workers (5 percent) earn as little as $6.00 to $6.19, while another 5 percent make $7.60 to $7.79 an hour. The area under the frequency distribution sums to 1 (100 percent).

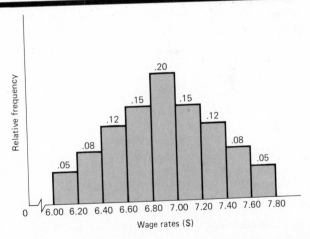

to $7.80 range. Likewise, .05 or 5 percent of all wages will be between $6.00 and $6.19, 8 percent will lie between $6.20 and $6.39, and so forth.

What causes a wage distribution such as that depicted in Figure 12-5? The answer is imperfect information and costly searches. Some workers and firms simply will be unaware that greater or lesser wages are being paid to similar workers. Other employees may recognize that there is a variance in pay but also will realize that it is costly to discover which employers of this type of labor are paying the higher amounts. In technical terms, many workers will judge the marginal cost of obtaining the necessary information to be more than the expected marginal gain from the higher wage. Under conditions of imperfect, costly information, (1) wage variability is likely, even in markets where jobs are homogeneous, and (2) these differentials can persist.

2. Lengthy adjustment periods. A second implication of imperfect, costly information is that long-run supply adjustments to wage differentials created by changes in demand may take months or even years to occur. Suppose, for example, that the demand for labor in occupation X rises sharply. Given an upward-sloping short-run labor supply curve, this will produce a wage increase in occupation X. But information concerning this new wage is likely to be only incompletely disseminated. Persons making choices on the types and amounts of human capital to obtain will learn *gradually* of the higher wage in occupation X. Of course, as more time transpires, more information will become known. But even then some potential labor suppliers to X will wonder if this is indeed a permanent wage differential relative to other occupations or one that will quickly evaporate by the time they become qualified.

Once people *do* begin to recognize that the wage rate in occupation X is permanent, then some will respond and eventually create a flow of labor into X and away from, say, Y and Z. This will cause the wage narrowing predicted by the pure theory. But recall from our discussion in Chapter 4 (Figure 4-3) that in some occupations requiring long training periods, for example, law and engineering, the supply response may be so great that the wage differential not only is eliminated but turns in the opposite direction. Then, in the next period, still another overadjustment may occur, reducing labor supply so dramatically that a positive wage differential *again* arises. Hence, as shown by the wage rate adjustment path in Figure 12-6, some wage rates may for a time oscillate above and below the long-run equilibrium wage W_e. Note from the diagram that the wage rate shifts from W_0 to W_1 to W_2, and so forth, as units of time transpire. To summarize: Labor markets in which information is imperfect and costly will be characterized by many **transitional wage differentials** which exist because of lengthy and occasionally oscillating adjustment paths to final equilibriums.[12]

[12]For evidence of these "cobweb" adjustments, see Richard B. Freeman, "A Cobweb Model of the Starting Salary of New Engineers," *Industrial and Labor Relations Review*, January 1976, pp. 236–248 and "Legal Cobwebs: A Recursive Model of the Market for New Lawyers," *Review of Economics and Statistics*, May 1975, pp. 171–180. For a discussion of "cobweb" models and alternative wage rate adjustment paths, see Belton M. Fleisher and Thomas J. Kniesner, *Labor Economics: Theory, Evidence, and Policy*, 3rd ed. (Englewood Cliffs, N.J.: Prentice-Hall, Inc., 1984), pp. 186–191.

Immobilities. *Labor immobilities,* defined simply as impediments to the movement of labor, constitute another major reason why wage differentials occur and sometimes persist. For convenience we will classify these barriers to labor mobility as geographic, institutional, and sociological.

1. Geographic immobilities. We shall discover in Chapter 14 that wage differences between geographic areas provide an incentive for workers to migrate. By moving to the high-wage location a worker can enhance lifetime earnings. But moving also involves costs—for example, transportation expenses, forgone earnings during the move, the inconvenience of adjusting to a new job and community, the negative aspects of leaving family and friends, and the possible loss of seniority and pension benefits. If these costs deter migration to the extent that an insufficient number of migrants are attracted to the higher-paying locale, geographic wage differentials will persist.

2. Institutional immobilities. Restrictions on mobility imposed by such institutions as government and unions may reinforce geographic immobilites. We previously noted in Chapters 6 and 10 that government licensing of occupations can restrict the movement of qualified workers among jobs. Also, differing licensing requirements in various states can limit worker mobility geographically. Craft unions also are a factor here; they impede mobility by limiting the access of nonunion workers to union-controlled apprenticeship programs and union-filled jobs. Other institutional immobilities involve pension plans and seniority rights which reduce people's incentives to move from one job to another.

FIGURE 12-6 WAGE RATE ADJUSTMENT PATH
An increase in labor demand initially may cause a substantial wage increase to, say, W_0, in occupations which require long training periods. But the supply response to the higher wage may create a surplus of labor to the occupation in the subsequent period, driving the wage rate lower, say to W_1. For a time the wage rate may oscillate above and below the long-run equilibrium wage rate W_e before equilibrium in the market is finally restored. During the transition periods, wage differentials between this occupation and others paying W_e will be observed.

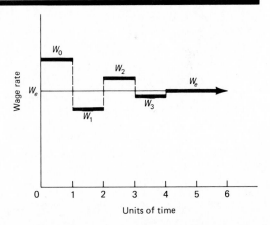

3. Sociological immobilities. Finally, there are numerous sociological barriers to labor mobility. In Chapter 11 we examined theories of labor market discrimination by race and gender. You may recall, for example, that females appear to be "crowded" into certain occupations. This drives down the equilibrium wage in these occupations and raises it elsewhere. Certainly, to the extent that there are barriers which keep qualified women from moving from these lower-paying positions to higher-paying occupations, wage differentials between the sexes can persist. In the same vein, blacks historically were excluded from certain higher-paying occupations either through informal understandings by employers or through formal prohibitions by unions. As an example of the latter, over twenty national unions had constitutional provisions barring blacks from membership in 1930. In fact, some unions such as the Locomotive Engineers and the Railway Conductors still excluded blacks from membership in 1964 when the Civil Rights Act was passed.[13]

CYCLICAL AND SECULAR CHANGES IN THE WAGE STRUCTURE

We have established that wage differentials can and do exist and in many cases persist over time. But, it is also important to note that wage differences vary over the course of a business cycle and some seemingly "permanent" differentials change over long periods of time.

Cyclical Changes. Empirical evidence indicates that wage rate differences between skilled and unskilled occupations tend to rise during recessions and decline with economic expansions and tight labor markets.[14]

What explains this phenomenon? Several plausible explanations have been provided, but perhaps the simplest is that changes in demand for skilled and unskilled workers differ greatly during a recession as compared to an expansion. During a recession the demand for low-skilled workers drops much more rapidly than the demand for skilled people. For instance, few firms will dispense with top- or middle-level executives during a business downturn which is not expected to be permanent. Personnel directors, corporate vice-presidents, legal staff, and accountants will be needed irrespective of the decline in sales. Additionally, firms will be reluctant to furlough workers in whom they have invested much job training. If they do, these skilled people may take employment elsewhere, causing the firm which temporarily discharged them to lose its ability to capture a return on its human capital investment.

---

[13]F. Ray Marshall, Vernon M. Briggs, Jr., and Allan King, *Labor Economics,* 5th ed. (Homewood, Ill.: R. D. Irwin, Inc., 1984), p. 567.

[14]For example see Michael Wachter, "Cyclical Variation in the Interindustry Wage Structure," *American Economic Review,* 1970, pp. 75–84, and D. S. Hamermesh and Albert Rees, *The Economics of Work and Pay,* 3rd ed. (New York: Harper & Row, Publishers, 1984), p. 386.

On the other hand, recessions normally produce large-scale layoffs of unskilled production workers. Therefore, labor markets for lower-skilled workers often experience substantial excess supplies of labor during downturns, and this causes either actual declines in wage rates for unskilled workers or *slower increases* in these wages relative to skilled workers. Thus the skilled-unskilled wage rate ratio rises. During the recovery and expansion phases of the cycle this process reverses itself and the wage differential narrows.[15]

Secular Changes. Wage structures also change over long time periods. These secular changes may either be changes in equilibrium wage differentials—ones caused by autonomous shifts in labor supply or demand—or they may simply be long-run adjustments from disequilibrium to equilibrium positions in a labor market. Two examples are the historical narrowing of the "skill differential" and the narrowing of the north-south wage gap.

1. The narrowing of the "skill differential." Economists refer to the wage differential between skilled and unskilled workers as the *skill differential*. Empirical studies indicate that this differential declined steadily in the United States between 1900 and 1950. In other words, the average hourly earnings for unskilled workers rose more rapidly than for skilled employees over these decades.[16] This implies that (*a*) the supply of skilled workers increased more rapidly than the supply of unskilled employees, or (*b*) the demand for skilled employees rose less rapidly than the demand for unskilled laborers, or (*c*) some combination of (*a*) and (*b*) occurred.

Of these three possibilities, the supply explanation appears most plausible. Becker has pointed out that if technological change is assumed to be neutral— that is, if the *ratios* of marginal physical products (MPs) of all the factors of production remain constant—the *demand* for skilled and unskilled workers will increase proportionately through time. Hence, taken alone this will leave the *ratio* of skilled to unskilled wages unchanged. But, a proportionate rise in both wages *will* increase the *absolute* difference between skilled and unskilled wages. For example, suppose that initially the skilled wage was $4 and the unskilled $2. The wage gap obviously would be $2. Now let the real wages of skilled and unskilled labor rise to $10 and $5, respectively, due to neutral changes in technology which increase the marginal physical products (MPs) of each type of labor. Clearly, the skilled-unskilled ratio will remain 2 (= $10/$5 = $4/$2), but the absolute wage difference is now $5 (= $10 − $5) compared to $2. What impact will this increase in the absolute wage difference have on the *supply* of skilled workers? To answer this question we must recall the human capital

---

[15]For an equally plausible but alternative explanation of this phenomenon, see Melvin Reder, "The Theory of Occupational Wage Differentials," *American Economic Review*, December 1955, pp. 833–852.

[16]See Paul G. Keat, "Long Run Changes in Occupational Wage Structure 1900–1956," *Journal of Political Economy*, December 1960, pp. 584–600.

model presented in Chapter 4, specifically equation (4-3). Because the $5 wage differential is greater than the previous $2 difference, the incremental earnings will be greater from investing in education and skill training than before. This will increase the rate of return on education or, stated alternatively, shift the demand curve for human capital outward (Figure 4-5). This will lead more people to acquire education and skill. Hence, the supply of skilled workers will increase relative to the supply of unskilled and the skill differential will fall.[17]

At least four other factors likely complemented the relative decline in the supply of unskilled workers. First, government made school attendance through age 16 compulsory, and this reduced the supply of unskilled workers. Second, changes in the immigration laws reduced the inflow of unskilled workers more sharply than that of skilled laborers during the period discussed. More precisely, the immigration laws of 1921 and 1924 gave preference to skilled immigrants (Chapter 14). Third, government increased subsidies to higher education by making direct appropriations to state universities, providing federal grants to public and private colleges, and making student loans available at relatively low interest rates. This undoubtedly increased the *private* rate of return on investments in education which then increased the relative number of college-trained *skilled* workers. Finally, child labor legislation reduced the supply of *unskilled* laborers.

2. The north-south differential. During the past 40 years wage differentials between the south and north have narrowed appreciably. Whether this represents a movement from a disequilibrium situation to a market equilibrium or simply is the net outcome of various autonomous shifts in labor supply or demand curves is difficult to determine. But this much is clear. In the 1930s and 1940s a wide north-south wage disparity existed. During the 1950s and 1960s nearly 3 million blacks emigrated from the south. One view is that the north-south differential for similarly educated, trained, and employed workers may have ended as early as the 1960s. In the late 1960s and 1970s, the observed 10 percent regional wage premium paid in the north was offset by a 10 percent difference in price levels. Therefore, the real wages paid in each region reached a rough equilibrium. In fact, in the 1970s and 1980s blacks began to join thousands of others in a *reverse* migration to the south.[18]

SUMMARY

1. Theoretically, if *all* workers and jobs were homogeneous and all labor markets were perfectly competitive, then workers would move among the various jobs until the wages paid in all markets were identical.

[17]Gary S. Becker, *Human Capital*, 2nd ed. (National Bureau of Economic Research, 1975), pp. 75–77.

[18]Donald Bellante, "The North-South Differential and the Migration of Heterogeneous Labor," *American Economic Review*, March 1979, pp. 166–175.

2. Casual and sophisticated examinations of wage rates and weekly earnings reveal that a variety of wage differentials do exist and that many of them persist over time.

3. One major source of wage differentials is heterogeneous jobs. Such nonwage aspects of jobs as (1) risk of job injury and death, (2) fringe benefits, (3) job status, (4) job location, (5) the regularity of earnings, (6) the prospect for wage advancement, and (7) the extent of control over the work pace influence labor supply decisions in ways which generate "compensating wage differentials." Jobs also differ greatly as to their skill requirements. Other things being equal, in order to attract a sufficient flow of laborers to an occupation that requires considerable prior investment in human capital, employers must pay these workers more than they pay less-skilled employees.

4. Another major source of wage disparities is heterogeneous workers. Specifically, workers possess greatly varying stocks of human capital and differing preferences for various nonwage aspects of work. Consequently, the overall labor market is composed of numerous submarkets consisting of groups of workers who offer little competition to other groups.

5. The hedonic theory of wages hypothesizes that workers who possess differing subjective preferences for wages versus nonwage job amenities seek to find optimal matches with employers who differ in their costs of providing those nonwage attributes. Among a wide variety of implications which flow from this model is the basic one that labor markets will generate sustained wage differentials, even among persons who have similar stocks of human capital.

6. Such labor market realities as imperfect and costly market information and barriers to labor mobility constitute a third major source of wage differentials. Imperfect and costly information creates ranges of wage rates, independent of other factors, and explains why transitional wage differentials often are long-lasting.

7. Labor market immobilities—geographic, institutional, and sociological—also help explain persistent earnings differences among workers.

8. Wage differences between skilled and unskilled occupations tend to increase during recessions and decline during periods of tight labor markets.

9. The so-called "skill differential," which is the pay gap between skilled and unskilled workers, declined secularly in the United States over the first half of the twentieth century. The major reason is thought to be the increased relative supply of skilled workers, which in turn can be explained by increased incentives to invest in human capital; improved access to financing of these investments; and child labor, immigration, and school attendance legislation.

QUESTIONS AND STUDY SUGGESTIONS

1. Key terms and concepts to remember: homogeneous workers and jobs; wage structure; heterogeneous workers and jobs; compensating wage differentials; noncompeting groups; hedonic theory of wages; isoprofit curve; equilibrium wage differentials; transitional wage differentials; labor immobilities; skill differential.

2. Suppose that all workers and jobs in a hypothetical economy are homogeneous. Explain why there will be no wage differentials if this economy is perfectly competitive and information and mobility are costless. Explain why wage differentials would arise if, on the other hand, information and mobility were imperfect and costly.

3. Analyze why college professors generally earn less than their professional Ph.D. counterparts who are employed by corporations.

4. Discuss: "Many of the lowest-paid people in society—for example, short-order cooks—also have relatively poor working conditions. Hence, the theory of compensating wage differentials is disproved."

5. Explain why it may be in a worker's *short-term* best interest to have job titles upgraded for purposes of adding status, say becoming a mixologist rather than a bartender, or being referred to as a sanitation engineer rather than a garbage worker. Why may such title changes not be in the *long-term* best interest of these workers, however?

6. Explain how the theory of investment in human capital relates to the notion of noncompeting groups and how the latter relates to the presence of equilibrium wage differentials.

7. What is the hedonic theory of wage differentials? Discuss the characteristics of isoprofit curves. Combine isoprofit curves with worker indifference curves to explain how two workers with identical stocks of human capital might be paid different wage rates.

8. Speculate as to why the average hourly wage rate paid by manufacturing firms to production workers is so much lower in North Carolina than in Michigan (Table 12-3).

9. Explain how each of the following relate to wage differentials: (*a*) seniority provisions, (*b*) varying state licensing requirements for occupations, (*c*) racial segregation, and (*d*) regional cost-of-living differences.

10. Explain why "pay comparability" legislation (Chapter 9), which requires that the public sector remunerate government employees at wages equal to private-sector counterparts, might create excess supplies of labor in public-sector labor markets.

11. Cite and explain several reasons why the "skill differential" narrowed between 1900 and 1950 in the United States. Relate this narrowing to the decline in the *rate* of return to investments in college education observed by some economists for the past two decades.

12. Suppose that (*a*) employers must pay higher wages to attract workers from wider geographic areas and hence that higher wages are associated with longer commuting distances (less of the amenity "closeness of job to home"), and (*b*) females have greater tastes for having jobs close to their homes than males. Use the hedonic wage model to show graphically why a male-female wage differential might emerge, independently of skill differences or sexual discrimination.

SELECTED REFERENCES

EHRENBERG, RONALD G., and ROBERT S. SMITH, *Modern Labor Economics*, 2d ed. (Glenview, Ill.: Scott, Foresman and Company, 1985), Chap. 8.

MABRY, BEVARS D: *Economics of Manpower and the Labor Market* (New York: Intex Educational Publishers, 1973), Chap. 14.

ROBACK, JENNIFER: "Wages, Rents and the Quality of Life," *Journal of Political Economy,* December 1982, pp. 1257–1278.

SMITH, ADAM: *The Wealth of Nations* (New York: The Modern Library, 1957), pp. 99–106.

SMITH, ROBERT S.: "Compensating Wage Differentials and Public Policy: A Review," *Industrial and Labor Relations Review,* April 1979, pp. 339–352.

VISCUSI, W. KIP: *Employment Hazards: An Investigation of Market Performance* (Cambridge, Mass.: Harvard University Press, 1979).

T I M E   A N D   O N E - H A L F

WAGE DIFFERENTIALS: MARRIED VERSUS SINGLE MALES

What explains the significantly higher wage rates received by married males relative to single males?

One of the more puzzling wage rate differentials observed in the labor market is that between married and unmarried men. Average wage rates received by married males are anywhere from 8 to 30 percent greater than the hourly pay received by single males.[1] For example, one study discovered that young married men earn about 10 percent higher wage rates and 33 percent more annual earnings than their unmarried counterparts.[2] Another study found that, as compared to never-married men, married males had about 27 percent higher wages and that divorced or separated males had 9 percent higher wages.[3]

What accounts for this wage differential? At least four explanations have been offered.

1. *Differing incentives to marry.* The wage rate premium received by married males may simply reflect a sorting process by which higher-wage males seek marriage—and are sought as marriage partners—to a greater extent than lower-wage males. According to Becker, marriage allows for a greater specialization of skills and thus increases the combined well-being of the marriage partners.[4] Because of the interrupted labor force activity associated with bearing and raising children, many women devote fewer lifetime hours to market work than do males. These women, therefore, may perceive a lower rate of return on human capital, get less education and training, and have lower wage rates than males. Consequently, females may seek out marriage partners who, other things being equal, earn high wages and thus can contribute more to the total gain that role specialization within marriage allows. Similarly, higher-wage males can gain more than lower-wage men by specializing in market work (working more hours) and matching up with females who specialize in home production. Put bluntly, the greater the differences in the comparative advantages between two people, the greater the *incentive* to marry and achieve the gains from specialization and exchange. Therefore, lower-wage males may not only be less attractive as potential marriage partners, but may also have less of an incentive to get married. Their opportunity costs of working in the home and engaging in time-intensive leisure activities are lower, and therefore, they may foresee fewer benefits from specializing in market work. This could explain why, on the average, unmarried males work 260 *fewer* hours a year than married males.[5] If this controversial view of role

[1]Lawrence W. Kenny, "The Accumulation of Human Capital During Marriage by Males," *Economic Inquiry*, April 1983, pp. 223–231.

[2]Zvi Griliches, "Wages of Very Young Men," *Journal of Political Economy*, August 1976, part 2, pp. 69–85.

[3]Geoffrey Carlinger, "Wages, Earnings, and Hours of First, Second, and Third Generation American Males," *Economic Inquiry*, January 1980, pp. 87–102.

[4]Gary S. Becker, *A Treatise on the Family* (Cambridge, Mass.: Harvard University Press, 1981).

[5]Donald O. Parson, "Health, Family Structure, and Labor Supply," *American Economic Review*, September 1977, pp. 703–712.

specialization and marriage is valid, the higher wage rate is the *cause* of the greater incidence of marriage among high-wage males, as compared to the other way around!

2. *Differing personal attributes.* Personality, physical attractiveness, reliability, and other such personal attributes may simultaneously contribute to a male's likelihood of being married *and* to his chances of having a high wage, independently of his level of education and training. Those personal characteristics which make one a good (bad) employee may at the same time make one an attractive (unattractive) marriage partner. An unreliable, unmotivated male is neither a desirable employee nor an appealing mate. Marriage and higher wage rates, therefore, may not be related in any *causal* way, but instead be joint outcomes of hard-to-measure personal characteristics that lead *both* to a higher probability of marriage *and* to a higher wage rate.

3. *Differing incentives to accumulate human capital.* Perhaps males who anticipate being married most of their lives have more of an incentive to accumulate education and training than do men who do not contemplate, or are uncertain about, getting married. If those anticipating being married and having families to support also expect to work more hours over their careers, they will perceive a greater return on human capital. Given the same cost of financing this human capital, they will rationally choose to accumulate relatively more education and training than will people expecting to work fewer hours over their lifetimes. For the same reason, married men may have a greater incentive to *add* to their human capital during marriage. In this explanation, then, the anticipation of marriage and the marriage itself together *cause* the observed higher wage rates for married males.[6]

4. *Differing costs of acquiring human capital.* It is equally plausible that married men tend to acquire relatively more human capital while married because they have lower *costs* of financing such investments. Males may be able to borrow from household income at lower implicit interest rates (forgone interest on savings) than the bank rates charged to single males. This conforms to the observation that many wives "put their husbands through school" by temporarily working in the labor market. Given equal incentives to invest in human capital (equal internal rates of return), a married male who faces lower financing expenses will choose to accumulate more education and training than a single male. This greater accumulation of human capital will produce higher wage rates.

A study by Kenny supports this hypothesis. Kenny compared the accumulation of human capital by males while married to their accumulations while single and concluded that ". . . most of the unexplained wage differential associated with marital status . . . is the product of additional investment in human capital during marriage; very little of the differential appears to be associated with individual differences in the initial level of human capital. . . . Furthermore, the evidence supports the hypothesis that marriage facilitates the financing of human capital."[7]

[6]Kenny, op. cit., p. 224.

[7]Ibid., p. 230.

THE PERSONAL DISTRIBUTION OF EARNINGS

I n the previous chapter we examined the structure of wages in the U.S. economy. There we discovered that the labor market generates differences in wage rates and earnings that are based on such things as level of education and training, occupation, nonwage attributes of jobs, race and gender, and union status. Our interest now turns to the *size*, or *personal*, distribution of wage and salary income among individual workers. More specifically, we now describe the national pattern of individual earnings and analyze the degree of inequality in this distribution.

In pursuing this topic we first discuss alternative ways of describing the earnings distribution and measuring the degree of observed inequality. Second, we examine theories which help to explain the pattern of the distribution of U.S. earnings. Our focus then turns to the topic of personal earnings mobility, or movement within the aggregate earnings distribution. Fourth, we review our earlier discussion (Chapter 8) of the impact of unions on the degree of earnings inequality. We then conclude with a discussion of how the pay structure in the public sector and the legally mandated minimum wage affect the overall distribution of earnings.

DESCRIBING THE DISTRIBUTION OF EARNINGS

We can describe the degree of inequality in the distribution of earnings in several ways. Let us examine two graphic portrayals: the frequency distribution and the Lorenz curve.

The Frequency Distribution. The distribution of annual earnings received by full-time U.S. workers in 1982 is shown in Figure 13-1. This absolute *frequency distribution*—or *histogram*—shows the number of employees (measured on the vertical axis) whose annual earnings fell within each $5,000 earnings range shown on the horizontal axis. For example, the third bar from the left represents earnings within the $10,000 to $15,000 range. One would then know from the height of this bar that about 14.3 million people had annual earnings in this category in 1982. Or, as a second example, the bar representing the wider $30,000 to $40,000 range tells us that 6.2 million—3.1 million per each of the two $5,000 subranges—received work income between $30,000 and $40,000 in 1982.

It is equally common to represent the distribution of income in terms of *relative* frequencies, in which case the vertical axis simply is converted to percent of total earners, rather than being the *absolute* number of such workers, as shown here.

Three measures of location, or central tendency, are commonly used to summarize histograms or absolute frequency distributions such as the one in Figure 13-1. The *mode* is simply the income category occurring with the greatest frequency. The *mean* is the arithmetic average, obviously obtained by dividing the total earnings by the number of workers. Finally, the *median* is the amount of annual work income received by the individual who stands at the midpoint of the array of earnings. By definition, one-half of those earning wages and salaries receive more than the median, while the other one-half receive less. With these definitions in mind, note from Figure 13-1 that the distribution of annual earnings for full-time U.S. workers is concentrated around a single leftward mode ($10,000—$15,000 in 1982), has a median level of earnings ($17,671 in 1982)

FIGURE 13-1 THE DISTRIBUTION OF ANNUAL EARNINGS FOR FULL-TIME WORKERS, 1982
The personal distribution of annual earnings is highly unequal and is skewed to the right. The histogram (absolute frequency distribution) of earnings is characterized by (1) much bunching around the leftward mode, (2) an extended rightward tail, and (3) a mean (arithmetic average) that exceeds the median (one-half above, one-half below). *Derived from U.S. Bureau of the Census, Money Income of Households and Persons in the United States, 1982; Current Population Reports, ser. P-60, no. 142, table 51.*

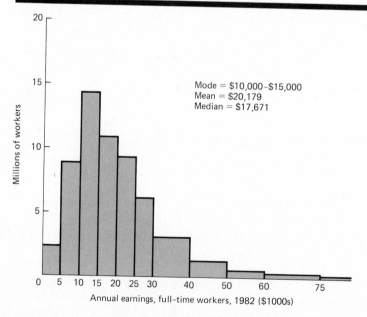

Mode = $10,000–$15,000
Mean = $20,179
Median = $17,671

Millions of workers

Annual earnings, full-time workers, 1982 ($1000s)

which is to the right of the mode, and possesses a mean, or average ($20,179 in 1982), which is greater than both the mode and median. The mean exceeds the median because the average is pulled upward by the extremely high earnings of the relatively few workers who have earnings in the long rightward tail of the histogram. Notice that this tail is so long that our truncated diagram prevents it from reaching the horizontal axis. These characteristics correctly suggest that most U.S. workers receive earnings in the leftward two-thirds of the overall distribution, but that a few people receive extraordinarily large annual earnings relative to the median and average.

The Lorenz Curve and Gini Coefficient. The degree of earnings inequality can also be shown by a *Lorenz curve* such as the one portrayed in Figure 13-2. This curve indicates the *cumulative* percent of all wage and salary earners (part-time and full-time) from left to right on the horizontal axis and the corresponding *cumulative* percent of the total earnings accruing to that percent of earners on the vertical axis. If each worker received the average income, the Lorenz curve would be the diagonal (45°) line which bisects the graph in the figure. Why is this so? The answer is that 20 percent of all earners would receive 20 percent of all earnings, 40 percent of the workers would get 40 percent, and so forth. All of these points would fall on the diagonal line which we appropriately label "perfect equality."

The actual Lorenz curve in Figure 13-2 is derived by plotting the data for 1982 from Table 13-1. This table shows the percent of total earnings accruing to

FIGURE 13-2 THE LORENZ CURVE FOR ANNUAL EARNINGS
The Lorenz curve is a useful way of summarizing the distribution of earnings. Line *af* represents perfect equality in the distribution, while the Lorenz curve *abcdef* illustrates the actual earnings distribution for 1982. The greater the area between the line of perfect equality and the Lorenz curve, the more unequal the distribution of earnings.

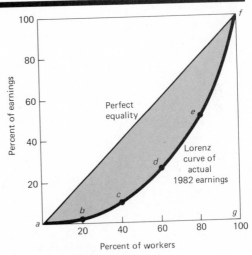

five numerically equal groups, or *quintiles*. For 1982 we see that the bottom 20 percent of all workers (part-time as well as full-time) received 1.9 percent of the total earnings, which plots as point *b* on the Lorenz curve. The bottom 40 percent of the earners received 10 percent (= 1.9 + 8.1) of the total earnings, which gives us point *c* on the curve, and so forth. The shaded area between the diagonal line of perfect equality of earnings and the Lorenz curve provides a visual measure of the extent of earnings inequality. The larger this area, the greater the degree of disparity in annual earnings. If there were complete inequality—if one person had 100 percent of total earnings—the Lorenz curve would coincide with the horizontal and right vertical axis, forming a 90° angle at point *g*.

The visual measure of earnings inequality just described can be easily transformed into a mathematical measure. The **Gini coefficient** (equation 13-1) is simply the *ratio* of the shaded area of Figure 13-2 to the entire triangle southeast of the diagonal.

$$\text{Gini coefficient} = \frac{\text{area between Lorenz curve and diagonal}}{\text{total area southeast of diagonal}} \qquad (13\text{-}1)$$

If there were complete equality of earnings, the distance between the diagonal and the Lorenz curve would be *zero* and therefore the Gini coefficient also would be zero (= 0/*afg*). On the other hand, if one person had all the income, the area between the Lorenz curve and the diagonal would be equal to *afg* and the Gini coefficient would be 1 (= *afg/afg*). Obviously, the larger the Gini coefficient, the greater the degree of earnings inequality. The Gini coefficient for the 1982 data shown in Table 13-1 and the Lorenz curve displayed in Figure 13-2 is .44.

TABLE 13-1

The Distribution of Annual Wage and Salary Earnings for Individuals, 1982

Quintile	Percent
Lowest 20 percent	1.9
Second 20 percent	8.1
Third 20 percent	16.0
Fourth 20 percent	26.2
Highest 20 percent	47.8
Total	100.0

Source: Derived from U.S. Bureau of the Census, *Money Income of Households and Persons in the United States, 1982; Current Population Reports,* ser. P-60, no. 142, table 51.

Cautions. Great care must be exercised in interpreting frequency distributions, Lorenz curves, and Gini coefficients. First, annual earnings are a product of both wages per hour *and* the number of hours worked in a year. Hence, a distribution which includes part-time workers and people who work full-time only portions of the year will display greater variability than distributions which include only full-time workers. You might note that the histogram in Figure 13-1 includes only full-time wage and salary earners, while the data in Table 13-1 and the corresponding Lorenz curve include both full- and part-time workers.

A second problem of measurement and interpretation is the failure of most earnings data to include fringe benefits (Chapter 8). The addition of these benefits increases the skewness of the frequency distribution of earnings or, stated differently, increases the southeast sag of the Lorenz curve and raises the Gini coefficient. Workers who have above-average annual earnings also tend to have higher-than-average fringe benefits as a percentage of their total compensation.[1]

A third warning is that earnings distributions can be shown by either *individual* or by *family* wages and salaries. Although the general *shape* of the family distribution is similar to that for individual workers, the median and average incomes obviously are higher in the latter formulation. Also, the family distribution is tighter; that is, the Gini coefficient is less. The reason is that the income effect (Chapters 2 and 3) produced by the high incomes of some males reduces the likelihood that their wives will be labor force participants. This income effect is offset somewhat by the tendency for males with higher earnings to marry females who earn more than the average female salary when they do choose to work.[2]

A fourth caveat is that frequency distributions, Lorenz curves, and Gini coefficients are all *static* portrayals or measures of earnings inequality. They do not provide information about the extent of personal movement within the distribution from year to year or over people's lifetimes. We discuss this important topic later in the chapter.

A final important caution is that annual *earnings* are only one of several possible sources of individual or family *income*. Twenty-five percent of the national income accrues in the form of rent, interest, profits, and proprietory income. The personal distribution of each of these income shares is even more unequal than the personal distribution of wages and salaries. Are we then to conclude that the distribution of family income is more unequal than the distribution of earnings? There are "yes and no" aspects to our answer. The size distribution of family income, *before* government taxes and transfers, *is* more

[1]Timothy M. Smeeding, "The Size Distribution of Wage and Nonwage Compensation: Employer Cost versus Employee Value," in Jack E. Triplett (ed.), *The Measurement of Labor Cost* (Chicago, Ill.: The University of Chicago Press, 1983), pp. 237–277.

[2]James Smith, "The Distribution of Family Earnings," *Journal of Political Economy*, October 1979, pp. S163–S192, Evelyn Lehrer and Marc Nerlove, "A Life-Cycle Analysis of Family Income Distribution," *Economic Inquiry*, July 1984, pp. 360–374, and David Betson and J. VanDerGagg, "Working Married Women and the Distribution of Income," *Journal of Human Resources*, Fall 1984, pp. 532–543.

unequal than the distribution of earnings. This can be seen by comparing the first column in Table 13-2 with quintile data for earnings displayed earlier in Table 13-1. But, note from Table 13-2 that the distribution of family income *after* taxes and transfers is substantially less unequal than both the distribution before taxes and transfers *and* the personal distribution of earnings (Table 13-1). It is apparent that government tax and transfer policies reduce *income* inequality. Furthermore, the data in Table 13-2 do *not* include as income the value of such *in-kind* transfers as food stamps, government-financed medical care, housing subsidies, and so forth. If we counted the monetary value of these items as income, the distribution of family income after taxes and transfers would be even less unequal.[3]

EXPLAINING THE DISTRIBUTION OF EARNINGS

It is more difficult to *explain* the distribution of earnings than to describe it. Human characteristics that we might associate with earnings—intelligence, physical strength, motivation, determination—are thought to be distributed according to the familiar bell-shaped normal curve. So why then are earnings not also distributed in this manner? There are numerous theories which attempt to explain this paradox.[4] Rather than simply describing each of these theories, we will approach this topic as follows. First, we will discuss the basic human capital explanation for earnings inequality. We will then explore the diversity of alter-

[3]For evidence of this see Edgar Browning, "The Trend Toward Equality in the Distribution of Net Income," *Southern Economic Journal,* July 1976, pp. 912–923. Keep in mind, however, that the value of noncash perquisites such as the use of corporate airplanes and memberships in private clubs also are not included as income in Table 13-2.

[4]For a review of these theories, see Gian S. Sahota, "Theories of Personal Income Distribution: A Survey," *Journal of Economic Literature,* March 1978, pp. 1–55.

TABLE 13-2

The Distribution of Family Income

Quintile	Before Taxes and Transfers (%)	After Taxes and Transfers (%)
Lowest 20 percent	0.6	6.5
Second 20 percent	8.0	12.1
Third 20 percent	16.4	16.9
Fourth 20 percent	26.7	24.6
Highest 20 percent	48.2	39.8
Total	100.0	100.0

Source: G. William Hoagland, "The Effectiveness of Current Transfer Programs in Reducing Poverty" (Washington: Congressional Budget Office, 1980), p. 19.

native explanations by *synthesizing* several of them into a modified, multifactor human capital model of the earnings distribution.

Human Capital Theory. The human capital theory discussed initially in Chapter 4 provides valuable insights into why the personal distribution of earnings is unequal and has a long rightward tail. Recall that human capital investments take various forms, the two most critical for present purposes being *formal education* and *on-the-job training.* Let us explain how each relates to the earnings distribution.

   1. Formal education: amount and quality. Formal education has an investment component in that it requires present sacrifice for the purpose of enhancing one's future productivity and therefore one's lifetime earnings. A review of Figure 4-2 reminds us that a given investment will be undertaken only if the present value of the expected stream of enhanced earnings (area 3) equals or exceeds the present value of the sum of the direct and indirect costs (areas 1 + 2). Other things being equal, the greater the amount of one's formal schooling and the better its quality, the higher will be the investment costs (areas 1 + 2), and therefore the greater must be the enhancement of productivity and the future earnings stream *in order to justify the investment.* Hence, we have a rudimentary theory of earnings inequality. If other things such as ability, nonwage aspects of jobs, uncertainty of earnings, and life expectancies are held constant, earnings will be systematically and positively related to the *amount* and *quality* of one's formal education. An unequal distribution of educational attainment will produce an unequal distribution of personal earnings.

   Table 13-3 offers at least superficial evidence of the link between the *amount* of education undertaken and mean annual incomes. Numerous statistically

TABLE 13-3	
Mean Earnings of Full-Time Male Workers by Educational Attainment, 1982	
Mean earnings, males, total	$23,653
Elementary school:	
Less than 8 years	13,439
8 years	16,066
High school:	
1–3 years	17,025
4 years	20,480
College:	
1–3 years	23,093
4 years	29.547
5 or more years	36,079

Source: U.S. Bureau of the Census, *Money Income of Households and Persons in the United States, 1982; Current Population Reports,* ser. P-60, no. 142, table 48.

sophisticated studies confirm the basic positive relationship between education and earnings shown in the table. And, although fewer in number, empirical tests also find a direct relationship between the *quality* of formal education and subsequent earnings.[5] One must take care, however, not to *overstate* the importance of the link between education and earnings. Formal schooling explains only an estimated 7 to 12 percent of the observed differences in individual earnings.

2. On-the-job training. The explanatory power of the basic human capital model rises appreciably once on-the-job training is added to our analysis. On-the-job training varies from simple "learning-by-doing" to formal apprenticeships and training programs and, as indicated in Chapter 4, may either be *general* or *specific* to the firm. In the case of *general* training, the worker will bear the investment cost through a reduced wage. The worker's expected *gain* in future wages, therefore, must be sufficient to produce a rate of return on the investment cost (reduced present wage) equal to what the worker could obtain through alternative investments. In the case of nontransferable *specific training*, the firm will be forced to pay the investment expense. The employer obviously will undertake this investment only if the expected *increase* in the worker's productivity justifies it. Hence, training is undertaken in both cases on the expectation of an increase in productivity and earnings in the future. Therefore, one would expect to observe a direct relationship between the amount and quality of on-the-job training and a person's annual earnings.

Mincer has shown that about one-half to two-thirds of the variation of personal earnings are explained once postschooling on-the-job investment is included in the definition of human capital.[6] This inclusion adds so much explanatory power for at least two reasons. First, taken alone, formal schooling does little to explain why people's earnings typically *rise* with age. That is, education explains why postschooling earnings exceed preschooling pay, but it does not alone explain why earnings *rise* more rapidly for educated people over their work lives. After all, most people conclude their formal education relatively early in their lives. On-the-job training, on the other hand, provides a basic explanation for the age variations in earnings which are so apparent in the distribution. As one accumulates more training on the job, one's productivity and earnings rise. Furthermore, evidence clearly shows that people who possess greater amounts of formal education *also* tend to receive more on-the-job training from employers. Those people with the most formal education have demonstrated their abilities to absorb training and tend to be the people firms choose for on-the-job training. Hence, those who have more education have *disproportionately* greater earnings than less-educated workers.

A second reason postschooling investment helps explain the observed inequality in the distribution of earnings is through its impact on hours of work.

---

[5]Paul Taubman and Terrence Wales, *Higher Education and Earnings* (New York: McGraw-Hill Book Company, 1974) and George E. Johnson and Frank Stafford, "Social Returns to Quantity and Quality of Schooling," *Journal of Human Resources,* Spring 1973, pp. 139–155.

[6]Jacob Mincer, *Schooling, Experience, and Earnings* (New York: Columbia University Press, 1974).

Assuming that in the aggregate the substitution effect dominates the income effect (Chapter 2), people who have more schooling and on-the-job training will not only have higher hourly wage rates, but will choose to work more hours annually than less-educated and less-trained workers. This will mean that the annual earnings—wage rate × hours worked—will be *disproportionately* greater than the differences in schooling and on-the-job training, implying that the earnings distribution will be skewed to the right.

A Modified Human Capital Model: A Multifactor Approach. The basic human capital explanation of earnings disparities is not without its critics. Of particular interest to our topic is the criticism that schooling and on-the-job training do not sufficiently explain the long, extended rightward tail of the earnings distribution. Many economists believe that we can better understand why the earnings distribution is skewed rightward by expanding the human capital model to include additional factors such as (1) ability, (2) family background, (3) risk-taking, and (4) random elements related to the aforementioned factors of schooling and on-the-job training.

1. Ability. Ability is broadly defined as "the power to do" and consists of something *separate* and *distinct* from the skills gained through formal education or on-the-job training. Ability is difficult to isolate and measure but is thought to be normally distributed. In addition, ability is multidimensional; that is, it takes several forms, including native intelligence (IQ), physical dexterity, motivation, and so forth, and it may be *either* genetic *or* environmental in origin. Our interest in this discussion is not so much in the *source* of observed differences in ability as it is in the *consequences* of these differences for the distribution of earnings. As we will see, ability can influence earnings *directly*, in other words, independently of human capital investments, and *indirectly*, through its impact on the optimal amount and quality of human capital acquired.

Those who envision a direct impact of ability on earnings argue that in a market economy people are rewarded in a general way according to their ability to contribute to a firm's output. Other things being equal, the greater one's ability, the greater one's productivity and therefore earnings. At the extreme, critics of the human capital theory contend that the observed positive relationship between formal education and earnings *largely* reflects *self-selection* which is based on differences in ability. People who possess higher intelligence are simply more likely to choose to attend college than those with less intelligence. Even if these highly intelligent people did not go to college they could be expected to have larger earnings than those who actually decided not to go to college. In other words, if we could somehow control for the skills and knowledge gained during college, this high-ability group still would have substantially higher earnings than their less able counterparts. Consequently, according to this view, much of the inequality of earnings normally attributed to differences in education and training is actually the result of differences in ability.

A related possibility is that *elements* of differences in ability are complements to one another in the "production" of earnings. This implies that the addition of one factor will increase the productivity of other elements of ability. In other words, ability differences may act *multiplicatively* to generate the exceptionally high earnings that some people receive. To illustrate this idea let us suppose that ability consists of several normally distributed complementary elements, two of which are *intelligence* and the **D-factor,** where D represents drive, dynamism, doggedness, or determination.[7]

Given these assumptions, a person who is fortunate enough to be located in the rightward tail of both the normal distribution of intelligence *and* the normal distribution of the D-factor will have earnings that are disproportionately greater than the relative position in either of the two distributions. This idea can be illustrated by a simple example. Suppose that we could place a cardinal value on intelligence and the D-factor. Next suppose that Adams' intelligence is 4 on a scale of 1 to 5 (where 5 is high and 1 is low) while Bates' is 1 *and* that Adams' D-factor also is 4 compared to a rating of 1 for Bates. If intelligence and the D-factor interacted in an *additive* way to determine earnings, we would simply add 4 + 4 for Adams (= 8) and 1 + 1 for Bates (= 2) and note that Adams could be expected to earn 4 times as much as Bates (= 8/2). But we have speculated that the two factors might interact *multiplicatively* to determine earnings; that is, Adams' score will be 16 (= 4 × 4) while Bates' will be 1 (= 1 × 1). In this case, Adams' earnings will be 16 times those of Bates (= 16/1)! The point is that if elements of ability are positively correlated and interact in a complementary fashion, a skewed distribution of earnings is entirely consistent with normal distributions of the elements.

Perhaps of even greater significance is the notion that ability can influence earnings through its effect on the human capital investment decision. You may recall from Figure 4-6 that greater ability enables some people to translate any given investment in human capital, say a year of college or a year of on-the-job training, into a larger increase in labor market productivity and earnings than others. Therefore, the *rate of return* on each year of schooling or training will be higher for those who possess greater ability.[8] Consequently, these people will have a greater demand for formal education *and* their employers will possess a stronger desire to train them on the job than will be the case for less able people. The result? People possessing greater ability will tend to have disproportionately greater stocks of human capital and earnings than simple differences in abilities would suggest. Stated simply, people who do well in school because of inherent ability tend to get more schooling and people who get more

[7]Howard F. Lydall, "Theories of the Distribution of Earnings," in A. B. Atkinson (ed.), *The Personal Distribution of Income* (Boulder, Colo.: Westview Press, 1976), p. 35.

[8]This conclusion must be viewed cautiously. Greater ability also may imply larger forgone earnings during the investment period, in which case the observed greater postinvestment earnings may *not* yield higher rates of return. See John Hause, "Ability and Schooling as Determinants of Lifetime Earnings, or If You're So Smart, Why Ain't You Rich?" in F. Thomas Juster (ed.), *Education, Income and Human Behavior* (New York: McGraw-Hill Book Company, 1975), pp. 123–149.

education, in turn, tend to receive more on-the-job training than others. These tendencies skew the overall distribution of earnings to the right.

2. Family background. Differences in family background—indicated by such variables as family income, father's and mother's years of education, father's and mother's occupations, number of children, and so forth—also influence earnings both directly and indirectly.

The direct effect of family background on earnings often comes through employment of family members in family-owned businesses. A youth born into a family owning a prosperous Mercedes dealership stands a good chance of earning a sizable income later in life! Also, family "connections" may enable sons and daughters of the wealthy to gain high-paying positions in firms which are owned or managed by close friends or business associates. Sometimes these networks simply increase a job seeker's access to information about job openings, but in other instances they generate jobs for adult children through intricate reciprocity arrangements among those who interact both socially and commercially with one another.

Of perhaps greater significance, however, is the role of family background in influencing the decision of how much formal education to obtain. This influence affects both the demand for human capital and the supply price of investment funds. High-income families tend to provide more preschool education for children, are more likely to live in areas which have better schools, and tend to stress the importance of higher education as a route toward a professional career. Their children also may be socialized to think in terms of attending higher-quality educational institutions. Consequently, high-income parents tend to have a greater *demand* for human capital for their children and, therefore, these offspring tend to obtain more formal education.[9]

Family background may also provide easier financial access to higher education. Wealthier families may be able to finance their children's education from annual earnings or personal savings and thereby incur only the opportunity cost of forgone goods or interest. Lower-income families most probably will need to borrow funds from imperfect financial markets at higher interest rates. Because of these differing supply prices for human capital, the children of wealthier parents will find it optimal to obtain more formal education than children of poorer families (Figure 4-7).[10] These differences in education will combine with

---

[9] The mathematically minded reader who desires a more detailed presentation of this general perspective should see Gary Becker and Nigel Tomes, "Child Endowments and the Quality and Quantity of Children," *Journal of Political Economy*, August 1976, pp. 143–162 and Nigel Tomes, "The Family, Inheritance and the Intergenerational Transmission of Inequality," *Journal of Political Economy*, October 1981, pp. 928–958.

[10] Care must be taken not to *overstate* this effect, however. Financial aid—low-interest loans, scholarships, and so forth—received by students from lower-income families reduces the supply price for this group. Also, the *implicit* borrowing costs to the rich may not be that much lower than the *actual* borrowing costs to the poor. For evidence of this latter possibility, see Edward Lazear, "Family Background and Optimal Schooling Decisions," *The Review of Economics and Statistics*, February 1980, pp. 42–51.

direct family influences to produce an unequal, rightwardly skewed distribution of earnings.

3. Chance and risk-taking. Some economists have incorporated the role of random elements into theories of the distribution of earnings and income. These **stochastic theories** demonstrate how the cumulative impacts of random fortune tend to produce a long rightward tail in the distribution of such *nonwage* income as profits, rents, and capital gains. Because this is a text in *labor* economics, our interest, of course, is strictly in the distribution of *earnings,* and thus many of the stochastic theories have little relevance.

Nevertheless, according to some economists, stochastic elements offer important insights as to why *earnings* are unequal and why the earnings distribution is skewed to the right. Three examples of ways in which luck might enter into the earnings determination process are as follows. First, suppose that at a specific instant all persons possess a given level of *normally* distributed earnings *plus* an opportunity to participate in a lottery. Further suppose that the lottery winnings consist of opportunities to be a premier professional athlete, a rock star, a motion picture celebrity, a major corporate executive, or a best-selling author. These positions are *few* in number but pay *considerably* more than the average salaries in society. But there is a catch: You must incur *risk* if you wish to play the lottery; that is, you must buy a lottery ticket. The ticket price may be, say, the cost associated with advocating bold business ventures to your employer only to have one of them fail, the direct and indirect costs of refining your acting, musical, or athletic skills only to discover that the investment does not result in stardom, or the cost of forgoing present job security to become a writer whose uncertain earnings derive from book royalties.

Will all workers of equal ability participate in this lottery? Obviously not! Some people simply are much too averse to risk. Only those who are less averse to risk will decide that the chance of winning the few big prizes is worth the price of the ticket. How then might the distribution of earnings be affected by the lottery? Three distributions, each individually symmetrical, would be observable. First, there would be a distribution of earnings for the many nonparticipants in the lottery. Secondly, we would observe a distribution, possibly lying to the left of the one for nonparticipants, indicating the earnings of lottery losers. Finally, there would be a distribution lying to the right of that for nonparticipants displaying the very large average earnings of the relatively few lottery winners. Even though each of these three distributions might be normally distributed, the composite distribution of earnings would be skewed to the right.[11]

In Chapter 12, we implied a second way chance may account for differences in personal earnings. In Figure 12-5 it was observed that differences in pay for the *same type of work* can exist under circumstances of imperfect wage informa-

---

[11]This example is based upon a more complex model presented by Milton Friedman, "Choice, Chance, and the Personal Distribution of Income," *Journal of Political Economy,* August 1953, pp. 273–290. For a highly technical criticism of Friedman's article see S. M. Kanbur, "Of Risk Taking and the Personal Distribution of Income," *Journal of Political Economy,* August 1979, pp. 769–797.

tion and costly job search. Who receives which wage in the frequency distribution shown in the figure is in part determined randomly. For example, suppose that Gomez and Green are equally qualified job seekers who both have the same acceptance wage (minimum acceptable wage). Also, assume that each is searching in a random fashion for job openings in the frequency distribution shown in Figure 12-5. Through good luck, Gomez may receive the highest wage offer in the distribution on her first try, while the less fortunate Green may get an offer above her acceptance wage, but well below the pay received by Gomez.

A final example of the role of chance in theories of personal earnings is provided by Thurow. He contends that "marginal products are inherent in jobs and not individuals. The individual will be trained into the marginal productivity of the job he is slated to hold, but he does not have this marginal productivity independent of the job in question."[12] The implication of this thesis is that workers possessing a particular set of general background characteristics, that is, being equally trainable, will make up a labor pool from which employers will draw randomly. Those who are fortunate will get selected for jobs which have high marginal productivity and annual earnings, but because such jobs are few, other equally qualified people will end up in lower-paying occupations. Hence, according to Thurow, "similar individuals will be distributed across a range of job opportunities and earnings. In effect, they will participate in a lottery."[13]

A Schematic Summary. Figure 13-3 summarizes the major determinants of earnings just discussed.[14] The *basic* human capital explanation of earnings is represented by the thick solid line connecting *education and training* with earnings. The more comprehensive multifactor explanation is portrayed by the entire figure. Notice that *ability* affects earnings directly, as shown by the thick line connecting the two, and indirectly via its impact on the optimal amount and quality of education and training (thin line). Likewise, *family background* has direct and indirect effects on personal earnings. The solid arrow between them represents the role of family firms, family connections, and so forth, while the thin line from family background to education and training illustrates the impact of family education and wealth on the demand for, and supply price of, human capital. Finally, the role of *chance* is portrayed by the broken line that leads directly to earnings.

One could easily add more complexity to Figure 13-3. For example, we could connect chance with family background and ability, for in a sense both are partly products of luck! Also, we could add a *feedback loop* from earnings to education and training inasmuch as present earnings may help determine how

---

[12]Lester C. Thurow, *Generating Inequality: Mechanisms of Distribution in the U.S. Economy* (New York: Basic Books, Inc., Publishers, 1975), p. 85. Thurow's "job competition" model of the labor market is summarized in Chapter 15's Time and One-Half section.

[13]Ibid., p. 92.

[14]For a fuller discussion of this representation see A. B. Atkinson, *The Economics of Inequality,* 2d ed. (Oxford: Clarendon Press, 1983), p. 122.

much subsequent education one might find optimal. Also, and very importantly, we might acknowledge that *race* and *gender* influence earnings because of discrimination in hiring, pay, and promotion (Chapter 11). Then, too, we could recognize the role of compensating wage premiums in causing earnings differences (Chapter 12). Finally, as pointed out by Lydall, Rosen, and others, hierarchial structures of organizations may create large earnings disparities.[15] But even without these important considerations, Figure 13-3 adequately summarizes the major determinants of the personal distribution of earnings.

MOBILITY WITHIN THE EARNINGS DISTRIBUTION

The aggregate personal distribution of earnings is quite rigid from one year to the next and changes only slightly from one decade to the next. But this fact masks the degree of individual movement within that fixed distribution. As Schiller colorfully points out:

On the one hand, individuals may be highly mobile across discrete points of the aggregate distribution, suggesting a conventional game of musical chairs (to the tune of the human capital school fight song) in which the position of

[15]Howard Lydall, *The Structure of Earnings* (London: Oxford University Press, 1968) and Sherwin Rosen, "Authority, Control, and the Distribution of Earnings," *Bell Journal of Economics,* Autumn 1982, pp. 311–323.

FIGURE 13-3 FACTORS AFFECTING PERSONAL ANNUAL EARNINGS
The basic human capital explanation of the personal distribution of annual earnings is shown by the heavy solid arrow which connects education and training to annual earnings. The multifactor approach adds ability and family background as variables which can directly influence earnings (heavy lines) or indirectly affect earnings by having an impact on the amount and quality of education and training that a person receives (thin lines). Luck, or chance, also plays a role in affecting annual earnings (broken line). [*Adapted from A. B. Atkinson, The Economics of Inequality, 2nd ed. (Oxford: Oxford University Press, 1983), p. 122.*]

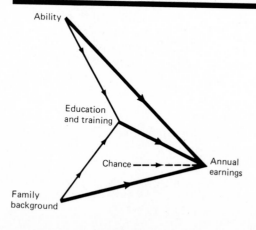

the chairs themselves is the only thing that never changes. On the other hand, the rigid shape of aggregate distribution is equally compatible with a total lack of personal mobility—a game, as it were, that individuals play by remaining in their chairs until the music (played by dual labor market theorists . . . [Chapter 15]) is over.[16]

Which of these two possibilities best describes reality? The answer appears to be the musical chairs scenario. The evidence suggests that there is considerable movement or mobility within the rather rigid static distribution. This *earnings mobility* is of two main types: (1) life-cycle mobility, and (2) a "churning" which is independent of age.

Life-Cycle Mobility. We know from our previous discussions of age-earnings profiles (Figure 4-1) that people's earnings typically vary systematically with age over the course of the life cycle. More precisely, most people have relatively low earnings when they are young; later, during their prime earning years, their earnings rise substantially; and finally, their earnings tend to fall at the time of retirement. Thus, even if everyone had an *identical* stream of earnings over her or his lifetime, we still would observe age-related inequality in the distribution of earnings. In any specific year, the static annual distribution of earnings would include, say, young (low-earnings) workers just beginning their labor force participation, middle-aged (high-earnings) employees in the prime of their careers, and older workers who were phasing into retirement. This inequality of *annual* earnings for a specific year would be present despite complete equality of *lifetime* earnings!

The evidence suggests that there is much **life-cycle mobility** of earnings *and* that this mobility contributes to more equality in *lifetime* earnings than is observed using static cross-sectional *annual* data. The degree of inequality of lifetime earnings may be as much as 45 percent less than the annual inequality shown earlier in Table 13-1.[17]

Churning within the Distribution. Is there movement within the earnings distribution that is *independent* of age itself? In other words, do people's *relative* age-adjusted earnings positions change during their lifetimes? Is there sufficient *churning within the earnings distribution* to allow the "cream" to rise? To answer this question, Schiller drew a sample from Social Security records of

---

[16]Bradley R. Schiller, "Relative Earnings Mobility in the United States," *American Economic Review*, December 1977, p. 926.

[17]Lee A. Lillard, "Inequality: Earnings vs. Human Wealth," *American Economic Review*, March 1977, pp. 42–53. Also, see Peter Friesen and Danny Miller, "Annual Inequality and Lifetime Inequality," *Quarterly Journal of Economics*, February 1983, pp. 139–155. For a discussion of how age affects the Gini coefficient of family *income*, see Morton Paglin, "The Measurement and Trend of Inequality: A Basic Revision," *The American Economic Review*, September 1975, pp. 598–609.

nearly 75,000 males who were 16 to 49 years of age and earned at least $1000 in 1957. He divided the sample into 20 earnings categories (ventiles), each containing 5 percent of the workers, and then observed the movements of individuals among the categories between 1957 and 1971. *Controlling for the effects of age*, Schiller found that about 70 percent of the workers were mobile across at least two earnings categories and that on the average workers moved about four categories, or one-fifth of the way from one end of the earnings distribution to the other. Schiller concluded that "the longitudinal earnings data . . . unambiguously demonstrate that individuals are highly mobile across relative positions in the earnings distribution."[18]

The finding that people are mobile within the earnings distribution is significant in that it implies that this churning joins with the age factor to reduce the degree of lifetime inequality. In terms of Schiller's "chair" analogy, the same workers *do not* always remain in the same earnings chairs. For example, a salesperson may have relatively small commissions and earnings in the first year of a new job, yet receive considerably larger annual commissions in subsequent years. Or a manager may get promoted to a job which pays considerably more than the job previously held. Or, as an example of churning in a downward direction, a performer who is highly paid one year may earn much less annually during following years. And, as stated by Blinder, "Americans seem quite willing to tolerate gross disparities in [earnings] so long as there is a reasonable chance that low-income families in one year can become high-income families in another. . . . While ghetto dwellers rarely trade places with Rockefellers, ours is not a stratified society."[19]

Nevertheless, one must not *overstate* the extent of churning in the earnings distribution. Schiller, for example, found that (1) there was lower mobility in and out of the *lowest* and *highest* 5 percent (ventile) categories than to and from other categories, and (2) although blacks were also mobile, their *rate* of mobility was less than that for whites. Conclusion? Although evidence confirms that there is much churning within the earnings distribution, the extent of this type of mobility is neither uniform throughout the distribution nor equal for all groups of workers.

UNIONS AND THE DISTRIBUTION OF EARNINGS: A REVIEW

In our discussion of the economic impacts of unions (Chapter 8), we examined in some detail how unions affect the distribution of earnings. Because this *net* effect may be significant, let us review the union impact at this point.

---

[18]Schiller, op. cit., p. 938.

[19]Alan S. Blinder, "The Level and Distribution of Economic Well-Being," in Martin Feldstein (ed.), *The American Economy in Transition* (Chicago: University of Chicago Press, 1980), p. 454.

Recall that the spillover model of unionism (Figure 8-2) implies that unions achieve wage increases partially at the expense of lower nonunion wages. The higher wage rate achieved by unions results in displacement of workers who then seek reemployment in the nonunion sector. Consequently, labor supply increases in the nonunion sector, depressing wages there. Another factor which might lead one to think that unions make the distribution of earnings *more* unequal is that unionization is more extensive among skilled, higher-paid workers than it is among less-skilled workers. The wage gains secured by unions, then, ought to widen the earnings differential between skilled and unskilled workers. Finally, high union wages may increase the long-run demand for high-quality workers who justify the high pay. This will decrease the demand for low-quality workers and tend to widen the earnings distribution.

But recall from Chapter 8 that, according to Freeman and Medoff, three other factors more than offset these tendencies for the earnings distribution to widen. First, unions promote and achieve uniform wages *within* firms by negotiating union scales and salary schedules *and* by requesting *absolute* pay increases, rather than relative—that is, percentage—increases. Second, unions contribute to uniformity of wages *among* firms. Finally, evidence suggests that unions narrow the earnings differential between white- and blue-collar workers.

The net effect, according to Freeman and Medoff, is a significant compression of the earnings distribution. Or stated in terms of the Lorenz curve for earnings (Figure 13-2), unions lessen the southeasterly sag of the curve and reduce the Gini coefficient.[20]

THE PUBLIC SECTOR AND THE DISTRIBUTION OF EARNINGS

There are myriad routes through which government affects labor supply, labor demand, bargaining power, or all three and thereby has an impact on wage rates and the earnings structure (Chapters 9 and 10). For example, although government transfer programs reduce *income* inequality in society, they also increase *earnings* inequality by creating incentives for recipients to work fewer hours. As a second example, by promoting unionism, passage of the Wagner Act (1935) likely tightened the earnings distribution in the United States. A little-researched question is whether or not the *sum* of government activities which relate to the labor market narrows, widens, or leaves unchanged the before-tax personal distribution of *earnings*. We will have to await further research to make this determination. Nevertheless, it is instructive to analyze two major aspects of this broad topic: (1) the impact of the government pay distribution on the overall personal distribution of earnings, and (2) the affect of the minimum wage law on the aggregate distribution of earnings.

[20]Richard B. Freeman and James L. Medoff, *What Do Unions Do?* (New York: Basic Books, Inc., Publishers, 1984), chap. 5.

Government Employment and the Earnings Distribution. One out of six U.S. workers is employed by government. How do the wages paid to these employees affect the distribution of earnings? The answer is that government employment and remuneration tend to narrow the overall earnings distribution.

Government agencies and government contractors usually adhere to a prevailing wage rule under which the wages paid to public employees are comparable to the earnings of similar workers in the private sector. But this rule tends to be modified at both the bottom and top ends of the government pay structure. Blue-collar public employees are paid more than their private-sector counterparts, while white-collar workers in government—particularly executives—are paid much less. As a consequence, the personal distribution of earnings in the public sector is more egalitarian than in the private sector, causing the overall distribution in society to also be less unequal.[21]

The reasons for the compression of earnings in the public sector are many. For example, elected officials may pay low-wage workers more than their private-sector counterparts to avoid the potentially politically embarassing circumstance of having full-time government workers qualifying for government cash and in-kind welfare benefits. Also, it seems probable that low- to middle-wage earning employees who are large in number and strong politically are more likely to secure wage increases than are higher-paid managers and professionals who are few in number. Furthermore, it may be that the large salaries paid to executives in corporations simply are not politically feasible when paid to top governmental administrators and elected officials. In this regard, we might note that in 1984 the total of the *combined* salaries and bonuses of the *ten* highest-paid corporate executives in the United States was more than the *combined* salaries of the following government officials: the President of the United States, the Vice-President, the 100 U.S. senators, the 50 state governors, the 9 Supreme Court justices, and the 50 heads of major regulatory agencies.

Table 13-4 provides more specific information on this topic. Column 2 combines into a single quintile distribution the earnings of government employees *plus* the earnings of workers in the private sector who owe their employment to government purchases. Column 3, on the other hand, shows the quintile distribution of earnings generated by private sector demand. Notice that the distribution of earnings resulting from government was considerably less unequal than the quintile distribution deriving from private purchases. More specifically, observe that the lowest 60 percent of the workers in column 2 accounted for 33 percent (= 2.9 + 9.8 + 20.3) of that group's total earnings, while the lowest 60 percent of the workers in column 3 accounted for only 25.4 percent (= 2.3 + 7.4 + 15.7). Additionally, observe that the top quintile in the government column earned 41.7 percent of total wages and salaries paid to this group as compared to 49.1 percent paid to the private demand group. Table 13-4

[21]Walter Fogel and David Lewin, "Wage Determination in the Public Sector," *Industrial and Labor Relations Review*, April 1974, pp. 410–431.

thus extends our generalization: Government employment—direct *and* indirect—exerts an equalizing effect on the overall personal distribution of earnings.[22]

The Minimum Wage Revisited. Although much research attention has been given to the *employment* effects of the federal minimum wage (Chapter 10), considerably less has been devoted to the effect of the minimum wage on the distribution of *earnings*. Our discussion of this topic is therefore somewhat speculative.

You may recall from Chapter 10 that the minimum wage fails to reduce significantly the inequality of *family income* because many recipients are members of middle- or even high-income families. Also, as noted in our earlier discussion of Table 13-2, much of the income received by families in the lowest quintile of the family income distribution is derived from government transfers. Because *wage* income is relatively small for these families, the minimum wage has a small impact on their total income.

Our interest in this chapter, however, is the distribution of *earnings* rather than the distribution of family *income*. It is logical therefore to inquire about the impact of the minimum wage on earnings differences. Does the minimum wage make the earnings distribution *less* or *more* unequal? Unfortunately, we can not provide an unequivocal answer. Some effects of the minimum wage compress the distribution; others create more inequality. For convenience we will label the former as *narrowing effects* and the latter as *widening effects*.

[22]Lester C. Thurow, *The Zero-Sum Society* (New York: Basic Books, Inc., Publishers, 1980), pp. 166–167.

TABLE 13-4

Government-Generated versus Privately Generated Earnings, by Quintile

(1) Quintile	(2) Government (%) (Direct + Indirect)	(3) Private (%) (Generated by Private Demand)
Lowest 20 percent	2.9	2.3
Second 20 percent	9.8	7.4
Third 20 percent	20.3	15.7
Fourth 20 percent	25.3	25.4
Highest 20 percent	41.7	49.1
Total	100.0	100.0

Source: Lester C. Thurow, *The Zero-Sum Society* (Basic Books, Inc., Publishers, 1980), p. 167. Data are calculated from U.S. Bureau of the Census, *Current Population Reports, Consumers Income 1976*, Census tapes and U.S. Department of Labor input-output tables.

1. Narrowing effects. Several effects of the minimum wage are thought to interact to narrow the distribution of earnings. First, and most apparent, the imposition of the minimum wage raises the hourly pay of those workers who previously received wages below the minimum wage, provided they *remain employed*. Assuming that these workers continue to work as many hours as before, the result will be a tightening of the earnings distribution.[23] Second, the minimum wage can reduce earnings inequality by raising the wage rates and earnings of other low-wage workers and more-skilled workers relative to the pay received by supervisors and executives. How is this possible? One possibility is that firms will wish to substitute higher-skilled workers for some of the minimum-wage workers, since the latter must now be paid more than they were previously. This will increase the demand for, and wages paid to, higher-skilled employees. This effect will not extend to supervisors, midmanagement, and executives because they are not substitutes for the minimum-wage workers. A second reason why wages might rise for non-minimum-wage workers is due to a "ripple" effect. If a worker values his or her wage for both its purchasing power *and* for the relative status it provides, then the firm may find it profitable to increase the wage rates paid to those who receive wages above the minimum. This will maintain the wage rate hierarchy and thereby dissuade workers from becoming disgruntled and reducing their work effort.[24]

But will not this upward ripple effect extend to supervisory personnel and management? Perhaps not. The minimum wage and ripple effect on the wages of other workers may result in a surplus of workers in blue-collar markets, allowing the firm to screen for and employ those workers who need the least supervision. Hence, the optimal number of managers may fall, and this translates into less demand for, and earnings paid to, this high-earnings group. Consequently, the earnings distribution may narrow.[25]

2. Widening effects. Other effects of the minimum wage tend to disperse rather than to compress earnings. Recall from our discussion in Chapter 10 that an above-equilibrium minimum wage reduces employment for some workers; that is, firms will not choose to employ as many hours of low-productivity labor at the minimum wage as they did before its imposition. This reduced employment may take two forms: discharges or reduced hours.

Workers who are discharged because of the minimum wage may seek employment in the sector of the economy which is not covered by the minimum wage (Figure 10-5). This will increase the supply of labor in the uncovered

---

[23]This increase in earnings may be partially or fully offset by a decline in fringe benefits, however. See Walter J. Wessels, "The Effect of Minimum Wages in the Presence of Fringe Benefits: An Expanded Model," *Economic Inquiry*, April 1980, pp. 293–313.

[24]Jean B. Grossman, "The Impact of the Minimum Wage on Other Wages," *Journal of Human Resources*, Summer 1983, pp. 359–378.

[25]This explanation is closely related to that provided by G. A. Calvo and Stanislaw Wellisz, "Hierarchy, Ability, and Income Distribution," *Journal of Political Economy*, October 1979, pp. 991–1010.

sector and thereby reduce the market wage for other extremely low-paid employees. In this respect the distribution of earnings will become more unequal.

The unemployment impact of the minimum wage may alternatively take the form of reduced hours of work for *some* minimum-wage workers. If this reduction in hours is greater in percentage terms than the increase in pay per hour, the *earnings* for these people will fall. Therefore, we would discover that, while the minimum wage increased earnings for those low-skilled workers who remain fully employed, it would *reduce* earnings for others and thus cause greater inequality of earnings.[26]

We see then that the *net* effect of the minimum wage on the distribution of earnings as measured by, say, the Gini coefficient is ambiguous. Further research will be needed to clarify the relative importance of the various effects.

SUMMARY

1. The degree of inequality in personal earnings can be shown either by a histogram (absolute frequency distribution), a relative frequency distribution, or a Lorenz curve. A frequency distribution shows either the absolute or relative number of employees whose annual earnings fall within various ranges of annual earnings. The Lorenz curve portrays the cumulative percentage of all wage and salary earners and their corresponding cumulative percentage of total earnings.
2. The frequency distribution for U.S. earnings evidences considerable bunching around a single leftward mode which is to the left of the median and mean, and displays a long rightwardly skewed tail, indicating rather wide disparities in personal earnings.
3. The Gini coefficient measures the degree of earnings inequality on a scale of zero (complete equality) to one (complete inequality). It can be found graphically by comparing the area between the diagonal line and the Lorenz curve to the entire area southeast of the diagonal.
4. Frequency distributions, Lorenz curves, and Gini coefficients of *personal earnings* must be interpreted cautiously because they (*a*) differ depending upon whether part-time workers are included or excluded, (*b*) fail to include fringe benefits, (*c*) do not provide information on *family* earnings, and (*d*) display more inequality than income after taxes and transfers.
5. According to human capital theorists, approximately one-half to two-thirds of earnings inequality is explained by the interactive differences in people's formal education and on-the-job training.
6. Ability (*a*) is thought by some economists to influence earnings *directly* through enhancement of productivity, (*b*) may take several forms which interact multiplicatively to produce the observed skewed distribution of earnings, and (*c*) may *indirectly* have an impact on earnings by determining the return from—and hence the optimal amount of—investment in human capital.
7. Family background, extent of risk-taking, and degree of luck also are variables

[26]Support for this possibility can be found in a study by Peter Linneman, "The Economic Impact of Minimum Wage Laws: A New Look at an Old Question," *Journal of Political Economy*, June 1982, pp. 443–469.

which help explain earnings inequality and the rightwardly skewed tail of the earnings distribution.

8. There is considerable movement by individuals within the overall distribution of earnings. This mobility is related to the life cycle, reflecting the generally positive relationship between age and earnings, and can also be of a "churning" nature, through which people with more education, training, ability, or luck rise from lower to higher levels of age-adjusted earnings.

9. Available evidence suggests that *on balance* unions lessen earnings inequality by (*a*) establishing uniform wages for given jobs *within* firms, (*b*) producing uniform wages *among* firms, and (*c*) achieving higher wage gains for relatively low-paid blue-collar workers than for relatively high-paid white-collar workers.

10. The distribution of earnings among government employees is more egalitarian than the distribution in the private sector and therefore contributes to a tighter overall distribution of earnings.

11. The net impact of the minimum wage law on the distribution of earnings is ambiguous.

QUESTIONS AND STUDY SUGGESTIONS

1. Key terms and concepts to remember: histogram; frequency distribution; Lorenz curve; Gini coefficient; human capital model; multi-factor approach to earnings determination; D-factor; stochastic theories; earnings mobility; life-cycle mobility; "churning" within the earnings distribution.

2. Suppose that a hypothetical economy consists of 20 nonunionized, private-sector workers who have the following annual earnings: $18,000, $9,000, $82,000, $12,000, $13,000, $76,000, $61,000, $14,000, $22,000, $23,000, $21,000, $46,000, $59,000, $26,000, $27,000, $37,000, $6,000, $41,000, $3,000, $24,000.
   a. Using annual earnings ranges of $10,000; that is, 0–$10,000, $10,000–$20,000, and so forth, construct a histogram (absolute frequency distribution) of this nation's distribution of personal earnings. What is the mode of the histogram? What is the average (mean) level of earnings? What is the median level of earnings? Characterize the distribution as being (1) normal, (2) skewed leftward, or (3) skewed rightward. Explain.
   b. Construct a Lorenz curve showing the quintile distribution of earnings for this economy.
   c. What would be the likely impact of unionization of this entire work force on the Lorenz curve? Explain.

3. Speculate about why a given Gini coefficient is compatible with more than one particular Lorenz curve. Illustrate graphically.

4. Why is it that people who have more formal education than others also in general tend to receive more on-the-job training during their careers? What is the implication for the distribution of earnings?

5. Critically evaluate: "Lifetime earnings are less equally distributed than annual earnings."

6. How might successful attempts by government to tighten the distribution of family *income* through transfers inadvertently make the distribution of *earnings* more unequal?

7. Suppose that the government adopts a subminimum wage for teenagers (Chapter 10), that is, it allows employers to hire teenagers at some fixed wage rate that is

below the adult minimum. Assess the likely impact of this on the personal distribution of earnings.

8. Explain how both *ability* and *family background* can *directly* influence earnings, independently of education and training. How do ability and family background *indirectly* determine earnings through the human capital investment decision?

9. Explain why the distribution of earnings in the public sector is compressed inward at both ends relative to the private-sector distribution.

10. In the light of new information presented in this chapter, answer question 11 at the end of Chapter 4.

SELECTED REFERENCES

ATKINSON, A. B.: *The Economics of Inequality*, 2d ed. (London: Oxford University Press, 1983).

ATKINSON, A. B. (ed.): *The Personal Distribution of Income* (Boulder, Colo.: Westview Press, Inc., 1976).

BLINDER, ALAN S.: *Toward an Economic Theory of Income Distribution* (Chicago: University of Chicago Press, 1974).

MINCER, JACOB: *Schooling, Experience and Earnings* (New York: Columbia University Press, 1974).

OSBERG, LARS: *Economic Inequality in the United States* (Armonk, N.Y.: M. E. Sharpe, Inc., 1984).

SAHOTA, GIAN S.: "Theories of Personal Income Distribution: A Survey," *Journal of Economic Literature*, March 1978, pp. 1–55.

THUROW, LESTER C.: *Generating Inequality: Mechanisms of Distribution in the U.S. Economy* (New York: Basic Books, Inc., Publishers, 1975).

T I M E   A N D   O N E - H A L F

IS THE MIDDLE CLASS DECLINING?*

Robert Z. Lawrence disputes the popular perception that, as the U.S. economy shifts away from traditional manufacturing and toward services and high technology, the relative number of mid-level jobs will appreciably decline.

We are hearing these days, from a variety of observers, that the middle class in the United States is or soon will be shrinking. As the U.S. economy shifts away from basic manufacturing and towards high-technology and service industries, the number of mid-level jobs will decline—or so the argument goes. Some commentators, leaping from presumption to prescription, have urged that the middle class be safeguarded by initiatives—such as protectionist trade measures and selective industrial policies—designed to prop up basic manufacturing industries and forestall the structural changes that are taking place in the economy.

*Extracted from Robert Z. Lawrence, "Sectoral Shifts and the Size of the Middle Class." From *The Brookings Review*, Fall 1984, pp. 3–11. Copyright © 1984 by the Brookings Institution, Washington, D.C.

Those who anticipate the dwindling of the middle class contend that the industries in which employment is decreasing—the automobile and steel industries, for example—have traditionally been characterized by a profusion of mid-level jobs. High-technology and services industries are seen as offering mostly high-paying and low-paying jobs—the former for professionals and managers, the latter for clerical and assembly-line workers. Thus, the flow of employment away from basic manufacturing is seen as auguring the contraction of the middle class.

The evidence adduced in support of this line of reasoning is typically anecdotal or selective. In this article, I will examine more comprehensive data to determine how much the distribution of earnings in high-technology and services industries differs from the distribution of earnings in basic manufacturing. . . .

The median usual weekly earnings of males employed full-time in 1983 was $379 per week ($19,708 per year). Earnings data for 1983 are reported only in terms of rather large brackets. For purposes of this analysis, therefore, middle-class earnings are defined

TABLE 1

Earnings Distribution* across Sectors, Categorized by High, Middle and Low Earnings, 1983

Sector	Distribution in 1983(%)		
	High	Mid	Low
Total	21	46	33
Goods producing	24	46	30
Agriculture	3	27	69
Mining	48	42	9
Construction	28	45	27
Manufacturing	23	48	29
Durables	26	50	24
Nondurables	19	44	37
Services	19	42	40
Transportation, communication, and public utilities	36	49	15
Trade	14	38	48
Finance, insurance, and real estate	22	43	35
Private households	2	8	90
Miscellaneous services	16	43	41
Public sector	23	55	23

*Income categories established using median male weekly earnings of $379 in 1983 as a middle benchmark. The categories are defined as follows: high = $500+; mid = $250–499; low = $0–249.

Source: Bureau of Labor Statistics; unpublished data, *Usual Weekly Earnings of Employed Full-Time Wage and Salary Workers, 1983.*

as those between $250 and $499 per week ($13,000 to $25,948 per year); the median figure just mentioned is almost exactly at the midpoint of this range. Earnings above and below the middle bracket are defined as upper-class and lower-class respectively.

Table 1 reports the distribution of usual weekly earnings in the United States by economic sector. It shows that, contrary to the common perception, the proportion of full-time workers earning middle-class incomes in the production of goods—46 percent—is exactly the same as the proportion for the rest of the economy. Durable goods manufacturing does rank second among all sectors in the proportion of its workers receiving middle-class earnings (50 percent). However, the public sector has the most intensively middle-class workforce (55 percent), and in third place is a services sector: transportation, communication, and public utilities (49 percent). There is virtually no difference between the proportions of middle-class earners in non-durable manufacturing (44 percent) and in such categories as finance, insurance, and real estate (43 percent) and miscellaneous services (43 percent). In fact, if the entire manufacturing workforce were to be reemployed with earnings patterns typical of the rest of the economy, the aggregate distribution of earnings would change very little. The numbers of workers receiving upper-class and middle-class earnings would decline by only 3.0 and 1.7 percent respectively. . . .

A different data base and a slightly different definition of middle-class earnings were used to examine earnings patterns at a more disaggregated level. Table 2 shows these patterns in the major high-technology sectors. The data reported here, just released from the 1980 census, include both part-time and full-time earnings. They flatly refute the contention that high-technology industries offer relatively few middle-class job opportunities. All of the major high-technology sectors have smaller shares of lower-class jobs than manufacturing in general has, and almost all of them have larger shares of middle-class jobs. The disaggregated data do confirm that the automobile and steel industries are important sources of upper-class jobs, but the proportion of their workers receiving

TABLE 2

Earnings Distribution* of the Experienced Civilian Labor Force, Selected Industries, 1979

	Distribution in 1979 (%)		
	High	**Mid**	**Low**
High technology†	34	37	29
Manufacturing	29	34	38

*Earnings categories established using median male annual earnings of $14,442 in 1979 as a middle benchmark. The categories are defined: high = $18,748.7+; mid = $10,095.4–18,748.6; low = $0–10,094.4.

†Machinery except electrical; electrical machinery, equipment and supplies; chemicals and allied products; aircraft and parts; professional and photographic equipment.

Source: Bureau of the Census, prepublication data, *Earnings of the Experienced Civilian Labor Force by Industry in 1979,* table 290.

middle-class earnings is actually lower than the proportion for most of the high-technology industries.

In short, therefore, we should expect, first, that everything else being equal, declines in the share of total employment accounted for by manufacturing would yield only small reductions in the proportion of workers in the middle-class earnings bracket and, second, that continued shifts of employment within manufacturing towards the high-technology industries would have little impact on the earnings distribution.

MOBILITY, MIGRATION, AND EFFICIENCY

n previous chapters we observed that labor markets perform a variety of economic functions, including providing information to labor market participants. Knowledge of alternative wage rates and job options allows workers to assess the opportunity cost of their present employment, while knowledge of market wage rates for alternative types of labor enables firms to hire resources in cost-minimizing combinations and at profit-maximizing levels. When such things as product demand, labor productivity, levels of investment in human capital, family circumstances, or general economic conditions change, some *workers* find it advantageous to change employers, occupations, geographic locations, or some combination of all three. On the other hand, *employers* respond to changing economic circumstances by hiring, transferring, or discharging workers; closing or expanding present facilities; or moving operations to new locations. Taken together, these actions by workers and firms generate considerable movement or mobility of labor resources from job to job and place to place in the economy. Such labor mobility is the central focus of the present chapter.

The discussion proceeds in the following fashion. First, we define various *types* of labor mobility. Second, we select geographic mobility for special attention and examine migration as an investment in human capital. Following that, we take a closer look at the *determinants* of migration, that is, the factors which promote and impede mobility. Fourth, the efficiency and distributional consequences of migration and immigration are discussed. Finally, we examine U.S. immigration law and discuss the economic effects of illegal aliens.

TYPES OF LABOR MOBILITY

The boxes in Figure 14-1 categorize several important kinds of labor mobility. The *columns* of the boxes identify locational characteristics of the employment change while the *rows* indicate occupational characteristics. Let us describe the kind of labor mobility associated with each box.

Box I: Job Change/No Change in Occupation or Residence. Box I indicates a type of mobility in which neither the worker's occupation nor residence changes. This form of mobility occurs frequently, for example when electrical engineers switch employers within California's "Silicon Valley" or automobile salespersons quit one dealership to work for another. This category also includes trans-

379

fers of employees from one of a firm's units to another in the same local area, for example when a bank employee is reassigned from one branch of a local bank to another.

Box II: Occupational Change/No Change in Residence. This box identifies changes in occupation which are not accompanied by changes in residence. Much of this **occupational mobility** involves moves to closely related occupations, for example when a carpenter takes a job in a lumberyard. But in other cases, this mobility is characterized by a significant occupational change. For example, a part-time warehouse employee who completes college might accept a job as a securities broker in the same town. Approximately one out of ten workers in the United States is employed in a different occupation than he or she was in the previous year. About 70 percent of these changes in occupation are accounted for by people who are 35 years old or younger. Many of these changes also involve geographic mobility (box IV).

Box III: Geographic Change/No Change in Occupation. **Geographic mobility** pertains to movements of workers from a job in one city, state, or nation to another. In one 3-year period—1975 to 1978—over 6 percent of all adults moved from one state to another, while an additional 7.5 percent moved between counties of the same state. Company transfers of employees have ranged between 300,000 and 500,000 annually since 1979. Furthermore, annual flows of *legal* immigrants to the United States were roughly 250,000 in the 1950s, 320,000 in the 1960s, and 400,000 during the 1970s. Also, as many as 500,000 *illegal* aliens entered the United States during some years in the 1980s. Many of these moves involve changes in jobs but not occupations. Examples: An executive for an aerospace firm gets transferred from Wichita to Seattle; a farm worker

FIGURE 14-1 TYPES OF MOBILITY

Mobility can take several forms, four of which are summarized by boxes I through IV. Specifically, it can involve a job change, but no change in occupation or residence (box I); an occupational change, but no change in residence (box II); a geographic move to a job in the same occupation (box III); or geographic migration accompanied by a change in occupation (box IV).

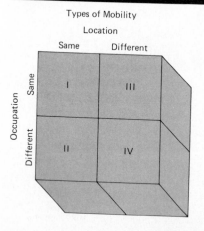

moves from Mexico to the United States; a corporate lawyer leaves a New York City law firm to join one in Boston; a professional football player gets traded from New Orleans to Cleveland.

Box IV: Geographic Change/Change in Occupation. Approximately 30 percent of geographic job-related moves are accompanied by changes in occupations. Hence, these changes represent both geographic and occupational mobility. For example, a discharged steelworker might leave Pennsylvania to take a job as a construction worker in Arizona. Or perhaps a high school teacher might move from a small town to take a position as an insurance claims adjuster in a distant urban area.

To limit our focus and retain clarity, we will confine our attention to *geographic* mobility (boxes III and IV) in the remainder of the chapter. But be advised that much of the analysis that follows can also be directly transferred to the other forms of labor mobility.

MIGRATION AS AN INVESTMENT IN HUMAN CAPITAL

Labor migration has been extensively studied by economists, sociologists, demographers, and geographers. One important way that economists have contributed to the understanding of geographic mobility is through the development and testing of the human capital model of migration. Recall from Chapter 4 that human capital consists of the income-producing skill, knowledge, and experience embodied within individuals. This stock of capital can be increased by specific actions—investments in human capital—which require *present* sacrifices but increase the stream of *future* earnings over one's lifetime. Such actions include obtaining more education, gaining added training, and maintaining one's health. Migration to a higher-paying job is also a human capital investment in that it entails present sacrifices in order to obtain higher future earnings.

Will migration occur in all situations where there is a potential for increased lifetime earnings? The answer is "no," because there are *costs* associated with the migration investment which must be weighed against the expected *gains.* The main costs are transportation expenses, forgone income during the move, psychic costs of leaving family and friends, and the loss of seniority and pension benefits. According to our analysis of Chapter 4, *if* the present value of the expected increased earnings exceeds the present value of these investment costs, the person will choose to move. If the opposite is true, the individual will conclude that it is not worthwhile to migrate, even though the earnings potential in the destination area may be higher than in the present location.[1]

---

[1] The classic article on this topic is by Larry A. Sjaastad, "The Costs and Returns of Human Migration," *Journal of Political Economy*, suppl., October 1962, pp. 80–93. For reviews of a wide variety of labor mobility models see Michael J. Greenwood, "Research on Internal Migration in the United States: A Survey," *Journal of Economic Literature*, June 1975, pp. 397–433 and Charles F. Mueller, *The Economics of Labor Migration: A Behavioral Analysis* (New York: Academic Press, 1982), pp. 1–70.

Equation (14-1)—a modification of equation (4-3) in Chapter 4—gives the net present value of migration.

$$V_p = \sum_{n=1}^{N} \frac{E_2 - E_1}{(1 + i)^n} - \sum_{n=1}^{N} \frac{C}{(1 + i)^n} - Z \tag{14-1}$$

where:

V_p = present value of net benefits
E_2 = earnings from new job in year n
E_1 = earnings from existing job in year n
N = length of time expected on new job
i = interest rate (discount rate)
n = year in which benefits and costs accrue
C = direct and indirect monetary costs resulting from move in the year n
Z = net psychic costs of move (psychic costs minus psychic gains)

In terms of equation (14-1), if $V_p > 0$, implying that the earnings gain is expected to exceed the combined monetary and psychic investment costs, the person will choose to migrate. If, conversely, $V_p < 0$, the person will decide to remain in his or her present job and location. Assuming that all else is equal, the greater the annual earnings differential $(E_2 - E_1)$ between the two jobs, the higher the present value of the net benefits (V_p), and the greater the likelihood that an individual will choose to migrate.

THE DETERMINANTS OF MIGRATION: A CLOSER LOOK

Various factors in addition to the annual earnings differential $(E_2 - E_1)$ influence the discounted present value of the total earnings and costs streams in equation (14-1) and thereby affect the present value of the net benefits and the decision to migrate. These factors or **determinants of migration** include age, family circumstances, education, distance, and unemployment.

Age. Migration studies consistently find that age is a major factor determining the probability of migration. All else being equal, the greater a person's age, the less likely he or she is to migrate. There are several reasons for this which have to do with either reducing the gain in net earnings from migrating or increasing the costs of moving. Let us examine these reasons in some detail.

First, older migrants have fewer years to recoup their investment costs. Alternatively stated, given a specific cost of migrating, the shorter the time period one has to gain the annual earnings advantage, the smaller the V_p term in equation (14-1). A young person may view a relatively small wage differential to be significant over his or her lifetime; a person who is two or three years away from retirement is not likely to incur migration costs to achieve this short-lived annual differential.

Second, older people tend to have higher levels of human capital which is *specific* to their present employers. Age, length of time on a job (job tenure), and annual wages are all positively correlated. The longer a person's job tenure, the greater is the amount of on-the-job training and employer financed investment of a *specific* variety he or she is likely to have. This human capital, by definition, is *not* transferable to other jobs (Chapter 4). Hence, the wage one receives after several years of job tenure partially reflects a return on a specific investment in human capital and is likely to be higher than the wage that one can get elsewhere. Therefore, regardless of the length of time available to recoup the investment costs, older people may be less likely to migrate.[2]

The cost of moving is a third age-related consideration which affects migration. Older people often have higher migration costs than younger people. For example, a young person may be able to transport possessions across the country in a 4' by 8' U-haul trailer, whereas an older person may need to hire a professional mover who uses a moving van. Or, as another example, a younger person who migrates may lose little seniority or future pension benefits, while an older person may incur very large costs of this type.[3] Also, it is possible that the psychic costs of migration rise with age. Older people are more likely than younger workers to have roots in their present community, children in the local school system, and an extensive network of workplace friends. The higher these net psychic costs—Z in equation (14-1)—the less likely one is to migrate.

Finally, the inverse relationship between age and migration exists partially because people are most mobile upon completing lengthy investments in human capital. Many people begin "job shopping" at the end of high school—ages 18 to 19—which may result in geographic moves.[4] Migration is even more pronounced for college graduates, who enter labor markets which are regional and national in scope. It therefore is not surprising to discover that the peak age for labor migration in the United States is 23.

Family Factors. The potential costs of migrating tend to multiply as family size increases. Therefore, we would expect married workers to have less tendency to

---

[2]Jacob Mincer and Boyan Jovanovic, "Labor Mobility and Wages," in Sherwin Rosen (ed.), *Studies in Labor Markets* (Chicago: The University of Chicago Press, 1981), pp. 21-63. There are exceptions to this generalization, however. Charles Mueller found that for people who have *high* incomes, the longer one's job tenure, the *greater* the likelihood of migration. "In the high-paying jobs, it may be that either better opportunities lie with firms other than one's own as experience accumulates or the tendency of job transfer is greater as one's own tenure with a firm increases." See Charles F. Mueller, *The Economics of Labor Migration,* p. 143. Also see Ann P. Bartel, "The Migration Decision: What Role Does Job Mobility Play?" *American Economic Review,* December 1979, pp. 775–786.

[3]For evidence that the prospect of leaving behind an employer-provided pension constitutes a high cost of changing jobs, see Olivia S. Mitchell, "Fringe Benefits and the Costs of Changing Jobs," *Industrial and Labor Relations Review,* October 1983, pp. 70–78.

[4]William Johnson, "A Theory of Job Shopping," *Quarterly Journal of Economics,* May 1978, pp. 261–278.

migrate than single people, other factors such as age and education being constant. Furthermore, it seems logical to expect higher migration rates for married workers whose spouses either do not work or work at low pay. If both spouses currently earn a high wage, the family's cost in forgoing income during the move will be high, and when combined with the possibility that one spouse will not find a job in the destination location, this cost reduces the net present value to the family from migration. Finally, the presence of school-aged children can be expected to reduce the likelihood of migration. The parents and children simply may conclude that the psychic costs associated with the move are too great relative to the expected monetary gain.

These particular predictions from the human capital model are borne out by empirical evidence. Jacob Mincer found that (1) unmarried persons are more likely to move than married ones, (2) the wife's employment inhibits family migration, (3) the longer the wife's job tenure, the less likely that a family will migrate, and (4) the presence of school-aged children in the family reduces migration.[5]

Education. Within age groupings, the level of educational attainment beyond high school is a major predictor of how likely one is to migrate within the United States. The higher one's educational attainment, all else being equal, the more likely it is that one will migrate.[6] Several reasons have been offered for this relationship. College graduates and those with post-graduate training—MBAs, PH.D.s, lawyers, CPAs—search for employment in *regional* and *national* labor markets in which employers seek qualified employees. These markets often are characterized both by substantial job information and by participants who possess excellent ability to analyze and assess the available information. The potential for economic gain from migration also may be increased because of the heterogeneity of many of the workers and positions (Chapter 12). Union wage scales and minimum-wage rates reduce wage differentials within occupations which do not require college training. On the other hand, the wide disparities of pay for professional and managerial employees provide them more opportunity to move to jobs entailing greater responsibility and pay. Less-specialized workers may have a greater opportunity to increase their earnings through *occupational* mobility within their present locale (box II in Figure 14-1). That route may not be open to highly specialized workers who therefore may use *geographic* migration to achieve gains in earnings.

---

[5]Jacob Mincer, "Family Migration Decisions," *Journal of Political Economy,* October 1978, pp. 749–774. Julie DaVanzo also found that the labor force participation by wives has a negative effect on mobility. The higher the *percentage* of total family income earned by the wife, however, the greater the likelihood of family migration. See *Why Families Move: A Model of the Geographic Mobility of Married Couples,* Monograph 48, Employment and Training Administration, U.S. Department of Labor, 1977.

[6]Larry H. Long, "Migration Differentials by Education and Occupation: Trends and Variations," *Demography,* May 1973, p. 245.

Other factors are also at work here. College-educated workers are more apt to get transferred to new geographic locations and, if not transferred, are more likely than those with fewer years of schooling to have new jobs already in place upon migrating. Thus, the probability of their failing to find a job once they move to the new area is zero, and the expected earnings gain over their lifetimes is increased. Finally, people who have college degrees may attach fewer psychic costs, Z, to leaving their hometowns. Many college students initially migrate to new areas to attend school in the first place, and this experience may make it easier for them to move again when new economic opportunities are present. Or, perhaps the fact that these people moved geographically to attend college indicates that they have lower innate psychic costs of, or stronger preferences for, migration than do those who did not make that same choice initially. For whatever reasons, studies show that people who move once are more inclined to migrate again.

Distance. The probability of migrating is inversely related to the distance a person must move. The greater the distance, the less information a potential migrant is likely to possess about the job opportunities available. Also, transportation costs usually increase with distance. Finally, the longer the physical distance of the move, the more probable it is that psychic costs will be substantial. With respect to such costs, it is one matter to move across town, another to move to a nearby state, and still another to migrate across the country or to another nation. Psychic costs may be partially reduced, but not necessarily eliminated, by following "beaten paths" and congregating in specific neighborhoods within the destination area. That is, migrants often follow the routes previously taken by family, friends, and relatives. These earlier migrants ease the transition for those who follow by providing job information, employment contacts, temporary living quarters, and cultural continuity. But the longer the distance of the move, the less available is the information about wage disparities and the greater is the psychic cost. Hence, there is less likelihood that one will migrate.[7]

Unemployment Rates. Based on the human capital model, high unemployment rates in an "origin" location should increase the net benefits from migrating and *push* workers away. That is, an unemployed person must assess the probability of gaining employment in the *origin* location relative to the probability of gaining employment at the potential *destination*. While evidence on this matter is surprisingly mixed, recent studies find that (1) families headed by *unemployed* persons *are* more likely to migrate than others, and (2) the rate of unemployment at the origin *does* affect out-migration.[8] Such out-migration may

---

[7]Henry W. Herzog, Jr. and Alan M. Schlottmann, "Labor Force Migration and Allocative Efficiency in the United States: The Roles of Information and Psychic Costs," *Economic Inquiry*, July 1981, pp. 459–475.

[8]See DaVanzo, op. cit., and "Does Unemployment Affect Migration?—Evidence from Micro Data," *Review of Economics and Statistics*, November 1978, pp. 32–37.

not always be as great as might be expected, however, when the decision makers are mainly older and less-educated workers or when unemployment compensation and other income transfers are relatively high.

Does the unemployment rate at the possible destination influence the migration decision by affecting the probability of getting employment and therefore increasing the *expected value* of discounted net benefits? No definitive conclusion can be reached on this question. For one thing, the general unemployment rate does not always reflect the probability that a specific *individual* will find employment. Also, in-migration itself can increase unemployment rates at the destination. Nevertheless, one generalization is possible: Currently unemployed workers tend to migrate to destinations which are characterized by lower-than-average unemployment rates.

Other Factors. Many other factors may influence migration. We list only a few of them here. First, studies show that home ownership tends to deter migration.[9] Second, occupational licensure reduces migration by impeding the flow of licensed practioners among states that have differing requirements.[10] Third, state and local government policies often influence labor migration. Examples of these policies include (1) tax laws which affect the disposable income of individual citizens, (2) per capita government expenditures for government services in an area, and (3) policies which have an impact on the location of industries.[11] Fourth, federal defense contracts appear to shift labor regionally in the United States.[12] Fifth, in the case of international migration, the language spoken at the destination is a prime factor affecting mobility. Immigration quotas and emmigration prohibitions also greatly influence international migration. Additionally, many international migrants are pushed from their present places of residence by political repression and war. Sixth, union membership may be a determining factor. By providing workers with a voice with which to change undesirable working conditions, unions may reduce voluntary "exits" and thereby reduce mobility and migration (Chapter 8). Or, from a different perspective, perhaps the wage gains that unions secure for workers reduce the incentive for members to migrate to new jobs. Seventh, some scholars suggest that people increasingly have placed a high priority on environmental quality in their migration decisions.[13] Although extremely diverse, these factors share a common feature in that they all influence V_p in equation (14-1) by affecting either the expected gains from migrating, or the expected costs, or some combination of both.

[9]DaVanzo, *Why Families Move.*

[10]For the effect of occupational licensing on the mobility of lawyers, see B. Peter Pashigian, "Occupational Licensing and the Interstate Mobility of Professionals," *Journal of Law and Economics,* April 1979, pp. 1–26.

[11]R. J. Cebula, "A Survey of the Literature on the Migration-Impact of State and Local Government Policies," *Public Finance,* vol. 34, no. 1, 1979, pp. 69–84.

[12]Philip L. Rones, "Moving to the Sun: Regional Job Growth, 1968–1978," *Monthly Labor Review,* March 1980, p. 15.

[13]Larry H. Long and Kristen A. Hansen, "Reasons for Interstate Migration," *Current Population Reports, Special Studies,* no. 81, Bureau of the Census, March 1979, p. 78.

THE CONSEQUENCES OF MIGRATION

The consequences of domestic and international migration have several dimensions. Initially, we will examine the *individual* gains from migration by asking: What is the return on this form of investment in human capital? We then will analyze the increased output accruing to *society* from migration. There we will also attempt to sort out the *distribution* of net gains. Who benefits? Who loses?

Personal Gains. People obviously expect to increase their lifetime utility when they *voluntarily* decide to migrate from one area to another. One interesting way to conceptualize this expected gain is to ask: What amount of money would we have to pay to entice the migrant to reject the job opportunity? This dollar amount is an estimate of the migrant's expected gain from moving to the new location.

Empirical studies confirm that migration increases the lifetime earnings of the average mover.[14] The estimated rate of return is similar to that on other forms of investment in human capital, which means it generally lies in the 10–20 percent range. But at least five caveats and complications must be recognized in this regard.

1. Migration decisions are based on *expected* net benefits, and most are made under circumstances of uncertainty and imperfect information. High *average* rates of return do not imply returns which are positive for *all* migrants.

In many instances, the expected gain from migration simply does not materialize—the anticipated job is not found at the destination, the living costs are higher in the new area than anticipated, the psychic costs of being away from family and friends are greater than expected, the anticipated raises and promotions are not forthcoming. Hence, it is not surprising to discover the presence of major *backflows* in migration patterns. Although this return migration is costly to those involved, it does perform a useful economic function: It increases the availability of information about the destination to other potential migrants, thereby enabling *them* to assess better the benefits and costs of moving. This makes subsequent migration more efficient.

We should also be aware that not all return migration indicates an unprofitable investment in human capital. Some people temporarily migrate as a way to accumulate wealth or enhance their stock of human capital via on-the-job training or after-work education. Most return to their original locations upon reaching their financial or human capital goals. For example, many of those who built the Alaskan pipeline returned to the lower forty-eight states upon completion of

---

[14]For example, see John B. Lansing and J. N. Morgan, "The Effect of Geographical Mobility on Income," *Journal of Human Resources*, Fall 1967, pp. 475–494. For a more recent article on this subject see Stephen C. Farber, "Post-Migration Earnings Profiles: An Application of Human Capital and Job Search Models," *Southern Economic Journal*, January 1983, pp. 693–705.

their task. Also, many illegal aliens who cross the U.S.-Mexican border return to Mexico.[15]

2. Lifetime income gains from migration do not necessarily mean that migrants receive gains from earnings during the first few postmigration years.

Studies show that some migrants experience earnings that are lower than previous earnings in the first few years after moving. These reductions, however, tend to be followed by more than commensurate increases in earnings in later years. Stated differently, some migrants accept a short-term postmigration *reduction* in earnings as an investment cost for faster rate of growth of future earnings.

3. Increases in lifetime earnings do not imply that migrants necessarily will receive annual earnings equal to those received by people already at the destination.

The skills which migrants possess are not always perfectly transferable between regions (because of occupational licensure), between employers (because of specific training), or between nations (because of language and other factors). This lack of *skill transferability* may mean that migrants—although perhaps improving their own wage—may be paid less than similarly trained, educated, and employed workers at the destination. But, on the other hand, migration tends to be characterized by *self-selection*. Because some migrants choose to move while others with similar skills do not, it is possible that the former have greater motivation for personal economic achievement and greater willingness to sacrifice current consumption for higher levels of later consumption. As Chiswick has pointed out:

> Such self-selected immigrants would tend to have higher earnings than the native born in the destination, if it were not for the disadvantage of being foreign born. Combining the [negative] effects of skill transferability and favorable self-selection suggests that the earnings of the foreign born may eventually equal and then surpass those of the native born.[16]

This in fact *is* the case for foreign-born persons who immigrate to the United States. For example, given equal amounts of education and premigration labor experience, male immigrants on the average achieve earnings parity with their native-born cohorts after 11 to 15 years, and after that have higher earnings by as much as 5 percent.[17]

4. A gain in family earnings from migration does not necessarily imply a gain in earnings for *both* working spouses.

Several studies have discovered that, on the average, migration increases the

---

[15]Michael J. Piore, *Birds of Passage: Migrant Labor and Industrial Societies* (Cambridge, England: Cambridge University Press, 1979), pp. 149–154.

[16]Barry R. Chiswick, ''Immigrant Earning Patterns by Sex, Race, and Ethnic Groupings,'' *Monthly Labor Review*, October 1980, p. 22.

[17]Ibid., p. 23. Also see Chiswick's ''The Effect of Americanization on Foreign-Born Men,'' *Journal of Political Economy*, October 1978, pp. 897–921 and James Long, ''The Effect of Americanization on Earnings: Some Evidence for Women,'' *Journal of Political Economy*, June 1980, pp. 620–629.

earnings of husbands but tends to reduce the earnings for wives, at least over the following 5-year period.[18] Apparently the higher average earnings and stronger labor force attachment of husbands relative to wives entices families to migrate in response to improved earnings for the husband. These moves, on the average, increase the family's income but they also reduce either the wife's incentive to work (income effect), her market opportunities, or some combination of the two.

5. A positive rate of return to migration does not necessarily imply higher earnings than would have accrued had past wage rates continued to be earned.

Some migrants are pushed into moving by job loss or political repression. For these persons job mobility is not totally voluntary. For example, suppose that Smith, a 50-year-old Ohio steelworker, earns $18 an hour in wages and fringe benefits, has children in college, and has lived all of his life in the same locale. If Smith is displaced from his job because of a factory shutdown, exhausts his unemployment benefits, and eventually finds a job at $12 an hour in a new occupation in the southwest, can we conclude that migration enhanced his well-being? Considerable misunderstanding exists on this very point. The job loss and its consequences for Smith and his family are indeed severe in that income from work falls to zero. But once this event occurs, Smith faces a new set of prospective earnings streams over the remainder of his work life. For illustrative purposes, let us assume that the highest paying job he can find in his present locale is at $8 an hour. Therefore, by migrating to the southwest where he can earn $12 an hour, Smith *does* increase his lifetime earnings, other things being equal, even though these earnings are considerably lower than those that *would have accrued* in the absence of the job loss. To repeat: Migration increases lifetime earnings for most movers; it does not always increase earnings above levels which existed prior to a job loss.

Wage Narrowing and Efficiency Gains. Economic efficiency is said to exist when a nation achieves the greatest possible real national output or income from its available land, labor, capital, and entrepreneurial resources. Labor mobility is a *crucial* factor in approaching this goal. To demonstrate this proposition, let us make several simplifying assumptions. First, suppose that there are only two labor markets, each perfectly competitive and each situated in a different geographic locations. Second, suppose that each labor market contains a fixed number of workers and that there is no unemployment in either market. Third, let us assume that nonwage job amenities and locational attributes are the same in both areas. A fourth assumption is that capital is immobile. Finally, we assume that workers possess perfect information about wages and working conditions in both markets and that migration between the two markets is costless.

[18]For example, see Solomon Polachek and Francis Horvath, "A Life Cycle Approach to Migration," in Ronald G. Ehrenberg (ed.), *Research in Labor Economics* (Greenwich, Conn.: JAI Press, 1977), pp. 103–149 and Stephen Sandell, "Women and the Economics of Migration," *Review of Economics and Statistics,* November 1977, p. 410.

1. Numerical illustration. Let us first approach this topic numerically and then examine it graphically. Columns 1_A and 2_A in Table 14-1 display the demand for labor in market A, while columns 1_B and 2_B show it for B. Notice that the wages are given in *annual* terms and that, because of our assumption of perfect competition in the product and labor markets, these wages equal the value of the marginal product (VMP) of labor.[19] Columns 3_A and 3_B cumulate the VMP data to show the value of the total product (VTP) associated with each level of employment. Also, notice that the VMP is greater for each labor input in labor market A than in B. This difference in the strength of labor demand is not crucial to our analysis but presumably arises from a greater capital and technological endowment in A than in B, so that the marginal product of labor is higher in market A.

Now let us suppose that *initially* 2 workers are employed in market A and each earns $23,000 annually (boxed figure), while 8 workers, earning $7,000 apiece, are working in B (boxed figure). Next, we relax the assumption that these are separate markets and observe that, given our *other* assumptions, workers in B will migrate to labor market A in pursuit of higher earnings.

What will happen to annual earnings in the respective markets as this migration occurs? The number of workers in A will *increase,* causing the market wage there to fall. In region B, the corresponding *decline* in the quantity of labor will increase the equilibrium wage. Migration will continue until the wage advantage in A is totally eliminated. This occurs in Table 14-1 at $15,000 (cir-

---

[19]If this is not clear, the reader may want to review the discussion pertinent to Table 5-2.

TABLE 14-1

Allocative Efficiency: The Role of Labor Mobility

	Labor Market A			Labor Market B	
(1_A)	**(2_A)** VMP$_A$	**(3_A)**	**(1_B)**	**(2_B)** VMP$_B$	**(3_B)**
Workers	**Annual Wage**	**VTP$_A$**	**Workers**	**Annual Wage**	**VTP$_B$**
1	$25,000	$ 25,000	1	$21,000	$ 21,000
2	23,000	48,000	2	19,000	40,000
3	21,000	69,000	3	17,000	57,000
4	19,000	88,000	4	15,000	72,000
5	17,000	105,000	5	13,000	85,000
6	15,000	120,000	6	11,000	96,000
7	13,000	133,000	7	9,000	105,000
8	11,000	144,000	8	7,000	112,000
9	9,000	153,000	9	5,000	117,000
10	7,000	160,000	10	3,000	120,000

cled data). At this annual wage, employers in the highly capital-endowed region
A will hire 6 workers, while those in the less-endowed area B will hire 4
workers. To generalize: Assuming perfect competition, costless information, and
costless migration, market wages will equal the value of the marginal product of
labor ($W = VMP$), and labor will relocate until VMPs are equal in all labor
markets ($VMP_A = VMP_B$).

Does this migration of labor enhance the total value of output in our hypothetical nation? To determine the answer, again note Table 14-1, columns 3_A
and 3_B. Before migration transpired, the value of the total product (VTP) was
$48,000 in labor market A and $112,000 in B. Thus the combined premigration
GNP was $160,000 (= $48,000 + $112,000). And after migration? A glance at
the table shows it to be $192,000. The 6 workers in A produce a combined
output valued at $120,000, while the 4 workers in B produce $72,000. In this
simple model then we observe that wage differentials create an incentive for
labor to move from one market to another. This mobility, or migration, equalizes
wages and results in allocative efficiency; that is, it generates the highest possible
value of total output.

2. Graphic portrayal. We can easily show graphically both the wage narrowing and efficiency gains from migration. For variety and to extend our focus,
let us now employ an international, rather than an interregional, example.
Figure 14-2 (a) shows the demand for labor in the United States, and graph (b)
portrays the labor demand curve for Mexico.

FIGURE 14-2 THE EFFICIENCY GAINS FROM MIGRATION
The migration of labor from low-wage Mexico (b) to high-wage United States (a) will increase the
national output and reduce the average wage rate in the United States and produce the opposite
effects in Mexico. The output gain of $DBCE$ in the United States exceeds the loss of $JHIK$ in Mexico;
therefore, the net value of the combined outputs from the two nations rises.

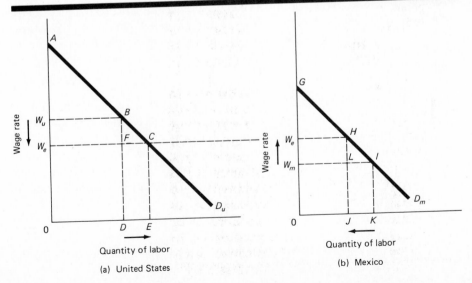

(a) United States

(b) Mexico

Suppose that the employment and wage levels in the United States and Mexico are $0D$, W_u, and $0K$, W_m respectively. Because information is assumed to be perfect and migration is assumed to be costless, labor will flow from Mexico to the United States until the equilibrium wage of W_e is achieved in each nation. Notice the positive efficiency gains accruing to the "world" from this migration. The United States *gains* national output equal to the area $DBCE$ in graph (a), and Mexico *loses* national output equivalent to the area $JHIK$ in graph (b). Because the U.S. gain exceeds the Mexican loss, the total value of the combined output produced by the two nations rises. Stated differently, the sum of the areas $0ACE$ in graph (a) and $0GHJ$ in (b) exceeds the premigration areas $0ABD$ plus $0GIK$. Conclusion? Given our assumptions, wage-induced labor migration—whether internal or international—tends to increase the total income and output in the *combined* origin and destination. Quite simply, migration enables a larger total real output to be achieved from a given amount of resources.

External Effects. The generalization drawn from Table 14-1 and Figure 14-2 raises an important question: If the efficiency gains from migration are so direct and evident, why do so many people in origin and destination locales view migration negatively? Although numerous noneconomic factors are also at work, much of the explanation *is* economic in character and can be understood by analyzing **migration externalities**, or third-party effects. These externalities can be "real" or "pecuniary" and either positive or negative.

1. Real negative externalities. Real negative externalities are effects of private actions which spill over to third parties and create misallocations of resources (economic inefficiency). You may recall the example of water pollution. If a firm produces a product and in the process pollutes a river used by downstream municipalities, recreational enthusiasts, and industries, then the firm fails to cover all the costs of its actions. As a consequence, the price of the product the firm produces is too low, more resources are devoted to producing this output than is socially optimal, and downstream users incur costs which absorb further resources. In some circumstances, mass migration generates similar negative spillovers. As Thurow points out:

> Private incomes may increase enough to more than make up for the costs of moving, but the social costs of accommodating in a crowded urban area may exceed the net private gain. More public services must be provided, and congestion may increase. Excess capacity, and hence waste, may develop in the production of social services (schools, etc.) in areas from which people are moving, and new investment in social services may be needed in areas to which they are moving.[20]

[20]Lester C. Thurow, *Investment in Human Capital* (Belmont, Calif.: Wadsworth Publishing Company, 1970), p. 231.

Put simply, where negative externalities from migration are substantial and diffuse, the private gains to migrants and employers will overstate the net gain to society. Under these circumstances, more migration will occur than is consistent with achieving an optimal allocation of society's resources. For example, this outcome occasionally occurs when substantial migration to a "boom town" creates increases in congestion, crime, and other external costs.

2. Pecuniary externalites: income redistribution. Most of the expressed opposition to emigration and immigration, however, arises not from these potential real externalities but rather from numerous pecuniary—or financial—ones. Pecuniary externalities may be defined as acts which do not affect total output but instead redistribute income among individuals and groups. Such redistributive effects typically give rise to active resistance on the part of adversely affected groups and engender heated political debate. Careful analysis of Figure 14-2 reveals several redistributive impacts of migration.

First, note that, while immigration from Mexico to the United States *increases* the total product in the United States, it *reduces* it in Mexico. Stated more generally, migration increases the value of the total product produced in the combined economies of the origin and destination but, under most conditions, these gains accrue to the destination. There are exceptions, of course. As an extreme example, if the *JK* workers who migrate to the United States are unemployable (value of marginal product = 0), then no increased output is forthcoming and the destination nation will end up being the loser by virtue of having to support the migrants. Conversely, the origin nation will gain in that its fixed national output will be shared among fewer people. Also, many migrants save a large portion of their wages and either send these funds home or bring them back as a lump sum at the end of their temporary stay. In these cases the origin nation captures a share of the efficiency gains. But when migration is permanent, is in response to higher wages in the destination nation, and involves migrants who leave jobs in the origin nation, the destination nation experiences an increase in national income while the origin nation loses. These distributional impacts partially explain why "brain drains"—the emigration of highly skilled workers—are a source of economic concern for some nations of the world.[21]

A second income distribution consequence of migration is also evident from Figure 14-2. Immigration increases the supply of labor in the United States from $0D$ to $0E$, which drives down the average wage rate from W_u to W_e and reduces the wage bill *to native U.S. workers* from $0W_uBD$ to $0W_eFD$. Notice that immigration may or may not increase the total wage bill in the United States—that depends on the elasticity of labor demand (Figure 5-6). It is clear, however, that the influx of the *DE* workers reduces the wage bill accruing to the $0D$ native U.S. workers. In Mexico, the reduction in labor supply *increases* the wage rate (W_e

---

[21]"Brain drains" also are viewed negatively because the origin nation loses the return on investments in human capital which it may have either paid for in full or partially subsidized. For a relatively recent discussion of brain drains see Viem Kevok and Hayne Leland, "An Economic Model of the Brain Drain," *The American Economic Review*, March 1982, pp. 91–100.

rather than W_m) for those who remain. Another generalization thus emerges: Immigration is likely to be opposed by laborers at the destination (region or nation) while workers in the place of origin (area) are likely to support emigration. These differing perspectives again reflect the reality that, although migration generates net efficiency gains, it also creates redistributional effects which result in income gainers and losers.

A third potential for opposition to migration by some groups in origin and destination locales arises from the impact of migration on labor income relative to capital income. We again return to Figure 14-2, graph (a). Immigration increases the total *nonimmigrant* national income in the United States by the triangle *FBC*. To see why, note that the value of the total product rises from 0*ABD* to 0*ACE* in the United States. Of the total gain (*DBCE*), migrants receive *DFCE*. This leaves triangle *FBC* as the increase in total *nonimmigrant* income. Now recall that in the previous paragraph we concluded that the wage bill to native U.S. workers *falls*. So who receives the gain that native workers lose? The answer, of course, is U.S. businesses. They gain area W_eW_uBF at the expense of native U.S. workers and also obtain the added product shown by the triangle *FBC*. Thus this simple model suggests that "business interests" gain added income from immigration—at least in the short run—and conversely actually lose income when substantial out-migration occurs. This helps explain why some U.S. businesses historically have recruited foreign workers to come to the United States. For example, Chinese workers were recruited to help build the railroads, and migrant agricultural workers presently are recruited to help harvest U.S. crops and produce.

The conclusion that businesses gain from migration at the expense of domestic workers must be tempered by the fact that this is a short-run, partial-equilibrium model. The theoretical possibilities become more complicated when a long-run, general-equilibrium approach is used and when various assumptions are relaxed. For example, the new migrants are likely to spend portions of their earnings in the United States. This will increase the *demand* for many types of labor and may increase wages for workers who are not close substitutes for the specific immigrant labor. Additionally, the gain in business income relative to the stock of U.S. capital increases the rate of return on capital. This tends to increase domestic investment spending and consequently enlarges the stock of U.S. capital. In situations where capital and labor are complements, the marginal product of labor will rise and hence labor demand will increase. Thus, in the long run, part of the negative impact of immigration on the wage rate may be lessened. But the basic point is quite clear: Differing views of the desirability of open migration policies, illegal alien problems, and "brain drains" can partially be understood in the context of the actual and perceived redistributional effects of migration.

One final distributional outcome merits discussion. An inflow of immigrants can affect the distribution of disposable income in a destination nation or area through its effect on transfer payments and tax collections. If the immigrants to the United States in Figure 14-2 are highly educated and skilled professionals, for example, we would expect little opposition from the general U.S. public.

These workers most probably will be net taxpayers and not major recipients of cash and in-kind transfer payments. However, if the immigrants are illiterate, low-skilled individuals who are not likely to find permanent employment in the United States, then this influx may necessitate increased government spending on transfer and social service programs. As a consequence, this specific immigration may produce higher taxes for U.S. citizens, lower average transfer payments to native low-income persons, or some combination of each. Thus both taxpayers and low-income residents in the United States may oppose the migration. A real externality might even result from the increased taxes and transfers through a disincentive impact on labor supply (Chapters 2 and 9). This rests on the assumption, of course, that the immigrants are eligible for the transfer programs and heavily use them. In fact, empirical evidence indicates that immigrants tend to be less likely than the native U.S. population to receive welfare payments.[22]

It may be worthwhile at this point to summarize our analysis. We have observed that migration (1) raises the lifetime earnings of the average migrant; (2) increases the value of the combined total output and income of the places of origin and destination; (3) causes wage narrowing among similar workers; and (4) creates externalities which, if real, may reduce the efficiency gains of migration and if pecuniary may produce income redistribution effects.

CAPITAL AND PRODUCT FLOWS

Table 14-1 and Figure 14-2 overstate the probable extent of labor migration between two regions or nations for reasons other than those associated with the costs of obtaining information and migrating. In reality, through differing rates of investment, capital itself is mobile in the long run. Also, products made in one locale are sold in many others. These facts have considerable significance for labor migration.

The impacts of *capital mobility* and interregional or international trade on wage differentials and therefore on labor migration are illustrated in Figure 14-3. Here we use the United States and South Korea in a simplified example. Notice initially that given the labor demand curves D in each nation, wages in the United States, W_u, exceed those in South Korea, W_k. Our previous analysis implied that this wage differential would induce Korean workers to migrate to the United States. But other forces are also at work. The lower Korean wage rate might cause some U.S. producers to abandon production facilities in the United States and construct new facilities in Korea. We would expect this increase in capital in Korea to increase the marginal product (MP) and value of marginal product (VMP) of labor there. The labor demand curve therefore would shift outward, say to D_1 as shown in graph (b) of Figure 14-3. Conversely, the lower stock of capital in the United States would result in a reduction in labor demand from D to D_1 here (graph a).

[22]Francine Blau, "The Use of Transfer Payments by Immigrants," *Industrial and Labor Relations Review*, January 1984, pp. 222–239.

Note in the figure that the increase in labor demand from D to D_1 in South Korea raises the market wage from W_k to W_e. In the United States, the decline in demand from D to D_1 lowers the wage from W_u to W_e. Capital mobility thus has removed the wage disparity in our model and eliminated the incentive for labor to migrate. But as is true with labor mobility, migration of capital is very costly and is impeded by many real-world economic, political, and legal obstacles. For example, U.S. producers of meat products would not be likely to find it profitable to move to South Korea to realize savings in labor costs. Other costs such as transporting livestock to Korean production facilities and shipping meat products to U.S. markets would simply be too high. Thus, while significant flows of capital *have* occurred (for example, from the northeast in the United States to the south and southwest and from the United States to South Korea, Mexico, and elsewhere), their role in narrowing wage differentials has been limited. But the key point is that, to the extent that capital is mobile, wage differentials between areas tend to be smaller and thus less labor migration will occur than if investment is confined to the domestic economy.[23]

Interregional and international trade have a similar potential effect on wage differences and labor mobility. Again return to Figure 14-3. Let us now suppose that capital and labor are immobile, U.S. and South Korea workers are homogeneous, and the costs of transporting goods between the two nations are zero.

[23]For a recent critical discussion of American capital exports, see Seymour Melman, *Profits without Production* (New York: Alfred A. Knopf, 1983), chap. 1.

FIGURE 14-3 THE IMPACT OF CAPITAL AND PRODUCT FLOWS ON WAGE DIFFERENTIALS

A high wage rate in the United States, W_u, and a low wage rate in South Korea, W_k, may cause either (1) flows of capital from the United States and toward South Korea, or (2) a price advantage for Korean-produced goods. In either case, the demand for labor is likely to increase in South Korea and decline in the United States. Thus the wage rate differential will narrow and consequently no labor migration will occur.

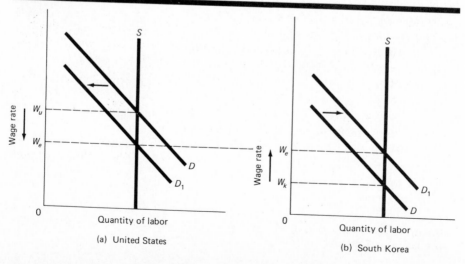

(a) United States

(b) South Korea

What effect will the low Korean wage W_k compared to the high U.S. wage W_u have on the relative competitiveness of Korean versus U.S. goods? Assuming that competition forces product prices down to marginal costs in both nations, U.S. consumers would reallocate their expenditures toward the lower-priced Korean goods. This would increase the total demand for these imports and eventually increase the derived demand for Korean labor. As shown by the outward shift of the labor demand curve from D to D_1 in Figure 14-3 (b), this would cause the Korean wage rate to rise. The opposite chain of events would occur in the United States. Here, reduced product demand would cause the derived demand for U.S. labor to shift inward from D to D_1 and the wage to fall to W_e. This wage narrowing via product flows diminishes the extent of labor migration, once we relax the assumption that labor is immobile.

But, in reality, transportation costs are so high for many goods and services that shipping them long distances is not economical. Hence, trade can be expected to narrow, but not equalize, wages in the long run. Conclusion: Labor migration, capital mobility, and trade between regions and nations all complement one another in promoting an efficient allocation of resources. Labor mobility simply is one aspect of the broader mobility of resources and commodities in the economy. In fact, the U.S. government has at times promoted investment in undeveloped nations and has reduced trade barriers as ways to slow immigration from those nations into the United States. In other instances, however, the government has penalized investment by U.S. firms abroad and enacted tariffs and import quotas to protect domestic employment and wage rates (Chapter 10).

U.S. IMMIGRATION POLICY AND ISSUES

The foregoing analysis of the motivations for migration, the efficiency gains produced by this mobility, and the problem of gainers versus losers provides the tools necessary for understanding some of the controversies surrounding U.S. immigration patterns and policies.[24]

Before World War I, immigration to the United States was virtually unimpeded. The great influx of foreign labor which occurred in the nineteenth century contributed to economic growth and to rising levels of per capita income. The flow of immigrants was slowed by World War I and the restrictive Immigration Acts of 1921 and 1924. These acts established immigration quotas for various nationalities based on the number of foreign-born persons of that nationality in the United States in specific census years. Additionally, the laws allowed several categories of nonquota immigrants to enter the United States. Between 1921 and 1965, only 10 million foreigners entered the United States, and over

---

[24]The reader who is interested in a broader examination of U.S. immigration policy and issues should see Mary M. Kritz (ed.), *U.S. Immigration and Refugee Policy: Global and Domestic Issues* (Lexington, Mass: Lexington Books, 1983).

one-half were nonquota immigrants, including 900,000 Canadians, 500,000 Mexicans, and thousands of spouses and children of U.S. citizens.

In 1965, the Immigration and Nationality Amendments to the 1952 Immigration and Nationality Act shifted the preferences of the quota system away from northern and western European immigrants and toward a more evenly balanced set of nationalities. Further amendments established the present world-wide annual ceiling of 270,000 immigrants, set an annual limit of 20,000 persons per nation, and developed a six-point preference system which gives priority to family members and people who have specific job skills. Furthermore, the present law allows 50,000 political refugees to enter the United States annually. The president and Congress can adjust this refugee limit upward and have frequently done so for special situations. For example, almost 140,000 political refugees arrived from Cuba and Haiti in 1980. Hence, as observed in Table 14-2, it is not uncommon for over one-half a million quota and nonquota immigrants to enter the United States legally in a given year.

To these totals we must add the annual number of illegal aliens who arrive mainly from Mexico, the Caribbean, and South America. Also, government officials estimate that 10 to 20 percent of the 7 million foreign nationals who reside in the United States under student and other nonimmigrant visas fail to leave by the expiration date. A small percentage of these people become permanent undocumented aliens. According to the U.S. Census Bureau, there were 5 to 7.5 million illegal residents in the United States in 1984.

The large inflow of refugee immigrants from Southeast Asia and Cuba, together with the illegal alien problem, has made immigration and immigration policy a major public issue in the United States. The main reason for the general concern is that many recent immigrants and most undocumented aliens are unskilled workers. People fear that these individuals and their families reduce employment opportunities for the existing work force, depress wage rates in already low-wage labor markets, and put a financial strain on United States taxpayers via their receipt of transfer payments and use of social service programs. Are these concerns justified? Unfortunately, a simple "yes" or "no"

TABLE 14-2

Net Legal Civilian Immigration to the United States, Selected Years

Year	Total (Thousands)	Year	Total (Thousands)
1960	327	1978	508
1965	373	1979	539
1970	438	1980	787
1975	449	1981	624
1976	353	1982	532
1977	394	1983	517

Source: U.S. Bureau of the Census, *Statistical Abstracts of the United States*, 1985, p. 9.

answer cannot be provided. But let us attempt to assess each of the three concerns as they relate specifically to the *illegal alien* component of the immigration issue.

Illegal Immigration: Employment Effects. Some observers contend that the deportation of illegal aliens would increase domestic employment on a one-for-one basis. That is, they argue that a given number of jobs exist in the economy, and that if one of these positions is taken by an illegal worker, then that job is no longer available for a legal resident. At the other extreme, some people claim that illegal aliens only accept work which resident workers are unwilling to perform. As we will demonstrate, both views are overly simplistic.

Figure 14-4 illustrates a market for unskilled agricultural workers. The curve D is the typical labor demand curve with which we are familiar. Supply curve S_d portrays the labor supply of *domestic* workers, while curve S_t reflects the *total* supply of domestic *and* illegal workers. Hence, the horizontal distance between S_t and S_d is the number of illegal aliens who will offer their labor services at each wage rate.

Given the presence of the illegal aliens, the market wage and level of employment are W_t and Q_t. Notice that at this low wage, *no* domestic workers are willing to work. In this case the minimum acceptable wage of domestic workers is simply too high. Perhaps this is due to the availability of nonwage income, a

FIGURE 14-4 THE IMPACT OF ILLEGAL ALIENS ON DOMESTIC JOBS AND WAGES
The presence of illegal aliens in this low-wage labor market shifts the labor supply curve to S_t and reduces the market wage from W_d to W_t. At W_t, all workers hired are illegal aliens. If the illegal aliens were deported, however, Q_d domestic workers would be employed. Thus it is misleading to conclude that illegal aliens accept jobs which domestic workers will not take. It is also misleading to conclude that the deportation of illegal aliens would create employment for native workers on a one-for-one basis.

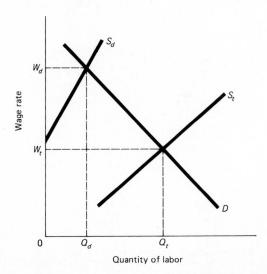

Quantity of labor

high marginal value or opportunity cost associated with leisure, or a perceived lack of possibilities for advancement in the job. Can we therefore conclude that "illegal aliens take work which U.S. workers do not want"? Clearly in Figure 14-4 the answer is "yes," *but* only if we add "at the low wage W_t." If all the illegal aliens were deported, the wage would rise to W_d in this market, and *some* U.S. workers, specifically $0Q_d$, would indeed be willing to do this work. The point is this: So-called "undesirable" work will attract U.S. workers *if* the wage rate is sufficiently high (Chapter 12). If the illegal aliens are deported and if employers continue to offer wage rate W_t, there will be a shortage, $0Q_t$. But this shortage occurs because the wage rate has not been allowed to rise to its equilibrium, not because U.S. workers are unwilling to do work which illegal aliens are willing to perform. The willingness to work at any given job depends partly on the wage rate being paid.

The opposite argument, that illegal aliens reduce domestic employment by an amount equal to the employment of illegal aliens, is also misleading. As shown in Figure 14-4, the presence of the undocumented laborers *increases* the total number of jobs in this low-skilled labor market. In the presence of the illegal migration the number of jobs is Q_t; without the inflow it is only Q_d. It is erroneous to contend that deportation of the Q_t illegal migrants would result in an increase in domestic employment of Q_t. But it *is* correct to say that native employment would increase by the amount Q_d in this labor market. We conclude that illegal immigration does cause *some* substitution of illegal aliens for domestic workers but that the amount of displacement most likely is less than the total employment of the illegal aliens.[25]

Illegal Immigration and Wage Rates. There is little doubt that large inflows of migrants—be they legal or illegal—can depress some wage rates. Note in Figure 14-4 that the increase in labor supply reduces the U.S. market wage from W_d to W_t. In this regard, Smith and Newman found that real wage rates in towns in Texas that border Mexico were about 8 percent lower than in Texas towns further inland.[26]

Organized labor recognizes the negative impact of illegal immigration on the wage rate and therefore strongly supports measures to eliminate it. For example, unions have led the battle to impose fines on firms which knowingly or unknowingly hire undocumented Mexican workers.

The *overall* effect of illegal immigration on the average wage rate in the economy is less clear. Some native workers and illegal immigrants are complements in the production process. This implies that illegal immigration raises the marginal product of these native employees and thus increases the demand for

[25]For an empirical investigation of the extent of job displacement see George E. Johnson, "The Labor Market Effects of Immigration," *Industrial and Labor Relations Review,* April 1980, pp. 331–341.

[26]Barton S. Smith and Robert Newman, "Depressed Wages along the U.S.–Mexico Border: An Empirical Analysis," *Economic Inquiry,* January 1977, pp. 51–66.

their labor services. More concretely, it is possible that illegal immigration raises the wage rates for, say, workers who help transport fruit. Also, spending by illegal aliens in the United States adds to the demand for products and therefore increases the derived demand for labor. For example, the demand for many workers in the barrios of Los Angeles may be greater because of the presence of illegal workers. On the other hand, this impact is reduced because many illegal aliens remit large portions of their pay to their families living abroad.[27]

So what can we conclude concerning the impact of illegal immigration on wage rates? The safest conclusion—given the complexities of the real world—is that *large-scale* illegal immigration does reduce the wage rate for substitutable low-skilled domestic workers. But illegal immigration probably has little *net* impact on the average level of wages in the United States.

Fiscal Impacts of Illegal Immigration. Finally, what are the effects of undocumented aliens upon tax revenues, transfer expenditures, and public services? Illegal migrants do not qualify for public assistance from such programs as Supplemental Security Income (aid for the aged, blind, and disabled), Aid to Families with Dependent Children, and food stamps. Furthermore, fraudulent participation is risky, since it increases the likelihood of discovery and deportation. Also, most illegal aliens are young working males without families, while eligibility for the major transfer programs depends on such characteristics as old age, illness, disability, or position as female head of the household. Studies indicate that most male illegal aliens are net taxpayers. Illegal aliens do use public services such as schools and parks, but most also pay social security taxes, user fees, and sales taxes.[28] Most scholars of the illegal immigration problem conclude that these fiscal effects of illegal immigration are of lesser consequence than the employment and wage effects discussed previously.

SUMMARY

1. Mobility takes numerous forms, including occupational mobility and geographic mobility.
2. The decision to migrate can be viewed from a human capital perspective, by which the present value of expected gains in lifetime earnings are compared to investment costs (transportation expenses, forgone income during the move, and psychic costs).
3. Various factors can influence the decision to migrate. Age is inversely related to the probability of migrating, family status influences the migration decision in several

[27]For evidence on these large remittances see David North and Marion Houstown, *The Characteristics and Role of Illegal Aliens in the U.S. Labor Market: An Exploratory Study* (Washington, D.C.: Linton and Co., Inc., 1976).

[28]Walter Fogel, "Illegal Alien Workers in the United States," *Industrial Relations*, October 1977, p. 255. To the extent that illegal immigrants displace American workers, they may impose indirect costs upon U.S. welfare and income maintenance programs.

ways, educational attainment and mobility are positively related, and unemployment rates in destination areas reduce the probability that an *unemployed* worker will migrate there.

4. The *average* lifetime rate of return on migration is positive and is estimated to be in the 10 to 20 percent range.

5. Labor mobility contributes to allocative efficiency by relocating labor resources away from lower-valued and toward higher-valued employment. Under conditions of perfect competition and costless migration, workers of a given type will relocate until the value of the marginal product of labor (VMP) is the same in all similar employments ($VMP_a = VMP_b = \ldots = VMP_n$), at which point labor is being allocated efficiently.

6. Mass migration of labor generates negative externalities which if real may reduce the efficiency gains of migration, and if pecuniary may alter the distribution of income among various individuals and groups in origin and destination areas.

7. Wage differentials may generate capital and product flows which tend to equalize wages in the long run and reduce the extent of labor migration.

8. U.S. law limits world-wide legal immigration to the United States to 270,000 people annually and places a ceiling of 20,000 on immigrants from a single country. In addition, thousands of political refugees are allowed to enter the country each year.

9. Illegal aliens in the United States do not reduce native employment by the full extent of the employment of the illegals, but they do depress wage rates in some labor markets.

QUESTIONS AND STUDY SUGGESTIONS

1. Key terms and concepts to remember: occupational mobility; geographic mobility; determinants of migration; self-selection; skill transferability; efficiency gains from migration; external effects (real vs. pecuniary); capital mobility; illegal immigration (employment, wage rate, and fiscal impacts).

2. Use equation (14-1) to explain the likely effect of each of the following on the present value of net benefits from migration: (a) age, (b) distance, (c) education, (d) marital status, and (e) the discount rate (interest rate).

3. What is meant by the term "beaten paths"? How do such paths increase V_p in equation (14-1) and thereby increase the likelihood of migration?

4. Why are people who possess *specific* human capital less likely to change jobs, other things being equal, than persons who possess *general* human capital? Does this imply that people who possess large amounts of specific human capital will never migrate? Explain.

5. Use Table 14-1 to determine the impact of wage-induced labor migration on:
   a. the combined output of the two regions
   b. capital versus wage income in the destination region
   c. the average wage rate in the origin region
   d. the total wage bill for the native workers in the destination region

6. Use the variables in equation (14-1) to cite at least two reasons why it may be rational for a family to migrate from one part of the country to another, even though the hypothetical move produces a decline in family earnings in the first year of work following the move.

7. How might a wage differential between two regions be reduced via movements of capital to the low-wage area?
8. Comment: "If we deported the 5 million illegal aliens who are now in the United States, our total national unemployment would decline by 5 million."
9. How might labor mobility and migration affect the degree of monopsony power (Chapter 6) in labor markets?
10. Is it consistent to favor the free movement of labor *within* the United States and be opposed to immigration *into* the United States?
11. If one believes in free international trade, then to be consistent must one also advocate unrestricted international migration of labor?

SELECTED REFERENCES

BRIGGS, VERNON M: *Immigration and the American Labor Force* (Baltimore: The Johns Hopkins University Press, 1984).

CHISWICK, BARRY R. (ed.): *The Gateway: U.S. Immigration Issues and Policies* (Washington, D.C.: American Enterprise Institute for Public Policy Research, 1982).

GREENWOOD, MICHAEL J.: "Research on Internal Migration in the United States: A Survey," *Journal of Economic Literature,* June 1975, pp. 397–433.

KRITZ, MARY M. (ed.): *U.S. Immigration and Refugee Policy* (Lexington, Mass.: D.C. Heath and Company, 1983).

MUELLER, CHARLES F.: *The Economics of Labor Migration: A Behavioral Analysis* (New York: Academic Press, 1982).

PIORE, MICHAEL J.: *Birds of Passage: Migrant Labor and Industrial Societies* (Cambridge, England: Cambridge University Press, 1979).

SJAASTAD, LARRY A.: "The Costs and Returns of Human Migration," *Journal of Political Economy,* October 1962, pp. 80–93.

TIME AND ONE-HALF

LONG-TERM JOBS IN THE U.S. ECONOMY*

While the U.S. labor market is characterized by a high degree of occupational and geographic mobility, there also is a surprising amount of stable, long-term job tenure.

Our discussion of labor mobility in this chapter may conjure up an image of a U.S. work force whose members are repeatedly leaving one employer for a job with another. This image is not entirely accurate. Many changes in occupations do not entail changes in

---

*This is a summary of Robert E. Hall's "The Importance of Lifetime Jobs in the U.S. Economy," *American Economic Review,* September 1982, pp. 716–724.

employers. For example, a football coach at a high school may become an administrator within the same school district, or a production worker may obtain a college degree and be promoted to a supervisory position in the same firm. Also, as indicated previously, much of the geographic mobility in the economy consists of intracorporate transfers of employees. Finally, the often-cited statistic that the median number of years of job tenure is only 3.5 years is misleading. Young workers who make up a large proportion of the labor force cannot possibly have long job tenures. Their short tenures dramatically pull down the median.

To gain a better picture of the degree of long-term jobs in the United States, Hall projected what he calls the "eventual tenure" of jobs currently being held. He defines a job as continuous employment with the same employer or, for those self-employed, continuous activity in the same line of work. Job tenure simply is the number of years since the worker's present job began. Eventual tenure is determined by summing actual present tenure and the projected additional time on the job. Hall estimates the latter by analyzing the number of workers in one age-tenure category who advance to higher age-tenure categories. Table 1 shows the distribution of eventual tenure across all age and tenure categories. It reveals that a significant proportion of workers *do* change jobs quite frequently. Notice that 23.5 percent of the workers have eventual job tenures of less than two years. But the table also discloses other interesting facts. Nearly 60 percent of U.S. workers are currently employed on jobs which eventually will last 5 years or more. More strikingly, almost 28 percent of the work force is in jobs which will last 20 years or more. Seventeen percent of present workers have jobs which, when ended, will be 30 or more years in length. Further analysis by Hall shows that, among workers who are 30 years or older, about 40 percent are in employment which eventually will last 20 or more years. Hall also finds that job tenure for blacks is nearly identical to that for whites.

Conclusion: While ours is definitely a mobile society, it also is a society characterized by stable, near-lifetime employment for a significant proportion of the labor force.

TABLE 1

The Distribution of Eventual Job Tenure

Years	Percent			
0–0.5	9.8			
0.5–1	6.7	23.5		
1–2	7.0			
2–3	5.0			
3–5	13.5			
5–10	14.8			
10–15	10.4			
15–20	4.7			
20–25	4.7	58.0		
25–30	6.2		27.9	
30–35	10.0			
35+	7.0			17.0

Source: Robert E. Hall, "The Importance of Lifetime Jobs in the U.S. Economy," *American Economic Review,* September 1982, p. 720.

CRITIQUES OF ORTHODOX WAGE THEORY

Our analysis of wage determination has centered upon the marginal productivity theory. In its simplest form this theory envisions rational sellers and employers of labor coming together in a competitive market in which their combined decisions yield an equilibrium wage rate and an equilibrium level of employment. Suppliers and demanders of labor are both presumed to be motivated to maximize their well-being or profits. Specifically, on the supply side households make decisions with respect to the amount of time they are willing to devote to labor market activity. These labor supply decisions are part of a household's desire to maximize its utility in a context in which utility depends upon earned income (work), nonmarket work, and leisure. Furthermore, human capital theory is merely an extension of the marginal productivity model. In the long run workers make rational human capital investment decisions, as described in Chapter 4, which increase their productivity and determine both their place in the hierarchy of job skills and their earnings. Labor demand decisions reflect the efforts of employers to hire labor and other inputs in profit-maximizing amounts. The simplest portrayal of orthodox marginal productivity theory is that of Figure 6-4. In this model wage rates function as a market-clearing mechanism. Hence, shifts in labor demand or supply elicit changes in wage rates so that there are no unsatisfied buyers or sellers of labor.

This orthodox interpretation of the labor market has long been a subject of controversy and debate. It is important in our examination of labor markets and wage determination to be familiar, not only with the mainstream or orthodox position, but also with the various critiques of, and alternatives to, that view. Hence, this chapter presents summaries of several of the better-known critiques of orthodox theory.[1] Specifically, we seek to outline (1) the institutionalist conception of the labor market, (2) the notion of internal labor markets, and (3) the theory of dual or segmented labor markets. The reader will find that these three theories are closely related in that they overlap and build upon one another. The

---

[1]The interested reader will find a comprehensive critique of orthodox theory in Lester C. Thurow, *Generating Inequality* (New York: Basic Books, Inc., Publishers, 1975), chap. 3 and app. A. Chapters 4 and 5 of *Generating Inequality* summarize Thurow's "job competition model" as an alternative to the marginal productivity theory.

institutionalist portrayal of labor markets, which was developed after World War II, was in effect the intellectual springboard from which the notions of internal labor markets and labor market duality evolved in the 1960s and 1970s. Similarly, we shall discover that the theory of dual labor markets is primarily concerned with contrasting "good" jobs found in internal labor markets with "bad" jobs located in what are called secondary labor markets. In short, these three unorthodox views have much in common and, in particular, they share the basic idea that institutional factors—unions and collective bargaining, customs and habit, administrative rules and procedures, and the institution of discrimination—greatly dampen and alter the impact of economic forces upon the determination of wage rates, employment, and the allocation of human capital investments.

We will proceed as follows. After a brief survey of the institutionalist conception of labor markets, we will develop the notion of internal labor markets in some detail. What are internal labor markets? Why have they evolved? How do they function? Do they foster or impede economic efficiency? Our attention will then shift to dual labor market theory where some of the basic differences between dualism and orthodox theory will be stressed. The chapter will end with a brief critique of the dual theory.

INSTITUTIONAL ECONOMICS AND WAGE DETERMINATION

The *institutionalist view of labor markets* evolved during the 1940s at a time of rapid union growth (Chapter 7) and the spread of centralized collective bargaining. To the institutionalists the presence of strong unions and collective bargaining had the effect of rendering orthodox wage theory largely irrelevant. In the words of the leading institutionalist spokesman, Arthur M. Ross, "Among all the participants in economic life, the trade union is probably least suited to economic analysis."[2] Collective wage determination under unions is fundamentally different from competitive wage setting, and the difference is not merely one of degree, but of kind. Hence, the institutionalist critique was an effort to provide an alternative construct for understanding wage determination. As such, the institutionalist critique of orthodoxy stressed the following interrelated points.

Conscious Human Decisions. According to the institutionalists, the evolution of collective bargaining has had the effect of making the wage rate an administered rate rather than a market rate. Wages are determined by the "conscious

[2]Arthur M. Ross, *Trade Union Wage Policy* (Berkeley: University of California Press, 1948), p. 7. See also Clark Kerr, "Labor Markets: Their Character and Consequences," *American Economic Review,* May 1950, pp. 278–291 and Paul J. McNulty, *The Origins and Development of Labor Economics* (Cambridge, Mass.: The MIT Press, 1980), chap. 7.

human decisions'' made by union and management representatives around the bargaining table, rather than by the impersonal market forces of supply and demand. Organized labor and the large corporations with which unions bargain seek to alter market forces and in fact have the power to do so. Institutionalists argue that it is more accurate to say that supply and demand adjust to wage rates than it is to assert the reverse.

Unions as Political Institutions. In the judgment of the institutionalists, labor unions are fundamentally political, as opposed to economic, institutions. Collective bargaining is a "pressure game," and the union as a participant is subject to forces of a political nature. For example, union leaders are subjected to pressures from union members, from rival leaders within the union, from rival unions, from employers, and from government. Union leaders try to adjust to these crosscurrents of pressure in a way which will ensure their own survival as leaders and the survival and growth of the unions which they represent. Because of the political character of unions, the economic analysis embodied in the marginal productivity theory is irrelevant or, in Ross' words, "an alien logic." Economic forces are significant only to the extent they generate political pressures with which union leaders must cope. Hence, in the institutionalist view an adverse shift in consumer demand or a recession influences wage and employment determination, not by shifting the demand curve shown in Figure 6-4, but rather through their impact upon employer bargaining attitudes and the pressures exerted by union members upon their leaders. Furthermore, in the political context which dominates the bargaining process, the wage rate becomes an instrument which is manipulated in the interest of furthering the reputations of the union leaders and the security, growth, and prestige of the union as an institution. The wage rate is "a tool for manipulating the loyalty of workers and the approval of the public, and a symbol of victory or defeat in the contest between union and management."[3]

Inappropriateness of Maximizing Assumption. Contrary to orthodox theory, the institutionalist position is that an understanding of union wage policy will "not be found in the mechanical application of any maximization principle."[4] The reader may recall from Chapter 7 the problems involved in models of union behavior which rely on simple maximizing rules. While the formal objective of a business enterprise may be fairly stated as that of profit maximization, a union's purpose is multidimensional and more difficult to define.

> The formal purpose of the union is vaguer than that of the business firm. Profit can be measured in one dimension. "Economic welfare" is a congeries of discrete phenomena—wages, with a dollar dimension; hours of work,

---

[3]Ross, op. cit., p. 100.
[4]Ibid., p. 8.

with a time dimension; and physical working conditions, economic security, protection against managerial abuse, and various rights of self-determination, with no dimension at all. Therefore, the union leader has considerably more discretion in interpreting the formal purpose.[5]

Furthermore, it is impossible to attribute a wealth- or income-maximizing assumption to unions because unions are merely *agents* and not *sellers* of labor. Unions are wage-fixing institutions and, as such, are concerned only partially, if at all, with the employment implications of their wage policies. "The volume of employment associated with a given wage rate is unpredictable before the fact, and the effect of a given rate upon employment is undecipherable after the fact."[6] The reason, according to the institutionalists, is that a "sea of external forces" in the form of productivity changes, shifts in consumer preferences, and changes in overall business conditions cloud and conceal the wage rate–employment relationship. Hence, unions do not act like other sellers; unions are *not* simultaneously concerned with both price (the wage rate) and quantity sold (employment). Because price and quantity are both critical variables in wealth- or income-maximizing behavior, unions cannot be regarded as maximizers in the same sense as business enterprises.

Equitable Comparisons. If the maximization principle is rejected, how then is union wage policy to be explained? In the institutionalist view "it does not require any profound theoretical analysis to understand union wage policy . . . ."[7] What is of critical importance in formulating union wage policy and in determining the structure is **equitable comparisons** based upon ideas of fairness and justice. That is, whether or not a given wage settlement is satisfactory to workers, to the union as an institution, or to the employer is strongly determined by how that wage compares with what other comparable workers are getting and other employers are paying.

> Comparisons are important to the worker. They establish the dividing line between a square deal and a raw deal. He knows that he cannot earn what he would like to have, but he wants what is coming to him. In a highly competitive society, it is an affront to his dignity and a threat to his prestige when he receives less than another worker with whom he can legitimately be compared.[8]

[5]Ibid., p. 27.

[6]Ibid., p. 80.

[7]Ibid., p. 8.

[8]Ibid., p. 51. The brief discussion of pattern bargaining in Chapter 7 is pertinent to this point. We will also discover in Chapter 19 that this "wage imitation" or tendency to base pay demands upon equitable comparisons may foster wage-push inflation.

Such comparisons also reveal how well one union has done as compared to others, thus demonstrating to the union members whether they are getting a fair return for their union dues. In the institutionalist view, comparisons or "wage relativities" are as important—indeed, perhaps more important—than absolute wage rates in determining whether workers are satisfied with their earnings. And, similarly, employers desire to avoid wage bargains which are out of line compared to other employers. If the settlement is too high, employers will lose business to others; if it is too low, worker morale may suffer, causing declines in productivity and profits.

To recapitulate: The institutionalist concept of the labor market holds that such markets are uniquely different from product markets. The twin institutions of unions and collective bargaining make largely irrelevant orthodox theory's notion of individual choices rendered in a utility-maximizing framework. The orthodox view is replaced by the view that collective decisions and market power result in wage rates which are administered, rather than determined by the market. Unions are essentially political, not economic, institutions which pursue various and multidimensional goals. Wage policy is governed, not by the maximization principle, but rather by standards of equity and fairness.

This group of interrelated notions provides the intellectual roots of more recent challenges to the marginal productivity theory. It is to these challenges which we now turn.

INTERNAL LABOR MARKETS

A strict interpretation of neoclassical theory evokes the notion of an auction market in which workers are openly and continuously competing for jobs *and*, conversely, firms persistently bid to attract and retain labor services. Orthodox theory assumes that the firm, as an institution, poses no obstacle or barrier to the competitive pressures of the labor market. That is, it is assumed that the wage rates of every type of labor employed by the firm are determined by market forces. Hence, the wage structures of all firms which happened to employ the same types of workers would be identical. Workers would have access to jobs at all skill levels for which they are qualified, and mobility between firms would be unimpeded and extensive.

But critics of orthodox theory contend, and mainstream economists increasingly agree, that this portrayal is sorely at odds with the real world. The public school teacher, the skilled machinist, and the government bureaucrat, to cite but a few, are *not* faced with the daily prospect of being displaced from their jobs by someone who is equally capable and who is willing to work for a slightly lower salary! Workers, on the one hand, enjoy "job rights," and employers, on the other hand, seek to maintain stable work forces. Although, as indicated in Chapter 14, there is considerable occupational and geographic mobility in our economy, the average worker's employment is in fact quite stable. A recent study concludes that today the typical worker is holding a job which will last for 8 years. A quarter of all workers hold jobs which will last 25 years or more! Even for women—who we know have problems in achieving access to more desirable jobs (Chapter 11)—some 15 percent hold jobs that will last 20 years or more.[9] Indeed, perhaps as much as 80 percent of the labor force participates in "internal labor markets" in which they are substantially shielded from the competitive pressures of the "external labor market."[10]

Characteristics of Internal Labor Markets. What is an internal labor market? How and why do they evolve? What are their implications? An *internal labor market* is "an administrative unit, such as a manufacturing plant, within which the pricing and allocation of labor is governed by a set of administrative rules and procedures" rather than by economic variables.[11] Within many firms we find more or less elaborate hierarchies of jobs, each of which centers upon a certain skill (machinist), a common function (building maintenance), or a single focus of work (the computer). Furthermore, each job hierarchy entails a sequence or progression of jobs which thus forms what is called a mobility chain or *job ladder.* As suggested by Figure 15-1, a new worker will typically enter this job ladder as a trainee in the least skilled job at the bottom of the ladder. The position at which workers gain access to the job ladder is called, for obvious reasons, a *port of entry.* It is through the port of entry that the sequence of jobs which constitute the job ladder makes contact with the *external labor market.* This external labor market is the "auction market" of orthodox theory. That is, in recruiting workers to fill vacancies for the least-skilled position in a job ladder, the firm must compete with other firms who are hiring the same kind of labor. While the market forces of supply and demand may thus be paramount in determining the wage rate paid for the port-of-entry position, market forces are held to be superseded by administrative rules and procedures in explaining the wages paid for other jobs which constitute the job ladder of the internal labor market. The point to be stressed is that within the internal labor market it is institutionalized rules and procedures, along with custom and tradition, which

---

[9]Robert E. Hall, "The Importance of Lifetime Jobs in the U.S. Economy," *American Economic Review,* September 1982, pp. 216–224.

[10]Peter B. Doeringer and Michael J. Piore, *Internal Labor Markets and Manpower Analysis* (Lexington, Mass.: D. C. Heath and Company, 1971), pp. 41–42. A more recent estimate by David M. Gordon, Richard Edwards, and Michael Reich, *Segmented Work, Divided Workers* (Cambridge, England: Cambridge University Press, 1982), pp. 211–212, suggests that about two-thirds of all workers are employed in internal labor markets. John T. Dunlop's, "The Task of Contemporary Wage Theory," in George W. Taylor and Frank C. Pierson (eds.), *New Concepts in Wage Determination* (New York: McGraw-Hill Book Company, 1957), pp. 128–139, is a pioneering statement on the structure of jobs and wages within firms. The Doeringer and Piore book is a comprehensive discussion of the evolution and character of internal labor markets.

[11]Doeringer and Piore, op. cit., pp. 1–2.

are foremost in determining how workers are allocated in the job hierarchy and what wage rates they are paid.

Reasons for Internal Labor Markets. Why do internal labor markets exist? The basic answer to this question is that firms typically encounter significant costs in the recruiting and training of workers and that these costs can be minimized by reducing labor turnover. Let us first consider the matter of training. Internal labor market theorists contend that many job skills tend to be unique and specific to individual enterprises.

> Almost every job involves some specific skills. Even the simplest custodial tasks are facilitated by familiarity with the physical environment specific to the workplace in which they are performed. The apparent routine operation of standard machines can be importantly aided by familiarity with a particular piece of operating equipment. . . . Moreover, performance in some production and most managerial jobs involves a team element, and a critical skill is the ability to operate effectively with the given members of the team. This ability is dependent upon the interaction of the personalities of the

FIGURE 15-1 AN INTERNAL LABOR MARKET
A worker typically enters an internal labor market at the least-skilled port-of-entry job in the job ladder or mobility chain. While the wage rate of the port-of-entry job will be strongly influenced by the forces of demand and supply in the local external labor market, wage rates and the allocation of workers within the internal labor market are governed primarily by administrative rules and procedures. [Adapted from Robert M. Fearn, Labor Economics: The Emerging Synthesis (Cambridge, Mass.: Winthrop Publishers, Inc., 1981), p. 142.]

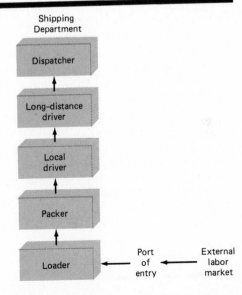

members, and the individual's work "skills" are specific in the sense that skills necessary to work on one team are never quite the same as those required on another.[12]

The specificity of job skills and technology to individual firms means that workers require *specific training* which is most efficiently acquired on the job. The cost of such training, you will recall from Chapter 4, is borne by the employer. But to obtain a return on this investment in human capital, the employer must *retain* specifically trained workers *over a period of time*. The job ladder—the core characteristic of internal labor markets—is the mechanism by which the desired work force stability is achieved.

The mutual advantageousness of the internal labor market to both the firm and to workers merits further comment. As just noted, the reduction of worker turnover increases the return the firm receives on its investments in specific training. Furthermore, the amount of training that a firm needs to provide will be reduced by the presence of the internal labor market. If the firm fills a vacancy from the external labor market, it will have to finance *all* of the specific training which the worker requires. It can avoid much of this cost by simply promoting an internal applicant who, by virtue of having worked for the firm for some time, has already acquired a portion of the specific training that is prerequisite to the job opening. Similarly, recruitment costs will be larger if a position is filled from the external labor market. The firm—even after interviewing and screening—will have only limited knowledge about the quality of workers in the external labor market. But it will have accumulated a great deal of information about members of its present work force. Thus, promoting from within will greatly reduce recruitment and screening costs and lessen the chances of making an error in filling the job. A final advantage of the internal labor market to the firm is that the existence of a clearly defined job ladder will provide an incentive for its existing work force to be disciplined, productive, and continuously motivated to seek new skills.

Internal labor markets also confer advantages upon workers who are accepted into them. Workers who are admitted receive benefits in the form of enhanced job security and built-in opportunities for job training and promotion. Workers need not leave the firm to secure better jobs, but rather may ascend a well-defined sequence of jobs which constitute the job ladder. Furthermore, those in the internal labor market are shielded from the competition of workers in the external labor market. In addition, the formalization and codification of the rules and procedures which govern both worker allocation and wage rates within the internal labor market protect workers from favoritism and capricious managerial decisions. Workers in internal labor markets are more likely to enjoy due process and equitable treatment with respect to layoffs, promotion, and access to training opportunities.

---

[12]Ibid., pp. 15–16.

The Role of Unions. Although the presence of a labor union can accelerate the development of internal labor markets, the cause-effect relationship is rather complicated. Internal labor markets tend to invite unionization; conversely, unions promote or accelerate the evolution of internal labor markets. On the one hand, there are several reasons why the emergence of an internal labor market is conducive to unionization. First, the enhanced stability of the labor force resulting from an internal labor market promotes unionization. A fluid, unstable work force is an obstacle to organization, but a stable group of workers develops a community spirit and perhaps a common set of grievances which leads to formalization through a union. Second, workers in internal labor markets possess specific training which endows them with considerable bargaining power. Remember: Employers must retain specifically trained workers in order to realize a return on their human capital investments. It is only natural that workers might want to express this bargaining power collectively through a union. Finally, the administrative rules and procedures which prevail in the internal labor market tend to define quite clearly the scope and character of managerial decisions. Unionization is a logical response to those instances where managerial actions are at odds with customary rules and procedures. Conversely, the presence of a union can be important in reinforcing the development of an internal labor market. A written collective bargaining agreement codifies, formalizes, and makes more rigid the rules and procedures which prevail in the functioning of an existing internal labor market.

Labor Allocation and the Wage Structure. Let us consider in more detail the promotion process, that is, the allocation of labor, *and* the determination of wages within the internal labor market. The critical point to recall is that in the internal labor market the pricing and allocation of labor are determined, not by the forces of supply and demand, but rather by administrative rules and procedures. Thus in the case of promotions the typical administrative rule is that, other things being roughly equal, the worker who has been on a particular rung of a job ladder for the longest period of time will be promoted to the next rung when an opening occurs. That is, promotions are generally determined on the basis of *seniority*. Seniority is typically tempered, however, by the presumed ability of the individual to perform the job satisfactorily after a trial period. In short, the rules indicate that the "right" to the promotion resides with the most experienced worker, not necessarily the most able worker available from either the internal or external labor market. Similarly, layoffs are allocated on the basis of reverse seniority; the newest workers are laid off first (Chapter 18).

The wage structure within an internal labor market is also determined by administrative procedures, through custom and tradition, and by the pattern of mobility which is sought. In terms of Figure 15-1, how should the wage rate of a packer in the shipping department, for example, compare with that of a local driver? Very frequently a system of job evaluation is used to establish the wage rate attached to each job in a job ladder. *Job evaluation* is essentially a procedure by which jobs are ranked and wage rates assigned in terms of a set of job characteristics and worker traits. Table 15-1 shows an illustrative job evaluation scheme whereby points have been assigned, undoubtedly with some degree of arbitrariness, to various job characteristics and traits. Thus, using this system, the actual points assigned to a packer's job and a driver's job might be 50 and 75 respectively. This ranking implies that the wage rate of a driver should be 50 percent higher than that of a packer. For example, if packers receive $5.00 hourly, then drivers should be paid $7.50 per hour. Note in particular that in the internal labor market wage rates frequently are attached to jobs rather than individuals. Internal labor market theorists are suggesting in effect that productivity often resides in jobs rather than in workers. Also observe the obvious point that administrative procedure has supplanted the forces of demand and supply.

Once established, custom and tradition come into play to make the internal wage structure rigid: "Any wage rate, set of wage relationships, or wage setting procedure which prevails over a period of time tends to become customary; changes are then viewed as unjust or inequitable, and the work group will exert economic pressure in opposition to them."[13] Recalling the previously discussed notion of equitable comparisons, we should note that custom and rigidity tend to evolve around wage *relationships* as opposed to specific wage *rates*.

The wage structure is not determined in isolation from the allocative function of the internal labor market. One of the important constraints which applies is that the wage structure must foster and facilitate the internal allocation of labor which the employer seeks. "The wage on every job must be high enough

[13]Ibid., p. 85.

TABLE 15-1

Model Job Evaluation System

Factor		Maximum Points
Working conditions		15
Noise	5	
Dirt	5	
Smell	5	
Responsibility for equipment		25
Responsibility for other workers		20
Skill		20
Manual dexterity	10	
Experience	10	
Education		35
Physical effort		10
Total points		125

Source: Peter B. Doeringer and Michael J. Piore, *Internal Labor Markets and Manpower Analysis* (Lexington, Mass.: D. C. Heath and Company), p. 67.

relative to the job or jobs from which is it supposed to draw its labor and low enough relative to the jobs to which it is supposed to supply labor to induce the desired pattern of internal mobility."[14] Thus in Figure 15-1 the wage of a packer must be sufficiently higher than that of a loader so that the latter will aspire to become the former!

The Efficiency Issue. At the hazard of digressing, it is intriguing to pause a moment to consider the question whether internal labor markets are efficient. The basic premise of orthodox economics is that competitive pressures result in the efficient use of labor and other inputs. When competition prevails, workers and other productive resources are paid in terms of their marginal productivity with the result that any level of output is produced with the least-cost (most-efficient) combination of inputs (Chapter 6). But the critical feature of the internal labor market is that, aside from port-of-entry jobs, workers are shielded from competition. Wages in internal labor markets are determined, not by market forces, but by rather arbitrary administrative procedures embodied in job evaluation, through custom and tradition, and so forth. Thus it would only be by chance that the various kinds of workers would be paid in accordance with their productivities. Furthermore, workers are promoted (allocated) largely on the basis of seniority, rather than in terms of worker ability (productivity). These characteristics imply that the existence of internal labor markets conflict with society's interest in allocative efficiency.

But most internal labor market theorists and some mainstream economists rebut this line of reasoning. Internal labor markets and the wage structures embodied in them may exist precisely because they efficiently allocate labor! In the first place, recall that the internal labor market reduces labor turnover, thereby reducing the costs of training, recruitment, screening, and hiring. Of particular significance is the fact that the job ladders of internal labor markets provide the employer with abundant *information* as to the quality of its workers. Hence, the firm is less likely to promote an unproductive worker if it selects that worker from within the internal labor market. In comparison, hiring from the external labor market is based upon more limited information, which may increase the risk of obtaining an unproductive worker. It is also noteworthy that the use of seniority in the allocation of labor is *not* necessarily at odds with efficiency. The worker who has been on the job the longest is probably a suitable candidate for promotion. Furthermore, only in a very few instances is internal labor market promotion based *solely* on seniority. The senior worker with the requisite ability and an acceptable performance record typically gets promoted rather than simply the most senior employee.

A second reason why internal labor markets may be efficient centers upon the distinction between static and dynamic efficiency. *Static efficiency* refers to the combining of labor and other resources *of given quality* in the most efficient

---

[14]Ibid., p. 78.

(least costly) way. **Dynamic efficiency,** on the other hand, has to do with increases in productive efficiency which arise from *improvements in the quality* of labor and other resources. For present purposes the relevant contention is that internal labor markets promote dynamic efficiency, which is held to be of greater consequence than realizing static efficiency. The gain from utilizing *existing* skills of workers more efficiently is a "one-shot" gain, while the gains from *improving* worker knowledge and skills can go on indefinitely.[15] Furthermore, internal labor markets are conducive to dynamic efficiency because, by providing security to more-skilled senior workers, it makes those workers willing to pass along their knowledge and skills to less-skilled colleagues. Put bluntly, a highly skilled senior worker will want to conceal his or her knowledge from less-skilled junior workers *if* the latter can become competitors for the former's job! But seniority rules and other security provisions embodied in internal labor markets guarantee that this will not happen. If senior workers are assured that they have priority with respect to promotions, that their wages will not be reduced as more workers acquire knowledge of their job, and that they will be the last to be laid off, then senior workers will be amenable to sharing their skills with fellow workers. Internal labor markets may provide these assurances.

Finally, orthodox economists point out that the pay structures within typical internal labor markets may be effective incentive-generating devices, particularly in large firms where it is difficult to monitor the work effort of employees. More specifically, the wage structure of the internal labor market may be such that not only are senior workers paid more than junior workers, but senior workers are paid more than their marginal revenue products (MRPs), while junior workers are paid less than their MRPs.[16] The "premium" paid senior workers is an inducement for younger employees to work hard. By being productive, young workers demonstrate to employers that they deserve to be retained and to progress up the job ladder to higher-paying jobs in which they, too, will enjoy the "premium" of a wage rate in excess of their MRPs. Young workers presumably accept wages which are initially less than their MRPs for the privilege of participating in a labor market where in time the reverse will be true! This wage structure is also appealing to young workers in that it offers the prospect of higher lifetime earnings. The greater work effort and higher average worker productivity which results from this wage structure increases the firm's profits in which workers may share through wage bargaining.[17]

To recapitulate: Some economists feel that internal labor markets contribute to inefficiency because wages are determined by rigid administrative procedures

---

[15]Thurow, op. cit., pp. 194–195.

[16]This implies a relationship between wage rate and MRPs which is just the opposite of that shown in Figure 4-8(b).

[17]Edward P. Lazear, "Agency, Earnings Profiles, Productivity, and Hours Restriction," *American Economic Review,* September 1981, pp. 606–620; Lazear, "Why Is There Mandatory Retirement?" *Journal of Political Economy,* December 1979, pp. 1261–1284; and Lazear and Sherwin Rosen, "Rank-Order Tournaments as Optimum Labor Contracts," *Journal of Political Economy,* October 1981, pp. 841–864.

and rules, rather than on the basis of worker productivity. Other economists take the opposite position, arguing that (1) internal labor markets reduce recruitment, screening, and training costs; (2) the security provided by the internal labor market induces senior workers to share their skills and knowledge with junior workers; and (3) the wage structure of the internal labor market may provide young workers with greater incentives to work productively.

DUAL LABOR MARKET THEORY

Let us now use the institutional conception of wage determination and our understanding of internal labor markets as building blocks to consider the dual labor market theory and the challenge it poses for orthodox labor market analysis. Some labor economists have extended the internal labor market concept to the point where they envision two distinct types of labor markets: primary and secondary labor markets. This notion that a dichotomization of labor markets has occurred is alternatively labelled the theory of labor market segmentation or the *dual labor market theory.*[18]

Primary and Secondary Labor Markets. *Pimary labor markets,* by definition, are where the "good" jobs are. *Primary labor market jobs are generally the kinds of jobs envisioned in the foregoing discussion of internal labor markets.* More specifically, jobs in primary labor markets are characterized by (1) employment stability and job security; (2) high and rising wage rates; (3) the presence of job ladders, that is, good and clearly defined opportunities for occupational advancement; (4) the use of relatively advanced, capital-intensive technologies and the presence of efficient management; and in many cases (5) the presence of a strong and effective labor union. In vivid contrast, *secondary labor markets* embody "bad" jobs and have essentially the opposite characteristics of primary labor markets. In secondary labor markets (1) employment is unstable and worker turnover is high; (2) wage rates are low and relatively stagnant; (3) jobs are "dead end"; that is, job ladders are nonexistent or severely restricted; (4) production technology is relatively primitive and labor-intensive; and (5) unions are absent and management is therefore able to follow archaic and capricious practices in dealing with its labor force. Workers in secondary labor markets can be thought of as

[18]The following is a sampling of important contributions to the theory of dual labor markets: Michael Reich, David M. Gordon, and Richard C. Edwards, "A Theory of Labor Market Segmentation," *American Economic Review,* May 1973, pp. 359–365; Thomas Vietorisz and Bennett Harrison, "Labor Market Segmentation: Positive Feedback and Divergent Development," *American Economic Review,* May 1973, pp. 366–376; David M. Gordon, *Theories of Poverty and Underemployment* (Lexington, Mass.: D. C. Heath and Company, 1972); Richard C. Edwards, Michael Reich, and David M. Gordon (eds.), *Labor Market Segmentation* (Lexington, Mass.: D. C. Heath and Company, 1975); and David M. Gordon, Richard Edwards, and Michael Reich, *Segmented Work, Divided Workers* (Cambridge, England: Cambridge University Press, 1982).

workers who, for one reason or another, do *not* pass the screening process which would allow them access to a job ladder in an internal market.

Mutually Supportive Characteristics. Dualists contend that the features of both primary and secondary labor markets tend to be mutually supportive and reinforcing. For example, in primary markets high and rising wages put pressure upon management to raise productivity in order to offset the cost impact of higher wages. These productivity-increasing efforts typically entail the use of more and technologically superior capital. This in turn produces the need to upgrade the labor force and simultaneously generates advancement opportunities for workers. Employers are motivated to provide additional on-the-job training for their personnel; workers are motivated to acquire new skills because of the job advancement and higher wages which accompany these skills. Furthermore, as they invest in the specific skills of their workers, employers recognize that employment must be stabilized in order to realize a return on these human capital investments. We thus envision a self-reinforcing process of progress and development in primary labor markets. Furthermore, the employment stability of primary labor markets is conducive to unionization. And unions may reinforce and accelerate the process of development by exerting pressure for wage increases and by formalizing the rules and administrative procedures which determine the occupational advancement of workers.

The characteristics of the secondary labor market are also interrelated and mutually supportive. The payment of low and poverty-level wage rates means there is no particular pressure upon management to introduce labor-saving machinery and equipment. As a result, worker productivity stagnates and so do wages. Furthermore, a stagnant technology means that there are no opportunities or incentives to upgrade worker skills. Skill requirements are so modest that current employees and available unemployed workers are more or less interchangeable. Secondary labor market jobs entail simple, menial, repetitive tasks which can be quickly learned by virtually anyone. In contrast to primary labor market jobs there is little or no specific training required to perform these jobs. As noted, job ladders are extremely limited or nonexistent; these are dead-end jobs. Indeed, the employment relationship tends to be casual; worker turnover and job instability are high because of the unskilled character of secondary labor market jobs. There is virtually no investment in specific training by employers, and hence there is no reason to reduce worker turnover. Employers might even look favorably upon a high level of employee turnover because labor force volatility discourages unionization, on the one hand, and allows the employer to avoid the cost of such fringe benefits as paid vacations and retirement pay, on the other.

Examples of secondary labor market jobs include: domestic jobs; dishwashing jobs in restaurants; menial jobs in hospitals (as orderlies, nursing aids, cleaning workers); stitching and pressing jobs in apparel plants; lower-level clerical jobs, and so forth. As some of our examples imply, "good" primary labor market jobs and "bad" secondary labor jobs may exist side by side in the same firm or institution. Most of a large corporation's production work force may have primary jobs, but its janitorial workers are likely to have dead-end secondary jobs. And while most employees of a college or university have primary jobs, the food service workers and groundskeepers have secondary jobs.

Job-Worker Feedbacks. Dual labor market theorists also argue that there is a critical interdependence between workers and jobs in both primary and secondary labor markets. Through a kind of feedback process, workers in both markets tend to develop behavioral patterns and worker traits which are appropriate to their particular labor market. In primary labor markets, for example, employment is stable and workers tend to become "reliable" and have stable work habits. Primary labor market workers are dependable in that they report for work regularly, are punctual, and handle company equipment and materials conscientiously. Furthermore, these workers adhere to the rules and procedures of the primary labor market and are anxious to learn new skills which will allow them to move up the job ladder.

A similar feedback process is allegedly at work in secondary markets. The lack of upward mobility, that is, the absence of job ladders, induces poor work habits and weak job attachment on the part of workers. The low wage rate and unattractive working conditions which characterize a secondary labor market job are also conducive to a high rate of labor turnover. As noted earlier, employers may encourage a casual employment relationship to prevent unionization or long-term financial commitments to their workers. Therefore, absenteeism and tardiness are not penalized and, hence, tend to become common worker traits. One of the very unfortunate consequences of this feedback process between job and worker is that workers who initially might have the characteristics to function successfully in a primary labor market can lose those characteristics as a result of a period of employment in a secondary labor market.

Sources of Dualism. Thus far our discussion of the dual labor market theory has begged a fundamental question: Why has labor market dualism evolved? What factors have been responsible for the simultaneous existence of primary and secondary labor markets?

1. Industry structure. One explanation is that dualism in labor markets is a reflection of dualism in product markets. At the most mundane level this explanation asserts that different industries are faced with different degrees of production variability and that this variability is reflected in their labor markets. These output variations stem not only from seasonal and climatic factors, but also from fluctuations associated with the business cycle. To use an extreme example, the manufacture of artificial Christmas trees or children's Halloween costumes is an inherently volatile productive activity. It is no surprise that the manufacture of such products results in a casual, unstable relationship between employer and workers. Conversely, industries which enjoy substantial seasonal and cyclical

stability in the demand for their products provide the stable employment relationships characteristic of primary labor markets.

This line of reasoning can be put into a broader historical context with the
contention that labor market dualism is intimately related to the evolution of the
business sector of our economy. Thus, for example, Galbraith[19] has envisioned
the development of a dichotomy in the business sector which is made up of a
"planning sector" and a "market sector." The planning sector consists of some
1000 giant corporations which carry on the bulk of our society's economic
activity. These firms, protected by various barriers to entry, possess considerable
monopoly power. They are also capital-intensive and technologically progressive and enjoy substantial economies of scale and high rates of profit. Freed from
the day-to-day rigors of competition, these firms are more concerned with planning for their long-run security and growth. To this end the large corporations of
the planning sector attempt to insulate themselves from the uncertainties of the
market. Hence, they shape and stabilize consumer demand through advertising
and other forms of product promotion. Foreign markets are controlled through
direct investment in foreign productive facilities, participation in cartels, and the
solicitation of favorable public policies.

The critical point for present purposes is that the stability and profitability of
the major corporations which make up the planning sector are conducive to a
stable derived demand for labor, capital-intensive and technologically progressive production techniques, rising productivity and real wages, and a need for
skilled labor. In short, the labor markets associated with the planning sector
have those characteristics which define primary labor markets.

The market sector which constitutes the remainder of the economy involves
some 12 million or so small firms and farmers. Here competition is strong,
economies of scale are few, technology is relatively primitive, and firms are
subject to all of the uncertainties and vicissitudes of market forces. It is in the
market system that secondary labor markets are common. In short, General
Motors provides the "good" jobs of the primary labor market; Joe's Diner provides the "bad" jobs of the secondary labor market.

2. Divide and conquer. Radical economists who embrace the dual labor
market theory argue that dualism or segmentation has been consciously propa-
gated as a means of offsetting the evolution of a unified, class-conscious labor
movement which might threaten capitalist control of the economy. In abridged
form, the argument is as follows. In the competitive phase of capitalism prior to
1890 the American economy changed from handicraft to factory production.
This fundamental shift promoted the homogenization of the labor force.

The factory system eliminated many skilled craft occupations, creating large
pools of semiskilled jobs. Production for a mass market and increased mech-

---

[19]John Kenneth Galbraith, *The New Industrial State* (Boston, Mass.: Houghton Mifflin Company,
1967). See also Robert T. Averitt, *The Dual Economy* (New York: W. W. Norton and Company, Inc.,
1968).

anization forged standardized work requirements. Large establishments drew greater numbers of workers into common [urban] working environments.[20]

This homogenization of the labor force posed a potential threat to capitalist power and control of the economy. An essentially "deskilled" labor force with common problems and interests, concentrated in urban areas, provides the basis for a class-conscious labor movement capable of wrenching power from the capitalist class.

Radical economists contend that during the 1890–1920 period monopoly capitalism evolved, and the giant corporations which were increasingly dominating the economy purposely developed strategies designed to supplant the homogenization of the labor force with stratification, segmentation, or, in other words, dualism. A most obvious form of dualism or segmentation was to create internal labor markets, that is, hierarchical job ladders centered upon some specific technology or job skill. The funnelling of workers into these various internal labor markets would presumably divert worker consciousness away from the common interests of the working class and toward individual interest in progressing up the job ladder. More specifically, from the employer's standpoint the creation of job ladders had two distinct advantages.

First, it gave workers a sense of vertical mobility as they made their way up the ladder, and was an incentive to workers to work harder. . . . The other advantage of the job ladder arrangement was that it gave the employers more leverage with which to maintain discipline. The system pitted each worker against all the others in rivalry for advancement and undercut any feeling of unity which might develop among them.[21]

It is also worth noting that, according to dualists, the segmentation and disunification of the labor force was promoted in a variety of other ways. For example, various piece-rate schemes were developed which linked the wages of workers to their *individual* productive efforts, thereby undermining the collective identity of the work force. Furthermore, the larger corporations provided a variety of paternalistic "welfare" programs for their workers. Such paternalism took the form of pension and disability funds, stock purchase plans, and company housing and recreational facilities. "By increasing the ties between workers and their employer, they [employers] hoped to weaken the ties between workers and their class."[22] Finally, radicals contend that the employers of monopoly capitalism deliberately "exploited race, ethnic and sex antagonisms in order to undercut unionism and break strikes."[23] For example, historically blacks were

[20]Reich, Gordon, and Edwards, "A Theory of Labor Market Segmentation," op. cit., p. 360.

[21]Katherine Stone, "The Origins of Job Structures in the Steel Industry" in Edwards, Reich, and Gordon, (eds.), *Labor Market Segmentation,* pp. 46–47.

[22]Ibid., p. 53.

[23]Reich, Gordon, and Edwards, "A Theory of Labor Market Segmentation," op. cit., p. 362.

often brought in as strikebreakers in order to "deflect class conflicts into race conflicts." And employers sometimes transformed previously "male jobs" into "female jobs" for the purpose of making those jobs less susceptible to unionization.

Barriers to Mobility. One final feature of labor market duality merits emphasis. While there is mobility *within* both the primary and secondary labor markets, there is little mobility *between* the two. According to dualists, a variety of interrelated forces seriously curtail mobility. The institution of discrimination—based on such factors as race, sex, and ethnic background—is of paramount importance in allocating workers among primary and secondary labor markets. In particular, dualists argue that discrimination forces many blacks, women, Hispanics, and illegal immigrants into secondary markets. But once a worker takes a secondary labor market job he or she may become trapped in that market. Recall that secondary workers tend to acquire "bad" work habits as a consequence of holding "bad" jobs. Hence, an individual with a history of secondary labor market work is likely to be regarded as an "inferior," "low status," or "unreliable" worker and therefore not a desirable employee by a primary labor market employer. Remember, too, that a secondary labor market worker will have acquired no industry- or firm-specific skills of value to primary employers. Mobility may also be impeded by the fact that, while overall economic and technological progress gets reflected in rising average skill levels for primary labor market jobs, secondary labor markets continue to be characterized by menial "raw labor" jobs. Hence, it becomes increasingly difficult over time for secondary workers to bridge the growing skill gap between the two labor markets.

Comparing Orthodoxy and Dualism. It is informative to explore a number of major distinctions between orthodox and dual labor market theory. These interrelated points pertain not only to differences in labor market conceptions, but also to economic policies.

1. Nature of labor markets. To orthodox theorists such factors as racial and sexual discrimination, labor union activities, the roles of custom and habit, and so forth are comparatively minor qualifications to the functioning of labor markets. Competitive market forces are presumably dominant and ultimately override such considerations. (Recall from Chapter 11 the argument that competitive pressures will eliminate labor market discrimination in the long run). In contrast, dualists stress that such considerations are central to an understanding of how labor markets operate. The very structure and characteristics of labor markets depend upon the presence or absence of unionization, the degree to which discrimination is practiced, and so on. Unionization and discrimination are not mere aberrations, but key determinants of the character of labor markets. Perhaps it is fair to say that orthodoxy envisions market forces as determining the character of labor market institutions, while dualists contend that labor market institutions dominate market forces.

2. Worker-job relationship. A related point is that orthodox theory focuses upon *workers,* while the dual theory stresses *jobs.* Thus orthodox theory suggests that "bad" workers—those with little human capital—end up with "bad," low-paying jobs. This in turn implies that it is within the individual's range of choice to improve his or her labor market situation by acquiring more education and training as means of obtaining a "better" job. But dualists see labor market opportunities—the chance to get a "good" primary labor market job with training opportunities which lead to high wages—as being controlled by primary labor market employers. These employers ration or allocate training opportunities to workers who apply for port-of-entry positions. We know from Chapter 11 that discrimination based upon race, sex, or ethnic background may be critical in determining the allocation of training opportunities and therefore accessibility to high earnings. Hence, in the dualist view the individual worker does *not* control his or her labor market destiny. One's productivity and earnings depend, not so much upon the human capital acquired through schooling and formal vocational training, but rather upon successful entry to a "good" job ladder in a primary labor market.

3. Poverty and policy. The fact that orthodox theory focuses upon workers while dualism emphasizes jobs leads to a fundamental policy difference. The two theories differ sharply on the problem of assisting low-wage, poverty-level workers. As envisioned from the standpoint of orthodox theory—or, more precisely, of human capital theory—workers receive low earnings because their productivity is low. And their productivity is low for the simple reason that they have been unable or unwilling to invest in sufficient quantities of human capital. Hence, orthodox theorists make the obvious recommendation that low-wage workers be provided with additional human capital in the form of general education and vocational training so that they may improve their productivity and acquire higher-income jobs.

But dualists see the problem much differently. To them the low-income worker's problem is frequently *not* the need for more education and training, but rather the inability to gain access to a "good" primary labor market job.[24] The problem of poverty-level workers lies not so much in the individual worker's shortcomings, but rather in the dualistic structure of labor markets. Thus dualists and orthodox economists embrace a fundamentally different conception of labor productivity. To the orthodox economist productivity resides essentially in the *worker.* Hence, to raise the earnings of poor workers one must provide them with more human capital. But to the dualists productivity lies primarily in the

---

[24]The roots of the dual labor market theory go back to the 1960s, at which time economists studying urban ghetto labor markets found that indicators of worker productivity, such as years of schooling or vocational training, seemed to have little or no impact upon the employment prospects or the quality of jobs attained by secondary workers. See Gordon, op. cit., pp. 44–46.

job. Secondary labor market workers can raise their earnings only by achieving greater access to primary labor market jobs. "The reason why secondary workers cannot get into the primary segment is not because they lack the ability or productive potential, but rather because of the refusal of workers and employers in the primary segment to accept them into their work groups."[25] Dualists back their position that productivity resides in jobs rather than in workers with the following observations. On the one hand, the educational and manpower training programs made available to disadvantaged workers in the 1960s and 1970s failed to provide an effective remedy for poverty or to eliminate the working poor. On the other hand, while the United States has substantially reduced inequality in the distribution of educational attainment over time, this has not been matched by less inequality in the distribution of earnings.

What policies do dualists recommend to aid low-wage workers in gaining greater access to primary labor market jobs? First, antidiscrimination legislation (Chapter 11) should be more vigorously pursued to ameliorate this institutional barrier to the good jobs of primary markets. A second strategy is to encourage the growth of labor unions through prolabor legislation. The idea here is that the unionization of secondary markets will hasten the development and formalization of the administrative rules, job ladders, and other structural features which characterize primary labor markets. The presence of a union, in other words, will tend to hasten the evolution of a secondary labor market into a primary labor market. A third recommendation is to impose a substantial increase in the level and coverage of the minimum wage. The argument here is that secondary labor market employers will react via the shock effect (Chapters 8 and 10). In particular, confronted with higher labor costs, employers will be obligated to substitute capital for labor. This substitution will generate the need for specific on-the-job training and the upgrading of workers. Given this investment in worker training, the employer will seek to lower labor turnover. In short, a higher minimum wage will induce those developments which tend to change secondary into primary labor markets.[26] Finally, dualists recommend the creation of "good" public sector jobs to utilize more fully the productive potentials of secondary labor market workers and to allow them to achieve above-poverty earnings. Such governmentally provided jobs will also offer on-the-job training to those untrained workers now in dead-end secondary labor markets.

4. Unemployment. Orthodox and dual labor market theorists hold somewhat different views of the unemployment problem and how it should be corrected. Rejecting the labor market dichotomy of the dualists, orthodox theorists envision a continuum of jobs or, alternatively, a national labor market queue wherein we can imagine workers being arrayed from "best" to "worst." The

---

[25]Caroline Joll, Chris McKenna, Robert McNabb, and John Shorey, *Developments in Labour Market Analysis* (London: George Allen & Unwin, 1983), p. 383.

[26]See Thomas Vietorisz, "We Need a $3.50 Minimum Wage," *Challenge*, May–June 1973, pp. 49–62.

level of aggregate demand determines how far down the queue employers find it profitable to hire workers. Those workers with the least human capital (formal education, labor market experience, and so forth) who are located at the rear of the labor queue will necessarily bear the brunt of unemployment. The rate of unemployment can be reduced by increasing aggregate demand so that employers find it profitable to hire "disadvantaged" workers near the end of the queue.

Dualists interpret the unemployment problem differently. In their view the labor turnover—the "frictional unemployment" (Chapter 18)—associated with secondary labor markets is endemic to such markets. Employment stability is sought by neither employers nor workers in secondary labor markets. Workers can always quit such jobs and later acquire similar "bad" jobs when they choose. Secondary labor market employers are confronted with low training and recruitment costs and therefore have little incentive to encourage employment stability. Indeed, as noted earlier, they may favor labor force instability as a deterrent to unionization! Hence, dualists point out that, when full employment is achieved for the economy as a whole, those workers associated with secondary labor markets will be experiencing high unemployment rates (see Table 18-2). The solution to their unemployment problem is not a further increase in aggregate demand, but an increase in primary labor market job opportunities and a decline in the number of secondary labor markets. The specific policies mentioned in connection with our earlier discussion of the poverty issue are relevant.

Criticisms of Dualism. Proponents of the orthodox conception of the labor market have offered a variety of criticisms in discounting the significance of labor market dualism.[27]

1. Orthodox economists contend that dualism does *not* amount to a rigorous economic theory of labor markets. Dual labor market theories "are sketchy, vague, and diverse if not internally conflicting. Description, narratives, and taxonomies crowd out model development."[28] Dualists, it is argued, are perhaps more effective in criticizing orthodox theory than they are in advancing a coherent, internally consistent alternative. An example of inconsistency: Dualists argue that many secondary labor market workers are trapped into such jobs because of discrimination and in fact possess the human capital requirements to function successfully in primary labor markets. But they also contend that adverse feedback effects cause secondary labor market workers to become "bad"

---

[27]See, in particular, Michael L. Wachter, "Primary and Secondary Labor Markets: A Critique of the Dual Approach," *Brookings Papers on Economic Activity,* no. 3, 1974, pp. 637–680 and Glen G. Cain, "The Challenge of Segmented Labor Market Theories to Orthodox Theory: A Survey," *Journal of Economic Literature,* December 1976, pp. 1215–1257. In contrast, see Michael J. Piore, "Labor Market Segmentation: To What Paradigm Does It Belong?" *American Economic Review,* May 1983, pp. 249–253 and Irvin Sobel, "Human Capital and Institutional Theories of the Labor Market: Rivals or Complements?" *Journal of Economic Issues,* March 1982, pp. 255–272.

[28]Cain, op. cit., p. 1221.

workers because they hold "bad" jobs. Which dualist assertion is correct? Are secondary labor markets populated by *good* workers in bad jobs or by *bad* workers in bad jobs?

2. A related point is that in practice the concepts of primary and secondary labor markets are difficult to delineate. The identification of "good" primary labor markets jobs and "bad" secondary labor market jobs in the real world is extremely difficult to accomplish short of subjective, and therefore arbitrary, judgments. Does an urban garbage collector—represented by an aggressive union, paid $15 an hour, and enjoying considerable job security—have a primary or secondary labor market job? What about longshoremen and automobile production workers? Both are well-paid, but the former are faced with unstable work and the latter persistently complain of undesirable working conditions. Are these good or bad jobs? The problem of clearly distinguishing between primary and secondary labor market jobs complicates the problem of empirically testing the notion of dualism, an issue to which we now turn.

3. Orthodox economists contend that empirical evidence should substantiate a number of rather obvious hypotheses *if* the concept of labor market dualism is valid.[29] First, if workers are in fact segmented into two distinct markets, the resulting distribution of earnings should be bimodal or "double-peaked." That is, a frequency distribution of wage earners should be clustered around one peak in the low-wage secondary market and another peak in the high-wage primary market. But in fact earnings are distributed on a unimodal or single-peaked basis (see Figure 13-1), suggesting a continuum of jobs rather than a dichotomy. Second, for a variety of reasons summarized earlier, dualism asserts that there is little mobility between secondary and primary labor markets. Once again, although it is difficult to define an "adequate" or "reasonable" amount of mobility between the two markets, available evidence does *not* suggest that, for example, low-wage and black workers are encumbered by serious job immobilities.[30] Third, given the job ladders of primary labor markets and the dead-end nature of secondary labor market jobs, dualism would lead us to expect that human capital investment (for example, years of education) would contribute more to a worker's earnings in the former market than in the latter. While there is some support for this generalization, the methodology of the research is questionable and thus the conclusion unclear.[31] In short, we can say that overall there is no strong empirical support for the dual theory.

[29]See Wachter, op. cit., pp. 650–651 and John T. Addison and W. Stanley Siebert, *The Market for Labor: An Analytical Treatment* (Santa Monica, Calif.: Goodyear Publishing Company, Inc., 1979), p. 190.

[30]For details see Cain, op. cit., pp. 1231–1232 and Wachter, op. cit., pp. 658–659. Mobility within the personal distribution of earnings was discussed in Chapter 13.

[31]The methodological problem is rather complex, but can be illustrated by this hypothetical example. Suppose a government program provides additional schooling for workers now in secondary labor markets. In two or three years we attempt to measure the impact of this additional human capital investment by determining the relationship between years of education and the earnings *of secondary market workers*. The problem is that any secondary labor market sample of workers will be biased in that those workers who have benefited most from the extra education are likely to have moved on

4. More positively, orthodox economists feel that most of the allegedly unique findings and implications of labor market dualism can be readily explained within the aegis of orthodox analysis. For example, while dualists would view the administrative rules and procedures which determine wage rates and labor allocation within primary labor markets to be at odds with economic efficiency and therefore inconsistent with orthodoxy, we saw earlier that an alternative interpretation holds them to be efficient and consistent with orthodox theory. Similarly, the concept of noncompeting groups of workers (Chapter 12) has long been an accepted notion of orthodox theory. Dualism can thus be regarded as an extreme statement of the concept of noncompeting groups embellished by questionable descriptions and interpretations.

5. Finally, it is worth noting that the "divide and conquer" explanation of dualism espoused by radical economists has encountered criticism. In particular, recall that radicals argue that internal labor markets are generated at the initiative of employers to create disunity among workers. Critics point out that there are many historical examples which illustrate that internal labor markets have been established at the instigation of labor rather than management. The establishment of unions and formalized internal labor markets in such core industries as automobiles and steel in the 1930s is relevant. In short, causality may be the opposite of that assumed by radical dualists: "while it is true that internal labor markets can be imposed from above as part of an antilabor strategy, they also can result from a struggle from below by workers for whom the system of job rights and regulation is a desired improvement."[32]

Given the relative newness of the dualistic approach, no simple and definitive comparison of the relative merits of orthodoxy and dualism is possible. One can certainly argue that dualism has raised a variety of pertinent questions for consideration. Why has discrimination persisted over time in contradiction to Becker's orthodox taste-for-discrimination model (Chapter 11), which suggests that competitive pressures will eliminate it? Why is it that, despite less inequality in educational attainment, the distribution of earnings in the United States has *not* narrowed as orthodox theory would suggest? And, similarly, why have human resource development programs involving vocational training had only modest impact upon the employment and earnings prospects of "disadvantaged" workers and upon the incidence of poverty?[33] And there is no doubt that

---

to better jobs in primary markets and therefore will be excluded from our study! Those who remain in the secondary labor market are generally those who have benefited little or not at all from additional education. Hence, our research will *incorrectly* tell us that education does *not* increase the earnings of workers *in secondary labor markets*. The interested reader should see Paul Osterman, "An Empirical Study of Labor Market Segmentation," *Industrial and Labor Relations Review*, July 1975, pp. 508–521 and William J. Kruse, "An Empirical Study of Labor Market Segmentation: Comment," and Paul Osterman, "Reply," both in *Industrial and Labor Relations Review*, January 1977, pp. 219–224.

[32]Paul Osterman, "The Nature and Importance of Internal Labor Markets," in Paul Osterman (ed.), *Internal Labor Markets* (Cambridge, Mass.: The MIT Press), p. 11.

[33]Joll et al., op. cit., p. 379.

dualism embodies some unique and intriguing perspectives on labor markets, including the idea that jobs provide feedback which has an impact on worker quality and the notion that human capital is not a sufficient condition for upward socioeconomic mobility. At a minimum dualism makes it evident that orthodox theory—upon which the bulk of this textbook is based—is not the only analytical game in town and that the impact of social and institutional constraints upon the labor market options of some groups of workers are critical to an understanding of how labor markets function.

SUMMARY

1. The institutionalist view of the labor market holds that (*a*) wages are determined by bargaining decisions rather than market forces, (*b*) unions are fundamentally political institutions whose behavior eludes economic analysis, (*c*) union goals are multi-dimensional and not understandable in terms of a simple maximizing assumption, and (*d*) union wage policies stress equitable comparisons with peer employees.
2. Most firms and plants embody internal labor markets in which wages and the allocation of labor are determined by administrative rules and procedures rather than by supply and demand.
3. Internal labor markets entail hierarchies of jobs called job ladders which focus upon a certain job skill, function, or technology. Once entering the job ladder through a port of entry, internal labor market workers are largely shielded from the competitive pressures of external labor markets.
4. Internal labor markets exist because they generate advantages for both employers and workers. For employers internal labor markets reduce worker turnover and thereby increase the return on specific training and reduce recruitment and training costs. For workers internal labor markets provide job security, opportunities for training and promotion, and protection from arbitrary managerial decisions.
5. By providing labor force stability internal labor markets attract unions; conversely, unions promote and accelerate the development of internal labor markets.
6. It is unclear whether internal labor markets diminish or enhance productive efficiency.
7. Dual labor market theorists argue that a labor market dichotomy exists. Primary labor markets are associated with well-defined internal labor markets. Primary labor market jobs are characterized by employment stability and job security, high and rising wages, opportunities for advancement, capital-intensive technologies and efficient management, and the presence of unions. Secondary labor markets embody the opposite characteristics: employment instability and insecurity, low wages, little or no opportunity for advancement, labor-intensive technologies and archaic management, and the absence of unions.
8. The specific characteristics of both primary and secondary labor markets tend to be mutually supportive.
9. Feedback from jobs to workers exists, so that workers holding "good" jobs in primary markets become "good" workers and those with "bad" jobs in secondary markets tend to become "bad" workers.
10. Dualism may reflect (*a*) the existence of a dualistic structure in product market or (*b*) the desire of capitalists to thwart the evolution of a homogeneous class-conscious labor movement.

11. Discrimination, feedback from jobs to workers, and diverging skill levels combine to restrict mobility between secondary and primary labor markets.
12. Orthodox and dual labor market theory differ on the following points. Dualists view discrimination, union activities, and custom and habit as major structural factors in labor markets, while orthodox theorists do not. Dualists emphasize job acquisition, rather than human capital acquisition, as the critical determinant of earnings. While orthodox economists advocate increases in the availability of human capital and the expansion of aggregate demand to reduce poverty and unemployment, dualists stress policies which increase the number and accessibility of primary labor market jobs.
13. Orthodox economists argue that (a) dualism is not a mature theory of labor markets, (b) in practice primary and secondary labor market jobs are difficult to distinguish, (c) empirical evidence does not support basic hypotheses implied by dualism, (d) the findings and implications of dualism are more adequately explained by orthodox theory, and (e) the implied causality of the radical explanation of dualism is questionable.

QUESTIONS AND STUDY SUGGESTIONS

1. Key terms and concepts to remember: institutionalist view of labor markets; equitable comparisons; internal labor market; job ladder; port of entry; external labor market; seniority; job evaluation; static and dynamic efficiency; dual labor market theory; primary and secondary labor markets.
2. Explain how the institutionalist conception of the labor market, the idea of internal labor markets, and dual labor market theory relate to one another. Specifically, what are the common ideas or lines of thought?
3. How do you explain the existence of internal labor markets? What are their advantages to employers? To workers?
4. Explain: "Unions are both a consequence and a cause of internal labor markets." Why might the presence of internal labor markets in a firm encourage unionization?
5. Do you think internal labor markets enhance or detract from efficiency? How might one argue that the realization of dynamic efficiency is more important than achieving static efficiency? Do you agree?
6. Outline the basic features of the dual labor market theory. Contrast the characteristics of primary and secondary labor markets. Demonstrate how the specific characteristics within each market might reinforce each other.
7. According to the dualists, why has labor market dualism evolved in the United States? Are primary and secondary markets converging or diverging?
8. Why do dualists contend that there is little mobility between secondary and primary labor markets?
9. Classify the following as primary or secondary labor market workers: a typist in a large corporation's typing pool, a file clerk, an apprentice machinist, a union carpenter, a cook at a fast-food chain, an automobile mechanic, a Ford production-line worker, a junior high school teacher. In each instance explain the reasoning underlying your classification.
10. "Human capital (orthodox) and institutionalist theories of the labor market are complementary rather than competing." Do you agree?
11. How would (a) poverty and (b) unemployment be explained by a dualist? By an orthodox economist?

SELECTED REFERENCES

Cain, Glen G.: "The Challenge of Segmented Labor Market Theories to Orthodox Theory: A Survey," *Journal of Economic Literature,* December 1976, pp. 1212–1257.

Doeringer, Peter B., and Michael J. Piore: *Internal Labor Markets and Manpower Analysis* (Lexington, Mass.: D. C. Heath and Company, 1971).

Edwards, Richard C., Michael Reich, and David M. Gordon (eds.): *Labor Market Segmentation* (Lexington, Mass.: D. C. Heath and Company, 1975).

Gordon, David M.: *Theories of Poverty and Underemployment* (Lexington, Mass.: D. C. Heath and Company, 1972).

Osterman, Paul, (ed.): *Internal Labor Markets* (Cambridge, Mass.: The MIT Press, 1984).

Ross, Arthur M.: *Trade Union Wage Policy* (Berkeley, Calif.: University of California Press, 1948).

Wachter, Michael L.: "Primary and Secondary Labor Markets: A Critique of the Dual Approach," *Brookings Papers on Economic Activity,* no. 3, 1974, pp. 637–680.

Wilkinson, Frank (ed.): *The Dynamics of Labour Market Segmentation* (London: Academic Press, 1981).

TIME AND ONE-HALF

THE JOB COMPETITION MODEL

In his *Generating Inequality*,* Lester C. Thurow develops a "job competition" or "labor queue" model of the labor market which builds upon and extends the concept of internal labor markets.

According to Thurow, the supply and demand or "wage competition" labor market model of orthodox economics conceives of workers who acquire skills by means external to labor markets; that is, workers presumably obtain skills from formal programs of general and vocational education. Employers bid for these skills, varying wage rates in accordance with the productivity of workers. Thurow's job competition model presents a sharply contrasting view: "The labor market is not a market where fully developed skills bid for jobs. Rather, it is primarily a market where supplies of trainable labor are matched with training opportunities that are in turn directly associated with the number of job openings that exist."†

To Thurow cognitive job skills are not acquired before a worker enters the labor market, but are realized largely on the job. Wage rates are not variable in Thurow's job competition model, but are fixed by collective bargaining or unilateral decision by the employer. How then are potential workers allocated to the number of training slots or job opportunities which an employer has available? The answer is that the employer establishes a *labor queue* in which potential employees are ranked in terms of their relative trainability for the available jobs. A complex of *background characteristics* including formal

*Lester C. Thurow, *Generating Inequality* (New York: Basic Books, Inc., Publishers, 1975).
†Ibid., p. 79.

education, work experience, personality traits, age, race, sex, and so forth are used by employers to determine each worker's relative position in the labor queue. The "best" potential employees are the ones who an employer believes can be trained for a given job—or a lifetime sequence of jobs—at the least cost. Those who appear to be the most trainable will be the first chosen for available port-of-entry jobs in internal labor markets where extended job ladders exist. Less trainable workers—those further back in the labor queue—will be hired for an internal labor market where promotional opportunities are more limited, shunted to a secondary labor market, or not hired at all.

In the job competition model productivity is inherent in jobs, rather than in individuals. Workers are trained into the marginal productivity of the jobs they are to hold; workers do not possess a certain marginal productivity independent of the given job. Indeed, the job competition model puts greater emphasis upon on-the-job training and, in fact, certain important features of labor markets stem largely from the training function. Specifically, most labor markets (even those wherein unions are absent) are characterized by (1) the absence of wage competition and (2) a variety of forms of worker security, for example, promotion and layoff on the basis of seniority. These features arise because experienced skilled workers will be unwilling to communicate their knowledge and capabilities through on-the-job training unless they are assured that new trainees will not usurp their jobs.

Thurow contends that his labor queue model is useful in understanding certain observable phenomena which are at odds with the predictions of orthodox theory. For example, Thurow notes that it has long been observed that workers with highly similar background characteristics (education, age, race, sex) earn very different incomes. The orthodox model implies that the earnings of such individuals should be equal or nearly so. Thurow explains these earnings inequalities in terms of what he calls the "lottery aspect" of the national labor queue. Recall that, according to the job competition model, productivity resides in jobs rather than individuals. More specifically, Thurow argues that the productivity of a worker is generally dependent upon the voluntary cooperation of groups or teams of workers in the production process. It follows that two workers with identical background characteristics might realize substantially different earnings because by chance one obtains a position with a high-productivity (high-wage) work team and the other with a low-productivity (low-wage) team. To use Thurow's illustration, "Raw unskilled labor makes a very different wage, depending on whether it works for General Motors or for a Mississippi plantation."‡ In short, two workers with identical background characteristics—workers whom orthodox theory would predict to have identical or highly similar earnings—may earn substantially different incomes in the job competition model depending upon where, when, and for whom they are queuing in the labor market. There is in effect a kind of lottery for training slots; some workers with given background characteristics happen to obtain slots where group productivity and therefore their earnings are high, while others do not.

Furthermore, orthodox labor market theory would suggest that an increase in the education levels of low-income workers would tend to lessen the degree of inequality in the distribution of personal income. More education would change unskilled workers into more skilled workers and directly raise their incomes. In addition, the consequent decline in the supply of unskilled workers would tend to raise their wage rates and earnings, while the increase in the supply of skilled workers would tend to reduce their earnings. These changes would obviously tend to lessen income inequality. But Thurow

‡Ibid., p. 109.

observes that in fact the more widespread availability of educational opportunities since World War II has *not* made the distribution of earnings more equal, a finding which he feels is perfectly understandable in terms of his queue model.

Thurow contends that in his model the relative upgrading of the skills and earning potential of one worker or some group of workers in the queue via education will necessarily mean a relative downgrading of the skills and earning potential of other workers. If Jones's acquisition of the MBA degree moves him ahead in the national labor queue, the relative position of Smith who holds only the B.S. degree will be worsened. If you move ahead in the job line, someone else is moved back. Similarly, if more education transforms "grade school" workers into "high school" workers, the distribution of earnings need not become less unequal. The additional high school workers will be likely to take the best (highest-paying) jobs which heretofore had been available for grade school workers. Therefore, the average earnings of grade school workers will decline because they have been pushed further back in the national labor queue. The average earnings differentials between the two groups of workers are likely to be preserved.

LABOR PRODUCTIVITY: WAGES, PRICES, AND EMPLOYMENT

Previous chapters emphasized the determination of wage rates for specific types of workers and explained the complex cluster of individual wages which constitutes the wage structure. The focus of attention now shifts to the long-term trend of the average level of real wages. We shall find that the secular expansion of the level of real wages is intimately linked to the growth of labor productivity. Hence, much of the present chapter is devoted to productivity growth and its various ramifications.

In more specific terms, this chapter is organized as follows. First, the concept of labor productivity is introduced and its measurement is briefly discussed. Second, the various economic implications of productivity growth are examined, with the emphasis being on the relationship between productivity and real wages. A third and major segment of the chapter examines the primary factors which contribute to the growth of labor productivity. Next, cyclical changes in labor productivity are briefly considered. Fifth, the relationship between productivity and employment growth is analyzed. Finally, we survey explanations of the slowdown in the rate of productivity growth which began in the mid-1960s.

THE PRODUCTIVITY CONCEPT

In essence, productivity is a simple concept. It is merely a relationship between real output—the quantity of goods and services produced—and the quantity of input used to produce that output. Productivity, in other words, is a measure of resource or input efficiency expressed in terms of a ratio:

$$\text{Productivity} = \frac{\text{output}}{\text{input}} \qquad (16\text{-}1)$$

Productivity, then, tells us how many units of output we can obtain from a unit of input. If output per unit of input increases, productivity obviously has risen.

As you might sense from this definition, there is in practice a whole family of productivity measures which vary depending upon the specific data one chooses to insert in the numerator and denominator of the productivity equation. For example, the output in the numerator might be the real GNP, the real output of the private sector, or the real output of a particular industry or plant. It is to be emphasized that the output in the numerator must be stated in *real* rather than money terms. The production of more goods and services per unit of input constitutes an increase in productivity, not higher prices on a fixed or even declining quantity of output. As for the denominator, some productivity specialists combine inputs of both labor and capital to derive a measure of *total factor productivity*. Because labor is the focal point of our discussion, we will be concerned with **labor productivity**, in which worker hours are related to total product, or real GNP.[1]

Measurement. Figure 16-1 provides information which enables us to calculate labor productivity for each of two specific years for a hypothetical economy. The figure shows two aggregate production functions, TP$_1$ and TP$_2$, each of which represents a specific year and relates quantities of worker hours to total annual real GNP for that period. We will initially focus our attention on the aggregate production function labeled TP$_1$. This curve reflects two assumptions—first, that the quality of labor, amount of capital, and the methods of production are fixed,

[1]For a brief survey of available productivity measures see Jerome A. Mark, "Productivity Measurement," in Jerome M. Rosow (ed.), *Productivity: Prospect for Growth* (New York: Van Nostrand Reinhold Company, 1981), pp. 54–75.

FIGURE 16-1 THE AGGREGATE PRODUCTION FUNCTION AND LABOR PRODUCTIVITY
The aggregate production functions TP$_1$ and TP$_2$ portray the relationship between worker hour inputs and total product, or real GNP, for two time periods and differing capital stocks. Assuming no change in labor hours, the upward shift of the production function portrays a 50 percent increase in labor productivity.

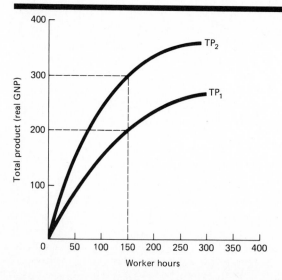

and second, that diminishing marginal returns occur over the entire range of the curve. In other words, TP_1 indicates the relationship between worker hours and total product, *other things being equal,* and shows that total product rises at a diminishing rate as added units of labor are used in conjunction with the fixed capital stock.

The input-output information provided by curve TP_1 allows us to measure labor productivity for this hypothetical economy for this particular year. Specifically,

$$\text{Labor productivity} = \frac{\text{total product (real GNP)}}{\text{number of worker hours}} \qquad (16\text{-}2)$$

Equation (16-2) confirms that labor productivity is simply the average productivity of labor inputs for the economy as a whole. For illustrative purposes, let us assume that the number of worker hours—the denominator in equation (16-2)—is 150. The aggregate production function tells us that total product is 200. Dividing 200 by 150, we conclude that labor productivity is 1.33. Equation (16-3) allows us to convert this labor productivity figure to an index number, using this specific year as the base year.

$$\text{Productivity index}_{\text{base year}} = \frac{\text{productivity}_{\text{year 1}}}{\text{productivity}_{\text{base year}}} \times 100 \qquad (16\text{-}3)$$

Equation (16-3) simply sets labor productivity equal to 100 for the base year. That is, $100 = (1.33/1.33) \times 100$.

We now can turn our attention to the upward shift of the aggregate production function from TP_1 to TP_2 in Figure 16-1. In the long run, other things are *not* equal; that is, labor quality can improve, the capital stock can increase, and resources can be combined more efficiently. For example, suppose that this economy enlarged its stock of capital goods, which in turn enabled workers to use more machinery and tools in the production process. As illustrated by the upward shift of the aggregate production function from TP_1 to TP_2, this would increase output per unit of labor input. Assuming that the number of worker hours remain constant at 150, total product would rise to 300, and labor productivity would increase to 2 (=300/150). By comparing this new productivity level, 2, to productivity for the base year, 1.33, we can determine the productivity index in year 2.

$$\text{Productivity index}_{\text{year 2}} = \frac{\text{productivity}_{\text{year 2}}}{\text{productivity}_{\text{base year}}} \times 100 \qquad (16\text{-}4)$$

Hence, the new index is 150 [=(2/1.33) × 100], which represents a 50 percent increase relative to the base year.

The BLS Index. The Bureau of Labor Statistics (BLS) publishes an official index of labor productivity for the United States economy. Table 16-1 shows the course of the BLS index of output per worker hour since 1960 and indicates the percentage change in productivity from the previous year. Note that 1977 is the base year for the index.

Because this **BLS productivity index** is widely used and cited, it is important to be familiar with its characteristics. First, the index is calculated by dividing constant dollar (real) GNP originating in the private sector by the number of worker hours employed in the private sector. The public sector is excluded from the BLS index for a very practical reason: The social goods and services provided by government—such things as national defense, flood control, police and fire protection—are not sold in a market to individual buyers. Therefore, it is extremely difficult to estimate the economic value of the public sector's output.

TABLE 16-1

Index of Labor Productivity* and Percentage Change over Previous Year, 1960–1984

Year	Output per Worker Hour	Annual Percentage Change
1960	65.2	1.5
1961	67.4	3.3
1962	69.9	3.8
1963	72.5	3.7
1964	75.6	4.3
1965	78.3	3.5
1966	80.8	3.1
1967	82.6	2.3
1968	85.3	3.3
1969	85.5	0.2
1970	86.2	0.8
1971	89.3	3.6
1972	92.4	3.5
1973	94.8	2.6
1974	92.5	−2.4
1975	94.6	2.2
1976	97.6	3.3
1977	100.0	2.4
1978	100.5	0.5
1979	99.3	−1.2
1980	98.8	−0.5
1981	100.7	1.9
1982	100.9	0.2
1983	103.7	2.7
1984	107.0	3.2

*Business sector

Source: *Economic Report of the President, 1985*, Tables B-40 and B-41, and Bureau of Labor Statistics.

Productivity experts believe that productivity has grown less rapidly in the public sector than it has in the private sector. For this reason the BLS data tend to overstate the entire economy's productivity growth. Second, the index understates productivity growth in that improvements in the *quality* of output are not taken into account. This, of course, is merely a reflection of a shortcoming involved in calculating real output or GNP for the private sector; GNP measures changes in the quantity, but not the quality, of output. Third, the use of output per worker hour subtly implies that labor alone is responsible for rising productivity. This is obviously not true. As we already implied in our discussion of Figure 16-1, the factors which affect labor productivity are manifold and diverse. They include improvements in the quality of labor, the use of more capital equipment, improvements in production technologies and managerial organizational techniques, increased specialization as the result of expanding markets, shifts in the structure of the economy, public policies, and societal attitudes. The point is that, while the BLS index of labor productivity provides information about changes in labor productivity, it does not explain the *causes* of these changes.

Despite the limitations and biases noted above, the BLS index of labor productivity provides a reasonable approximation of how private-sector efficiency has changed through time. Indeed, the official BLS measure has certain notable virtues. First, the index is conceptually simple and can quite easily be calculated from available data. Second, because it is calculated on a per worker *hour* basis, the index automatically takes into account changes in the length of the workweek. In contrast, an index of output per worker per year would understate the growth of labor productivity if the length of the average workweek decreased through time. Finally, as a measure of hourly output, the index can be directly compared with hourly wage rates.[2]

IMPORTANCE OF PRODUCTIVITY INCREASES

The growth of labor productivity is important for at least two reasons.

1. Productivity growth is the basic source of improvements in real wages and living standards.
2. Productivity growth is an anti-inflationary force in that it tends to offset or absorb increases in money wages.

Let us consider these two points in the order stated.

Productivity and Real Wages. Real wage rates have increased in the United States over the past century at an average annual rate of 2 to 3 percent. Figure

---

[2]For a succinct discussion of the problems involved in measuring productivity, see Sar A. Levitan and Diane Werneke, *Productivity: Problems, Prospects, and Policies* (Baltimore: The Johns Hopkins University Press, 1984), pp. 12–23.

16-2 provides an accurate but somewhat superficial explanation for that secular trend. The figure shows that increases in real wages, for example, from $(w/p)_1$ to $(w/p)_2$ to $(w/p)_3$, occur when the demand for labor rises more rapidly than labor supply. As seen in the figure, these rising real wages are fully compatible with increases in the number of worker hours (Q_1 to Q_3).

The supply and demand explanation for rising real wages naturally raises a more penetrating question: Why has labor demand increased over the decades? Figure 16-3 identifies the primary source of this increase: rising labor productivity!

Notice the extremely close relationship which actually exists between the increase in output per worker hour and the growth of average real hourly earnings.[3] Put simply, increases in labor productivity have increased the demand for labor relative to labor supply and therefore have boosted the average real wage rate. When one recognizes that society's real output *is* its real income, the close relationship between productivity and real wages is no surprise. Real income per worker per hour can only increase at the same rate as real output per worker per hour; more output per hour means more real income to distribute for each hour worked. The simplest case is the classic one of Robinson Crusoe on the deserted island. The number of coconuts he can pick or fish he can catch per hour *is* his real income or wage per hour.

The importance of the contribution which the growth of labor productivity has made to the overall growth of our economy can hardly be overstated. We

---

[3] The vertical axis of Figure 16-3 embodies a ratio, or logarithmic, scale which displays equal percentage changes as equal distances. For example, the distance from 50 to 60 is the same as the distance from 100 to 120; both are 20 percent increases.

FIGURE 16-2 REAL WAGE INCREASES: LABOR SUPPLY AND DEMAND EXPLANATION

Increases in real wages occur when the demand for labor rises more rapidly than labor supply.

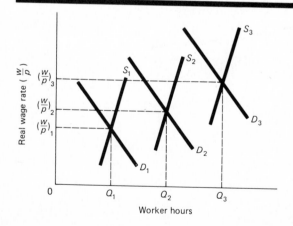

can rearrange the labor productivity equation (16-2) as follows:

$$\text{Real GNP} = \text{worker hours} \times \text{labor productivity} \qquad (16\text{-}5)$$

Equation (16-5) simply states that real output can increase because of an increase in inputs of worker hours *or* because each of those hours of work generates more output. In other words, total product as shown in Figure 16-1 can rise because of a rightward movement along an existing aggregate production function or as a result of an upward shift of the function. Data indicate that rising productivity has clearly been the more important of the two contributors to a growing real GNP. Over the 1947–1984 period, for example, real output increased by 245 percent. During this same period, labor productivity rose by 145 percent, while worker hours of labor increased by only 40 percent.

Inflation and Productivity. Although the causes of inflation are complex and controversial, most economists acknowledge a link between the rate of productivity growth and the rate of inflation. Other things being equal, rapid productivity growth helps limit the rate of inflation, and slow productivity growth causes the inflation rate to be higher than otherwise. More specifically, productivity gains offset increases in money wages and thereby help restrain increases in unit labor costs and ultimately product prices. Equation (16-6) is a useful approximation in understanding the relationship between increases in money wages, productivity, and unit labor costs.

FIGURE 16-3 LABOR PRODUCTIVITY AND THE AVERAGE LEVEL OF REAL WAGES
Because real output *is* real income, the growth of real output per worker hour and the growth of real wage rates are very closely related.

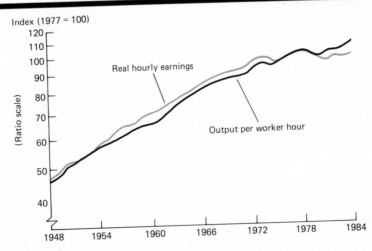

$$\frac{\text{Change in}}{\text{money wages (\%)}} - \frac{\text{change in}}{\text{productivity (\%)}} = \frac{\text{change in}}{\text{unit labor costs (\%)}} \quad (16\text{-}6)$$

If, for example, hourly money wages are currently $5.00 and a worker produces 10 units per hour, then unit labor costs—that is, labor cost per unit of output—will be $.50. Now, if money wages increase by 10 percent to $5.50 per hour and productivity also increases by 10 percent to 11 units per hour, then unit labor costs will be unchanged. That is, $5.00/10 = $5.50/11 = $.50. In terms of equation (16-6), 10 percent minus 10 percent equals no increase in unit labor costs. Similarly, if money wages rise by 10 percent and labor productivity does not rise at all, unit labor costs will rise by 10 percent. That is, if the wage is $5.00 initially and output per hour is 10 units, unit labor costs will be $.50. But with wages now at $5.50 and output still at 10 units per hour, unit labor costs will be $.55, which is a 10 percent increase. In equation (16-6), 10 percent minus 0 percent equals a 10 percent increase in unit labor costs. Columns 1 through 3 of Table 16-2 show the indicated relationship between changes in the hourly compensation of workers, productivity, and unit labor costs for the 1955–1984 period.

Given that labor costs on the average constitute 70 to 75 percent of total production costs and assuming that higher production costs eventually cause higher product prices, the link between productivity increases and the rate of

TABLE 16-2

The Relationship Between Changes in Wages, Productivity, Unit Labor Costs, and the Price Level, 1955–1984 (Annual Percentage Changes)

Year	(1) Compensation per Hour Worked	minus	(2) Output per Hour Worked (Productivity)	roughly equals	(3) Unit Labor Costs	(4) Price Level*
1955	2.5		4.0		−1.4	−0.4
1957	6.5		2.5		3.9	3.6
1959	4.3		3.2		1.0	0.8
1961	3.8		3.3		0.5	1.0
1963	3.7		3.7		0	1.2
1965	3.9		3.5		0.3	1.7
1967	5.3		2.3		3.0	2.9
1969	7.0		−0.2		6.7	5.4
1971	6.6		3.6		2.9	4.3
1973	8.0		2.6		5.3	6.2
1975	9.6		2.2		7.3	9.1
1977	7.7		2.4		5.1	6.5
1979	9.4		−1.2		10.7	11.5
1981	9.4		1.9		7.3	10.2
1983	4.3		2.7		1.6	3.0
1984	4.2		3.2		1.0	3.4

*Consumer Price Index

Source: Bureau of Labor Statistics. Data are for the private business sector.

inflation is clear. If we assume that labor costs are 70 percent of total costs, then, other things being equal, the 10 percent increase in unit labor costs in our example would translate into a 7 percent increase in product prices.

As the data in Table 16-2 suggest, with important exceptions, changes in unit labor costs and the rate of inflation do track quite closely. As a rough rule of thumb, in most years changes in unit labor costs are associated with similar changes in the rate of inflation.

One must be careful not to infer from Table 16-2 that the relationship between the growth of money wages and the increase in labor productivity is necessarily a primary cause of inflation. Many other factors—the money supply, inappropriate fiscal policy, expectations, price "shocks"—are all held by various economists to be of significance. Indeed, as we shall see in Chapter 19, monetarists would argue that the relationship between the growth of real output and increases in the money supply is the primary determinant of changes in the price level. They contend that excessive growth of the money supply causes all prices to rise, including the nominal price of labor or the money wage. But most economists argue that both demand and supply (cost) factors can cause inflation, at least in the short term. They believe that the relationship between money wages and productivity shown in equation (16-6) is an important determinant of the price level. In fact, as we point out in Chapter 19, the U.S. government has at times implemented wage-price policies designed to restrict money wage increases to the average labor productivity increase as a means of controlling inflation.

The question of whether increases in unit labor costs cause inflation or are simply a symptom of inflation is subject to great debate (Chapter 19). For now, suffice it to say that given the rate of increase in money wage rates, the higher the rate of labor productivity, the smaller the rate of inflation.

LONG-RUN TREND OF LABOR PRODUCTIVITY[4]

It will be useful to examine the long-run trend of labor productivity over two periods: 1889–1969 and 1970–1982. Available data suggest that over the eight decades from 1889 to 1969 the average annual increase in output per worker hour was about 2.4 percent. While this figure may not seem particularly impressive, the "miracle" of compounding translates this annual increase into very large increases in hourly output and income over a period of time. Specifically, a

---

[4]Among the numerous economists who have contributed to the economic literature on productivity trends, Edward F. Denison and John W. Kendrick stand out. See, for example, Denison's *Accounting for United States Economic Growth, 1929–1969* (Washington, D.C.: Brookings Institution, 1974) and *Accounting for Slower Economic Growth: The United States in the 1970s* (Washington, D.C.: Brookings Institution, 1979). Also see Kendrick's *Productivity Trends in the United States* (Princeton: Princeton University Press, 1961); *Postwar Productivity Trends in the United States, 1948–1969* (New York: Columbia University Press, 1973), and (with Elliot S. Grossman) *Productivity in the United States: Trends and Cycles* (Baltimore: The Johns Hopkins University Press, 1980).

2.4 percent annual increase in hourly output will cause output per worker hour to double in about 29 years. During the 1970–1982 period, however, productivity growth slowed to a 1.2 percent average annual rate. This slowdown is analyzed in the final section of the chapter.

Focusing on the 1889–1969 period for empirical support, let us delineate and discuss the causes of productivity growth. Generally speaking, the critical determinants of productivity growth can be classified under three headings: (1) the average quality of the labor force, (2) the amount of capital goods employed with each worker hour of labor, and (3) the efficiency with which labor and capital inputs are combined.

Average Quality of Labor. The average quality of labor depends upon the stock of human capital in the society and the degree of effort expended by workers. Specifically, it is evident that, other things being the same, a better-educated, better-trained work force can produce more output per hour than can a less-educated, inadequately trained one. Indeed, Chapter 4's discussion of education and training as investments in human capital which increase labor productivity and earnings is highly relevant at this point. Table 16-3 provides a general overview of the increases in formal educational attainment of the population (25 years of age and older) since 1940.

Investments in human capital which enhance the health and vitality of workers also improve the average quality of labor. Improved nutrition, more and better medical care, and better general living conditions improve the physical vigor and morale of the labor force. These same factors enhance worker longevity and contribute to a work force which is more productive because it is more experienced.

Finally, changes in the composition of the labor force have been a less

TABLE 16-3

Years of School Completed by the Population, 1940–1983 (25 Years of Age or Over)

Year	Percent High School Graduates or More	Percent College Graduates or More	Median Years of School Completed
1940	24.5	4.6	8.6
1950	34.3	6.2	9.3
1960	41.1	7.7	10.6
1970	55.2	11.0	12.2
1975	62.5	13.9	12.3
1980	66.5	16.2	12.5
1983	72.1	18.8	12.6

Source: U.S. Bureau of the Census, *Statistical Abstract of the United States, 1985,* p. 134.

obvious factor in enhancing the stock of human capital, increasing the average quality of labor, and thereby improving productivity. In particular, increasingly stringent child labor and school attendance legislation has kept potential young workers—workers who would be unskilled and relatively unproductive by virtue of their lack of education and work experience—out of the labor force. This exclusion has tended to increase the *average* quality of the labor force.

A benevolent circle of feedback and self-reinforcement may evolve historically with respect to labor quality. If the productivity of labor rises, real wages also rise. These enhanced earnings in turn permit workers to improve their health and education, which leads to further improvements in labor quality and productivity. And so the cycle repeats itself. This circular interaction may be strengthened by the fact that the demand for education and health care are both elastic with respect to income. This means that rising national income generates more than proportionate percentage increases in expenditures on these items.

Quantity of Physical Capital. The productivity of any given worker will depend upon the amount of capital equipment with which he or she is equipped. A construction worker can dig a basement in a much shorter period of time with a bulldozer than with a hand shovel! A critical relationship with respect to labor productivity is the amount of capital available per unit of labor or, more technically, the capital-labor ratio. This ratio has increased historically. For the aforementioned 1889–1969 period the stock of capital goods is estimated to have increased sixfold and, over the same period, labor hours are estimated to have doubled. Thus the quantity of capital goods per labor hour was three times as large in 1969 as it was in 1889. Stated differently, the capital-labor ratio increased threefold over this 81-year period.[5] The total physical capital stock (machinery and buildings) per worker in 1979 was approximately $21,500.

Improved Efficiency. The third and quantitatively most important source of rising productivity is greater efficiency in the use of labor and capital. In the present context "improved efficiency" is a comprehensive term which includes a variety of both obvious and subtle factors which enhance labor productivity. At a minimum, improved efficiency encompasses (1) technological progress, including that which is embodied within improved capital, (2) improved business organization and managerial techniques, (3) greater specialization as the result of expanding markets, (4) the reallocation of labor from less to more productive uses, and (5) changes in a society's institutional and cultural setting and its public policies.

Let us comment briefly on each of these factors. First of all, technological progress involves the development of more efficient techniques of production. The evolution of mass-production assembly-line techniques immediately comes

---

[5]Solomon Fabricant, *A Primer on Productivity* (New York: Random House, Inc. 1969), chap. 5.

to mind, as do computers, biotechnical developments, xerography, robotics, and containerized shipping. The switch from the old open-hearth process of steel-making to the oxygen method enhanced productivity in that industry, as did the supplanting of the distillation process by the newer cracking process in petro-leum refining. Improved managerial techniques—time and motion studies and the creation of new systems of managerial control of production—have similarly enhanced productive efficiency. Currently a variety of "worker participation" and "job enrichment" plans are being experimented with in the hope that they will enhance worker productivity. The growth of markets has allowed firms to become mass producers, and this in turn has permitted greater specialization in the use of labor and therefore greater output per worker hour. Productivity has also been stimulated by the reallocation of labor from less productive to more productive employments. Thus, for example, productivity gains have been real-ized historically by the reallocation of labor from agriculture—where the aver-age productivity of labor is relatively low, to manufacturing—where the aver-age productivity of labor is relatively high.

Finally, the cultural values of a society, the nature of its institutions, and the character of its public policies affect labor productivity in myriad ways. The simple fact that American values condone material advance and that the suc-cessful inventor, innovator, and business executive are accorded high levels of respect and prestige are important for productivity growth. Similarly, the "work ethic" is generally held in high esteem. Equally critical is the existence of a complex array of financial institutions which marshall the funds of savers and make them available to investors. On the other hand, recall from Chapter 8 that the impact of unions upon productivity is unclear.

Public policies and social attitudes provide a mixed picture with respect to their implications for productivity. For example, while the long-run trend to-ward freer international trade and the general policy of promoting domestic competition bode well for productivity growth, the many exceptions to free trade and procompetition policies do not. Tariffs and import quotas shelter American producers from competition and can have the effect of retaining labor and other inputs in relatively inefficient industries. Similarly, we know from Chapter 11 that discrimination based on race, gender, or age is an artificial impediment to allocative efficiency and therefore a barrier to productivity growth.

Relative Importance. Assessing the relative quantitative importance of the vari-ous causes of productivity growth is a difficult undertaking. Drawing upon his own research and the work of others, Fabricant made the rough estimates shown in Table 16-4. For the period 1889–1969, he estimated that approxi-mately one-sixth of the long-term annual increase in productivity was due to both improvements in the quality of labor and increases in the capital-labor ratio. The remaining two-thirds of the increase was associated with the collec-tion of factors we have termed "increased efficiency." As mentioned earlier, the 1970–1982 period witnessed a major stagnation in productivity growth. Economists are still sorting out the relative importance of the factors which caused the small increases which did occur.

CYCLICAL CHANGES IN PRODUCTIVITY

Emphasis thus far has been upon the long-term trend of labor productivity. Given the close relationship between productivity growth and real wages, this attention is entirely appropriate. However, productivity also exhibits a rather systematic short-run or cyclical pattern around the long-term trend. The character and consequences of this pattern merit comment.

Labor productivity generally displays a procyclical pattern. That is, productivity growth falls below the long-term trend during a cyclical downturn or recession and rises above the trend during an economic upturn or recovery. Over the 1889–1969 period total real output declined in 17 years and increased in the remaining 63 years. In the 17 years of declining real output the rate of productivity growth was *negative,* averaging −0.6 percent per year; in the 63 years of expanding aggregate output, labor productivity rose by 3.4 percent per year. The weighted average of these figures yields the 2.4 percent figure for the period which was cited earlier.[6]

The reasons for these cyclical changes in productivity are quite detailed. We shall simplify the discussion by considering just three factors: (1) changes in the utilization of labor, (2) changes in the utilization of plant and capital equipment, and (3) changes in the composition of aggregate output.

Utilization of Labor. As the economy moves into a downturn or recession, a firm's sales and output will decline more rapidly than its inputs of labor.

Specifically, during cyclical contractions, employers normally are loath to fire workers—preferring instead to shunt labor into maintenance and other

[6]Ibid., p. 90.

TABLE 16-4	
Relative Importance of the Causes of Productivity Growth, 1889–1969	
Improved labor quality	0.5%
More capital per worker hour	0.4
Increased efficiency	1.5
Average annual productivity increase	2.4%

Source: Solomon Fabricant, *A Primer on Productivity* (New York: Random House, 1969), pp. 52, 66, and 73.

less essential tasks rather than the production of goods—until they are convinced that the downturn is not a temporary aberration. As a consequence, *measured* productivity (the ratio of output to *employed* labor) declines. Analogously, once a recovery starts, employers put these underutilized labor resources back on the production line. So output can expand briskly with little need for new hiring, and measured productivity registers dramatic gains.[7]

Why the reluctance to fire workers during a downswing? Why is labor a quasi-fixed, rather than a completely variable, input? Some employees, of course, are salaried workers or "overhead" labor. Few firms will dispense with top- or middle-level executives during a downturn. An internal auditor, a marketing manager, and a personnel director will be needed even though output is currently down. In addition, the typical firm will have invested in the specific training of its skilled and semiskilled workers. Remember from Chapter 4 that such workers must be retained in order for the firm to realize a return on its human capital investment. If these workers are furloughed, the firm runs the risk of losing them to other employers. Finally, there are also layoff and rehiring costs to contend with, and within limits, it may be less expensive to retain and underutilize workers if layoff and rehiring costs can be avoided by so doing. Hence, firms find it to be in their long-run profit-maximizing interest to hoard labor during recession and, from a social perspective, use labor less productively than previously.

But during the upswing or recovery phase of the cycle, output can be increased substantially by simply correcting this underutilization. That is, within limits firms can increase output by taking up the slack in their currently employed labor forces. More output can be obtained from the number of worker hours now being employed so that productivity will rise sharply.

Utilization of Plant and Equipment. A similar point can be made with respect to capital equipment. Competition forces firms to design their plants so that they operate with maximum efficiency during "normal times." This means that, during a recession, falling output will cause the plant and equipment to be used at less than the optimum level, and productivity consequently falls. Conversely, during recovery plant utilization moves back in the direction of the most efficient level of output, and productivity tends to rise.

Composition of Output. Cyclical fluctuations affect the various sectors of the economy with differing degrees of severity. Specifically, the demand for durable manufactured goods—machinery and equipment and such consumer goods as

---

[7]Alan S. Blinder, *Economic Policy and the Great Stagflation* (New York: Academic Press, 1981), pp. 65–66.

automobiles, refrigerators, and television sets—is very sensitive to cyclical changes. By way of contrast, the demand for most services is much less responsive to cyclical changes. Thus, the *relative* share of manufactured goods in national output declines during cyclical downswings and increases during upswings. Because the level of productivity in manufacturing is among the highest of all sectors of the economy, it follows that the relative decline in manufacturing during a recession will cause overall labor productivity to fall. Conversely, the relative expansion of manufacturing as a proportion of total output during recovery causes average labor productivity to rise. Note that this effect is independent of other cyclical influences upon productivity. Even if no individual firm or industry experienced a productivity change due to a change in the utilization of labor and capital, the indicated relative shift in the composition of output would cause average labor productivity to vary procyclically.

Implications. Of what consequence are these cyclical changes in productivity? In the first place, they are not merely the result of cyclical fluctuations, but rather are an integral part of the business cycle. When the economy lapses into a recession, productivity falls sharply, and this tends to increase unit labor costs. If money wage rates continue to rise during the recession, unit labor costs will rise by an even larger amount. Rising costs typically squeeze business profits. This profit decline tends to deter investment spending in two ways: It diminishes the financial resources (undistributed profits) which firms have for investing *and* it generates pessimistic business expectations. Falling investment, of course, serves to intensify the cyclical downswing. Conversely, rising productivity during recovery tends to stimulate the upturn. Rapidly increasing productivity keeps unit labor costs down and contributes to rising profits. Profit growth is conducive to expanded investment spending, which accelerates the economic expansion.

A second and not unrelated point is that cyclical changes in productivity have important implications for economic policy. For example, some economists are more or less resigned to the view that it is necessary to create a recession through the application of restrictive monetary and fiscal policies to arrest rapid inflation. But an understanding of cyclical changes in productivity suggests that any such recession may have to be deep and long to produce its intended effects. Specifically, the decline in productivity which accompanies recession may contribute to rising unit costs which in turn may contribute to supply, or cost-push, inflation. On the other hand, if the economy is already in a recession and unemployment is high, then the rapid labor productivity increase which occurs in the early stages of recovery may permit policy makers to increase output and employment through expansionary monetary and fiscal measures with less fear of generating added inflation. The reason is that high productivity growth tends to limit cost and price increases.[8]

[8]A more detailed discussion of cyclical changes in productivity can be found in John W. Kendrick, *Understanding Productivity: An Introduction to the Dynamics of Productivity Change* (Baltimore: The Johns Hopkins University Press, 1977), pp. 87–89.

PRODUCTIVITY AND EMPLOYMENT

Let us now consider the impact of productivity growth upon the level of employment. Do employees "work themselves out of their jobs" as they become more productive?

Superficial consideration of the relationship between productivity and employment often leads people to conclude erroneously that productivity growth causes unemployment. The reasoning normally is that an increase in labor productivity means that fewer workers are needed to produce any given level of real output. For example, if a firm employs 50 workers whose average productivity is $10 worth of real output per hour, then $500 worth of output can be produced. If the productivity of the 50 employees were to increase by 25 percent to $12.50 worth of output per hour, the same output could now be produced with only 40 workers (= 40 × $12.50).

But this illustration is too simple because it ignores society's desire for additional output. Recall from Chapter 1 and your principles course that society's wants tend to exceed its available resources. Productivity increases allow society to achieve higher levels of output, that is, to fulfill more wants, given these limited resources. In terms of the previous example, the 25 percent productivity increase enables society to gain $125 worth of output. The 50 workers now can produce $625 worth of output (= 50 × $12.50) as compared to $500 (= 50 × $10 = $500). The long-term historical trend of productivity growth in the United States has *not* given rise to a growing stockpile of unemployed workers. Rather, increases in labor productivity have been associated in the aggregate both with higher real wages *and* higher levels of employment.

Does this positive relationship between productivity and employment also apply on an industry-by-industry basis? In answering this question it will be useful to (1) ascertain the relationship between productivity growth and changes in employment in an industry, *given the locations and elasticity of the product demand curves,* (2) indicate the complexities once these demand assumptions are relaxed, and (3) present actual data on the relationship between industrial productivity and employment growth in the United States.

Demand Factors Constant. Let us analyze how productivity growth and employment changes in an industry would be related in the *absence* of shifts in, and varying elasticities of, product demand. We must first establish that wage rates in various U.S. industries tend to move more in accord with *national* productivity than with *industry* productivity. That is, as indicated in the right-hand column of Figure 16-4, compensation per hour rises more or less evenly in all industries, even though output per worker hour varies greatly by industry (left-hand column). Why is this the case? If wages began to diverge—rising rapidly in high-productivity-growth industries and increasing slowly in low-productivity-growth industries—the wage structure would be pulled apart. Workers would respond to the growing wage differentials by leaving the low-growth, low-wage industries to seek the higher wages in the high-growth industries. Similarly, new labor force entrants would choose employment in the high-growth industries and shun the low-growth industries. The increased labor supply would tend to reduce wages in the high-productivity industries, and the diminished labor supply would tend to increase wages in the low-productivity industries. In short, labor supply responses would tend to prevent wages from diverging in the various industries. To repeat: The trend of wages paid by specific industries is dominated by the nationwide trend of productivity primarily because workers are responsive to wage differentials (Chapter 12).

With this fact in mind, let us now reconsider equation (16-6) in the context of a simple numerical example designed to illustrate the relationship between productivity growth and employment changes in an industry, *all else being constant*. Assume that (1) the annual rate of productivity growth for the economy as a whole is 3 percent; (2) industry X realizes a 6 percent annual productivity

FIGURE 16-4 OUTPUT PER WORKER HOUR AND COMPENSATION PER WORKER HOUR, SELECTED INDUSTRIES, 1967–1980

Changes in labor productivity vary considerably by industry on an annual basis, but compensation increases per hour of work tend to be closely matched *across* industries. Hourly increases in pay per year are more closely related to the average increase in labor productivity for the entire economy than they are to the change in productivity within specific industries. (*Bureau of Labor Statistics, Productivity and the Economy: A Chartbook, June 1983, p. 39.*)

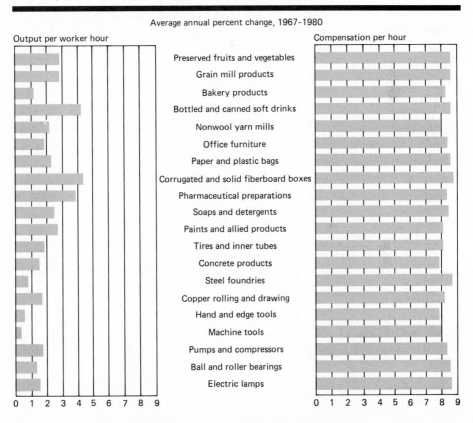

Average annual percent change, 1967-1980

increase, while productivity growth in industry Y is 0 percent; and (3) wage rates and earnings in both industries increase by 3 percent in accordance with the economy's overall rate of productivity growth. Substituting these numbers in equation (16-6), we find that unit labor costs will *decrease* by 3 percent in industry X and *increase* by 3 percent in industry Y. Further assuming that changes in unit labor costs result in roughly equivalent price changes, we can expect prices to *fall* by about 3 percent in industry X and to *rise* by about 3 percent in industry Y. *Given the locations and elasticities of the product demand curves* for the two industries, output and sales would rise in industry X and decline in Y. Provided that the increase in sales more than compensates for the fact that each unit of output can now be produced with a smaller quantity of labor, an expansion of employment in industry X would result. Conversely, the price increase for industry Y's product would reduce output and sales, implying the need for fewer workers. Therefore, other things being the same, industries with rapid productivity growth would tend to employ more workers, while industries with slow productivity growth would provide less employment.

Demand Factors Variable. It is *not* realistic to expect that product demand conditions are similar and unchanging for various industries in the economy. In terms of our numerical example, the demands for the products of industries X and Y may have different elasticity characteristics *and* may be changing (shifting) through time in such a way as to undermine the generalization that productivity growth and employment growth are positively related. The price and income elasticities of, and shifts in, product demand curves can and do have profound effects upon the cause-effect chain which links productivity and employment.

Once again, consider industry X, where productivity is rising by 6 percent and product price is *falling* by 3 percent. The consequent increase in output and employment would be especially large *if* the demand for its product is elastic with respect to both price and income. If demand is elastic with respect to price, then the 3 percent price decline will generate a larger (for example, 8 or 10 percent) increase in sales. This suggests a relatively large increase in employment. Similarly, if demand is elastic with respect to income,[9] then the growth of income in this economy will tend to cause relatively larger increases in the demand for product X. For example, a 3 percent increase in income—which is the amount by which real income is increasing in our hypothetical two-industry economy—might shift the demand curve to the right so that perhaps 9 or 10 percent more of the product would be purchased at any given price. Of course,

[9]Income elasticity is measured as the percentage change in quantity demanded relative to a given percentage change in income. If the percentage increase in the quantity demanded is greater than the percentage increase in income which triggered the increase in the amount demanded, then we say that demand is "income elastic" or "income sensitive." If the percentage increase in quantity demanded is less than the percentage increase in income, then demand is "income inelastic" or "income insensitive." In the special case of an *inferior good,* an *increase* in income *decreases* the demand for the product.

industry X's demand curve may shift rightward for reasons other than rising incomes. For example, consumer preferences for the product may become stronger, or the imposition of tariffs or quotas on competing foreign products may have deflected consumer purchases from imports and in favor of domestic production. The point is that increases (rightward shifts) in product demand will enhance output and therefore employment in the industry. In contrast, if the demand for industry X's product is inelastic with respect to both price and income, the increases in output would tend to be small. If sufficiently small, the increase occasioned by the enhancement in sales may fail to offset the fact that rising productivity has reduced labor requirements per unit of output. In this case employment in industry X will decline, despite the high rate of productivity growth.

The worst scenario in terms of adverse employment effects would occur if product X were an *inferior good*—a product which people buy *less* as their incomes rise—because the resulting decrease (leftward shift) of the product demand curve would tend to reduce employment even though product price is falling. Enhanced foreign competition or declines in the prices of substitute goods are other developments which could also cause decreases in demand and diminished output and employment. To recapitulate: The conditions most conducive to employment growth in an industry experiencing rapid productivity growth are (1) a price- and income-elastic product demand curve and (2) fortuitous circumstances which increase product demand.

Conversely, recall that industry Y, achieving no productivity growth, would find that the price of its product is *rising* by 3 percent. The adverse effect of this price increase on output and employment will be minimized, or perhaps completely offset, if product demand is inelastic with respect to price and elastic with respect to income. The employment-diminishing effect would be aggravated, however, if demand is price elastic and income inelastic. Once again, changes in product demand stemming from a variety of causes other than rising real income may intensify or alleviate the impact upon output and employment.

Our analysis can be used to gain insight into the waxing and waning—particularly the waning—of various industries in our economy. For example, productivity in higher education—particularly in teaching—has been relatively constant. The result has been rising educational costs and rising tuition. But the demand for higher education is inelastic with respect to price and elastic with respect to income. As a consequence, higher education has absorbed an expanding proportion of per capita income. Furthermore, the production of certain highly crafted goods—fine pottery, glassware, and furniture—has also experienced little or no productivity growth. This has resulted in sharply rising prices for such products. But the demand for these products is price elastic, and the result has been that the total production of such quality products has tended to fall. A similar analysis applies to the performing arts. (Given the size of the audience, how does one increase the productivity of a string quartet?) Live theater performances entail very high prices and prosper without subsidization only in a handful of large cities. The symphonies and community theaters of most cities and towns are dependent upon public and private subsidization.

Furthermore, the financial problems of many large cities may be intimately tied to the fact that they provide services—of police, hospital workers, social workers—for which it is difficult to raise productivity. As the wages of public employees rise in accordance with the (higher) productivity growth of the national economy, the cost of government services will necessarily increase. The source of soaring government budgets may lie much more in the low productivity growth associated with public services than with bureaucratic mismanagement or malfeasance.[10]

[10]These examples are from William J. Baumol, "Macro-economics of Unbalanced Growth: The Anatomy of Urban Crisis," *American Economic Review,* June 1967, pp. 415–426.

FIGURE 16-5 OUTPUT PER WORKER HOUR AND EMPLOYMENT, SELECTED INDUSTRIES, 1960–1981

Average annual percentage changes in employment within industries are not systematically related to industry annual productivity changes. (*Bureau of Labor Statistics, Productivity and the Economy: A Chartbook, June 1983, p. 47.*)

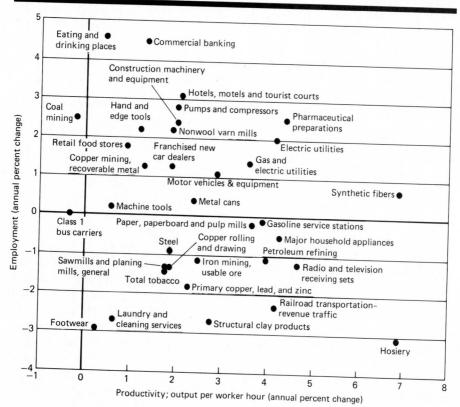

Observed Relationship: Selected Industries. Figure 16-5 compares for a 21-year period the average annual percentage changes in employment with the average annual percentage changes in productivity for some 35 industries. You will observe that the scattering of industry data points is random; one simply cannot generalize upon the relationship between productivity growth and employment growth by industry!

While productivity increased for 33 of the 35 industries over the 1960–1981 period, we note that employment increased in 18 industries, declined in 16, and remained unchanged in 1. In some industries rapid productivity growth is associated with declines in employment (hosiery, radio and television sets, and railroad transportation), while other industries experienced both rapid productivity growth and employment growth (electric utilities, pharmaceuticals). Similarly, some industries which have been comparatively stagnant with respect to productivity growth have experienced large employment increases (eating and drinking places, commercial banking), while employment has declined in others (footwear, laundry and cleaning services).

It is challenging to speculate about the productivity and employment changes shown for specific industries in Figure 16-5. For example, one might surmise that the decline in employment experienced by the hosiery industry, despite its rapid productivity growth, is associated with the fact that foreign imports have decreased the demand for domestic production. Similarly, the large rise in employment in the "eating and drinking" industry, where productivity growth has been negligible, might well reflect large increases in consumer demand related to changing labor market participation rates for married women. If we recall the time allocation model of Chapter 3, we can see how the increasing value of women's time in the labor market may have induced families to substitute time-saving meals in restaurants for time-intensive meals prepared in the home. The reader is urged to use his or her general knowledge of the economy to ponder the production and employment changes of various other industries shown in Figure 16-5.

RECENT PRODUCTIVITY SLOWDOWN

As mentioned earlier, the 1970–1982 period witnessed a major stagnation of productivity. Data make it clear that the rate of productivity growth began to slow in the mid-1960s and continued to decline through the 1970s and early 1980s. In the 1948–1966 period labor productivity rose at an average annual rate of 3.3 percent. That figure fell to 2.1 percent in the 1966–1973 period and then to only 1.1 percent in 1972–1978. Between 1978 and 1982, output per worker hour increased at an average annual rate of less than 0.2 percent.

The effects of this severe slowdown are those discussed earlier. The standard of living in the United States rose less rapidly than it had in the past and less rapidly than in several other nations. For example, real compensation per hour rose by 39 percent over the 1958–1970 period, but over the equally long 1970–1982 time span it increased by only 7 percent. For the 1973–1980 period, the annual average productivity growth was 0.1 percent in the United States compared to 3.4 percent in Japan and 3.2 percent in West Germany.[11] Also, according to many economists, the slowdown in productivity growth contributed to the unusually high inflation rate of the 1970s.

Possible Causes. There is no consensus among experts as to why American productivity growth has slowed and fallen behind the rates of Japan and western Europe.[12] Indeed, the fact that so many factors may bear upon a country's productivity performance may preclude a simple explanation of the slowdown. Given this caveat, let us survey some of the possible causes of the slowdown which have been put forward by various analysts. It will be helpful to distinguish between economic and institutional factors. Economic factors, to which we turn first, entail investments in new plants and equipment, the experience and training of the work force, and the development of new technologies.[13]

Economic factors. There is a high positive correlation between the percentage of a nation's GNP devoted to investment goods and the productivity increases it achieves. As Figure 16-6 indicates, the United States has been investing a smaller proportion of its GNP and realizing a lower rate of productivity growth than other western capitalist countries. Why has investment in recent years been relatively low in the United States?

A number of plausible reasons have been offered. First, the uncertain stagflation environment of the 1970s tended to dampen business incentives to invest. Indeed, the fact that stock prices were depressed while construction costs soared tended to induce firms to expand by buying existing businesses rather than by building *new* plants and equipment. Inflation also tended to squeeze *real* after-tax profits and thereby impinged upon the ability to invest. And the overall sluggishness of the economy in the 1970s undoubtedly acted as a depressant upon investment. Businesses are not anxious to add to their capital facilities when existing machinery and equipment are being underutilized!

---

[11]*Economic Report of the President, 1980.*

[12]There is also disagreement as to whether a slowdown has actually occurred. Michael R. Darby has recently contended that "the productivity panic is based on statistical myopia" and that in fact the long-term trend of productivity in the United States has been quite constant. See his "The U.S. Productivity Slowdown: A Case of Statistical Myopia," *American Economic Review,* June 1984, pp. 301–322.

[13]For empirical analysis of causes of the slowdown see Denison, *Accounting for Slower Economic Growth;* J. R. Norsworthy, Michael J. Harper, and Kent Dunze, "The Slowdown in Productivity Growth: Analysis of Some Contributing Factors," *Brookings Papers on Economic Activity,* no. 2, 1979, pp. 387–421; and John W. Kendrick, "Productivity Trends and the Recent Slowdown; Historical Perspectives, Causal Factors, and Policy Options," in William Fellner (ed.), *Contemporary Economic Problems* (Washington, D.C.: American Enterprise Institute for Public Policy Research, 1979), pp. 17–69.

In addition to the decline in investment spending as a percentage of GNP, the composition of investment spending changed in the late 1960s and 1970s. For example, the expansion of government regulation of businesses in the areas of pollution control and worker health and safety diverted some investment spending away from output-increasing capital goods and toward capital which may have increased total utility in society, but did not directly increase output itself. A firm which must spend $1 million on a new scrubber to meet government standards for air pollution obviously does not have that $1 million available to spend on capital which would add to its productive capacity.[14] Stated differently, the composition of investment may have shifted toward uses that do not increase *measured* productivity.[15] In addition, some economists suggest that high marginal, corporate, and personal tax rates have reduced after-tax profitability and therefore discouraged the undertaking of new investment projects. Finally, the dramatic increases in the price of energy which occurred in the 1970s may have caused highly productive, capital-intensive techniques to become relatively less attractive. In particular, high energy prices increased the costs of operating capital equipment. This in effect raised the price of capital

[14]This raises an important point. Workplace safety, clean air and water, and the general "quality of life" may come at the expense of productivity. But the converse is also true. That is, we cannot assume that productivity advances automatically enhance society's welfare; they may come with opportunity costs of other things which we value more highly. Productivity measures output per hour of work, not utility per hour of work.

[15]The interested reader should consult Edward F. Denison, "Effects of Selected Changes in the Institutional and Human Environment upon Output per Unit of Input," *Survey of Current Business,* January 1978, pp. 21–44.

FIGURE 16-6 INVESTMENT AND THE GROWTH OF PRODUCTIVITY
The larger the proportion of GNP which a nation invests, the greater will be its rate of productivity growth. (*Testimony of Michael K. Evans in Joint Economic Committee, Special Study on Economic Change, Part 2, 1978, p. 603. Data are for 1960–1976.*)

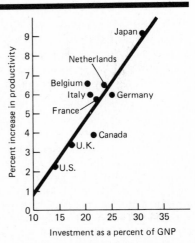

relative to the price of labor. Producers were therefore more inclined to use less productive, labor-intensive techniques.[16]

We must also recall that the critical relationship for productivity growth is the capital-labor ratio, which is the amount of capital available per worker hour. In the late 1960s and in the 1970s the labor force grew unusually fast as post-World War II "baby boom" workers entered the labor force and as women increased their participation rate. Specifically, in the 1948–1966 period the annual increase in worker hour *input* was 0.4 percent, but between 1966 and 1978 it averaged 1.4 percent. The stock of capital simply did not expand during this period at a sufficient rate to keep the capital-labor ratio from declining.

Aside from its rapid expansion, the average *quality* of the labor force may have diminished in the late 1960s and 1970s. The large number of young baby boom workers who entered the labor force had little experience and training and therefore were less productive. Similarly, we know from Chapter 3 that the labor force participation of women increased significantly over the 1955–1982 period. Many of these entrants were married women who had little or no prior labor force experience and therefore also had relatively low productivity. Finally, the average level of educational attainment of the labor force has been increasing more slowly in recent years. The median number of years of school completed by the civilian labor force was 12.2 in 1966 and increased to only 12.6 by 1983.

Technological advance—usually reflected in improvements in the quality of capital goods and improvements in the efficiency with which inputs are combined—may also have faltered. Technological progress is fueled by expenditures for formal research and development (R & D) programs, and R & D spending in the United States declined as a percentage of GNP between the mid-1960s and the late 1970s. Specifically, R & D outlays rose steadily in the postwar period to a peak of 3 percent of the GNP by the mid-1960s, only to decline to about 1 percent by the late 1970s. This decline was partly the consequence of decreasing federal support and partly the result of businesses' reaction to the economic instability and uncertainty associated with the 1970s.[17]

Institutional and behavioral factors. A very different view of the productivity slowdown stresses that forces of an institutional nature—the way work is organized, the attitudes and behavior of workers and managers, communication between labor and management, and the division of authority among managers and workers—account for much of our poor productivity performance vis-a-vis Japan and western Europe. The argument here is that American industrial relations are characterized by an adversarial relationship between managers and

---

[16]See Dale W. Jorgenson, "Energy Prices and Productivity Growth" in Rosow, *Productivity: Prospects for Growth,* chap. 2. Also see John A. Tatom, "The Productivity Problem," *Federal Reserve Bank of St. Louis Review,* January 1982, pp. 3–16.

[17]For the varying views on the role of the R & D slowdown in reducing productivity, see Zvi Griliches, "R & D and the Productivity Slowdown," *American Economic Review,* May 1980, pp. 343–348, and Frederic M. Scherer, "R & D and Declining Productivity Growth," *American Economic Review,* May 1983, pp. 215–218.

their employees. Feeling alienated from their employers, workers do not participate in the decisions which govern their daily work lives; they do not identify with the objectives of their firms, and they therefore are not motivated to work hard and productively. Managers are judged, rewarded, and motivated by short-term profit performance and thus, it is argued, give little attention to long-term plans and strategies which are critical to the realization of high rates of productivity growth. Japanese industries, by way of contrast, provide lifetime employment security for a sizeable portion of their work force, allow for worker participation in decision making, and use bonuses to provide a direct link between the economic success of a firm and worker incomes. Furthermore, the direct interest that workers have in the competitiveness and profitability of their enterprise reduces the need for supervisory personnel. The result of all this is a commonality of interest and cooperation between management and labor, greater flexibility in job assignment, and enhanced willingness of workers to accept technological change. Lifetime employment is also conducive to heavy investment by employers in the training and retraining of their workers.[18] The implication is that an overhaul of our industrial relations systems is a key to revitalizing our productivity growth.

A Resurgence? There is some evidence to suggest that the United States may have turned the corner with respect to its productivity slowdown.[19] Productivity growth rose to 2.7 percent in 1983 and to 3.2 percent in 1984. While it remains to be seen whether these improved figures reflect only a short-run cyclical improvement or a more permanent trend, it is quite evident that many of the factors which depressed productivity growth have dissipated or been reversed. For example, inflation has been brought under control, and therefore its depressing effect upon investment has been reduced. Similarly, business tax rates have been reduced and regulatory controls have been relaxed. Since 1977 research and development spending has been increasing as a percentage of gross national product. Important new innovations involving computerization and robotics may be providing a significant stimulus to productivity. The inexperienced baby boom workers who flooded labor markets in the 1960s and 1970s are now rapidly moving into the 25- to 54-year-old prime labor force as more mature, more productive workers. While American industrial relations remain distinctly different from the cooperative "shared vision" of Japanese managers and workers, the problems imposed by recession and increasing foreign competition are pushing American workers and managers in that direction. "Quality circles" and "employee involvement" plans are increasingly common in American industry. But to repeat: Whether the recent revival of productivity is transitory or permanent is unclear at this point.

[18]For an interesting elaboration of these points, see Levitan and Werneke, op. cit., chap. 3.

[19]See, for example, "The Revival of Productivity," *Business Week*, Feb. 13, 1984, pp. 92–100, and John W. Kendrick, "Productivity Gains Will Continue," *Wall Street Journal*, Aug. 29, 1984.

SUMMARY

1. Productivity is the relationship between real output and inputs. The "official" Bureau of Labor Statistics (BLS) index of labor productivity is the ratio of real GNP originating in the private sector to the number of worker hours employed in the private sector.
2. The BLS index overstates productivity growth because it excludes the public sector. On the other hand, it understates productivity growth in that quality improvements in output are ignored. The BLS index measures, but does not reveal the causes of, productivity growth.
3. The advantages of the BLS index are that (a) it is conceptually simple, (b) it automatically takes changes in the length of the workweek into account, and (c) it is directly comparable to hourly wage rates.
4. Economists are interested in labor productivity primarily because changes in productivity correlate very closely with changes in real wage rates.
5. Other things being equal, productivity growth tends to offset increases in money wages and thereby restrains increases in unit labor costs and product prices.
6. The basic factors which determine productivity growth are (a) improvements in the quality of labor, (b) increases in the capital-labor ratio, and (c) improved efficiency in the use of labor and capital inputs. Improved efficiency is quantitatively the most important factor.
7. Labor productivity falls below the long-term rate of growth during recession and rises above that rate during recovery. Causal factors include cyclical changes in the utilization of labor and capital and in the relative importance of the manufacturing sector.
8. There is no easily discernible relationship between productivity growth and employment changes in various industries. Price and income elasticities of product demand, coupled with demand shifts due to changes in such factors as consumer tastes or public policy, make it virtually impossible to predict whether a productivity increase will be associated with increasing or declining employment in any given industry.
9. The rate of productivity growth has slowed dramatically since the mid-1960s. Possible causal factors include (a) a relatively low level of investment spending, (b) demographic changes in the composition of the labor force, (c) a relative slowing of research and development spending, and (d) the adversarial relationship which typically exists between workers and managers.

QUESTIONS AND STUDY SUGGESTIONS

1. Key terms and concepts to remember: labor productivity, BLS productivity index.
2. How is labor productivity defined? Comment upon the shortcomings and advantages of the Bureau of Labor Statistics index of labor productivity.
3. How do you account for the close correlation between changes in the rate of productivity growth and changes in real wage rates for the economy as a whole? Does this relationship hold true on an industry-by-industry basis? Explain.
4. Discuss the relationship between productivity growth and price inflation.
5. Briefly comment in quantitative terms upon the long-term (1889–1969) trend of labor productivity in the U.S.; cite the three primary factors which contributed to that growth and indicate the relative quantitative importance of each. Discuss the

specific factors which have contributed to increased efficiency in the use of labor and capital.

6. Describe and explain the cyclical changes which occur in labor productivity. Of what significance are these changes?

7. Explain the relationship between changes in (a) money wage rates, (b) productivity, (c) unit labor costs, and (d) product price. What does this relationship suggest about the expected impact of productivity growth upon employment in a particular industry? Can you reconcile your generalization with Figure 16-5?

8. Assume labor productivity is rising by 6 percent in the economy as a whole, but only by 1 percent in industry X. Also assume that money wages for all industries rise in accordance with the economy's overall rate of productivity increase. Labor costs are 90 percent of total costs in industry X. The demand for industry X's product is highly elastic with respect to price and inelastic with respect to income. Assuming no shifts in demand curves for products in the economy other than those associated with changes in income, forecast the future growth or decline of industry X, specifying all of the steps in your reasoning.

9. Comment upon each of the following statements:
   a. "While most highly productive companies are profitable, not all profitable companies are highly productive."
   b. "Increased public demand for such amenities as clean air and safer workplaces has complicated the difficulties of comparing productivity rates over time."
   c. "Rising productivity means that it takes fewer workers to produce a given level of output. Productivity increases are therefore a source of unemployment."

10. The rate of increase in the productivity of American labor has been declining since the mid-1960s. How do you account for this slowdown? What specific policy changes do you think might help to reverse this trend?

11. What do you think would be the long-run impact of each of the following upon labor productivity?
    a. A decision by the Federal Reserve System to lower interest rates
    b. A sharp curtailment of military spending

SELECTED REFERENCES

DENISON, EDWARD D.: *Accounting for Slower Growth: The United States in the 1970s* (Washington, D.C.: The Brookings Institution, 1979).

GRILICHES, ZVI (ed.): *R & D, Patents, and Productivity* (Chicago: University of Chicago Press, 1984).

JOINT ECONOMIC COMMITTEE: *Productivity and Inflation* (Washington, D.C., 1980).

KENDRICK, JOHN W.: *Understanding Productivity* (Baltimore: The Johns Hopkins University Press, 1977).

KENDRICK, JOHN W., and ELLIOT S. GROSSMAN: *Productivity in the United States: Trends and Cycles* (Baltimore: The Johns Hopkins University Press, 1980).

LEVITAN, SAR A., and DIANE WERNEKE: *Productivity: Problems, Prospects, and Policies* (Baltimore: The Johns Hopkins University Press, 1984).

NELSON, RICHARD R.: "Research on Productivity Growth and Productivity Differences: Dead Ends and New Departures," *Journal of Economic Literature*, September 1981, pp. 1029–1064.

NEW YORK STOCK EXCHANGE: *Reaching a Higher Standard of Living* (New York, 1979).

ROSOW, JEROME M. (ed.): *Productivity: Prospects for Growth* (New York: Van Nostrand Reinhold Company, 1981).

T I M E   A N D   O N E - H A L F

PRODUCTIVITY: INTERNATIONAL COMPARISONS AND TRADE IMPLICATIONS

What are the implications of differing national rates of productivity growth for competitiveness in international trade?

Let us consider two questions. First, how does the productivity of the United States and its rate of productivity growth compare quantitatively with other major capitalist economies? Second, how do differences in productivity growth among countries affect international competitiveness?

Quantitative comparisons. Figure 1 indicates that American productivity growth has lagged behind that of its major international trading partners. Over the 1950–1981 period, U.S. productivity per worker increased at about 1.5 percent per year, as compared to approximately 2 percent for Canada and the United Kingdom, 4 to 4.5 percent for France and Germany, and over 6 percent for Japan. While all of these nations experi-

FIGURE 1 TRENDS IN LABOR PRODUCTIVITY, 1950–1981

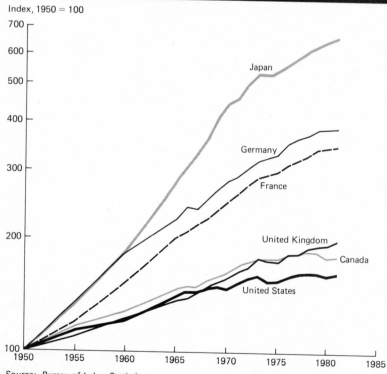

Index, 1950 = 100

Source: Bureau of Labor Statistics

enced a slower rate of productivity growth after 1973, the slowdown was the greatest for the United States and Canada. On the other hand, Figure 2 reveals that, while the productivity gap is closing, the United States still enjoys the highest absolute level of output per worker. Despite the rapid growth of output per Japanese worker shown in Figure 1, we observe in Figure 2 that Japanese workers produce almost 30 percent less per hour than do American workers.

Implications. Does the U.S. lead in the absolute level of productivity give it a competitive advantage in selling goods abroad? Does the lagging productivity growth in the United States doom it to reduced exports and increased imports? Somewhat surprisingly, the answer to both questions is "not necessarily." The relationship between a nation's productivity growth and its competitiveness in world markets is complex and unclear. In particular, high levels of productivity generally are accompanied by high real hourly pay, *and* high rates of productivity growth usually generate high rates of wage increases. With respect to the latter, in the 1973–1980 period the output of U.S. manufacturing workers grew by 1.1 percent annually, but real hourly compensation rose by only 1.8 percent per year. In comparison, output per manufacturing worker for the European Economic Community nations increased by 2.7 percent per year, while real compensation per hour there increased at an annual rate of 4.1 percent. Hence, despite slower productivity growth in the United States, European workers—not U.S. workers—tended to price

FIGURE 2 RELATIVE LEVELS OF PRODUCTIVITY, 1960–1981

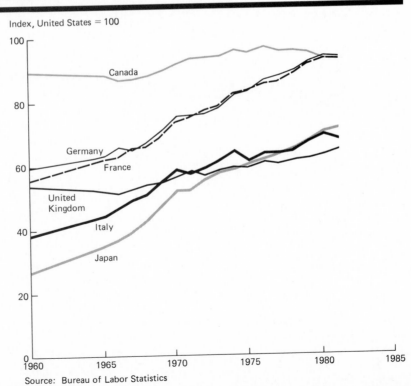

Index, United States = 100

Source: Bureau of Labor Statistics

themselves out of world markets through rising unit labor costs and higher product prices.*

If not lagging productivity growth, what was responsible for the much-publicized increases in the U.S. trade deficit during the mid-1980s? First, the international exchange value of the dollar appreciated and a "strong dollar" made American products more expensive and thus less attractive to foreign buyers. Second, debt-troubled developing countries were forced to curtail their imports of American goods. Finally, the United States experienced more rapid growth in national income, and therefore in imports, than did Japan and Europe.† In short, the generalization that a high absolute level of productivity enhances a nation's international competitiveness and that a slow rate of productivity growth generates trade deficits is only one-half of the story. Absolute levels of real wages and increases in real wage rates must also be considered, since unit labor costs are based upon both wages and productivity.

*Economic Report of the President, 1983, p. 53.
†Economic Report of the President, 1984, p. 43.

LABOR'S SHARE OF THE NATIONAL INCOME

The distribution of income has long been a major concern of econo-mists. Distinction is made between the (1) size or personal distribution of income and (2) functional distribution of income. The *size distribution of income* is concerned with the division of income among households and individuals classi-fied by income brackets and was considered in Chapter 13. The *functional distribution of income* focuses upon the division of national income among the productive factors—labor, land, capital, and entrepreneurship—which combine to produce that national income. In other words, the functional distribution of income shows how the national income is apportioned as wages, rent, interest, and profits.

This chapter examines the functional distribution of income. We first indi-cate several reasons why this is a topic of importance. Second, we present empirical data on functional shares and indicate a number of difficulties in-volved in using and interpreting these data. Third, we examine several theories of functional shares which purport to explain how the national income is di-vided in the long run. These include (1) a micro-oriented marginal productivity theory, (2) a theory based upon the bargaining power of labor unions, and (3) a Keynesian macro-based theory. Finally, brief consideration is given to short-run or cyclical changes in shares of the national income.

THE STUDY OF FUNCTIONAL SHARES

Why are economists interested in functional shares? First, the *alleged* constancy of wage and salary income as a share of national income has intrigued econo-mists and demanded an explanation. In a social science characterized by frequent changes in critical variables, a seemingly constant share of national income paid to labor resources invites investigation.[1] Second, the relative shares of the na-

---

[1] John Maynard Keynes once observed that "the stability of the proportion of the national dividend accruing to labor . . . is one of the most surprising, yet best-established facts in the whole range of economic statistics. It is the stability of this ratio for each country which is chiefly remarkable, and

tional income accruing to labor and property provide insights as to the relative importance of these two types of economic resources. Third, the relative sizes of property and labor income relate to the degree of inequality in personal income. Data show that income from property is more unequally distributed than income from work. Many of those with the highest incomes in our economy obtain large portions of their income from the ownership of property; those with the lowest incomes receive little or no income from property ownership. Fourth, the functional distribution of income may have significant macroeconomic implications. That is, the way the national income is shared may affect employment and inflation rates in the short run and growth rates in the long run. For example, if the functional shares accruing as rent, interest, and profits are relatively large, the economy's rates of saving and investment—and, hence, its rate of growth— might be greater than otherwise. Finally, economists have been interested in whether unions have been able to increase the share of national income received by employees. While one would surmise that the growth of a relatively strong labor movement in the United States would increase the wage and salary share, we shall discover shortly that it is not clear that this has occurred.

MEASUREMENT AND INTERPRETATION

Table 17-1 provides a long-run view of the various income shares as derived from national income accounting statistics. "Employee compensation" is essentially wage income. It consists of wages and salaries and a variety of wage and salary supplements, including payments by employers into social insurance funds and a variety of private pension, health, and welfare funds for workers. Economists refer to this wage and salary income as labor's share of national income. "Proprietors' income" is the income received by the owners of unincorporated businesses, that is, sole proprietorships and partnerships. "Corporate profits," "rents," and "interest" are virtually self-defining. These three income shares are frequently aggregated and designated as "business income" or "capital income."

Conceptual Problems. Before interpreting these figures, it is important that we be aware of limitations inherent in these income classifications which affect their usefulness in measuring and analyzing income shares. *The basic problem is that these empirical measures of income shares do not neatly fit the economist's theoretical concepts of the functional shares.* More precisely, the national income measures are partly a matter of accounting convenience, and hence, most are some mixture of wage, rent, interest, or profit income. Let us consider a few illustrations.

---

this appears to be a long-run, and not merely a short-period, phenomenon." J. M. Keynes, "Relative Movements of Real Wages and Output," *Economic Journal*, March 1939, p. 48. Note that we say "alleged" constancy of labor's share because, as we shall discover momentarily, some authorities contend that labor's share has increased over time.

The economist defines "rent" as the return paid to nonreproducible resources (land) which are provided in fixed quantities by nature.[2] But the rental share in the national income accounts includes payments for the use of housing and leased buildings, both of which are obviously reproducible and expandable. Similarly, one can argue that the employee compensation, or wages, category in the national income accounts reflects not only "pure" wage income paid to "raw labor," but also "interest" paid on investments in human capital (Chapter 4). Furthermore, because the salaries of business executives are included in this category, one can make a case that a portion of it is entrepreneurial or profit income. Similarly, corporate profits include not only entrepreneurial income, but also interest and rental income. Another more subtle problem stems from the way the income originating in the governmental sector is measured in national income accounting. Specifically, because the goods and services of government (national defense, police and fire protection, streets and highways, and so forth) are not sold on the market, they cannot be valued at their market price. Hence, in national income accounting, the value of government output is simply calculated as the value of the labor employed. Stated differently, government production is treated as being 100 percent labor-intensive, and no attempt is made to estimate the output contributions of public land and capital. Because the role of government has increased historically, this treatment of the value of public sector output may exert an upward bias with respect to labor's share.

[2]Economists consider rent on land to be a *surplus,* that is, a payment which is unnecessary to ensure that land will be available to the economy as a whole. Recall our related definition of "economic rent" in Chapter 10.

TABLE 17-1

Functional Shares, Percentage of Total in U.S. National Income, 1900–1984 (Period Averages of Shares for Individual Years)

			Property (Capital) Income			
(1) Decade	(2) Employee Compensation	(3) Proprietors' Income	(4) Corporate Profits	(5) Interest	(6) Rent	(7) Total
1900–1909	55.0	23.7	6.8	5.5	9.0	100
1910–1919	53.6	23.8	9.1	5.4	8.1	100
1920–1929	60.0	17.5	7.8	6.2	7.7	100
1930–1939	67.5	14.8	4.0	8.7	5.0	100
1939–1948	64.6	17.2	11.9	3.1	3.3	100
1949–1958	67.3	13.9	12.5	2.9	3.4	100
1954–1963	69.9	11.9	11.2	4.0	3.0	100
1963–1970	71.7	9.6	12.1	3.5	3.2	100
1971–1981	75.9	7.1	8.4	6.4	2.2	100
1982–1984	74.8	4.8	8.7	9.9	2.1	100

Source: Irving Kravis, "Income Distribution: Functional Share," *International Encyclopedia of Social Sciences* (New York: The Macmillan Company and Free Press, 1968) vol. 7, p. 134, updated.

Perhaps the most troublesome functional income category is proprietors' income. Proprietors—people in business for themselves—typically provide at least some of the labor and property resources used in their business in addition to their entrepreneurial talent. Consequently, their earnings are a mixture of wage, rent, interest, and profit income. The issue is how proprietor's income should be disaggregated between wage and capital income. Some economists contend that because many proprietors—for example, lawyers, dentists, barbers—are generally highly labor-intensive, it is a reasonable approximation to count *all* of their income as wages. Others disagree and propose alternative means of dividing this income between wage and capital shares. For example, one might impute an average income to each self-employed proprietor equal to the average annual wages of workers, multiply by the number of proprietors, and assign the resulting wage bill to the employee compensation share and the residual to the capital income category. Alternatively, one could split proprietors' income between employee compensation and capital income in the same proportion that wages bear to capital income in the rest of the economy. For example, note in Table 17-1 that for the 1982–1984 period capital income accounted for approximately 21 percent and employee compensation for about 75 percent of the national income. Hence, comparing employee compensation to the sum of employee compensation plus capital income, that is, to national income less proprietors' income, yields .78 [= 75 percent/(75 percent + 21 percent)]. Similarly, capital income as a percent of the sum of employee compensation and capital income is .22 [= 21 percent/(75 percent + 21 percent)]. Using this approach, we would therefore assign .78 of proprietors' income to employee compensation or wages and the remaining .22 to capital income.

Regardless of how we count proprietors' income, we cannot conclude that an observed increase in labor's share of national income necessarily reflects changed functional shares within *industries*. Rather the increase may simply result from a relatively faster growth of highly labor-intensive service industries, such as legal services, relative to the growth of capital-intensive industries, such as steel. Indeed, some economists factor out these changes in the *industrial mix* before examining the labor share trends.

The conclusion to be drawn from this discussion is that a great deal of caution and tentativeness must be used in interpreting the course of income shares on the basis of the national income accounts. One is never certain whether an apparent trend of, say, labor's share is the consequence of economic forces—for example, technological progress, changes in the structure of industry, or the varying strength of the labor movement—as opposed to measurement biases.

Interpreting the Data. The data in Table 17-1 can be variously interpreted, depending upon whether labor's share is viewed narrowly or broadly. On the one hand, if we define labor's share narrowly as "employee compensation" (column 2), the data indicate that labor's share has increased substantially in the long run from about 55 percent to 75 percent of the national income. The only apparent interruption in the relative growth of employee compensation in this century occurred in the 1939–1948 period, but as we shall see later, this is probably explainable in terms of the cyclical increase in labor's share which occurred during the Great Depression of the 1930s. Examination of the other shares suggests that the capital share (corporate profits *plus* interest *plus* rent) was quite constant during this century, declining by only a percentage point or two. Hence, the expansion of employee compensation has come primarily at the expense of proprietors' income. The dramatic decline in proprietors' income from about 24 percent to only 5 percent largely reflects the evolution of the corporation as the dominant form of business enterprise in the United States. Thus individuals who would have operated their own corner grocery stores in the 1920s perhaps now are paid employees in corporate supermarkets.

On the other hand, suppose one interprets labor's share more broadly. To simplify, let us accept the contention that proprietors' income is largely made up of payments to labor and combine columns 2 and 3—employee compensation and proprietors' income—as an approximate measure of labor's share. Now the situation changes considerably, and we find that labor's share has been virtually stable during this century! Labor's share broadly defined has fluctuated only 2 or 3 percentage points around 80 percent of the national income. Indeed, as an approximation one might say that labor's share (columns 2 and 3) and capital's share (columns 4, 5, and 6) of the national income have roughly been divided on an 80 percent–20 percent basis throughout this century. Conclusion? Labor's share can be variously interpreted as suggesting either an historically increasing or a relatively constant proportion of the national income accruing to labor.

THEORIES OF LABOR'S SHARE

At the outset we must stress that there is no generally accepted theory of functional shares. Numerous forces—including, among others, changes in the prices and quantities of inputs, technological change, the growth of labor unions, changes in the structure of industry—might be reasonably expected to affect income shares. In what follows we accept the modest goal of presenting the basic framework of three of these theories: (1) the micro-based marginal productivity theory which is associated with John Bates Clark (among others), (2) a bargaining power model which attempts to assess the impact of unions upon income shares, and (3) British economist Nicholas Kaldor's Keynesian-oriented macroeconomic theory.[3]

---

[3]Our discussion here is far from comprehensive. Aside from theories which are primarily of historical interest, the main omissions are the Marxian theory and the monopolistic pricing theory. The interested reader might consult E. H. Phelps Brown, *Pay and Profits* (Manchester, England: Manchester University Press, 1968) and Jan Pen, *Income Distribution: Facts, Theories, Policies* (New York: Praeger Publishers, 1971). More advanced volumes on the subject include Martin Bronfenbrenner, *Income Distribution Theory* (Chicago: Aldine-Atherton, Inc., 1971), and K. R. Ranadive, *Income Distribution: The Unsolved Puzzle* (Bombay: Oxford University Press, 1978).

The Marginal Productivity Theory. The essence of Clark's "factor pricing" or *marginal productivity theory of income shares* is essentially Chapter 5's marginal productivity theory expanded so as to apply to the economy as a whole.[4] Clark assumed that competition prevailed in both product and labor markets. Furthermore, to avoid the problem of dealing with the whole structure of wages, he assumed that all workers were homogeneous or, in other words, that there was only one type of labor. As demonstrated in Figure 17-1, the wage rate W paid to each of these homogeneous workers and the quantity of workers employed Q will be determined by the intersection of the labor demand and labor supply curves. Note that the assumption of competitive product markets makes the labor demand curve synonymous with the value of marginal product (VMP) curve. It follows that the total value of the output produced—that is, the national output or national income—is simply the total area under the aggregate labor demand (VMP) curve up to the equilibrium amount of labor employed. In other words, area 0AEQ is the national output and income. The total wage bill, or labor's *absolute* share, is obviously 0WEQ, the wage rate W multiplied by the number of workers employed Q. The remainder or residual WAE represents the absolute share of the national income accruing to owners of property resources

---

[4]John Bates Clark, *The Distribution of Wealth* (New York: Kelley & Millman Inc., 1956, originally published in 1899). See also K. W. Rothschild, *The Theory of Wages* (Oxford, England: Basil Blackwell, 1956), chap. 5.

FIGURE 17-1 THE MARGINAL PRODUCTIVITY THEORY OF INCOME SHARES
The intersection of labor demand and supply determines the average level of wages W, the level of employment Q, and hence labor's absolute share 0WEQ. Assuming competition, the labor demand curve is also the VMP curve. By summing the VMPs of the 0Q workers we can obtain the national income of 0AEQ. The property income absolute share WAE is found by subtracting labor's share from the national income.

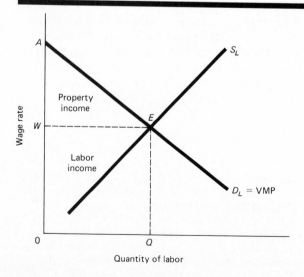

(capital and land). In terms of *relative* shares, labor receives $0WEQ/0AEQ$ and the property share is $WAE/0AEQ$.[5]

We might note in passing that implicit in Clark's simple model of Figure 17-1 are those changes which would affect the average level of wages, W. First, given the demand (VMP) for labor, a decrease (increase) in the supply of labor will increase (decrease) the average wage rate. The interest that many of the less-developed countries have in controlling population and ultimately labor force growth is evident in this generalization. Second, given the supply of labor, an increase in productivity would shift the labor demand curve rightward, or upward, and thereby increase the average level of wages. This generalization is already familiar to us; we found in Chapter 16 that there is a close relationship between the growth of labor productivity and increases in real wages.

Changes in absolute shares. Simple extensions of Clark's basic model make it possible to offer two propositions concerning changes in *absolute* functional shares.[6]

Proposition one: *An increase in the supply of any input (say, labor) will increase (decrease) the absolute share accruing to that factor, provided the demand for that input is elastic (inelastic).* The proposition follows from the total wage bill (wage income) rules for elasticity discussed in Chapter 5. In Figure 17-2 the increase in labor supply from S_1 to S_2 has two opposing effects upon labor's absolute share. On the one hand, the decline in the wage rate from W to W' tends to reduce labor's absolute share. But, on the other hand, the increase in employment from Q to Q' tends to increase labor's absolute share. By definition, an elastic demand for labor means that the increase in employment is relatively greater than the decline in wage rates. Hence, the net result is an increase in labor's absolute share.

From a geometric viewpoint we observe in Figure 17-2 that labor's absolute share is rectangle $0WEQ$ *before*, and rectangle $0W'E'Q'$ *after*, the increase in labor supply. Noting that the area $0W'BQ$ is common to both rectangles, we observe that the "loss" of $W'WEB$ is more than offset by the "gain" of $QBE'Q'$. Hence, there is a net increase in labor's *absolute* share; the new wage bill $0W'E'Q'$ exceeds the old wage bill $0WEQ$ by the excess of $QBE'Q'$ over $W'WEB$. No simple observation can be made about *relative* shares, however, because the national income has also increased from $0AEQ$ to $0AE'Q'$.

---

[5]Clark and other marginal productivity theorists held that the marginal productivity notion was also applicable to capital. This raised an intriguing and quite technical question: If labor and capital are both paid amounts equal to their respective marginal products, will the resulting absolute shares going to labor and capital precisely exhaust the available total output? Or will there be a residual? Or, alternatively, will there be insufficient output to go around? The answer to this so-called "adding-up problem" is that total output would be precisely exhausted only when the economy was operating under conditions of "constant returns to scale"; that is, when the inputs of capital and labor are increased by a given percentage, output will increase in the same percentage.

[6]These two propositions and the ensuing more complex analysis of *relative* shares are from John R. Hicks, *The Theory of Wages*, 2d ed. (London: Macmillan & Company, Ltd., 1963), pp. 114–120.

Proposition two: *An increase in the supply of any input (labor) will always increase the absolute share going to all other inputs taken together.* This generalization is apparent in our two-input economy of Figure 17-2, where we observe that the increase in the supply of labor from S_1 to S_2 increases the absolute property income share from WAE to $W'AE'$. You may recall that we provided a concrete application of this proposition in our earlier discussion of the distributional effects of immigration (Chapter 14).

Relative shares: price and quantity changes. Of perhaps greater interest is the question of what happens to *relative* shares in the long run in which the prices and quantities of the various inputs change. To get at this rather complex issue let us continue to think in terms of a two-input (labor and capital) economy.

In panel (a) of Figure 17-3 we portray the demand for and supply of labor in 1900 by D_{L1} and S_{L1}. Similarly, in panel (b) D_{K1} and S_{K1} represent the demand for and supply of capital in 1900. By multiplying the quantity of labor Q_{L1} by its price P_{L1} we observe that the rectangle $0P_{L1}aQ_{L1}$ in panel (a) shows labor's *absolute* income share in 1900. Similarly, the rectangle $0P_{K1}bQ_{K1}$ in panel (b) represents capital's absolute share in 1900. The sum of these absolute shares constitutes the total national income in our two-factor economy and we can determine *relative* shares by comparing the absolute shares of labor and capital with that national income. Using the hypothetical price and quantity figures shown in parentheses, we find in the left half of Table 17-2 that the absolute

FIGURE 17-2 ELASTICITY OF DEMAND AND CHANGES IN LABOR'S ABSOLUTE SHARE
An increase in labor supply will increase labor's absolute share when labor demand is elastic. In this case the increase in supply from S_1 to S_2 increases labor income from $0WEQ$ to $0W'E'Q'$. The lower wage rate W', which accompanies the increase in labor supply, reduces labor income by $W'WEB$, but the increase in employment to Q' adds the larger amount $QBE'Q'$ to labor's absolute share.

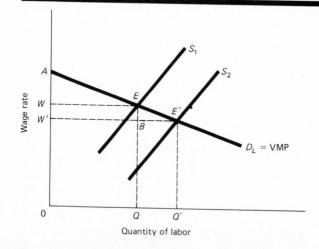

shares received by labor and capital are $80 and $20, and these constitute 80 and 20 percent of the $100 national income.

Given the long-run growth which has occurred in our economy, we would expect the demands for and supplies of both labor and capital to have increased over time. The extent to which the price and quantity of labor has increased relative to the price and quantity of capital as a result of these shifts in demand and supply will determine new absolute shares and also tell us how the relative shares of the two inputs have changed. In panel (a) of Figure 17-3 we show that labor supply has not increased as dramatically as has labor demand over this period. Why the relatively small increase in labor supply? The answer is that increases in the supply of labor are constrained by rates of population growth and increases in labor force participation rates (Figure 3-1). Compared to other nations, population expansion has been modest in the United States and, as we found in Table 3-1, the aggregate participation rate in the United States has been relatively stable. You might also recall from Chapter 3 that the workweek and workyear declined prior to World War II. In any event, as a result of the relatively small increase in labor supply, we find that the price of labor has increased greatly over the 85-year period, while the increase in the quantity of labor employed has been comparatively modest. We purposely portray a much different supply response in the capital market of panel (b). Here the increase in the demand for capital is accompanied by a very large supply response, with the result that the increase in the price of capital has been relatively small and the

FIGURE 17-3 THE EFFECTS OF SHIFTS IN INPUT DEMAND AND SUPPLY CURVES UPON RELATIVE INCOME SHARES

Increases in the demands for and supplies of labor and capital have increased the absolute incomes of both. In this case the price of labor has increased relative to the price of capital, but the quantity of capital utilized in the production process has increased relative to the amount of labor. As shown in Table 17-2, the magnitudes of these changes are such that relative income shares remain constant.

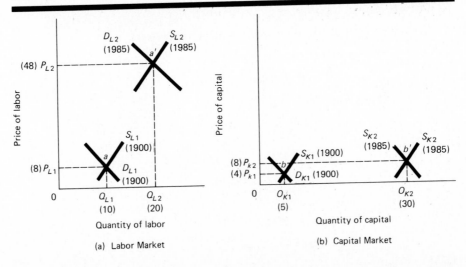

(a) Labor Market

(b) Capital Market

increase in the quantity of capital used relatively large. The large increase in the supply of capital simply reflects the absence of the constraints pertinent to labor.

The 1985 absolute shares going to labor and capital are $0P_{L2}a'Q_{L2}$ and $0P_{K2}b'Q_{K2}$, respectively. Using the hypothetical price and quantity figures for 1985, we can again calculate absolute and relative shares. In the right-hand half of Table 17-2 we find that the absolute shares are $960 and $240 for labor and capital, respectively. Comparing these absolute shares with the $1200 national income, we find in this instance that relative shares remain at 80 and 20 percent.

What is the purpose of this exercise? Basically, it provides us with a plausible interpretation of what has actually happened historically in the United States. First, real wages have increased in comparison to the real price of capital (as approximated by the real rate of return on investment). Second, a long-run substitution of capital for labor in the productive process has occurred. For example, you may recall from Chapter 16 that the capital-labor ratio increased about threefold over the 1889–1969 period; that is, the number of worker hours doubled during this period while the stock of capital rose about sixfold. This is not unexpected; the discussion of the least costly combination of inputs in Chapter 6 indicates that relatively cheap inputs (capital) will be substituted for relatively expensive inputs (labor). A third and closely related point is that the increase in the price of labor relative to the price of capital may well have been a factor that stimulated producers to discover and implement new capital-using (labor-saving) technologies. Finally, and most pertinent for our present discussion, all of these developments and adjustments are consistent with the concept of constant relative shares which, as we know, is one way of perceiving the national income data of Table 17-1.

Generalizing: the elasticity of substitution. It is important to understand *why* relative shares remain unchanged in our example. In this illustration the price of labor has risen relative to the price of capital. Other things being equal,

---

TABLE 17-2

Changes in the Income Shares of Labor and Capital (Hypothetical Data)

	Year: 1900			Year: 1985		
	Absolute Shares					
	Price	Quantity			Price	Quantity	
Labor	$8 × 10	= $ 80	Labor	$48 × 20	= $ 960
Capital	$4 × 5	= 20	Capital	8 × 30	= 240
National income		$100	National income		$1200
	Relative Shares					
Labor	$80/$100	= 80%	Labor	$960/$1200	= 80%
Capital	$20/$100	= 20%	Capital	$240/$1200	= 20%
National income		100%	National income		100%

this would cause *labor's* relative share to increase. However, other things are not equal; the higher relative price of labor induces the substitution of capital for labor in the production process. This tends to increase *capital's* relative share. The net outcome with respect to relative shares clearly depends upon which effect— the relative increase in the price of labor or the relative increase in the utilization of capital—is dominant. Or, stated more simply, the overall impact upon relative shares depends upon the ease with which producers can substitute capital for labor when labor becomes relatively more expensive.

The extent to which capital can be substituted for labor when the latter becomes relatively more costly is measured by the ***elasticity of substitution,*** which under competitive conditions is as follows:

$$E_s = \frac{\% \text{ change in } (K/L)}{\% \text{ change in } (P_L/P_K)} \tag{17-1}$$

In this formula K and L refer to the amounts of capital and labor, while P_K and P_L indicate the prices of capital and labor, respectively.

The alert reader will recognize the general similarity between this formula and the simple formula for the elasticity of labor demand presented earlier in equation (5-1). The essential difference is that here we are comparing percentage changes in quantity and price *ratios* rather than percentage changes in the quantity and price of a single input.

Let us use the elasticity of substitution to delineate three general cases, beginning with the circumstance of constant relative shares which we have already examined.

Constant relative shares: $E_s = 1$. In Figure 17-3 and Table 17-2 we observed that the ratio of the price of labor to the price of capital rose from \$8/\$4 or 2 in 1900 to \$48/\$8 or 6 in 1985 (a 200 percent increase). Similarly, because of this increase in the relative price of labor, firms increased the ratio of the quantity of capital to the quantity of labor in the production process from 5/10 or 1/2 to 30/20 or 1 1/2 over the same period of time. This change in the capital-labor ratio from 1/2 to 1 1/2 is also a 200 percent increase. Substituting these percentage changes in the price and quantity ratios in the denominator and numerator respectively of equation (17-1), we find that the elasticity of substitution is equal to one. *Generalization:* If the elasticity of substitution equals one, any proportional change in relative input prices will be exactly offset by the proportional change in the quantities of the inputs employed, and therefore relative income shares will be unchanged.

Increasing labor share: $E_s < 1$. What if technology was such that it was more difficult to substitute capital for labor? Specifically, what if the 200 percent increase in the capital-labor price ratio had been accompanied by an increase in the capital-labor ratio from 5/10 or 1/2 to only 20/20 or 1. In this case the proportional increase in the capital-labor ratio is just 100 percent. As a result, labor's relative income share will rise, and capital's relative share will fall. To verify this assertion simply substitute 20 for 30 units as the 1985 quantity of capital figure in Table 17-2. This decreases capital's 1985 absolute share from $240 to $160 and also reduces the national income from $1200 to $1120. Labor's relative share increases from 80 percent (= $960/$1200) to approximately 86 percent (= $960/$1120), while capital's relative share decreases from 20 percent (= $240/$1200) to about 14 percent (= $160/$1120). *Generalization:* If the elasticity of substitution is less than one (in this case 100%/200% = ½), the input whose relative price has increased (labor) will experience an increase in its relative income share. The relative share of the other input (capital) will obviously decline. Why does labor's share increase? Because the substitution of capital for labor is small in comparison to the relative increase in wages.

Decreasing Labor Share: $E_s > 1$. Finally, what if technology had permitted an even greater substitution of capital for labor than embodied in Figure 17-3 and Table 17-2? Suppose that the assumed increase in the relative price of labor had given rise to an increase in the capital-labor ratio from ⁵/₁₀ or ½ to ⁴⁰/₂₀ or 2 (a 300 percent increase). The result would be a decline in labor's relative share and an increase in capital's relative share. By substituting 40 for 30 as the 1985 quantity of capital figure in Table 17-2, we find that capital's absolute share in 1985 is $320 rather than $240 and that the national income is $1280 rather than $1200. As a result, labor's relative share falls from its original 80 percent (= $960/$1200) to 75 percent (= $960/$1280), while capital's relative share rises from 20 percent (= $240/$1200) to 25 percent (= $320/$1280). Note in terms of equation (17-1) that the 200 percent increase in the relative price of labor generates a 300 percent increase (⁵/₁₀ or ½ to ⁴⁰/₂₀ or 2) in the capital-labor ratio. *Generalization:* If the elasticity of substitution is greater than one (300%/200% = 1½ in this instance), the input whose relative price has increased (labor) will incur a decline in its relative income share. This means that capital's relative share will increase.

The top portion of Table 17-3 is a convenient summary of the generalizations we have derived from our discussion. The bottom portion simply restates

---

TABLE 17-3

Income Shares and the Elasticity of Substitution

| Direction of P_L/P_K Change | Elasticity of Substitution, E_s | | |
	$E_s > 1$ (Elastic)	$E_s = 1$ (Unit)	$E_s < 1$ (Inelastic)
Increase	Labor's share decreases Capital's share increases	Income shares are unchanged	Labor's share increases Capital's share decreases
Decrease	Labor's share increases Capital's share decreases	Income shares are unchanged	Labor's share decreases Capital's share increases

these generalizations when it is assumed that the price of labor has *decreased* relative to the price of capital. The table merits careful study by the reader.

Bargaining Power Theory: The Role of Unions. The marginal productivity theory of income shares assumes that there is competition and that the prices of both products and inputs are therefore determined by the market. In contrast, the *bargaining power theory* postulates that labor unions might have the power to alter market wage rates and thereby obtain an enlarged share of output for their constituents. Indeed, we found in Chapter 8 that studies for the 1950s suggest that union workers achieved an estimated relative wage advantage of 10 to 15 percent over nonunion workers in the same occupation, while more recent studies suggest that this differential may have widened to 20 or 30 percent in the 1970s.

The critical question is whether the ability of unions to raise wage rates is reflected in a rising national income share for labor. The answer provided by most researchers is that unions have *not* been able to increase labor's relative share. Consider three complementary explanations of this conclusion.

First, we know from Chapter 8 that the attainment of higher wages by unions reduces employment opportunities in unionized labor markets. According to the spillover effect (Figure 8-2), workers thus tend to reallocate themselves to nonunion labor markets as they seek employment. This increase in the supply of labor will tend to reduce wage rates in nonunion labor markets. In short, simple economic analysis suggests that higher wages for organized workers may come at the expense of the wages of unorganized workers. Hence, the average wage level and therefore the overall share of the national income going to labor may very well remain unchanged. Union workers apparently gain at the expense of nonunion workers, not at the expense of the capital share.

A second scenario emphasizes the substitution of capital for labor. As unions succeed in raising wages, affected employers will be prompted to substitute capital for labor in order to minimize production costs. Indeed, if capital is highly substitutable for labor, the demand for labor may be relatively elastic (Chapter 5). When this is the case, an increase in the wage rate will *reduce* the wage bill. In comparing the income shares of predominantly unionized sectors of the economy (manufacturing, mining, construction, transportation, and communications) with predominantly nonunion sectors (agriculture, wholesale and retail trade, finance, and services) for the 1919–1956 period, Cartter found that labor's share *declined* in the unionized and *increased* in the nonunionized sectors. Cartter attributed the declining labor share in the unionized sectors largely to shifts to capital-intensive production methods.[7] More recent data suggest that labor's share in the highly unionized sectors has been virtually constant, while labor's share in the essentially unorganized sectors has continued to trend upward.

[7]Allan M. Cartter, *Theory of Wages and Employment* (Homewood, Ill.: Richard D. Irwin, Inc., 1959), pp. 167–171.

Finally, Kerr has offered what might be termed the ***pursuit-and-escape scenario*** to explain the apparent inability of organized labor to increase labor's relative share. Kerr envisions labor and management as being engaged in a contest of pursuit and escape. Organized labor attempts to encroach upon profits by increasing money wages. But management can escape this encroachment in either of two ways: (1) by increasing productivity, which has the effect of absorbing money wage increases and preserving profits, and (2) by increasing product prices as a means of passing increases in wage costs on to consumers. Kerr argues that it has been the effective use of these two escape techniques by management which explains the perceived historical stability of labor's share.[8]

Phelps Brown cites two rather remarkable episodes of money wage inflation which lend support for the pursuit-and-escape scenario. The first involves the so-called "Blum Experiment." In 1936–1937 in France the government of Leon Blum undertook policies which within 9 months raised the hourly cost of labor to French industry by some 60 percent! Within a short period the prices of industrial products had also increased by 60 percent and profit margins were restored. The second case occurred in Australia shortly after the outbreak of the Korean war in the early 1950s. The weekly earnings of workers rose by 20 percent or more in each of 2 successive years. Within 2 years the profit margins of manufacturers were reestablished at their initial levels.[9]

The overall conclusion is that, because of (1) their indirect wage-reducing effects in nonunion labor markets, (2) the substitution of capital for labor, and (3) the ability of management to raise productivity and product prices, unions probably have *not* had an observable effect upon labor's share of the national income.

Kaldor's Macro-Based Theory. Given that functional shares are essentially aggregative concepts, it is no surprise that some economists have drawn upon the concepts of macroeconomics or, more precisely, Keynesian economics to explain income shares. One of the better known models is ***Kaldor's macro-based model***, which attempts to demonstrate that labor's share varies inversely, and the profit or capital share of the national income varies directly, with the investment-income ratio.[10]

Assumptions and relationships. The key assumptions and relationships embodied in Kaldor's model are as follows. In the first place, he envisions a private (no-government) economy which is operating at the full employment level. In this economy the entire national income Y consists of wage income W

[8]Clark Kerr, "Labor's Income Share and the Labor Movement," in George W. Taylor and Frank C. Pierson (eds.), *New Concepts in Wage Determination* (New York: McGraw-Hill Book Company, 1957), pp. 260–298.

[9]Phelps Brown, *Pay and Profits*, pp. 17–21.

[10]Nicholas Kaldor, "Alternative Theories of Distribution," *Review of Economic Studies*, 1955–1956, pp. 83–100.

and profit or capital income P. Relative shares are therefore W/Y and P/Y for labor and capital respectively. The equilibrium national income will occur where planned or intended investment I is equal to saving S. Recall from your introductory economics that the production of any level of national output generates an identical amount of income. But a portion of that income is saved, causing consumption to be insufficient to purchase the entire national output. National output will only remain stable (that is, be in equilibrium) if investment expenditures are sufficient to fill the "consumption gap" created by saving. To repeat: Equilibrium occurs where investment and saving are equal or, stated relative to the national income, where I/Y equals S/Y.

Kaldor makes additional stipulations concerning the nature of saving and investment. In the case of the former he indicates that total saving in the economy is the sum of saving by wage earners and by owners of capital. Kaldor further assumes that (1) the propensities to save of both wage earners and capitalists are constant; that is, the fractions of their incomes which they save do *not* vary as their incomes change and (2) the propensity to save of wealthier profit receivers is greater than that of less affluent wage earners. With respect to investment, Kaldor assumes that it does *not* vary with the level of national income, but rather is determined by such factors as business expectations, technological change, and so forth.

The model. Figure 17-4 is a useful way of bringing together these assumptions and relationships. The vertical axis shows the saving-income *and* invest-

FIGURE 17-4 THE EQUILIBRIUM SHARES OF PROFITS AND WAGES
In Kaldor's model the relative shares of national income received as profits and wages are determined by the intersection of the I/Y and S/Y lines or, in other words, where investment equals saving. An increase (decrease) in I/Y will decrease (increase) the wage share and increase (decrease) the profit share. [*John T. Addison and W. Stanley Siebert, The Market for Labor: An Analytical Treatment (Santa Monica, Calif.: Goodyear Publishing Company. Inc., 1979), p. 278.*]

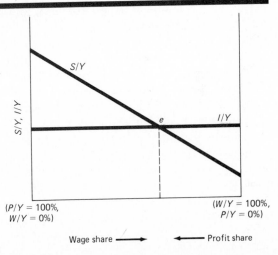

ment-income ratios. The horizontal axis shows relative income shares with the wage share increasing as we move left to right and the profit share increasing as we move right to left. The S/Y line rises northwesterly as P/Y rises (and W/Y falls). The reason for this, of course, is that the propensity to save of profit income receivers exceeds that of wage income receivers. Hence, as we move from right to left on the horizontal axis, the resulting redistribution of a given national income from wages to profits results in a larger volume of saving and a rising saving-income ratio. The horizontal I/Y line reflects the earlier noted assumption that investment is independent of the level of national income.

Equilibrium occurs where investment equals saving ($I = S$) or, in this portrayal, where the investment-income ratio equals the saving-income ratio ($I/Y = S/Y$) at point e. The critical conclusion of Kaldor's model is that an increase in the investment-income ratio—that is, an upward shift in the I/Y line—will lower the wage share and increase the profit share of national income as indicated on the horizontal axis. Stated simply, an increase in I/Y requires a functional redistribution of the national income from wage to profit receivers in order to achieve the higher S/Y required to restore equilibrium ($I = S$). Conversely, a decline in the investment-income ratio will increase labor's share and reduce the profit share of national income. In short, labor's share varies inversely, while the profit share varies directly, with the investment-income ratio.

The redistributional process. Figure 17-4 is useful in demonstrating what will happen to the wage and profit shares of the national income as the investment-income ratio changes. What it does *not* reveal is the specific nature of the *process* by which this redistribution occurs. How, for example, does the national income get reapportioned from wage to profit receivers when I/Y increases? The answer, according to Kaldor, is through changes in the price level. Let us suppose an increase occurs in I/Y. Recalling Kaldor's assumption that the economy is at full employment, the increase in investment spending cannot induce an increase in *real* national income. But the added spending can and does bid up the *money* national income. Stated differently, the increase in investment generates demand-pull inflation (Chapter 19). This supposedly causes product prices to rise faster than money wages, so that profits increase relative to wage income. In other words, the profit share rises relative to the wage share. Because the propensity to save of profit receivers exceeds that of wage receivers, the aggregate S/Y ratio increases as it must to restore equilibrium. A decline in I/Y will trigger the opposite scenario. Prices will presumably fall ahead of money wages, causing a redistribution of income from profits to wages and a decline in saving and S/Y.

How then does Kaldor's model relate to the observed trend in the functional distribution of income shown earlier in Table 17-1? Again, recall the two possible interpretations of that data. If we accept the view that labor's share has been relatively constant, then this would imply a relatively stable I/Y ratio over the years. On the other hand, if labor's share has increased secularly as some believe, then we should observe a decline in the I/Y ratio as well. The evidence indicates that the I/Y ratio has remained reasonably constant over the long secular trend in the United States, although some economists perceived a slight decline in the ratio in the 1970s.

Criticisms. Kaldor's pioneering Keynesian-based model has not been without its critics. First, the model assumes the distinctly *non*-Keynesian premise that the economy is operating at full employment. The model does *not* provide a clear picture of what would happen to income shares as investment increased in an economy with less than full employment and therefore failed to create demand-pull inflation. Second, as we shall see in the ensuing section on cyclical changes in income shares, there is no general agreement that wage increases always lag behind price increases during periods of demand-pull inflation. If they don't, the redistribution of income predicted by Kaldor will not occur. Third, the assumed constancy of the savings propensities has been challenged. A basic premise of Keynesian theory is that *average* propensities to save of all income receivers increase as their incomes increase. Fourth, the assumption that investment is independent of the other variables in the model has also been questioned. In Kaldor's model investment determines the profit share. But critics argue that causation may run the other way. Businesses may be expected to adjust their levels of investment to the level of profits (undistributed business earnings). Or firms may adjust the proportion of their profits which they retain (save) to fulfill their investment plans. The point is that most economists feel that the relationship between saving, investment, and profits is in reality much more complex and uncertain than that portrayed in Kaldor's model. Finally, the model clearly suggests that empirical data should confirm a fairly stable relationship between changes in investment and changes in profits. In fact, data indicate that no such relationship exists. But irrespective of these criticisms, considerable interest remains in Kaldorian-type explanations of functional shares.[11]

CYCLICAL CHANGES IN LABOR'S SHARE

Data reveal a rather marked anticyclical movement of labor's share. That is, labor's relative share seems to rise during recession and to fall during prosperity. The profit share behaves in the opposite, procyclical fashion; it falls during recession and rises during economic recovery and expansion. These changes are conspicuously evident in Table 17-1's comparison of the 1930–1939 Great Depression decade with the booming 1920–1929 decade which preceded it. Economists have generally explained these cyclical shifts in income shares in terms of (1) the capacity effect and (2) the wage-lag effect.[12]

[11]For more detailed accounts of these criticisms see Jan Pen, *Income Distribution: Facts, Theories, Policies,* pp. 186–190 and E. H. Phelps Brown, *Pay and Profits,* chap. 4.
[12]For a more detailed treatment of this topic see Robin Hahnel and Howard J. Sherman, "Income Distribution and the Business Cycle: Three Conflicting Hypotheses," *Journal of Economic Issues,* March 1982, pp. 49–71.

Capacity Effect. The more widely accepted hypothesis is that the procyclical behavior of the profit share—and hence the anticyclical behavior of the wage share—is the consequence of cyclical changes in the levels of plant utilization. The basic thrust of the *capacity effect* is that, by using their plants at "normal" capacity during prosperity, firms earn larger profits than when their plants are underutilized during recession.

Figure 17-5 is a useful focal point for our discussion. Recall from your introductory economics that a firm's average or unit cost curve, AC, is U-shaped.[13] To simplify we assume in Figure 17-5 that the firm is selling its product at price P_p. The essence of the capacity effect is that during prosperity most firms enjoy high levels of output and sales at Q_p and therefore a wide profit margin as shown by *ab*. But during recession, output and sales fall far short of capacity, at Q_r, and rising unit costs cause per unit profits to fall to *a'b'*. Observe that during prosperity profits expand because per unit profits increase *and* sales expand. Conversely, during recession profits contract because per unit profits are squeezed *and* fewer units are sold. This rise of profits during prosperity is such as

[13]If your memory is a bit hazy, the explanation is as follows. The short-run average cost curve falls with output for essentially two reasons. First, fixed costs (for example, rent, interest on bonded indebtedness, contractual wages, property taxes) per unit of output decline as they are spread over a larger and larger number of units of output. Second, variable costs (for example, most labor, raw materials, power) per unit decline because of *increasing* returns (rising marginal productivity) encountered in the early stages of production. Ultimately, however, unit variable costs rise because of *diminishing* returns, and when rising unit variable costs increase sufficiently to offset the effect of falling unit fixed costs, the average or unit (total) cost curve will rise.

FIGURE 17-5 THE CAPACITY EFFECT: AVERAGE COSTS AND PROFITS IN PROSPERITY AND RECESSION

The capacity effect holds that, when firms are operating at or near a prosperity or capacity output Q_p, their unit and total profits will be large. Hence, the profit share of national income will be large and labor's share will be small. Conversely, at a less-than-capacity recession output Q_r, per unit and total profits will be small, causing the profit share to be small and labor's share to be large.

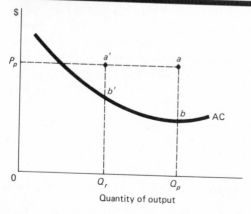

to cause the profit share of national income to rise and labor's relative share to fall. The opposite occurs during recession.

Other, more complex, forces are also at work here. Specifically, the price and cost curve shown in Figure 17-5 might well change over the cycle. For example, during economic expansion the price might rise as the demand for products increases. Furthermore, we know from Chapter 16 that labor productivity rises at above-average rates during expansion, which would cause the unit cost curve to shift downward. Both of these developments would tend to enhance the growth of profits as firms moved from below-capacity (recession) levels of production toward capacity (prosperity) levels. A possible offsetting factor is that, during the later phases of an economic expansion, wage rates may rise more rapidly than productivity growth, causing the unit or average cost curve to shift upward. Proponents of the capacity effect feel that these real-world complications do not alter the overall explanatory value of their hypothesis.

Wage-Lag Effect. A more controversial and less well-accepted explanation of cyclical changes in income shares is based on the *wage-lag effect*. The contention here is that wages are relatively inflexible compared to prices in both cyclical upswings and downswings. Hence, the profit share rises and labor's share falls during upswings as prices increase more rapidly than money wages. The opposite occurs during cyclical downswings. But why do wages lag? First, an inflationary expansion based upon an increase in aggregate demand normally affects product markets—and therefore product prices and profits—before it affects labor and other resource markets. Second, the unionized sector is characterized by relatively long-term wage contracts which slow the adjustment of money wages to inflation. Finally, it may also be that many individual workers and nonunion workers simply do not realize that rising prices have reduced their real wages until significantly after the fact.

The wage-lag effect tells us that real wages should fall during inflationary periods. Does this really happen? Direct empirical investigation of a number of important inflationary episodes yields basically inconclusive findings. Furthermore, in those instances where real wages actually did decline, it is often possible to attribute the decline to considerations other than inflation. For example, a decline in average real wages during an inflation might be due to a change in the size or location of the labor force, not to an increase in the price level ahead of money wages. One important test of the wage-lag effect produced the "wrong" results and has cast some doubt about the validity of the concept. The test was based on the hypothesis that for the wage-lag effect to be valid, firms with larger relative wage bills should have a greater increase in profits during inflation than those with smaller wage bills. The results did not support the hypothesis.[14]

---

[14]See R. A. Kessel and A. A. Alchian, "The Meaning and Validity of the Inflation-Induced Lag of Wages Behind Prices," *American Economic Review*, March 1960, pp. 43–66.

SUMMARY

1. Because the various national income accounting measures do not coincide with the economist's concepts of functional shares, these data do not yield an unambiguous view of the secular trend of labor's relative share. While "employee compensation" (the wage share narrowly defined) has increased in the long run, the sum of "employee compensation" and "proprietors' income" (the wage share broadly defined) has been fairly constant.

2. The marginal productivity theory of labor's share is the basis for two generalizations concerning labor's absolute share. First, an increase in the supply of labor will increase labor's absolute share if the aggregate demand curve for labor is elastic. Second, an increase in the supply of labor (capital) will always increase the absolute share going to capital (labor).

3. The impact of secular changes in the relative prices and quantities of labor and capital upon relative shares depends upon the elasticity of substitution. The elasticity of substitution measures the percentage change in the relative amounts of capital and labor used in comparison to the percentage change in their relative prices. An increase in the relative price of labor will increase (decrease) labor's relative income share if the elasticity of substitution is less (more) than one. If the elasticity of substitution equals one, a change in the relative price of labor will leave relative income shares unchanged.

4. The bargaining power theory, which suggests that the apparent ability of unions to gain a relative wage advantage will increase labor's relative share, has not been substantiated. The main reasons are that (a) higher union wage rates may come at the expense of nonunion workers, (b) union wage pressure induces employers to substitute capital for labor, and (c) employers are often able to offset union encroachment on profits through increases in labor productivity or product price.

5. Kaldor's macro-based theory envisions that the profit share of national income varies directly, and labor's share varies inversely, with the investment–national income ratio. Given a full employment equilibrium and an increase in the investment-income ratio, it is the process of demand-pull inflation which redistributes income from wage to profit receivers, thereby generating the added saving required to restore equilibrium.

6. Labor's relative share rises during recession and tends to fall during prosperity. Economists have attempted to explain this anticyclical movement in terms of the capacity effect and the wage-lag effect. The former suggests that during prosperity firms move toward full-capacity production where lower unit costs relative to product price cause the profit share to increase and labor's share therefore to decrease. The latter holds that wages are relatively inflexible as compared to prices; therefore the profit share increases (and the wage share decreases) during prosperity when prices are rising ahead of wages. The opposite occurs during recession.

QUESTIONS AND STUDY SUGGESTIONS

1. Key terms and concepts to remember: size and functional distribution of income; marginal productivity theory of income shares; elasticity of substitution; bargaining power theory; pursuit-and-escape scenario; Kaldor's macro-based model; capacity effect; wage-lag effect.

2. State and discuss the major statistical and conceptual problems involved in using the national income accounts to measure the trend of functional shares. What has been the trend of labor's share as narrowly measured by "compensation to employees"? What has been the trend as broadly measured by "compensation to employees" plus "proprietors' income"?

3. Portray the marginal productivity theory of functional shares diagrammatically and indicate the absolute shares going to labor and capital. What must happen in this model for the average level of wages to increase?

4. Evaluate each of the following statements in terms of the marginal productivity theory:
    a. "An increase in the supply of labor will increase capital's absolute share regardless of whether the demand for labor is elastic or inelastic."
    b. "An increase in the supply of labor will decrease labor's absolute *and* relative shares if the demand for labor is inelastic."

5. What is the elasticity of substitution? How is it measured? If an increase occurs in wages relative to the price of capital, what will happen to relative income shares when the elasticity of substitution is (*a*) greater than one and (*b*) less than one?

6. "If unions are effective as wage-increasing institutions—and there is strong evidence that they are—then the growth of unions in our economy must have caused labor's relative share to rise." Do you agree?

7. What are the basic assumptions and relationships underlying Nicholas Kaldor's "Keynesian" theory of income shares? What is the relationship between the investment-income ratio and the relative shares going to labor and capital? Explain the process by which income shares change as the result of an increase in the investment-income ratio. What criticisms have been made of Kaldor's model?

8. How do labor and profit shares vary cyclically? How might these variations be explained?

9. Assume that in 1910 the prices of labor and capital were $5 and $3 and the quantities employed were 12 and 5 units respectively. By 1980 the prices of labor and capital were $30 and $6 and the quantities employed were 24 and 50 units respectively. Determine the absolute and relative shares going to labor and capital for both years. Calculate the elasticity of substitution. What general relationship exists between the elasticity of substitution and the indicated changes in relative shares?

SELECTED REFERENCES

Atkinson, A. B.: *The Economics of Inequality,* 2d ed. (London: Oxford University Press, 1983), chap. 9.

Bronfenbrenner, Martin: *Income Distribution Theory* (Chicago: Aldine-Atherton, Inc., 1971).

Davidson, Paul: *Theories of Aggregate Income Distribution* (New Brunswick, N.J.: Rutgers University Press, 1960).

Humphrey, Thomas M.: "Income Distribution and Its Measurement," *Monthly Review* (Federal Reserve Bank of Richmond), August 1971, pp. 7–16.

Pen, Jan: *Income Distribution: Facts, Theories and Policies* (New York: Praeger Publishers, 1971).

Phelps Brown, E. H.: *Pay and Profits* (Manchester, England: Manchester University Press, 1968).

Ranadive, K. R.: *Income Distribution: The Unsolved Puzzle* (Bombay: Oxford University Press, 1978).

T I M E   A N D   O N E - H A L F

LABOR CAN'T GET MORE*

Canadian economist W. H. Pope argues that in basically capitalistic economies, such as Canada and the United States, labor (earners of wages and salaries) will, over the course of the business cycle, get the income, and only the income, that the capitalists (earners of profit, rent, and interest) think is appropriate.

In the longer run—at the most, in a decade, say—it is not profit, rent, and interest that are the residual: wages and salaries are the residual. Certainly, it is possible for individual professional associations and unions to increase their share of the national pie in both the short and long run. But they do not do so at the expense of the capitalists.

They do so at the expense of those in less powerful associations and of the unorganized, the disabled, the retired, and the unemployed. Forced to pay higher wages and salaries by a powerful professional association or union, and determined to maintain capital's share, management simply increases prices: increased prices that reduce the share of real income going to the two-thirds of the population that is neither capital nor strong labor.

Labor can price itself out of the market. And that is what the accompanying figure shows. Quite remarkable is the close correlation between wages, salaries, and supplementary labor income as a percentage of net national income and the unemployment rate

*Extracted from W. H. Pope, "Labor Can't Get More," *Policy Options* (Halifax: Institute for Research on Public Policy), March/April 1983, p. 18. Reprinted by permission.

FIGURE 1 THE RELATIONSHIP BETWEEN LABOR'S SHARE AND UNEMPLOYMENT IN CANADA

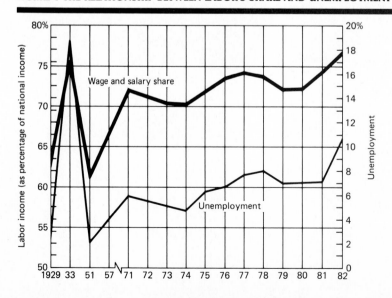

over the past dozen years: A decrease in the percentage of national income going to capital—which necessarily means an increase in the share going to labor—leads to increased unemployment.

That this relationship has existed for over fifty years is evident from the four earlier years selected. At the depth of the Depression, in 1933, labor's share achieved a high of 76.8 percent for the simple reason that the return to capital in that and the previous year were at historic lows.

The recent situation is even worse than appears at first sight: Within the capitalist share the percentage of net national income absorbed by interest payments and miscellaneous investment income has continuously increased year by year from 6.6 percent in 1975 to 10.7 percent in 1982. Therefore, the proportion of national income going to corporations and entrepreneurs as profits, already squeezed by the increasing share going to labor, has been squeezed again by the sharply increased share going to the rentier.

While individual professional associations and unions can increase their share of national income at the expense of society as a whole during all phases of the business cycle, labor as a whole can gain an increased share only at its own expense, and only during recession, for capital reacts to its own diminished share by withdrawing the services of capital from production, by laying off workers, by closing factories; in a word: by striking.

It is a Pyrrhic victory, indeed, for labor to gain a percentage point or two in its share of the national income when the cost is a proportionately far greater increase in the unemployment rate and a drop in total production and real incomes. Even the most successful professional associations and unions in Canada in 1982, as in 1933, ended up with lower real incomes than they had gained in previous years.

EMPLOYMENT AND UNEMPLOYMENT

I n earlier chapters we discussed the microeconomics of employment; that is, we analyzed how individuals make short- and long-term labor supply decisions and how firms determine their profit-maximizing levels of employment under varying market circumstances. We now wish to address several broader questions involving employment. What factors determine the *aggregate* level of employment in the economy? Why is there considerable unemployment even when government considers the economy to be fully employed? What causes total employment periodically to fall short of the full employment level? What are the policy options for promoting fuller use of labor resources?

In answering these and related questions we first examine the procedures and problems associated with measuring unemployment and defining full employment. Next, we develop a macroeconomic model which allows us to analyze how total U.S. employment is determined. This model is used later in the chapter to examine unemployment of the type which accompanies recessions and then again in the following chapter to analyze the role of labor markets in the inflationary process. Third, we delineate *types* of unemployment, taking care to distinguish between unemployment caused by job search, structural changes in labor supply and demand, and cyclical downturns in total spending. In this section we develop a theory of sequential job search and discuss how unemployment rates are affected by (1) differences between actual and expected rates of inflation and (2) the unemployment insurance program. Next, the overall unemployment rate is disaggregated and examined by such group characteristics as occupation, age, sex, race, and duration of unemployment. Finally, we focus attention on public policies designed to reduce unemployment.

EMPLOYMENT AND UNEMPLOYMENT: DEFINITIONS AND MEASUREMENT

Employment statistics—in particular unemployment rates—are widely used to assess the macroeconomic health of the economy. Therefore, it is important to examine how unemployment is measured and to understand the limitations of the data as indicators of economic hardship and guides to public policy.

Measurement. Each month the Bureau of Census conducts a Current Population Survey (CPS) in which approximately 72,000 households located in over

625 sampling areas are interviewed to determine who is employed, unemployed, or not in the labor force. The Bureau of Labor Statistics (BLS) of the U.S. Labor Department then uses the sample data from this **Household Survey** to estimate the total number of people officially employed and unemployed in the survey week. A person is considered *employed* if at any time during the survey week she or he (1) was employed by a firm or government, (2) was self-employed, or (3) had a job but was not working because of illness, bad weather, a labor dispute, or a vacation. A person is considered officially *unemployed* if during the survey week he or she was 16 years old or over, was not institutionalized, and did not work, *but* was available for work and (1) had engaged in some specific job seeking activity during the past *four* weeks, (2) was waiting to be called back to a job from which he or she had been laid off, (3) would have been looking for a job but was temporarily ill or, (4) was waiting to report to a new job within 30 days.

How are people who do not fall within either the employed or unemployed category classified? The answer is that they are either (1) under age 16 or institutionalized (hospitalized, incarcerated, and so forth) *or* (2) not in the labor force. Hence, the *potential* members of the labor force are either employed, unemployed, or not in the labor force. And as indicated in equation (18-1) the labor force itself simply consists of all those employed and unemployed.

$$\text{Labor force} = \text{employment} + \text{unemployment} \qquad (18\text{-}1)$$

The **unemployment rate** then is the percentage of the labor force that is unemployed.

$$\frac{\text{Unemployment}}{\text{rate (\%)}} = \frac{\text{unemployment}}{\text{labor force}} \times 100 \qquad (18\text{-}2)$$

To clarify how the total population is broken down into various components *and* how we compute the values for equations (18-1) and (18-2), let us examine Figure 18-1. The numbers in the boxes are in millions and are actual U.S. data for 1984. Notice from the figure that in 1984 the total population was 236.63 million people, of which (1) 62.84 million were not in the labor force because of home responsibilities, school attendance, illness and disability, old age, and so forth; (2) 58.55 million were under 16 or institutionalized; and (3) 115.24 million were in the labor force. Of those in the labor force, 106.70 million were employed (either working or absent from work because of vacations, strikes, and so forth) and 8.54 million were unemployed. The unemployed consist of people who were laid off or discharged from, or quit, previous jobs and people who were either reentrants or new entrants to the labor force.

The total labor force [equation (18-1)] then is simply found by adding those employed and unemployed (= 115.24 = 106.70 + 8.54). The unemployment rate (equation 18-2) in 1984 was 7.4 percent, calculated by dividing the number of people unemployed (8.54) by the size of the labor force (115.24) and multiplying by 100.

Table 18-1 provides information on employment and unemployment for selected years since 1960. Notice in particular that the absolute level of employment increased considerably over these years and that the unemployment rate varied from a low of 3.5 percent in 1968 to a high of 9.5 percent in 1982 and generally drifted upward over the years shown.

A Critique of the Household Data. The official employment-related statistics based on the CPS household interviews and reported by the BLS possess several notable virtues which make them useful to economists. First, the sampling technique is uniform throughout the nation and, with the exception of minor changes, has remained consistent over the years. Therefore, economists can compare employment and unemployment rates between periods and track cyclical and secular trends. Second, the time lag between the survey and the reporting of the data is short, and the information is highly accessible through government publications. Third, the data are reported in disaggregated as well as overall forms; for example, unemployment rates are provided by race, age, sex, marital status, occupation, reason for unemployment, and duration of unemployment. This aids in analyzing the distribution of the burden of unemployment. Finally, the data provide useful clues as to the direction of the overall economy during the course of a business cycle.

Unfortunately, however, these official statistics also have numerous limitations. For example, the official data include all *part-time workers as fully employed* when in reality some of these people desire to work full time. Also, to be counted as unemployed, a person must be actively seeking work. But studies show that

FIGURE 18-1 TOTAL POPULATION, LABOR FORCE, EMPLOYMENT, AND UNEMPLOYMENT, IN MILLIONS, 1984
Of the total population of 236.63 million people in the United States in 1984, 115.24 million were in the labor force. Of the latter, 106.70 million workers were employed and 8.54 million people were unemployed. The unemployment rate for 1984 therefore was 7.4 percent.

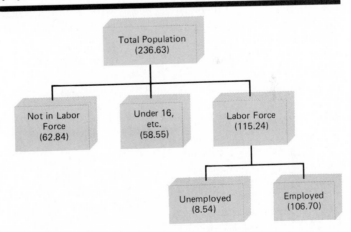

many people unsuccessfully look for work for a time, become discouraged, and then abandon their job search. Hence these **discouraged workers** (Chapter 3) constitute "hidden unemployment." Still another problem is that the data do not measure the **subemployed;** that is, the statistics fail to include people who are forced by economic circumstances to accept employment in occupations that pay lower wages than those they would qualify for in periods of full employment. In each of these respects the official unemployment statistics *understate* the extent of underutilization of labor resources and the degree of economic hardship associated with a particular "official" overall rate of unemployment.

Other problems with the data, however, cause some observers to conclude that the true extent of economic hardship in the nation may be *overstated* by the "official" unemployment rate. For example, it is likely that some respondents to the monthly household survey provide *false information* which increases the official unemployment rate. In order to present a good image of themselves and family members, interviewees may indicate that household members are actively seeking work when in fact they are not in the labor force. A second problem is that each unemployed person is counted equally whether he or she is, say, a normally full-time worker who has a strong attachment to the labor force, a semiretired person who wishes to work part time, or a teenager seeking an after-school job. To the extent that the unemployment statistics include people in the latter two categories, the official unemployment rate may be somewhat misleading.[1]

---

[1]Well over one-half of all teenagers who are unemployed are enrolled in school and seeking only part-time work.

TABLE 18-1

Employment and Unemployment, Selected Years

Year	Employment* (Millions)	Unemployment (Millions)	Unemployment† Rate (%)
1960	67.6	3.8	5.4
1962	68.8	3.9	5.4
1964	71.3	3.8	5.0
1966	75.0	2.9	3.7
1968	78.2	2.8	3.5
1970	80.8	4.1	4.8
1972	84.0	4.9	5.5
1974	88.5	5.2	5.5
1976	90.4	7.4	7.6
1978	97.7	6.2	6.0
1980	100.9	7.6	7.0
1982	101.2	10.7	9.5
1984	106.7	8.5	7.4

*Includes resident armed forces.

†All workers, including resident armed forces.

Source: Economic Report of the President, 1985.

Nor do the household data contain information on the *minimum acceptable* wages (reservation wages) for those unemployed, some of whom may have recently been discharged from high-paying jobs in declining sectors of the economy. These people may remain unemployed until they accept the reality that they no longer can command their initial reservation wages. Unemployment insurance benefits, supplemental unemployment benefits (SUBs) provided by firms, and severance pay probably increase the length of this adjustment period. A closely related criticism of using the official data as an indicator of the social impact of unemployment is that the increase in the number of multi-earner families over the past few decades has reduced the amount of poverty corresponding to any specific level of unemployment. The loss of a job by one family member substantially lessens the standard of living of most families, but it does not push as many families into poverty as it once did.[2]

The Stock-Flow Model. One final limitation of the overall unemployment rate requires comment. This rate does not distinguish between people who are experiencing short—perhaps less serious—unemployment spells and those who are going through long periods of unemployment. Suppose, as a simple illustration, that an economy has only 12 members in the labor force. In situation A, each person is unemployed for one separate month during a year, while in situation B, one person is unemployed and the rest employed for the entire year. The Household Survey would discover that in each case 1 out of 12 workers is unemployed *in each month* and therefore that the annual employment rate is 8.3 percent ($\frac{1}{12}$). Yet most observers would judge situation B to be of greater social concern.

This example points out an important fact: The household data measure *stocks* of people in each of the three important labor force categories—employed, unemployed, and not in the labor force—but does not indicate the continuous movement—or *flows*—of people *between* the various categories. This movement is captured in the **stock-flow model** of unemployment shown in Figure 18-2. Two things to note from this diagram are that (1) the unemployment rate [= $U/(E + U)$] can remain constant even though the *specific* people in the unemployment "pool" change, and (2) several distinct flow factors can act independently or interact with one another to cause the unemployment rate to change. As one example of the latter, suppose that the rate of inflow to the unemployment category U by way of layoffs, flow 2, increased, while all other flow rates remained constant. Obviously, this would increase the absolute number of people who are unemployed while leaving the size of the labor force ($E + U$) unchanged, thereby causing the unemployment rate to rise. As a second and more complex example, suppose that the rate of exit from the *employed* category E via retirements and withdrawals, flow 4, increased while all other flow rates re-

[2]S. L. Terry, "Unemployment and its Effect on Family Income," *Monthly Labor Review,* April 1982, pp. 35–43.

mained unchanged. Once again the unemployment *rate* would rise, but in this case the *absolute* number of unemployed persons would remain at its previous level. Restated, the size of the labor force $(E + U)$ would shrink, and since unemployment (U) would remain constant, the unemployment *rate* $[= U/(E + U)]$ would rise.

An analysis of the flows between the categories of labor force status helps us understand the length of unemployment spells of individuals and the reasons why unemployment rates rise and fall. The following is a sampling of insights gleaned from the stock-flow analysis of unemployment rates: (1) Empirical evidence suggests that a considerable amount of unemployment is due to prolonged spells of unemployment for relatively few people.[3] (2) During recessions the rates of layoffs and discharges rise, and the rates of "new hires" and "recalls" fall, more than compensating for the decline in voluntary job quits. Consequently, the overall unemployment rate rises. (3) First-time labor force entrants and people reentering the labor force from the "not in the labor force" category typically constitute over one-third of the unemployed. (4) Unemployment rates stay higher than expected during earlier phases of an economic recovery because improved job prospects entice people who are out of the labor force to seek work, that is, become officially unemployed.

[3]Kim B. Clark and Lawrence H. Summers, "Labor-Market Dynamics and Unemployment: A Reconsideration," *Brookings Papers on Economic Activity,* no. 1, 1979, pp. 13–60.

FIGURE 18-2 THE STOCK-FLOW MODEL OF UNEMPLOYMENT
At any point in time, there is a measurable *stock* of people in each of the three boxes which represent categories of labor force status. But these stocks are simultaneously being depleted and replenished by numerous *flows* into and out of each category. Changes in the rates of these flows can have significant impacts on the unemployment rate.

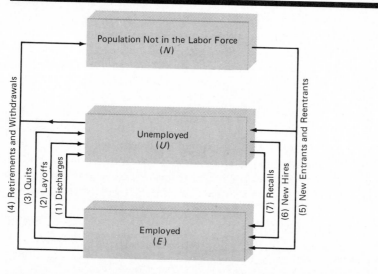

Defining Full Employment. Should society set a goal of achieving a zero rate of unemployment? Clearly not! Not only is a zero rate of unemployment unachievable in a dynamic market economy, it may be undesirable. Later in this chapter we will discover that some *voluntary* unemployment is a way by which individuals increase their personal earnings and part of the process through which society enhances its national output and income. We also will observe that some *involuntary* unemployment is an *unavoidable* by-product of changes in tastes, population shifts, and technological advance. These changes create structural mismatches between labor demand and supply and require adjustments in the allocation of labor resources from some occupations and regions to others.

How much voluntary and unavoidable involuntary unemployment is there in the U.S. economy? What rate of unemployment constitutes *full employment?* In the 1960s, economists concluded that a 4 percent unemployment rate was an achievable full-employment policy goal. But in the 1970s and 1980s numerous factors led economists to revise this figure upward to 5.5 or even 6 percent. Two of the more important factors were (1) a changed composition of the labor force such that groups having high unemployment rates—teenagers, for example—constituted a larger fraction of the overall labor force, and (2) evidence that rates of unemployment in the 4 percent range tended to be associated with accelerating rates of inflation.

Today the consensus appears to be that a 6 percent unemployment rate constitutes "practical" full unemployment and that attempts to reduce the rate below this level through policies which increase aggregate demand will cause the existing rate of inflation to accelerate. Hence, this rate is sometimes called the equilibrium or *natural rate of unemployment* and is defined variously as (1) the unemployment rate at which no excess demand or supply exists in the overall labor market, (2) the rate at which job vacancies equal the number of people unemployed, or (3) the unemployment rate that will occur in the long run if expected and actual rates of inflation are equal. We will defer explanations of the economic rationales for these definitions to later in this chapter and to Chapter 19.

MACROECONOMIC OUTPUT AND
EMPLOYMENT DETERMINATION

The macroeconomic model shown in Figure 18-3 is central to much of the discussion in this and the following chapter. Note in graph (a) that the vertical axis shows the *price level* for a hypothetical economy and the horizontal axis measures *real national output.* Conceptually, real output always equals real income; that is, one dollar of output generates one dollar of income in the form of wages, rent, interest, and profits. Consequently, the horizontal axis also measures real national income.

Next note the *aggregate demand and supply* curves in graph (a). Aggregate demand is shown as curve D_0 and indicates the total quantity of output that domestic consumers, businesses, government, and foreign buyers will collectively desire to purchase at each price level. As the price level falls, the quantity of goods and services demanded rises. The negative slope of the aggregate demand curve exists for two reasons. First, as the price level declines, the demand for money drops because fewer dollars are needed to purchase the same *quantity* of goods and services. If the money supply is fixed, this decrease in money demand will cause interest rates to fall, which then will increase spending on such interest-sensitive commodities as new autos, homes, and plants and equipment. Thus, other things being equal, the lower the price level, the greater the quantity of output demanded. A second explanation for the shape of the D_0

FIGURE 18-3 REAL OUTPUT AND TOTAL EMPLOYMENT DETERMINATION
The intersection of the aggregate demand and supply curves D_0 and $S_k AS_c$ in graph (a) produces equilibrium price and real output levels P_0 and Q_n. Given Q_n and the aggregate production function shown in graph (b), an equilibrium level of total employment E_n is determined.

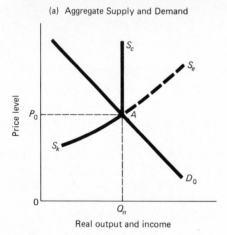

(a) Aggregate Supply and Demand

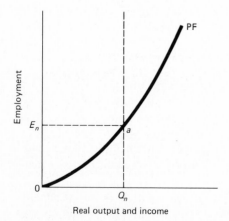

(b) Aggregate Production Function

curve is that lower price levels increase the *real value* of such assets as currency, checking deposits, and savings deposits whose values are fixed in money terms. As the price level falls, the purchasing power of dollar-denominated wealth held by consumers rises, and people tend to increase their spending on normal goods and services.

The aggregate supply curve in Figure 18-3 (a) synthesizes varying interpretations of the relationship between the price level and the total quantity of output that producers will be willing to sell. The solid curve labeled S_kAS_c incorporates traditional Keynesian (S_kA) and classical (AS_c) assumptions about the working of the economy. The rather flat slope of the curve's segment S_kA is explained as follows: As aggregate demand falls (D_0 shifts leftward), firms experience declines in sales and increases in inventories of unsold goods. Because wages are inflexible downward, firms respond by laying off or discharging workers and reducing production. Consequently, output falls. On the other hand, the AS_c segment of the aggregate supply curve shows that when labor and capital resources are being fully used, as is assumed to be the case at output level Q_n, increases in aggregate demand cause only the price level to rise; that is, the greater demand and higher prices cannot generate greater output. The *monetary* value of the Q_n output increases because of the higher price level, but *real* output remains constant at Q_n.

Other economists envision a short-run aggregate supply curve as shown by S_kAS_e. They assume that in the long-run the economy generates a natural level of output Q_n but that in the short run, output can be less or greater than that amount depending on the relationship between the actual and expected price levels. We must defer a full discussion of this interpretation to later, but the following constitutes its essence. Suppose that the price level is P_0 and that this is where workers expect it to remain. Then suppose that unanticipated inflation occurs so that the price level rises above P_0. As a result, the prices that firms receive for their products will rise, while wage rates, at least temporarily, will remain fixed at their previously contracted levels. This will mean that *real* wages will fall, causing firms collectively to attempt to increase their employment and output. Meanwhile, unemployed workers who are searching for jobs will begin to receive inflation-induced higher *money wage* offers and mistakenly think that they are being offered higher *real wages.* Consequently, they will begin to accept job offers more quickly; the level of *employment* will rise, *unemployment* will fall, and national output *temporarily* will rise above Q_n. Hence, the aggregate supply curve will extend upward as shown by the broken line AS_e.

The lower graph (b) in Figure 18-3 indicates the level of employment which will correspond to each possible level of real output. Close inspection reveals that the curve PF is the economy's aggregate production function, presented with the axes reversed as compared to the normal representation (Chapter 16). This procedure allows us to maintain direct correspondence between the horizontal axes in graphs (a) and (b).

The intersection (point A) of aggregate demand and supply in graph (a) produces price level P_0 and real output level Q_n. Dropping directly down to graph (b), we see from point a that Q_n is associated with employment level E_n. Since E_n

happens to be the *full*—or natural—level of employment, we simply assume that the unemployment rate associated with Q_n is about 6 percent.

Recall from Table 18-1 that the actual unemployment rate in the United States often has been greater than this natural rate. For example, unemployment was 7.6 percent in 1976 and 9.5 percent in 1982. Therefore, our attention next turns to causes of unemployment. Our task in this discussion is to ascertain in more detail why the natural rate of unemployment is so high and also why unemployment rates occasionally are greater or less than the natural rate. In approaching this topic, it will be convenient to categorize unemployment as either frictional, structural, or demand-deficient. Throughout this discussion bear in mind that the boundaries between unemployment categories are not absolute and that the extent of one type of unemployment may be a function of the amount of one of the other types.

FRICTIONAL UNEMPLOYMENT

Even when aggregate demand is sufficiently great to employ all of the labor force and when those who are unemployed possess skills which match those required by firms having job openings, the nation's unemployment rate will remain positive. As implied in our stock-flow model (Figure 18-2), people continuously (1) quit present jobs to shop for new ones, (2) enter the labor force to seek work for the first time, (3) reenter the labor force after periods of absence, and (4) move from one job to take another within the next 30 days. Likewise, employers continuously (1) search for replacements for workers who quit or retire, (2) discharge some employees in hopes of finding better ones, and (3) seek new workers to fill jobs created by expansion of their firms. Thus, unlike "auction" markets such as security and wheat exchanges, the overall labor market never fully "clears." At any moment there is considerable *frictional unemployment;* that is, not all active job searchers will have yet found or accepted employment and not all employers will have yet filled their job vacancies.

Job Search. Two major characteristics of the labor market contribute to the need for presently unemployed people to *search* for the best job offer, and for firms to *search* for employees to fill existing job vacancies. First, as we indicated in our earlier discussion of the wage structure (Chapter 12), workers and jobs are highly heterogeneous. The personalities, levels of motivation, innate capabilities, and places of residence of individuals differ greatly even though they may possess similar general levels of education, training, and experience. Jobs also are often unique; employers pay differing wages, offer varying opportunities for advancement, and provide a variety of working conditions, even for like types of workers. Second, market information about such differences in individuals and jobs is imperfect and takes time to obtain. Therefore, job seekers—many of whom currently are not working elsewhere—and prospective employers discover that it is in their respective interests to search for information about each other as a way to improve the terms of the transaction. People who are not presently employed and who are actively seeking work or "job shopping" are officially unemployed. And because there are continuous *flows* to and from the labor force and between jobs, the *stock* of frictionally unemployed persons is simultaneously being diminished and replenished (Figure 18-2).

There are both expected gains and costs associated with acquiring job information. Let us examine each in terms of a ***job search model.*** Suppose that an unemployed person is seeking work and recognizes that the heterogeneous nature of jobs and employers, together with imperfect market information, gen-erates a wide variance of likely wage offers for his or her occupation. Fur~ assume that this person faces the distribution of wage offers shown i~ 18-4. This frequency distribution is interpreted as follows. The h~ measures the various wage offers, higher offers being further to t¹ tical axis indicates the relative frequency of offers at each of th~ example, the frequency with which wage offers in the *a* to *b* ra~ be .05. Stated differently, 5 percent of the wage offers will b similarly, 15 percent of the wage offers will fall within the *b* ~ percent in the *c* to *d* range, and so on.

Next, let us make the simplifying assumption that this person c~ estimate the mean and variance of the frequency distribution of wage c~ has no way of knowing which employer has a job opening or which emp~

FIGURE 18-4 WAGE OFFERS, THE ACCEPTANCE WAGE, AND FRICTIONAL UNEMPLOYMENT
Given this frequency distribution of monetary wage offers and the person's acceptance wage W_a, s~ or he will reject all offers lower than *c* and accept any offer between *c* and *g*. The probability that a specific offer will exceed the acceptance wage is 80 percent (.30 + .30 + .15 + .05). During the period of search for an acceptable wage offer this person is frictionally unemployed.

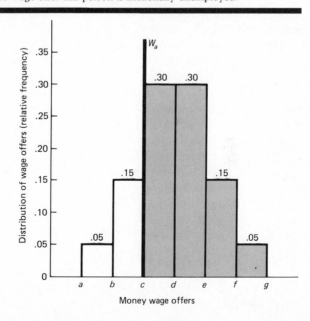

offering which wage. In other words, assume that the worker knows the cards in the deck but recognizes that it has been thoroughly shuffled.[4]

How will a job search benefit this worker? Because this person is unemployed, he or she does not have an immediately available wage opportunity. A job search makes it possible to obtain wage offers and increase the likelihood of discovering wage opportunities in the rightward areas of the distribution shown in Figure 18-4.

And what are the costs of gaining job information? They include costs of such obvious things as "for hire" notices in newspapers and other publications, fees paid to employment agencies, and transportation to and from interviews. But the cost of job search also includes significant opportunity costs. For instance, suppose that this person searches for one job offer at a time, either getting an offer or not, and if the former, either accepting it or rejecting it before continuing to search for other offers. If this person receives and rejects an offer, that wage opportunity is lost, because most wage offers cannot be "stored." Therefore, *a major cost of continued job search is the forgone earnings of the previous best opportunity*. As higher wage offers are received and rejected, the *marginal* cost of continued search rises.

What decision rule might this person employ in accepting or rejecting a particular wage offer? One approach is to establish an ***acceptance wage*** and reject any wage offer that falls below it. But how would one rationally select such a wage? Theoretically, if a person knows the frequency distribution in Figure 18-4 and can estimate the cost of generating new job offers, she can find the wage which equates the *expected* marginal benefit (MB) and *expected* marginal cost (MC) from search. If the job seeker is offered an hourly wage above this acceptance wage, she will conclude that it is not worthwhile to continue searching (MB < MC); if offered a wage below this amount, the person will reject the offer and continue to look for new offers, because the expected marginal benefit of the activity exceeds the expected extra cost (MB > MC).

This optimal acceptance wage is shown as the vertical line W_a in Figure 18-4. The shaded area of the frequency distribution indicates the probability that any single offer will be above the reservation wage. In this case the probability is 80 percent (= .30 + .30 + .15 + .05). The probability that this person will accept any wage offer in the c to g range is 100 percent, and the probability that she will accept offers in the 0 to c range is zero. And to reiterate the main point: During the period of searching for a wage offer which exceeds her acceptance wage, this person is frictionally unemployed. Because of the continuous nature of the labor force flows in the economy, this type of frictional unemployment is always present to one degree or another.[5]

[4]Arthur M. Okun, *Prices and Quantities: A Macroeconomic Analysis* (Washington, D.C.: The Brookings Institution, 1981), p. 27.

[5]Not all frictional unemployment is "search unemployment." For example, many economists consider *seasonal unemployment* to be a type of frictional unemployment. Seasonal unemployment—for example, time lost by construction workers in winter—is often more of a "wait" than a "search" phenomenon.

Several important implications arise from the search model just presented. We will examine two in detail and then briefly list several others.

Inflation and Search Unemployment. Will inflation have an impact on the length of time people search for jobs? To answer this question let us assume initially that the rate of inflation is zero and that the economy is operating at its natural levels of output and employment. Now suppose that expansionary fiscal and monetary policies increase aggregate demand such that the general price level rises by 5 percent. Also assume that increases in money wage offers match this increase in the price level so that *real* wage offers remain unchanged.

Figure 18-5 (a) repeats the frequency distribution of wage offers discussed previously, indicating again that, given the acceptance wage W_a the probability that the job searcher will accept any specific offer is 80 percent. But now observe from graph (b) that the entire frequency distribution has *shifted rightward* because money wage offers are now 5 percent higher than previously. What impact will this shift have on a person's length of job search? Let us examine two distinct circumstances.

1. Expected inflation. If the job searcher represented by Figure 18-5 (a) and (b) fully anticipates the 5 percent rate of inflation, she will simply raise the

FIGURE 18-5 THE IMPACT OF UNEXPECTED INFLATION ON FRICTIONAL UNEMPLOYMENT
Unexpected inflation results in higher monetary wage offers, and the frequency distribution shifts from that shown in (a) to that seen in (b). Because this person's acceptance wage initially remains at W_a, he or she is more likely to accept the next wage offer—a probability of 95 percent versus 80 percent—and hence frictional unemployment falls. But once people recognize that the money wage offers are no higher in real terms than previously, they adjust their acceptance wages (for example, W_a to W_a'), and the natural rate of frictional unemployment returns.

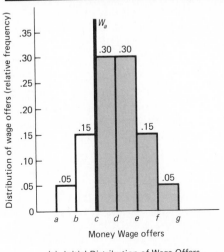

(a) Initial Distribution of Wage Offers

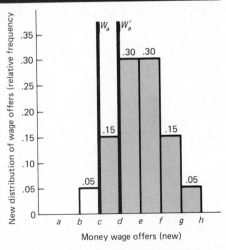

(b) Higher Distribution of Money Wage Offers

acceptance wage by 5 percent to keep it constant *in real terms*. This is shown in graph (b) as the rightward shift of line W_a to W'_a. In this case, the worker's expectation that inflation will rise by 5 percent offsets the 5 percent increase in the money wage distribution and leaves the probability that any specific wage offer will be accepted at 80 percent (= .30 + .30 + .15 + .05). To generalize: When the actual rate of inflation matches the expected rate, jobs searchers will *not* be influenced by the inflation. Their average length of job search will remain constant and, therefore, the unemployment level will stay at the natural rate.

2. Unexpected inflation. Suppose that the present rate of inflation is zero percent and that our job searcher expects this price stability to continue. Also, suppose that, in the short run, this person fails to adjust her expectation to the reality of higher inflation. Under these circumstances, the 5 percent inflation will cause our unemployed job seeker to reduce her search time. This will cause unemployment to decline temporarily below the natural rate. This is easily demonstrated in Figure 18-5. Expecting inflation to be zero, this individual holds her acceptance wage rate at W_a. But the 5 percent inflation causes the wage distribution to shift rightward as shown in Figure 18-5 (b). The probability that a new wage offer will be accepted increases from 80 percent to 95 percent (= .15 + .30 + .30 + .15 + .05). This person's duration of job search therefore falls, and if this pattern is wide-spread, frictional unemployment declines. But, according to this *adaptive expectations theory*, the unemployment decline will be short-lived. In the long run, unemployed job searchers will adjust their expectations of future inflation to the actual 5 percent rate. Consequently, they will increase their acceptance wages and lengthen their job searches, causing the unemployment rate to return to its natural level. Generalization: Actual rates of inflation which exceed expected rates may *temporarily* reduce unemployment below its natural rate.

Unemployment Compensation and Search Unemployment. A second major implication of our search model is that unemployment benefits provided by government, past employers, or both will increase the extent of frictional unemployment by enabling unemployed persons to search for higher wage offers at less *net* cost.[6] Recall that a person's acceptance wage is established at the level where the expected gain from more search just equals the expected cost. Quite understandably, the presence of unemployment compensation increases one's acceptance wage, because it *reduces* the expected *net* cost of searching for a higher wage offer. That is, the opportunity cost of continued search is reduced to the previously highest offer *minus* the unemployment benefits. For example, as

---

[6]This is *not* to suggest that such programs are undesirable; in fact, one expressed purpose of these payments is to allow workers to search for positions commensurate with their skills and experience, rather than being forced through economic necessity to take jobs in which they are subemployed. Also, much unemployment occurs in the form of layoffs, and unemployment compensation cushions the decline in earnings while workers wait to be called back.

portrayed in Figure 18-6, an individual who qualifies for unemployment benefits may have an acceptance wage W'_a rather than W_a, and given the distribution of wage offers, the probability that this person will accept the next job offer falls to 20 percent (= .15 + .05) compared to the previous probability of 80 percent (= .30 + .30 + .15 + .05). Hence, this person's optimal length of job search increases, and the overall rate of frictional unemployment in the economy rises. Numerous empirical studies confirm this prediction.[7] Other studies confirm that acceptance wage rates fall—one estimate is by 15 percent—when people exhaust their unemployment benefits.[8]

Other Implications of the Search Model. Let us briefly consider several other important implications that emerge from the job search theory. First, a prospective worker may not accept the initial job offer or even seek out available jobs

[7]For a review of these studies, see Sheldon Danziger, Robert Haveman, and Robert Plotnick, "How Income Transfers Affect Work, Savings, and the Income Distribution," *Journal of Economic Literature*, September 1981, pp. 975–1028.

[8]Raymond Fishe, "Unemployment Insurance and the Reservation Wage of the Unemployed," *Review of Economics and Statistics*, February 1982, p. 12–17.

FIGURE 18-6 THE IMPACT OF UNEMPLOYMENT BENEFITS ON FRICTIONAL UNEMPLOYMENT
Unemployment benefits reduce the *net* opportunity cost of rejecting wage offers and continuing to search for higher-paying employment, and thus allow people to increase their acceptance wages. For the person shown, the increase in the acceptance wage from W_a to W'_a means that the probability of receiving an acceptable wage offer in the next attempt falls from 80 to 20 percent (.15 + .05). Hence, the length of job search and the amount of frictional unemployment rises.

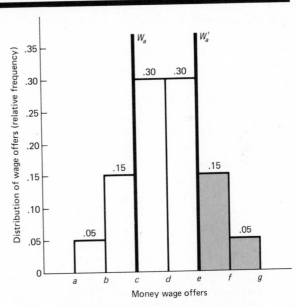

that pay below the acceptance wage. This fact may join structural factors in helping explain the presence of numerous unfilled job vacancies even in the presence of considerable overall unemployment. Second, the longer the expected length of tenure on the job, the higher a person's acceptance wage, all else being equal. For instance, suppose that a person expects to be employed on a new job for 20 years. The anticipated gain from searching for a high wage offer is greater in this case, and the acceptance wage higher, than if she expects to work only a month or two for the new employer. Third, random luck will play a part in the wage and earnings distribution in the economy (Chapter 13). One person may receive the highest wage offer in the frequency distribution on the first try; another may get a lower offer, continue to search, and finally accept an offer above her acceptance wage but below the highest wage in the distribution. Fourth, the level of search unemployment is partly a function of the overall demand for labor. During recessions, the length of time required to discover *each* wage offer rises because so few firms are hiring workers. Also, if job searchers perceive a recession to be *temporary,* they may retain their acceptance wages, thereby prolonging their job search and contributing to a rise in frictional unemployment.

STRUCTURAL UNEMPLOYMENT

Voluntary, frictional unemployment does not constitute *all* of the observed unemployment at the nation's full employment—or natural—rate of unemployment. Much of the unavoidable unemployment is **structural unemployment.** This unemployment involves many of the same features as frictional unemployment but possesses the differentiating characteristic of being caused by changes in the composition of either the demand for, or the supply of, labor. Structural unemployment is a "square pegs, round holes" phenomenon and has two dimensions. First, it may result from a mismatch between the skills needed for available jobs and the skills possessed by those seeking work. Second, structural unemployment may occur because of a geographic mismatch between the locations of job openings and job seekers. Examples of structural unemployment abound: Robotic technology and the increase in the market share of imports greatly reduced employment in the U.S. auto industry in the 1970s. Many of the workers who were displaced did not have the skills required for available positions which were open, for example, in accounting and computer programming. Similarly, changes in agricultural technology over the past 100 years caused job losses for many farm operators and laborers who did not possess readily transferable job skills in expanding areas of employment.

The extent of structural unemployment depends on the *degree* and *speed* of the compositional changes in labor demand and supply and the *speed* of the adjustments to the imbalances and mismatches. Training and retraining play a key role in this adjustment process, and efforts to shorten the duration of this type of unemployment normally involve retooling of skills to match job vacancies.

Several additional observations on this subject deserve mention. In the first place, higher levels of general education are associated with lower levels of structural unemployment. For instance, college graduates who are displaced from their existing employment because of changes in demand or technology have a wider range of job options and usually find retraining to be easier than persons who have little formal education.[9]

A second observation is that structural and recession-related (cyclical) unemployment overlap. When recessions occur, both the overall level of unemployment *and* the amount of structural unemployment increase. This is the case because firms no longer need to provide company-financed on-the-job training to fill their openings; instead they can draw skilled workers from the large unemployment pool. This contrasts to the situation which exists when the economy is rapidly expanding and fully employed. Under these latter circumstances, firms experiencing shortages of skilled workers often find it profitable to hire people who do not possess the required job skills but who can be trained while on the job.

A final observation is that futurists in nearly every historical period have warned of impending massive increases in technological unemployment. To date, however, the historical record indicates that, on the average, technological change creates more jobs than it destroys and does not greatly alter the overall rate of structural unemployment. As just one example, in 1910 the Bell telephone system handled 7 million calls, which amounted to 57 calls per Bell employee. By 1981, advances in technology and economies of scale had enabled Bell employees to handle 219 *billion* telephone calls—250,000 per worker! Nevertheless, Bell's total employment rose from 121,310 workers in 1910 to 874,000 employees in 1981. More generally, recall the discussion surrounding Figure 16-5 which suggested that there is no systematic relationship between productivity changes and employment changes on an industry-by-industry basis.

But might not the computer and robotic revolution change this pattern? Most economists doubt that it will. They point out that, although specific workers will lose their jobs and that many firms, communities, and perhaps even regions will suffer negative consequences, the new technologies will spur capital investment, spawn secondary industries, and generate output effects which will increase overall labor demand. To fill available positions in the expanding sectors, firms there may need to engage in more concerted on-the-job training. Hence, most economists view the current explosion of new technology as presenting a major challenge to society, but not one that is fundamentally different from previous challenges posed by other new technologies.

[9]W. R. Johnson, "The Demand for General and Specific Education with Occupational Mobility," *Review of Economic Studies*, October 1979, pp. 695–705.

DEMAND-DEFICIENT UNEMPLOYMENT

In many years the unemployment rate greatly exceeds the 6 percent natural rate. For example, unemployment was 8.3 percent in 1975 and 9.5 percent in 1982. In the depth of the Great Depression—1933—24.9 percent of the labor force was unemployed! These high unemployment rates are by-products of recessions and depressions and result from deficiencies in aggregate demand which force firms to lay off and discharge workers. The evidence strongly suggests that declines in aggregate demand, rather than, say, differences between expected and actual inflation rates, are the *primary* cause of cyclical unemployment.[10]

Again we return to the basic aggregate supply and demand framework developed previously. Notice the sharp decline in aggregate demand denoted as the movement from D_0 to D_1 in Figure 18-7. Keynesians view a decline in investment spending as the usual cause of such a shift. Monetarists look to a decline in the rate of growth of the money supply as the normal culprit. But irrespective of the cause, observe that real output declines from the natural level Q_0 to the less than full employment level Q_1, as shown by the movement from A to B in the upper graph and from a to b in the lower one. We also see that employment declines from E_0 to E_1 and, because most of the E_0E_1 persons laid off or discharged remain in the labor force, the unemployment rate rises. Because the cause of this unemployment is a decline in aggregate demand, economists call this either *cyclical* or *demand-deficient unemployment.*

To see why this unemployment may be *in*voluntary, note Figure 18-8, which portrays the quantities of labor demanded and supplied as a function of the *real* wage. The downward-sloping demand curve indicates that employers will hire more workers at lower real wages. The upward-sloping labor supply curve assumes that higher real wages will attract more workers to the labor force. Initially, the equilibrium real wage and output levels are W_0 and E_0 as shown by point a'. Suppose that this level of employment produces the natural rate of unemployment and corresponds to the E_0 in graph (b) of the previous Figure 18-7. But the decline in aggregate product demand shown in that figure results in output level Q_1. To produce this level of output only E_1 workers are required. This translates to Figure 18-8 as a decline in the demand for labor from D_{L0} to the vertical line XD_{L1}. This vertical line is the *effective demand curve for labor* because it shows the number of workers which firms collectively will employ at each real wage rate below X, given the fact that only Q_1 units of output can be sold. The presence of demand curve XD_{L1} produces a disequilibrium situation in the labor market. At real wage W_0, a' individuals desire work—and *were* previously working—but firms desire to hire only b' workers. Hence, distance $a'b'$ illustrates involuntary demand-deficient unemployment. Will

---

[10]Ronald S. Warren, Jr., "Labor Market Contracts, Unanticipated Wages, and Employment Growth," *American Economic Review,* June 1983, pp. 389–397.

money wages then fall faster than product prices so that the real wage drops to c', thereby eliminating involuntary unemployment? For reasons that we will explore soon, money wages are very "sticky" downward; that is, money wage cuts are the exception rather than the rule even during recessions. But, let us suppose that money wages did fall more rapidly than prices and that the real wage fell to c'. Employment *would not* rise beyond E_1 because of the deficient effective spending for products. Instead, $a'b'$ workers would quit seeking work because of the low real wage, and *voluntary* withdrawals from the labor force would replace *involuntary* unemployment. Nevertheless, it is evident that the

FIGURE 18-7 DEMAND-DEFICIENT UNEMPLOYMENT
Declines in aggregate demand such as D_0 to D_1 cause real output and total employment to fall; in this case, from Q_0 to Q_1 and E_0 to E_1. For obvious reasons the resulting increase in unemployment is called demand-deficient unemployment.

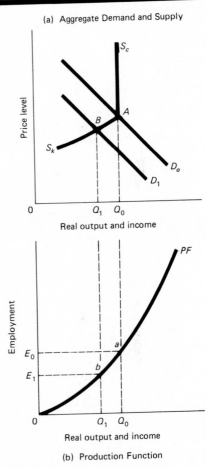

(a) Aggregate Demand and Supply

(b) Production Function

cause of the lower employment is *not* too high a real wage, but rather a deficiency of effective aggregate demand.[11]

But, as indicated, money wages in the aggregate do in fact tend to be inflexible downward in the United States. One reason is the presence of unions, which actively resist cuts in money wages, particularly since they are aware that prices are also inflexible downward. Such cuts are viewed as "givebacks" of previously hard-earned collective bargaining gains and thus create significant bargaining resistance. Also, unions appear to prefer layoffs to temporary wage reductions. The latter affect all workers, while layoffs usually affect only a small percentage of the firm's work force and normally involve people with little seniority. Hence, a *majority* of workers benefit by a layoff policy as contrasted to wage cuts, and elected union leaders are likely to be responsive to this majority when negotiating wage and layoff provisions.

Another reason why money wages are inflexible downward is that firms themselves may favor temporary selective layoffs to across-the-board temporary wage reductions. The latter might cause higher-skilled, more-experienced work-

---

[11]Figure 18-8 is based upon the model developed by Robert J. Barro and Hershel I. Grossman, "A General Disequilibrium Model of Income and Employment," *American Economic Review*, March 1971, pp. 82–93. For a discussion of shortcomings of this model, see Robert J. Barro, "Long-Term Contracting, Sticky Prices, and Monetary Policy," *Journal of Monetary Economics*, July 1977, pp. 305–316. Peter Howitt, on the other hand, has recently argued that the implications of the model are valid irrespective of these criticisms. See his "Transaction Costs and Unemployment," *American Economic Review*, March 1985, pp. 88–100.

FIGURE 18-8 DEMAND-DEFICIENT UNEMPLOYMENT: THE LABOR MARKET
Declines in aggregate demand for output reduce the quantity of new output produced, which in turn causes a decline in the demand for labor from D_{L0} to XD_{L1}. As a result, involuntary demand-deficient unemployment of an amount represented by the distance from a' to b' occurs.

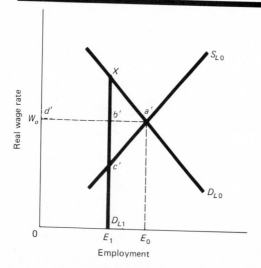

ers in whom the firm has invested large amounts of training to quit and take jobs elsewhere. The layoff strategy allows the firm to "inventory" or "hoard" this skilled labor and instead lay off workers who are more easily replaced if they happen to take alternative employment rather than wait for a callback. Furthermore, the existence of unemployment compensation and the way it is financed biases the decision toward layoffs. Those laid off experience a *net* loss of income which is less than the full decline in wages, and therefore they will be less likely to accept other permanent jobs during this period. In addition, because the tax payments paid by firms to the unemployment compensation program are not perfectly related to layoff experience, firms which dismiss *substantial* numbers of workers are subsidized by the tax payments of other firms. Stated technically, the unemployment benefits received by workers who are temporarily unemployed exceed the *incremental* tax cost to the firms which lay them off.[12]

A final and closely related reason why wages appear to be sticky downward during recessions is that explicit and implicit contracts govern many employment relationships. **Explicit contracts** are formal, legally binding agreements such as individual or "master" labor contracts, while **implicit contracts** are informal, often unstated, understandings which are in a sense "invisible handshakes."[13] One common feature of many implicit contracts is an understanding that the firm will maintain existing money wages and pay cost-of-living wage increases except under severe economic conditions such as impending bankruptcy. In return for this guarantee, employers obtain the right to lay off workers in response to cyclical declines in the demand for their products. In essence, by providing "insurance" against wage declines during recessions, employers can attract workers at a lower average wage. Additionally, the "fixed wage–variable employment" contract provides firms with certainty in the reduction of the wage bill (wage × number of worker hours) compared to the uncertainty associated with a wage reduction which might cause some highly valued workers to quit. Finally, these contracts may produce positive "reputation effects" which may allow firms to attract better-quality workers who require less supervision.

THE DISTRIBUTION OF UNEMPLOYMENT

The distribution of unemployment is uneven over the labor force and changes as demand-deficient unemployment rises and falls. In Table 18-2 we present disaggregated unemployment rates by race, age, sex, and duration of unemployment for two different years. These years were selected for purpose of contrast; in

---

[12]See Martin Feldstein, "The Importance of Temporary Layoffs: An Empirical Analysis," *Brookings Papers on Economic Activity*, no. 3, 1975, pp. 725–744 and Robert H. Topel, "On Layoffs and Unemployment Insurance," *American Economic Review*, September 1983, pp. 541–559.

[13]For early statements of implicit contract theory, see Martin N. Baily, "Wages and Unemployment under Uncertain Demand," *Review of Economic Studies*, January 1974, pp. 37–50 and Costas Azariadis, "Implicit Contracts and Unemployment Equilibria," *Journal of Political Economy*, December 1975, pp. 1183–1202.

1979, the economy was roughly fully employed with a 5.8 percent civilian unemployment rate, while in 1982, a major recession drove the overall rate to 9.7 percent.

Observation of the large variance in the disaggregated rates of unemployment *within each year* and comparison of the rates *between* the two years support several generalizations drawn from more extensive studies of unemployment data. First, the unemployment rates for people in occupations requiring less human capital tend to be higher than those for persons in positions requiring more skills. Notice, for example, that in 1979 the unemployment rate for blue-collar workers was 7 percent compared to the 3.3 percent rate for white-collar employees. As a corollary, the unemployment rate tends to rise more rapidly for lower-skilled workers during a recession. Observe in Table 18-2 that the unemployment rate for blue-collar workers was nearly 103 percent higher in 1982 than it was in 1979, while for white-collar workers the rise was only 57.6 percent. The reasons for the differential rates between workers of various skills and the rising relative rates for lower-skilled workers during recessions include the following: (1) Lower-skilled workers are often subject to more technologically caused unemployment and longer *spells* of structural unemployment, (2) higher-skilled workers are more likely to be self-employed, and (3) during periods of falling product demand, firms tend to lay off or discharge workers in whom they have invested the least amount of human capital over the years and to retain more-skilled workers, managers, and professionals.

TABLE 18-2

Unemployment Rates for Labor Force Subclassifications, 1979 (Full Employment) versus 1982 (Recession)

Category	Unemployment Rate, 1979 (%)	Unemployment Rate, 1982 (%)	Percentage Increase
Overall	5.8	9.7	67.2
Occupation			
Blue-collar	7.0	14.2	102.9
White-collar	3.3	5.2	57.6
Age			
16–19	16.1	23.2	44.1
Black, 16–19	33.2	48.0	30.8
White, 16–19	14.0	20.4	45.7
Males, 20+	4.2	8.8	109.5
Females, 20+	5.7	8.3	45.6
Race			
Black	12.3	18.9	53.7
White	5.1	8.6	68.6
Sex			
Female	6.8	9.4	38.2
Male	5.1	9.9	94.0
Duration			
15 Weeks +	1.2	3.2	166.7

Sources: Economic Report of the President, 1985; Employment and Earnings.

A second generalization concerning the disaggregated unemployment data shown in Table 18-2 is that the rate of unemployment for 16- to 19-year-olds is considerably higher than for adults. Additionally, the black teenage unemployment rate greatly exceeds that for white teenagers. Notice that the overall teenage unemployment rate was 16.1 percent in 1979 and 23.2 percent in 1982, but that the black teenage rates for the two years were 33.2 and 48.0 percent. Teenagers have low skill levels, high rates of job quits and discharges, little geographic mobility, and frequent transitions to and from the labor force. Hence, they have numerous spells of frictional and structural unemployment. Also, some teenage unemployment is attributable to the minimum wage (Chapter 10).[14]

The high relative incidence of unemployment for black teenagers is particularly striking and troublesome, and may be caused by: (1) overt and "statistical" discrimination (Chapter 11), (2) lack of adult job information "networks" for finding jobs, (3) and geographic isolation in central cities where newly created jobs are relatively few.

A third broad generalization based on Table 18-2 is that over the years, the unemployment rate for all blacks—teenage *and* adult—has been about two times that for whites. For example, in 1979 the black unemployment rate was 12.3 percent compared to the white rate of 5.1 percent. The reasons for the higher black rates of unemployment are complex and difficult to sort out, but one factor is that blacks are more heavily represented in lower-skilled occupations. Recall from our prior discussion that such occupations have high rates of frictional and structural unemployment. Also, blacks live disproportionately in declining inner cities where the demand for labor is often insufficient to employ all those seeking work. The possible contribution of discrimination to black unemployment was discussed in Chapter 11.

A fourth generalization that one can draw from the disaggregated unemployment data is that female unemployment rates are quickly approaching those for males. This has occurred over the past decade as females have moved into positions that are career-oriented and characterized by lower unemployment rates. We see in Table 18-2 that in 1979 the overall unemployment rate for females was 6.8 percent and for males, 5.1 percent. In 1982, the female unemployment rate actually was lower than that for males. This is explained by the impact of the 1981–1982 recession on unemployment rates in such specific industries as wood products, autos, construction, and steel, which have high male-to-female employment ratios.

A final generalization concerning the disaggregated data illustrated in Table 18-2 is that the number of persons unemployed for long periods—say 15 weeks or more—as a percentage of the labor force is much less than the overall unemployment rate, but rises during recessions. Notice that the unemployment rate for people without work for 15 weeks or longer was only 1.2 percent in 1979

---

[14]The Time and One-Half section at the end of this chapter examines youth unemployment in more detail.

compared to the overall rate of 5.8 percent. But also observe that this rate rose to 3.2 percent in 1982, indicating that recessions tend to create longer periods of idleness of labor resources and much more social hardship than do short-term frictional and structural unemployment.

REDUCING UNEMPLOYMENT: PUBLIC POLICIES

The U.S. government is officially committed to the goal of full employment. The Employment Act of 1946 proclaimed among other things that "it is the continuing policy of the Federal Government to use all practicable means consistent with its needs and obligations and other essential considerations of national policy . . . to promote maximum employment, production, and purchasing power." The Full Employment and Balanced Growth Act of 1978 reaffirmed this goal and required that government (1) establish 5-year employment and inflation goals and (2) formulate programs to achieve them.

Table 18-3 deserves careful examination for it summarizes the wide variety of government programs which in full or in part are designed to reduce frictional, structural, and cyclical unemployment. Analysis of each of these approaches is obviously impossible in a single chapter. Therefore, we will confine our attention to selected aspects of just three topics: fiscal policy, public service employment, and wage subsidies.

Fiscal Policy. As defined in Table 18-3, *fiscal policy* is the deliberate manipulation of expenditures and taxes by the federal government for purposes of promoting full employment, price stability, and economic growth. Keynesian economists view fiscal policy, when accompanied by accommodating monetary policy, as the major governmental tool for increasing aggregate demand and in that way reducing demand-deficient unemployment. The intended impact of fiscal policy on real income and total employment is shown in Figure 18-9. Suppose initially that the economy is characterized by aggregate demand and supply curves D_0 and S_kAS_c and that the price, real output, and employment levels are P_0, Q_0, and E_0, respectively. Also assume that the full employment level of output is Q_1. Distance E_0E_1 then represents demand-deficient unemployment.

Proper Keynesian fiscal policy would increase aggregate demand to D_1, which would raise national output to Q_1 and increase total employment to the full employment level E_1. This increase in aggregate demand could be accomplished through some combination of (1) tax cuts for individuals to increase personal consumption spending, (2) tax reductions or direct subsidies to firms to promote greater investment spending, and (3) increases in government expenditures.

But what appears simple in theory—shifting the aggregate demand curve rightward precisely to D_1—is much more difficult in reality. Let us explore three major complications. First, timing is crucial, and several time lags make the precise management of aggregate demand difficult. Once the administration has

TABLE 18-3

Government Policies and Programs to Reduce Unemployment

Frictional Unemployment

1. *Job information and matching:* government programs which increase the availability of information concerning job vacancies and skills of those seeking work and help match job applicants and employers. Examples: U.S. Job Service (state employment agencies).

Structural Unemployment

1. *Educational subsidies:* government programs and tax expenditures which reduce the investment costs of obtaining human capital and thereby enhance people's ability to obtain jobs that are less likely to become obsolete as new technology emerges. Examples: Pell Grants and Guaranteed Student Loans for college students; subsidies under the Vocational Educational Act; funding of primary and secondary schools, community colleges, and state-supported universities.
2. *Equal employment opportunity laws:* laws making it illegal to discriminate in hiring and promotion on the basis of race or gender, thus removing an institutional barrier which creates structural unemployment. Examples: Title VII of Civil Rights Act of 1964; Executive Order 11246.
3. *Job training and retraining:* programs designed to provide skills and work experience for those structurally unemployed. Examples: Manpower Development and Training Act (MDTA) institutional training at skill centers; MDTA on-the-job training programs; The Job Corps; Comprehensive Employment and Training Act (CETA) programs aimed at youth, Native Americans, displaced homemakers, etc.
4. *Public service employment* (PSE): direct government hiring and on-the-job training of the long-term structurally unemployed. Examples: CETA, Title II as amended in 1978.
5. *Directed wage subsidies or employment tax credits:* direct payments or tax credits to firms which hire members of specific disadvantaged groups which experience high rates of structural unemployment. Example: Targeted Employment Tax Credit program, 1979; AFDC-WIN program.

Demand-Deficient Unemployment

1. *Fiscal policy:* deliberate manipulations of expenditures and taxes by government for the purposes of increasing aggregate demand and thereby increasing national output and employment. Examples: tax cuts in 1964, 1970, and 1974.
2. *Monetary policy:* deliberate actions taken by the Federal Reserve to increase the nation's supply of money to reduce interest rates and increase aggregate demand for products and services. Examples: monetary expansions in 1974–1975 and 1982.
3. *Supply-side policies:* deliberate actions taken by the government to increase labor supply, savings, and investment and to reduce the costs of goods and services so that the aggregate supply curve shifts rightward. Examples: Reagan administration 1981 tax cuts, Individual Retirement Accounts (IRAs), deregulation.
4. *Public service employment:* direct government hiring of people unable to find jobs. Examples: Works Progress Administration (WPA) in the 1930s; Comprehensive Employment and Training Act (CETA); Title VII, Public Service Employment (PSE) in the 1970s.
5. *Wage subsidies or employment tax credits:* direct payments or tax credits to firms which expand their employment. Example: the New Jobs Tax Credit program of 1977.

recognized that aggregate demand has declined, it must formulate a fiscal policy and submit it to Congress. Next, Congress must hold hearings on the proposed policy and pass it as law. Then, once in place, the policy itself takes time to have full impact on the economy. During these lags, factors independent of the fiscal policy can shift the aggregate demand curve further inward or rightward. Hence, a specific dose of fiscal policy may turn out to be either inappropriately large or small.

Another complication of fiscal policy is that government borrowing to finance the deficits created by the fiscal policy may compete with private borrowing and cause interest rates to rise. These higher rates may crowd out private borrowing and investment spending during the expansion, causing the actual increase in aggregate demand to fall short of the expected D_0D_1 increase.

FIGURE 18-9 OVERLY EXPANSIONARY FISCAL POLICY

If the government incorrectly views Q_2 and E_2 as the full employment levels of real output and employment when the natural levels are Q_1 and E_1, it may take actions to increase aggregate demand from D_0 to D_2 and inadvertently cause inflation. Gains in output and employment beyond Q_1 and E_1 will occur only because the actual price level (P_2) exceeded the expected one (P_1). In the long run, output and employment will return to their natural levels of Q_1 and E_1, but the excess demand at P_2 will cause the price level to rise further, to P_3

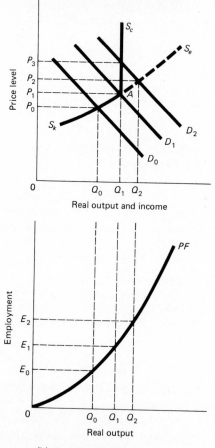

(a) Aggregate Supply and Demand

(b) Aggregate Production Function

A final complication relates to the problem of defining full employment. Suppose that government mistakenly targets Q_2 in Figure 18-9 as the full employment level of output, when in fact the natural, nonaccelerating inflation level is actually Q_1. If government increases aggregate demand from D_0 to D_2 to achieve the real output and employment levels Q_2 and E_2, it will cause the price level initially to rise from P_0 to P_2. In the short run, this may increase real output and employment above their natural levels; that is, the economy may move upward along the broken-line segment of S_e. But this only occurs because the actual rate of inflation exceeds the expected rate, causing frictional unemployment to fall temporarily (recall our previous discussion on this topic). But, once workers and firms recognize that the actual rate of inflation is higher than expected, they will readjust their search and hiring behavior so that employment and real output will return to their natural levels E_1 and Q_1. In the meantime, with aggregate demand at D_2, the price level will continue to rise to its equilibrium level at P_3.

Public Service Employment (PSE). The federal government occasionally initiates programs to reduce demand-deficient and structural unemployment through direct hiring of the unemployed. For example, in the 1930s the Roosevelt administration established the Civilian Conservation Corps (CCC) and the Works Progress Administration (WPA) to provide immediate employment to people out of work. Likewise, in the 1970s Congress established public service employment (PSE) programs under the Comprehensive Employment and Training Act (CETA).

Proponents of the PSE approach contend that these programs reduce demand-deficient unemployment during the lag between the implementation and final effect of more traditional fiscal and monetary policies. They also argue that if the programs are properly targeted toward disadvantaged low-wage workers who are displaced from occupations where there is much excess labor supply, the increase in labor demand caused by the PSE hiring will not create inflationary pressures. Therefore, the tradeoff between unemployment and inflation will be improved.[15]

Critics argue that PSE accomplishes nothing that tax cuts could not accomplish more efficiently. Both work mainly by increasing aggregate demand, the major difference between them being that PSE increases the ratio of public- to private-sector output and reduces the nation's capital-labor ratio. Furthermore, those opposed to PSE contend that in practice legislative and administrative lags reduce the rate of actual job creation, and consequently government begins its hiring about the time the recovery phase of the cycle is beginning. Thus the government competes with the growing private sector demand for labor. Other opponents point out that the budgetary costs of the PSE programs lead to either

---

[15]See Barbara Bergmann and Robert Bennett, "Macroeconomic Effects of a Humphrey-Hawkins Type Program," *American Economic Review*, May 1977, pp. 265–270.

increased taxes or more government borrowing and that in the long run either or both reduce the private investment needed to expand private-sector employment opportunities. Finally, critics of the PSE approach note that the local governments which often receive and administer the PSE funds have goals such as tax reduction, debt repayment, land acquisition, and purchase of capital which compete with the PSE goal of job provision. Some of the PSE money is often used to pay salaries of workers who would have been hired anyway or used to maintain a given level of employment and public services at *reduced tax expense* to those in the government's jurisdiction. Consequently, the *net increase* in public sector jobs may be far less than the stated number of PSE employees.

Several studies of the CETA PSE program concluded that such *fiscal substitution* did in fact occur and that only about 50 to 70 percent of federal job creation funds were used to *increase* state and local government employment. This fiscal substitution helps explain why many public-sector unions opposed the CETA PSE program. The program allowed local governments to hire new nonunion employees at the same time recession-caused budget cutbacks forced them to discharge experienced, unionized employees.

Although the Reagan administration allowed the CETA PSE to expire in the early 1980s, it is unlikely that this will end the policy debate. The idea of government guaranteeing jobs for all who want them has great political appeal, and most observers feel that massive amounts of unemployment created by major recessions clearly require some type of government action.

Wage Subsidies. Some economists advocate that government pay direct **wage subsidies** to firms or grant them tax credits when they hire previously unemployed workers. These subsidies can be either *general* or *targeted,* the former aimed at reducing demand-deficient unemployment and the latter designed to lessen the extent of structural unemployment. Our focus here will be on wage subsidies paid directly to employers who hire low-wage workers who are structurally unemployed. The rationale for such programs is that the *natural* rate of unemployment is not necessarily *optimal.* Put simply, actions to reduce structural unemployment may generate real output and income gains that exceed program costs. But will a wage subsidy increase employment and reduce the unemployment rate for a targeted category of workers? Will it increase overall employment and cause the natural rate of unemployment to decline?

Figure 18-10 helps us answer the first of these questions. Here we portray the labor market for the targeted group of low-wage workers and their potential employers. Prior to the wage subsidy, labor demand and supply were D_{L0} and S_{L0}, and the equilibrium wage and level of employment were W_0 and E_0. Suppose that a wage subsidy of $2 an hour is now granted to the employers for each worker hour of employment. This subsidy is shown as the *vertical* distance between D_{L0} and D_{L1} at each level of E—for example, distance AB or CD. From the perspective of those hiring workers, the extra revenue generated to the firm from hiring each worker hour will be $2 higher than before. That is, the firm will get the extra revenue from the added output that the worker helps to produce,

plus $2 of wage subsidy from the federal government. Hence, D_{L1} is the actual
demand curve for labor in this market, and at the old wage W_0 *excess demand EA*
will exist. This will increase the equilibrium wage and equilibrium employment
level to W_1 and E_1 respectively (point C). In this case, the targeted wage subsidy
causes (1) an increase in employment for the specific worker group (E_0 to E_1),
(2) a rise in the market wage (W_0 to W_1), and (3) a decline in the *net* wage paid
by the employer (W_0 minus W_s, where W_s is the new market wage W_1 minus the
wage subsidy CD).

In the long run, any observed increase in employment caused by a wage
subsidy is either caused by a substitution or an output effect. The wage subsidy
reduces the *net* price of labor relative to (1) the price of capital, (2)nontargeted
low-wage labor, and (3) skilled labor, and thereby encourages the firm to substitute subsidized labor for the unsubsidized factors. Also, the lower *net* wage
reduces the firms' costs, causing them to expand their output. As output rises,
more targeted labor will be required. The *extent* to which employment increases
for the targeted group depends upon several factors. First, and most obviously,
the greater the wage subsidy the greater the employment impact. Second, the
more elastic the *supply* of labor, the greater the increase in employment. Third,
the more elastic the *demand* for this type of labor, the more the increase in
employment. The reader should use Figure 18-10 to confirm these assertions.

Although it appears likely that a wage subsidy will increase employment for
those in the targeted category, it is less certain that it will reduce the overall
unemployment rate or the natural rate of unemployment. The reason? For one,
it is possible that the low-wage, subsidized employment will be substituted for

FIGURE 18-10 THE IMPACTS OF A TARGETED WAGE SUBSIDY
A wage subsidy of AB effectively shifts the demand for labor for the targeted group from D_{L0} to D_{L1}.
Following the subsidy, the firm's average wage cost is W_s, the subsidy is $W_1 - W_s$, the market wage is
W_1, and the employment level is E_1. The greater the wage subsidy and the more elastic the labor
supply and demand curves, the larger the increase in employment for the targeted group.

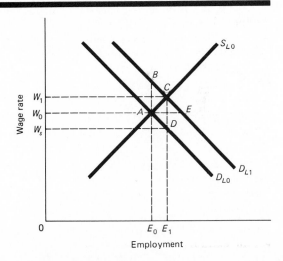

nontargeted low-wage labor or for higher-skilled labor. If so, the unemployment rate for these groups could rise. Also, because the wage subsidy in this example applies only to low-wage workers, the firms' incentives to provide specific skill training and job advancement may be reduced. Such training might boost the skills and wages of these workers to the point that they are no longer qualified for wage subsidies. In effect, the net return to the firm on their investment in this human capital is the extra output *minus the lost wage subsidy*. Therefore, this program might retard workers' normal advancement and maintain a greater percentage of the targeted group in the low-wage ranks. Ironically, this would be expected to increase the targeted group's long-term likelihood of experiencing renewed spells of structural unemployment as technology changes.[16]

Several actual wage subsidy programs have been tried over the past two decades. For example, a Targeted Jobs Tax Credit plan was put into effect in 1979 which provided tax subsidies for firms hiring unemployed youth (18 to 24), handicapped persons, and welfare recipients. Few economists view wage subsidies as the *sole* or even major solution to cyclical and structural unemployment, but many deem this approach preferable to the public service employment (PSE) alternative.

SUMMARY

1. A person is officially unemployed if she or he is 16 years or older, is not institutionalized, and is either actively seeking work, waiting to be called back to a job after being laid off, or waiting to report to a new job within 30 days.
2. The official unemployment data have several limitations as measures of economic hardship and as guides to public policy. The stock-flow model sorts out causes of changes in the unemployment rate and provides information on the duration of employment spells for individuals.
3. Unemployment rates at or near 6 percent appear to represent a "full" or natural rate of unemployment. At this rate there is neither an excess demand nor supply of labor, and the actual and expected rates of inflation are equal.
4. Frictional unemployment is a natural and often constructive occurrence in a dynamic economy characterized by heterogeneous workers and jobs, imperfect information, and continuous movements of people among the various categories of labor force status.
5. The rational job seeker forms an acceptance wage at a level where the expected marginal costs and benefits of continued search are equal and then compares this wage to actual wage offers.

---

[16]For a discussion of wage subsidies, see James R. Knickman, "Wage Subsidies and Employment," in Frank C. Pierson, *The Minimum Level of Unemployment and Public Policy* (Kalamazoo, Mich.: W. E. Upjohn Institute for Employment Research, 1980), pp. 171–186; Daniel S. Hamermesh, "Subsidies for Jobs in the Private Sector," in John L. Palmer (ed.), *Creating Jobs: Public Employment Programs and Wage Subsidies* (Washington, D.C.: The Brookings Institution, 1978), pp. 87–122; Robert Eisner, "A Direct Attack on Unemployment and Inflation," *Challenge*, July–August 1978, pp. 49–51; and John Bishop and Robert Haveman, "Selective Employment Subsidies: Can Okun's Law Be Repealed?" *American Economic Review*, May 1979, pp. 124–130.

6. Fully anticipated inflation has no impact on the optimal length of job search because job seekers will adjust their acceptance wages upward at the same rate as money wage offers rise. But if job searchers mistakenly view inflation-caused rises in money wage offers as real wage increases, they will shorten their job search and unemployment temporarily will fall below the natural rate.
7. Unemployment benefits extend the optimal length of job search by reducing the *net* opportunity cost of continuing to seek still higher wage offers.
8. Structural unemployment results from a mismatch between the skills needed for available jobs and the skills possessed by those seeking employment.
9. Declines in the aggregate demand for goods and services cause a deficiency in the aggregate demand for labor. Wage rates tend to be inflexible downward for a variety of reasons, including the presence of explicit and implicit contracts, and hence involuntary, demand-deficient unemployment arises.
10. Unemployment is distributed unevenly over the labor force. For example, the unemployment rate for blacks is about twice that for whites.
11. Fiscal policy is a major tool used to combat demand-deficient unemployment, but it is fraught with several complications, including: (*a*) time lags, (*b*) the crowding out of private investment spending, and (*c*) difficulties in determining the "full" employment target.
12. Wage subsidies can reduce structural unemployment for targeted groups. The greater the subsidy and the more elastic the supply and demand curves in the affected labor market, the greater the employment impact. The effect of such plans on the overall unemployment rate is less certain.

QUESTIONS AND STUDY SUGGESTIONS

1. Key terms and concepts to remember: Household Survey (CPS); unemployment rate; discouraged workers; subemployed; stock-flow model; full employment; natural rate of unemployment; aggregate demand and aggregate supply; frictional unemployment; job search model; adaptive expectations theory; structural unemployment; demand-deficient unemployment; effective demand curve for labor; explicit and implicit contracts; fiscal policy; public service employment (PSE); wage subsidies; acceptance wage.
2. What factors tend to *understate* the extent to which the official unemployment rate accurately measures the degree of economic hardship in the nation? What factors lead some observers to conclude that the official unemployment rate *overstates* economic hardship?
3. Use the following data to calculate (*a*) the size of the labor force, (*b*) the official unemployment rate, and (*c*) the labor force participation rate (Chapter 3) for a hypothetical economy: population = 500; population 16 years or older and noninstitutionalized = 400; persons employed full or part time = 200; persons unemployed and actively seeking work = 20; persons who have quit seeking work due to lack of success = 10; part-time workers seeking full-time jobs = 30.
4. Use the basic model shown in Figure 18-3 to illustrate graphically each of the following: (*a*) demand-deficient unemployment and (*b*) temporary increases in output and employment beyond their natural, or full employment, levels.
5. Explain how each of the following would affect the probability that a job searcher will accept the next wage offer and thus affect the expected length of the person's

unemployment spell: (*a*) a decline in the rate of inflation below the expected one and (*b*) a decrease in unemployment benefits.

6. Define the term structural unemployment and distinguish it from frictional and demand-deficient unemployment. Why might structural unemployment fall when demand-deficient unemployment declines?

7. Why are monetary wages inflexible downward? What is the implication of this characteristic for the ability of involuntary demand-deficient unemployment to persist for a considerable length of time?

8. Assume that the official national unemployment rate rises from 6 percent to 11 percent because of a major recession. What impact do you predict this would have on (*a*) the black-white unemployment rate ratio, (*b*) the labor force participation rate, (*c*) the teenage-adult unemployment rate ratio, and (*d*) the blue-collar–white-collar unemployment rate ratio? Explain.

9. Explain why public employee unions often oppose locally administered, federally funded public service employment programs.

10. Use graphic analysis to demonstrate the following propositions: (*a*) given the usual-shaped market labor demand and supply curves, the larger a wage subsidy the greater the employment impact; (*b*) given a wage subsidy and labor demand, the more elastic the labor supply, the greater the employment impact; and (*c*) given a wage subsidy and labor supply, the more elastic the demand for labor, the greater the employment impact.

11. Do you expect the *natural rate* of unemployment to (*a*) increase, (*b*) decrease, or (*c*) remain at the present level over the next decade? Explain your reasoning.

12. Explain why economists decided to revise the full-employment rate of unemployment upward in the 1970s.

13. Examine critically: "Unemployment in the United States can be resolved quickly and efficiently. The government should simply provide jobs for everyone who wants to work and cannot find suitable employment in the private sector."

SELECTED REFERENCES

Baily, Martin N., and Arthur M. Okun: *The Battle Against Unemployment and Inflation* (New York: W. W. Norton & Co., 1982).

Economic Report of the President: various years.

Fleisher, Belton M., and Thomas J. Kniesner: *Labor Economics: Theory, Evidence, and Policy,* 3rd ed. (Englewood Cliffs, N.J.: Prentice-Hall, Inc., 1984), chap. 12.

Gordon, Robert J.: *Macroeconomics,* 3rd ed. (Little, Brown and Company, 1984).

Korliras, Panayotis G., and Richard S. Thorne (eds.): *Modern Macroeconomics: Major Contributions to Contemporary Thought* (New York: Harper & Row, Publishers, 1979).

Okun, Arthur M.: *Prices and Quantities: A Macroeconomic Analysis* (Washington, D.C.: The Brookings Institution, 1981).

Palmer, John L. (ed.): *Creating Jobs: Public Employment Programs and Subsidies* (Washington, D.C.: The Brookings Institution, 1978).

Reynolds, Lloyd G., Stanley H. Masters, and Collette H. Moser: *Readings in Labor Economics and Labor Relations,* 3d ed. (Englewood Cliffs, N.J.: Prentice-Hall, Inc., 1982), readings 14–19.

T I M E   A N D   O N E - H A L F

YOUTH UNEMPLOYMENT*

How serious is the teenage unemployment problem? What are the determinants and consequences of high rates of teenage unemployment?

The unemployment rate for teenagers (16 to 19 years old) greatly exceeds the rate for adults. In 1984, for example, the civilian unemployment rate was 7.5 percent while the rate for teenagers was 18.9 percent. Furthermore, the unemployment rate for black male teenagers was 43 percent! Let us examine the teenage employment problem in more detail.

1. *Seriousness of the problem.* Although youth unemployment is a significant difficulty for thousands of teens, it is *not* a crisis for youth as a group. Most teenagers do not work or seek work while attending school, and the great majority of youth who desire after-school jobs and summer employment *do* find work after short periods of job search. Of those who are unable to obtain employment, nearly one-half attend school while they are unemployed. Typically, only about 5 percent of all teenagers are simultaneously both unemployed and not in school. Additionally, the teenage *employment rate*—total teenage employment divided by the total teenage population—actually has *increased* over the past two decades. Finally, the evidence suggests that most teens move into and out of the labor force with relative ease and suffer only short spells of unemployment. For example, the rapid surge of teenagers into the labor force during the summer actually *reduces* the teenage unemployment rate relative to this year-long average! The reason? The employed portion of the teenage labor force rises faster than the unemployed portion. Additionally, the high rate of teenage unemployment relative to adult unemployment does not result from longer duration of average unemployment spells, but rather from the substantially higher rate at which teenagers quit or are fired from jobs *and* the higher rate at which they move into and out of the labor force.

These comments conceal several disturbing facts, however. The employment rate for black teenagers has fallen since 1955, and the unemployment rate for black teenagers has significantly increased. Also, evidence suggests that a small percentage of teenagers do experience long periods of serious unemployment. In fact, 10 percent of all youth aged 16 to 19 account for more than one-half of all teenage unemployment. Teenagers in this group are disproportionately black, disproportionately high school dropouts, and disproportionately from high-poverty areas.

2. *Determinants of teenage employment status.* The likelihood that a teenager will find employment depends on *market* and *personal* factors. Three important market determinants are (*a*) the general state of the economy, (*b*) the industrial mix in a particular area, and (*c*) the level of the minimum wage.

When the economy expands and overall unemployment falls, teenage employment increases and teenage unemployment rates decline. When the economy goes into a

---

*This discussion draws heavily upon and updates an overview of the teenage unemployment problem provided by Richard B. Freeman and David A. Wise (eds.) in their *The Youth Labor Market Problem: Its Nature, Causes, and Consequences* (Chicago: University of Chicago Press, 1982), pp. 1–16.

recession, the opposite happens. Research indicates that a 1 percent decrease (increase) in the *unemployment* rate for adult males is associated with a 5 percent increase (decrease) in the *employment* rate for male teenagers.

The industrial mix in a particular locale is an important factor in explaining differences in teenage employment and unemployment rates across the nation. Teenage employment is greater in locations which have major industries employing significant numbers of unskilled laborers.

The minimum wage also influences the level of teenage employment and unemployment. A 10 percent increase in the minimum wage is associated with a 1 to 3 percent reduction in teenage employment. Overall, the minimum wage is estimated to reduce male teenage employment by about 7 percent.†

Several personal characteristics also produce differences in employment and unemployment rates among teenagers. Education, family background, and race are three factors which merit comment. High school dropouts have higher unemployment rates than do high school graduates and also are employed fewer weeks per year. Somewhat surprisingly, family background as measured by family income does *not* appear to be related to teenage employment. Perhaps any employment advantages accruing from family connections are offset by income effects which reduce the incentive of wealthier children to become or remain employed. Finally, there are significant differences in both employment and unemployment rates between black and white youth. The reasons for these differences are not clearly understood, but recent research points to several possible explanations. These range from discrimination to the higher rates of discharge of blacks from present employment, often due to absenteeism and to the lack of employed adult role models within many intercity black families.‡

3. *The consequences.* The widely expressed fear that teenage unemployment "scars" teenagers in such a way as to adversely affect their employablity in future years appears to be unfounded. The best evidence to date indicates that early unemployment does not increase the probability of subsequent unemployment as an adult, other things being constant. In fact, Becker and Hills conclude from their research that job switching during the teen years—and the resulting unemployment while job shopping—has *positive* long-run payoffs. In tracking specific individuals, they find that short periods of teenage unemployment are associated with *higher* average wages some 8 to 10 years later, and that teen labor market experience actually *narrows* the subsequent black-white wage differential.§

Irrespective of the long-term impact, of course, teenage unemployment sometimes imposes serious *immediate* economic burdens. This is particularly true for teens from low-income families which can ill afford to "transfer" income to their teenage daughters and sons. Furthermore, unemployed teenagers have more time and perhaps incentive to engage in illegal street activities. Thus, although teenage unemployment may not produce long-term adversity, the short-term costs are likely to be real for both the affected individuals and the communities in which they reside.

---

†David A. Wise and Robert H. Meyer, "The Effects of the Minimum Wage on the Employment and Earnings of Youth," *Journal of Labor Economics,* January 1983, pp. 66–100.

‡Richard B. Freeman, "Minority Youth Unemployment," *National Bureau of Economic Research Reporter,* Fall 1983.

§Brian E. Becker and Stephen M. Hills, "The Long-Run Effects of Job Changes and Unemployment among Male Teenagers," *Journal of Human Resources,* January 1983, pp. 197–212.

INFLATION:
THE
ROLE
OF
LABOR
MARKETS

In the previous chapter we discussed the topics of employment and unemployment. We now direct our attention to the equally complex and important topic of inflation. Specifically, this chapter will analyze the *role of labor markets* in causing, exacerbating, or simply transmitting inflation. We will discover that this area of labor economics is complicated, unsettled, and controversial.

The chapter will unfold as follows. First, we will define inflation and examine the extent of increases in the general price level and hourly money wages during the past twenty years. Next, our attention will turn toward the topic of wage-push inflation. In that section we will explore the important relationship between wages, productivity, and average labor costs and explain the mechanics of wage-initiated and wage-perpetuated inflation. There we will examine the factors that enable workers to gain wage increases which drive up unit labor costs. In the third part of the chapter, consideration will be given to alternative theories, in which wage rate increases are simply symptoms, not causes, of inflation. Analysis of demand-pull inflation, short- and long-run Phillips curves, and adaptive and rational expectations will be central to our discussion. Fourth, we will examine some of the empirical evidence on "unions and inflation" and state a few general conclusions. Lastly, we survey the anti-inflation tools which economists refer to as *incomes policies*.

INFLATION AND HOURLY WAGES:
AN HISTORICAL OVERVIEW

Inflation is defined as a rising general level of prices in the economy. The general price level is measured through various price indexes, the best known of which is the Consumer Price Index (CPI). The Bureau of Labor Statistics (BLS) computes the CPI by determining the typical purchases of a middle-income family headed by an urban wage earner. It calculates a weighted-average price for this "bundle," or "market basket," of about 300 items for a specific base year and arbitrarily sets that price—CPI—equal to 100. It then recalculates the weighted-average price each month, divides it by the old one, and multiplies the outcome by 100 to determine the new CPI. Therefore, as seen in equation (19-1), annual percentage increases in the CPI measure the yearly inflation rate.

$$\text{Inflation rate in year X} = \frac{\text{CPI in year X} - \text{CPI in year X-1}}{\text{CPI in year X-1}} \times 100 \qquad (19\text{-}1)$$

For example, the CPI for 1984, was 307.6 compared to 297.4 in 1983; hence, the rate of inflation was 3.4 percent. That is, $3.4 = [(307.6 - 297.4)/297.4] \times 100$.

The government also calculates various indexes of changes in average hourly compensation. The most useful for our purposes is the Index of Compensation per Hour (ICH), which measures changes in average hourly compensation, including employer contributions to social security and private fringe benefit plans. Increases in hourly compensation such as those measured by this index are sometimes referred to as *wage inflation.* In employing this term, however, be aware that under some circumstances increases in money wages are fully compatible with zero rates of *price* inflation.

In Figure 19-1 we illustrate the *changes* in the CPI and ICH since 1950. With respect to price inflation, note that the CPI (1) increased in every year during the period, (2) tripled between the base year, 1967, and 1984, and (3) rose dramatically in the late 1970s before slowing its growth in 1983. The even greater steepness of the ICH curve indicates that average hourly compensation rose more rapidly than the CPI for most of the period. Also notice that hourly monetary compensation rose more rapidly during the 1970s than in the late 1960s and early 1970s.

Figure 19-1 poses several interesting questions. For example, can we con-

FIGURE 19-1 INFLATION AND HOURLY COMPENSATION TRENDS, 1967–1984
The general price level as measured by the Consumer Price Index (CPI) tripled between 1967 and 1984. Money compensation per hour as measured by the Index of Compensation per Hour (ICH) rose even more swiftly than the CPI. (*Derived from the Economic Report of the President, 1985, Tables B-40 and B-52.*)

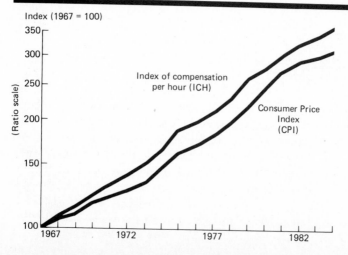

clude that rapid rises in hourly wages *cause* inflation? If not, do such increases *aggravate* or *perpetuate* ongoing inflation? Is it possible that the high rates of inflation observed in the figure cause *money wages* to rise? Or, do other factors cause *both* the CPI and ICH to rise simultaneously? As we will soon discover, there are several theories of the cause of inflation and of the role of labor markets in the inflationary process.

WAGE INCREASES AS A CAUSE OF INFLATION

Many economists contend that theory and evidence suggest that rapid rises in money wages *can*, and under many circumstances *do*, cause inflation in the U.S. economy. This does not imply that these observers view increases in money wages as the sole—or even the primary—cause of inflation. Rather, they argue that the general price level can rise either because of *increases* in aggregate demand or *decreases* in aggregate supply, and that the latter can occur when increases in money wages exceed productivity gains economywide. Under these circumstances, the wage increases will drive costs upward, creating cost-push inflation of a wage-push variety.

The Relationship between Wages, Productivity, and Labor Costs. To understand how increases in wage rates might produce inflation, let us return to the ***relationship between wages, productivity, and labor costs*** first discussed in Chapter 16. The latter is defined as follows.

$$\frac{\text{Unit labor}}{\text{cost}} = \frac{\text{total labor cost}}{\text{quantity of output}} \qquad (19\text{-}2)$$

The numerator in the equation—total labor cost—consists of the average money wage rate times the total hours of labor used. Hence, through substitution:

$$\frac{\text{Unit labor}}{\text{cost}} = \frac{\text{hourly wage rate} \times \text{worker hours}}{\text{quantity of output}} \qquad (19\text{-}3)$$

and by dividing both the numerator and denominator by labor hours:

$$\frac{\text{Unit labor}}{\text{cost}} = \frac{\text{hourly wage rate}}{\text{quantity of output/worker hour}} \qquad (19\text{-}4)$$

Recall that *productivity* is defined as output per worker hour, the denominator in equation (19-4). This equation thus provides a workable representation of how unit labor costs relate to wage rates and productivity. For example, suppose that the average productivity in the economy is 20 units of output per worker hour and that the average wage is $10 an hour. The average—or unit—labor cost would be $.50 (= $10/20).

But our interest here is in *changes* in wages, productivity, and unit labor costs, and not specifically their absolute levels. As we noted in Chapter 16, an approximation of the relationship of changes in these three variables can be calculated by employing the mathematical rule that the percentage change in the ratio of two variables—in this case, wages and productivity—equals the percentage change in the numerator minus the percentage change in the denominator. Therefore:

$$\text{Change in unit} \atop \text{labor cost (\%)} = {\text{change in} \atop \text{wage (\%)}} - {\text{change in} \atop \text{productivity (\%)}} \qquad (19\text{-}5)$$

An important conclusion can be drawn from equation (19-5): If wages rise faster than productivity growth, unit labor costs will rise; if they rise less rapidly than productivity, unit labor costs will fall; and if wages and productivity increase at an equal rate, average labor costs will not change.

Several examples will help demonstrate this proposition. First, suppose that average hourly wages in the economy rise from $10 to $10.30 per hour in a particular year and that productivity increases from 20 to 20.6 units of output per worker hour. How much will unit labor costs rise? The answer, of course, is zero. Workers are being paid 3 percent more each hour [= ($10.30 − $10.00)/$10.00], but they also are producing 3 percent more output per hour [(20.6 − 20.0)/20.0]. Thus unit labor costs remain constant at $.50 per hour ($10/20 = $.50 = $10.30/20.6). As a second example, suppose that productivity does not increase at all in the foregoing situation. Then unit labor costs will rise by the full 3 percent wage advance. Alternatively, if wages increase by 6 percent and productivity advances by 3 percent, then unit labor costs will rise by 3 percent.

So why is this important? The answer is twofold: (1) as indicated in Figure 19-2, annual percentage changes in hourly compensation *have* tended to exceed

FIGURE 19-2 HOURLY COMPENSATION, PRODUCTIVITY, AND UNIT LABOR COSTS, 1970–1984
It is not uncommon for increases in hourly compensation to exceed annual productivity gains. The result is increases in unit labor costs. (*From U. S. Bureau of the Census, updated.*)

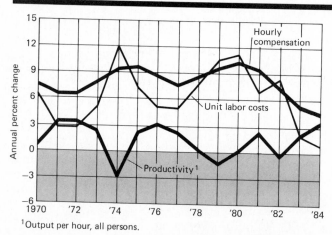

[1]Output per hour, all persons.

productivity gains in many years, and (2) because labor costs constitute about three-fourths of all product costs, increases in unit labor costs tend to increase the marginal and average costs of goods and services.

The Wage-Push Model. Thus far we have established that wage increases which exceed productivity increases cause production costs to rise. We next need to establish how higher costs might lead to increased prices. This can be accomplished through use of the aggregate supply and demand model first described in the previous chapter. In Figure 19-3, aggregate demand and aggregate supply are initially D_0 and S_0, respectively. The intersection of D_0 and S_0 generates a price level of P_0 and national output of Q_0. Now suppose that workers gain an average wage increase which greatly exceeds the national rise in productivity. This will increase unit labor costs, and assuming no offsetting reduction in other costs, will drive up the supply price of output. Consequently, the aggregate supply curve will shift leftward from S_0 to S_1 in Figure 19-3, indicating that producers will no longer be willing to offer as much output for sale at each price level. Stated differently, at each level of output, the equilibrium price level will be higher than previously. Now notice the disequilibrium in the product market. At the old price level P_0, buyers will desire to buy output level B, but suppliers, faced with higher costs, will only be willing to offer the output shown by point A. This *excess* demand for products (distance BA) will increase the equilibrium

FIGURE 19-3 WAGE-PUSH INFLATION
Increases in money wages which exceed national increases in output per worker hour drive unit labor costs upward. Consequently, the aggregate supply curve S_0 shifts inward to S_1. At the existing price level P_0, the amount demanded B exceeds the quantity of goods supplied A and the price level rises to P_1. The *rate* of inflation is $(P_1 - P_0)/P_0$.

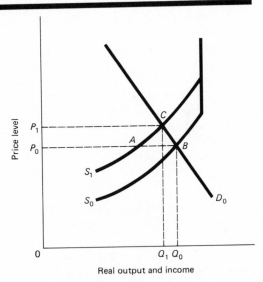

price level to P_1 (point C). The true cause of this inflation is excessive growth of money wages. But notice that observation of the adjustment process may lead one to mistake the excess demand for products (BA) to be the cause. The latter occurred only because the supply curve shifted leftward to S_1. An important point emerges: Sorting out demand versus supply (cost) causes of inflation is a difficult endeavor.

Wage-Push Inflation: Contributing Factors. Wage-push theorists cite several interconnected factors which under certain circumstances enable workers to advance their wages faster than productivity and thereby contribute to *wage-push inflation.* These factors include (1) union market power, (2) markup pricing, (3) wage imitation, (4) explicit and implicit contracts, (5) productivity declines, and (6) monetary accommodation.

1. Union market power. According to some economists, unions have increased the union-nonunion wage differential (Chapter 8) over the past two decades and in so doing have contributed to wage-push inflation.[1] Other economists contend that, in an economy characterized by oligopolistic industries, downwardly rigid money wages, protective tariffs, anticompetitive labor market rules, and wages set on the basis of "equitable comparisons," unions can cause wage-push inflation simply by gaining increases in hourly compensation *at the same rate as nonunion firms* but faster than the growth of labor productivity. They also can *perpetuate* demand-caused inflation through gaining "cost-of-living" wage increments which exceed productivity advances. Or, as shown later, they can *worsen* existing inflation by achieving "customary" yearly wage increases when productivity is slowing either cyclically or secularly.

But won't the backward shifts in the aggregate supply curve caused by union-induced increases in unit costs cause declines in output and increases in unemployment (Q_0 to Q_1 in Figure 19-3)? And won't this unemployment halt wage inflation? Perhaps not! The reason: Union contracts, government rules, and institutional customs greatly reduce *wage competition* in the economy. The very purpose of unionism is to fix wages by negotiating contracts and removing competition among workers for jobs. Persons who are unemployed and willing to work for less than existing wages are effectively restrained from competing with the employed on that basis. Also, where wages are set by custom rather than market forces, nonunion wages do not necessarily fall when union workers who are unemployed seek work in nonunion jobs. Hence, according to wage-push theorists, unemployment per se does not preclude union-caused wage-push inflation.

2. Markup pricing. Some economists argue that the economy has two broad types of product markets: competitive markets in which supply and de-

---

[1] For example, see Daniel J. B. Mitchell, *Unions, Wages, and Inflation* (Washington, D.C.: The Brookings Institution, 1980).

mand determine prices, and noncompetitive markets in which prices are *administered* through the use of **cost-markup pricing** principles.[2] In these latter markets, large corporations first determine their average production costs, of which labor costs constitute a large proportion, and then apply a set percentage markup to establish the product prices they will charge. This markup provides the margin which allows the firms to pay dividends and finance expansion. Because firms within oligopolistic industries compete with one another mainly on a nonprice basis, and because rivals have similar costs and markups, these oligopolists supposedly do not resist union wage demands—for example, by accepting a long strike—as vigorously as they might. Once the new labor contracts are signed, the firms simply recalculate their new unit labor costs, add in their average nonlabor expenses, and apply their percentage markup to determine their new higher prices. Because buyers normally view price increases caused by *cost* increases to the seller as "fair," they continue to purchase from their customary suppliers. In this way, then, workers consistently can demand and receive wage rate increases which exceed productivity advances.

3. Wage imitation. Another factor which is thought by some observers to interact with union market power and cost-markup pricing to cause wage-push inflation is **wage imitation**.[3] Unions, nonunion workers, and even employers may imitate others in demanding and providing wage increases. They may do this for several reasons. First, they may conclude that it is less expensive to imitate the wage increases being paid elsewhere in their industry, geographic area, or the overall economy than to *search* for a "correct" wage given the specific circumstances in their market for labor. According to this line of reasoning, it is costly to obtain information about product demand, demand elasticity, current and prospective economic conditions, productivity trends, and the like. Wage imitation therefore may be an *efficient* rule-of-thumb for wage setting. Second, wage imitation may occur simply because it appears to produce an equitable wage outcome. In essence, the utility which workers in one firm associate with their wages may be dependent on the wage rates similar workers in other firms are paid. This may give rise to wage imitation behavior.

> That is, unit A follows unit B because this is the "fair" thing to do. Workers in unit A are disappointed if their wages lag behind those of B. The wage of B [affects the utility] of unit A workers, since the B wage influences the satisfaction that A workers derive from their own wages. Behavior based on tradition can easily be put in the equity framework. It need only be assumed that people find the old way of doing things the equitable way. The equity framework can also encompass other forms of behavior. Workers in unit A

---

[2] See, for example, Alfred S. Eichner (ed.), *A Guide to Post-Keynesian Economics* (New York: M. E. Sharpe, Inc., 1979). Also see Sidney Weintraub, *Capitalism's Inflation and Unemployment* (Reading, Pa: Addison-Wesley Publishing Co., 1978).

[3] This section draws on the work of Mitchell, op. cit., pp. 163–207.

might suddenly discover that unit C was paying a higher wage and seek to emulate that unit. Such behavior . . . would easily fit into social norms such as "equal pay for equal work."[4]

Finally, nonunion firms may match union wage increases as a way to deter unionism—recall our earlier discussion of the "threat effect" (Chapter 8). In this way, firms may be able to avoid unionization and the cumbersome work rules which sometimes accompany union contracts.

How can wage imitation contribute to average wage gains which exceed economywide productivity advances? The answer is that major union settlements in *key industries* in which firms mark up their costs to determine prices may set off ripple effects emanating outward to other union and nonunion contracts. Hence, inflationary wage increases may occur in segments of the economy where we would not otherwise expect to find them. By failing to *demand* wage increases approximately equal to what others are receiving, workers may fear losing ground to them, and by failing to *provide* "fair" pay increases, employers may jeopardize their reputations as good places to work and therefore may find it difficult to attract and retain high-quality workers.

4. Explicit and implicit contracts. In the previous chapter, we explained why firms and workers find it mutually advantageous to reach understandings about future wages based on formal contracts and "invisible handshakes." These explicit and implicit contracts reduce the uncertainty which workers have about future wages; allow firms to reduce recruitment, screening, and supervision costs; and increase the probability that employers will capture returns from firm-financed investment in human capital. But these contracts also increase the possibility of wage-push inflation.[5]

For example, let us suppose that one implicit contract is as follows: We agree that under all but extremely adverse circumstances, wages shall rise such that they keep up with inflation and provide a real wage increment equal to the national average increase in labor productivity.

We can easily demonstrate how this implicit contract—if widespread— might perpetuate inflation even after the initiating causal factor is removed. Suppose, for example, that existing inflation is 7 percent and that labor market participants expect this rate to continue. Also, assume that productivity is expected to grow annually at 3 percent. This implies *annual* wage increases of 10 percent (7 percent inflation plus 3 percent productivity). Although this is consistent with the informal understanding, the 10 percent wage increase will also increase unit labor costs in the economy. Even if the driving force which caused

---

[4]Ibid., p. 165.

[5]See Arthur M. Okun, "The Invisible Handshake and the Inflationary Process," *Challenge*, January–February 1980, pp. 5–12 and *Prices and Quantities: A Macroeconomic Analysis* (Washington, D.C.: The Brookings Institution, 1981). This idea is discussed by Daniel Mitchell and Larry Kimbell, "Labor Market Contracts and Inflation," in Martin Neil Baily (ed.), *Workers, Jobs, and Inflation* (Washington, D.C.: The Brookings Institution, 1982), pp. 199–238.

the 7 percent inflation—say excessive aggregate demand—vanishes, inflation may continue for a time under the new impetus of wage-push forces.

This analysis also holds true for explicit contracts negotiated between firms and unions.

5. Productivity declines. A fourth factor which can cause a gap between the wage rate and productivity to open or widen is a decline in the trend rate of productivity. The lower the annual increase in output per worker hour, the more a given increase in money wages increases the rate of inflation. The long-term increase in productivity growth is only on the order of 2 or 3 percent annually. A simple model of the wage-price inflationary process which we have been discussing can be used to explain how, under some circumstances, an unexpected, permanent decline in the rate of productivity growth—say to 1.5 percent annually—can contribute to *accelerating* inflation. Specifically, let us again assume in Table 19-1 that union wage demands are composed of two elements: cost-of-living increases to offset any expected increase in the price level (row 1) and an improvement factor to capture labor's share of the average national annual productivity increase (row 2). We assume in period 1 that the price level and productivity both have been rising by 3 percent yearly, and unions therefore demand and receive a 6 percent increase in money wages (row 3). This produces a 3 percent increase in unit labor costs because actual productivity rises by only 3 percent (row 4). We assume that this increase in unit labor costs produces an equal increase in price inflation (row 5). Suppose now in period 2 that unions, anticipating that 3 percent inflation and 3 percent productivity growth will continue, dictate another 6 percent wage increase. But what if productivity growth actually falls to 1.5 percent in period 2? The result is that inflation will rise to 4.5 percent. Now, if in period 3 unions and firms incorrectly assume that productivity will return to its historical trend of 3 percent and recognize that

---

TABLE 19-1

Productivity Decline and Accelerating Inflation

	Period				
	1	**2**	**3**	**4**	**5**
(1) Assumed inflation	3%	3%	4.5%	6%	7.5%
(2) Expected growth in real income	3	3	3	3	3
(3) Wage increase	6	6	7.5	9	10.5
(4) Productivity gain	3	1.5	1.5	1.5	1.5
(5) Actual inflation (unit labor costs)	3	4.5	6	7.5	9

Source: Adapted from New York Stock Exchange, *Reaching a Higher Standard of Living* (1979), p. 26.

actual inflation is 4.5 percent, a 7.5 percent pay raise may result. But if the productivity increase is permanently reduced to 1.5 percent, these wage demands will generate a still higher 6 percent rate of inflation in period 3. By tracing the analysis through periods 4 and 5 we observe that the continuous underestimation of the rate of productivity gain can result in an *accelerating* rate of wage-push inflation. Only when unions and firms realize that the apparent below-normal rate of productivity is actually the new normal rate, will the acceleration stop.[6]

6. Monetary accommodation. A final contributing factor to wage-push inflation is that government often *accommodates* the wage-push actions of market participants. As indicated in the previous chapter, the federal government has accepted the responsibility for promoting full employment. If wage-push inflation is to be more than a one-time event, increases in money wages must exceed the average annual productivity advance on a repeated basis. That is, the aggregate supply curve in Figure 19-3 must continuously shift leftward relative to the location of the aggregate demand curve. *If* aggregate demand stayed constant at D_0, these supply decreases would generate a substantial decline in national output, rapidly rising unemployment in labor markets, and excess capacity of existing plant and equipment. These circumstances eventually would undermine union bargaining power and corporate pricing policies. Consequently, workers could no longer raise money wages faster than the productivity rate, firms would be unable to increase product prices, and the wage-push inflation would end.

But what if the federal government responds to the declining output by increasing aggregate demand via increases in its expenditures, tax reductions, and increases in the money supply? This, of course, would shift the aggregate demand curve rightward in Figure 19-3, adding demand elements to the wage-induced inflation. Stated differently, labor market participants create inflationary pressure when collectively they increase their wages more rapidly than productivity. But the government can keep this pressure from causing continued inflation by permitting the ensuing recession to occur. Instead, legislative mandates, political factors, and human concerns over rising unemployment normally lead government to accommodate the private-sector actions via expansionary fiscal and monetary policy. Wage-push theorists envision the following relationship between increases in money wages and changes in the money supply:

$$\begin{array}{ccc} \text{Excessive} & & \\ \text{increases in} & \rightarrow \quad \text{increases in} \quad \rightarrow & \text{increases in} \\ \text{money wages} & \quad \text{unemployment} & \text{money supply} \end{array}$$

---

[6]We are assuming that fiscal and monetary authorities are "accommodating" these wage and price increases, a matter discussed in the following section. For a more sophisticated presentation of this theory, see Joint Economic Committee, *Productivity and Inflation* (Washington: U.S. Government Printing Office, 1980).

They contend that excessive money wage gains cause unit labor costs, average production costs, and the general price level to rise. The latter causes the quantity of output demanded to fall and unemployment to rise. Because of the government's full employment objective, this ultimately leads to *monetary accommodation* (rightward shifts in aggregate demand) in the form of money supply growth. Typically, changes in the money supply are looked upon as autonomous policy decisions which lead to changes in output, employment, and the price level. But in the present formulation cause and effect are reversed. Increases in money wage rates which affect output, employment, and the level of prices cause or induce changes in the money supply!

WAGE INCREASES AS A SYMPTOM OF INFLATION

Although the wage-push theory of inflation just discussed has its supporters, the majority of U.S. economists contend that wage-push theorists mistakenly view increases in money wages as a cause of inflation when in fact most of these increases simply accompany inflation. According to this mainstream view, excessive aggregate demand creates demand-pull pressures which eventually raise all prices, including the prices of labor services. Hence, observed increases in money wages are a symptomatic response which lags behind the rise in the general price level.

The Demand-Pull Model. Figure 19-4 portrays the pure theory of *demand-pull inflation.* Suppose that initially the economy is at the full employment output level Q_0 and the general price level is P_0. Next, we introduce an increase in aggregate demand which is shown by the rightward shift from D_0 to D_1. At the old price level P_0, the amount of output demanded shown by point B exceeds the quantity that producers are able to supply (point A). The excess demand at P_0 (BA) then pulls prices upward as consumers, businesses, and government bid against one another for a fixed quantity of available goods and services. The price level rises to P_1 and the inflation rate over the particular period is $(P_1 - P_0)/P_0$. Note from the vertical movement from A to C on the aggregate supply curve that production costs rise at the same rate as inflation $[(C - A)/A]$. Assuming no change in the composition of these costs, we would discover that money wages rose by a percentage equal to the rate of productivity growth plus the rate of inflation.

While agreeing on this basic model, economists disagree on their answers to two questions related to demand pull. First, what is the cause of the demand shift shown in the graph? Second, once this inflation occurs, can it then be perpetuated via wage push?

The contending views on these two questions are easily distinguishable in their simplist forms.[7] Keynesian economists view aggregate demand in terms of categories of "effective" spending, specifically domestic consumption spending, investment spending, government spending, and spending by foreigners on net exports. Any one, or any combination, of these spending components can shift the aggregate demand curve rightward. Domestic or foreign consumers can draw down past savings or borrow to finance added spending, corporations can also borrow or use retained earnings to increase investment, and government can borrow or print money to finance deficits. All these groups then can be responsible for creating demand-pull inflation. Monetarists, on the other hand, contend that inflation is always a monetary phenomenon. They employ the familiar identity $MV = PQ$ to show that rates of growth of the money supply M which exceed increases in the growth of real output Q are accompanied by a rise in the price level P, assuming no change in velocity V. According to this perspective, rapid increases of the money supply expand the actual cash balances held by individuals and corporations beyond the levels desired. To reestablish the desired ratios of cash balances to other items in their portfolios, these market participants increase their spending on a full range of commodities and other assets. Hence, aggregate demand rises, and because the quantity of output rises

[7]In reality the arguments are much more sophisticated and the distinctions are increasingly blurred. The era of distinct Keynesianism and monetarism is past; most mainstream macroeconomists incorporate Keynesian analysis into their short-term macro-analyses and monetarism into their long-term analyses.

FIGURE 19-4 DEMAND-PULL INFLATION
When the economy is at its full employment output Q_0 and aggregate demand rises, an excess demand for commodities BA occurs at the existing price level P_0. Consequently, prices are pulled upward to a higher price level P_1. The rate of inflation is $(P_1 - P_0)/P_0$.

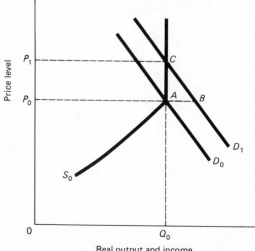

less rapidly, inflation occurs. To summarize: Keynesians and monetarists agree that excess aggregate demand can cause inflation; they disagree on whether or not demand-pull inflation is always a monetary phenomenon.

Let us now answer our second question: Can demand inflation be perpetuated via wage-push factors? Most, but not all, Keynesians would answer with a qualified "yes." They would cite the wage-push factors which we discussed previously. Monetarists, however, would disagree. At the extreme, they contend that there is no such thing as wage-push inflation. Suppose, for example, that unionized workers demand and oligopolistic industries grant a 12 percent annual wage increase and that these firms successfully pass on the resulting increase in unit labor costs to their customers. In the absence of growth of the money supply, the only way oligopolists could accomplish this is to restrict output (their product demand curves are fixed). This would result in a reduction of their work forces, and the newly unemployed would eventually be forced to seek jobs in the nonunion sector. This would increase labor supply there and, assuming downward flexible wages, would cause the competitive market wage there to fall. Meanwhile, if the demand curves for the union-produced products are inelastic, consumers of those products would discover that the higher prices left them with less *remaining* income to buy other goods and services. The demand for these latter commodities would fall, causing their prices to decline. Hence, only the *composition* of prices and wages in the economy would change, not the overall wage and price *levels*. The only way that wage and price inflation could occur is if the monetary authorities increased the money supply during the period of the 12 percent union wage increase. If this occurred, prices would indeed rise, but the inflation would be demand-pull, not wage-push. According to monetarists, causation between wage increases, price increases, and monetary growth lies in the following direction:

$$\text{Excessive growth} \atop \text{of the money supply} \rightarrow \text{increase in price level } \textit{and} \atop \text{increases in money wages}$$

Excess Demand and the Short-Run Phillips Curve. The impact of excess demand on money wages and prices can also be illustrated through the well-known *Phillips curve,* which shows the relationship between rates of money wage (or price) inflation and unemployment. One such curve is shown as PC in Figure 19-5 (b). The negative slope of the curve indicates the observed relationship between increases in money wages $\dot{W}$ and the rate of unemployment U. This inverse relationship and the convex nature of the curve can be understood through reference to the graph of the labor market shown to the left of the Phillips curve [Figure 19-5 (a)].[8]

---

[8]This model is a simplified version of one presented by Richard Lipsey, "The Relationship between Unemployment and the Rate of Change in Money Wage Rates in the United Kingdom, 1862–1957: A Further Analysis," *Economica*, February 1960, pp. 1–31.

Carefully note at the outset that the left-hand graph involves different variables from those measured by the Phillips curve. In graph (a) we are holding prices constant and measuring the *absolute* monetary wage W on the vertical axis—not money wage *increases*, $\dot{W}$, as in the Phillips curve. We are also measuring *total* employment on the horizontal axis in graph (a), as contrasted to the *rate of unemployment* in the Phillips curve graph. Also, be aware that we are assuming there is a basic asymmetry in the labor market which creates an upward "ratchet" effect on money wages. That is, money wages are freely flexible upward under conditions of excess demand for labor but, once having reached a particular absolute wage, they are inflexible downward.

With this background information in mind, let us examine three particular situations in the labor market shown in graph (a) and relate them to various segments of the Phillips curve shown in graph (b). First, suppose that the wage rate in the economy is W_4. Notice that the number of people seeking work at this wage, H, exceeds the quantity of people demanded, G. Clearly, the *excess supply* of labor (HG) indicates that the effective demand for products and labor must be depressed in the economy. Under these conditions of high unemployment in the labor market, increases in money wages will be low, at best. This situation—high unemployment and low increases in money wages—corresponds to points on the far rightward portion of the Phillips curve shown in (b). If we assume that U_2 is the full employment rate of unemployment, then we can conclude that points to the right of Y are analogous to situations in the labor market such as the

FIGURE 19-5 THE DEGREE OF EXCESS DEMAND AND THE PHILLIPS CURVE

The greater the excess demand for labor, the lower the unemployment rate and the higher the rate of increase in money wages. For example, if excess demand is high—such as BA in graph (a)—the unemployment rate will be low, say U_1, but money wages will rise rapidly ($\dot{W}_1$). At the other extreme, given that wages are inflexible downward, an excess supply of labor such as HG will be associated with points such as Z on the Phillips curve in graph (b). That is, unemployment will be very high and money wage increases will be slight or even zero.

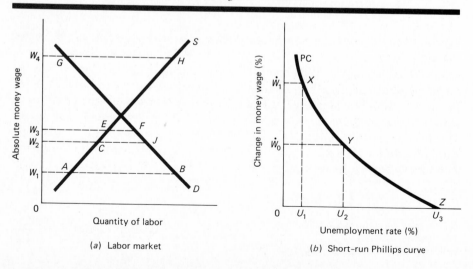

(a) Labor market

(b) Short-run Phillips curve

extreme one we just described; that is, there is excess labor supply to one degree or another.

Next, suppose that the absolute wage in graph (a) is W_1. Now substantial *excess demand BA* characterizes the situation. It is reasonable to assume that the greater the absolute excess demand relative to the level of employment $[(B - A)/A]$, the *faster* the rise in money wages. If we use the unemployment rate as an indication for the extent of excess demand, then we can conclude that the lower the unemployment rate, the more rapid the rise in money wages. Thus the labor market situation shown by excess demand BA corresponds to points such as X on the Phillips curve. Additionally, note that the excess demand circumstances shown by JC and FE in graph (a) will also produce money wage increases, but the *rate* of such rises will be less than for BA.

The negative slope of the Phillips curve then can be explained in terms of degrees of excess demand for labor. The curve is convex because successively larger increases in excess demand are needed to reduce the unemployment rate by each percentage point. This is because once demand-deficient unemployment is reduced, only structural and frictional unemployment remain (Chapter 18). These latter two types of unemployment do not yield readily to increases in excess demand in the economy. Also, the downward rigidity of money wages means that progressively greater increases in unemployment rates are required to slow wage inflation by each percentage point.

We have seen then that the short-run Phillips curve can be viewed in an aggregate demand framework. Supporters of the demand theory of inflation contend that the Phillips curve per se does not provide evidence for the existence of wage-push inflation. For example, $\dot{W}_0$ in Figure 19-5 (b) may be a money wage increase equal to the productivity advance and therefore consistent with a zero inflation rate.

Wage-push theorists counter this demand-pull perspective by pointing out that the Phillips curve certainly does not preclude the wage-push explanation. For example, as labor markets tighten, unions can more aggressively pursue their wage demands and, because of strong product demand, firms are more willing to grant increases in money wages which exceed productivity gains. The expanding aggregate demand in the economy allows corporations to use their market power to pass along increases in unit labor costs and perhaps even increase the percentage of their price markups. Furthermore, according to supporters of the wage-push perspective, the *location* of the Phillips curve—independent of its slope—is partially determined by the extent of wage-push inflation at *each* unemployment rate. In fact, public policy in the 1960s and early 1970s focused on methods of shifting the supposedly stable Phillips curve leftward to improve the tradeoff between inflation and unemployment. One policy that government implemented was wage and price guideposts. The purpose? To reduce money wage increases to the level of increases in productivity and thereby shift the Phillips curve leftward.

In retrospect, this policy was rather misguided. For as indicated in Figure 19-6, the actual Phillips data points during the 1970s lay far *upward* and *rightward* of those surrounding the presumed stable 1956–1969 curve (PC_1). Notice, for example, that the unemployment rates in 1963 and 1979 were both about 5.5 percent, yet inflation was 11.3 percent in 1979 compared to 1.2 percent in 1963! Did the Phillips curve shift outward from PC_1 to PC_2 to PC_3 as shown in the figure? If so, why? Numerous explanations have been offered and include the following: the productivity slowdown, increased wage push, higher oil prices, increased government regulation, and a changed composition of the labor force which increased the frictional and structural unemployment rates. Note that all but the last of these contentions reflect the general perspective that *cost increases cause inflation.* But economists who view cost increases as *symptoms* of inflation provide perceptive counterexplanations. Let us examine them in detail.

Adaptive Expectations and the Long-Run Phillips Curve. Figure 19-7 indicates how the Phillips data points during the 1970s and early 1980s can be explained without resorting to cost-push and structural interpretations. To

FIGURE 19-6 THE PHILLIPS DATA POINTS, 1956–1984

Between 1956 and 1969, there appeared to be a stable tradeoff between inflation and unemployment as seen by the grouping of Phillips data points around PC_1. After 1969, however, the points tended to lie above and to the right of PC_1. Did the Phillips curve shift outward to positions such as PC_2 and PC_3, or was the original Phillips curve concept conditioned upon the expectation of a constant rate of inflation?

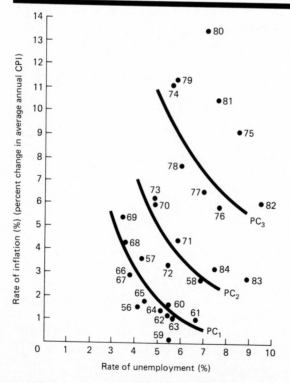

achieve greater clarity, we will divide the analysis into two components: an explanation of *specific* short-run Phillips curves and an examination of why the curves *may shift upward* to produce a vertical long-run Phillips curve.

1. The short-run Phillips curve revisited. Our initial attention will focus on Phillips curve $SRPC_1$, in Figure 19-7. Suppose that the economy is experiencing a mild rate of inflation P_1 and a *natural rate of unemployment U_n*. Recall from Chapter 18 that one definition of this natural rate is the level of unemployment which will occur when *expected* inflation equals the *actual* rate of inflation.

According to this perspective, such curves as $SRPC_1$ exist because people *expect* the existing rate of inflation to continue *and in fact it often does not*. To understand this, let us establish three points on $SRPC_1$. We begin at point A where we assume people expect the P_1 rate of inflation to continue into the future. But now suppose the Federal Reserve increases the rate of growth of the money supply so that the actual rate of inflation is P_2.[9] This higher-than-anticipated inflation will reduce unemployment from U_n to U_1 for two reasons, both of which involve the labor market. First, firms will discover that their product

[9]It may do this because society has defined full employment to be at a lower rate of unemployment than the natural rate.

FIGURE 19-7 ADAPTIVE EXPECTATIONS AND THE LONG-RUN PHILLIPS CURVE
Each short-run Phillips curve such as $SRPC_1$ indicates the combinations of inflation and unemployment rates which are possible when the *actual* rate of inflation diverges from the *expected* rate. When inflation is greater than expected, such as P_2 rather than P_1, the economy moves from A to C and unemployment *temporarily* falls to U_1. But P_2 becomes the new *expected* rate, the short-run Phillips curve shifts to $SRPC_2$, and unemployment returns to the natural rate U_n at D. Hence, in the long run, any one of many rates of inflation is consistent with the natural rate of unemployment; that is, the long-run Phillips curve is vertical.

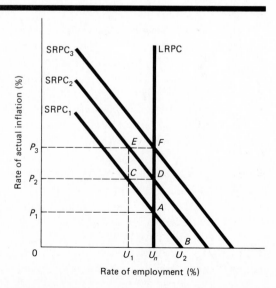

prices are rising under conditions of strong demand, but that their unit labor costs are rising less rapidly. Why is this so? Many employees are working for wage rates specified in long-run contracts which were negotiated on the *expectation* that inflation would continue to be P_1. But individual firms see the prices of *their* products rising relative to these money wages and hire more workers at the now lower *real* wage. Second, people engaged in job search will begin to receive rising money wage offers as firms begin to bid for new workers. Recall from the search model discussed in the previous chapter that, if workers view these money wage increases as real ones, they will reduce their search time, and again, unemployment will fall. To repeat: When inflation is greater than anticipated (P_2 rather than P_1), unemployment will fall (U_n to U_1). Hence, point C on SRPC$_1$ is established.

Now let us determine a third point on the short-run Phillips curve SRPC$_1$. Again we assume that the economy is initially at point A (P_1, U_n), but now suppose that monetary policy reduces the actual rate of inflation to zero. Firms, locked into long-term wage term contracts, will discover that their product prices do not increase as rapidly as the money wages they are contracted to pay. *Real* labor costs will rise, the firms will lay off workers, and unemployment will rise from U_n to U_2. At the same time, job searchers will find that money wage offers are lower relative to their acceptance wages, which are based on an *expected* P_1 rate of inflation, and will extend their search time. This will contribute to the increase in unemployment shown in the figure. We then have a third point on SRPC$_1$—B—and another principle: When inflation is less than expected (P_0 rather than P_1) unemployment will rise (U_n to U_2).

The short-run Phillips curve is simply derived by connecting all such points as C, A, and B. These points show the various levels of unemployment associated with rates of *actual* inflation which differ from the expected rate P_1. We can similarly derive curves SRPC$_2$ and SRPC$_3$; each reflects a *higher* initial expected rate of inflation at the natural rate of unemployment.

2. The long-run vertical Phillips curve. Let us now introduce an *adaptive expectations* scenario to our model. Specifically, let us return to point A on Phillips curve SRPC$_1$. Again suppose that the actual rate of inflation is P_2 compared to the expected rate P_1. Through the labor market actions previously discussed, the economy will move leftward along SRPC$_1$ to point C, and unemployment will *temporarily* fall to U_1. But people eventually will begin to recognize that the actual rate of inflation is P_2, and they will adapt their expectations for future inflation from P_1 to P_2. Once this occurs, the short-run Phillips curve shifts upward to $SRPC_2$. Remember that higher *expected* rates of inflation translate into higher *locations* of short-run Phillips curves. What happens to the unemployment rate? As old contracts expire, workers will demand increases in money wages to reflect the new, higher expected rate of inflation P_2, and job seekers will increase their search time because they now perceive the present money wage offers to be inadequate in real terms. As a result, real labor costs will rise, firms will discharge workers, and unemployment will rise from $C(U_1)$ to $D(U_n)$. Note that at D, the natural rate of unemployment is reestablished—*but now at a higher* *rate of both actual and expected inflation!* And we might add, *at a higher annual increase in money wages.* That is, money wages have increased *because* of the inflation.

The analysis easily can be continued from point *D*. Suppose that the government declares, "We achieved a low unemployment rate U_1 two years ago, so our present unemployment U_n indicates that aggregate demand is insufficient." It might then increase the money supply to stimulate aggregate spending. But, according to this adaptive expectations model, this would increase the actual rate of inflation to P_3. Unemployment would again temporarily fall until individuals and firms recognized that actual inflation was once again higher than anticipated. The economy would then move from point *E* to point *F*. Hence, in the *long run,* there is no tradeoff between unemployment and inflation; the long-run Phillips curve is vertical at the natural rate of unemployment. Any one of several rates of inflation—such as *A, D,* and *F*—is compatible with U_n.

This particular perspective thus purports to explain the Phillips data points in Figure 19-6. According to this adaptive expectations model, these points were produced by overly stimulative government fiscal and monetary policies. The northerly points reflect *accelerating* inflation and *fluctuating* unemployment rates.

Rational Expectations in Labor Markets. Some economic theorists hypothesize that workers do more than simply take into account the present observed rate of inflation in formulating their bargaining positions and conducting their job search. They also incorporate information about government deficits and money supply growth into their thinking to form ***rational expectations*** about the *future* course of inflation.[10] As stated by McCallum:

> [The rational expectations hypothesis] presumes that individual economic agents use all available and relevant information in forming expectations and that they process this information in an intelligent fashion. It is important to recognize that this does not imply that consumers or firms have "perfect foresight" or that their expectations are always "correct." What it does suggest is that agents reflect upon past errors and, if necessary, revise their expectational behavior so as to eliminate regularities in these errors. Indeed the hypothesis suggests that agents *succeed* in eliminating regularities involving expectational errors, so that the errors will on the average be unrelated to available information.[11]

In our previous discussion of Figure 19-7, the short-run declines in unemployment were caused by policies which produced higher-than-expected rates of

[10]The concept of rational expectations originated with John F. Muth. See his "Rational Expectations and the Theory of Price Movements," *Econometrica,* July 1961, pp. 315–335. The major recent contributors to this theory are Robert Lucas, Thomas Sargent, and Neil Wallace.

[11]Bennett T. McCallum, "Rational Expectations," in Martin N. Baily and Arthur M. Okun (eds.), *The Battle Against Unemployment and Inflation,* 3d ed. (New York: W. W. Norton & Company, 1982), p. 146.

inflation. These policies worked only because economic agents were misled by the government into thinking that inflation would be lower than it turned out to be. But, according to the rational expectations theory, workers and firms will take into account available information about stimulative government policy when forming their expectations about future inflation. In short, government will be unable to use expansionary policies to produce *systematic* errors in inflation expectations. Workers will respond to announced changes in macroeconomic policy by changing their behavior. More specifically, as we indicated in Chapter 18, job searchers will adjust their monetary acceptance wages upward and therefore will not be misled by rising monetary wage offers into reducing their search time. Also, unions which happen to be in the process of negotiating contracts will demand higher wages in the expectation that inflation will increase. As a result of these actions, even the temporary reductions in unemployment that would occur under the assumption of *adaptive* expectations will fail to materialize.

In terms of Figure 19-7, expansionary government policies will move the economy from points *A* to *D* to *F*. In the case of perfectly anticipated inflation, the only Phillips curve will be the long-run vertical one. Once again, the observed increases in money wages and increased unit labor costs will simply be *symptoms* of inflation—caused by government-produced increases in demand which do not create systematic errors in expectations—rather than distinct *causes* of inflation.

WAGES AND INFLATION: EVIDENCE AND CONCLUSIONS

What, if anything, can we conclude concerning the role of wages in causing, perpetuating, or merely transmitting inflation? The theories just discussed obviously provide contrasting views on this issue. Can empirical evidence clarify matters? Unfortunately, because this issue has a "chicken and egg" dimension, constructing statistical tests in this area is extremely difficult.[12]

Once inflation begins it becomes nearly impossible to sort out whether wages are pushing prices upward or whether wages are being pulled upward by prices. Statistical testing that involves the 1970s and early 1980s is particularly formidable. During that period, oil prices rose sharply; wage and price controls were imposed, modified, and lifted; productivity growth declined secularly; and major changes in economic policy "regimes" transpired. Still, economists have made notable attempts to test the validity of the various theories. The following are mainstream conclusions drawn from the growing body of research findings on this general topic. Be aware that not all economists accept these conclusions

---

[12]Some economists contend that demand-pull and cost-push inflation forces simply cannot be isolated. See F. D. Holtzman, "Inflation: Cost-Push and Demand-Pull," *American Economic Review,* March 1970, pp. 24–42.

and that new studies may generate evidence that could modify or invalidate them.

1. Over the long term—which we will arbitrarily define as 5 years or more—increases in the growth of the money supply appear to be the most significant factor in determining the rate of inflation. However, the existing empirical evidence does not clearly establish that increases in the *money supply* cause the price and wage levels to rise or that *real labor and product market factors* exert upward pressure on prices through excess demand. Remember, excess demand can occur either because of a rightward shift of the aggregate demand curve *or* a leftward shift of aggregate supply curve. In the latter situation, a recession may occur and the monetary authorities may increase the money supply to stimulate the economy. Therefore, the money supply growth may be a *consequence* of the real labor and product market factors. But, irrespective of interpretation, economists are reaching a consensus that slower long-term rates of growth of the money supply either directly, or through less "accommodation" of wage inflation, produce lower rates of inflation.[13]

2. Unions do *not* appear to be an *initiating* cause of inflation. Stated differently, unions do not seem to cause initial bursts of inflation or major increases in the rate of existing inflation, independently of other causes. The major episodes of rapid inflation in U.S. history were started by expansion of aggregate demand, lifting of wage and price controls, or dramatic rises in oil prices.[14]

3. Unions *do* appear to *perpetuate* existing inflation and make it more costly to reduce inflation once it has begun. Evidence is contradictory as to whether wage imitation of union wage settlements is a major mechanism at work here.[15] Additionally, there is little empirical evidence to date which supports the extreme form of the rational expectations view that unions and firms perfectly incorporate expectations about the impacts of present economic policies into wage determination in anticipation of inflation. Rather, the available evidence suggests that unions perpetuate inflation through the long-term contracts which they negotiate. These agreements reflect expectations of the future rate of inflation and labor market conditions based on the existing circumstances. One

[13]For the classic studies on the monetary theory of inflation see Milton Friedman, "The Role of Monetary Policy," *American Economic Review*, March 1968, pp. 1–17 and Anna J. Schwartz, "Secular Price Changes in Historical Perspective," *Journal of Money, Credit, and Banking*, pt. II, February 1973, pp. 243–269. For a study which lends credence to the "accommodation" perspective see John Geweke, "Feedback between Monetary Policy, Labor Market Activity, and Wage Inflation, 1955–1978" in Baily, op. cit., pp. 159–198.

[14]For evidence of the latter two causes as they relate to the 1970s, see Alan Blinder, *Economic Policy and the Great Stagflation* (New York: Academic Press, 1979).

[15]For evidence suggesting that wage imitation is not a significant factor, see Robert J. Flanagan, "Wage Interdependencies in Unionized Labor Markets," *Brookings Papers on Economic Activity*, 1976, pp. 635–673 and Y. P. Mehra, "Spillovers in Wage Determination in U.S. Manufacturing Industries," *Review of Economics and Statistics*, August 1976, pp. 300–312. For evidence which contradicts the Flanagan findings, see Susan Vroman, "The Direction of Wage Spillovers in Manufacturing," *Industrial and Labor Relations Review*, October 1982, pp. 102–112.

significant study concludes that union and nonunion wage increases are equally responsive to the existing labor market conditions *in the first year* of union contracts. But in second and third contract years, scheduled union wage increases plus cost-of-living adjustments do not respond nearly as much to labor market conditions such as unemployment and quit rates as do wages in the nonunion sector. Because union contracts do not begin and expire concurrently with one another, in any *single* year, wages are less responsive to labor market conditions than they would be in the absence of unions.[16] Consequently, unions perpetuate existing inflation even after the initiating cause—say a surge in aggregate demand—no longer is present. Unions also appear to increase the degree of monetary and fiscal restraint, and thus the extent of unemployment, necessary to reduce inflation. The extent to which unions perpetuate existing inflation, however, is limited by the fact that only about 15 percent of the U.S. labor force is unionized.

Automatic cost-of-living adjustments (COLAs) reinforce the tendency for unions to perpetuate inflation. The percentage of major contracts containing these provisions rose from about 20 percent in the mid-1950s to approximately 50 percent in the 1980s. But these provisions do not initiate inflation, and because of fractional adjustment formulas and "caps" which place maximums on wage increases, they do not increase money wages on a dollar-for-dollar basis with increases in the CPI. Also, evidence quite clearly shows that unions which have COLA protection negotiate lower scheduled money wage increases than unions which do not have COLAs in their contracts. Hence, the union contract, not the COLA itself, appears to be the key inflationary feature.[17]

To recapitulate: The empirical evidence has not settled the theoretical dispute over the role of wages in the inflationary process, but it does indicate that while unions do not initiate inflation, they help maintain its momentum by adjusting wages to existing rates of inflation and by agreeing to multiyear contracts, some of which contain COLAs. Once increases in unit labor costs take on a life of their own, the government is faced with the dilemma of allowing a major recession, accommodating the wage advances through stimulative fiscal and monetary policy, or experimenting with supply-side or direct wage and price strategies. In the long term, however, it appears that the rate of growth of the money supply remains the major policy tool for promoting price and wage stability.

INCOMES POLICIES

Restrictive monetary and fiscal policies slow economic growth and may generate higher than politically acceptable rates of unemployment. Consequently, economists search for policies which might either reduce the rate of inflation at any

[16]See Flanagan, op. cit.

[17]Edward Wasilewski, "Scheduled Wage Increases and Escalator Provisions in 1980," *Monthly Labor Review*, January 1980, pp. 9–13. In 1980, the average scheduled wage increase was 3.8 percent for pre-1980 negotiated contracts containing COLAs and 6.8 percent for contracts without the clauses.

level of unemployment or reduce the extent of unemployment at any level of inflation. Policies to achieve the former include incomes policies, and programs to achieve the latter are referred to as employment and training policies (discussed in the previous chapter). Our interest here is in **incomes policies,** which consist of direct or indirect governmentally imposed restraints on increases in factor and product prices. Three broad and related categories of incomes policies are wage and price guideposts, mandatory wage and price controls, and incentive-based incomes programs.

Wage and Price Guideposts. Also referred to as wage and price guidelines or standards, **wage and price guideposts** are distinguished by the fact that compliance is chiefly voluntary. An example is the Kennedy-Johnson guideposts of 1962–1966. In 1962, the Council of Economic Advisors (CEA) formulated a voluntary incomes policy consisting of two major guideposts for noninflationary wage and price behavior. The wage guidepost stated that money wages in *all* U.S. industries should rise at an annual rate equal to the national secular trend rate of productivity (3.2 percent). The CEA recognized that productivity rates varied across industries and that where productivity rose faster than 3.2 percent, a wage increase of 3.2 percent would produce a decline in unit labor costs. On the other hand, where the industry rates were lower than the national average, the 3.2 percent wage hike would cause unit labor costs to rise. Hence, the CEA stated the price guidepost as follows: Prices in each sector in the economy should change in accordance with changes in industry unit labor costs. For example, suppose that productivity increased by 1.2 percent in industry A and 5.2 percent in B. If each paid a wage increase equal to the national average productivity increase of 3.2 percent, unit labor costs would rise by 2 percent (= 3.2 − 1.2) in industry A and fall by 2 percent (= 5.2 − 3.2) in industry B. If each adhered to the price guideline, prices would rise by 2 percent in industry A and fall by 2 percent in B. Economywide, however, price rises would be offset by price reductions and no inflation would occur.

The wage and price guideposts appeared to be effective in the 1962–1965 period, but when aggregate demand began to expand under fiscal and monetary stimulus in 1965 and 1966, inflation accelerated and the Johnson administration abandoned the program. Critics quickly pointed out that the guideposts seemed to work earlier precisely because they were not needed.[18]

Mandatory Wage and Price Controls. Legally binding wage and price controls were used in World War II and the Korean conflict. Then in 1971, the Nixon administration employed powers newly granted by Congress to impose the first peacetime **mandatory wage and price controls.** The goal was to reduce inflation

---

[18]For a discussion of conflicting empirical findings on the effectiveness of the guideposts see George Perry, "Inflation in Theory and Practice," and Robert Gordon "Comment" in *Brookings Papers on Economic Activity,* 1980, No. 1, pp. 207–242 and 249–257.

from the 1970 rate of 5.9 percent to a targeted 2.5 percent rate while simultaneously increasing aggregate demand through tax cuts to help the economy recover from the 1970–1971 recession. The controls began with Phase I, a 90-day freeze of all wages, prices, and rents, and then entered Phase II, in which a Price Commission and Pay Board were authorized to establish minimum legal wage and price increases. The Price Commission set a 2.5 percent limit, and the Pay Board established a maximum wage increase of 5.5 percent. The logic underlying the figures rested squarely on our familiar relationship between wages, productivity, and prices. The agencies assumed that productivity would rise by 3 percent, and given the 5.5 percent increase in wages, unit labor costs and inflation would rise by only 2.5 percent. After going through a "voluntary" Phase III, a new 60-day freeze, and a Phase IV, the Nixon experiment ended.

Most economists—including many who cautiously supported the concept of wage and price controls at the time—now conclude that the 1971–1974 program was a failure. The controls did reduce *price* increases (not wage increases) during the first 16 months when the economy was operating with considerable excess production capacity. But viewed over the long period of the 1970s, the evidence suggests that the program at best repressed inflation temporarily and, at worst, may have accelerated it by creating numerous allocative distortions.[19]

It is misleading, however, to imply that *all* economists oppose wage and price controls under *all* circumstances. Defenders argue that controls can quickly alter inflationary *expectations* and thereby reduce wage and price increases which are accelerating largely independently of excess aggregate demand. They also point out that, by countering allocative distortions caused by powerful unions, oligopolists, or both, wage and price controls may actually improve the nation's allocation of resources. This debate will surely continue, but at this stage of U.S. economic history supporters of mandatory wage and price controls clearly are relatively few in number.

Incentive-Based Incomes Policies. A final category of incomes policies rests on the premise that noninflationary wage and price behavior can be promoted by providing sellers of labor services and products an incentive not to raise their prices *and* by giving buyers of labor an incentive not to pay higher wages. Many specific incentive-based programs have been proposed, but the **tax-based incomes policy (TIP)** seems to have generated the most interest. For example, consider the following simple plan. Suppose that government announced a wage guidepost of a maximum annual hourly compensation increase of 3 percent and also enacted a tax surcharge on corporate profits of firms which grant pay increases (including fringe benefits) that exceed the 3 percent figure. More specifically, let's assume that the tax surcharge is set as some specific multiple— say 2—which is to be applied to the percentage point difference between the

---

[19]Blinder, op. cit., pp. 132–133. Chapter 6 of Blinder's work contains a review of the empirical findings of the effects of the 1971–1974 wage and price controls.

actual wage increase granted and the 3 percent rate set as the guidepost. To clarify how the plan would work, suppose that a firm and union negotiate a contract in which the first-year wage increase is 8 percent. The excess wage increase in percentage point terms would therefore be 5 (= 8 − 3), which would be multiplied times 2 to get 10. Rather than paying the usual corporate net income tax of 46 percent, this firm would pay 56 percent (= 46 + 10). The incentive to comply with the wage standard is obvious; failure to do so would reduce after-tax profits. Yet, the plan would be sufficiently flexible to allow for wage increases which exceed productivity gains where specific circumstances warrant them.

Advocates of tax-based incomes policies point out that such plans do not require large increases in federal expenditures to administer; do not require radical dismantling of unions or corporations; and work within the framework of the market system. Critics counter that the plans are often structured to be antiunion; that the tax penalty will contribute to inflation because firms will shift it forward to consumers via price hikes; and that TIPs, like all incomes policies, direct attention away from the major source of inflation in the U.S. economy—excessive aggregate demand.[20]

The debate on incomes policies will surely continue. Innovative plans such as TIPs (and the plans discussed in the end-of-chapter Time and One-Half section) have generated renewed interest in the general topic. But a major lesson in this chapter is that one's position on the desirability of an incomes policy— irrespective of type—ultimately reflects one's view of the role of *labor markets* in the inflationary process. Incomes policies hold little attraction for those economists who view labor markets as mere transmitters of inflation, rather than as a causal factor.

SUMMARY

1. Economists disagree on whether labor market activity causes or simply transmits inflation.
2. If average hourly compensation in the economy increases more rapidly than national productivity, unit labor costs will rise. These increased costs produce leftward shifts in the aggregate supply curve which in turn push the general price level upward.
3. Wage-push theorists cite several interconnected factors which enable workers to increase wages faster than the increase in national productivity. These include (1) union market power; (2) cost-markup pricing; (3) the imitation of key wage settlements; (4) the existence of explicit and implicit employment contracts; (5) unantici-

---

[20]For details of tax-based incomes plans see Laurence Seidman, "Tax-Based Incomes Policies," *Brookings Papers on Economic Activity,* 1978, No. 2, pp. 363–389 and David C. Colander (ed.), *Solutions to Inflation* (New York: Harcourt Brace Jovanovich, Inc., 1979). Also see Colander's "Incomes Policies: MIP, WIPP, and TIP," *Journal of Post Keynesian Economics,* Spring 1979, pp. 91–100. For criticism of TIPs see Larry L. Dildine and Emil M. Sunley, "Administrative Problems of Taxed-Based Incomes Policies," and Albert Rees, "New Policies to Fight Inflation: Sources of Skepticism," both in *Brookings Papers on Economic Activity,* 1978, No. 2, pp. 363–389 and 453–477, respectively.

pated declines in the trend rate of national productivity; and (6) fiscal and monetary policies which accommodate wage increases.

4. Many economists view wage increases as simply a symptom of demand-pull inflation. Although disagreeing on the mechanisms through which demand-pull inflation is generated, Keynesians and monetarists agree that excessive spending in the economy relative to available output will cause both wages and prices to rise.

5. The Phillips curve can be explained either in terms of degrees of excess demand in the labor market or the emergence of wage-push forces as markets tighten. For the period 1956–1969, the Phillips curve appeared to show a stable, predictable tradeoff between rates of inflation and unemployment. The Phillips curve points for the years in the 1970s and early 1980s, however, suggest the curve has shifted rightward and upward.

6. According to the adaptive expectations view, short-run Phillips curves exist because people expect the existing rate of inflation to continue. When inflation is greater than expected, unemployment temporarily falls; when inflation is less than anticipated, unemployment temporarily rises.

7. According to the adaptive expectations perspective, in the long run market participants adjust their expectations of inflation to the new observed rate. This causes the short-run Phillips curve to shift upward or downward, unemployment returns to the natural rate, and as a result, the long-run Phillips curve becomes vertical.

8. Some economists claim that people form their expectations rationally and adjust their behavior in response to new fiscal and monetary policies which they believe will eventually change the rate of inflation.

9. Empirical evidence indicates that unions do not initiate bursts of inflation but can perpetuate inflation caused by other factors.

10. Various types of incomes policies have been proposed and implemented as tools to reduce cost-push inflation. These include wage and price guideposts, mandatory wage and price controls, and incentive-based incomes policies.

QUESTIONS AND STUDY SUGGESTIONS

1. Key terms and concepts to remember: wage inflation; the relationship between wages, productivity, and labor costs; wage-push inflation; cost-markup pricing; wage imitation; explicit and implicit contracts; monetary accommodation; demand-pull inflation; short-run Phillips curve; adaptive versus rational expectations; the vertical long-run Phillips curve; incomes policies; wage and price guideposts; mandatory wage and price controls; tax-based incomes policy (TIP).

2. Suppose that the following data exist for a hypothetical economy: average money wage = $8 an hour, total worker hours = 100, total output = 1600 units. What is this nation's average level of productivity? What are its unit labor costs? If the number of labor hours remains constant, but the average wage rate and average productivity rise by 5 and 3 percent, respectively, what will be the new level of *total* money wages, the new level of total output, and the new level of productivity? By what percentage will unit labor costs rise?

3. Use Figure 19-1 to determine whether *real wages* rose, fell, or remained constant during the 1967–1984 period. Explain.

4. Show and explain, using graphic analysis, how excess demand in the nation's product market can occur either because the aggregate demand curve shifts rightward or the aggregate supply curve shifts leftward. What is the implication for inflation in each case?

5. Explain how an implicit contract might benefit both workers and employers. How could it contribute to wage-push inflation?

6. Explain how a permanent, unexpected *increase* in national productivity could contribute to a declining rate of inflation.

7. Contrast the relationship between money wage increases and money supply increases in (*a*) the pure wage-push theory of inflation and (*b*) the monetary theory of inflation.

8. Use each of the following three views to explain why the short-term Phillips curve displays a negative relationship between inflation and unemployment: (*a*) the excess-demand theory, (*b*) the wage-push theory, (*c*) the adaptive expectations theory.

9. Explain how COLAs might speed the upward shifts of the short-term Phillips curves envisioned in the adaptive expectations model.

10. Will the share of national income going to labor (Chapter 17) increase, decrease, or remain unchanged if money wages rise at a pace equal to national productivity? Explain.

11. Explain the Kennedy-Johnson wage-price guideposts, indicating in detail the relationship between money wages, productivity, unit labor costs, and product prices. What specific problems are associated with the use of wage-price guideposts or controls? Would you favor a special tax surcharge on firms which grant money wage increases in excess of productivity increases?

12. Use Figure 19-7 to explain how a high rate of inflation, such as P_3 at the natural rate of unemployment U_n, might be reduced by the use of restrictive monetary and fiscal policies.

SELECTED REFERENCES

Baily, Martin Neil (ed.): *Workers, Jobs, and Inflation* (Washington, D.C.: The Brookings Institution, 1982).

Baily, Martin N., and Arthur M. Okun: *The Battle against Unemployment and Inflation,* 3d ed. (New York: W. W. Norton & Company, 1982).

Blinder, Alan S.: *Economic Policy and the Great Stagflation* (New York: Academic Press, 1979).

Friedman, Milton: "Nobel Lecture: Inflation and Unemployment," *Journal of Political Economy,* June 1977, pp. 451–472.

Lerner, Abba, and David C. Colander: *MAP: A Market Anti-Inflation Plan* (New York: Harcourt, Brace, Jovanovich, Inc., 1980).

Meade, James E.: *Wage Fixing* (London: George Allen and Unwin, 1982).

Mitchell, Daniel J. B.: *Unions, Wages, and Inflation* (Washington, D.C.: The Brookings Institution, 1980).

Reynolds, Lloyd G., Stanley H. Masters, and Collette H. Moser (eds.): *Readings in Labor Economics and Labor Relations,* 3d ed. (Englewood Cliffs, N.J.: Prentice-Hall, Inc., 1982), Readings 20–25.

TIME AND ONE-HALF

NOVEL PRESCRIPTIONS FOR CURING WAGE INFLATION

Several unorthodox forms of incomes policy were proposed during the past decade. Two which merit elaboration are the market-based anti-inflation plan (MAP) and a proposal which calls for "centralized wage fixing."

Market Anti-inflation Plan (MAP).* According to Lerner and Colander, wage-price spirals occur because firms and workers do not take into account the inflationary impacts of their wage and price decisions. The basic idea of MAP is to translate "the social harm from the inflationary element in price and wage increases into a private cost that the firm will try to avoid, and to do this through the market mechanism so as to avoid all administrative control or regulation of wages and prices."† The goal of MAP is to eliminate increases in the average price level without interfering with the changes in relative prices and wage rates which cause labor markets to clear and resources to be allocated efficiently.

How would MAP work? Although the actual plan is complex, the following simplified version captures its essence. An agency of government would establish a new commodity—anti-inflation credits—which firms would be required to pay in order to increase their prices. The agency would allocate to firms a supply of these credits just sufficient to allow for a targeted rate of overall inflation, say 2 percent. Firms desiring to raise their prices beyond this rate would need to purchase credits from firms which had excess credits. Excess credits would accrue to companies which held price increases below 2 percent annually. Furthermore, the government agency would grant additional credits to firms which reduced their product prices. Hence, a market for credits would emerge in which supply and demand would interact to generate an equilibrium price. This price would create an incentive to sell credits (reduce product prices or at least hold increases below 2 percent) and a disincentive to buy credits (increase product prices by more than 2 percent). By equating the quantity of credits bought and sold, the market price would ensure that increases in prices above 2 percent on individual products would be fully offset by lesser price hikes or price declines elsewhere in the economy. In other words, inflation would be at the 2 percent rate.

In terms of the labor market, firms could be expected to increase their resistance to excessive wage increases because the resulting higher unit labor cost could be passed forward to customers only by purchasing costly anti-inflation credits. This added expense would obviously reduce profits.

While acknowledging that a market-based incomes policy might be preferable to, say, wage and price controls, critics point out that MAP would create an accounting nightmare for the agency issuing the credits and for firms attempting to comply with the plan's rules. These coordinating, monitoring, and compliance costs might greatly out-

---

*Abba Lerner and David C. Colander, *MAP: A Market Anti-inflation Plan* (New York: Harcourt Brace Jovanovich, Inc., 1980).

†Abba Lerner and David C. Colander, "MAP: A Cure for Inflation" in David C. Colander (ed.), *Solutions to Inflation* (New York: Harcourt Brace Jovanovich, Inc., 1979), p. 213.

weigh any anti-inflationary benefits from the plan. Furthermore, some detractors contend that MAP, like other incomes policies, directs policy attention toward the symptoms of inflation—rising wages and prices—rather than the alleged true cause—excessive growth of aggregate demand.

Centralized Wage Fixing.‡ Britain's Nobel prize–winning economist James Meade advocates what he calls a "not-quite-compulsory arbitration" system as part of a broader plan to achieve full employment and price stability. He suggests that authorities create a steady, consistent noninflationary rate of growth of aggregate demand and then promote full employment by controlling the rate of wage inflation and the relative prices of various types of labor.

Meade argues for a permanent arbitration panel or pay commission to monitor rates of pay in all sectors of the economy. Any wage bargain freely achieved between employers and workers would be permitted to stand, but all unresolved disputes over wage issues could be taken by either party to arbitration. This option supposedly would reduce the likelihood that a firm would grant an inflationary wage increase voluntarily, because the pay commission would be directed to design all awards primarily to promote full employment in the overall economy. More precisely, industries characterized by severe excess supplies of workers would receive a low or zero wage increase while industries in which labor shortages were evident would be given a higher wage rate increase. Employer or union actions in the form of lockouts or strikes would be permitted in opposition to the terms of the award. But such actions would be accompanied by substantial penalties—for example, monetary "fines." In terms of the Chamberlain model (Chapter 7), this would increase the "cost of disagreeing" for the party taking the action and therefore increase the other side's bargaining power.

As might be imagined, the centralized arbitration concept has numerous critics. They point out that the idea wrongly assumes that some type of incomes policy is required to achieve noninflationary full employment. They also argue that this plan unduly centralizes wage setting authority in the hands of government and seriously undermines the right of free collective bargaining, along with its attendant right to strike. Finally, some contend that a central arbitration board simply could not obtain sufficient information about long-run labor demand and supply to accomplish its stated goal of setting economywide pay efficiently and equitably. Nevertheless, even Meade's critics agree that his novel proposal has generated useful discussion and debate on solutions to inflation and unemployment, particularly in Great Britain.

‡James E. Meade, *Wage Fixing* (London: George Allen and Unwin, 1982).

CHAPTER 20

LABOR IN THE SOVIET ECONOMY

Our goal in this chapter is to gain a basic understanding of the labor sector in the Union of Soviet Socialist Republics (U.S.S.R.). We undertake this endeavor for three reasons. First, the labor practices and problems of the Soviet Union are unique and quite intriguing per se. Second, by examining the labor sector in the Soviet Union—wherein ideology, institutional arrangements, and governmental and economic structures are so vividly in contrast with our own—we cannot help deepening our understanding of labor markets and labor issues in the United States. Third, examination of the Soviet labor sector provides us with an opportunity to demonstrate the general applicability of various concepts introduced in previous chapters to circumstances much different from those prevailing in the United States. In other words, we shall find that such concepts as labor supply and demand, human capital investment, participation rates, wage differentials, labor productivity, and so forth, are not peculiar to the United States but apply also in the U.S.S.R.

The discussion is arranged around the following topics. After acquiring an overview of the Soviet economy, we describe the combination of freedom and central direction which exists in the labor sector. The next task is to consider how the central planners tailor the wage structure to achieve the allocation of labor appropriate to the fulfillment of planned production goals. Third, the role of labor unions is examined and contrasted with that of American trade unions. Fourth, the working conditions which confront Soviet industrial workers are discussed. Fifth, we explore the issues of unemployment and labor scarcity in the U.S.S.R. Next, we direct our attention to Soviet productivity problems. Finally, the role of female labor is briefly examined.

THE SOVIET SYSTEM

To understand the labor sector of the Soviet economy—wage determination, the role of unions, working conditions, and an assortment of labor problems and issues—one must have a basic grasp of that nation's ideology, institutions, and economic goals.

Ideology. The Soviet government—which we can safely identify with the Communist party—views itself as a dictatorship of the proletariat, or working class. Following Marxism-Leninism, the Soviet leadership envisions its system as the inevitable successor to capitalism, the latter being plagued by internal contradictions stemming from the exploitation, injustice, and insecurity which it allegedly embodies. Especially important for our purposes is the Marxian notion of a *labor theory of value;* that is, the idea that the economic or exchange value of any commodity is determined solely by the amount of "socially necessary" labor time required for its production. Because of the capitalistic institution of private property, capitalists own the machinery and equipment necessary for production in an industrial society. The propertyless working class is therefore dependent upon the capitalists for its employment and livelihood. Given the worker's inferior bargaining position and the capitalist's pursuit of profits, the capitalist will exploit labor by paying a daily wage which is much less than the value of the worker's daily production. That is, the capitalist can and will pay workers a subsistence wage and expropriate the remaining fruits of their labor as profits or what Marx termed *surplus value.* The function of the Communist party was to overthrow this system and to replace it with a classless society within which human exploitation is absent. The Soviet government thus views itself as the vanguard of the working class; its actions are held to be in keeping with the legitimate goals of the proletariat.

Institutions. At the risk of oversimplification, the two critical institutional characteristics of the Soviet economy are (1) state ownership of property resources and (2) authoritarian central economic planning.

The Soviet state owns all land, natural resources, transportation and communication facilities, the banking system, and virtually all industry. Most retail and wholesale enterprises and most urban housing are governmentally owned. In agriculture many farms are state-owned; most, however, are government-organized collective farms, that is, essentially cooperatives to which the state assigns land "for free use for an unlimited time." Implements and small tools used by craftsmen are privately owned. About one-half of the total Soviet population, and about one-fourth of the urban population, live in privately owned housing.

The government is totalitarian and operates the economy on the basis of central planning. Its constitution makes this clear: "The economy of the U.S.S.R. is a single national-economic complex embracing all elements of social production, distribution, and exchange. . . . Management of the economy is carried out on the basis of state plans of economic and social development."

Markets play a peripheral role in the command economy of the Soviet Union. In capitalistic systems markets are the basic mechanism through which decisions concerning the composition of output, methods of production, the allocation of resources, and the distribution of income are determined. In the U.S.S.R. these decisions are the consequence of directives embodied in the central plan. Governmentally determined decisions concerning prices and wages are used to implement the goals of the plan.

Economic Goals. Soviet economic goals have stressed rapid industrialization and economic development. Soviet planning, as embodied in a series of Five-Year Plans, has focused upon the goal of transforming a basically underdeveloped agrarian society into an industrially advanced economic power. And, it is fair to say, this goal has been substantially accomplished. A closely related objective is military strength. Soviet ideology envisions the U.S.S.R. as being encircled by hostile capitalist countries. Military power is therefore viewed as essential to sustaining the Soviet system. While a society of consumer abundance is persistently forecast for the future, in fact the production of consumer goods and services has been, to say the least, a matter of secondary priority.

FREEDOM AND DIRECTION IN THE LABOR SECTOR

Labor markets in the Soviet Union are a curious blend of free choice and governmental direction. Subject to constraints enumerated below, workers in the U.S.S.R. are free to move, that is, to quit one job in favor of another and to move geographically. This freedom is much less circumscribed today than it was during the Stalinist era (1930–1953). Labor turnover, along with absenteeism and tardiness, was subject to criminal sanctions until 1956. Stalin attempted to reduce labor turnover and mobility by requiring each worker to have a "labor book" which was, in effect, a type of passport for workers. When taking a job a worker was required to surrender his labor book to the plant manager. The book was returned to the worker only if the plant manager allowed the worker to leave his job. In an economy characterized by persistent labor shortages, the labor book could freeze workers to their current jobs and effectively prohibit voluntary mobility. Furthermore, during the Stalinist period, plant managers were given the responsibility for issuing ration cards to employees. This meant that, if a worker quit or was dismissed, his ration card for food and other consumer items would be sacrificed. Workers who changed jobs would also face eviction from housing owned by the employing enterprise.[1] But since the Stalinist period labor market policies and practices in the U.S.S.R. have clearly moved away from coercion and toward positive incentives; the carrot has largely replaced the stick. While Soviet workers today still have "labor books," the criminal sanctions which Stalin applied to mobile and "undisciplined" workers no longer exist. One important practical consideration—the very limited availability of housing in the most desirable urban areas—does impose a very serious

[1]For an interesting discussion of such coercive techniques, see Harry Schwartz, *Russia's Soviet Economy*, 2d ed. (New York: Prentice-Hall, Inc., 1954), pp. 523–532.

impediment to labor migration. Hence, to some extent the political liberalization regarding labor mobility is a moot issue.

Although workers are now generally free to move and therefore to allocate themselves occupationally, industrially, and geographically, there are a number of important exceptions where "direction" or "command" supersedes free choice.

1. Forced labor. The Soviet Union has a history, particularly under Stalin, of using concentration camp labor for construction, mining, and forestry in the harsh climates of Siberia and the Far North to which free labor could not be readily attracted. This *gulag* population was initially composed of peasants who resisted the collectivization of agriculture and later of victims of political purges, prisoners of war, political dissidents, and so forth. The economic benefits of forced labor may have been significant during Stalin's initial collectivization and industrialization drive in the 1930s and 1940s. But given the low productivity of forced labor, it is generally agreed that the state currently derives modest benefit from it, and today it is regarded to be of relatively small economic consequence.

2. Assignment of graduates. An important exception to free choice for workers entails the state's "right" to assign the graduates of technical schools and universities to a specific location for 3 years. Hence, a graduating physician or engineer may be assigned to a remote village in the Western Siberian plain or to Murmansk in the north, although his or her preference may have been for the urban amenities of Leningrad, Moscow, or Kiev. This procedure, as some readers will no doubt be aware, is not unlike one's obligation upon graduation from an American ROTC program. As is true of the ROTC, the state's "right" to assign students geographically is viewed as a means by which students can pay back society for their free education. However, anecdotal evidence suggests that non-compliance with state assignments is quite high in the U.S.S.R. Graduates "pull strings," invent excuses, and in the extreme simply do not show up at their assigned destinations.

3. Mobilization campaigns. The Communist party or the Komsomol (Communist Union of Youth) frequently engage in the semivoluntary recruitment of workers and students to carry out special tasks such as a specific construction or agricultural project or to aid in the harvest. Soldiers who are being demobilized will often be approached to participate in such undertakings.

4. The draft. All Soviet men are subject to 2 years of compulsory military service, with the exception of those who are enrolled in certain high-priority educational programs.

5. Geographic mobility. Given that urban incomes and amenities are much superior to those of rural areas *and* that agricultural production has been seriously deficient, the Soviet authorities sought for a time to restrain the migration of peasants from rural to urban areas through a system of "internal passports."

Never very effectively enforced, this restraint was generally lifted on a regional basis during the 1970s. However, special permission is required to move to Moscow, Leningrad, Kiev, and some thirty other major population centers. Again, evasion of these restrictions on geographic mobility are common.

6. General admonitions to work. The choice of an able-bodied adult not to participate in the labor market is also constrained in the Soviet Union. Workers are not only guaranteed the "right" to work but also have a positive obligation to do so. Indeed, the old Soviet constitution of 1936 flatly stated, "Work in the U.S.S.R. is a duty and a matter of honor for every able-bodied citizen, in accordance with the principle 'He who does not work, neither shall he eat.'" Article 60 of the 1977 constitution is a bit more subtle: "Conscientious labor in one's chosen field of socially useful labor and the observance of labor discipline are the duty and a matter of honor for every able-bodied U.S.S.R. citizen. The evasion of socially useful labor is incompatible with the principles of socialist society." It is pertinent to note that the Soviet Union does *not* have a system of unemployment insurance; unemployed workers are therefore exposed to more severe financial exigencies than are their American counterparts. Furthermore, a Soviet "parasitism" law specifies that any able-bodied individual who is unemployed for more than 4 months a year may be liable for 2 years of imprisonment.[2] Given these pressures to work, it is not surprising that participation rates in the Soviet Union are higher than any other industrialized nation in the world. For all men between the ages of 16 to 60 the Soviet labor force participation rate is 87 percent; the comparable figure for women is 80 percent.

If direction and coercion are *not* the dominant mechanisms in the Soviet labor sector, how do central planners achieve an occupational, industrial, and geographic allocation of labor which is reasonably consistent with the production goals specified in each Five-Year Plan? The basic answer is that the composition and allocation of labor are strongly influenced by (1) state control over the educational system, that is, over the structure of human capital, and (2) state determination and manipulation of wages.

The Soviet government has virtually total control over the educational system and exerts considerable pressures, directly and indirectly, upon students to choose those curricula and careers which are consistent with the output goals of the plans. If, for example, the perceived need of the national economy is for more oil, then the number of openings for geology students in higher education will be expanded and the stipends paid to such students will be increased by state directives. The kinds of education and training received by Soviet citizens are clearly subject to much greater state direction and control than is the case in the west. Stated differently, the Soviet government is actively and deeply involved in determining the quantity and the composition of human capital acquired by the labor force and hence the location of the labor supply curves of the

---

[2]Joseph Godson, "The Role of the Trade Unions," in Leonard Schapiro and Joseph Godson (eds.); *The Soviet Worker* (New York: St. Martin's Press, 1981), p. 117.

various occupations. The role of the wage structure in determining the composition and allocation of the labor force merits more detailed discussion.

WAGE STRUCTURE AND LABOR ALLOCATION

The fact that a market system does not exist is critical in understanding wage determination and wage differentials in the U.S.S.R. In a market economy such as the United States labor is allocated among various industries, firms, and regions largely on the basis of job opportunities and wage differentials. As we found in our earlier discussion of migration (Chapter 14), workers tend to move toward those regions (industries, firms) which pay high wages and have job openings. Put simply, if there is a shortage of workers in labor submarket X and a surplus in submarket Y, then wages will tend to rise in X and to fall in Y. The resulting wage differential will prompt a reallocation of workers from Y to X (and of capital from X to Y), and the surplus and shortage in the respective submarkets will automatically tend to be corrected.

The Planners' Task. As indicated, free markets do not exist in the Soviet Union; prices and wages are determined by the central planners and *not* by supply and demand. Nevertheless, central planners have long been aware that wage differentials have an allocative function and that wages should be determined in terms of the desired allocation of labor rather than on the basis of equality.[3] Hence, the pattern of wage differentials—the governmentally determined wage structure—in the Soviet Union is designed to achieve that industrial and geographic allocation of labor which is appropriate to the fulfillment of planned production goals. Thus, if the state wants to increase output in, say, the steel and hydroelectric industries, then it will raise wage rates to attract more workers to these industries. If it desires to increase oil exploration or timber production in Siberia, it attempts to establish a compensating wage differential (Chapter 12) to induce the required number of workers to bear the harsh climate and general lack of amenities in the area. Similarly, if the production and distribution of consumer goods are assigned a low priority in the plan, the wages of workers in these sectors will be set at relatively low levels.

Wage-Determination in Practice. While labor markets do not exist in the U.S.S.R. in the same sense that they do in the United States, it is revealing to use simple demand and supply analysis to explain how Soviet planners might alter the occupational composition of the labor force to meet planned production goals. In Figure 20-1 we assume initially that the number of oil well riggers

---

[3]Problems associated with poverty and income inequality are met largely through the welfare system in the U.S.S.R., rather than by adjustments in the wage structure.

required by the current Five-Year Plan is Q_1. We draw the labor demand curve D_1 here as being perfectly inelastic on the assumption that, given technology, achieving the level of oil production stipulated by the plan requires a fixed number of workers. Stated differently the demand for riggers is determined by planners without regard to the wage rate. The labor supply curve S_1 slopes upward, reflecting rising marginal opportunity costs and the fact that Soviet workers are free to change occupations. We further suppose that by trial and error the planning authorities have established the planned wage rate W_1, at which initially there is neither a shortage nor a surplus of riggers. In other words, the number of riggers who make their services available is equal to the number required by the plan.

Now let us assume that a new Five-Year Plan calls for an increase in oil production and therefore the need for Q_1Q_2 additional riggers. In Figure 20-1 this has the effect of shifting demand from D_1 to D_2. What actions might the planners take to accomplish this desired outcome? The answer is essentially twofold: (1) increase the planned wage rate paid to riggers and (2) invoke human capital directives which have the effect of shifting the labor supply curve of riggers rightward. By increasing the planned wage rate from W_1 to W_2, some Q_1Q' additional workers who now possess the requisite qualifications will shift from alternative occupations to become riggers. In addition, government directives can be used to increase the openings in vocational schools for students willing to become riggers, and the party and Komsomol bureaucracies can be used to

FIGURE 20-1 IMPLEMENTING A PLANNED INCREASE IN A PARTICULAR OCCUPATION
In the Soviet Union the demand for labor is determined without regard to the wage rate as shown by the perfectly inelastic labor demand curves. If planners decide to increase the number of workers in this occupation (D_1 to D_2), they may either increase the wage rate or influence the human capital decisions of workers. In this case a combination of a higher wage rate (W_1 to W_2) and an increase in the number of workers who choose to enter this occupation (S_1 to S_2) would result in the desired expansion (Q_1 to Q_2) of this occupation.

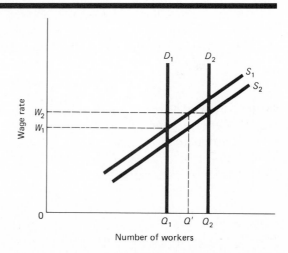

Number of workers

encourage youths to enter this line of work. The effect is to shift the labor supply curve of riggers from S_1 to S_2, providing an additional $Q'Q_2$ riggers.

In a market economy the indicated adjustments would tend to occur *automatically*.[4] An increase in the derived demand for a particular type of labor would raise the wage rate and create job openings. Workers now having the requisite skills would enter this occupation and others would undertake to acquire the needed skills. But, as indicated, the desired labor force adjustments in a planned economy require appropriate decisions by the planning authorities. If planners misjudge either the elasticity of the labor supply curve or the responsiveness of workers to training opportunities, too many or too few riggers may become available. Hence, if the increase in planned wage rates and the rightward shift of the labor supply curve were less than indicated in Figure 20-1, then a shortage of riggers would result and the plan's production target for oil would be in jeopardy. Conversely, if the increases in planned wage rates and labor supply were greater than shown, then a surplus of riggers would occur, implying the overfulfillment of oil production goals perhaps at the expense of other production targets.

Historically, in the Soviet Union, there have been cycles of constricting and then widening wage and earnings differentials. For example, a dramatic equalization followed the 1917 Revolution, but the distribution of wages widened again in the early 1920s. A marked decline in wage inequality characterized the latter half of the 1920s, but in 1931 Stalin introduced substantially greater wage differentials. The reasons for Stalin's action are of interest. The wage structure inherited by Stalin was so compact that pay differentials between skilled and unskilled workers and between easy and difficult work had virtually disappeared. In pursuing his plan for rapid industrialization and economic growth, Stalin sought to change a largely unskilled rural labor force into a skilled industrial labor force. His new wage structure, which geared wages to skills and productivity, was designed to provide incentives for workers to make the desired transition. Once again, the point is that the structure of wages in a centrally planned system must be appropriate to the goals of the plan. It is worth noting that wage inequality declined significantly under Khrushchev in the late 1950s, and this narrowing of wage differentials continued until the late 1960s. Since then a modest reversal has occurred, though earnings inequality remains dramatically less than in the Stalinist period.

To say the least, "the task of determining relative earnings of millions of workers and other employees, scattered over a vast area and operating under a greater variety of technical and economic circumstances, is a task of great complexity."[5] What specific considerations or criteria do planners take into account in constructing the wage structure? One authority has summarized the process as follows:

---

[4]This is not to say that free markets negotiate perfect adjustments. Recall, for example, the market for college graduates discussed in Chapter 4.

[5]Alec Nove, *The Soviet Economy*, rev. ed. (New York: Praeger, 1969), p. 208.

Marx's labor theory of value maintains that the value of a product is determined by the quantity of socially necessary labor required to produce it. In an effort to translate that formula into a comprehensive wage system binding wages to the value of the labor performed, Soviet economists have identified half a dozen dimensions of work that should be considered in the formulation of an individual worker's wage: time, complexity, working conditions, skill, location, industry, and enterprise. Out of this theoretical formulation have arisen a base rate (*stavki*) establishing the amount payable to the least skilled worker in a given industry, and three skill scales (*tarifnye setki*) establishing coefficients which, in the end, determine the pay rate of a given job at a specific enterprise. Additional coefficients relate the wage to working conditions and geographic region. Finally, various bonus systems are established by individual enterprises.[6]

In general, we can think of a Soviet industrial worker's total wage as being composed of two parts: (1) a basic wage rate determined by industry and skill level and (2) a variety of supplementary payments related to job characteristics and worker performance. Thus, if the job is located in the Far North, Siberia, or another remote area, special wage supplements are provided. Supplements are also provided for especially arduous or dangerous jobs such as underground mining. Finally, additional wage supplements in the form of bonuses are paid to workers whose enterprises fulfill or overfulfill their assigned production goals. It is not uncommon for a substantial portion—perhaps as much as a third—of an industrial worker's total wage to be in the form of supplements.

Table 20-1 provides data on average monthly earnings (including bonuses) by industry. These data merit two comments. First, despite recent trends towards greater equalization, there are considerable differences in wages and earnings in the U.S.S.R. Although international comparisons are difficult, a recent comprehensive survey of earnings concludes that there is a "rather striking similarity" in the degree of earnings inequality found in the U.S.S.R. and in the western countries.[7] Second, Stalin's interest in developing heavy industry continues to be reflected in the wage structure. We observe that workers in the seven basic industries listed first in the table receive higher wages than those in light industries (textiles, clothing, shoes, and so forth) and in food industries (milling, meat, beverages, and so forth). The wage structure is designed to attract the most able and ambitious workers into the priority sectors of the economy.

But even a diverse and well-designed wage structure cannot be so finely tuned that every enterprise acquires the precise amounts of each type of labor needed to fulfill its production assignment. Thus we find that plant managers, within limits, evade official wage scales to overcome existing or potential shortages of labor. For example, a plant manager faced with the prospect of losing

[6]Blair A. Ruble, *Soviet Trade Unions: Their Development in the 1970s* (Cambridge, England: Cambridge University Press, 1981), p. 79.

[7]Abram Bergson, "Income Inequality under Soviet Socialism," *Journal of Economic Literature*, September 1984, pp. 1052–1099.

unskilled workers may arbitrarily regrade them as semiskilled workers at a higher rate of pay. Or the manager may restructure the bonus scheme or piece-rate system so as to increase the earnings of workers who are in particularly short supply. Finally, a Soviet factory manager may also enhance the real incomes of desired workers by manipulating in-kind goods and services, including factory-operated housing and food stores.

These comments on labor regrading and restructured bonus schemes imply that plant managers have the capacity to circumvent the wage scales set by the state plan. But the state does exert overall control of each plant by determining its *fixed wages fund*. That is, the central plan will allocate a *fixed* amount of funds to pay the wage bill of, say, the Leningrad Tractor Plant. Hence, to the extent the plant's manager regrades some workers and increases bonuses to overcome a shortage of this type of worker, wage payments for other types of labor must be curtailed.

What conclusions can be drawn from this discussion? First, it is an extremely difficult task for planners to approximate a rational wage structure which will avoid shortages or surpluses of particular types of labor. Second, market forces *do* enter the wage structure through their influence on planners' wage-setting decisions and through evasion of official wage scales by plant managers. Third, evasion of the system is restricted by central planners through their overall control of each plant's total wages fund.[8]

---

[8]For details, see Nove, op. cit., pp. 205–212.

TABLE 20-1

Average Earnings of Workers and Salaried Employees, by Branch of Industry, U.S.S.R., 1975

	Rubles per Month
All industry	162.2
Electric energy	167.3
Coal mining	274.9
Ferrous metallurgy	188.0
Chemicals	165.2
Machinery	164.1
Wood and paper	169.3
Construction materials	165.4
Light industries	124.6
Food industries	145.9

Source: Blair A. Ruble, *Soviet Trade Unions: Their Development in the 1970s* (Cambridge, England: Cambridge University Press, 1981), p. 85, from sources cited therein.

ROLE OF LABOR UNIONS

Unions in the U.S.S.R. are organized on an industrial basis and include all grades of labor, including plant directors or managers. Everyone employed in a given factory—janitor, assembly-line worker, engineer, supervisor—is a member of the same national union, as are all workers employed in plants throughout the Soviet Union which are considered to be part of the same industry. Currently there are some thirty-one national unions, each associated with a single or combined group of industries. Although union membership is not compulsory, it is estimated that about 98 percent of all Soviet workers do belong. The basic reason for membership is essentially pragmatic: Union membership results in substantially increased social welfare benefits, preferential access to housing and to vacation resorts, and so forth.

Labor unions in the Soviet Union have little in common with American unions. Since the Communist party has declared itself to be the "vanguard of the proletariat," an *independent* labor movement would necessarily be redundant and, indeed, a counterrevolutionary threat to the party. Hence, labor unions in the Soviet Union are subservient to the state and its objectives.

Trade unions are given the function of developing communist attitudes among working people, promoting cooperation in the building of communism, and encouraging a total effort in developing the technical/material base of communism. Taken together, these are referred to in Soviet literature under the rubric of "trade unions are schools for communism." On the other hand, trade unions are *not* given any authority to negotiate with enterprise managers on basic wages, hours, pensions, and the like, for these are fixed by law: what may be negotiated are agreements on how terms and conditions of employment are to be lawfully administered.[9]

In short, unions are primarily "transmission belts" for party policy and therefore attempt to mobilize workers to reach or surpass centrally determined production goals. Hence, unions organize "socialist competitions" among individuals, groups of workers, or various factories to stimulate output. Additionally, they help enforce policies to reduce worker turnover, absenteeism, tardiness, and so forth. On the other hand, unions have the power and responsibility to protect workers from illegal or questionable practices by plant managers. For example, under pressure to fulfill ambitious production goals, plant directors may resort to illegal overtime work, rest-day work, or the denial of leave for sickness or injury. At least in principle, unions are to protect workers from such actions. But, as our illustration indicates, the "transmission belt" function and

---

[9]Dan C. Heldman, *Trade Unions and Labor Relations in the U.S.S.R.* (Washington, D.C.: Council on American Affairs, 1977), p. 50.

the "protective" function are often in conflict. Almost invariably, union officials assign higher priorities to their party loyalties and obligations than they do to their responsibilities to union members. Therefore, it is common to find union officials backing the decisions of plant managers even when they are at the expense of workers.

In contrast to the west, life is more oriented toward one's place of work in the U.S.S.R.; social life and work are often closely interlocked. The reason for this is that the Communist party envisions a clear link between one's social and private life, on the one hand, and one's effectiveness as a worker, on the other. A worker whose private life is characterized by drunkenness and a general lack of discipline will not be a conscientious worker. Hence, unions are involved in providing sports, cultural events, and other leisure-time activities for workers. The unions are also involved in administering social insurance funds and the housing which most factories provide.

WORKING CONDITIONS

In the mid-1950s the official Soviet workweek was approximately 48 hours, but since then it has been reduced to about 40 hours. Although the Soviet constitution specifies a workweek of 41 hours, there is substantial anecdotal evidence which indicates that overtime work is quite common, and hence an accurate measure of the typical workweek eludes us.

Storming. Overtime work stems in large part from the phenomenon of *storming* to fulfill production goals. Storming is the practice of working long hours and with great intensity during the last few days of each production period (say, a month or quarter) to realize production targets and the associated bonuses. According to Smith, storming is the "national phenomenon of crash programs and the wildly erratic work-rhythm of Soviet factories, large and small, civilian and military. Storming to fulfill the monthly, quarterly, or annual plans turns every month into a crazy industrial pregnancy, sluggish in gestation and frenzied at the finish."[10] At the start of a month an enterprise's production is virtually at a standstill. Why so? Because workers are recovering from the highly intense work effort required in the final days of the previous month to meet production targets. Some workers may have had to work double shifts or Saturdays and Sundays (normally rest days) and are simply exhausted. Others may have celebrated the end of the storming period and are recovering from the effects. Furthermore, enterprises find it difficult to operate at normal capacity early in the month because other enterprises which supply them with materials and components are similarly recovering from storming. Hence, it may not be until the tenth or twelfth day of the month that all components needed to achieve normal

---

[10]Hedrick Smith, *The Russians* (New York: Ballantine Books, 1976), p. 286.

production rates are available. It follows that a large proportion of the month's production quota must be realized in the final days of each month. One Soviet economist has recently noted that in the last 9 days of each month far more is produced than in the first 14 days. For example, 2.6 times more machine tools and 1.8 times more tractors and combines were produced in the last 9 than in the first 14 days![11] Stated differently, employees are frequently grossly overworked at the end of the month and then underemployed at the start of the next month.

This erratically paced production is hardly conducive to product quality. Because Soviet price tags indicate production dates, wary consumers seek out goods produced during the middle of the month and avoid those manufactured after the twentieth of each month.

Strikes. Although strikes are not illegal as such, they are strongly discouraged and pose considerable risk to participants. Soviet ideology views strikes as meaningless and counterrevolutionary because in theory state enterprises are owned by, and operated in the interest of, workers. Therefore, it is reasoned that it makes no sense for workers to strike because they are in fact striking against themselves! Reliable statistics on strikes do not exist because the Soviet government suppresses such information. But there is ample anecdotal evidence to indicate that worker protests—reflected in either strikes or slowdowns—do occur with some frequency. Worker strikes may reflect concerns with unsafe working conditions, managerial corruption, the boosting of work norms, and so forth. In other cases strikes may reflect tensions arising from broader economic problems such as food shortages and price increases.

> Beginning in May, 1980, strikes were reported at several locations in the Soviet Union. The first strike, protesting food shortages, occurred at the Togliatti Auto Plant, where over a two-day period, about 70,000 workers joined in a protest. This was followed by a similar two-day stoppage at the auto and truck plant in Gorky. Similar strikes were then reported to have taken place at the Kama River Truck Plant at Naberezhnye Chelny (Brezhnev) and at the tractor plant at Cheboksary, as well as at a tractor factory in Estonia, at a Donetsk coal mine in March 1981, at Kiev in March, April, May and June, 1981, and Ordhonikidze in October 1981. There were even reports of a general strike in Odessa in the fall of 1980 provoked as usual by food shortages.[12]

Workers who find plant managers and their local union officials to be unresponsive to specific complaints concerning unsafe working conditions or unreasonable work norms may seek to have these grievances redressed by appealing

[11]Cited in Nove, op. cit., p. 228.
[12]Marshall I. Goldman, *U.S.S.R. in Crisis; The Failure of an Economic System* (New York: W. W. Norton & Company, 1983), p. 111.

to the upper echelons of the unions and to the government and the party. But Communist ideology asserts that oppression has been eliminated from Soviet society; therefore, to pursue such complaints is an extralegal activity, and those who protest are viewed as being dissidents. There are many stories of dissident workers who have incurred the same treatment and fate as intellectual and political dissidents: harassment, psychiatric detention, geographic relocation, or imprisonment.[13]

UNEMPLOYMENT AND LABOR SHORTAGES

Western economists are in agreement that Soviet economic planning has been successful in eliminating the cyclical unemployment which plagues market economies. In fact, the tautness of the Five-Year Plans tends to generate chronic labor shortages. The Soviet Union publishes no figures on unemployment, pointing out that unemployment was "liquidated" in 1930! One western economist has estimated that unemployment in the U.S.S.R. may be on the order of 1 or 2 percent of the labor force.[14]

Frictional Unemployment: Labor Turnover. The major unemployment problem in the Soviet Union involves frictional or job search unemployment. It is fair to say that Soviet authorities have been greatly preoccupied with the problem of labor turnover, which creates frictional unemployment. How severe is this problem? Apparently it is no more serious than in the west. About 20 percent of all Soviet workers change jobs each year, a figure which is comparable with turnover in the United States and the United Kingdom. But the Soviet government has been greatly concerned with the consequent loss of work time and correctly perceives that a worker's productivity will be below average while breaking in on a new job. Worker turnover therefore conflicts with the attainment of planned production goals. More generally, Soviet leadership may regard labor turnover as reflecting a general deterioration of social discipline in the U.S.S.R. Official concern with reducing turnover may be a manifestation of the yearning of an older generation of leaders for more order and predictability in Soviet society.

Why is labor turnover as high as it is in the U.S.S.R.? First, given that the central plans overcommit human resources and thereby generate more or less chronic labor shortages, workers know that they can readily obtain another job if they quit their current one. Hence, paradoxically, the plans' "guarantee" of full employment encourages turnover and contributes to search or frictional unemployment. Second, Soviet labor unions are generally ineffective in resolv-

---

[13]For a series of fascinating case studies, see David K. Shipler, *Russia: Broken Idols, Solemn Dreams* (New York: Times Books, 1983), pp. 203–208.

[14]P. J. D. Wiles, "A Note on Soviet Unemployment on U.S. Definitions," *Soviet Studies*, April 1972, pp. 619–628.

ing worker grievances, and this contributes to turnover. Using the terms we introduced in Chapter 8, the ineffectiveness of Soviet labor unions as "voice institutions" leaves unhappy workers with the "exit mechanism" as the only means of resolving their grievances. Because strikes are strongly condemned, worker turnover often serves as a substitute. Finally, Soviet labor turnover may be a reflection of the fact that workers are generally poorly paid and are under considerable pressure to fulfill production quotas. Hence, Soviet workers are apparently quite willing to change jobs in the prospect of achieving higher pay, better housing, and improved working conditions.

Labor Shortage. The chronic labor shortage[15] stemming from the ambitiousness of the Soviet Five-Year Plans will be greatly aggravated in the 1980s by a significant slowing down of labor force growth. While the annual average increase in the labor force was 1.5 percent in the 1971–1981 decade, it is predicted to be only 0.6 percent in the 1981–1991 period. This drop is the consequence of the two demographic developments portrayed in Figure 20-2: (1) fewer young people are reaching working age and (2) more adults will be retiring from the labor force. The former development is a reflection of a rather dramatic decline in birth rates during the 1960s. The latter is complicated by a rising mortality rate among

---

[15]We use the word "shortage" here in a nontechnical sense. That is, we do *not* mean a market shortage in the sense that a below-equilibrium wage rate will cause the quantity of labor demanded to exceed the quantity supplied. In the present context we simply mean that future increments to the labor force will be appreciably smaller than in the past.

FIGURE 20-2 INCREMENTS TO THE SOVIET WORKING-AGE POPULATION
The Soviet Union is faced with a significant decline in the growth of its working-age population as a result of (1) a decrease in young people reaching working age and (2) an increase in the number of workers retiring from the labor force. [From *Ann Goodman and Geoffrey Schleifer, "The Soviet Labor Market in the 1980s," in Joint Economic Committee, Soviet Economy in the 1980s: Problems and Prospects, Part 2 (Washington, 1982), p. 327.*]

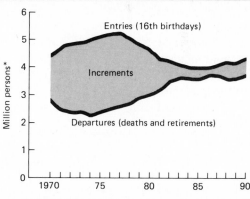

*Males 16–59 and females 16–54.

Soviet males, attributable to the increasing incidence of alcoholism, industrial accidents, and cardiovascular disease.[16] The problem of greatly diminished labor force growth is a particularly acute one for the Soviet Union because past growth of the national output has been much more dependent upon labor force growth than it has been upon productivity growth. Restated, historical growth of the Soviet GNP has been largely attributable to more inputs of labor as opposed to more output per worker.

Let us survey some of the policies which Soviet planners have invoked, or might consider, to deal with the labor shortage. First, child care facilities have been expanded to increase the participation rates of women with young children. In terms of the simple work-leisure choice model (see Figure 2-7 in particular) Soviet planners hope that the availability of day care centers will reshape (flatten) the indifference curve of some women to the extent that they will now decide to engage in labor-market work rather than be nonparticipants. The problem is that the participation rate of Soviet women is already very high. An estimated 90 percent of Soviet adult women are already working or studying full time. Hence, there is little room to increase their labor force participation. Second, pension laws have been revised to increase the yearly benefits of older workers who agree to work beyond the normal retirement age, and this policy has increased the participation rates of this group somewhat. Third, in the 1960s the government promoted part-time employment and part-time schooling for teenagers to enhance the labor supply. The result was a relative abundance of unskilled and relatively unproductive teenage workers and a perceived deterioration in the quality of education such workers received. Hence, this policy was abandoned. In the spring of 1984, however, the Soviet government approved educational reforms which link the educational system more closely to labor market needs. Most importantly, the reforms put increased emphasis upon vocational education at the expense of academic subjects. At the secondary school level, some 40 percent of all students are to be enrolled in vocational schools attached to local factories. Fourth, an untried option is to increase labor supply by increasing the length of the workweek. But such a policy would undoubtedly be unpopular among workers: "Soviet workers have grown accustomed to the current pattern of work and leisure, and would be unlikely to acquiesce placidly in any drastic change."[17] It would also be expensive, because Soviet law requires time and one-half for the first 2 hours of overtime and double time thereafter. Fourth, historically the U.S.S.R. has accelerated its industrial growth by reallocating underemployed labor from rural to urban areas. This option is increasingly limited by the need to sustain and increase Soviet agricultural production. Furthermore, most of the available underutilized agricultural manpower is in

---

[16]Ann Goodman and Geoffrey Schleifer, "The Soviet Labor Market in the 1980s," in Joint Economic Committee, *Soviet Economy in the 1980s: Problems and Prospects, Part 2* (Washington, D.C., 1982). pp. 326–327. See also Philip Grossman, "Labor Supply Constraints and Responses," in Holland Hunter (ed.), *The Future of the Soviet Economy: 1978–1985* (Boulder, Colo.: Westview Press, 1978), pp. 142–166.

[17]Grossman, op, cit., p. 158.

Central Asia, where cultural considerations and language differences may make such labor inappropriate for industrial production in the western Soviet Union. A long-run policy is to encourage Soviet couples to have more children. The Soviet government seems to be moving in the direction of a pronatalist policy, including lump-sum payments for first, second, and third children and partially paid 1-year leaves for working mothers.[18] The problem with this policy, as we know from Chapter 3, is that higher birthrates tend to reduce female participation rates. Long-run increases in the labor force achieved through higher birthrates may have the immediate or short-run effect of reducing the size of the labor force! Still another option is to increase labor productivity, a possibility to which we now turn.

LABOR PRODUCTIVITY

While productivity comparisons are difficult to make, it is fair to say that the average productivity of Soviet workers is substantially less than that of American workers. A recent estimate for 1982 suggests that the Soviet worker produces about 40 percent as much each hour as does an American worker.[19] Furthermore, as in most western countries, the Soviet Union has recently experienced a slowdown in its rate of productivity growth. Table 20-2 shows the rather dramatic decline in the productivity of Soviet labor which occurred in the 1970s.

How can the Soviet Union's productivity problems be explained? First, it is well known that the Soviet system of planning is not conducive to innovation and technological change. "Bureaucratic conservativism" apparently makes it comfortable for the planning hierarchy to produce the same products with the same production methods year after year. Thus, in the 1960s "old guard" central

---

[18]Goodman and Schleifer, op. cit., pp. 342–343.
[19]Cited in Andrew Zimbalist and Howard J. Sherman, *Comparing Economic Systems* (Orlando, Fla.: Academic Press, Inc., 1984), pp. 186–187.

TABLE 20-2

Growth of Soviet Labor Productivity (Average Annual Percentage Change)

	1971–1975	1976–1980
Total economy	2.1	1.2
Industry	4.4	2.8
Construction	2.4	1.1
Transportation	3.5	1.0

Source: Ann Goodman and Geoffrey Schleifer, "The Soviet Labor Market in the 1980s," in Joint Economic Committee, *Soviet Economy in the 1980s: Problems and Prospects, Part 2* (Washington, 1982), p. 335, from CIA estimates.

planners resisted planning innovations designed to introduce a limited price-profit system in the hope of increasing efficiency. The reforms were viewed as alien to the system and a threat to the existing power structure. Thus the Soviet system continues to emphasize steel and machine tools as it did in the 1930s, rather than the computers and other sophisticated capital goods it really needs.[20] Second, the input supply system is notoriously unreliable. Enterprise A cannot produce efficiently because enterprises B and C have failed to provide it with needed inputs, or a transportation bottleneck has delayed delivery. A further consideration is that the Soviet Union is having to resort increasingly to inferior and less accessible natural resources. In particular, ores, petroleum, electric power, and timber are all becoming increasingly costly because reserves in the industrialized western Soviet Union are being depleted, and it is costly to develop and transport such resources from Siberia and other remote areas.

But there is also evidence to suggest that some portion of the Soviet productivity problem is attributable to labor itself and to the reactions of workers and managers to the incentive system. Thus some observers claim that the average Soviet worker simply does not choose to work very hard. "Although Russians are capable of great exertion if pressed to produce, sustained hard work is not a national characteristic. They do not have the work ethic of Americans, Germans, or Japanese."[21] If, in fact, Soviet workers are not inclined to exert themselves, this may well be the consequence of a lack of adequate material incentives. Because of the low priority which the Five-Year Plans assign to production of consumer goods, there is only a limited array of relatively low-quality goods and services available to Soviet worker-consumers. (The price of an automobile is far beyond the means of the average factory worker and, for those able to buy, the waiting period may be 1 to 5 years!) Thus, while harder work might result in bonuses and promotions, the consequent increase in *money* income does *not* translate into a proportionate increase in *real* income. After decades of lofty promises, the system has failed to produce a reasonably high standard of living for the masses of Soviet workers. "All future and no present, certainly as in the U.S.S.R. after six decades, begins to appear after a while more like a long-term confidence game than a meaningful program of economic development."[22] Hence, according to one observer, a new freedom has developed in recent years, the "freedom not to work too hard."[23] As a Soviet worker once remarked to a western journalist: "The government pretends to pay us and we pretend to work."

Certain characteristics of the planning system may also negatively affect the

---

[20]The major theme of Marshall Goldman's *U.S.S.R. in Crisis,* cited earlier, is that the current inappropriateness of the Stalinist planning model has generated deteriorating economic conditions and growing unrest in the Soviet Union.

[21]Smith, op. cit., p. 295. See also Heldman, op. cit., p. 24.

[22]Goldman, op. cit., p. 175.

[23]Blair A. Ruble, "Soviet Trade Unions and Labor Relations after 'Solidarity'," in Joint Economic Committee, op. cit., p. 359. This article is recommended for a perceptive discussion of current labor conditions and worker morale in the U.S.S.R.

productivity of workers. For example, the aforementioned practice of storming to meet monthly production quotas may well reduce labor productivity. "Running machinery overtime without maintenance speeds its deterioration: crash work lowers quality, dragooning workers against their will demoralizes their spirit and causes deep antagonisms which cannot be fully expressed."[24] Productivity targets are almost invariably stated in terms of gross output and, as a result, quality is largely ignored. This suggests that a relatively large portion of an enterprise's output may not be usable. Furthermore, neither plant managers nor workers are anxious to accept innovation. Stopping production to retool may mean loss of bonuses in the short run and the prospect of higher production quotas in the long run. In addition, while Soviet workers are motivated to fulfill their assigned production quotas in order to realize associated bonuses, their goal is *not* to be as productive as they might be. The best outcome for a Soviet worker is to exceed the quota *slightly*, because *substantial* overfulfillment is an invitation for the planning authorities to raise or "ratchet up" the quota. Similarly, Soviet plant managers, subject to the same incentive system, are interested in concealing the true production capacities of their enterprises. To this end many plant managers "hoard" redundant labor. Just as it is handy for a plant manager to hoard materials and spare parts in an economy where taut plans make the supply system unreliable, so it is desirable to hoard labor. To the extent that managers are successful in overstaffing their plants, there obviously occurs a negative effect upon productivity. The unreliability of the supply system also gives rise to another effect which diminishes productivity. Enterprises often resort to producing their own needed inputs. Thus it is a widespread practice in Soviet enterprises to create "dwarf-workshops" in which plants produce essential supplies (for example, nuts, bolts, small castings, and so forth). The problem is that the production of such inputs is highly unspecialized, and productivity is therefore very low.[25]

The Soviet government is not without policies and programs designed to offset or counterbalance these tendencies toward low labor productivity. The Communist party promotes "socialist competitions" between brigades of workers or factories, provides awards and decorations for exemplary workers, and generally exhorts workers to be disciplined and conscientious. A favorite party device is the "counterplan" whereby workers "spontaneously" put forward a production plan entailing output quotas in excess of those indicated in the official Five-Year Plan. A more recent policy—called the **Shchekino experiment**—attempts to deal with the problem of hoarding redundant labor. First introduced in the Shchekino chemical combine in 1967, this program allows plant managers to use 50 percent or more of the wages saved by releasing redundant workers to increase the incentive bonuses paid to other workers. Although the Soviets claim that the Shchekino experiment has been successful in reducing both redundant labor and labor turnover, the program is only applicable to some 3 percent of the

---

[24]Murray Seeger, "Eye-Witness to Failure," in Schapiro and Godson, op, cit., pp. 84–85.
[25]David A. Dyker, "Planning and the Worker," in Schapiro and Godson, op, cit., p. 65.

entire labor force. Reluctance to apply this program more broadly apparently reflects the government's fear such widespread use might create a western-type unemployment problem.[26] The program also may have been subverted by entrenched bureaucratic interests such as the trade unions who would lose their ability to control worker dismissals.

FEMALE LABOR IN THE U.S.S.R.

As suggested earlier, the Soviet economy is highly dependent upon female labor force participation. Fifty-one percent of the Soviet labor force is female, and the participation rate of working-age (16–55) Soviet women is approaching 80 percent. By way of comparison, 43 percent of the U.S. labor force is composed of women, and the participation rate of American working-age women is only 52 percent. In this section we want to explain the high participation rates of women in the U.S.S.R. and to comment upon the extent to which economic inequality exists between Soviet men and women.[27]

High Female Participation Rates. The very high labor force participation rates of women in the Soviet Union can be explained in terms of a number of interrelated factors.[28] First of all, Soviet ideology views women's entry into the labor market as an important factor in achieving a genuinely socialist society. Soviet ideology emphasizes the intrinsic value of work, stressing the contributions it makes to one's social status and self-esteem. Furthermore, because a working woman is not dependent upon marriage for economic support, she can presumably enter marriage on an equal basis with her husband and thereby realize a more egalitarian pattern of family life. Recall that "parasitism" is frowned upon by Soviet officials; all able-bodied persons in the Soviet Union are expected to be employed. Second, the establishment of rapid industrialization and growth as the Soviet Union's primary economic goal in the 1930s created both the opportunity and the need for women to work. A third and closely related factor is the

---

[26]Ibid., pp. 58–60.

[27]This section draws heavily upon Gail W. Lapidus, "The Female Industrial Labor Force: Dilemmas, Reassessments, and Options," in Arcadius Kahan and Blair A. Ruble (eds.), *Industrial Labor in the U.S.S.R.* (New York: Pergamon Press, 1979), pp. 232–279. Alastair McAuley's *Women's Work and Wages in the Soviet Union* (London: George Allen & Unwin, 1981), is also highly recommended.

[28]It is interesting to observe that recent research suggests that Soviet married women react in the same general way as do wives in nonsocialist countries to the key variables which affect labor force participation. In particular, the participation rates of Soviet wives vary directly with (a) their educational attainment and (b) the level of wages they can obtain *and* inversely with (a) their husbands' income and (b) the presence of small children. See Gur Ofer and Aaron Vinokur, "Work and Family Roles of Soviet Women: Historical Trends and Cross-Section Analysis," *Journal of Labor Economics,* January 1985, pp. S328–S354, and Ofer and Vinokur, "The Labor-Force Participation of Married Women in the Soviet Union: A Household Cross-Section Analysis," *Journal of Comparative Economics,* June 1983, pp. 158–176.

demographic imbalance which has existed between males and females. World War I, the Revolution and ensuing civil war, the political purges of the 1930s, and World War II all contributed to a serious shortage of males. "In 1946, there were only 59 men for every 100 women in the 35–59 age group."[29] This meant, on the one hand, that the economy's human resource needs had to be met increasingly by women and, on the other, that many Soviet women had no choice but to become entirely self-supporting. Finally, economic incentives contribute to high female participation rates. State-determined wage rates are at sufficiently low levels that most families with dependents cannot live decently with only one breadwinner.

One of the more profound consequences of the very high participation rates of Soviet women is low birth rates. A recent Soviet study[30] indicates that the average Soviet working woman devotes some 30 hours per week to homemaking chores. The reason for this inordinate burden is essentially threefold. First, as in the United States, men do not assume a significantly greater amount of domestic work when their wives enter the labor force. Second, in comparison to the United States, household capital goods are relatively scarce; the typical Soviet woman is *not* aided by microwave ovens, dishwashers, and food freezers. Finally, shopping is notoriously antiquated and very time-consuming in the U.S.S.R. A great deal of time is spent standing in lines for consumer goods or travelling to peasant markets to obtain needed farm products. Female resistance to the combined pressures of labor market work and homemaking may well take the form of a conscious decision to have fewer children. Thus an ironic tradeoff seems to exist between high female participation rates and the diminished growth of the Soviet labor force. The high participation rates which are essential to plan fulfillment and economic growth in the short run may contribute to labor shortages in the long run.[31]

Male-Female Income Gap. The official stance of the Soviet government is that women have equal access to educational and employment opportunities. But, as in the United States, there is a substantial income gap between male and female workers. Specifically, on the average females earn an estimated 65 to 70 percent as much as males in the U.S.S.R. This leaves a 30 to 35 percent income gap, only slightly less than the U.S. gap of 35 percent discussed in Chapter 11. Indeed, the causes of this sex differential are not unlike those prevailing in the United States.

First, there is considerable occupational and industrial segregation of female workers in the Soviet Union. Women are underrepresented in the key high-

[29]Lapidus, op. cit., p. 236.

[30]Cited in Seeger, op. cit., p. 100. See also Smith, op. cit., pp. 76–90.

[31]For more on the tradeoff between fertility and participation rates, see Anna Kuniansky, "Soviet Fertility, Labor-Force Participation, and Marital Instability," *Journal of Comparative Economics*, June 1983, pp. 126–128. Ms. Kuniansky's estimates suggest that a 1 percent increase in labor force participation reduces fertility by 7 percent.

wage industries of Table 20-1 and overrepresented in the low-wage industries. "Although half of all industrial workers are women, three industrial branches— machine building and metalworking, textiles, and the food industry—account for 70 percent of all female industrial employment; women comprise over 80 percent of food and textile workers and over 90 percent of garment workers, but less than 30 percent of the workers in coal, lumber, electric power, and mineral extraction."[32] Furthermore, reversing the situation prevailing in the United States, blue-collar workers are generally better paid than white-collar workers in the U.S.S.R. Women are concentrated in the white-collar occupations. Incidentally, it is well publicized that most (over 70 percent of) medical doctors in the Soviet Union are women, but the fact is that medicine is an occupation of below-average income!

Aside from occupational segregation, the second cause of the male-female income gap is that women are concentrated in the lower echelons of each occupational category. Although Soviet women have a higher level of educational attainment than men *and* tend to have more continuous labor force participation than women in other industrially advanced economies, women are underrepresented in executive-type positions. As in the United States, Soviet women are noticeably absent from positions of managerial authority.[33] And similar to many American women, Soviet females are frequently overqualified for the positions they hold.

SUMMARY

1. The Soviet system is a dictatorship of the working class and is characterized by state ownership of property resources and central economic planning. The Five-Year Plans have emphasized industrialization and military strength.
2. Soviet workers are generally free to change jobs and to move geographically. Exceptions to these freedoms include penal labor, compulsory military service for young males, the 3-year job assignments of technical school and university graduates, and some restriction on movement to the larger urban areas.
3. Soviet economic planners use wage differentials to seek an allocation of labor consistent with their economic goals. Wage rates for individual workers are composed of (a) a basic wage determined by industry and skill level and (b) supplementary payments and bonuses based upon job characteristics and production performance.
4. Within limits determined by a plant's fixed wages fund, managers can regrade labor and revise bonus schemes to cope with shortages of particular kinds of labor.
5. Soviet labor unions are subservient to the state. Their primary functions are to encourage worker fulfillment of production targets and to protect workers from illegal actions by plant managers.

---

[32]Lapidus, op, cit., p. 125.

[33]Available data do suggest, however, that Soviet women have made greater progress than American women in acquiring managerial positions. See Kathryn M. Bartol and Robert A. Bartol, "Women in Professional and Managerial Positions: The United States and the Soviet Union," *Industrial and Labor Relations Review*, July 1975, pp. 524–534.

6. Storming denotes the uneven pace of industrial production in the U.S.S.R., whereby a large proportion of output is accomplished in the final days of each month. While strikes are discouraged and are relatively rare, they do occur.

7. Although central planning has virtually eliminated cyclical unemployment in the Soviet Union, frictional unemployment does exist. Furthermore, underemployment arises from the tendency of plant managers to hoard labor.

8. The chronic labor shortage caused by the ambitiousness of the Five-Year Plans is becoming more acute in the 1980s because of a significant decline in labor force growth. This decrease is the consequence of a decrease in young people entering the labor force and an increase in the number of adults reaching retirement age.

9. Labor productivity is relatively low in the U.S.S.R., and as in the west, the rate of productivity growth has declined in recent years. Although these productivity problems may arise in large measure from planning difficulties and the need to use inferior and less accessible natural resources, some portion is attributable to labor incentive problems, resistance to innovation, and the tendency of plant managers to hoard labor.

10. The very high labor market participation rate of almost 80 percent for Soviet women is a consequence of (*a*) ideological considerations, (*b*) persistent emphasis upon economic growth, (*c*) a deficit of male workers, and (*d*) the need for most families to have two or more breadwinners. Soviet women earn 30 to 35 percent less than men because of (*a*) occupational and industrial segregation and (*b*) the concentration of women in the lower echelons of each occupational category.

QUESTIONS AND STUDY SUGGESTIONS

1. Key terms and concepts to remember: labor theory of value; surplus value; fixed wages fund; storming; Shchekino experiment.

2. Comment upon the following two statements:
   a. "Coercion is not a key element in the process of labor planning in the contemporary Soviet Union."
   b. "Labor supply in the Soviet Union has been, to a very considerable extent, unplanned."

3. How does labor get allocated among geographic areas, industries, and firms in the United States? In the U.S.S.R.? Given the increase in labor demand shown in Figure 20-1, explain the adjustments through which a new equilibrium would be achieved in the United States *and* in the Soviet Union.

4. Why is union membership very high in the Soviet Union? What are the basic functions of Soviet labor unions? How do they differ from American unions?

5. Why is storming a characteristic of Soviet industrial production? What is the effect of storming upon (*a*) labor productivity and (*b*) product quality?

6. What is the estimated rate of aggregate unemployment in the U.S.S.R.?

7. Account for the high labor market participation rates in the Soviet Union, particularly for women.

8. Using Figure 2-7 as a reference point, demonstrate how each of the following might affect the labor force participation of Soviet women:
   a. the absence of nonwage (property) income
   b. the use of ideological education to "shape" tastes in favor of labor market work
   c. low birth rates
   d. the increasing availability of child care centers

    e. the relatively low earnings of Soviet males
9. Why is the Soviet labor shortage expected to be more acute in the 1980s? What policies might be invoked to reduce the shortage of labor?
10. Explain the relatively low level of Soviet labor productivity.
11. Evaluate: "Soviet women face essentially the same barriers to economic equality as do American women."

SELECTED REFERENCES

HELDMAN, DAN C.: *Trade Unions and Labor Relation in the U.S.S.R.* (Washington, D.C.: Council on American Affairs, 1977).

JOINT ECONOMIC COMMITTEE: *Soviet Economy in the 1980s: Problems and Prospects, Part 2* (Washington, D.C., 1982), papers by Ann Goodman and Geoffrey Schleifer and by Blair A. Ruble.

KAHAN, ARCADIUS, and BLAIR A. RUBLE (eds.): *Industrial Labor in the U.S.S.R.* (New York: Pergamon Press, 1979).

LANE, DAVID, and FELICITY O'DELL: *The Soviet Industrial Worker* (Oxford, England: Martin Robertson, 1978).

MCAULEY, ALASTAIR: *Women's Work and Wages in the Soviet Union* (London: George Allen & Unwin, 1981).

RUBLE, BLAIR A.: *Soviet Trade Unions* (Cambridge, England: Cambridge University Press, 1981).

SCHAPIRO, LEONARD, and JOSEPH GODSON (eds.): *The Soviet Worker* (New York: St. Martin's Press, 1981).

YANOWITCH, MURRAY: *Work in the Soviet Union* (Armonk, N.Y.: M. E. Sharpe, Inc., 1985).

T I M E A N D O N E - H A L F

BUILDING SOCIALISM

Do Soviet workers subscribe to the values of the Soviet system?

Casual examination of the ideology, institutions, and procedures relevant to the Soviet labor sector conjures up a vision of workers who are continuously pressed to work harder, to increase production, and to "build socialism." Thus we find a school system whose curriculum is highly oriented to the needs of the economy and which indoctrinates students to be disciplined and motivated workers. Workers are confronted with ambitious production targets and, through bonus systems, their incomes are linked to the fulfillment of those output goals. Factory management, the Communist party, and the trade unions all exhort workers to greater effort. Conversely, a variety of negative sanctions may face the undisciplined worker. The overall impression is one of a "sweat and strain" work environment, epitomized perhaps by the phenomenon of storming which characterizes the conclusion of each production period.

    While the Soviet government and press provide little information concerning working conditions and worker attitudes toward their jobs, there is anecdotal evidence to indicate that this nose-to-the-grindstone portrayal may not be totally accurate. Consider the following synopsis of a work day of a three-man brigade of machine operators at a factory in Perm as reported in *Pravda:**

7:45	Start work (only one member of the brigade was there on time)
9:20–9:40	Break for a smoke
9:40–9:55	Work
9:55–10:20	Break for a smoke
10:20–11:05	Lunch break
11:05–11:20	Aimless wandering around the shop
11:20–11:40	Tuning a press
11:40–13:00	Working
13:00–14:00	Smoking and aimless wandering around the shop
14:00–14:30	Cleaning up
14:30	Finish work

This portrayal of a brigade which works hard for only 3 or 4 hours a day no doubt is extreme in that it warranted newspaper publicity. Yet it does provide insights into work life in the U.S.S.R. According to one young Soviet Jew: "The Soviet Union is the greatest society in the world for malingering. No one has to work here. You just keep your head down and show up where you are supposed to be and you can survive at a low standard of living. Most people are satisfied with that."†

The lack of labor discipline is also revealed in evidence that Soviet workers engage in illegal work. Illegal moonlighting is apparently motivated by a desire to supplement incomes, but it implies that the primary jobs of such workers may not be very demanding. Thus low-paid teachers tutor the children of well-to-do families for examinations which determine entry to universities and technical institutes. Some doctors and dentists, abetted with "borrowed" state equipment and medicines, carry on lucrative private practices. Skilled construction workers, known as "finishers," can be hired to paint an apartment, repair faulty plumbing, or retile a floor. Some suggest that the notoriously shoddy construction which characterizes Soviet housing is premeditated! Workers deliberately engage in substandard construction because it creates an immediate private market for them to correct the defects.

To summarize: Most Soviet workers seem to be more interested in their own welfare than in "building socialism"; they are frequently successful in circumventing pressures for increased production; and some unknown number engage in illegal private labor.

---

*Cited in David A. Dyker, "Planning and the Worker," in Leonard Schapiro and Joseph Godson (eds.), *The Soviet Worker* (New York: St. Martin's Press, 1981), p. 55.

†Cited in Murray Seeger, "Eye-Witness to Failure," in Schapiro and Godson, op. cit., p. 101.

INFORMATION SOURCES IN LABOR ECONOMICS

O ur discussion of contemporary labor economics is now virtually complete. But learning is a *process,* not an *outcome.* Not only is there much more to learn about labor economics, but today's knowledge also sometimes has a way of becoming tomorrow's myth! How might one *augment* the knowledge of labor economics gained from studying this textbook? How might one *maintain* one's stock of knowledge in this field in the face of normal depreciation and threatened obsolesence?

Our goal in this final chapter is to survey some avenues by which the interested reader might continue the learning process. The chapter should prove useful to those preparing term papers in this or subsequent courses. In this regard note the list of potential term paper topics in Table 21-1. Those who at some later date wish for personal or professional reasons to update their knowledge of labor economics should also find this chapter to be valuable.

Our discussion is organized as follows. First, we discuss sources of labor statistics such as those used throughout this book and then indicate how one might proceed to update or extend tables and figures. Second, we call the reader's attention to various publications which contain articles on labor economics and policy. Here we annotate bibliographic indexes, professional journals, compendia of invited essays, and nontechnical publications. Next, several advanced textbooks in the "new" labor economics are briefly described. Finally, mention is made of textbooks and key journals that cover closely related fields such as labor law, collective bargaining, labor relations, and labor history. We provide specific Library of Congress classification numbers throughout the discussion to facilitate the reader's library search.

SOURCES OF LABOR STATISTICS

Statistical sources can be classified as being either primary or secondary and as providing either time-series or cross-sectional data. A ***primary statistical source*** is an original source of data such as that generated from the U.S. Bureau of Census's *Current Population Survey* (CPS) and reported by the U.S. Bureau of Labor Statistics (BLS). You may recall from Chapter 18 that this particular survey samples about 72,000 households nationwide each month to obtain information on labor force participation, employment, and unemployment. The CPS data are replicated or summarized in numerous *secondary statistical sources* such as handbooks of statistics, business periodicals, and textbooks. Secondary sources are normally reliable, but the reader should be aware that they usually present truncated versions of the data. Therefore, one can often obtain more information by going to the primary source.

TABLE 21-1

A Selected List of Term Paper Topics

Worker Absenteeism

Multiple Job Holding ("Moonlighting")

Income Maintenance Experiments

The Retirement Decision

Female Labor Force Participation Rates

Discouraged- versus Added-Worker Effects

Cyclical and Secular Changes in the Average Workweek

Racial Differences in Labor Force Participation

Educational Attainment and Earnings, Hours of Work, and Unemployment

Trends in Labor Force Participation of Older Males

Criticisms of Human Capital Analysis

The Firm's Investment in Human Capital: On-the-Job Training

Mandatory Retirement

Effectiveness of Public-Sector Training Programs

Monopsony in Labor Markets

Occupational Licensing

The Decline of Unionism

Determinants of Union Membership

Deregulation and the Labor Market

Theories of Collective Bargaining

The Economics of Seniority

Labor-Owned Enterprises

Incentive Pay Systems

Compulsory Arbitration

Effects of Right-to-Work Laws

The Growth of Fringe Benefits

Unions and Job Turnover

Economic Impacts of Strikes

Trends in Government Employment

Public versus Private Pay

Tax Cuts and Labor Supply

The Future of the Voluntary Army

Teen Subminimum Wage Proposals

Effects of the Minimum Wage

Labor Market Impacts of OSHA

Earnings Disparities by Race

Trends in the Female-Male Earnings Ratio

Occupational Discrimination

The Comparable Worth Issue

Effectiveness of Anti-discrimination Laws

Compensating Wage Differentials

Firm Size and Pay Levels

The North-South Wage Differential

The Earnings of "Superstars"

Family Background and Human Capital Investment in Children

Trends in the Size of the Middle Class

Unions and the Distribution of Earnings

Occupational Mobility

Earnings of Recent Immigrants

Illegal Aliens: Labor Market Issues

Displaced Workers

Are Internal Labor Markets Efficient?

Trends in Real Wage Rates

International Comparisons of Real Wages

The Productivity Slowdown

International Trends in Productivity Growth

Trends in Self-Employment

What is "Full" Employment?

Theories of Job Search

Technological Unemployment

Implicit Contracts: Theory and Implications

Teenage Unemployment

Black Unemployment

The Public Service Employment Issue

Wage Subsidy Programs

Adaptive versus Rational Expectations in Labor Markets

Tax-Based Incomes Policies

Labor Market Effects of Unemployment Insurance Benefits

International Differences in Unemployment Rates

Alternative Work Arrangements: Compressed Work, Flextime, and Work Sharing

Labor Force Participation in the Soviet Union

Lifetime Employment in Japan

Cost-of-Living Adjustment Clauses (COLAs)

Labor statistics are reported as time-series data, cross-sectional data, or some combination of the two. **Time-series data** are ordered chronologically, that is, by some period of time such as month or year. Examples are Table 3-1, which lists the labor force participation rates by sex for selected years, 1947–1985; Table 8-5, which shows the number of work stoppages in the United States for each year since 1960, and Table 16-1, which chronicles the BLS's annual labor productivity index since 1960.

Cross-sectional data, on the other hand, are measurements of a particular variable at a specific time, but for different economic units or groups. For example, Table 10-2 reports occupational fatalities and injuries in 1983 *by industry.* Similarly, Table 12-3 presents data on the average hourly wage of production workers in 1984 *by selected state,* and Table 18-2 summarizes unemployment rates for two specific years *by occupation, race, sex, age, and duration.*

What are the major (primary and secondary) sources of time-series and cross-sectional labor statistics? We will approach this topic by initially annotating bibliographies of statistical sources, then the sources of general U.S. statistics, and finally sources that are specific to labor economics. Where possible, we paraphrase the descriptions supplied by the sources themselves.[1]

Bibliographies of Statistical Sources. Bibliographies of statistical publications index sources of statistical series by topical heading much as the familiar *Reader's Guide to Periodical Literature* lists magazine articles. Just as the *Reader's Guide* contains no articles itself, bibliographies of statistical sources contain no statistical series themselves. These bibliographies or indexes often are a good place to begin one's search for statistical series. For labor economics one might fruitfully seek out listings under such topics as unions, employment, labor, and productivity. Of the several bibliographic guides, the following are particularly useful.

American Statistics Index (Washington: Congressional Information Service). Annual with Monthly Supplements. [Z 7554 U5 A46]

This index provides the most comprehensive access to U.S. government statistical publications available. It indexes and abstracts all of the statistical publications issued by federal agencies and therefore provides a starting point in searching for specific statistical series.

U.S. Bureau of the Census. *Directory of Federal Statistics for Local Areas: A Guide to Sources* (Washington: U.S. Government Printing Office). [HB 2175 U54]

This directory lists sources of federal statistics for metropolitan statistical areas (MSAs). An MSA is a geographic area containing either (1) one city having 50,000 or more inhabitants, or (2) an urbanized area of at least 50,000 people *and* a total MSA population of at least 100,000.

---

[1]Our organization of statistical sources follows that used by Charles Helppie, James Gibbons, and Donald Pearson, *Research Guide in Economics* (Morristown, N.J.: General Learning Press, 1974) pp. 69–91.

U.S. Bureau of the Census. *Statistical Abstract of the United States* (Washington: U.S. Government Printing Office). Appendix, "Guide to Sources of Statistics." [HA 202]

Alphabetically arranged by subject, this appendix contains references to the primary and secondary sources of data summarized in the body of this national data book. Publications listed under each subject are divided into two main groups: "U.S. Government" and "Other."

General Summary Statistics. Several excellent volumes contain summaries of statistical series on a full range of political, economic, social, and demographic variables. These "data books," "statistical abstracts," or "statistical handbooks" contain numerous tables of interest to students of labor economics. A few of the more significant works are:

U.S. Bureau of the Census. *Statistical Abstract of the United States* (Washington: U.S. Government Printing Office). Annual. [HA 202]

This previously cited annual edition provides comprehensive summaries of statistics on the social, political, and economic organizations of the United States. It draws both on government and private sources, and many of the over 1500 tables present statistics relevant to labor and labor markets. A section of particular significance is titled "Labor Force, Employment, and Earnings." Other useful sections are "Immigration and Naturalization," "Education," and "Federal Government Finances and Employment."

U.S. Bureau of the Census. *Historical Statistics of the United States, Colonial Times to 1970* (Washington: U.S. Government Printing Office). Issued 1976. [HA 2020 A385]

This book contains more than 12,500 statistical time series, largely annual, on American social, economic, political, and geographic developments covering periods from 1610 to 1970. This is excellent source for back dating series found in the *Statistical Abstract*.

U.S. Office of the President. *Economic Report of the President* (Washington: U.S. Government Printing Office). Annual. [HC 106.5 A272]

This annual report has an extensive appendix containing statistical data relating to income, the labor force, employment, and production. Two sections of the appendix that are of particular usefulness to labor economists are "Population, Employment, Wages and Productivity" and "International Statistics." Furthermore, the text of the *Report* usually contains sections or chapters pertaining to recent labor market developments.

Labor-Specific Statistical Sources. Considerable overlap of tables occurs in the various statistical sources. For example, the *Statistical Abstract of the United States* contains many labor-related series also found in the more specialized sources which we are about to annotate. But, in general, labor-specific sources tend to contain a wider range of data and statistical series that relate directly to labor economics. Awareness of these specialized sources is therefore critical for finding data that may not be presented elsewhere. Let us examine several excellent publications.

U.S. Department of Labor, Bureau of Labor Statistics. *Handbook of Labor Statistics* (Washington: U.S. Government Printing Office) Annual. [HD 8064 A3]

This publication presents the major series of statistics generated annually by the Bureau of Labor Statistics. It contains tables grouped into the following categories: (1) labor force, (2) employment, (3) hours, (4) productivity and unit labor costs, (5) compensation, prices and living conditions, (6) unions and industrial relations, (7) occupational injuries and illness, (8) foreign labor statistics, and (9) general economic data.

Directory of U.S. Labor Organizations (Washington: The Bureau of National Affairs, Inc.). Annual. [HD 6504 D64]

In addition to providing aggregate union membership data for American labor, this publication presents detailed statistics concerning the membership of individual unions and the demographic, occupational, industrial, and geographic characteristics of union members.

U.S. Department of Labor, Bureau of Labor Statistics. *Monthly Labor Review* (Washington: U.S. Government Printing Office). Monthly. [HD 8051 A78]

This periodical is a source of current statistics on labor force participation, productivity, employment, unemployment, and consumer prices. Its appendix reports the results of the (1) Current Population Survey, (2) Establishment Payroll Survey, and (3) Consumer Price Survey, all of which are conducted monthly.

U.S. Department of Labor, Bureau of Labor Statistics. *Employment and Earnings* (Washington: U.S. Government Printing Office). Monthly. [HD 5723 A25]

Employment and Earnings is a monthly publication which provides current information on employment status, characteristics of the employed and unemployed, hours and earnings, productivity, and state and area labor force data. It is worth noting that in 1985 this publication introduced a valuable new series showing union membership by age, race, sex, occupation, and industry.

International Labor Office. *Yearbook of Labor Statistics* (Geneva, Switzerland: ILO Publications). Annual. [HD 4826 I63]

This international yearbook contains time series of labor-related data classified by over 180 countries or territories.

U.S. Department of Labor, Employment and Training Administration. *Employment and Training Report of the President* (Washington: U.S. Government Printing Office). Annual through 1982. [HD 5723 U5 E4]

This useful report includes an extensive statistical appendix which contains many statistics not summarized elsewhere. Major headings include Labor Force, Employment, and Unemployment; Special Labor Force Data (marital status, school enrollment, dual job holders); Employment Hours, Earnings, and Labor Turnover; Employment Projections; Employment and Training Program Statistics; and Productivity. The body of the *Report* contains detailed analyses of employment and unemployment, public employment and training programs, the economic status of particular demographic groups (veterans, Hispanics, women who head households, etc.), and other related topics. Unfortunately, this publication was discontinued in 1983.

U.S. Department of Labor, Employment and Training Administration. *National Longitudinal Survey* (NLS). Conducted by the Center for Human Resource Research, Ohio State University.

This is a source of primary data for people doing original research. The NLS collects information from the same group of people periodically over an extended period of time. It provides information on union status, wages, fringe benefits, job separations, and job satisfaction. The availability of extensive personal information allows researchers to control for such factors as education, age, and parents' income.

Survey Research Center, Institute for Social Research, University of Michigan. *Panel Study on Income Dynamics.*

This is a primary data source used mainly by researchers. Nearly 5000 families were first surveyed in 1968 and interviewed annually each year thereafter. When family members leave home and set up new families, the latter also become part of the annual surveys. This survey provides information on employment, earnings, unemployment, fringe benefits, and so forth.

Updating and Augmenting Tables. Most of the statistical tables found in *Contemporary Labor Economics* are drawn from the general abstracts or labor-specific statistical sources just discussed. One can update most of these tables simply by noting the source cited for each and then finding the most recent edition of that particular publication. Normally, series found in earlier editions are included somewhere within the new ones.

For such purposes as writing term papers, tables in the text may not be sufficiently specific to meet one's needs. But keep in mind that the source cited in the table likely contains much more data than that summarized in the table. For example, Table 14-2 provides statistics on net civilian immigration into the United States for selected years. By referring to the source, *Statistical Abstract of the United States,* one would discover a wealth of additional information on immigration, for example, (1) immigrants by country of birth, (2) immigrants by selected personal characteristics, and (3) the relocation of southeast Asian refugees by state. Furthermore, one would discover there that a *primary* source of immigration data is the *Statistical Yearbook of the Immigration and Naturalization*

Service (Washington: U.S. Government Printing Office), which contains still more information.

APPLICATIONS, NEW THEORIES, EMERGING EVIDENCE

Our attention now turns to those sources in which new developments in labor economics are reported. We will annotate numerous professional journals, compendia of invited essays, and nontechnical publications in the discussion that follows. But first let us highlight works which provide indexes or bibliographies of labor-related publications.

Indexes and Bibliographies. Several publications help direct interested persons toward specific books and journal articles that treat labor economics. Three of the more useful sources are:

American Economic Association. *Index of Economic Articles* (Homewood, Ill.: Richard D. Irwin). Updated via new volumes. [Z 7164 E2A57]
    This series contains bibliographic citations to articles from over 250 economics journals, with each volume covering a particular period. For example, Volume I covers the 1886–1924 period while Volume XIX indexes articles published in 1977. This index is not current, however, and hence those interested in recently published articles should consult the source which follows.

American Economic Association. *Journal of Economic Literature (JEL)*. Quarterly. [HB 1 J62]
    This useful publication contains (1) review articles of research on particular topics, (2) an annotated listing of new books in economics, (3) reviews of selected books, (4) a listing of recent issues of economics journals and the titles of articles therein, (5) a listing of the most recent journal articles, indexed by topic, and (6) abstracts of selected journal articles, also categorized topically. The 800 numbers in the *Journal of Economic Literature classification system,* shown in Table 21-2, define subtopics in labor economics.
    The *Journal of Economic Literature* and *Index of Economic Articles* are also available through DIALOG Information Retrieval Service (DIALOG file 139: Economic Literature Index). This computer file can be searched by such items as author, journal, subject index, geographic area, and *JEL* index number.

New York State School of Industrial and Labor Relations, Cornell University. *Industrial and Labor Relations Review.* Quarterly. [HD 4802 I53]
    This journal, discussed in more detail in the following section, devotes a sizable portion of each issue to listing recent books and articles in labor economics, labor law, and labor relations. It also reviews selected books and summarizes research in progress.

Professional Journals. Scholarly journals contain articles in which economists report new theories, new evidence, new techniques for testing established theories, and the like. The main audience for these articles are other specialists in economics. Therefore, most undergraduates will find the mathematical models and econometric techniques employed to be formidable. However, the basic conclusions of articles can be gleaned through careful reading.

Articles on labor economics are found in *general* economics journals and labor-specific journals. Examples of the former include *The American Economic Review* [HB 1 E26], *Journal of Political Economy* [HB 1 J7], *Review of Economics and Statistics* [HB 1 R35], *Quarterly Journal of Economics* [HB 1 Q3], *Brookings Papers on Economic Activity* [HC 101 B785], *Economic Inquiry* [HB 1 W472], *Journal of Economic Issues* [HB 1 J68], *Southern Economic Journal* [HC 107A13A67], *Canadian Journal of Economics* [HC 111 C225], and *Oxford Economics Papers* [HB 31 0771].[2]

The following are important *labor-specific* journals.

New York State School of Industrial and Labor Relations, Cornell University. *Industrial and Labor Relations Review.* Quarterly. [HD 4802 I53]

This previously cited source is an interdisciplinary journal which contains articles on a wide variety of labor topics. For example, the April 1984 issue featured articles on the impact of unions on absenteeism, the effects of unions on

---

[2]For a listing of 107 economics journals, see S. J. Liebowitz and J. P. Palmer, "Assessing the Relative Impacts of Economic Journals," *Journal of Economic Literature,* March 1984, p. 80.

TABLE 21-2

Journal of Economic Literature Classification Systems: 800 Numbers

800   Manpower; Labor; Population
     810   Manpower Training and Allocation; Labor Force and Supply
         811   Manpower training and development
         812   Occupation
         813   Labor force
     820   Labor Markets; Public Policy
         821   Theory of labor markets and leisure
         822   Public policy; role of government
         823   Labor mobility; national and international migration
         824   Labor market studies; wages; employment
         825   Labor productivity
         826   Labor markets; demographic characteristics
     830   Trade Unions; Collective Bargaining; Labor–Management Relations
         831   Trade unions
         832   Collective bargaining
         833   Labor–management relations
     840   Demographic Economics
         841   Demographic economics
     850   Human Capital
         851   Human capital

teacher productivity, the silicosis problem of western miners, the economics of labor's share in the printing industry, and the labor force participation of older workers.

University of Chicago. *Journal of Labor Economics.* Quarterly. [HD 4802 J64]
This relatively new journal publishes theoretical and applied research on the supply and demand for labor services, compensation, labor markets, the distribution of earnings, labor demographics, unions and collective bargaining, and policy issues in labor economics.

University of Wisconsin. *The Journal of Human Resources.* Quarterly. [HD 5701 J6]
This quarterly publishes articles on the role of education and training in enhancing production skills, employment opportunities, and income, as well as human resource development, health, and welfare policies as they relate to the labor market.

International Labour Office, Geneva, Switzerland. *International Labour Review.* Monthly. [HD 4811 I65]
This journal contains articles, comparative studies, and research reports on such topics as employment and unemployment, wages and conditions of work, industrial relations, and workers' participation. Authors are scholars from all countries.

George Mason University. *Journal of Labor Research.* Quarterly. [HD 4802 J68]
Articles on labor unions, labor economics, labor relations, and related topics appear in this quarterly. Interdisciplinary studies are common and many papers have a public policy orientation. Occasionally it includes papers from symposia, conferences, and seminars sponsored by the journal.

University of California, Berkeley. *Industrial Relations.* Three issues each year. [HD 695 I5]
This journal includes articles on a variety of industrial relations topics. It publishes symposia papers and original articles, as well as research notes and "current topic" articles.

Industrial Relations Research Association. *Proceedings of the Industrial Relations Research Association.* Twice yearly. [HD 4815 I55]
These proceedings consist of addresses by distinguished labor experts, contributed papers, and invited papers on topics of interest to industrial and labor relations specialists and practitioners.

Commerce Clearing House. *Labor Law Journal.* Monthly. [HD 7806 L3]
This journal contains a survey of important legislative, administrative, and judicial developments in labor law. Articles on subjects pertaining to legal problems in the labor-relations field are featured.

London School of Economics. *British Journal of Industrial Relations.* Three issues each year. [HD 6951 B7]

Articles on labor economics, labor relations, and collective bargaining are published in this British journal. For example, a relatively recent issue contained articles titled "Management Strategy and the Reform of Collective Bargaining: Cases from the British Steel Corporation," "Product and Labour Markets in Wage Determination: Some Australian Evidence," and "The U.S. Automobile Collective Bargaining System in Transition."

New York University. *Labor History.* Quarterly. [HD 4802 L435]

This journal is concerned with research in labor history, the impact of labor problems on ethnic and minority groups, theories of the labor movement, comparative analysis of foreign labor movements, studies of specific unions, and biographical portraits of important labor leaders.

University of South Wales, Australia. *The Journal of Industrial Relations.* Quarterly. [HD 4811 J63]

Articles on labor relations and labor economics that are of interest to an international readership are presented in this Australian quarterly. It also prints speeches delivered on labor topics and publishes book reviews.

Compendia of Invited Essays. Several organizations and publishers release edited books on a regular basis which contain invited papers or chapters on current aspects of labor economics. Two examples are as follows.

Research in Labor Economics: An Annual Compilation of Research (Greenwich, Conn.: JAI Press). Annual. Ronald G. Ehrenberg, series editor.

Contributions to this series consist of original papers which are longer than the normal journal articles but shorter than traditional monographs. The series began in 1977 and continues to the present. Contributors include many of the more prominant researchers in labor economics.

Industrial Relations Research Association Series. Annual.

The Industrial Relations Research Association (IRRA) annually publishes a book made up of papers on a specific topic. Examples include *Public Sector Bargaining,* edited by B. Aaron, J. Grodin, and J. Stern and *Industrial Relations Research in the 1970s: Review and Appraisal,* edited by T. Kochan, D. Mitchell, and L. Dyer.

Nontechnical Publications. Although articles in professional journals are useful, their specialized language and esoteric statistical techniques often diminish their accessibility to undergraduate students. Sometimes of greater usefulness are nontechnical books, journals, magazines, and even newspapers which report and summarize recent theory and research.

1. Nontechnical books. Many important books in labor economics are directed to wide audiences, not just other labor specialists. Most of the works listed in the "Selected References" at the end of each chapter in this book can be comprehended by readers who are taking, or have completed, the undergraduate labor economics course. Also, undergraduate readings books are a good source of less technically presented information. Two excellent readers are:

Reynolds, Lloyd G., Stanley H. Masters, and Collette H. Moser (eds.), *Readings in Labor Economics and Labor Relations,* 3d ed. (Englewood Cliffs, N.J.: Prentice-Hall, Inc., 1982). [HD 4901 R389]
      This popular book of readings covers several topics in the "new" labor economics along with the more traditional topics of labor relations and labor law. New editions have appeared every four years.

Rowan, Richard L. (ed.), *Readings in Labor Economics and Labor Relations,* 5th ed. (Homewood, Ill.: Richard D. Irwin, Inc., 1985). [HD 6508 R655]
      This widely used book reproduces entire articles, rather than exerpts, and groups them into six parts: labor force characteristics, the American labor movement, the state of the unions, collective bargaining, labor market issues, and technology and human resource policy.

2. Hearings testimony. Testimony before Congressional committees is a valuable source of information on important research in labor economics. These volumes, published by the U.S. Government Printing Office, are located in libraries which are depositories of federal government publications. While numerous committees hold hearings on legislation relating to labor, two of the more relevant ones are the Senate Human Resources Committee and the House Education and Labor Committee (and subcommittees of each).

3. Nontechnical journals. A few nontechnical journals are also of interest to students of labor economics. The *Monthly Labor Review* mentioned earlier is of particular importance in this regard. It contains informative and readable articles on such topics as labor markets, wages and earnings, fringe benefits, mobility, unionism, and collective bargaining. Articles on particular topics can be found through the use of the *Monthly Labor Review Index* [HD 8051 A62]. Also, the AFL-CIO *Federationist* is a good source of information on organized labor's position on policy issues. Finally, the May issue of the *American Economic Review* (previously cited) contains papers delivered at the annual meeting of the American Economics Association. Usually one or two sessions of the conference pertain to labor economics and, because presentors are instructed to keep their papers noneconometric, these discussions usually are accessible to undergraduates.

4. Magazines and newspapers. The "economics" or "labor" sections of popular magazines such as *Business Week, Newsweek, Time,* and *U.S. News and World Report* occasionally contain stories on current labor economics issues.

By mentioning economists who have done research on a particular topic, these articles serve as helpful starting points for identifying academic sources. This is also true of newspaper articles, particularly those found in financial papers such as the *Wall Street Journal*. Listed below are a nontechnical magazine devoted exclusively to economics and two important indexes through which one can identify specific nontechnical magazine and newspaper articles.

Challenge: A Magazine of Economic Affairs. Bimonthly. [HC 101 N 533]

Among other things, *Challenge* contains invited articles on economic policy issues, interviews with leading economists, and a comment section called "The Growlery." It is not uncommon for an issue to contain one or two articles pertinent to labor economics. The articles are written by economic experts, but are directed toward all persons interested in the topics, not just specialists in the field.

Reader's Guide to Periodical Literature, 1900–present. [AI 3 R48]

This familiar reference source provides a cumulative topical index for articles in over 160 U.S. nontechnical, general, and popular magazines.

The Wall Street Journal Index. [HG 1 W26]

Wall Street Journal articles are listed by topic and corporation in this index.

TEXTBOOKS

There are several advanced textbooks in the "new" labor economics and numerous texts in closely related fields. The former strengthen one's *depth* of understanding of labor economics, while the latter add *breath* beyond the topics included in this textbook.

Advanced Texts. Advanced textbooks presume more knowledge of mathematics, econometrics, and economic theory than does this text. Nevertheless, the diligent reader whose preparation in those areas is modest can gain much from them. The following three books are used mainly in graduate courses in labor economics.

Addison, John T., and W. Stanley Siebert. *The Market for Labor: An Analytical Treatment* (Santa Monica, Calif.: Goodyear Publishing Co., 1979). [HD 4901 A35]

This book covers many of the topics found in *Contemporary Labor Economics,* but treats them with considerably greater analytical rigor. Mathematical appendixes follow several chapters.

Joll, Caroline, Chris McKenna, Robert McNabb, and John Shorey. *Developments in Labour Market Analysis* (London: George Allen and Unwin, 1983) [HD 5706 D43]

This British publication employs a rigorous graphical approach to analyze recent developments in labor economics. It presupposes that the reader has had several courses in economics, including intermediate microeconomic theory.

Fleisher, Belton M., and Thomas J. Kniesner. *Labor Economics: Theory, Evidence, and Policy*, 3d ed. (Englewood Cliffs, N.J.: Prentice-Hall, Inc. 1984). [HD 4901 F47]

Exceptionally well-written, this advanced textbook assumes that readers have completed intermediate microeconomics and are familiar with quantitative research techniques. Of special interest are the sections entitled "Frontiers of Labor Economics" and the extensive citations in the end-of-chapter "References and Selected Readings" sections.

Texts in Related Fields. High-quality textbooks abound for courses of study related to labor economics. One good way to discover them is to browse in your college bookstore for textbooks required for courses in such fields as collective bargaining, labor law, labor history, labor relations, human resource economics, and social insurance. Table 21-3 lists several such books by topic. Numerous other texts are available in each of these subject areas and could be identified by visiting with a professor who specializes in the particular field. These textbooks typically are revised on 3- to 5-year cycles.

TABLE 21-3

Representative Textbooks, Subjects Related to Contemporary Labor Economics

Collective Bargaining

Beal, E. F., and J. B. Begin. *The Practice of Collective Bargaining*, 7th ed., Richard D. Irwin, Inc., 1985.

Kochan, T. A. *Collective Bargaining and Industrial Relations*, Richard D. Irwin, Inc., 1980.

Labor Economics and Labor Relations

Bloom, G. F., and H. R. Northrup. *Economics of Labor Relations*, 9th ed., Richard D. Irwin, Inc., 1981.

Reynolds, L. G. *Labor Economics and Labor Relations*, 8th ed., Prentice-Hall, Inc., 1982.

Human Resource Economics

Levitan, S. A., G. Mangum, and R. Marshall. *Human Resources and Labor Markets: Employment and Training in the American Economy*, 3d ed., Harper and Row, Publishers, 1981.

Labor Law

Gregory, C. O. and H. A. Katz. *Labor and the Law*, 3d ed., W. W. Norton and Co., 1979.

Taylor, B. J., and F. Witney. *Labor Relations Law*, 4th ed., Prentice-Hall, Inc., 1983.

Social Insurance

Rejda, G. E. *Social Insurance and Economic Security*, 2d ed., Prentice-Hall, Inc., 1984.

Williams, C. A., J. G. Turnbull, and E. F. Cheit. *Economics of Social Security*, 5th ed., Ronald Press, 1982.

Labor History

Cohen, S. *Labor in the United States*, 4th ed., Charles E. Merrill Books, Inc., 1975.

Taft, P. *Organized Labor in American History*, Harper and Row, Publishers, 1964.

Dulles, R. F. *Labor in America*, 3d ed., Thomas Y. Crowell, 1966.

SUMMARY

1. Statistical sources are classified as being either primary or secondary and as providing time-series or cross-sectional data.
2. Bibliographies of statistical sources include the *American Statistics Index*, the *Directory of Federal Statistics for Local Areas*, and "The Guide to Sources" section of the *Statistical Abstract of the United States*.
3. Good sources of general summary statistics include the *Statistical Abstract of the United States*, *Historical Statistics of the United States*, and the *Economic Report of the President*.
4. Labor-specific statistical sources include the *Handbook of Labor Statistics*, *Directory of U.S. Labor Organizations*, *Monthly Labor Review*, *Employment and Earnings*, *Yearbook of Labor Statistics*, *Employment and Training Report of the President*, *National Longitudinal Survey*, and the *Panel Study of Income Dynamics*.
5. Indexes of professional journal articles are included in the *Index of Economic Articles*, the *Journal of Economic Literature*, and the *Industrial and Labor Relations Review*. Professional articles on labor topics are found in general journals on economics as well as in the specialized labor journals.
6. Additional routes by which one can stay current on labor economics topics include nontechnical publications such as (*a*) books that summarize sophisticated research in laymen's language, (*b*) testimony before Congressional hearings, (*c*) periodicals such as the *Monthly Labor Review*, and (*d*) "economics" or "labor" sections of such magazines and newspapers as *Business Week* and the *Wall Street Journal*.
7. Students desiring to *deepen* their knowledge of the "new" labor economics should consult one or more of the advanced texts in the field; students desiring to *extend* their knowledge to related fields may wish to gain access to standard textbooks in such subjects as collective bargaining, labor law, labor relations, social insurance, human resource economics, and labor history.

QUESTIONS AND STUDY SUGGESTIONS

1. Key terms and concepts to remember: primary statistical source; secondary statistical source; time-series data; cross-sectional data; *Journal of Economics Literature* classification system.
2. In what major way do the *American Statistics Index* and the *Handbook of Labor Statistics* differ?
3. Update the following tables in this textbook: Table 8-4, Table 10-2, and Table 12-2.
4. Use any relatively recent issue of the *Journal of Economic Literature* to:
   a. find and list the contents of a particular issue of the *Journal of Labor Economics* described therein
   b. identify and list the author(s), title, and professional journal of any *three* articles that deal with human capital (Hint: see Table 21-2)
5. Scan the annotations of labor-specific statistical sources listed in this chapter to determine where you would be most likely to find information on the number of first-time participants in employment and training programs. Use that source to identify the number of such participants for fiscal year 1980.
6. Where would one find statistics on total employment in the United States in 1820?
7. Use the *Statistical Abstract of the United States* to determine the labor force participation rate for females for 1980 in the United States, Canada, France, West Germany, Italy, Japan, Sweden, and the United Kingdom.

SELECTED REFERENCES

Azevedo, Ross E.: *Labor Economics: A Guide to Information Sources* (Detroit: Gale Research Company, 1978).

Helppie, Charles, James Gibbons, and Donald Pearson: *Research Guide in Economics* (Morristown, N.J.: General Learning Press, 1974).

Hoel, Arline A., Kenneth W. Clarkson, and Roger L. Miller: *Economics Sourcebook of Government Statistics* (Lexington, Mass.: Lexington Books, 1983), chap. 4.

T I M E   A N D   O N E - H A L F

REGRESSION ANALYSIS*

Many of the articles in the journals listed in this chapter report findings of econometric studies. In the following extract, Harvey S. Rosen skillfully highlights the main features of one commonly used statistical technique: regression analysis.

Econometrics is the statistical analysis of economic data. It does not rely upon asking people for their opinions or subjecting them to experiments. Rather, the effects of various policies are inferred from the analysis of observed behavior. While economists are unable to control historical events, econometrics makes it possible to assess the importance of events that *did* occur.

In a simple labor supply model, annual hours of work (L) will depend upon the net wage rate (w_n). [By definition, $w_n = (1 - t)w$, where t = tax rate.] A bit of thought suggests that variables like nonlabor income (A), age (X_1), and number of children (X_2) may also influence the hours of work decision. The econometrician chooses a particular algebraic form to summarize the relationship between hours of work and these explanatory variables. A particularly simple form is:

$$L = \alpha_0 + \alpha_1 w_n + \alpha_2 A + \alpha_3 X_1 + \alpha_4 X_2 + \varepsilon \tag{1}$$

The α's are the *parameters* of the equation and ε is a *random error*. The parameters show how a change in a given right-hand side variable affects hours of work, L. If $\alpha_1 = 0$, the net wage has no impact on hours of work. If α_1 is greater than 0, increases in the net wage induce people to work more. The substitution effect dominates. If α_1 is less than 0, increases in the net wage induce people to work less. The income effect dominates.

The presence of the random error ε reflects the fact that there are influences on labor supply that are unobservable to the investigator. No matter how many variables are included in the study, there is always some behavior that cannot be explained by the model.

Clearly, if we knew the α's, all debate over effect of taxes on labor supply would be settled. The practical side of econometrics is to estimate the α's by application of various

*Extracted from Harvey S. Rosen, *Public Finance* (Homewood, Ill.: Richard D. Irwin, Inc., 1985), pp. 39–42. © Richard D. Irwin, Inc. Reprinted with permission.

FIGURE 1 A SCATTER DIAGRAM

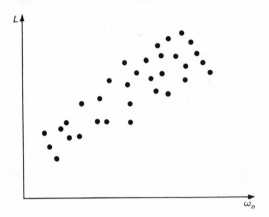

FIGURE 2 A REGRESSION LINE

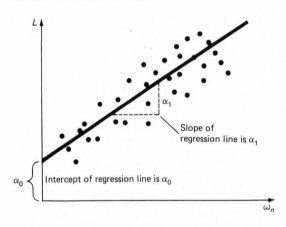

FIGURE 3 A REGRESSION LINE IN A SCATTER DIAGRAM WITH INCREASED DISPERSION

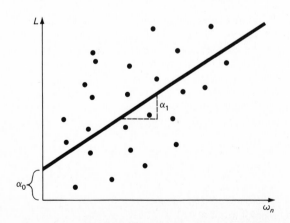

techniques. The most popular method is called *multiple regression analysis*. The heat of the debate over labor supply indicates that this technique does not always lead to conclusive results. To understand why, we consider its application to the labor supply example.

For this purpose, ignore for the moment all variables in equation (1) other than the net wage. Assume that hours of work decision can be written simply as

$$L = \alpha_0 + \alpha_1 w_n + \varepsilon \tag{2}$$

Equation (2) is characterized as *linear* because if it is graphed with L and w_n on the axes, the result is a straight line.

Suppose now that information is obtained on hours of work and on after-tax wages for a sample of people. Plotting those observations gives a scatter of points like that in Figure 1. Obviously, no single straight line can fit through all these points. The purpose of multiple regression analysis is to find the parameters of that line which fits "best." The best line is that which minimizes the sum of the squared vertical distances between the points on the line and the points in the scatter. Such a *regression line* is illustrated in Figure 2. The regression line is a geometric representation of equation (2), and its slope is an estimate of α_1.

After α_1 is estimated its "reliability" must be considered. Is it likely to be close to the "true" value of α_1? To see why this is an issue, suppose that our scatter of points looked like that in Figure 3. The regression line is identical to that in Figure 2, but the scatter of points is more diffuse. Even though the estimates of the α's are the same as those in Figure 2, there will be less faith in their reliability. Econometricians calculate a measure called the *standard error* which indicates how much an estimated parameter can vary from the true value. When the standard error is small in relation to the size of the estimated parameter, the coefficient is said to be *statistically significant*.

This example assumed that there is only one explanatory variable, the net wage. Suppose that instead there were two variables in the equation: the net wage and nonlabor income. In analogy to fitting a *regression line* in a two-dimensional space, a regression *plane* can be fitted through a scatter of points in a three-dimensional space. For more than two variables, there is no convenient geometrical representation. Nevertheless, similar mathematical principles are applied to produce estimates of the parameters for any number of explanatory variables (provided that there are fewer variables than observations). The actual calculations are done with high-speed computers.

With estimates of the α's in hand, inferences can be made about the changes in L induced by changes in the net wage. Suppose that $\alpha_1 = 100$. Then if a tax increase lowered the wage by 50 cents, it can be predicted an individual would work 50 hours ($100 \times \$.50$) less per year.

SUBJECT INDEX

601